CANADIAN PUBLIC ADMINISTRATION

CANADIAN PUBLIC ADMINISTRATION

Problematical Perspectives

Robert F. Adie
University of Winnipeg

Paul G. Thomas
University of Manitoba

PRENTICE-HALL CANADA INC., SCARBOROUGH, ONTARIO

Canadian Cataloguing in Publication Data

Adie, Robert F.
Canadian Public Administration

Bibliography: p.
Includes Index.

ISBN 0-13-112946-5

1. Canada — Politics and government. I. Thomas, Paul G. II. Title
JL108.A34 354.71 C81-095021-9

Prentice-Hall, Inc., Englewood Cliffs, New Jersey
Prentice-Hall of Australia, Pty., Ltd., Sydney
Prentice-Hall of India Pvt., Ltd., New Delhi
Prentice-Hall International, Inc., London
Prentice-Hall of Japan, Inc., Tokyo
Prenctice-Hall of Southeast Asia (PTE.) Ltd., Singapore

ISBN 0-13-112946-5

Production Editor: Deborah Burrett
Designer: Gail Ferreira

Typeset by Compositor Associates Limited
Printed in Canada by T.H. Best Printing Company Limited
1 2 3 4 5 THB 86 85 84 83 82

To:
Linda, Adam, Chris, Jo
and
Roberta, Hugh, Neal, Bryan

Contents

CANADIAN PUBLIC ADMINISTRATION

CHAPTER ONE

Introduction

Because of the complex, interdisciplinary nature of public administration, attempts to define it must remain arbitrary and inconclusive. Traditionally in the domain of political science, it is also taught by geographers, economists, sociologists, psychologists and accountants. As a result, those who teach public administration are liable to do so with a certain discipline bias. Awareness of this has led to the creation of institutes and schools of public administration where faculty are hired from a variety of disciplines, and thus students are exposed to a variety of perspectives. The same is true of schools of business which offer public administration in their programs. Furthermore, public administration impinges on all areas of life through the activities of government, and so, in turn, it is affected by the knowledge generated in many disparate fields. For example, the study of geography *per se* is not the concern of public administration, but obviously geographic factors such as the location of natural resources and the size of Canada have a direct bearing on various government policies concerning resources and the question of centralized or decentralized organizations to carry out policies. The study of marital customs and child-rearing practices is not itself the concern of public administration, but has an obvious relevance to it – witness, for example, current concern for equality of women in employment and interest in attitudes of youth toward the legitimacy of formal authority. Similarly, studies of atoms and bacteria are not themselves relevant to public administration, but consider governmental as well as general societal interest in such things as the sale of nuclear reactors and pollution of Canadian waters. And, finally, perhaps to belabor a point, the study of politics as such is not the concern of public administration, but obviously politics has a constant impact on governmental services. Even some areas of political science previously more-or-less ignored by those interested in public administration are becoming increasingly relevant. International relations and comparative politics, for example, were two such sub-disciplines, but there is today growing interest in international administration and developmental administration, and meaningful study of these is impossible without a basic grasp of the more general sub-disciplines.

All this, of course, begs the basic question: What is public administration? Many answers have been attempted over the years, but none has been universally accepted. Public administration is many things to many people, depending on discipline perspectives, and negative or positive attitudes toward the concept. Our definition too, must be arbitrary. The study of public administration would seem to concern the executive branch of government, commonly called the public, civil, or civic service, including all matters of concern within itself, all matters which impinge on it, and all matters on which it impinges.

The intent here is not to attempt discussion of all or even many of the large number of topics which most obviously belong under the heading of "public administration." Rather, the purpose is to examine in fair depth several topics on which a good deal of interest and concern have been expressed both publicly and academically, and a reasonably sophisticated knowledge of which is requisite to a basic understanding of public administration. The approach synthesizes the thoughts of a variety of writers on each of the topics, thereby acquainting the reader with some of the many problems, prospects, and ramifications of these aspects of the general field of public administration. Furthermore, since the writers in each topical area contradict one another in their basic assumptions, arguments, evidence and conclusions, an effort is made to present the material in controversial and even dichotomous terms, allowing the reader to arrive at a personal conclusion on the basis of personal values and/or intuition. Moreover, it should be noted that the topics selected and the way they are presented must obviously at times reflect a certain discipline bias and even personal bias on the part of the authors.

It should also be noted that the term "problematical," which appears frequently throughout this text, has a distinct meaning for the authors. It tries to capture and emphasize the ongoing controversy involved in each topical area. The term "issue" as it is commonly used suggests a much shorter and more intense controversy, with the issue being resolved by government action and/or by decline in interest and public debate. For example, an issue may exist over whether residents are to have a dominant voice in deciding on certain zoning laws regarding their community. The problematical nature of citizen participation concerns generalized views on the extent to which citizens can/should participate in making public choices of this nature. Similarly, an issue may arise over whether a government agency acted properly when it withheld information on its activities from affected citizens. The problematical perspective concerns the ongoing controversy over whether and/or under what circumstances government agencies should be allowed to withhold information from citizens. An issue, then, is resolvable, while problematical perspectives cannot easily if at all be resolved because the viewpoints are so disparate as well as generalized that significant disagreement will always prevail.

Chapter 2 deals with the ever-verdant jungle of management/organization theory. Viewpoints in this area are quite divergent and have long traditions, since many of the assumptions and the arguments following from them are microscopic (i.e., organization-based) renderings of political-philosophical controversies which have existed in Western culture over the centuries. Of essential concern here is the "proper" relationship between the organization and the individual who works for it. Differences in views of writers in this area seem to a great extent to be based on differing assumptions about human nature and the nature of organizations. These assumptions are in turn based on the individual's personal ideology which is the sum total of one's values, beliefs, habits, attitudes, and life experiences — that is, the end result of one's personal socialization. Any random group of people (e.g., a class studying public administration) will almost certainly have members who hold a generalized, rather pessimistic view of human beings as well as members who tend to be more optimistic.

Our discussion starts with management and organization theorists writing in the late 19th and early 20th centuries. It includes, for example, some of the ideas of Max Weber on bureaucracy, Frederick Taylor on Scientific Management and Luther Gulick on Administrative Science. These ideas are then contrasted with those of the human relations school (e.g., Elton Mayo) which achieved great popularity in the 1930s and 1940s. The ideology of the first group of writers led them to rather pessimistic assumptions about the nature of man, whereas the second group was much more optimistic.

The two schools of thought, although modified in various ways over the years, are very much with us today both in the theory and practice of public administration. Virtually any government or large private organization will show fairly strong approximation to Max Weber's "ideal type" bureaucracy. One need only read a few editions of, for example, *Canadian Business*, to discover strong elements of Scientific Management and, for that matter, strong elements of the humanistic challenge to that school of thought. The ideas of Administrative Science are reflected in the current emphasis on rationality in public budgeting and government planning in Canada. Many of the writers in the field of Modern Human Resource Management (or Motivation Theory) reflect Mayo's conclusion that somehow management must make life meaningful for the employee. The university graduate entering upon a career will carry along a bundle of personal assumptions about fellow human beings that will ultimately affect, for example, the way he or she responds to superiors and treats subordinates.

Discussion of this topic ends with some consideration of what appear to be current socio-economic trends in Canadian social thought. Some questions are raised concerning the values underpinning arguments about management's proper role in a society increasingly characterized by large organizations. On the very shaky assumption that agreement can be reached on this role, there remains the very complex, practical question of how to go about achieving the desired results.

This final discussion leads to the concerns of Chapter 3 which addresses the relationship between the organization and society. On the one hand, writers point toward the positive aspect of organizations, arguing that large-scale organization is the only effective way to achieve social goals, that our freedom from want and drudgery, our increasing leisure time and many other aspects of modern life commonly accepted as good are due to the administrative revolution which created modern organizations. On the other hand, there is a growing body of literature which emphasizes problems arising from large-scale organization — growing impersonality and lack of meaningful personal relationships, lack of congruency between government programs and the clientele they are directed toward, and the "tyranny of bureaucracy." Again, the variant viewpoints seem to be based on differing assumptions about the nature of man and of organizations. Both the anti- and pro-bureaucracy literatures have long traditions based either on general fear and distrust of government, or belief in the need for government and in its generally benevolent nature.

The arguments continue today, their various proponents often finding incongruous support. The anti-bureaucratic views of George Wallace in the United States have something in common with the Manitoba Liberal Party's (early 1970s) slogan "self-control, not state-control," and both have something in common with various student groups attempting to buck the establishment. All have some relationship with the ideas of Karl Marx and Robert Michels. Thomas Hobbes's views are reflected to some extent every time a public opinion leader or citizen group demands government action to cure a nasty social situation. When the government responds to new public concerns it predictably creates another complex organization (e.g., Environment Canada or the Department of Consumer and Corporate Affairs) and just as predictably other public opinion leaders or other citizen groups, or even the same ones, decry "bureaucratization" and/or lack of relationship of the agency or its programs to the problem area with which it was designed to cope.

The attitudes portrayed and arguments developed in Chapters 2 and 3 pervade subsequent discussion. Again, the intent is to present viewpoints in a fairly dichotomous fashion — that is, somewhere short of gross exaggeration — so as to show the differences and the significance of differences in the study of public administration. The assumption here is that people tend to lean toward one extreme or another, the side they favor being determined by their current situations, their particular socialization, and their general cultural milieu — that is, by their "ideology." This is not intended to suggest that most or even many people fall into extreme categories, or the "lunatic fringe." Rather, the argument is that most people lean one way or another, and this is quite important for both the study and the practice of public administration.

Furthermore, people can easily, even if unconsciously, be quite inconsistent in their views. An individual can work happily in a government agency, be closely identified with and proud of its programs and their goals, yet condemn government bureaucracy because of a significant reduction in the refund he expected on his income tax return. The head of a private corporation employing thousands of people may nevertheless express concern about bureaucratization in government. Students can become incensed over a certain university policy, be successful in fighting it and become proud members of the new establishment. A person with a very anti-government and/or anti-bureaucratic ideology may become particularly concerned over something he or she identifies as a social ill and demand government action (and therefore further bureaucracy) to cope with it. A university professor may vehemently advocate treating individuals as individuals rather than as categories, and yet, at the end of term, consciously or unconsciously categorize his students in assigning final grades.

Still, despite illogic and inconsistency, all of us do tend to have a generalized attitude toward people and organizations, and this will be reflected to a considerable extent in our views on the topics in these and the following chapters.

Chapter 4 deals with the theory and practice of public policy-making. It commences with discussion of differing approaches to studying public policy, and then proceeds to examine the policy role of bureaucrats by describing alternative theories of public policy-making. Such theories are often presented both as a *description* of how decision-making actually occurs in government and as a *prescription* of how it ought to occur. Disagreements exist over how rational government decision-making can or should be, and even over what is meant by rationality in public policy-making. The debate is usually presented as a polarized clash between *rationalists*, who emphasize that the clarification of goals and a wide survey of alternative choices is central to successful policy-making, and *incrementalists*, who insist that agreement on goals cannot be achieved in a pluralist society and that only a narrow range of options, incrementally different from past policies and limited to what is politically feasible, can and should receive the attention of decision-makers. Other writers take up a position in the middle on the continuum between rational-comprehensive policy-making and incrementalism, arguing that pure efficiency analysis should be integrated with political analysis. Still others denounce all decision-making theorists for being essentially technocratic in their concerns, showing an excessive preoccupation with the "how" of policy-making to the virtual neglect of the substance of policies.

Policy-making in Canadian government seems to fall in the middle ground between comprehensive rationality and incrementalism. A rational philosophy of policy-making came to the fore during the first term of the Liberal government led by Prime Minister Trudeau. A series of institutional reforms were introduced to ensure that elected politicians rather than appointed public servants made the basic policy decisions, that governments anticipated rather than simply responded to events, and that actions were based on an explicit assessment of performance in relation to stated goals. Trudeau's record in implementing his rationalist philosophy of policy-making has drawn mixed reviews. Many observers allege that incrementalism remains rampant in the government of Canada and that the much celebrated "priorities exercises" of the Liberal government were a waste of time and money. Others argue that while the structures for rational policy-making were created, incrementalism or, at best, some combination of rationalism and incrementalism predominated within them. Still others hold that the Trudeau decade witnessed a basic change in the way that Canadian governments analysed and approached policy problems. The second half of Chapter 4 describes and assesses the institutional reforms that are at the center of this debate. Some of the major structures (actors) in policy-making in Canada are described and analyzed with particular attention given to the public bureaucracy. The chapter concludes with some thoughts on the role of Parliament and democratic government in modern society, helping to set the stage for later discussion in Chapter 10 on the relationship between government and citizens in the administrative state.

The Trudeau government's efforts to obtain more rational policy-making resulted in certain basic changes in the federal expenditure budget process, discussed in Chapter 5. Rising public concern about the size and efficiency of governments has led to increasing study of budgetary procedures as a possible solution to the mixed bag of alleged evils called Big Government. The chapter begins by analyzing the extent to which governments have, in fact, grown in Canada. It also presents a cursory review of several of the more popular explanations for the increased scope of government activity in post-war Canada and then turns to the existing federal budgetary procedures which many observers have singled out as an important contributing factor to the rise in government spending. The main institutions and processes of budgeting within the government of Canada are described. It is stressed that the budgetary process is to a great extent secretive, changeable and subject to the influence of such imponderables as the play of personalities, making it a poor subject for reliable generalizations.

"Better budgeting" is the Holy Grail of public administration, and in the past 20 years certain new approaches have arisen to challenge the traditional, incremental style of budgeting. In the mid-1960s, the United States introduced the Planning, Programming, Budgeting System (PPBS) as a more rationalist approach to spending, and several years later the Canadian government followed suit. PPBS subsequently ran into very serious ideological and operational obstacles on both sides of the border, although it appears to have had a somewhat larger measure of success in Canada.

No sooner was PPBS in disrepute than the budgetary reform movement found two new banners to march under. Zero-based budgeting (ZBB) and sunset laws reflected the mood of retrenchment and consolidation in governments in the late 1970s and early 1980s. Whereas in the 1960s and early 1970s PPBS was to be the budgetary vehicle for policy analysis and program innovation, ZBB and sunset laws are seen as the means to check runaway spending, to terminate ineffective programs and to control unaccountable, even irresponsible, bureaucracies. The second half of this chapter seeks to provide a balanced assessment of the potential and actual accomplishments of PPBS, ZBB, and sunset laws in Canada and the United States. The comparisons made with the United States are partly intended to suggest the general complexity of public budgeting in modern society. In addition, it is illustrative of the link between budgeting and politics to consider the extent to which budget reform ideas, born elsewhere and subsequently imported into Canada, have to be modified to conform to the basic features of the Canadian political system.

In Chapter 6 the concept of "merit" is examined — its historical origins, its various applications to the public service and its intrinsically conflict-ridden character. The "merit principle" is rather sacrosanct today, in that to speak disparagingly of it is somewhat akin to attacking motherhood. Despite this and despite the fact that the public service is supposedly governed by the merit principle, many who cherish the idea are unable to define it in other than vague, very subjective terms. The question of who is best qualified or most capable is open to many different interpretations, even when basic selection criteria have been agreed upon by all parties making the selection. Otherwise, why have research studies revealed that trained and experienced personnel selection officers can disagree greatly on the merit of a candidate for appointment within the public service? Why have merit systems emphasized formal education and seniority at the expense of demonstrated job-related performance? And, why have our merit systems not produced a work-force that represents the best qualified from the vast numbers of people of various origins and beliefs who make up the total population? Or have they? We do not attempt definitive answers to these perplexing and enduring questions but we do try to uncover some of the reasons behind the continued existence of the questions.

A major concern of this chapter is the political environment in which the merit principle exists. Merit systems were originally established to eradicate political patronage as a method of appointment to the public service. In the process, however, it was necessary to remove the politician from active participation in the hiring and promotion of public servants, because the politician was supposedly concerned only with bestowing rewards for political support rather than with selecting the most competent person for the public service job. Implicit in the argument was the fact that the politician could not be trusted and that partisanship and competence were mutually exclusive. Contemporary public service commissions are vestiges of those earlier times when politics and administration were mechanistically viewed as separate entities, somehow independent from each other. And yet today commissions are alive and well, dutifully maintaining their vigilance over a system which attempts to inhibit partisan intrusions into administration but leaves the administrators free to make significant inputs into matters of public policy.

The final sub-topic to be discussed in this chapter is that of "representative bureaucracy" and its impact on the concept of merit. Initiatives undertaken by governments in the past two decades to bring about equal employment opportunities through affirmative action programs (e.g., bilingualism, or women in management) have resulted in a re-examination, and in some cases a redefinition, of the merit principle. The question is whether the public services, which function for all citizens, should be so constituted as to approximate proportionately all the major groups which comprise Canadian society. Quite aside from any practical implications, is such an idea compatible with the merit principle, or is the merit principle inherently opposed to such a democratic emphasis? Can preferential treatment be used to redress balances deemed to be improper in a representative sense? It will be noted that in this specific area of discussion there is a constant problematical overtone in that no answer can be attempted that is not easily attacked.

Practically every public policy adopted in Canada today is mediated through an elaborate network of intergovernmental meetings and committees. Chapter 7 draws attention to the development of extensive formal machinery for federal-provincial consultation, involving at the summit elected politicians and below them a wide array of appointed officials from various levels in the administrative hierarchy. It examines the historical evolution of intergovernmental relationships in Canada, in the process raising several major questions. Is the relationship primarily one of cooperation, of conflict and competition, of bargaining? Does most of the interaction among officials occur in formal, open meetings, or are the important decisions really reached at closed meetings and through informal contacts? To what extent can we generalize about intergovernmental relations or must we distinguish among issues and over time? What is the impact of intergovernmental relations on the internal operation of individual governments? That is, as most governments have created agencies responsible for the overall coordination of federal-provincial dealings, do the regular departments resent those agencies? And does the existence of full-time federal-provincial relations specialists contribute to heightened conflict within the federal system when such individuals become devoted to the protection and expansion of the jurisdiction of their governments?

The final part of the chapter looks at the implications of executive federalism for some of the more traditional concerns of public administration. Does the need for joint decision-making in many areas enhance bureaucratic influence at the expense of control by elected politicians? While public servants are deeply involved in the intergovernmental processes of policy formulation and implementation, Cabinet ministers supposedly possess ultimate control over decisions. However, in order to facilitate negotiations, ministers must grant their officials considerable discretionary authority and may be reluctant to challenge tentative agreements because of the balancing of interests involved and the technical content of the proposed compromises. Increased political involvement and identification of public servants with the policies of their respective governments may be another consequence of federal-provincial decision-making. This has implications for the traditional notion of political neutrality and anonymity of public servants. Increased joint decision-making also compounds the problem of accountability in modern government. If legislatures already represent a feeble check on executive action in other areas of government activity, in the realm of federal-provincial business they seem to be absolutely excluded. It has, for example, been argued that the decisions of federal-provincial meetings are reached in secrecy and presented by the individual governments to their respective legislatures as virtual *faits accomplis*. Again, this provides the basis for further discussion in Chapter 10 on the relationship between government and citizen in modern society.

Chapter 8 deals with "administrative accountability" and provides more extensive treatment of points raised in earlier chapters. Canada and the United States have different approaches to the problem of controlling the bureaucracy, each approach reflecting the system of government and the society in which it operates. Both systems seem to involve myths and inadequacies caused by the extensive scope and technical nature of modern government. As a result, reform seems necessary to many. Each society also appears to admire features of the other, but because of the different constitutional traditions success in transferring institutional features from one system to the other appears very uncertain.

Central to Canada's system of accountability is the concept of ministerial responsibility which requires that ministers, individually and collectively, be responsible to Parliament. Public servants, through ministers, are only indirectly accountable to Parliament. As a result, several questions arise: Do ministers really make policy and control their departments in the manner implied by the traditional, constitutional doctrines? Are ministers in turn effectively accountable to Parliament and thus to society? To whom and for what is the senior public servant, such as a deputy minister, responsible? Is he responsible solely to the minister he serves? To the Prime Minister who appoints him? To the goals of the government as a whole? To his professional conscience? To his clientele in the society? If he owes a responsibility to all these sources, which should be given greater weight in the event of conflict?

Circumstances have clearly changed since the development of the doctrine of ministerial responsibility in the 19th century. Public policy has broadened in scope and become much more technical. Departments have become large, very complex organizations. Crown corporations and regulatory boards have proliferated and are not subject to the same degree of direct ministerial supervision as regular departments. In the light of such changes, the chapter assesses the viability of Canada's accountability system and suggested reforms to that system.

Arising out of the debate over ministerial responsibility is the more specific issue of administrative secrecy, which is examined in Chapter 9. Ottawa is alleged to be one of the most secretive capitals in the Western world compared to, for example, Sweden, and even the United States. A large part of the explanation for the closed nature of Canada's policy-making and administrative processes is said to be our constitutional doctrines of ministerial responsibility and the related concept of an anonymous, permanent public service. The chapter examines these and other reasons for the degree of confidentiality surrounding government operations.

In the last several years in Canada there has been considerable debate over the need for and the content of a Freedom of Information Act similar to that which has existed in the United States for more than a decade and in Sweden since the last century. How should such an act operate in a country like Canada which is based upon different constitutional principles? What are its potential political and administrative costs? What are the potential benefits and who will enjoy them? Should the political value of openness override other political values dear to Canadians? As with so many other concerns in Canadian public administration, the questions are many, as are the answers—what is lacking is common agreement on the relative importance of the questions and the acceptability of the answers.

Chapter 10 addresses the role of the citizen in the context of modern government in general and public administration in particular. Literally everything that is included in the domain one labels the public sector, including its interdependence with the private sector, can somehow be related to the role of the citizen. When, for example, demands for increased citizen participation are directed specifically at tradition-defined public policy-making institutions, such as Cabinet and Parliament, they really involve the entire public sector, including public bureaucracy in all its aspects, because public policies pervade the public sector. If emphasis on citizen participation involves public bureaucracy in the first instance—for example, demands for a new, "proper" bureaucracy-clientele relationship — they once more impact ultimately on the entire public sector because the bureaucracy, as an actor, acts within a much larger context in which it cannot realistically be viewed as an independent variable.

Another way of portraying the wide scope and complex nature of citizen participation is to say that it involves the entire historical as well as current controversy between democracy and authoritarianism. There has never been in Western civilization agreement on the merits of either. In earlier centuries authoritarianism prevailed both in theory and in practice, but there always existed the democratic counterpoint. In later centuries the democratic perspective has tended to prevail, but no society is without its critics on this point.

Nor can we agree on what we really mean by either term. In the case of democracy, for example, we have alleged Canadian democracy and alleged Russian democracy. Many of us see ourselves as democratic and the Russians as dominated by Communist authoritarianism, while presumably many Russians see themselves as democratic and consider Canadians to be dominated by capitalist authoritarianism. And within our own country we cannot agree on exactly what we mean when we say "democracy." In efforts at clarification, we turn to adjectives and thus underline the lack of overall agreement. We have, for example, majoritarian democracy, representative democracy, pluralist democracy, grass-roots democracy, participatory democracy, and consociational democracy. We do not agree on these terms either as to their validity as descriptions of reality or as normative ideals to be sought.

Somewhere in all this is "citizen participation." As an ideal to be sought, it clearly belongs in the democratic camp. However, while it can be praised for its democratic nature it can also be deplored because of its impact on matters citizens in general do not and cannot understand.

In dealing with this topic of citizen participation, the approach here is quite limited, both in scope and depth, due to the complexity of the controversies and the nature of this text. The chapter begins with a consideration of "benevolent" or "paternalistic" authoritarianism which reflects genuine concern for humanity, but little faith in our ability to do what is best for ourselves. Following this is a discussion of citizen participation, which some claim has taken on the dimensions of a "movement." This movement attempts to open both the political and administrative components of government to citizen influence and/or control. However, the movement appears to have mutually contradictory specific goals and thus the question is raised whether it can have significant success in changing the current distribution of influence in the Canadian political system.

Chapter 11 summarizes the major concerns of the preceding chapters and attempts to relate these concerns to one another. The discussion emphasizes the need to view each topical area as part of a coherent whole. That is, the various factors discussed in each topical area must ultimately be seen as interacting with many other factors, and a realistic assessment of any one topical area must give some consideration to this interdependence.

At the end of each topical chapter (2-10) there is a list of books, reports and articles suggested for further reading. The items included in each list have been selected on the basis of a) their solid relevance to the area and b) their representation of different views in the area.

CHAPTER TWO

The Personal Meaning of Organizational Life

Introduction

The purpose of this chapter is to look at some of the major developments in administrative and management theory and practice that have occurred during the last 80 to 100 years. This historical perspective will show the mutually contradictory theories and practices that have arisen in the relationship between the organization and the individual. These contradictions may to some extent explain the ambivalences, frustrations, and dissatisfactions so often experienced by the individual at work today. If the individual finds organizational life at times puzzling and even difficult, the reason for this may lie in the conflicting views and practices of administration that remain with us as one part of our cultural heritage.

The history begins with discussion, in fair detail, of early thinkers such as Frederick Taylor, Henri Fayol, and Max Weber. It then proceeds, with less detail, to more recent theories that challenged theirs. The lesser detail is made possible not because these writers are less important than their forerunners but because they were reacting to them and the groundwork for the arguments has been laid in earlier discussion. From this second group of arguments discussion proceeds to the present, describing some of the most recent developments of generalized theory and practice in a Canadian context. What will emerge is a picture of the confusion and controversy which are due to sets of inherently contradictory ideas and their attendant practices.

Historical discussion of the impact of large organizations on the individuals who work within them typically commences in the late 19th and early 20th centuries. It was at that time that the large organization was becoming an increasingly visible phenomenon, with commercial and government activities being conducted on an ever-larger scale. Further, although the Industrial Revolution began much earlier, it had not until this period generated such an obvious need for an Administrative Revolution to accompany it. That is, the Industrial Revolution as we know it and however we might value it, could not possibly have proceeded to its present stage of development without a revolution also occurring in the way production was organized. In crude terms, for example, the assembly line was not a technological innovation, but rather an administrative device designed to maximize the production of new technology-based produce.[1]

It was this perceived phenomenon and the benefits accruing from it that led academics such as Max Weber, industrialists such as Henry Ford, and technocrats or "efficiency experts" such as Frederick Taylor to emphasize the development and utilization of newer, "better," more "rational" and "efficient" ways of organizing for success in a wide field of endeavors. Ford's assembly line, then, was a major administrative change from earlier ways of producing first carriages and then cars. Weber saw bureaucracy as inevitably dominating other modes of production due to its technical superiority in administration. Taylor's scientific management emphasized new techniques for organizing and training people to produce according to their potential.

Administrative theory is often stated as though the assumptions, arguments, and conclusions are entirely new, and have never occurred previously or at least simultaneously in other contexts. However, the major, constant underlying concerns in this area, both in the past and in the present, had their origins far back in the development of Western civilization.

The organization is a sub-society, part of a much larger society. As such, it has its internal system of government, its rulers and ruled, and its culture, including the attitudes, beliefs, habits and technologies of its citizens. However, it should not be expected that its government and citizens remain unaffected by the value controversies prevailing in the macrosociety.[2] To ignore this interaction between lesser and larger society is to preclude much broader understanding of what life in large organizations is all about.

Many of the most enduring philosophical-political questions through the centuries remain with us today in the general society and manifest themselves at the micro-level in administrative controversies. What is the *proper* use of force, or coercion, against the individual by the State? Does the State exist only under negative moral-legal imperatives with a list of things it must not do *to* the subject, or are there also positive moral-legal obligations which the State must meet *for* the subject? Conversely, does the individual have to perform certain duties *for* the State, or does he operate only on the basis of what he must not do *to* the State? Is man, as man, basically egocentric or does he have inherent interest in the well-being of his fellows? Is man basically good, needing only the proper environment for the goodness to be apparent, or is he basically evil, bearing careful watch?

On the pessimistic side, for example, Seneca and early Christian writers argued that government is the necessary remedy for man's proclivity to wickedness. Machiavelli urged strongly that human nature is essentially selfish, and the only really effective motive on which the ruler can rely is the desire of the individual and the masses for security above all. Thomas Hobbes held a similar view, attempting to validate it on scientific grounds and urging the constant need for coercion to hold men to their covenants. Calvin emphasized the absolute need for obedience to authority.

Opposing assumptions and the philosophies based on them have also been advanced through the centuries, although they had tough sledding in earlier years due to the early Christian insistence on man's inherent wickedness. Aristotle, for example, through his concern for the good State governed by laws, at least acknowledged that the State too had to be carefully watched. Later theorists such as Rousseau and John Stuart Mill developed such ideas, emphasizing the basic goodness of mankind and de-emphasizing, even denying, the need for control through coercion. Anticipating much of the group-based administrative theory of today, they argued that man realizes himself only as a member of society.

A great deal of current administrative literature heavily stresses the idea of the individual's basic goodness, his need for meaningful interpersonal relationships and also his need for what is today termed "self actualization," with the accompanying assumption that what he attempts to achieve will be "good" rather than "evil." In this current literature the organization is also assigned a quite positive role, just as is given to the State today in macro-theory. Rather than having only an essentially negative, coercive role, management is assigned the responsibility for creating an environment in which the individual is allowed the chance to demonstrate his inherent goodness. Management, in essence, becomes a "savior" of the micro-society, and, in the view of some, appears destined to be the savior of the macro-society as well.

The arguments remain problematical, as that term is defined here. The great majority of adult male and an increasing number of adult female Canadians spend approximately one-third of their "productive" lives working in relatively large, complex organizations. In this regard, there are some controversial questions: What benefits *do* Canadians enjoy from their membership in organizations and what benefits *should* they enjoy? What *do* they have to pay for their continued membership, and what *should* they pay? In order to get people to work maximally or even optimally, is the carrot or the stick the best means? Or are both degrading? And, since the organization exists in a broader social milieu where value controversies abound, one must expect administrative literature to reflect positions on these broader political questions. Thus, for example, the inculcation in the young of attitudes toward formal authority will have both general political meaning and more particular organizational meaning. In the organization one person will advance and another will accept or reject or modify an idea or practice on the basis of more generalized attitudes and values. We all, that is, view administrative matters from our particular ideological perspectives.

The Mechanists

Administrative theorists as well as practising management of the late 19th and early 20th centuries tended to see the individual as compelled, even duty-bound, to give up a very great deal of himself to obtain his wage — and a wage was all that was tendered to him. He had to give up to organizational imperatives not just large portions of his time and mental and physical energy, but to a great extent he had to concede his "individuality" as well. This was based on the idea of man in a work setting as an *interchangeable part* and this view has led to theorists of this era being classified as belonging to the *mechanistic tradition*. That is, this school of thought saw man in his work environment as a cog in a machine which, if kept adequately lubricated by money, would automatically perform as expected by management — the more money, the faster went the machine. Within this mechanistic tradition, two sub-schools have been identified — structuralist and proceduralist — the first emphasizing organization structure and the second stressing organization procedure.[3]

Max Weber epitomizes the *structuralist* school of thought through his writing on the ideal-construct he termed "bureaucracy." Many writers argue that the vast majority of large organizations today in varying degrees approximate the ideal type as propounded by Weber, and perhaps most would add that it is this approximation which has such a deleterious effect on the people who work within the organization.[4]

On the subject of bureaucracy, Weber begins his argument by distinguishing among three types of authority.[5] There is *traditional authority*, under which, as the term implies, A obeys B due to rights and status accorded to B by custom. An example here would be the authority of the patriarch in the extended family or that of a tribal chief. There is *charismatic authority*, under which A obeys B due to some "personality" projection of B with which A identifies positively. An example here is the devotion of fan club members or the enthusiasm of teenie-boppers for Pierre Elliot Trudeau in earlier years. And there is *legal authority*, under which A obeys B because A recognizes the legal competence, the "right" of B to tell him what to do. It was this legal authority upon which Weber based the ideal-construct he termed bureaucracy. The best example of it is the universal incidence of positions of formal authority one finds in today's organizations. It refers to the person who tells you what to do, and whom you obey willingly or not, simply because he is the boss.

Weber did not argue that any one of these types of authority could consistently operate without some incidence of the others, at least at times. However, he did insist that the purest type of legal authority was exercised when a bureaucratic staff was present.[6] In this bureaucracy there is a clearly defined layering of authority, a hierarchy, with each person under the control and supervision of a superior. Each person in the organization fills an "office," or position, on the basis of free, contractual agreement, and following from a division of labor based on specialization of function, each person is appointed to his position on the basis of competence demonstrated to superiors. Each office has a specified sphere of competence in that duties are specifically attached to it along with the necessary authority to carry them out. Each person obeys authority because that authority is attached to the position above his own: Each person obeys another only because the other has the "legal" right to give him orders. At the same time, a person is not entitled to give orders to others unless his office clearly gives him that right, and the orders he gives must pertain to the functions of his office. At all times, however, the individual is subject to strict and systematic supervision and discipline based on the principle of hierarchy. To avoid arbitrary, personalistic use of authority, it is clearly stated that the individual is always free to resign but that the employing authority can end his appointment only under certain circumstances, e.g., dereliction of duty.[7]

Weber argued, as have many since, that the growth of the modern organization was synonymous with the elaboration and spread of bureaucracy, and was the single most important phenomenon of the modern Western world. This, he felt, was due to bureaucracy's technical superiority in attaining rationality and efficiency in administration in every field of endeavor, whether capitalist- or socialist-based.[8] This superiority lies in the exercise of control through hierarchy with individuals gaining continually greater expertise as they advance through the ranks on the basis of demonstrated competence rather than on the basis of personalistic or other criteria.

Weber concluded this discussion on the internal consequence of legal authority with the observation that, because of its nature, it is dominated by a spirit of "formalistic impersonality" which leaves it without hatred or passion, but also without affection or enthusiasm. Individuals function without regard to personal considerations; their behavior at all times is governed by strict rules and regulations specified in the name of efficiency and rationality. However, these rules and regulations become emphasized and perpetuated due to the bureaucrats' concern for personal security in the organizations.[9]

While there is considerable disagreement over Weber's ideas, it is commonly held that he was not arguing that the ideal type of bureaucracy did or ever could exist in reality. Rather, drawing upon historical accounts, and on what he saw occurring around him, he concluded that the ideal type was the logical ultimate of organization development. Peter Blau has suggested that the ideal-construct as a methodological tool does not represent an average of the attributes of all existing bureaucracies, but rather is derived by abstracting the most characteristic aspects of all known organizations and combining them into the ideal type.[10]

Methodological points aside, it has been urged that it is impossible to plan an organization structure without at least an implicit concept of the *nature of man* in mind,[11] and this would appear true when devising an ideal structure. There is in Weber's writing on bureaucracy a constant emphasis on the need for discipline and control. He sees bureaucracy itself as a product of human striving for power and self-gain, which harks back clearly to ideas advanced by Machiavelli and Hobbes and, without the moral overtone, echoes much of Christian thought on man's nature. Furthermore, the individual in his personalistic seeking for security and power is seen by Weber as divorced from social ties and institutions, becoming one with the organization and thus losing real individuality. As a recent evaluation of Weber puts it, the impact of bureaucracy on the individual is the extreme limitation of his personal freedom and spontaneity, and his increasing incapacity to understand his own activities in relation to the whole organization.[12] He becomes a cog in a machine.

All this does not mean that Max Weber liked what he saw in the process of bureaucratization. Indeed, he was pessimistic about its ultimate consequences for society and for individuals, despite his belief in its inevitable predominance. The point of concern here is: If Weber did in fact produce the most significant statement to date on bureaucracy,[13] then we must take account of his views on the nature of man in organizations. He saw bureaucracy as having profound negative implications for democracy in the general society; but more importantly for present purposes, bureaucracy, if his views of it are ultimately correct even in a general sense, makes impossible any internal democracy in the organization. Democracy implies a feeling of belonging, of meaningful, positive identification with the social entity. Workers will be essentially alienated from such group feelings, and therefore will not desire what today is termed "participative management." Management for its own reasons will not allow real participation by employees in such matters as decision-making. If such is the case, then much current administrative literature oriented toward participative management is quite unrealistic. One cannot accept very much of Weber's view on the nature of bureaucracy and the nature of man in bureaucracy without being forced to reject the possibility of implementing much of modern motivation-to-work theory. We will return to this point near the end of the chapter.

The ideas of Frederick Taylor epitomize the *procedural* sub-school of the mechanistic tradition, in that Taylor concentrated on process as opposed to structure. As were Weber's ideas on bureaucracy, Taylor's *Principles of Scientific Management*, published in 1911, appears subject to various interpretations — perhaps depending on which part of the book the speaker has in mind. Taylor, for example, believed that the very existence of unions indicated poor management, so if a union leader uses the term "Taylorism" he is almost certainly speaking pejoratively. However, because Taylor stressed productivity, his image is not automatically negative to a businessman.

Taylor began his argument for scientific management by insisting that, although waste of natural resources was both prevalent and undesirable, the less obvious and unacknowledged waste of human energy in work settings was just as bad.[14] He sincerely believed that proper application of his principles would overcome this wastage of human resources by achieving the ultimate worker—"competent man."[15]

Under the best kind of ordinary management, which is called management of initiative and incentive, each worker bears almost the entire responsibility for his general work as well as for each detail of that work.[16] Management's role is to encourage initiative in workers by proffering hope of rapid promotion, higher wages, shorter hours, better working conditions, and so forth. Above all, this type of management operates on a basis of personal consideration for and friendly contact with workers; i.e., management has a genuine, kindly interest in their welfare.[17]

Under scientific management, work and responsibility become more-or-less equally divided between worker and manager. It is management's task to plan out fully the worker's task at least one day in advance, and each worker receives, in most cases, detailed written instructions describing exactly what he is to accomplish as well as how to accomplish it. The worker, of course, remains responsible for achieving what has been scientifically determined he should achieve.[18]

Taylor emphasized that productivity would profoundly benefit from this approach to managing people at work, and used various case studies to justify the contention. And he was very precise in his scientism. For example, when pig-iron (92 pounds) is being loaded, the "first class worker" can only be under load 43 percent of the time and for the other 57 percent must be entirely free from load.[19] Furthermore, the first class man is originally very carefully selected as to particular competence for the job at hand. In the case of loading pig-iron, what is needed is a "stupid," "oxlike" individual;[20] if the task demands greater intelligence, the individual is selected accordingly. The objective was the training and development of each individual so that he could, at his fastest pace and with maximum efficiency, do the highest class of work for which his natural abilities fitted him.[21]

Although some of Taylor's blunt categorizations of people – e.g., "ignorant" and "mentally sluggish"—today do his arguments little good,[22] he was not anti-worker or inhumane. At various points in his book a genuine concern for workers as human beings is apparent, and while the ultimate aim of scientific management was to obtain maximum productivity from the worker, he was never to be asked to work at a rate injurious to his health. Ideally, competent man was to be both happy and healthy.

Taylor clearly made certain assumptions about the nature of man to arrive at his "principles." First, the average worker, he felt, is quite short-sighted and must see his reward in the most immediate future, even the same day, if he is to do his job properly.[23] This implies that the worker is immature or child-like.

Second, Taylor clearly felt that the average worker is basically lazy, and that this is exacerbated by group pressures. "Soldiering," as he called it, comes about from (a) the natural instinct of man to take it easy (natural soldiering) and (b) interacting with others (systematic soldiering).[24] While natural laziness is a serious problem, systematic soldiering is much worse. It occurs from both an individual and group desire to keep management ignorant of just how much could actually be accomplished if workers really tried. In fact, Taylor argued that soldiering is so universal that is is difficult to find an individual who does not devote a considerable part of his day to figuring out just how slowly he can work while convincing his employer that he is working hard indeed.[25]

Third, the only real motivating or reward factor Taylor saw for people in work settings was money, or money-related items such as shorter work days. This assumption of "economic man" is quite apparent throughout Taylor's writings, and every example cited of actual or hypothetical increased productivity, rests on giving money for better performance. Further, Taylor explicitly withdrew from the worker much of the responsibility for his work which today's motivation-to-work theorists stress is a prerequisite for getting people to produce.

While Weber concentrated on administrative structure and Taylor on administrative process, another line of thought was developing which included strong elements of both and which was to have a specific impact on public administration and on administration in general. This school of thought, perhaps best known as the Science of Administration, is said to have its origins in the writings of Henri Fayol.

A French mining engineer and mine manager, Fayol began theorizing on management around the turn of the century, with most of his writing devoted to the idea that a general theory of management, valid for all large organizations, was possible.[26] His major work, *Administration industrielle et générale*, first presented as a lecture in 1908, became a very successful publication in France, and was translated into English and published in 1929 and again in 1949. Another, shorter work, "Administrative Theory in the State," was printed in English in Gulick and Urwick (eds.), *Papers on the Science of Administration* in the mid-1930s.

Fayol's 14 "principles of management" concerned Division of Work, Authority and Responsibility, Discipline, Unity of Command, Unity of Direction, Subordination of Individual Interest to General Interest, Personnel Remuneration, Centralization, Scalar Chain of Command, Order, Equity, Stability of Tenure, Initiative, and Morale.[27] Unlike Taylor, who was primarily concerned with the shop- or worker-level of the organization, Fayol concentrated on the management level, assuming that if this was functioning properly the sub-level would also. His principles were devoted to achievement of *efficiency*, the idea being that if the principles were properly applied in actual situations then efficiency would be maximized. Fayol was not himself generally dogmatic, clearly stating that principles of administration are and should be flexible, capable of being adapted to every need depending on circumstances.[28] He was not consistent in this view, however, for he also argued that a management code must be developed in order to carry out human endeavors in commerce, industry, politics, religion, war, and philanthropy. This code was to be comprised of the "acknowledged truths regarded as proven."[29]

Fayol's ideas had a distinct impact on administrative theory and practice. Just as examples, The Centre for Administrative Studies which he founded had a profound influence on French business, the Army, and the Navy;[30] Lyndall Urwick, who so strongly argued along related lines in the English language, makes specific reference to Fayol's contributions.[31] His principles were adopted and adapted in the United States, particularly in public administration, finding an especially fertile field for their growth due to the statement and elaboration of the politics/administration dichotomy.

Most simply stated, this latter concept insisted that politics was politics and administration was administration. Politicians made policy, whereas administrators simply implemented policy. There was no overlap. This dichotomy was regarded as both an ethical and operational principle in that it ought to exist, could exist, and did exist.

It is easy to see that if public administration consists of a neutral, entirely objective, dispassionate application of policies, then it is much more susceptible to neutral, objective, "scientific" study and to the application of "scientifically" derived principles of administration. In other words, if public servants are believed to be more-or-less automatons in the performance of their duties, then they, their activities, and their organizations will lend themselves more easily to rigorous scientific study. It is only when one acknowledges the humanness of public servants that it becomes difficult to think of them in such categorical fashion.

In the United States two men were particularly influential in promoting the principles of administration. Luther Gulick and Lyndall Urwick, members of the President's Committee of Administrative Science established under Franklin D. Roosevelt, published a collection of essays they edited for presentation to the Committee, entitled *Papers on the Science of Administration* (1937). In the Foreword Gulick stated that if those concerned scientifically with administration proceeded along the lines suggested by the various articles, then a valid and accepted theory of administration was possible. Even more strongly, Urwick urged in his article, "Organization as a Technical Problem"[32] that there are universal principles of administration which should govern arrangements for human organizations. These principles are relevant no matter the purpose of the organization, the personnel involved, or the constitutional, political, or social theory underlying the organization's creation.[33] In other words, to these men and to many others of their time, the administrative principles that had been derived from experience and study were, or at least could be, "laws" differing little in nature from the laws of the natural sciences.

A good example of these principles is contained in the term POSDCORB, an acronym in such wide use at the time that it led to the description of theory and practice of administration in that era as "POSDCORB administration."[34] It stood for Planning, Organizing, Staffing, Directing, Coordinating, Reporting, and Budgeting. Borrowing from Fayol, Gulick, in advancing POSDCORB, argued that this concept not only did include each of the major activities and duties of any chief executive, but also that all the elements of POSDCORB should be included in the activities and duties of any chief executive.[35] By sub-dividing the various elements for analytical as well as for practical purposes, all of administrative reality could be comprehended.[36] As with Weber and Taylor, achievement of efficiency was the prime goal. Gulick, for example, argued that in the Science of Administration, the basic "good" being sought was the attainment of efficiency, defined as the accomplishment of work with the least expenditure of human and material resources.[37] Further, they tended strongly to see people in organizations as cogs in a machine, as easily interchangeable parts, not a human problem (as is well illustrated by both the title and tenor of Urwick's well-known article, "Organization as a Technical Problem"[38]). And they tended to view man in the economic-rational sense, although, particularly in Fayol's case, this was not stressed as much as in Taylor.

In summary, although the Mechanist writers had differing viewpoints and proceeded from different starting points, they nevertheless had certain assumptions and conclusions in common, for example about the nature of man. They essentially viewed man as an economically rational being always intent on maximizing his material gains. They saw him as needing a strong element of control and discipline if he was to produce at reasonable levels. And they tended to see him as a given, as a cog in a machine and an easily interchangeable part. Mason Haire has summarized this view of man by suggesting he is lazy, short-sighted, selfish, error-prone, lacking in judgement and probably dishonest.[39]

Furthermore, given the controllability and predictability of man, they tended to see administration as capable of being not only scientifically studied, but also as being capable of generating more-or-less scientific "truths" by which all organizations could be rationally governed in order to achieve maximum efficiency (defined in simple terms of lowest ratio input to output). While then, as now, government operations posed some measurement problems not faced by private organizations, there was reciprocal influence from the two sectors. Taylor, for example, had a distinct impact on public administration,[40] and Gulick and Urwick had like influence on the private sector.[41] Many, it has been argued, owed a considerable intellectual debt to Max Weber.[42]

The Humanists

These various ideas had no sooner reached their peak of theoretical expression and practical acceptance than they came under serious attack. From about 1930 to 1950 all had come under fire and, at least in an academic sense, had been considerably discredited. This does not mean, however, that they are unimportant today. As will be seen, strong vestiges of them remain with us in both administrative theory and practice.[43]

Elton Mayo is commonly credited as the foremost writer in what came to be called the Human Relations school of administrative or management thought. His major work was *The Human Problems of an Industrial Civilization*, first published in 1933. It exposed the inadequacy of studying the individual as an isolated unit of production and of taking account only of the physical environment of the work setting,[44] and came to constitute a frontal attack on the whole idea of Scientific Management in particular and on the mechanistic tradition in general.

In 1927 an experiment was begun at the Hawthorne Works of the Western Electric Company in Chicago in collaboration with Harvard University. The experiment commenced quite orthodoxly for the time by attempting to establish a relationship between the amount of lighting in the work setting and worker output. Also orthodox were the initial assumptions held by the experimenters. These were: factory organization is a technological not a human problem; man is a rational-economic being; and output is a direct and simple result of the relationship between working conditions and the physical state of the worker.[45] We will not here go into the details of this and subsequent experiments, as they have been discussed and analyzed, praised and criticized in a vast body of social science as well as industrial literature. The end result of the initial experiment was the discovery that output could not be correlated with the environmental factor. Output increased when the amount of light was increased, but it also increased when the amount of light was decreased. This led to more elaborate, long-term experimentation out of which Mayo ultimately developed his ideas on industrial society. It was found, for example, that the mental attitude of workers was a crucial variable in production, and that this attitude in turn was related to such things as the strictness of supervision and the degree to which workers were allowed to vary from a fixed pace without reprimand.[46] That is, workers' output increased as workers experienced more pleasant, freer, happier working conditions.[47] Pay incentives were not an irrelevant factor in creating greater productivity, but it was the mental attitude that was crucial.

Related to this was the major finding that the work group could have great meaning to the worker, affect his happiness, and therefore influence his productivity. The group achieves much more meaning for itself and for its members if supervisors allow the group to set, or at least help set, its own work conditions. This group freedom allows the individual to experience the sense of freedom he so greatly desires. This was, in Mayo's view, a natural, inevitable human need. Individuals in all societies need a "non-logical" social code which regulates their attitudes and their interrelationships with others. If a purely economic (rational) code is imposed upon them – on the basis of assumptions, for example, like those of Taylor—people will experience a sense of defeat and at a lower, informal level, opposed to the economic code, will develop their own group, non-logical code. The end result of this is restriction of output.[48] In short, treating the individual as if he is an economically rational, isolated unit of production for purposes of creating greater productivity is self-defeating. The individual is a member of the group and needs the group in order to find self-meaning, without which he will be unhappy. Mayo, as one writer ironically suggests, replaced the "rabble" hypothesis with the "herd" hypothesis.[49]

While up to this point Mayo's theorizing essentially reflected an orthodox concern for industrial productivity, he more humanistically proceeded to broad generalizations on the nature of industrial society, its meaning for the individual, and the roles of government and management in that society. Drawing on very disparate sources – for example, Freud, Durkheim, a study of South Sea Islanders, and a contemporary study of delinquency in Chicago — he concluded that industrialization has broken down old, very necessary communal relationships which involved meaningful collaboration with others. This left the individual only the recourse of pursuing economic gain.[50] A vicious circle is thus created, as the latter pursuit only leads to further social disintegration.[51] Political action can do nothing to change this situation because, according to Mayo, effective political action in a community requires a sense of community on the part of its citizens — the desire and ability of a number of individuals to work together.[52] This desire and ability, as he asserted, have become increasingly less evident as industrialization has proceeded.

Since industrial society is a fact, the only solution Mayo saw was somehow to restore effective human collaboration and thus re-create meaningful human relationships. This, he felt, could only be achieved through the creation and recognition of an administrative elite whose enlightened management of large organizations would provide meaning to people's life through their membership in them.[53] This elite would be created through education, although Mayo was far from precise in suggesting exactly how this would work. In effect, however, management was to become the savior of society.

The end result of the Hawthorne experiments was to change profoundly management theory and, to a considerable extent, management practice. The demonstration that man is a social animal led easily to the view that there are distinct organizational, as well as humane, advantages to treating him as a responsible human being rather than as a cog in a machine.[54] This was all obviously in direct conflict with the major theoretical underpinnings of Scientific Management and to a considerable extent with the bases of the Science of Administration. (It is interesting to note that *The Human Problems of an Industrial Civilization* was published prior to *Papers on the Science of Administration*.) Mayo's ideas were to become the basis upon which the Human Relations school of administrative theory and practice subsequently developed. Although, as will be discussed below, the Human Relations school has undergone considerable change to the present, a constant element in most modern theory is the assumption of responsible man, and, much less explicit, the assumption of management as some sort of savior of society.

Barely had Max Weber's ideas on bureaucracy become generally known through translation to English-speaking scholars of administration (in the mid-1940s) when he came under attack from several directions. For example, Carl Friedrich questioned the entire logic of the ideal type, pointing to illogic and inconsistency on Weber's part in his elaboration of it. He also pointed out that Weber used such normative terms as "fully developed," "effectiveness of legal authority," and "acceptance of validity" as if they were unquestionable absolutes.[55] Frederic Burin questioned the idea of bureaucracy's inevitability and its on-going nature despite political and social change by pointing to the collapse of Weberian-described bureaucracy in Nazi Germany.[56] Alvin Gouldner argued that bureaucracy was not at all as impersonal as Weber suggested, that there is not a consistent impersonal application of rules within it—for example, rules are less and less strict as one moves up the bureaucratic levels.[57] And Herbert Simon, along the lines of his general critique of administrative principles, suggested that Weber used terms much too simplistically — for example, it is not sufficient to talk merely of specialization of function, one also must specify what manner of specialization, and along what lines, to achieve administrative efficiency.[58]

The attack against Weber's ideas on bureaucracy (as well as his views on numerous other subjects) continues today, although he also has his supporters. For example, critics of modern bureaucracy insist, like Weber, that there is a great deal of homogeneity within given bureaucracies, and some insist this homogeneity exists between bureaucracies. This is often deplored, depending on the writer, due to its strong tendency toward lack of initiative and creativity, lack of compassion and empathy, unwillingness to accept responsibility, inability to cope with clientele who adhere to other values and see reality differently. On the other hand, numerous studies can be cited which purport to demonstrate that this homogeneity does not exist, that one can find more differences than similarities in the attitudes and behavior of people within a bureaucracy, and certainly between bureaucracies. Actually, Weber's writings on bureaucracy have become a major bone of contention among a number of sociologists. Some say there's no validity at all to Weber's theories; others insist there is (although many of this group appear to use his ideas on bureaucracy only in order to declaim against its inhumanity[59]).

The attack against the Science of Administration was aimed at both the concept of the politics/administration dichotomy as well as the principles of administration. The dichotomy concept, which will be mentioned only briefly here as it is dealt with in a later chapter, was obviously in retreat by the mid-1940s. It was becoming increasingly apparent that not only were administrators already involved in policy formulation, but that, because of the ever-more complex nature of the government matters and because of the bureaucracy's growing expertise in these matters, administrators should be involved in policy formulation.[60]

The principles of administration were attacked on both logical and practical grounds. Herbert Simon is generally credited with being the first to make an elaborate, definitive attack against them in an article published in *Public Administration Review* in 1946. This was followed in 1947 in the same journal by Robert Dahl's article entitled "The Science of Administration: Three Problems"[61] and in the same year by Dwight Waldo in his book *The Administrative State*.

Using Simon's argument, "The Proverbs of Administration"[62] as the example of the attack, he argued forcefully and effectively that administration was not scientific in the sense that it had "principles." Those so-called principles that had been developed, he suggested, were quite analogous to proverbs in the sense that they usually came in mutually contradictory pairs—for example, "Look before you leap" is countered by "He who hesitates is lost." Similarly, no matter how plausible an administrative principle may appear, there will be an equally plausible contradictory principle, the two leading to opposite conclusions and actions while at the same time there will be no way of determining which is the right one to apply. One of the examples that Simon used concerned "span of control." One principle in this regard was: administrative efficiency is increased by limiting the span of control at any point of the hierarchy to a small number. Another principle stated: Administrative efficiency is enhanced by keeping at a minimum the number of organizational levels through which a matter must pass before it is acted upon. As Simon argued, pursuance of restricted span of control will perhaps achieve greater control over subordinates but will also lead to excessive red tape as matters for decision have to be carried up through numerous layers of authority until a common superior is found, and then downward in the form of orders and instructions—all of which is cumbersome, time-consuming, and "inefficient." On the other hand, the principle based on wider span of control may circumvent the red-tape problem but it runs the risk of the supervisor's being unable to effectively control actions of subordinates. A modern, somewhat whimsical example of the clash of principles concerns the Peter Principle and the Great Shelf Principle. The first states that every individual reaches his level of incompetence, while the second argues that the individual is generally "shelved" somewhere in the organization long before he has achieved his potential contribution to the organization. In short, commonly accepted principles lead to radically different conclusions and actions, and there is no way given to us to choose among them.

Thus, by 1950 several decades of administrative theory and practice were substantially discredited.[63] In general, it was more and more emphasized that administration is very complex and is not susceptible, or at least not easily susceptible, to "scientific" application as that term had been used. A new, humanistic and optimistic view of man emerged, a view that saw him as very complex but also at the very least capable of self-direction and self-control, even if not always achieving them. It also saw man in a much less individualistic sense, not as an atom or isolated unit of production but as a human being with a variety of motivations other than chance of material gain and involved in complex interrelationships with others.

As noted previously, however, the older ideas were never entirely discredited in theory, and certainly not in practice, and in modern guise many of them are with us today. This point will be returned to after a brief look at some of the developments since the 1940s.

The Neo-Humanists

The new conception of man at work suggested the basic need for a new philosophy of management as well as new practices built upon that philosophy. This philosophy came to be known as the "Human Relations" school of thought and has been defined as the study of the integration of people into work situations through knowledge and understanding of their attitudes, sentiments, and interrelationships.[64] And what came to be known as the "Human Relations Approach" to administrative practice has been defined as the application of this knowledge and understanding of people's attitudes, sentiments, and interrelationships to actual work situations.[65]

This latter point raises a basic question that has plagued both the theory and practice of Human Relations in organizations since their beginning: What is the *essential* point underlying Human Relations? Is it genuine concern for people as human beings? That is, is the main thrust of Human Relations humanitarian in nature? Or is the primary concern maximizing, or at least optimizing, productivity? Is the essential purpose of Human Relations an attempt to manipulate people so as to get them to work harder? This question, and the varying answers to it, are what today make this entire area of "people in organizations" so problematical.

There is no doubt that Mayo himself was production-oriented. For that matter, the Hawthorne Experiments themselves commenced not only with Taylorian assumptions but also with Taylorian purpose – how to increase productivity. Mayo, however, seems to have gone beyond simple concern for production in his arguments for restoration of meaning to the individual's life, although whether this second concern was dominant with him is impossible to say. Furthermore, even if Human Relations researchers were interested neither in bettering the lives of people nor in increasing productivity *per se*, but only in gaining knowledge of people for its own sake, it can still be claimed that the research was used for selfish organizational purposes– i.e., it was used to manipulate people.[66]

A common charge laid against Human Relations, not only by scholars of a humanitarian bent but also by tough-minded union leaders, is that management cynically uses non-material incentives merely in order to increase or at least maintain production levels without having to give employees greater material benefits. For example, participation by employees in decision-making affecting their jobs has always been advocated by Human Relations theorists. However, the charge can be, and has been, easily made that management's solicitation of employee opinions is really based on the Machiavellian expectation that employees will be much more likely to accept and implement decisions already made by management if they can be led to believe that they have participated in making those decisions.[67]

Another major criticism levelled against Human Relations was the charge that it was really an unworkable, unproductive way of achieving organization goals. The idea was that an organization exists for a purpose, and whatever that purpose may be, it must remain primary, and all concerned with achieving the purpose must remain secondary.[68] In this view, what Human Relations did was put the cart before the horse, with the result that the organization could no longer function effectively because its basic reason for existence was so de-emphasized.[69]

A related charge was that it was an error to assume that the practice of Human Relations – the creation, e.g., of greater morale – led to greater or at least sustained productivity. Instead, it was urged that the practice of Human Relations encouraged employees to feel sorry for themselves, to excuse failure, to act like children, and it encouraged executives to become so concerned with employee problems and excuses that they could no longer make organizationally-effective decisions.[70]

It is important to note that the problem with such arguments, then as now, was that they really could not be resolved. It appears quite reasonable to assume, for example, that some organizations and some managers cynically exploited the findings of Human Relations researchers. But must it also be assumed that all, or even most, did so? Were the exploiters the norm or the exception? On the basis of *evidence* available, as opposed to allegations, the question cannot be answered either way. Furthermore, it is also important to note the contradiction built into these illustrations of the controversy. For example, if indeed managers could not make effective decisions because of their concern for employee problems, then it would be difficult to assume that management was really concerned only with the manipulative potential of Human Relations theory. On the other hand, if Human Relations was disparaged because it tended to play down the organization's purpose, then perhaps Human Relations practice had the intent of only furthering that purpose with no genuine regard for employee benefit.

Despite any resistance to the idea, Human Relations has persisted. However, researchers have become increasingly sophisticated in their methodologies and techniques, as well as in their conclusions, and the emphasis has shifted somewhat from the earlier group basis to the individual *per se*. For want of a better term, this new direction in studying people in work situations can be labelled "motivation-to-work" theory which in turn can be subsumed under the more generic term "modern human resource management" theory. This field is extremely broad, it possesses a vast body of literature, and it rests to a great extent on the sub-discipline of psychology that was previously known as "industrial psychology" but that is increasingly being labelled "organization psychology." Due to the huge size of the subject, the work of only a very few of the major theorists can be discussed.[71]

The selection of the work of Abraham Maslow as a starting point seems reasonable due to his positive influence on most later motivation theorists. Even those theorists who do not base their ideas on his, generally go to considerable lengths to explain their rejection. Furthermore, it is difficult to conceive of a Canadian personnel manager in either the public or private sector who cannot provide some recounting of Maslow's "hierarchy of needs." For that matter, given the increasingly high level of education of Canadian employees, including public employees, probably millions have some knowledge of the hierarchy either from university courses or from the great variety of in-service courses provided by employers today.

Maslow published a major paper on this topic in 1943 entitled "A Theory of Human Motivation"[72] and in it proposed the "hierarchy of needs." This need hierarchy is typically represented as a pyramid, with the needs most important or primary to the individual lying on the bottom tiers of the pyramid, and with progression upward as the primary needs are gratified. Basically, his argument was that normal human beings all have these five categories of needs, and it is in their striving to fulfill a need that they are motivated to act. Acts, that is, do not occur in a vacuum; they are related to need fulfillment. Further, the idea of hierarchy is very important, as the higher-level needs will not generally become motivators of behavior until the lower-level needs are reasonably gratified. As a corollary of this, once a need is reasonably gratified, it will no longer be a motivator of behavior.

The physiological needs, according to Maslow, are clearly the most important of all and include food, drink, sleep, sex, and so forth. The safety needs involve personal security from threat and harm from weather, hunger, criminals, or whatever. These two categories of needs, physiological and safety, are primary to the individual and can dominate him to the exclusion of all influence on him of the other needs. Unless these primary needs are basically gratified, the other needs simply will not exist for the individual.

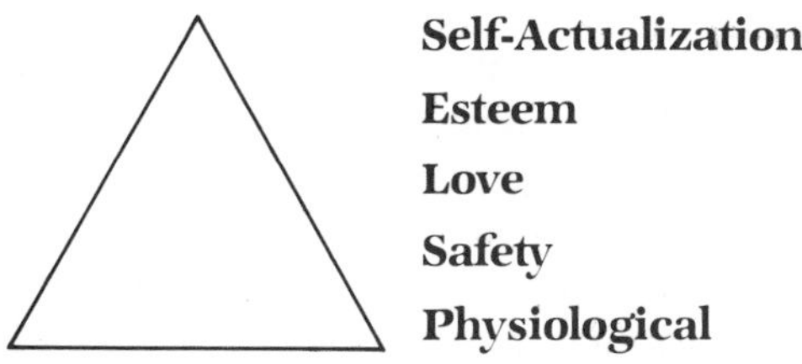

If the primary needs are gratified, then the love needs, which include the need to receive and give love and affection and to have a sense of belonging, will emerge as motivators of behavior. The individual will strive for affection and meaningful relationships. Again, once this need is gratified, the esteem needs will become motivators of behavior. These needs include the need for achievement, feeling of adequacy and confidence, independence and freedom, prestige and recognition, and importance. Finally, once esteem needs are reasonably gratified, the individual may come under the influence of self-actualization needs. These, as Maslow notes, cannot be generalized as they can take forms ranging from maternalism to athleticism to aestheticism. Perhaps they can be summed up crudely by saying that they involve the individual striving to become what he sees himself ideally to be.

Important to Maslow's thesis, and to much of later motivation-to-work theory, is his assertion that in our modern society the physiological and safety needs have already been met to a very great extent, and therefore cannot be looked to as motivators of behavior. And if this was true in 1943, it must be even more true today.[73]

There are many well-known writers in the field of motivation-to-work theory, as well as many more less well-known writers.[74] Theorists base their arguments on experimental studies they have conducted and, in a number of cases, on their successful and unsuccessful experiences as members of that growing industry known as "management consultancy." Quite arbitrarily two such theories will be briefly presented here, that of Chris Argyris who has conducted research in both government and business and who bases his ideas explicitly on Maslow's need hierarchy, and that of Frederick Herzberg who has strong overtones of Maslow but who has added his well-known "hygiene-motivator" thesis and whose extensive lecture tours have made him familiar to students, businessmen, and public servants across the United States and Canada.

Argyris sees the organization as a system with material as well as energy inputs, a conversion process, and outputs in the form of goods and/or services.[75] The human side of the energy input consists of physiological as well as psychological energy, which are interrelated. Putting aside physiological energy (which of course is extremely important), the argument is that psychological energy exists in all individuals, that its expression cannot easily be blocked, and that its amount varies with the individual's state of mind. This state of mind in turn depends upon the individual's ability to pursue and to fulfill those needs which are most important to him. That is, the more the individual can pursue and fulfill these needs, the more psychological energy he will have available. In organizational terms, then, the more the organization permits the individual to experience feelings of psychological success, the more energy he will have available to put toward organization goals.

This brings in Maslow's need hierarchy. Following Maslow's own assertions, Argyris argues that physiological and safety needs have, in today's society, largely been met in the case of people working for large organizations. People are not going to starve, they are not pushed anywhere near the limits of physical endurance, and they live in relative affluence with many material possessions for their enjoyment as well as security. Thus the two primary needs are no longer as potent as they once were in motivating people to work, while conversely the higher-level needs have become much more important.

While not totally ignoring the next two levels of the need hierarchy, love and esteem needs, Argyris concentrates on the idea of self-actualization in the work setting. Indeed, he, like many others, tends to collapse the three higher levels into one under the rubric "self-actualization." He argues that neither the individual nor the organization can realize any benefit from the creation of feelings of psychological success and the release of psychological energy due to: (a) specialization of function and work fractioning, to the extent that the individual often has no conception of the overall output he is engaged in; (b) responsibility for planning work, and for defining and controlling output rates belongs essentially to management rather than to those actually doing the work; (c) responsibility for issuing orders, changing work, and making shifts in assignments, belongs to management; (d) responsibility for performance evaluation, and determination of rewards and penalties belongs to management; and (e) management ultimately controls membership in the organization. There are several results of all this. First, few of the employee's abilities will be used, and those that are will tend to have the least potential for achieving for him feelings of psychological success. Second, the employee will tend to become dependent and subservient. And, third, the employee will undergo a decreasing sense of self-responsibility and self-control. In short, rather than creating opportunities for the employee to pursue psychological success by allowing him some fulfillment of his higher-level needs, the organization very typically guarantees that the employee will experience feelings of psychological failure, and neither the organization nor the individual gain from this condition.

This leads Argyris to three propositions. First, there is a lack of congruence between the demands of the pyramidal organization and the needs of individuals. Second, people in the organization will experience frustration, failure, short-time perspective, and conflict — all of which lead to deleterious consequences for both individual and organization. And, third, the degree of incongruency (first proposition) and therefore the degree of frustration and so forth (second proposition) will increase as people's desire for psychological success feelings increase, as dependence, subordination and so forth increase, as jobs become more specialized and fractionized, and as the organization attempts to implement traditional (e.g., Taylorian) management principles.

Argyris ironically concludes that while the organization has led in our society to the "good life" where physiological and safety needs no longer dominate us, it has at the same time created the conditions whereby the higher-level needs, which have become relatively much more important to us, are no longer capable of being meaningfully pursued except by the few — i.e., by those in the upper levels of the organization hierarchy. This means a basic loss to the individual, and also a basic loss to the organization because it is forced to rely on those motivators which today are the least potent in achieving desired behavior.

In the field of industrial-organization psychology Frederick Herzberg is renowned for the statement, elaboration, and "preaching" of his "motivation hygiene" thesis. There cannot be many managers in North America today who have not heard of him — whether or not they have understood his message or agreed with it. On the basis of studies first reported in *The Motivation to Work*,[76] as well as subsequent studies by himself and others, Herzberg argues that people in work situations face two sets of variables. One set, termed "motivation factors," relates to job satisfaction, while the other set, called "hygiene factors," refers to job dissatisfaction.

The hygiene factors concern the job environment and have considerable resemblance to what Maslowian theory terms "primary factors." The major hygiene factors are company policy and administration, supervision, salary, interpersonal relations, and working conditions.[77] On the basis of a medical analogy these factors are hygienic because proper attention to them can prevent illness, i.e., dissatisfaction — but they alone will not lead to health — i.e., satisfaction. Giving a worker more money or better working conditions, for example, may keep him from being dissatisfied, but will not lead to his satisfaction except perhaps at times on a short-term basis.

It is the motivation factors which lead to genuine worker satisfaction. Five factors have been identified as predominant: achievement, recognition, the work itself, responsibility and advancement, the last three in particular leading to a lasting change of attitudes. All, however, lead to personal growth and self-actualization, and it is the pursuance and realization of these factors that motivates the employee in the work situation. Put differently, the two sets of factors relate to two different need structures in the human being. Hygiene factors concern the need to avoid unpleasantness, while motivation factors relate to the need for personal growth, the latter being the characteristic distinguishing man from his fellow animals.

Today in Canada

As noted earlier, there are dozens of other writers in the area of motivation-to-work, but almost all present variations of a central theme — man's need in today's relatively safe, affluent society to pursue his higher-level needs, needs generally referred to as "self-actualization." This appears to be the underlying philosophy and working principle of most personnel work today. In the last decade innumerable seminars and workshops have been held at all levels of government for all levels of employees, propounding the basic message that man wants to self-actualize and that his job and his supervisors must allow him to do so.[78]

Earlier, "job enlargement" programs were the rage, involving a horizontal job-loading which essentially gave the employee more of similar things to do. When these proved not particularly useful, they were replaced with "job enrichment" schemes which involve vertical job loading, giving the employee more self-responsibility and more self-determination. Broader concepts such as MBO (Management by Objectives) which became popular several years ago in both industry and government had as one underlying motif the idea that people would not only accept but actually desired and would work better for considerable self-responsibility in their jobs. Most of the growing literature on OD (Organization Development) stresses the importance of the higher level needs of workers. Broad-based theories of QOL (Quality of Life) which involve general social concerns generally have strong QOWL (Quality of Work Life) components in them.[79] In short, "job satisfaction" and "self-actualization" are the "in" terms today in personnel administration.

Furthermore, it is commonly argued, with clear echoes of Mayo, that it is today's large employers, government and business, who have the terrible responsibility for providing people with more job satisfaction, first for themselves but ultimately because people who are more satisfied with their work are more satisfied with life in general and become better parents and better citizens.[80] More narrowly, it has been urged by Bryce Mackasey, then Minister of Labour, addressing the National Industrial Conference Board, that the root cause of industrial strife in Canada is to be found in the neglect of the motivational side of industrial relations.[81] Mackasey has also argued that the individual must learn how to make the organization and his job serve his ends, values, and desire to achieve. He quotes Prime Minister Trudeau as saying to a youthful segment of the work force: "You have been telling us that many of the employment opportunities in Canada are not meaningful to you. . . . You tell us what is meaningful, what is important, and we'll support you."[82] Along these lines motivation principles have been built into a wide variety of job situations in general, and Herzberg in particular has enjoyed considerable vogue in such agencies as Bell Canada, Canadian National Railways, and the Canadian Armed Forces. As one writer argues, the evidence is increasing that a growing number of public servants find their jobs lacking in satisfaction and that pressure is mounting for the implementation of job-enrichment schemes.[83] Certainly, all levels of government in Canada today have "personnel development" agencies staffed by people conversant with current behavioral theories, one of whose major functions it is to concern themselves with "employee satisfaction."[84]

Of course, all this theory has its critics, who argue from a variety of bases. The motivation-to-work field in general has been charged with lack of scientific humility, in that it emulates earlier theorists such as Mayo by making extravagant generalizations on the basis of insufficient and/or inconclusive data. It is accused of lack of coherence and integration in its theorizing. It ignores other basic psychological theory, such as that which argues that in most cases the individual's personality is essentially developed by the late teens, and therefore the ability to modify the personality strucutre at work is rather dubious. And because of its "in" nature, all sorts of people inadequately, if at all, conversant with the relevant literature are jumping on the bandwagon, using the jargon, and perhaps doing serious harm even if with the best of intentions.[85]

Another line of argument proceeds from ethical-moral grounds and concerns such concepts as "development." Individual development is a key term in all this literature, but it is almost invariably used with no clear, explicit meaning attached to it. Generally, when we use the term "development" we have in mind something along the lines of "change toward something better." We certainly do not usually mean "change toward something worse"; for that condition we employ terms such as "decay" and "regression." But use of the word "better" only confounds the problem, because what do we mean when we say "better"? Is "better" related to the production of more for the same or lesser cost? Is it connected to the realization of full human potential, regardless of any cost-production factors? If the latter, do we all agree on the elements of "full human potential"? It would obviously appear to be related, in work settings, to an optimistic view of the nature of man, since the various writers on the subject scarcely seem to be arguing that man's ability to laze should have its fullest expression.[86]

These are not idle questions. Unless we can agree on the answers to them, much of the motivation-to-work literature, which stresses self-actualization, cannot be understood and/or utilized. As noted earlier, Maslow himself argued that self-actualization could take many forms, but most subsequent writers seem to assume that the forms taken will be "good." Why this should be the case is not at all clear. The situation is analogous to much older political-philosophical literature dealing with the relationship between the individual and the State. For example, one definition of democracy implies the creation of conditions under which all individuals have an equal chance to achieve their potential as human beings. Obviously, certain potential outcomes are desirable, while others are not. A person should be free to realize his potential to become Prime Minister of Canada, but should not be free to realize his potential to become a Canadian Jack-the-Ripper. The first agrees with what we feel is "good," while the second relates to what we feel is "bad." Similarly, such terms in administrative literature as "self-actualization" are acceptable to us only if we assume that what people will strive for is acceptable or at least tolerable to our own values. But, are we agreed upon values? At the very least, we must make them explicit.

A closely related line of questions involves the concern about manipulation that some argue is inherent in current theory and practice as they have developed from the earlier Human Relations theory and practice; that is, what prompts the use of motivation-to-work theory? Is there a genuine concern for human beings as human beings, or is creation of job-satisfaction really a cynical attempt stated in modern social science terminology to get employees to produce more for less material reward? Is it really simply a case that any organization that can create feelings of being wanted, needed, responsible and happy, creates a "sense of loyalty and dedication that will be repaid with extraordinary effort"?[87] Are managers encouraged to be flexible so as to allow for employee satisfaction *per se*, or is this flexibility based on the manager's being "always mindful of his essential role of achieving *maximum productivity*."[88] In short, are we seeking to fulfill basic human needs or is this fulfillment only incidental to what Borden's discovered years ago, that Contented Cows Give More Milk?

Furthermore, whatever the answers to the above questions, does management have the "right" to engage in practices that involve modification of people's attitudes and behavior? On what moral-ethical grounds can we justify the direction of modification as the "proper" human direction? Of course, in child-rearing we all engage in behavior modification, whether or not we explicitly recognize that we are doing so. But this practice is based on centuries-old custom, and for that matter is not today entirely at the discretion of parents, as evidenced by child-welfare legislation as well as the recent Children's Rights movement. We also engage in behavior modification in areas such as law enforcement and mental health, but in these instances specific agencies are granted specific authority by specific legislation to carry out specific programs. These situations are not analogous to the use of behavior modification techniques and practices in organizations. Management has always been able to attempt to achieve desired behavior by coercion and reward; but this, some argue, is very different from management's determining what people should believe and how they should behave, and then hiring a battery of specialists to subtly, even covertly, manipulate them into believing and behaving "properly."[89]

Still another line of argument is pragmatically based and concerns material rewards. Any Canadian who reads newspapers or watches television could well ask: If Canadian employees today are really more concerned with self-actualization as opposed to money, why are wage and salary demands such a prevalent news item? Why do strikes, or the threat of strikes, which almost always involve material demands, occur every week in Canada, involving such disparate employee categories as school teachers and liquor store employees, nurses and dockworkers, letter carriers and air traffic controllers? If people today are more secure and less interested in money, why are hitherto unorganized groups such as university professors now forming unions to push their demands for salary and tenure? Why do medical associations resist government fee-setting? Why did the Anti-Inflation Board come into existence? Obviously there is abundant evidence to justify those who doubt the importance of self-actualization at work.[90]

Still another line of argument disparages the importance not of self-actualization itself, but the importance of it in the work setting. Thus, for example, a dean of a business and public administration school has suggested that we live in a society which from earliest childhood conditions us to accept work values or inculcates the work ethic. While in earlier years this was necessary for both personal and societal survival, the same stress on the ethic is today no longer necessary or desirable. We live in a time of contrived needs, busily working away at projects which will not benefit us and, given rapidly changing technology and society, have dubious benefit for the future. But we pursue these activities because the work ethic persists so strongly. Something is wrong if we are not working. Robert Coe suggests, why not begin to put work into its proper perspective? Why not see it as similar to a trip to the dentist, a necessary act performed as pleasantly and quickly as possible with the minimum human involvement?[91]

Related to this line of thought are some of the arguments against seeing the organization as some sort of savior of society or, more specifically, savior of the individual. This savior concept appears, for example, in Plato's *Republic* and later in the writings of St. Simon and Carlyle. In a generalized fashion it is connected to a long history of elite theory. Elton Mayo expressed it in modern administrative theory, and was attacked on the grounds that it was indefensible to see the work organization as the only institution capable of providing genuine meaning to man's life.[92] In more recent years numerous questions have been raised over current theories stressing the importance of the individual's finding meaning in his work. On what moral-ethical grounds do we assign the role of providing meaning in life to the work organization? Further, what is wrong with viewing the job in a utilitarian light, as providing the means whereby we can self-actualize elsewhere? Some of us perhaps enjoy work as such, but others may self-actualize on our own time in a wide variety of ways, from snowmobiling to charitable work, from electioneering to watching television, from philately to philandering. In short, the argument again is that the work ethic — not just the need to work but the need to find meaning in work — is far too greatly stressed today.

A final point to raise here is the possible futility of making the work organization meaningful to the individual except in a utilitarian, materialistic sense. This can be viewed from two aspects (a) the genuine receptivity of management to theories emphasizing self-actualization; and (b) the practical ability of management to put theory into practice, assuming it should genuinely wish to do so.

In the first instance, it can be argued that, while management may pay a great deal of lip service to modern motivation theory, its willingness to practise it is debatable. Such ideas as self-responsibility, participative management and democratic leadership have been so much vaunted that they have become part of our current work philosophy. In fact, they reflect, in organization terms, the strong current in our society today toward egalitarianism and individual worth. As one writer has suggested, to argue effectively against modern human resource management theory would be tantamount to shooting Smokey the Bear for sport.[93] It just isn't done.

Yet, is management really "democratically" oriented? There is a considerable body of literature along the lines of Robert Presthus' *The Organizational Society* which argues that the person who typically succeeds in organizations has a personality from which one would not expect much charity toward subordinates. That is, this "upwardly mobile" individual becomes a manager because he is ambitious, and to succeed must develop a considerable degree of ruthlessness toward his fellow competitors. If this is the case, while we can assume this individual will probably express himself in terms of current organization ideology, can we expect him to practise what he may preach? The common sense answer would seem to be "no." This point will shortly be returned to in another context.

Concerning the second aspect, a major contention in the controversy over motivation-to-work is that most such ideas are hopelessly limited in their perspective. The theories tend to view the organization in a sort of vacuum, rather than as a sub-society of a much larger society. Hence theorists perpetuate the same error in studying the organization that earlier thinkers committed concerning the individual, when they insisted on seeing him as an isolated unit of production. There are two interrelated factors to consider here.

First, an organization is a system which has numerous components all interacting and interdependent. One component, management, while important to the system's functioning, cannot be viewed as it so often is, as the single causal factor which determines the behavior of all other factors. So, for example, while all sorts of theories urge managers to trust employees to be self-responsible, they do not urge the employees to trust their bosses to do the best for them, the employees. The "trust" relationship, if it is to be functional must be reciprocal, and while conceivably management might somehow train itself along the lines suggested by motivation-to-work theory, this would appear somewhat pointless if at the same time employees cannot learn to trust management.

This leads to the second factor, something warned against in the introduction to this chapter. While at one level of analysis it is quite proper to see the organization as a system, at a more holistic level the organization must be seen as a sub-system of a much larger system, the general society. In this larger system certain things occur which have their impact on the sub-system and will be reflected in the sub-system's internal functioning. For example, if we assume that various socializing agencies, such as the family and school, generally teach young people to believe that a meaningful job in an organization is a valuable and realistic goal for which to strive, then they will want that meaningful job, will work to attain it and will be pleased when they do. However, the meaning of "meaningful" is also taught by the socializing agencies and the work organization has no direct control over the definition. On the one hand, children are taught to be cooperative, to be useful members of groups striving for common goals, to love others and to share with them. Meaningful jobs for them as adults will therefore have to accommodate these attitudes and attendant behaviors. On the other hand, our children are also taught in a wide variety of ways to be very competitive, to fight for grades, for goals, to fight, in fact, for love and social esteem. What is "meaningful" in a job will have to recognize this competitive element.

Perhaps the end result of our socialization process, then, is the creation of personalities who cannot easily, if at all, co-exist in job situations. If the "love thy brother" attitudes are dominant, then "meaningful job" will have one definition, while it will have another, quite different definition if the "climb on top of thy brother" attitudes prevail. What is certain is that management does not control the content of socialization; it can only attempt to work with the diverse products. Further, should there be any reality at all to this characterization of personality types, it would seem to follow that management cannot supply "meaningful jobs" to both.[94]

Max Weber in his discussion of bureaucracy made some of the first statements dealing with this situation when he talked of the bureaucrats' drive for power with attendant secretiveness and ruthlessness – they were people without hatred or passion and therefore without affection or enthusiasm. Some of the earliest North American commentators on Weber held on to this idea, pointing to some of the problems stemming from it, and there are many writers today who hold similar views. Essentially, this body of literature stands in contradiction to both the earlier Human Relations ideas as well as to much current motivation-to-work theory and practice.

The book *Reader in Bureaucracy*,[95] published in 1952 when the Human Relations movement was at its peak, has a variety of articles which specifically or incidentally echo Weber's views on the bureaucratic personality. Anthony Downs later developed a typology of officials based on their power orientations. There are purely self-interested officials motivated almost entirely by goals that benefit themselves – these are sub-categorized as climbers and conservers. The second type are the mixed-motive officials who combine self-interest and altruistic loyalty to larger values – sub-categorized as zealots, advocates, and statesmen. But, to repeat, the basis of the categorization according to Downs is that all seek power, even if for different reasons.[96] Robert Presthus in *The Organizational Society* talks of three types found in organizations – the Upward-Mobiles, the Indifferents, and the Ambivalents. As the name implies, it is the Upward-Mobiles who rise to the top and, according to Presthus, while these people can be very adept at playing various roles to achieve personal success, they have a need for dominance in inter-personal relations.[97] It is these people who must, if it is to be done at all, implement such practices as "democratic" management in order for other motivation theories to work. Furthermore, in terms of self-actualization at work, the Indifferents would seem to be somewhat beyond the whole idea, the Ambivalents would be at best marginal, and it is the Upward Mobiles who would most likely pursue self-actualization goals. Again, it is these people who have a hostility toward heterodoxy and who tend toward resentment should others escape from the discipline and sacrifice that ambition has required of them,[98] who would be called upon to foster feelings of psychological success in others with less drive. Referring back to Argyris, this type of person would seem most likely to create feelings of psychological failure in subordinates. In actual fact, it has been argued that the typical executive simply does not have the psychological capacity to relate much to any "democratic" urges of workers, because the executive is typically an authoritarian. Even paying lip service to such things as participative management is quite often beyond the executive.[99]

As noted, there is a large body of literature on the subject of "bureaupathology" – the sickness of bureaucracy – but it all takes a pessimistic view of bureaucratic man. This person is over-conforming, compulsively but superficially sociable, impersonal but hiding behind a facade of bonhomie, selfish and power hungry, ruthless and without sympathy and empathy. The literature ranges from the serious, such as the studies of Presthus and Hummel in the *Bureaucratic Experience*,[100] to the undocumented, such as Boren's *When in Doubt, Mumble*[101] and Bureaucrat X in *Cover Your Ass!*[102]

The point is that the literature today is both very confused and confusing, beginning from disparate perspectives and arriving at widely different conclusions. While the writers have been described here perhaps in more dichotomous terms than they themselves would acknowledge, it is difficult to discern how both groups can be right. The motivation-to-work theorists see man in favorable, optimistic light – to a great extent striving toward his own perfection in his work setting. The bureaupathology theorists see man at work in a skeptical, disparaging light – perhaps not worth saving, even if saveable (which they doubt).

This disagreement among the theorists finds its counterpart in practice in the governments of Canada. While a small host of "personnel development officers" pursue their merry way with an assortment of motivation-to-work theories and a bagful of Human Relations techniques, others in government seem to insist on a fairly strong adherence to the older mechanist school of thought.

Perhaps the most recognizable vestiges of these older ideas, possibly ones we would not wish to be without, concern the merit principle and the practice of job classification. Both of these theories, when pursued in practice, tend to take organization man as a "given," a cog in a machine just needing to be slotted in properly in order to function. The merit principle, as classically stated and often pursued in practice, assumes that individuals will be hired and promoted on the basis of their demonstrated competence to perform the job to be filled. However, the more governments insist that they are adhering to this principle in their personnel practices, the more they would seem to be insisting on pursuit of a basic tenet of the mechanistic tradition — people enter competitions, and in a very impersonal fashion which allows no unique, personalistic factors to favor or disfavor any individual, the "right" person is selected for the job. Taylor's competent man has been found. To the extent that governments follow this practice, and generally they insist that they do, they must ignore many elements considered crucial in modern personnel theory. The latter holds, for example, that the work group, supervisory attitudes and behavior, and a host of other factors must be considered in "properly" placing an employee — factors which the merit principle by definition cannot allow for. Similarly, governments tend toward rather elaborate job classification schemes — presumably to ensure fairness in salaries, less labor strife, and so forth — but job classification generally imposes significant constraints on the individual's performance in the job by limiting his ability to use initiative and creativity. Incentive schemes, such as job enrichment, promoted by modern theorists prove very difficult if not impossible to implement in the face of an elaborate, rigid job classification system. Lip service may be paid to the new idea of "fitting the job to the man," but the practice seems to remain "fitting the man to the job." It has been argued, for example, that we have hedged the public servant with so many constraints that public employment is not attractive to persons of initiative, vigor, and independence.[103]

But perhaps the most generalized indicator of the mechanistic tradition's presence in Canadian government today involves the strong adherence, at least in theory, to the principle of rationality. (This will be dealt with more fully in later chapters on public budgeting and policy-making.) Weber, Taylor, Fayol, Gulick and many others of earlier years stressed the need for "rationality" in administration, whether they emphasized that term itself or others such as "scientific" and "principles." This same concern for rationality pervades government services today and may be seen in the variety of literature on rational public budgeting, rational planning, rational programming, and so forth. A decade or so ago, following developments in the United States, certain catchwords came into use in Canada, such as PPB (Planning, Programming, Budgeting) and MBO (Management by Objectives). These were rationalist concepts and were enthusiastically hailed from the federal level to the local school board level. They have since lost some of their allure, but now a new set of magic letters has appeared from below the border. ZBB (Zero Base Budgeting) in its way attempts to out-rationalize the earlier rationalist concepts.

Some aspects of mechanist "principles" may be discerned in specific instances, although it is impossible to "prove" that this management philosophy is actually the basis of government administration. At a guess, probably it is not. More probably Canadian public services reflect a mixture of both the mechanist and humanist schools of thought, which may explain the confusion pervading government personnel administration today.

For example, the Royal Commission on Government Organization (commonly known as the Glassco Commission) in its Report in 1962 made recommendations on a wide range of personnel matters. They suggest little awareness of humanistic thinking, but there is much evidence of mechanistic thinking. The Report, clearly echoing Taylor, argued that there is waste of human resources due to the failure to give orderly consideration to the best methods of providing and utilizing people.[104] It clearly links morale and compensation policies, and compensation policies and productivity.[105] And it ends with approximately 15 recommendations, most with several sub-recommendations, but none of these indicate real awareness of humanist thought—they are quite mechanical in their orientation, and the key words are "productivity" and "efficiency."

Another specific indication of this kind of thinking is supplied by Treasury Board publications, in particular *A Manager's Guide to Performance Measurement* and *Operational Performance Measurements*, Volumes 1 and 2. These stress, to the virtual exclusion of all else, management's need to assess and demonstrate productivity. While such factors as effectiveness (client satisfaction) are certainly noted, the stress is on efficiency, the ratio of input to output. The schemes for measuring this are quite elaborate, and one would almost expect to find a great number of efficiency experts running around with stop-watches, clocking the movements of people as they go about their jobs. In fact, *A Manager's Guide to Performance Measurement* has a statement by Robert Andras, then President of the Treasury Board, which includes the argument: "The intelligent application of the principles and techniques of good management is thus more important than ever."

Other aspects of the mechanist philosophy are apparent. For example, much of the trouble in the Post Office is said to have arisen because of authoritarian management practices based on a negative view of man. One hears of one-way windows used to spy on employees; of doors taken off washroom stalls in order to discourage malingering; of washroom windows cranked open in mid-winter and the crank then removed in order to discourage loitering. And while the Post Office may be a particularly notorious example, it seems that almost every public servant can top such practices with his/her personal observations and/or experiences (all this despite the fact that Canadian governments really do spend millions of dollars on programs which are based on an entirely contrary view of man at work).

Summary and Conclusions

To briefly summarize and conclude this chapter, we all have our personal ideology based on our personal values — on our own socialization. This ideology places us somewhere along a continuum between a pessimistic view of our fellow human beings, characterized in administrative literature as the "mechanistic philosophy," and an optimistic view called the "humanistic philosophy." There is ample evidence, both in the literature and in actual situations to justify both views. If we *believe* people are basically lazy and need coercion in order to produce, we can easily point to numerous examples in real life situations. And if we *believe* that people are basically industrious and self-responsible, we can again point to a wide variety of examples. Of crucial importance is the fact that we tend to act upon our basic beliefs and therefore affect our interactions with peers, superiors and subordinates. Our beliefs tend to define our personal meaning of organizational life, and to the extent we influence others we define what organizational life means for them.

There is no common agreement on the various questions raised in this chapter of what life in organizations *is* all about, nor on what it *should be*. The entire area of our work life, where we spend approximately one-third of our "productive" years, is pervaded by problematical contentions.

For Further Reading

BOOKS AND REPORTS

Carson, John J. *Is the Personnel Administrator an Endangered Species?*. Kingston, Ontario: Industrial Relations Centre, Reprint Series 39, 1977.

Chung, Kae H. *Motivational Theories and Practices*. Columbus: Grid Inc., 1977.

Crozier, Michael. *The Bureaucratic Phenomenon*. Chicago: University of Chicago Press, 1964.

Dickson, Paul. *Work Revolution*. London: G. Allen & Unwin, 1977.

Downs, Anthony. *Inside Bureaucracy*. Boston: Little, Brown, 1967.

Dunn, J. D. and Elvis C. Stephens. *Management of Personnel: Manpower Management and Organizational Behaviour*. New York: McGraw-Hill, 1972.

Gellerman, Saul W. *Managers and Subordinates*. Hinsdale, Ill.: Dryden Press, 1976.

Landsberger, Henry A. *Hawthorne Revisited*. Ithaca, N.Y.: Cornell University Press, 1958.

Lyons, Terry. *The Personnel Function in a Changing Environment*. London: Pitman, 1971.

Levine, Charles H., ed. *Managing Human Resources: A Challenge to Urban Governments*. Beverly Hills, Calif.: Sage Publications, 1977.

Mankin, Don. *Toward a Post-Industrial Psychology: Emerging Perspectives on Technology, Work, Education, and Leisure*. New York: Wiley, 1978.

Miller, Lawrence M. *Behavior Management: The New Science of Managing People at Work*. New York, Wiley, 1978.

Owen, Trevor. *The Manager and Industrial Relations*. New York: Pergamon Press, 1979.

Presthus, Robert V. *The Organizational Society*, 2nd ed. New York: Knopf, 1978.

Srivista, Suresh, et. al. *Job Satisfaction and Productivity*. Kent State University, Comparative Administration Research, 1977.

von Mises, Ludwig. *Bureaucracy*. New Rochelle, N.Y.: Arlington House, 1970.

Wilks, Arthur Garland. *Forward Planning in Human Resources Management*. Edmonton: Queen's Printer, 1973.

ARTICLES

Allan, Gordon G. "A Case for Management Flexibility." *Optimum*, Vol. II, 2 (1971), pp. 56-65.

Argyris, Chris. "Organizational Illnesses: 1. An Analysis 2. Possible Cures." *Canadian Imperial Bank of Commerce Commercial Letter*. (October 1968), pp. 2-11.

Banner, David K. "Self Actualization: A Basic Human Need." *The Canadian Personnel and Industrial Relations Journal*, Vol. XXI, 3 (May 1974), pp. 42-45, 57.

Bladen, V. W. "Economics and Human Relations." *The Canadian Journal of Economics and Political Science*, Vol. 14 (1948), pp. 301-11.

Bobele, H. Kenneth and Peter J. Buchanan. "Look Again — Money *Can* Motivate." *Canadian Business Magazine*, Vol. XLIX, 2 (February 1976), pp. 55-57.

Bourne, C. Gordon. "A Personnel Manager Looks at the Behavioral Sciences." *The Canadian Personnel and Industrial Relations Journal*, Vol. XV, 3 (May 1968), pp. 43-51.

Boyd, A. D., A. C. Gross and E. G. Wertheim. "Worker Participation and the Quality of Life: A Behavioral Analysis." *The Labour Gazette*, Vol. LXXVII, 2, pp. 71-74.

Broedling, Laura A. "The Uses of the Intrinsic-Extrinsic Distinction in Explaining Motivation and Organizational Behavior." *The Academy of Management Review*, Vol. II, 2 (April 1977), pp. 267-76.

Cherns, Albert B. "Can Behavioral Science Help Design Organizations?" *Organizational Dynamics* (Spring 1977), pp. 44-64.

Cummings, L. L. and Chris J. Berger. "Organization Structure: How Does it Influence Attitudes and Performance?" *Organizational Dynamics* (Autumn 1976), pp. 34-49.

Dinan, Tom. "The Reality of the Workplace." *The Civil Service Review*, Vol. L, 1 and 2 (June 1977), pp. 25-28.

Earle, V. H. "Once Upon a Matrix — A Hindsight on Participation." *Optimum*, Vol. IV, 2 (1973), pp. 28-36.

Frederickson, H. George, "Human Resources in Public Organization." *International Review of Administrative Sciences*, Vol. XXXIII, 4, (1967), pp. 336-44.

Harker, H. J., "Motivation in the Public Service." *The Labour Gazette*, Vol. LXXII, 9 (1972), pp. 458-61.

Hartley, Brian. "Personnel Management in the Public Service of Canada: Is Progress a Reality or Illusion?" *Optimum*, Vol. I, 4 (1970), pp. 20-27.

Emerson, Eugene. "The Authoritarian Cultural Lag in Business." *Journal of the Academy of Management*, Vol. II, 2 (1959), pp. 111-26.

Johnson, Walter. "Assembly-Line Merry-Go-Round." *Canadian Forum* (July 1974), pp. 9-13.

Kinder, James F. "The Behavioural Sciences in Perspective." *The Canadian Personnel and Industrial Relations Journal*, Vol. XXII, 6 (November 1975), pp. 37-43.

Knowles, Ron. "Whatever Happened to Behavioral Science?" *The Canadian Personnel and Industrial Relations Journal*, Vol. XXIII, 4 (September 1976), pp. 18-22.

Lee, James. "Behavioral Theory vs. Reality." *Harvard Business Review* (March/April 1971), pp. 20-28, 157-59.

Little, Elliott M. "Some Management Responsibilities for Good Industrial Relations." *The Canadian Journal of Economics and Political Science*, Vol. XII (1946), pp. 356-60.

McAdam, Jim. "Behavior Modification as a Cost Effective System for Work Performance Management." *The Canadian Personnel and Industrial Relations Journal*, Vol. XXII, 6 (November 1975), pp. 50-54.

Meridith, Harry and Joe Martin. "Management Consultants in the Public Sector." *Canadian Personnel Administration*, Vol. VIII, 4 (1970), pp. 383-95.

Mowat-Chalu, Sidney. "Program Review and Evaluation in the Public Sector." *Optimum*, Vol. VII, 2 (1976), pp. 57-64.

Narayan, R. "Pay Referents and Pay Satisfaction: Test of a Hypothesis." *Optimum*, Vol. VII, 3 (1976), pp. 54-59.

O'Neill, J. G. "Are 'Principles' of Organization Still Valid?" *Optimum*, Vol. III, 2 (1972), pp. 14-25.

Oppenheimer, Martin. "Participative Techniques of Social Integration." *Our Generation*, Vol. VI, 3 (1969), pp. 100-09.

Pinder, Craig C., "Concerning the Application of Human Motivation Theories in Organizational Settings," *The Academy of Management Review*, Vol. II, 3 (July 1977), pp. 384-97.

Reddin, W. J. "Managerial Effectiveness in the Future." *Optimum*, Vol. VII, 2 (1976), pp. 50-56.

Seberhagen, Lance W. "What Motivates Civil Service Employees?" *Public Personnel Review*, Vol. XXXI, 1 (January 1970), pp. 48-50.

Subramaniam, V. "The Classical Organization Theory and its Critics." *Public Administration*, Vol. XLIV (Winter 1966), pp. 435-46.

Swan, H. F. "Personnel Induced Frustration: An Instrument for the Selection of Senior Executives." *Canadian Public Administration*, Vol. XIV, 4 (1971), pp. 621-36.

Thompson, Mark J. and Larry F. Moore. "Managerial Attitudes toward Industrial Relations — Public and Private Sectors," *Industrial Relations*, Vol. XXXI, 3 (1976), pp. 359-67.

Vaison, Robert. "The Culture of Business and Organization Thoery." *Optimum*, Vol. VI, 2 (1975), pp. 28-32.

Weinstein, Deena. "Bureaucratic Opposition: The Challenge to Authoritarian Abuses at the Workplace." *Canadian Journal of Political and Social Theory*, Vol. I, 2 (1977), pp. 31-46.

Wiggins, Ronald L. and Richard D. Steade. "Job Satisfaction as a Social Concern." *The Academy of Management Review*, Vol. I, 4 (October 1976), pp. 48-55.

Windmuller, John P. "Industrial Democracy and Industrial Relations." *The Annals of the American Academy of Political and Social Science*, Vol. 431 (May 1977), pp. 22-31.

ENDNOTES

1. Anthony Tillett, "Industry and Management: An Historical Perspective" in Anthony Tillett, Thomas Kempner, and Gordon Wills (eds.), *Management Thinkers* (Harmondsworth, Middlesex: Penguin, 1970), pp. 15-74.
2. See, for example, James L. Gibson, "Organization Theory and the Nature of Man" in Joseph A. Uveges, Jr. (ed.), *The Dimensions of Public Administration: Introductory Readings* (Boston: Holbrook Press, 1971), pp. 126-39; Tom Dinan, "The Reality of the Workplace," *Civil Service Review*, Vol. L, Nos. 1 and 2 (June 1977), pp. 25-28; and James Lee, "Behavioral Theory v. Reality," *Harvard Business Review* (March/April 1971), pp. 20-28 and 157-59.
3. The terminology is that used by Gibson, "Organization Theory and the Nature of Man."
4. It is argued to be dysfunctional for those outside the organization also, but that is the subject of the next chapter.
5. Max Weber, *The Theory of Social and Economic Organization*, trans. A. M. Henderson and Talcott Parsons (Glencoe: The Free Press, 1947), pp. 56-77 and p. 328.
6. *Ibid.*, p. 333.
7. *Ibid.*, p. 333-34.
8. *Ibid.*, p. 337-39.
9. *Ibid.*, p. 340.
10. Peter M. Blau, *Bureaucracy in Modern Society* (New York: Random House, 1956), p. 34.
11. Mason Haire, "What is Organized in an Organization?" in *Organization Theory and Industrial Practice* (New York: John Wiley & Sons, 1962), pp. 1-12.
12. Nicos P. Mouzelis, *Organization and Bureaucracy* (Chicago: Aldine Publishing Co., 1967), p. 19.
13. Martin Albrow, *Bureaucracy* (London: Macmillan, 1970), p. 45.
14. Frederick Winslow Taylor, *The Principles of Scientific Management* (New York: W. W. Norton and Co., 1967), p. 5.
15. *Ibid.*, p. 6.
16. *Ibid.*, p. 37.
17. *Ibid.*, p. 34.
18. *Ibid.*, p. 39.
19. *Ibid.*, p. 57.
20. *Ibid.*, p. 62.
21. *Ibid.*, p. 12.
22. For example, the library copy of *Scientific Management* used here has a number of rather violent, negative comments in a variety of hands, written in page margins wherever Taylor used such terms.
23. Taylor, *The Principles* . . . ., p. 23.
24. *Ibid.*, p. 19.
25. *Ibid.*, p. 26.
26. Norman Cuthbert, "Fayol and the Principles of Organization" in Tillett et al., *Management Thinkers*, pp. 108-39.
27. Henri Fayol, *General and Industrial Management*, trans. Constance Storrs (London: Pitman Publishing, 1949), Chapter 4.
28. *Ibid.*, p. 19.
29. *Ibid.*, pp. 41-42.
30. Cuthbert, "Fayol . . .".
31. See Lyndall Urwick, "Foreword" in Fayol, pp. v-xvii.
32. Lyndall Urwick, "Organization as a Technical Problem" in Luther Gulick and Lyndall Urwick (eds.), *Papers on the Science of Administration* (New York: Institute of Public Administration, 1937), pp. 47-88.

33. See also Lyndall Urwick, "The Need for a Science of Administration" and Luther Gulick, "Notes on the Theory of Organization" in J. E. Hodgetts and D. C. Corbett (eds.), *Canadian Public Administration* (Toronto: Macmillan, 1960), pp. 21-24 and pp. 38-66, respectively.
34. Dwight Waldo, "Scope of the Theory of Public Administration" in James C. Charlesworth (ed.), *Theory and Practice of Public Administration: Scope, Objectives, and Methods* (Philadelphia: American Academy of Political and Social Science, 1968), pp. 1-26.
35. Luther Gulick, "Notes on the Theory of Public Administration" in Gulick and Urwick, *Papers . . .* , pp. 1-46.
36. An excellent example of the "principles" orientation toward the executive is supplied by G. Gardner, "What Makes Successful and Unsuccessful Executives" in *Civil Service Review*, Vol. XXIV, 4 (December 1951), pp. 410 and 413-47.
37. Luther Gulick, "Science, Values and Public Administration" in Gulick and Urwick, *Papers . . .* , pp. 189-95.
38. *Ibid.*, pp. 47-88.
39. Mason Haire, "The Concept of Power and the Concept of Man" in George B. Strother (ed.), *Social Science Approaches to Business Behavior* (Homewood: Irwin-Dorsey, 1962), pp. 163-83.
40. See Dwight Waldo, "Public Administration" in Uveges, *The Dimensions . . .* , pp. 23-41.
41. Nicholas Henry, *Public Administration and Public Affairs* (Englewood Cliffs: Prentice-Hall, 1975), p. 8.
42. Gibson, "Organization Theory . . .".
43. It should be emphasized that the choice of both time periods and writers discussed here is to some extent arbitrary. For example, it has been claimed that Taylor built on Charles Babbage and that Captain Henry Metcalfe of the United States army was the first to argue that there could be a "science of administration." Similarly, in the early 1800s Robert Owen clearly anticipated some of Mayo's ideas, as did an associate of Taylor's, Henry Laurence Gantt, about a century later. See, for example, James F. Kinder, "The Behavioural Sciences in Perspective," *The Canadian Personnel and Industrial Relations Journal*, Vol. XXII, 6 (November 1975), pp. 37-43.
44. David Ashton, "Elton Mayo and the Empirical Study of Social Groups" in Tillett et al., *Management Thinkers*, pp. 294-304.
45. C. W. M. Hart, "The Hawthorne Experiments," *The Canadian Journal of Economics and Political Science*, Vol. IX (1943), pp. 150-163. In the same journal see also V. W. Bladden, "Economics and Human Relations," Vol. XIV (1948), pp. 301-311. The latter was the Presidential Address delivered at the Annual Meeting of the Canadian Political Science Association, June 18, 1948.
46. Elton Mayo, *The Human Problems of an Industrial Civilization* (New York: Viking Press, 1960), p. 65.
47. *Ibid.*, p. 67.
48. *Ibid.*, p. 116.
49. Gibson, "Organization Theory . . .".
50. Mayo, *The Human . . .* , p. 159.
51. *Ibid.*, p. 131.
52. *Ibid.*, p. 160.
53. *Ibid.*, pp. 175-80.
54. Ashton, "Elton Mayo . . .".
55. Carl J. Friedrich, "Some Observations on Weber's Analysis of Bureaucracy" in Robert K. Merton et al. (eds.), *Reader in Bureaucracy* (New York: Free Press, 1952), pp. 27-33.
56. Frederic S. Burin, "Bureaucracy and National Socialism: A Reconsideration of Weberian Theory" in Merton et al., *Reader . . .* , pp. 33-47.
57. Alvin W. Gouldner, "On Weber's Analysis of Bureaucratic Rules" in Merton et al., *Reader . . .* , pp. 48-51.
58. Herbert A. Simon, "Some Further Requirements of Bureaucratic Theory" in Merton et al., *Reader . . .* , pp. 51-58.

59. For an excellent comprehensive survey and commentary on recent writings on bureaucracy, see Peta Sheriff, "Sociology of Public Bureaucracies 1965-1975," *Current Sociology*, Vol. XXIV, 2 (1976), pp. 1-75. See particularly Section III, "Individuals Within Bureaucracies," pp. 46-72.
60. *See*, for example, V. O. Key, Jr., "Legislative Control" and Avery Leiserson, "The Formulation of Administrative Policy" in Fritz Morstein Marx (ed.), *Elements of Public Administration* (New York: Prentice-Hall, 1946), pp. 339-362 and pp. 365-380, respectively.
61. Dahl's article can be found reprinted in, among others, Hodgetts and Corbett, *Canadian Public Administration*, pp. 24-33.
62. *Public Administration Review*, Vol. 6, 1946. This can be found reprinted in W. D. K. Kernaghan (ed.), *Public Administration in Canada: Selected Readings*, 2nd ed. (Toronto: Methuen, 1971), pp. 27-35.
63. A summary of some of the criticism of the older school of thought can be found in: V. Subramanian, "The Classical Organization Theory and its Critics," *Public Administration*, Vol. 44 (Winter 1966), pp. 435-446; Nicholas Henry, *Public Administration . . .* , pp. 3-32; and Dwight Waldo, "Scope of the Theory of Public Administration."
64. Fred J. Carvell, *Human Relations in Business*, 2nd ed. (New York: Macmillan, 1970), p. 2.
65. *Ibid.*, p. 2.
66. See, for example, Martin Oppenheimer, "Participative Techniques of Social Integration," *Our Generation*, Vol. VI, 3 (1969), pp. 100-109. Oppenheimer suggests that the Human Relations approach was epitomized in Dale Carnegie's idea about influencing people by being nice to them.
67. See, for example, Ernest Dale, *Management: Theory and Practice* (New York: McGraw Hill, 1973), p. 34.
68. This clearly harks back to Fayol's concern for putting the general interest before private interest.
69. Eliot D. Chapple and Leonard R. Sayles, *The Measure of Management: Designing Organizations for Human Effectiveness* (New York: Macmillan, 1961), p. 6.
70. *Ibid.*, p. 6.
71. A current, lengthy summary of this area is supplied by Kae H. Chung, *Motivational Theories and Practices* (Columbus, Ohio: Grid Inc., 1974). This is one of approximately twenty in the Grid Series in Management.
72. Abraham Maslow, "A Theory of Human Motivation," *Psychological Review* Vol. L (1943), pp. 370-96.
73. It is important to note that Maslow's Need Hierarchy, and therefore subsequent motivation-to-work theories built on it, have far from total acceptance among scholars and, for that matter, among people in organizations. See, for example, Craig C. Pinder, "Concerning the Application of Human Motivation Theories in Organizational Settings," *The Academy of Management Review*, Vol. II, 3 (July 1977), pp. 384-397. For a current Canadian example of an attempt to operationalize the Need Hierarchy see Donald Patrick and T. Clift Read, "The Patrick-Read Needs Profile: a Practical Use of Behavioral Science Theory" *The Canadian Personnel and Industrial Relations Journal*, Vol. XXI, 1 (January 1974), pp. 13-19.
74. One Canadian theorist himself suggests that there is great confusion about motivation theory. There are, he says, about 20 personality theories, all well-developed and current, and all different. "Too many behavioral theories are grounded firmly in mid-air; they describe a Utopia, not reality." (W. J. Reddin, "Managerial Effectiveness in the Future," *Optimum*, Vol. VII, 2, 1976, pp. 50-56).
75. The following summary is based on Chris Argyris, *Integrating the Individual and the Organization* (New York: John Wiley and Sons, 1964), pp. 3-42. A more recent publication demonstrates that Argyris has not changed his basic ideas. See Chris Argyris, *On Organizations and the Future* (Beverly Hills: Sage Publications, 1973). See also Chris Argyris, "Understanding and Increasing Organizational Effectiveness" in *Commercial Letter* (Canadian Bank of Commerce), October 1968, pp. 1-11.

76. F. Herzberg, B. Mausner, and B. Snyderman, *The Motivation to Work* (New York: John Wiley and Sons, 1959).
77. The following is based on Frederick Herzberg, *Work and the Nature of Man* (New York: World Publishing, 1966), pp. 71-99, Chapter "The Motivation-Hygiene Theory." There has been some controversy over the extent to which Herzberg's motivation-hygiene thesis really differs from Maslow's Need Hierarchy thesis; some feel that the hygiene factors simply relate to the lower-level needs while the motivation factors relate to the higher-level needs. See, for example, Joseph J. Norwich, "Motivational Theories: How They Relate," *Canadian Business Magazine*, Vol. XLVII, 10 (October 1974), pp. 64-66.
78. See, for example, Philip Marchand, "Teaching Middle Management How to Cry," *Saturday Night*, Vol. XCII, 6, pp. 27-32; Richard W. Johnston, "Seeking the Answer to Herzberg's Question," in *Executive*, Vol. XVI, 6, pp. 51-52; and H. J. Harker, "Motivation in the Public Service," *The Labour Gazette*, Vol. LXXII, 9, pp. 458-461.
79. See, for example, Ronald L. Wiggins and Richard D. Steade, "Job Satisfaction as a Social Concern," *The Academy of Management Review*, Vol. I, 4 (October 1976), pp. 48-55.
80. See, for example, E. Szostak, "Job Enrichment Through Job Design" *Canadian Campus*, Vol. IX, 2 (October 1976), p. 18.
81. Cited by Harker, "Motivation . . .".
82. "Motivation and the Responsible Manager" in *The Labour Gazette*, Vol. LXXII, 10 (October 1972), pp. 532-535.
83. Harker, "Motivation . . .".
84. For example, a wide variety of in-service programs offered to federal employees include this idea. Among them would be: Career Assignment Program, Self-Development and Career Growth for Secretaries, and various MBO programs. See Bureau of Staff Development and Training, Public Service Commission of Canada, *Courses and Services 1975-1976*.
85. For a summary of this line of criticism see C. Gordon Bourne, "A Personnel Manager Looks at the Behavioral Sciences," *The Canadian Personnel and Industrial Relations Journal*, Vol. XV, 3 (May 1968), pp. 43-51.
86. This argument can be related to the idea of manipulation. It has been argued that most men do indeed enjoy some challenge in their jobs, but that the organization twists this natural desire into a divisive, humiliating competition for prestige and status. See Walter Johnson, "Assembly-Line Merry-Go-Round," *Canadian Forum* (July 1974), pp. 9-13.
87. "Job Enrichment," *Canadian Dimension*, Vol. XII, 3 (1977), pp. 29-32.
88. Gordon G. Allan, "A Case for Management Flexibility," *Optimum*, Vol II, 2 (1971), pp. 56-65.
89. For example, see: F. H. Kanfer, "Issues and Ethics in Behaviour Manipulation," *Psychological Reports*, Vol. 16 (1965), pp. 187-196; L. Krasner, "Behavior Control and Social Responsibility," *American Psychologist*, Vol. 17 (1962), pp. 199-294; C. R. Rogers and B. F. Skinner, "Some Issues Concerning the Control of Human Behavior: A Symposium," *Science*, Vol. 124 (1956), pp. 1057-1066.
90. "We were even given our very own pantheon of gods — McGregor, Maslow, Herzberg . . . . What practitioner had the gall to wonder about the relevance of Maslow's hierarchy of needs to the realities of the bargaining table?" R. Knowles, "Whatever Happened to Behavioral Science?" *The Canadian Personnel and Industrial Relations Journal*, Vol. XXIII, 4 (September 1976), pp. 18-22. See also: H. Kenneth Bobele and Peter J. Buchanan, "Look Again — Money *Can* Motivate," *Canadian Business*, Vol. XLIX, 3 (February 1976), pp. 55-57; and R. Narayan, "Pay Referents and Pay Satisfaction: Test of a Hypothesis," *Optimum*, Vol. VII, 3 (1976), pp. 54-59.
91. Robert K. Coe, "Implications of a Concept of Work on Management Theory and Practice," *Administrative Commentary*, Vol. II, 4 (November 1974), pp. 1-5. A Canadian study of a communications manufacturing unit found that workers had to be *forced* to get involved and that a scheme for participative management ended only in a "dictatorship of the proletariat." See V. H. Earle, "Once Upon a Matrix — a Hindsight on Participation," *Optimum*, Vol. IV, 2 (1973), pp. 28-36.

92. Gibson, "Organization Theory...".
93. Lee, "Behavioral Theory...".
94. For some views on the interaction between society and organization see: Lee, "Behavioral Theory..."; Dinan, "The Reality..."; L. R. Eastcott et al., "Constraints upon Administrative Behavior," *The Canadian Administrator*, Vol. XIII, 8 (May 1974), pp. 41-44; and Brian Hartley, "Personnel Management in the Public Service of Canada: Is Progress a Reality or Illusion?" *Optimum*, Vol. I, 4 (1970), pp. 20-27.
95. See particularly Merton's article, "Bureaucratic Structure and Personality," pp. 361-71.
96. Anthony Downs, *Inside Bureaucracy* (Boston: Little, Brown and Co., 1967), pp. 88 and 92-111.
97. Robert Presthus, *The Organizational Society* (New York: St. Martin's Press, 1978), p. 153.
98. Presthus, *The Organizational...*, p. 161.
99. Eugene Emerson Jennings, "The Authoritarian Cultural Lag in Business," *Journal of the Academy of Management*, Vol. II, 2 (1959), pp. 11-126.
100. Ralph P. Hummel, *The Bureaucratic Experience* (New York: St. Martin's Press, 1977).
101. James H. Boren, *When in Doubt, Mumble: A Bureaucrat's Handbook* (New York: Van Nostrand, 1972).
102. Bureaucrat X, *Cover Your Ass!: Or, How to Survive in a Government Bureaucracy* (Edmonton: Hurtig, 1977).
103. D. J. Collins, "Recruitment and Selection for Public Administration: The Last 10 Years," *Canadian Public Administration*, Vol. VII, 2 (1964), pp. 197-204.
104. Royal Commission on Government Organization, *Management of the Public Sector*, abridged ed. (Ottawa: Queen's Printer, 1962), p. 137.
105. *Ibid.*, p. 162.

CHAPTER THREE

The Social Meaning of Organizational Life

Introduction

The preceding chapter considered the impact on us of the organizations we work for. Here we are concerned with the fact that not only must the individual cope with working for a large organization but he must also cope with living in a complex society dominated by many other large organizations, the influence of which he cannot escape.

We awake each day to the dominant, constant fact of large organizations. The bed we sleep in and the cereal we eat for breakfast are manufactured and retailed by large organizations in the private sector; their quality and content are controlled by a vast number of government regulations to ensure, for example, that bedclothing is not too flammable or that there are not too many insect fragments in the cereal. The car we drive to work is produced and marketed in the private sector subject to myriad government rules and regulations concerning automobile manufacture and marketing; our use of it is governed by further very elaborate, complex services, regulations and standards set and administered in the public sector— traffic lights and speed signs, parking regulations, car licence, driver's licence, compulsory insurance, and a police force to ensure proper observance of it all. Our home is built by organizations in the private sector but its construction and location are governed by by-laws and regulations emanating from and enforced by all three levels of government. Sports we watch on television are almost certain to be highly organized, and to engage in a sport personally we must join other organizations called "leagues" or "teams." Should the rugged individual wish to get away from it all he will typically have to travel a considerable distance to do so; and should he wish to engage in a solitary pursuit such as hunting he may have to pass a safety course to use a gun, purchase a permit to possess it, and buy two different licences to use it. A cynic might argue that a guarantee of considerable government attention comes with an attempt to become a hermit. An official concerned with health would soon arrive, followed closely by another responsible for mental health and then by one for welfare. The official from forestry would come along, perhaps denouncing the lethargy of the environment officials. The Mountie interested in suspicious characters would be trailed by someone from the Human Rights Commission and/or someone from legal aid interested in the maintenance of individual freedoms, and both would be trying not to step on Revenue Canada. While this may seem a silly scenario, it is difficult to think of any area of one's life unaffected by large organizations in general and government organizations in particular.

Most of us do not sit around brooding about the highly regulated nature of our lives. In fact, as noted in the previous chapter, it is due to large organizations that most of us enjoy high levels of material comforts with much time for leisure. Still, in industrialized societies there does appear to be considerable disenchantment with certain aspects of modern life, and even alienation of many individuals from much of society as a result of large organizations.

Discussion of this unease, disenchantment, even alienation from bureaucracy will begin in this chapter with various anti-bureaucratic comments expressed "popularly" in Canada today. After the tone of present anti-bureaucratism is set, the discussion will return to some of the classical anti-bureaucratic theorists, beginning in the late 1800s when bureaucracy, as a negative theme, had the unique ability to unite conservative, liberal, and socialist critics of social trends.[1] The theme will be taken back to the present, offering explanations and arguments concerning the constant growth of bureaucracy, some of its more obvious social consequences, and the question of whether we can, or want to, escape from or at least mitigate its predominance. As in the preceding chapter, it will be seen that a seemingly straightforward topic has various significant dimensions, and that alleged problems and proferred solutions have many ramifications. That is, while bureaucracy may be a problem, there is considerable disagreement over the nature of that problem.

The Canadian "Monster"

There is definitely an anxiety in Canada today on the part of many citizens that bureaucracy will destroy much of what is politically and socially of value. It is intriguing to note the frequency with which the term "monster" is applied to bureaucracy. Arguments range from outright harangues to reasoned polemics to systematic studies, but they all share the idea of bureaucracy's pernicious influence. Actually, the common antipathy for government bureaucracy makes for strange although usually unconscious alliances. For example, President Ronald Reagan has argued that the federal bureaucracy of his country is a "crocodile" which will ultimately "eat" American businessmen.[2] Conversely, a "left-wing" Canadian magazine argues that the growth in government bureaucracy reflects the interests and power of a small class of corporate owners.[3] Both these statements hold in common a negative view of bureaucracy which was expressed by the slogan of the Manitoba Liberal Party under Izzy Asper, "Self Control, not State Control."

A rich source of anti-bureaucratic sentiments are the business magazines, that present all sorts of evidence that government bureaucracy is created and works for the benefit of bureaucrats and "welfare recipients" (more pejorative terms are also used) and to the detriment of honest, striving Canadians (in this case the various synonyms are eulogistic). A constant theme in such literature stresses the inefficient, incompetent, unrealistic, self-serving and red tape nature of government bureaucracy. So, for example, Douglas Fisher, a regular columnist in *Executive*, insists that bureaucracy, as it expands in numbers and budget, becomes insensitive, arrogant and flaccid. Bureaucrats engage in skullduggery and "boondoggling." Specialization of function allows for much buck-passing due to an attitude of: "It's not my department." In earlier years, according to Fisher, because of smaller size the bureaucracy posed fewer problems, and it was more susceptible to control by democratic forces. Today, on the other hand, its tremendous size and complexity have made it a menace to society. The ultimate plea is for smallness, a retreat to earlier, happier times when the bureaucracy was friendlier, more useful and more controllable.[4] Similarly, an article in *Canadian Business* discusses the swollen growth of public bureaucracy, the possibility of squandering public funds in unproductive ways, and points to reports of the Auditor General that indicate hundreds of cases of "flagrant misuse of public money." A Chamber of Commerce survey is cited which indicates that the primary concerns of its members are: mismanagement of unemployment insurance and the size of welfare packages; reduction of the numbers of public servants and an increase in their efficiency; abolition of local initiative programs and other such grants; elimination of duplication among various government services; reduction of emphasis on the costly bilingualism program; and, not least in emphasis, restraint on the salaries and wages of government employees.[5]

These are examples from only two magazines, but even superficial reading of other business publications with similar readerships will reveal that the anti-bureaucratic theme is fairly constant. However, it must not be thought that only businessmen express themselves negatively toward bureaucracy, as most socio-economic groupings in Canadian society at times flail out at bureaucracy in similar terms, although perhaps for different reasons. For example, Joseph Morris, ex-President of the Canadian Labour Congress, has argued that the bureaucracy in Ottawa has led to the demise of the constitutional principle and practice of parliamentary supremacy. It is the bureaucracy, defined as a "privileged and powerful group in the governmental apparatus," which controls information, influences Cabinet, and is the source of thousands of decisions affecting working people whose problems they have no sympathy for and do not understand. According to Morris, labor has a role to fill by strengthening the Opposition in Parliament through challenging the policies and advice of the bureaucracy.[6]

Newspapers also contribute significantly to the negative view many Canadians hold of bureaucracy. That is, if newspapers like other media do not actually create the view, they certainly would seem to reinforce it. The term "bureaucrat" is usually used in a pejorative sense in the newspapers, and bureaucracy tends to be a prime topic. Typical examples of negative headlines are: Monster creates worry, confusion; Ombudsman tees off on snail-like bureaucrats; The bureaucrat's bureaucrat; A bureaucrat's dream book; Trustee blames education hike on hiring of bureaucrats; Red-tape upsets M.P.; Bureaucracies try to make molehill out of mountain; Government staff near monster, many confused; Kicking out of prodigal civil servants proposed; and on, and on . . . .

Television also contributes to the negative image we hold of bureaucracy. A major example of this was the CBC's *Ombudsman* who fearlessly used to take on high-level bureaucrats and in scathing terms denounce the error of their ways, insisting upon redress for the complainant. Viewers were urged to send in complaints about treatment at the hands of bureaucrats.[7] Another good source of anti-bureaucratism is *The Fifth Estate*, which devotes a good deal of time to government operations and in excoriating terms paints a grim picture of Canadian bureaucracy. There are also the regular news programs which are only too happy to report on bureaucratic scandals or on a human interest story involving a cold-blooded bureaucrat. Similarly, radio contributes to this stream of criticism, particularly through its "action line" programs where citizen complaints pour in about bureaucratic arrogance and incompetence.

Another source of anti-bureaucratism worth mentioning is popular fiction; the impact a novel may have will be bolstered should it become the basis of a movie. J. E. Hodgetts, referring to the popular sport of "baiting the bureaucrat," has argued that the novelist has always been devoted to this sport because the bureaucrat is so open to satirization to which, of course, he cannot possibly respond in like fashion.[8] For the novelist, the bureaucrat is a sitting duck, and as examples Hodgetts cites Gogol's *Inspector General*, Mackenzie's *The Red Tapeworm* and Trollope's *The Three Clerks*. Such books have greatly increased today and now also include what might be called the mass consumption novel. The James Bond and Matt Helm books, for example, express a fairly constant anti-bureaucratic theme, implicitly and/or explicitly, in that the strong, silent men-of-action get the job done despite being hampered and constrained by the meaningless procedures, rigid thinking, buck-passing, and power-seeking of others within their organizations. That is, they often succeed despite organization, rather than because of it.

And, of course, there are those books whose sole intent is to satirize bureaucracy which have received considerable popular attention. Among these would be *Parkinson's Law*; *The Peter Principle*; *When in Doubt, Mumble*; *The Kidner Report*; *Cover Your Ass*; and *Ropes to Skip and Know*.

The bureaucracy is also a frequent target of politicians. This is inevitable and even desirable in the case of the Opposition, since two of its roles are to criticize government policy and government administration. However, the two roles often appear inseparable judging from politician's statements. As one example, Gerald Baldwin (PC — Peace River) argues that "modern government sits brooding over us like a great black vampire sucking our tax blood for its own special purposes." Parliament's ability to supervise this "monster" has been deliberately curtailed by new rules, and even in the supply of money the House of Commons and therefore the tax-paying public have no real voice. Governments, ministers and department officials cherish the feeling of "being lords of creation with other people's money," and resent any interference with spending as they see fit. In short, what is needed in Canada is more voice for the general society as opposed to the ivory tower intellects who advise the government, as well as a clear means of controlling the octopus-like, monolithic monster that is government.[9] (This is only one example of a politician speaking negatively about bureaucracy, but similar comments can easily be found in daily newspapers, magazines, and in the *Debates* of the House of Commons or those of the provincial legislatures.

The Auditor General, whether at the federal or provincial level, is often very critical of the public bureaucracy, and "inefficiency" tends to be a key word. His *Report*, which is given mass media coverage, must contribute significantly to the image of incompetence, or worse, on the part of public servants. The *Report* by Auditor General J. J. Macdonell in November, 1978 is illustrative of this. It states that public servants have looked upon the Treasury as a bottomless pit, and insists that they should be fired if they do not spend economically, efficiently, and according to Parliament's wishes — all of which suggests that they have not been doing so. It states that public servants annually dispense millions of dollars with little regard for dollar value to the taxpayer. The entire federal system, he argues, is conducive to empire building, with civil servants receiving promotion for innovative ideas about new spending programs, and not receiving promotions just because they have proved they can run programs efficiently and economically. A note of optimism is perhaps offered when he adds that due to new accounting procedures the Government may be approaching a degree of control over spending. Two years earlier he suggested that not only Parliament but also the Government had lost effective control over spending. The previously on-the-loose monster may now experience some restraint.

Actually, Macdonell's remarks about the inefficient, spend-thrift character of the federal bureaucracy were really quite in keeping with a general mood of 1978. The emphasis on government restraint had begun in the previous year and flowered in 1978. This was by no means confined to Canada, as it was a common theme in the Congressional elections in the United States in 1978. The reportage of those elections indicated many candidates emphasizing the need to reduce or at least slow down government spending, with California's Bill 13 receiving frequent mention. In Canada, provincial governments have heavily emphasized restraint, most notably perhaps the Government of Manitoba under Sterling Lyon who won an election in late 1977 based to a great extent on the issue of government overspending. The federal government is now clearly emphasizing restraint, and because of the inter-dependence of government financing, governments at all three levels have been taking very tough lines toward their programs and employees. Numerous cutbacks have occurred, as have personnel reductions, and others are clearly in the offing. The increasing talk of "sunset legislation" and of the new miracle approach to budgeting, Zero Base Budgeting, is part of this general mood.

A strong sub-theme throughout the discussion and implementation of restraint has been bureaucratic growth or, perhaps more accurately, the need to halt that growth, even to reverse it. Stated differently, various restraint policies have often been aimed at programs, which in difficult economic times are judged to be of low priority, or because of party ideology have no status at all. However, there appears to be a fairly strong assumption that the size of the bureaucracy per se is unnecessary, as opposed to dislike for or low evaluation of the programs the "Monster" administers. This is perhaps seen best in allegations of "bureaucratic fat," resulting in promises of reducing personnel (by say 10 percent) while maintaining the same level of services. The underlying assumption must be that the public servants involved have not been turning in a fair day's work for a fair day's pay. In this case, the negative view of bureaucracy is put into operational effect.

It is not our purpose at this point to explain why these negative views exist, nor to evaluate their validity. Rather, the intent is to indicate the far-from-favorable stereotypes of the bureaucrat and bureaucracy that exist in Canada. One writer, satirizing the satire aimed at the bureaucrat, suggests that the public stereotype of him is as follows: The bureaucrat arrives at the office between 9:15 and 10:30, the time of arrival depending on his status. He proceeds to spend his day writing progressively incomprehensible letters, gradually perfecting this exercise as his sense of humanity dissipates. He never makes a decision if he can possibly pass the buck, and will always postpone those decisions which appear inevitable in the hope that circumstances will change or that those who demand the decisions will give up due to the frustration of delay. When he is actually forced to action or decision, the bureaucrat will invariably discover that the pertinent file has gone astray and with relief will relax into customary repose. He is subservient to his superiors and intolerant toward subordinates and, if he feels safe enough, insolent to the public. He regards citizen complaints and arguments as a severe drain on his supply of Christian charity. Colleagues he regards as dangerous rivals. After his two-hour lunch he spends the afternoon devising strategy that will keep his subordinates on the job until official quitting time and which will allow himself to depart promptly once that moment arrives. Armed with newspaper and aspirins he returns home to seek release from his own futility by badgering his family.[10]

Comparing the tone and content of the above statements with the stereotype of the mechanistic tradition that was discussed in the preceding chapter, reveals a great deal of resemblance. If not man in general, then certainly public bureaucratic man is lazy and negligent, interested only in material gain and personal power, and needs to be coerced to perform adequately. The ruthless implementation of some recent restraint policies certainly does not indicate a view by "management" of public employees as responsible, self-motivated, dedicated human beings. The extent to which each of us accepts the stereotype of the bureaucrat, is the extent to which we do not hold a high view of the nature of man, even though we may think ourselves and our friends and work-mates to be exceptions to the rule. Perhaps it is a case of, "Of *course* there are good bureaucrats, but . . .," or "Some of my best friends are bureaucrats."

On the other hand, perhaps man is essentially good, but bureaucratic man is forced by his milieu to go against his basic nature. That is, bureaucracy *per se* may be the evil, impressing on employees behavior foreign to themselves, behavior which they may resent and resist but which they must adopt, given the lack of real alternatives in a society dominated by large, formal organizations.

The ramifications of each of these possibilities will, hopefully, emerge in the ensuing discussion of bureaucracy. However, if there is no likely third alternative, then the chance of actually implementing the ideas of human relations and motivation-to-work theorists discussed in the preceding chapter becomes rather remote.

Early Views on the Meaning of Bureaucracy

Much of the current controversy over the reason for bureaucratic growth and its meaning for society is reflected in the writings of theorists a century ago. While they held in common a concern about, a fear for, bureaucracy, they did not agree on the particulars. This is perhaps most clearly seen in the ideas on bureaucracy of Karl Marx, who himself appears to have had two conflicting views. Those who came after him and followed at least part of his broader theorizing also seem to be split as to which view he really meant to advocate. Some theorists (contemporary and later) have argued that Marx made significant contributions to the topic of bureaucracy, while others have insisted that he had a blind spot concerning it.

The "young Marx" in 1843 advanced ideas on bureaucracy which clearly anticipated arguments of writers such as Robert Michels, who repudiated Marx's later ideas. The problem seems to have been that these earlier comments were not published until 1927, and Michels and others had only the later, contrary views to consider. The earlier view insisted that bureaucracy is a circle from which no one can escape. Its general spirit is secret and mysterious, safeguarded internally by its hierarchical nature and externally by its nature as a closed corporation. For those within, the bureaucracy provides the essential meaning to their lives, while that which lies outside it becomes unreal. Because of this, perpetuation of bureaucracy becomes the goal of bureaucrats — that is, self-perpetuation of that which is real to them. In modern sociological terms, "goal displacement" occurs, whereby the original goal bureaucracy was created to achieve (the ends of the State) is displaced by the means to achieve that goal (self-perpetuation of bureaucracy), while at the same time the ends originally to be pursued become the justification for continuance of the means.

Because of this, bureaucracy comes to form a distinct and separate social stratum with its own particular interests. Created by the State it becomes separate from the State. It is not held together by the State, but rather the State is held together by the bureaucracy. As a result of this means-end inversion, bureaucracy becomes incapable of grasping reasons for social problems and therefore cannot cope with them. Even if officials have the best intentions, attempt to be humane, and are intelligent, their destiny – self-perpetuation – prevents them from coping with the great evidence of misery that is available to them. However, it is not likely that they will be humane, as the bureaucratic mentality, dedicated to material pursuits and veneration of authority, appears incapable of concern for humanity.[11]

This view of the separation of the bureaucracy from the State – the idea, that is, that bureaucracy has a life of its own – was not in later years mentioned by Marx. As his social theory developed, bureaucracy was infrequently referred to as simply a part of the State which would cease to exist when the State ceased to exist. This led to some vehement criticism from theorists such as Michels who, like the earlier Marx, saw bureaucracy as having a life of its own. The anarchist Bakunin, who fought with Marx over control of the International Workingmen's Association, felt that Marx was blind to the inevitable re-creation of bureaucracy. Martin Albrow suggests that Marx *had* to be forgetful of his earlier view of bureaucracy's self-life because it would not have been compatible with his general theory of the State as he subsequently developed it.[12] That is, if bureaucracy was simply part of the State, the problem of bureaucracy would automatically be resolved with the resolution of the problem of the State. However, if bureaucracy was an autonomous force, as argued in the earlier work, then the end of the State would not necessarily mean the end of bureaucracy.

Marx's discussion of bureaucracy is of particular interest because it points to the difficulty of evaluating bureaucracy's role in society. Since his two views are incompatible, which view is correct? As noted, the argument is far from resolved within Marxist-socialism itself. Djilas in *The New Class* pointed to how, in practice, a new bureaucratic class arose from the destruction of the old order under socialism. Hegedus, in *Socialism and Bureaucracy*, while acknowledging some problems with bureaucracy, insists that it can be controlled and put to useful socialist purposes. In Canada the question is quite relevant if stated this way: Does it really, in the long run, make any difference what party or regime is in power? Will the on-going bureaucracy dominate?

Max Weber saw no real escape from bureaucracy, but he placed it on a much broader social base than did Marx. Without bureaucracy, industrialized society in his view simply could not function. The entire pattern of daily life in such a society is cut to fit the framework of bureaucracy. While he felt that capitalism may have been particularly conducive to the growth of bureaucracy, he also believed modern socialist societies are just as dependent on it – and it was his guess that socialism would ultimately demand more bureaucracy than did capitalism. And should those subject to bureaucracy wish to resist it, this is really only possible by creating what is today termed a "counter-organization" which in turn will be subject to bureaucratization.[13]

Weber saw certain consequences for society following from the increasing predominance of bureaucracy. These consequences are "external" to the organization, as opposed to the "internal" consequences discussed in the preceding chapter. First, there was the tendency toward social levelling due to bureaucracy's need for the broadest possible base for recruitment of members. This follows logically from bureaucracy's need for technical competence. In a society with a small educated elite and uneducated masses, the potential competence for bureaucratic purposes is relatively limited as compared to a society where great numbers have reasonably high levels of education. Although Weber appears to have believed that this would be the likely outcome, he did suggest the possibility of a countertendency toward plutocracy arising from interest in the greatest possible duration of formal training. This possible tendency flows logically from the existing and probably ongoing class structure which would allow the children of wealthier parents to gain the greatest expertise through formal training.

These two tendencies — social levelling and government by the wealthy — which are not necessarily contradictory, have become part of both the pro- and anti-bureaucratic theories advanced since Weber. But there are two consequences of bureaucracy, also suggested by Weber, that have been more elaborated and are of central importance to discussion here. These are: 1) change of the general social ethos of the society; and 2) the possible incompatibility between democracy and bureaucracy.

Weber believed that the great emphasis on formalism and impersonality in organizations would eventually pervade their general environment — the society. As he stated it, there would be a spirit of formalistic impersonality, which would be without hatred or passion and therefore without affection or enthusiasm. Since people would not be able to relate positively in their dealings with organizations, they would become alienated from them and because of them and ultimately would become alienated from one another. An increasing number of writers argue that this alienation of people from socio-economic institutions and from one another has already occurred and that it provides the basis for much of today's anti-bureaucratic expression.

There is both explicit and implicit suggestion in Weber's ideas that bureaucracy might have consequences for democracy. The concept of social levelling seems contributive to democratic ideals, but other considerations cast doubt on it. Of primary interest in this context is bureaucracy's possession of knowledge and expertise, one of its dominant characteristics. Bureaucratic administration, according to Weber, meant fundamentally the exercise of control based on both technical knowledge and knowledge gained through experience, in particular from possession of a store of documentary material peculiar to the office. This puts bureaucrats into extraordinarily powerful positions in their relationships with others, especially when, as they so typically do, they practise "official secrecy." In their dealings with the elected representatives of the people the bureaucrats have an advantage, facing the non-specialized, temporary politicians. In Weber's view, the permanent official is much more likely to get his way in the long run than is his nominal superior, the minister.[14] While this may or may not be true, this belief certainly appears to have many adherents in our society, and contributes to the current anti-bureaucratic literature. For example, refer back to the statements of Fisher and Baldwin under the sub-heading "The Canadian Monster."

Robert Michels stated more clearly than Marx and more firmly than Weber the belief that organization, by definition, leads to preservation of organizational self-interest to the detriment of the people supposedly served. His much-cited Iron Law of Oligarchy is: Who says organization, says oligarchy.[15] Although his specific interest was political parties, he generalized to include all organizations under the Iron Law. He insisted that in order to pursue common goals people must form an organization of some sort and, due to specialization of function within the organization, a leadership necessarily emerges. While leaders at first may be voluntary and spontaneous, because of their need to pursue their beliefs and interests they become more and more "professional." It is at this point that leaders become stable and very difficult to remove — and if they are removed, the same phenomenon occurs again. This phenomenon, Michels argued, is partly due to a psychological transformation which the leader undergoes; the desire for personal prestige and power replaces the original desire to achieve group goals. But even more important is the "psychology of organization," with its technical and tactical needs, where the continued existence of the organization becomes the goal, rather than the means to a goal.

As was the case with Marx's earlier statements on bureaucracy, Michels was emphasizing the inevitability of "goal displacement" in organizations. Every organization is originally created to achieve a goal(s), but whatever that goal might be, due to a "universally applicable social law," the very inception of the organization creates interests peculiar to itself. In the pursuance of these special interests the original goal becomes ignored and the original means to that goal become advanced as the goal.[16]

Michels argued further that once the political oligarchy is determined, it needs a numerous and complicated bureaucracy to maintain itself. The bureaucracy is of particular use to the oligarchy, because not only does it impose and maintain the political order, whatever it may be, of the society, it also provides jobs for those who might otherwise threaten the predominance of the regime in power. By being admitted into the bureaucracy, potentially dangerous adversaries are transformed into defenders of the status quo because they have acquired a vested interest in it. In modern terms, opponents are "coopted by the establishment." However, according to Michels these potentially dangerous adversaries are basically members of the middle class, and therefore this device of syphoning off discontent ultimately works against the general interest of the society and to the advantage of the more educated members.

Furthermore, employment in the bureaucracy forces dependence on superiors, and bureaucratic employment therefore is characterized by a narrow, petty bourgeois and philistine nature. In fact, because of its inherent real interest in self-perpetuation, the more conspicuously a bureaucracy appears dominated by zeal, sense of duty, and devotion the more in reality it will be petty, narrow, rigid, and illiberal.[17] This is because the apparent devotion will be self-devotion. Once again, the means become the end, and the sole preoccupation becomes avoidance of anything which might clog the machinery.[18]

What emerges from these earlier writings on bureaucracy is a common concern for its pernicious consequences. This is despite the fact that the large organization as we know it today had only just begun its growth, and government functions and therefore size at that time were rather minute compared to today. Starting from disparate perspectives, arriving at different world views, and writing with varying degrees of emotion, these writers nevertheless saw problems for society in general as a result of bureaucratization. Weber and Michels saw the continuance and domination of bureaucracy as largely inevitable — unless there was a reversion to non-industrial society — while Marx, at least in later writings, foresaw the end of bureaucracy as contingent on the coming into being of the classless society. All saw bureaucracy as having an inherent thrust toward self-perpetuation and self-interest, ultimately alienating the people from itself.

The attack against bureaucracy has continued. While Scientific Management and Administrative Science advocates were not concerned about the possible social problems created by the large organizations about which they enthused, a theme of unease persisted even in their day. In general, the theme appears to have two major components (although they may be separable only for purposes of discussion). These are: 1) The destruction of cherished political values and institutions as the result of bureaucratization; and 2) the alienation of the individual from much of the society in which he must cope with bureaucracy.

Bureaucracy v. Democracy: The Legalists

In 1929, in a book entitled *The New Despotism*, Lord Hewart of Bury, then Lord Chief Justice of England, attacked the British bureaucracy for its supplantation of British parliamentary principles with non-legal methods. His ideas may be said to be of the conspiratorial or intentional elite persuasion, since he clearly argued that the New Despotism was occurring as a result of the efforts of an organized and skillful minority — champions of organized lawlessness.[19] It was obvious to Lord Hewart that for a number of years there had existed an organized minority holding despotic power and attempting to place government departments beyond the control of both Parliament and the

Courts. This was occurring to a great extent under the guise of a need for expertise in government, expertise dedicated to the best and most "scientific" way of ruling the country.[20] But despite this guise of expertise the movement was in reality a deliberate attempt to subordinate Parliament, to evade the Courts, and in general to undermine the entire system of self-government in Britain. The strategy of the despots was: get legislation passed in skeletal form; fill the gaps in legislation with their own rules, orders, and regulations; make it difficult or impossible for Parliament to check these; secure for them the force of statute; make their own decisions final; arrange that the fact of their decisions be conclusive proof of the decisions' legality; take power to modify the provisions of statutes; and prevent any sort of appeal to the Courts.[21]

Much of what Lord Hewart said appeared aimed at politicians as opposed to public servants. The "strategy" just described was actually based on the increasingly common delegation of power by Parliament to the Cabinet (the executive branch) which did in fact, then as now, through Orders-in-Council flesh out statutes with supplementary provisions, regulations and so forth. Much of the "conspiracy" aspect of the argument seems to relate to Cabinet domination of Parliament and Cabinet's subsequent ability to get legislation passed which not only allowed for the Orders-in-Council but also increasingly prevented appeals against the regulations thus made. Furthermore, he specifically noted that the public service was a fine body intent on diligent pursuit of duties.

However, Lord Hewart was not consistent in this view of the public service. Although he did not define the term "bureaucracy," his usage appears to include at least the upper echelons of the public service in addition to ministers. Furthermore, he felt that in all too many cases the Minister himself did not hear of administrative decisions, the actual decision-maker being anonymous and unascertainable.[22] Furthermore, even when the public servant acted in good faith to obtain a correct decision, his membership in the department concerned imposed on him an "official departmental mind" which did not allow him to think impartially. And although Lord Hewart felt that the public service was free of corruption, he nevertheless believed that the extension of the system of granting arbitrary powers to public servants could easily lead to corruption. In any event, the citizen stands helpless before the department, which influences the original legislation, makes subsequent regulations, prosecutes those regulations, and finally, because of provisions in that legislation, stands as judge over the citizen when he is in conflict with the department. Again, according to Lord Hewart all this was not a haphazard occurrence, but rather was quite purposive and systematic. The irresistible conclusion, he stated, was that the intended end result of this carefully devised plan was to give the department despotic powers.[23]

An article appearing in 1944 in the *Canadian Bar Review* argued along similar lines.[24] The author clearly acknowledged the rapid social change which had occurred in this century and which was continuing, and in particular pointed to the Great Depression and World War II as contributing to the growth in government bureaucracy. However, he argued, what was also occurring was a displacement of the "reign of law" by arbitrary government bureaucracy, operating without heed to established legal principles and beyond the control of the Courts. This was all coming about due to increasing delegation of authority by Parliament to the executive branch, through subsequent Orders-in-Council and departmental regulations, and by proliferation of Boards and Commissions. As a result, public servants were becoming the actual legislators, as well as the inquisitors, policemen, judges and executioners. The Order-in-Council and the regulation had become *substantive* law, "enforced by the blind and ruthless partisanship of bureaucratic red tape." A bureaucratic dictatorship was the inevitable outcome of this process. Echoing Lord Hewart's "administrative lawlessness," the author insisted that when delegated legislative authority becomes the norm, the reign of law is negated. At the whim of bureaucrats the daily lives of millions of citizens are regulated, limited and policed.

Bureaucracy v. Democracy: The Economists

Starting from another perspective and advancing different arguments, the ideas of some economists complement those of the legalists just cited. Frederick Hayek's *Road to Serfdom* stands as an excellent example of early reaction to the introduction of Keynesian economics into government, an introduction which was simultaneous with very rapid bureaucratic growth.[25] Appearing toward the end of World War II, it represents a defense of what has been termed "classical economic liberalism."

Basically, Hayek argued for retention of the free-market capitalist economy, insisting that only in the capitalist system is democracy possible. When democracy becomes dominated by a collective creed, it will inevitably destroy itself.[26] When state action becomes consciously aimed at achieving the good of the whole, the greatest good for the greatest number, no individual can plan his own existence and his rights are trampled upon.

The greatest evil for democracy appeared to Hayek to be "state planning," not because it is evil by nature, but because it goes against the free-market economy which he felt is the basis of democracy. Society reached its present stage of industrial growth, differentiation, complexity and flexibility as a result of the free market, and these, and attendant material benefits, would not have been possible if society had relied on conscious central planning. Benefits members of society enjoy, such as full employment, social security and freedom from want, simply cannot be attained by conscious, planned government policy. Solving economic problems by central direction is at best clumsy, primitive and of limited scope.

Hayek felt that the basic problem with the collectivism which so much of the world appears intent on pursuing is that it includes the urge to organize the whole of society and all its resources, while refusing to recognize autonomous spheres in which individual ends should be supreme. All real individualism becomes suppressed in the name of general welfare – a term whose vagueness and ambiguity Hayek felt only concealed the absence of real agreement on the ends of planning. What occurs under a collectivist philosophy, he urged, is that the experts, the planners take control. This leads to the belief that a Parliament, dominated by non-experts, is ineffective, and planning should be taken out of politics and placed in the hands of permanent officials and/or independent bodies. For that matter, due to its variety of opinion, Parliament cannot plan – it can at best agree that there ought to be plans. Then, as planners gain supremacy they inevitably impose their scale of values on the community for which they plan. Delegated legislation allows them to make arbitrary decisions, and democracy ends with an "economic dictatorship." In short, the rapid growth in government activities and attendant bureaucracy during the 1930s was to Hayek a signal of democracy's eventual demise.[27]

A contemporary American economist, Milton Friedman, indicates a similar unease about the constant growth in government.[28] This growth, he feels, is not in any way a conspiracy, an attempt to dominate the society for sinister purposes, but rather reflects the inevitable outcome of welfare systems. According to Friedman the fundamental fallacy of the Welfare State, a fallacy which leads to both financial crisis and the destruction of political freedom, is the attempt to do good at somebody else's expense. Using the disparate examples of Chile, Great Britain, and New York City, he argues that each crisis situation represents an attempt to accomplish high-minded objectives, but that each has ended in failure due to the inherent weakness of welfarism. Distinguishing between the political market and economic market, he argues that the former, which works on the majority principle to which politicians must cater, destroys the rights of the minority in that their preferences are overwhelmed. In the economic market, on the other hand, if 51 per cent of the people "vote" for red neckties, and 49 per cent for green ones, then 51 per cent get their preference, and so do the other 49 per cent. Each gets what he wants, rather than having someone else's preference imposed on him. Similarly, in the economic market a person's money is his to do with as he sees fit, whereas in the political market his money is simply taken from him to be done with as someone else sees fit. This reasoning leads to the conclusion that the economic market is, paradoxically, a more effective means for achieving political democracy than is the political market.

However, because of the constant trend toward welfarism, the political market is more and more negating the potential contribution of the economic market. The most extended period of freedom in Western Europe and the United States was, according to Friedman, the period of the 18th, 19th and early 20th centuries when government interference in the economic sphere was strictly limited. People were free, and in their freedom often did great things; for example, in the United States in the 19th century there were created many excellent universities, public libraries, eleemosynary hospitals, medical missions, societies for the prevention of cruelty to animals and so forth.

Opposed to this is the present situation where government, its bureaucracy with its rules and regulations, and its taxes are growing apace, as is also an attitude of intolerance. If government wants to do good for somebody, it has to take the money for the job from somebody else. This means that force, coercion and destruction of freedom lie at the very source of attempts to do good. Intent on their good works, politicians and bureaucrats become intolerant of any who speak out against their aims and policies. For example, a businessman at the head of a large corporation has to think carefully before speaking out on a major public issue. If he offends, there is the Internal Revenue Service ready to harass him, or the Department of Justice ready to launch an anti-trust suit against him, or the Federal Trade Commission standing by to investigate his products, perhaps with the aid of the Safety Council.

In short, although writing 30 years apart and using different arguments, Hayek and Friedman arrive at a similar "road to serfdom." This serfdom represents the end of political as well as economic democracy, and is the direct result of the constant growth in size and dominance of government and its bureaucracy.

Rejection of Legalist and Economist Arguments

Of course, it is not difficult to find arguments against those of Hewart, Johnson, Hayek and Friedman by people of varying political and economic persuasions. The two following examples have been chosen not only because they both oppose the reasoning just presented, but also because they differ so radically in all other ways.

Jacob Finkelman, a Canadian lawyer, in an article published in 1932 specifically rejected much of Lord Hewart's thesis and anticipated negatively the ideas of Hayek and Friedman by pointing to the inadequacies and problems of laissez-faire economics and government.[29] Finkelman suggested that what was occurring in Canada at that time was a shift in social philosophy, moving from laissez-faire into more positive government actions. Eighteenth-century government, which Friedman identifies as an era of much freedom for citizens and of great charitable undertakings, was characterized by Finkelman as a period when government was so inefficient and corrupt that it could not possibly solve social problems. Laissez-faire, he felt, developed only in the absence of anything better, and was bolstered by the emergence of Darwinism which stated for man what economists stated for the economy—survival of the fittest. The economists insisted that free competition had built industrial London, while the Darwinians argued that free competition had developed man. In either case, neither competitive area was to be tampered with. In this period, Parliament, having much time available, leisurely made its relatively few laws with great detail, attempting to provide for every possible contingency. The Courts, in their turn, kept steadfastly to the view that they quite objectively interpreted and applied the law in individual cases, divorced from governmental action as well as from social policy and a sense of the public at large. They were, that is, concerned only with individual offenders on an after-the-fact basis, and the public interest simply did not figure in deliberations.

However, the weaknesses in this scheme of things became more and more apparent. According to Finkelman, the untold misery, suffering and social waste arising from industrialization created a feeling of revulsion which undermined even the positive achievements of laissez-faire. People became ashamed of its negative excesses, and even firm adherents to the doctrine attempted to find ways and means to soften its harsh impact on the masses.

If laissez-faire was rejected, if the belief no longer could be held that society was so "divinely ordered" that each person received his just reward, then only the government could correct the actual situation. Under the new social philosophy, government became action-oriented, involved in the provision of social services, taking on a multitude of new concerns. However, the legislative system was unprepared and inadequate for this task and legislators, facing the need to meet the demands of the enfranchised masses in order to gain their support, "passed the buck" through devolution of their legislative power to the executive branch. Because of the new social philosophy, pronounced government growth occurred and delegating powers to public agencies became the norm. The latter was not a deliberate attempt to avoid responsibility, but rather was the response to an urgent need which Parliament simply was not suited to meet. Solutions to all sorts of social ills were needed, detailed legislation was needed, and the ever-increasing number of detailed statutes had to be administered. The only solution was reliance on administrative agencies to provide the time and expertise which Parliament lacked. Similarly, the Courts could not handle the vastly increased number of cases, the details of many of which required specific expertise in subject matter, and administrative agencies were given more and more judicial and quasi-judicial authority to decide on individual cases.

Finkelman insisted that the new system, as he saw it at that time, posed certain dangers. Parliament certainly could not abdicate its responsibilities; it had to continue to cope to the best of its ability. However, if Parliament simply could not handle the entire new work load, then other means just had to be found – and the only choice was to delegate power to the executive branch. And if the courts could not handle their new work load then some of the traditional judicial powers had to be given to administrative agencies. As long as the basics remained – no man may be judge in his own case; no party may be condemned unheard; and every party concerned is entitled to know the reason for a decision – then he did not see much difference in justice being administered by the Courts or by administrative agencies.

While Finkelman's argument may have been somewhat radical for its day, it in no way reflects current radical thought. One example of such thinking is provided by the periodical *Our Generation*.[30] The editor argues that a "social democratic liberal" view of the capitalist State prevails far too widely. This view, much like Finkelman's, sees the State as the means of reform, as the redistributor of wealth and provider of services. It is the means to the "just society." The expanding bureaucracy, the expanding "industrial public sector" and other government initiatives are the signs of the future good society.

The false assumption of this view according to *Our Generation* is that the resolution of the problems of capitalism lies in the growth of the public sector. The assumption is false because the real role of the State is to serve private capital, and therefore any real growth of the bureaucracy shows capital's increased strength. While a "few anachronistic businessmen" occasionally object to government growth, the State they say they fear has grown directly in response to their corporate needs in such areas as transportation, education, resource development, communications and scientific research. The growth in the so-called Welfare State, whose intent is to redistribute services and wealth to those at the lower levels of the capitalist order, is an exaggeration. As compared to GNP or total government expenditures, the expenditures by the State on social services have remained more or less constant. Furthermore, the additional state revenues required to finance the growing State bureaucracy have been disproportionately raised through increases in personal income and sales taxes. In short, the great majority of salaried employees in Canada have financed the creation of the vast bureaucracy whose basic role is to serve the needs of a small class of corporate owners.

Obviously, what are involved here are the very disparate world views leading to radically different conclusions concerning growth in government activities and the consequent growth in government bureaucracies. Since they cannot all be correct, we are left with the problem of deciding which has the most truth, which most accurately describes reality. This entire area is quite problematical. As members of our society, products of our culture, we cannot evaluate the problem in a vacuum. Any decision we make will be influenced by our personal ideology, just as the above described, disparate views were influenced by ideological biases.

One point that does seem clear is that there is a fairly strong anti-big-government sentiment in Canada, and that this sentiment is often expressed in anti-bureaucratic, ideological terms. It is quite possible that, while bureaucracy is condemned, it is really the policies which bureaucracy administers that are the source of concern. The large government bureaucracies in Canada to a great extent result from positive Government, which in turn derives from a social philosophy by no means universally subscribed to in this country. That the majority of anti-bureaucratic views expressed above appear to be related to a conservative ideological perspective is not coincidental, as conservatives are probably more prone to transfer their hostility in this fashion. For example, a study which examined attitudes toward "red tape" (a pejorative term closely connected to allegations of bureaucratic inefficiency) suggests that the epithet developed under conservative sponsorship. By condemning government bureaucracy, the individual expresses his dissatisfaction, his frustration, while at the same time he is spared the need to condemn duly legislated government policies. As a conservative his ideology makes him reluctant to condemn institutions such as Parliament, but he is allowed by that ideology "objectively" to point to the ineptness of government administrators, feeling better as a result of it.[31]

Herbert Kaufman[32] suggests that, in the case of the United States, this anti-bureaucratic view with its political, ideological basis has a long tradition, reflecting the struggles for power and/or dominance among the three branches of government — legislative, executive and judicial. Although in Canada we do not have such a formal, constitutional separation of powers, the various arguments against the bureaucracy suggest a fairly common concern that the executive branch as we know it has usurped the powers and rights of Parliament and the Courts. In the case of Finkelman, executive growth or bureaucratic expansion (whichever term one wishes to use) was not considered to be a problem, in fact it was viewed as a positive occurrence. This seems understandable, given the unsettled times, the apparent breakdown of the free market system and the advent of the Great Depression. Government was being asked to cope in areas it had previously shunned. Public servants, as not only the administrators of new policies but also the visible manifestations of those policies, could be viewed in a positive manner. Kaufman points out that bureaucrats in the United States in the 1930s were regarded by many as heroes in the struggle for a better social order. He further suggests that it was indicative of a much more general mood when Paul Appleby, a prominent New Deal official, dedicated his book *Big Democracy* to "Bill Bureaucrat". (The title and certainly the dedication seem very unlikely today.) Kaufman also argues that these shifts in emphasis for social salvation are never constant, and predicts that we are into an era when politics will revolve more and more around pro- and anti-bureaucratic ideologies. That this is occurring is perhaps indicated by our earlier discussion on the emphasis on "government restraint" prevailing in Canada today.

Anti-Bureaucratic Utopianism

It should not be assumed that only conservatives in general or businessmen in particular are anti-bureaucratic. Alfred Diamant suggests that we have entered an era where anti-bureaucratism has become commonplace in utopian thinking.[33] His argument is that proposed and/or pursued utopias are responses to existing conditions and that they flourish during times of upheaval and unrest. Past utopias tended to emphasize some form of organization, with the Perfect State being perfectly ordered and structured, creating individual fulfillment. The means to achieving these utopias were coercion, reasoning, or psychological manipulation, depending on the utopia proposed. Since the 1950s, however, utopias reject organization, order and stability precisely because they are a reaction to present domination by large organizations.

Diamant's thesis is that although life today is chaotic in many ways, it is nevertheless dominated by large organizations in production, consumption, education and even leisure and play. As a result, the good life or utopia has become one where individual and/or small group existence is the norm — an existence which stresses spontaneity over organization, and rejects specialization and division of labor. (Perhaps one example of this is the changing roles of men and women.) Such utopianists want at least some of the fruits of industrialization, but are unwilling to accept its other consequences.

There are several features of this trend, according to Diamant. First, it is a radical movement in the sense that it is against the established order of things. Second, although wide in scope, it is mainly limited to the industrialized societies. Third, it shows a deep aversion to organization in general and to organized leadership in particular. Fourth, it is a political as well as a cultural phenomenon, the political views intertwined with the particular desired life-style. Fifth, it stresses spontaneity, experimentation, open-endedness, and play. Sixth, it emphasizes sensuality, as opposed to the Puritanism by which the established order is alleged to be characterized. Seventh, it proposes to end the fractionalization of life which occurs under the present system. And, eighth, it is ambivalent about technology, in that some of its features are seen as worth having while others are not. Of these current utopian characteristics, Diamant suggests, the most central to the movement are spontaneity, sensuality and play, which replace order, puritanism and work.

If we accept Diamant's contentions even to a limited degree, they help explain the negative view of bureaucracy that is such a constant theme in our society. "Bureaucracy" becomes an all-embracing term for what people feel is wrong in their world. That is, the term is used much as Max Weber first employed it, denoting organization, order, stability, predictability, specialization and division of labor, impersonalism and so forth. It is not, then, the bureaucracy *per se* that people have in mind when they say "bureaucracy" with a sneer in the voice, but rather the entire way of life today. Thus, as Kaufman has suggested, radicals have definite feelings in common with conservatives, even if one tends toward future utopias as the solution while the other tends to retreat into a desire for the past.

Studies of Attitudes toward Bureaucracy

In addition to these broad-gauge explanations of the negative view held of bureaucracy, there has been research into specific attitudes and beliefs of people concerning bureaucracy with attempts to explain why these are held. Two such studies will be discussed here, one American and one Canadian. They are not intended to be proof of anything, but rather to stand as suggestions of possibilities.

In the case of the United States the study substantiates the idea that there is a generalized negative view of bureaucracy. Concentrating on client-centered organizations such as State Employment Services, Aid to Families with Dependent Children, and so forth, the study found that respondents were generally positive about their bureaucracy in general. Although ratings of the various agencies differed, it was found that, contrary to the popular negative image of the bureaucrat, the respondents were on the whole satisfied with services. Specifically, 43 per cent were "very satisfied," 26 per cent "satisfied," 13 per cent "somewhat dissatisfied" and 14 per cent "very dissatisfied." In a similarly positive vein, 16 per cent felt that bureaucrats had helped them more than they had to, and 57 per cent felt they had helped "about right," with only 12 per cent feeling they had helped less than they should have and 9 per cent that they had made no effort at all.

While the negative percentages were significant, the study concludes on this point that Americans have not found from their personal experience that bureaucratic encounters are all that bad. However, the study proceeds to point out that respondents consistently believed their own encounters to be better than what everyone else was experiencing. For example, 71 per cent said that their problems were taken care of, but only 30 per cent thought that government agencies do well at looking after problems. Eighty per cent felt they were treated fairly by bureaucrats, but only 40 per cent believed that government agencies treat most people fairly. Eighty per cent stated that they were treated considerately, while again only 40 per cent believed this to be the case for others. In short, the stereotype of the lazy, inaccessible, inconsiderate bureaucrat is so strong, that when people experienced the opposite face to face, they believed it must be an exception. But respondents' collective responses indicate many "exceptions."

Pursuing another line of questions, the study also found evidence that Americans have a disjointed set of political attitudes. They tend to cherish national symbols but are negative about national leadership. They are patriotic but mistrustful of government decisions. In short, they tend to be positive about their personal experiences but critical of government agencies in general and of politicians in particular. Perhaps, again, bureaucracy stands as a visible target for a general malaise in the society, guilty simply because it is part of government.[34]

Because American political culture, and therefore administrative culture, is different from Canada's, these findings can only be taken as suggestive of possibilities. The possibilities are reinforced by a somewhat older study of Canadian attitudes toward politicians, government and bureaucracy. This study helps to explain why the term "bureaucracy" has such a negative connotation in this country.

While responses varied from region to region, 17 per cent of all respondents said they expected "most fair" treatment from the federal government, 44 per cent expected "reasonably fair" treatment, 27 per cent said "just so-so," and only 9 per cent expected "unfair" treatment. However, the problem with these categories is that they can be interpreted in two quite different ways. Excluding the 9 per cent "unfair" group, it can be argued that the great majority of Canadians are at least somewhat positive toward the federal bureaucracy. On the other hand, excluding the 17 per cent "most fair" group, it can also be contended that the great majority of Canadians are at least somewhat negative toward the federal bureaucracy. However, taking the figures at face value, only the 9 per cent "unfair" group could in any way be considered hostile.

Concerning "prompt treatment," Canadians are much less likely to expect this than they are to expect "fair treatment." In this case 5 per cent of respondents expected "very prompt" treatment, 20 per cent said "reasonably prompt," 23 per cent "just so-so," 24 per cent "somewhat slow" and 17 per cent "very slow." This is similar to beliefs held about government "efficiency." Six per cent of all respondents thought that the government was "efficient," 18 per cent that it was "somewhat efficient," 31 per cent that is was "passable," 25 per cent that it was "somewhat inefficient" and 20 per cent that it was "inefficient." Taking all these figures strictly at face value, in simplistic majority terms Canadians expect to be treated fairly by a sluggish, inefficient bureaucracy. This apparent inconsistency seems to parallell the American study's finding that individuals can have positive encounters with bureaucracy but nevertheless retain the negative stereotype of it.

Grouping these findings in with answers to other questions, the study summarizes as follows: Somewhat over 60 per cent of us think that most public servants are courteous, intelligent and well-respected; 40 to 50 per cent think of most public servants as hardworking, efficient, enterprising and paid appropriately for their work; only 33 per cent believe most public servants are interested in people's problems; and 20 per cent feel that most public servants are able to redirect or otherwise assist people who go to the wrong department. Again, there is ambiguity present, in that most public servants are seen as intelligent and courteous, but only a minority are seen as interested in the individual's problems. In any event, although they may or may not be a majority, certainly many Canadians view bureaucrats on the negative side of a negative-positive continuum.

Relating these findings to others, the study could not arrive at clear answers as to *why* people feel the way they do about bureaucracy. However, there did appear to be some definite relationship between attitudes toward bureaucracy and feelings of political efficacy, the latter in turn depending on a number of variables. It suggests that members of the middle class are more likely to be interested in government affairs, to be knowledgeable about federal and provincial involvement, to use several sources of information about government programs, and to have positive views toward the bureaucracy. On the other hand, members of the lower class tend to be less interested in government affairs, to use available information sources less, to know less, and to describe their relationship with bureaucrats more negatively. The study suggests several reasons why middle class people are more knowledgeable, interested and positive in their attitudes toward bureaucracy. The middle class probably contains a higher proportion of public servants than do other classes. Middle class people's jobs are more likely to involve contacts with public servants, and knowledge of government activities is more likely to be an asset to them. They are also better equipped educationally to follow politics and to take action either as individuals or as members of organizations. They are more likely to realize that knowledge is necessary for successful political activity. And, they are more capable of being responsive and knowledgeable in dealing with bureaucracy. Lower class people as a group are not devoid of these attributes, but they do possess them to a lesser degree. However, the study concludes, quite enigmatically, that the relationship between public servants and the lower class is more pleasant and co-operative than might be imagined. This relationship will shortly be returned to in another context.[35]

Bureaucracy and Alienation

It was noted above that early discussions on bureaucracy emphasized its dangers for democracy and its potential for alienating the masses. It was also remarked that, while in discussion these two sub-themes in antibureaucratism can be distinguished only with difficulty, in practice they would appear to be inseparable. To this point, our discussion has stressed the bureaucratic-democratic aspect, although the element of alienation has been present (most clearly in such sub-topics as anti-bureaucratic utopianism, but also in others such as bureaucracy and the lower class). We will now leave the bureaucracy-democracy theme and concentrate on alienation itself, with the realization that the two themes are intermingled in reality.

It is possible that much of the anti-bureaucratic sentiment in our society is the result of individual alienation from bureaucracy because of negative experience with it. The American study on attitudes toward bureaucracy suggests that positive bureaucratic encounters do not affect the negative stereotype, while negative encounters reinforce it. If this is the case, then as bureaucracy continues to grow and as the potential for unsatisfactory encounters grows with it, the negative stereotype of bureaucracy will expand and strengthen.

Bureaucracy does work to a considerable extent the way Weber suggested it did. The impersonalism, the lack of emotional involvement with the client/citizen is a strong characteristic of government bureaucracy. Most of us have encountered it in various areas of our lives, whether in school, taking a driver's test, applying for unemployment insurance, trying to find a job, dealing with the police, discussing matters with Revenue Canada, applying for a waiver of a zoning requirement, complaining about a high water bill, adopting a child or even having one – the possibilities are endless. We can often come away from these encounters feeling that the bureaucrat is cold, insensitive, uncaring. If this happens several times, we will generalize that feeling and our personal negative stereotype of bureaucracy and bureaucrats will be created.

The bureaucrat, if he does his job properly, or "legally" in the Weberian sense of that term, must abide by the rules and regulations attached to his office. If, for example, the bureaucrat is involved with placing children for adoption, and if the legislation concerning adoption spells out the basic requirements that prospective parents must possess, then "legally" the child placement officer must refuse an application from a couple who do not meet these requirements. In fact, at the provincial level Ombudsman offices have been created to help ensure that the citizen is treated "properly" by the bureaucracy — that is, that he is treated legally and fairly rather then arbitrarily and unfairly.

The client, of course, wishes to be treated fairly, but his definition of "fair" is not necessarily the same as the bureaucrat's. If the two definitions are compatible, then the client "wins" and there is a good chance that he will consider the bureaucrat in a favorable light. However, if the two definitions of "fair" are incompatible, then the client will generally "lose" and think of the bureaucrat as officious, insensitive, incompetent, arrogant.

The crux of the matter is, of course, the definition of "fair." The bureaucrat tends to be strongly bound to the official definition, and while he can make mistakes and thus be officially unfair, his experience in his job, familiarity with relevant legislation and attendant rules and regulations, makes this not too common. The client, on the other hand, tends to view "fair" from another, personal perspective. He is personally involved in the decision in a way that the bureaucrat is not and "legally" may not allow himself to be. So the client brings to the encounter certain "exceptional circumstances" as well as perhaps subjective interpretations of the relevant regulations. He does not realize that the bureaucrat has probably seen such exceptional circumstances before, and according to the legal provisions under which he works must consider them as irrelevant to the issue at hand. The client's problem, which is so momentous to himself, is only one of many similar problems with which the bureaucrat has coped. If he is to be "fair" — that is, impartial — he must judge the case exactly as he has judged previous similar cases. The client, on the other hand, no matter how intelligent he may be, often finds it impossible to accept the bureaucrat's view of reality. "This is unique, exceptional, one-in-a-million me! Surely, these silly rules were never intended to apply in my case!" They almost always do, however, and so there is a very good chance that bureaucracy has gained another enemy.[36]

However, while impersonalism in bureaucracy is fundamental, it also has dysfunctional potential. A circumstance might indeed be exceptional. Habitually doing things "by the book" can lead to ignorance of reality — that the book is out of date. At the very least the bureaucrat might recommend a change to his superiors. In other words, impersonalism can lead to closed thinking, which benefits neither the client nor the organization.

Another factor to be considered here is the hierarchical nature of bureaucracy. Robert Merton points out that we believe that government employees are our public *servants*. In actual fact, due to the hierarchical nature of bureaucracy, the clientele constitute the bottom tiers of the hierarchy. All the internal rules and regulations of the organization, created for the sake of coordination, control and so forth, are imposed on the clientele in the sense that, if they want help, they must conform to them. Furthermore, the public sector differs from the private sector in that, in the latter, the dissatisfied client can take his custom elsewhere. Given the monopolistic nature of government services, this is not possible when the client is dissatisfied with the behavior and decisions of public bureaucrats. Generally, if a client wants help for a specific problem handled by the government, he *must* deal with the sole relevant agency.[37]

An important point to keep in mind in assessing the bureaucracy's orientation toward fair treatment is the view one holds of the nature of man in general and the nature of bureaucratic man in particular. As stressed in the preceding chapter, there are very disparate views held on these matters, and the "truth" of this problematic would appear to have great bearing on the other problematic of how bureaucracy treats clientele. There is a vast body of literature, emanating mainly from Organization Psychology, which sees bureaucratic man and bureaucracy in a rather favorable light, at the very least as having much potential for good. This was discussed in the preceding chapter in the context of motivation to work. There is another body of literature, in this case originating largely in sociology, that sees bureaucratic man and bureaucracy in a rather dim light. This was also discussed in the preceding chapter in the context of bureaupathology. It is this latter literature which prevails in discussion of bureaucracy-clientele relationships.

If indeed man, or just bureaucratic man, is basically self-oriented and self-seeking, suspicious of others, domineering toward inferiors and subservient to superiors then one can expect him to treat clientele in a very instrumental, non-self-involved fashion. He will view clients as problems the successful solution of which will lead to advancement in the organization, rather than regarding them as human beings in need of his help. Furthermore, because of organization imperatives and because he wishes to abide by these imperatives in order to advance himself, he will expend minimal resources on the solution of client problems — to do otherwise would be inefficient. According to Merton, this type of person is much more concerned with defending his entrenched interests than he is in really helping clientele[38]; any help he does extend is a means to preservation and/or advancement of self-interest.

Bureaucracy and the Lower Class

A number of studies of bureaucracy-clientele relationships stress the middle-class composition, norms, and values of bureaucracy. Among many others, Sjoberg *et al.*[39] point to the relatively high degree of formal education necessary to obtain government employment today, one result of which is that bureaucracy recruits largely from the middle class. (Refer to Michel's ideas on bureaucracy and the middle class earlier in this chapter.) If the individual does not have a middle-class background, he is quickly socialized by the organization to adopt and conform to its middle-class bias. For all employees, the bureaucracy, in a wide variety of ways, continuously reinforces middle-class orientations. What happens is that the individual, coming into the organization with a desire for personal success, will take on the trappings that will make him acceptable to existing members. He will dress and talk appropriately, read the right books and see the right movies, take out a mortgage on the right house in the right neighborhood, and even marry the right person or get rid of the wrong one.[40] It is often urged that the strength of this need to conform to middle-class norms in the organization should not be underestimated. Perhaps a good, practical (although middle-class) example of it can be seen in universities every year in early spring. Many students who are in their last year of study and who have throughout their stay worn blue jeans and scuffed shoes suddenly appear in classes and hallways in suits and ties and shiny shoes, or dresses and make-up. They are going for a job interview, and are recognizing the reality of the job market.

Although these and other middle class values and norms of bureaucracy are informal, they are nevertheless strongly adhered to and enforced in a variety of ways. According to a number of writers, this adherence has certain implications for the lower-class clientele of bureaucracies, and for society in general. It points to still another possible dimension of fair treatment.

It has been argued that the life-situation of lower-class people has certain common characteristics.[41] There tend to be long periods of unemployment and/or intermittent employment, which means that public assistance is often a major source of income. Jobs tend to be at the least-skilled and lowest-paid levels. There are high rates of marital instability, illegitimate births, unstable interpersonal relationships, and considerable suspicion toward anyone outside the immediate family. Residential areas have very poorly developed voluntary associations, and these have little participation. There is some general alienation from the larger society, little knowledge or interest in it. And there is a sense of hopelessness and fatalism, a low sense of personal efficacy, and low levels of aspiration.

It is argued that, as a result of this set of characteristics, the lower-class individual finds it very difficult to cope successfully with middle-class bureaucracy. The middle-class bureaucrat in turn finds it very difficult to cope successfully with such a client even when he sincerely wishes to help. The lower-class client lacks basic knowledge of the rules of the game (there are always some notable exceptions reported) and as a result he cannot manipulate rules to his own advantage nor can he attempt to gain special consideration through the informal aspects of bureaucracy. He is, in short, faced with an organization quite foreign to him, working in strange ways and insisting on many complex, incomprehensible rules.

Take, for a hypothetical example, the case of two children expelled from school for incorrigible behavior, and assume that one child is the son of an unmarried waitress and the other the son of a well-established university professor. It is doubtful whether the waitress would know how to begin going about reinstatement of her son. Furthermore, there is a good chance that she would not be too concerned with the expulsion, telling the boy that it is time for him to get a job anyway. The professor on the other hand, may attempt to move heaven and earth to achieve her son's reinstatement. Her position in the neighborhood will demand it, as will her friends, her basic values and her self-perception which greatly influences her perception of her son. At the very least she will probably attempt to have the decision reversed, and will "buck the system" with all her resources. She will argue with the teacher and principal, promise after-school treatment. She might even ask influential friends to write letters for her, threaten to take the matter to the School Board or to the Deputy Minister and Minister of Education. And, given the nature of the system, there would be a very good chance for her success. The impartial treatment becomes partial even if unconsciously so.

Clients dealing with bureaucracy tend to face its lower levels and it is the lower levels which are most dominated by rules and regulations and so can practise the least discretion. Therefore, the lower-class client, who has the least knowledge of the rules of the game begins and ends his bureaucratic encounters at this level. The middle-class client will often attempt to have the decision pushed upward in the hierarchy where the possibility of discretion is much greater.[42]

There is some argument that one overall effect of bureaucracy is reinforcement of the social class structure. Because of the emphasis on expertise, the richer areas of a city hire the best teachers. Teachers who serve in a poor area attempt to get out as quickly as possible.[43] As a result, socio-economic advancement of lower-class children is impeded not just by their cultural milieu but also by their receipt of the lowest quality of formal instruction. Schools also emphasize "standards" and these are established by the dominant middle-class groups. School "efficiency" demands that children live up to these standards. However, the "non-standard" needs of lower-class children tend not to be acknowledged, bureaucracy again not allowing for "special consideration." The alleged impartial rules have a built-in middle-class bias.

Sjoberg *et al.*[44] suggest that because of the differences in attitudes, values and norms between middle-class bureaucrats and lower-class clients, the former are often simply incapable of really understanding the latter's view of reality. Because of his own values the bureaucrat attempts to impose his view of reality on the client, either because he does not recognize that another view is possible or because he cannot accept that other view.[45] Thus, even the best-intentioned bureaucrat can easily fail in solving the problems of lower-class clientele.

Furthermore, if a bureaucrat does realize the problems of this situation, and attempts to step out of his formal role, the organization will probably discipline him for it, because he will be going against the established value system. A professional is placed under considerable pressure to conform to professional norms, simply by accusations of non-professional conduct. For that matter, such accusations can easily lead to loss of job. As Hummel[46] contends, functionaries who cannot accept the restrictions of bureaucratic service ultimately resign from, or are forced to leave, the bureaucracy. While success stories of mavericks do occasionally occur in organizations, and while the myth of the maverick has considerable popularity, it is certainly not the norm. In fact, its popularity could be argued to be a reflection of a desire to escape reality.[47]

A final item in this context involves the specialization that is so characteristic of modern bureaucracies. Assuming that the bureaucrat is totally committed to client service, he is nevertheless going to remain a specialist and his specific skills will tend to be quite narrow in perspective. However, the client may have several problems in conjunction, each reinforcing the other, none of which can be solved in isolation. For example, assume an individual who has a low level of formal education, is unemployed and in poor health. Unemployment may be partly a result of poor health (e.g., absenteeism), partly of too little education. Similarly, poor health may partly be due to lack of knowledge about good dietary habits compounded by a lower food budget; the low educational level cannot be bettered due to lack of funds and lack of energy. However, although these problems are interlocked, the experts who attempt to solve them work only on the basis of their own expertise. The medical officer sees the client as a poor health problem, the employment officer as an employment problem, and the education officer as an education problem. Each, separated by expertise, may earnestly wish to "solve" the client's problem, never fully if at all realizing that the total problem is not resolvable simply by attacking part of it, and that even one part of it cannot be successfully resolved without simultaneous attack on the other aspects. Expertise, in short, concentrates on single-problem solutions, while the client is often multi-problemal.[48]

The intent of this cursory discussion of bureaucracy and the lower class has been to suggest possible further explanation of the negative feelings toward bureaucracy in Canada. As the Canadian study on attitudes toward bureaucracy stated, the relationship between bureaucracy and the lower class in Canada is "more pleasant and cooperative than it might be." This suggests that the relationship could have been worse but is still not all that positive; this lack of positiveness is linked by the study to relatively low feelings of political efficacy on the part of the lower class. While this appears reasonable to a certain extent(substantiated by other studies of class and politics in Canada), it may also be the case that the lower class is negative toward the bureaucratic relationship because of factors that relate to, but are distinct from, feelings of political efficacy *per se*. It seems likely that the various factors just discussed concerning the middle-class bureaucracy and lower-class clientele preclude a positive relationship between them due to the class biases of each.

Alternatives to Bureaucracy

Because of alienation from bureaucracy on both a personal and class basis, and because of bureaucracy's anti-democratic nature, various alternatives to it have been proposed over the years. For example, there has been the anti-bureaucratic utopianism noted above, out of which some specific proposals have emerged. Related to this is the New Public Administration movement in the United States, an academic movement which has had some impact on Canada. It has been described as emphasizing relevance, postpositivism and confrontation, and it focuses on the "client-centered, street-level bureaucrat." The orientation is toward action to solve problems arising from bureaucracy, as opposed to study of bureaucracy from a value-neutral position.[49]

A good example of a non-bureaucratic organization is supplied by Orion White's "Dialectical Organization," an organization which, as its name implies, is at an extreme opposite from what is seen as the typical bureaucratic organization.[50] White attempts to justify this form of organization by attacking the basis of the bureaucratic organization. His argument is that, if the underlying justifications given for the typical bureaucratic organization are invalid, then insistence upon carrying on with such an organization is illogical. The two justifications he examines are the concept of "policy rationality," and the criterion of "efficiency."

According to White, "policy rationality" cannot justify the continued use of the bureaucratic form of organization, because bureaucracy is not rational in this sense. The making of policy is not rational because it is the result of political decisions involving less than a comprehensive evaluation of various alternatives. Expediency rather than rationality would appear to be its basis. And the application of policy is not rational because policy is applied differentially to clientele depending on their class position and so forth, as has just been discussed above. In short, rational policy is really not rational, but rather reflects only the "best way to do it." This, in turn, is defined by bureaucracies on other than rational grounds.

Similarly, White argues that the whole idea of "efficiency" in public organizations should be critically examined in the light of its ideological overtones. In his view, the degree of efficiency which an organization brings to bear in its relationship with the client should be a matter for political as opposed to administrative definition, since it often involves the question of how much personal freedom the client must surrender in the name of the "general good." Put differently, what and how much does the client have to "pay" in order to obtain a service? To use a hypothetical example, suppose there is an agency involved in helping single mothers to get jobs, and suppose there are two ways in which the agency can deal with these women: one, the workers can go to the women; or, two, the women can come to the workers. If the workers go to the women, then more effort is required of the workers, while the women receive help without having to leave their homes. On the other hand, if the agency decides that the women will come to the workers, then the women must do so in order to receive help. This will involve finding a babysitter or dressing the children to take them along, obtaining transportation. In this kind of situation who properly should determine the best way of handling things? Typically, the agency decides what is "best" on the basis of what is more "efficient." These questions, however, involve basic values, and should not be left up to administrative discretion hiding behind the far-from-value-free criterion of "efficiency."

The Dialectical Organization proposed by White would have characteristics completely opposite to those commonly alleged to typify bureaucratic organizations. In terms of structure, the two organizations compare as follows:

Bureaucratic Organization	**Dialectical Organization**
1. Layered authority relationships.	**1.** Lateral authority relationships.
2. Policy set at top.	**2.** Policy set consensually.
3. Organization operates inflexibly.	**3.** Organization operates flexibly.
4. Cohesive social structure, involving homogeneity, conformity, one view of the world.	**4.** Lack of definite social structure, involving heterogeneity, lack of norms, many views of the world.

Given this dialectical structure, personnel are encouraged to hold attitudes conducive to all-out service and to be intent on goal attainment, as opposed to attitudes of moderation and survival. They are also encouraged to adopt attitudes of sharing, cooperation and trust as opposed to attitudes of selfishness, competition and threat. Given these attitudes, the organization-client relationship would compare as follows:

Bureaucratic Organization	**Dialectical Organization**
1. Client treated as subordinate.	**1.** Client treated as equal.
2. Client viewed simplistically, segmentally.	**2.** Client treated as complex, as "whole."
3. Client expected to adapt to situation.	**3.** Attempt to change situation causing client problems.
4. Client treated impersonally.	**4.** Client treated with involvement.
5. Help is qualified, based on input-output "efficiency" calculations.	**5.** Help is unqualified; the goal is successful treatment.

White's argument, then, is against using the bureaucratic organizational form just because it has been and is the norm. Given its dysfunctional consequences, other organizational forms should be sought. Furthermore, we are urged to draw back from unhesitating acceptance of such terms as "rationality" and "efficiency" when these are attached to bureaucratic organizations, as they are far from value-free in nature, needing careful political as opposed to administrative evaluation.

Possible Consequences of Non-bureaucratic Forms of Organization

White insists that the Dialectical Organization is not an ideal form to be pursued in the abstract, but rather one that can be given substantive reality. As a result of a case study he conducted, he describes such an organization in actual practice, indicating its viability and its benefits. Assuming for purposes of argument that this form could be broadly implemented in the public service, there remains the question of its possible negative consequences. That is, its possible positive consequences are fairly apparent, but there would be no point in replacing bureaucracy with another form if the form's negative consequences equal or even outweigh those of bureaucracy.

First and foremost the use of such an organizational form implies a rather god-like nature on the part of personnel and assumes that man is basically "good" rather than having a proclivity toward wickedness. Unless this is assumed, how else can one justify removing the controls over workers which are such a strong characteristic of bureaucracy? Certainly, there is the assumption that staff members will use their freedom to the client's benefit, that they will begin to empathize with clientele and to really understand them; and that, given dedication to goal achievements, workers will devote unqualified resources to solution of problem situations for clients. Conversely, the assumption certainly is not that workers will utilize lack of restrictions to ride rough-shod over clients, to dominate them more than they are already dominated. To use a specific example from the Dialectical Organization, these workers trained in the client's problem area, these "experts," will treat clients as "equals," as having as valid a view of the problem area as they themselves have. However, as the preceding chapter points out, while the optimistic view of human nature receives considerable emphasis in administrative theory and practice today, it is still very seriously challenged.

To point again to a specific example, the Dialectical Organization would enphasize genuine involvement of the worker with the client. Impersonalism and objectivity would be replaced by personalism and subjectivity. With these, genuine sympathy and empathy for the troubled client would be possible. Weber's characterization of the bureaucrat as "without hatred or passion and therefore without affection or enthusiasm" would be invalid. In short, this subjective, personalistic treatment of the client, freed from bureaucratic rules, assumes that the treatment will automatically be "nice," and that it will be appreciated by the client. However, personalistic, subjective treatment does not by definition imply a particular relationship between worker and client, i.e., a relationship of love and trust. It could just as easily be one of hate and fear. Peter Blau, for example, insists that bureaucracy's attempts to be impersonal and impartial can be viewed as good to the extent that it helps overcome, for example, favoritism based on birth, social status and money.[51] Stated crudely, without bureaucracy there is no telling which form treatment would take, whereas according to many writers the tendency with bureaucracy is toward equal treatment even if the ideal is only approximated.

Taking another tack, Robert Michels insisted that people either organize themselves or they do not, and if they once begin to organize, then the process of tyranny with its attendant bureaucracy is also begun. In this view, organization means bureaucracy. To escape from bureaucracy, then, there must be no organization. This is what is advocated by certain anti-bureaucratic thinkers today – an emphasis on structurelessness, lack of formal leadership, lack of rules and regulations.

However, using the Women's Liberation Movement as an example, Sociologist Jo Freeman points to the "tyranny of structurelessness" which seems to have as many potential problems as the "tyranny of structure."[52] The Movement originated as an attempt at "consciousness-raising," and the means for this was the structureless "rap group." This group was quite informal, the informality encouraging participation in discussions leading to personal insight. As long as the goal was as unspecific as consciousness-raising, there was no problem with the method. But when goals become somewhat more specific, the limitations of structurelessness became evident. Such groups are subject to the process of informal organization. "Natural leaders" appear, to a great extent determined by their network of personal friendships, their membership in certain cliques, and also by virtue of unspecified but powerful personal criteria. Thus, the basis for elites is formed.

However, the cultivation and attainment of elite status demands much time, through attending meetings, fostering friendships with other influential people, and so forth. This automatically discriminates against any who, for whatever reason, cannot afford the amount of time and energy necessary to become influential in this fashion. The situation in Women's Lib was exacerbated by media and public devotion to "stars." Certain women were picked out by the media as "newsworthy" and these became spokespersons for the Movement. Even if the individual insists she is not speaking for others, the media treat her as if she were, and therefore she is as far as the public is concerned.

This kind of elitism has serious problems. First, people listen to others because they like them, rather than because they say significant things. Second, the informally-defined elite have no obligation to be responsible to the group at large. Their power is not given to them by the group, so the group cannot take it away. The elite cannot be directly influenced by the group, again because what influence the elite have is not determined by what they do for the group. In short, the group can in no way enforce responsibility on the part of its "leaders."

The point, as Freeman urges, is that insistence on no formal structure and therefore no formal leaders, led in this case of the Women's Liberation Movement to "elites by default." Structurelessness can lead to tyranny just as structure can.

Is There Any Escape from Bureaucracy?

The foregoing discussion indicates some of the fundamental tension existing between bureaucracy and democracy, and between bureaucracy and the individual, a tension that appears unresolvable and therefore problematical. As many point out, pursuit of common goals, democratic or otherwise, demands organizations. Organization, however, creates problems, the nature of which can be worse than the problems organization is intended to solve. There would appear to be no immediate way around this situation. To refuse to organize is at best a refusal to do anything, and could also lead to very elitist, uncontrollable situations. To organize, however, even to counter-organize to fight other organizations, poses another set of problems as difficult to accept as the first.

It is also possible that we, as citizens and as clients, create much of our own problem of bureaucracy. For example, if we are in a lineup waiting our turn for the attention of a government employee, we will not take it kindly if he takes someone out of turn. However, while he may be giving privileged treatment to a priveleged person (which is what we will tend to suspect) he may be acting compassionately. He may have knowledge, for example, that this person has health problems.

Another way in which we help to create our own "problem of bureaucracy" comes about from the demands for "efficiency" discussed earlier. The more Opposition Members and the media delight in catching out a bureaucrat, the more we push bureaucrats into defensive positions where paperwork multiplies, where delay occurs due to fear of error, and where every attempt is made to treat us strictly "by the book." For example, faced with it ourselves, or perhaps reacting in a general way to the plight faced by others, we decry the probing, exacting, suspiciousness of officers of the Unemployment Insurance Commission. We may avidly read a human interest story where an individual is not, according to the rules, entitled to benefits but who, on humanitarian grounds, we feel, deserves them. We deplore the heartlessness. However, we also deplore stories of how people suceed in receiving unemployment payments they are not entitled to. In the name of "more efficiency" we demand better performance, which of course requires more probing, exacting suspiciousness on the part of government employees.

Still another way in which we foster our own problem of bureaucracy is through constant demands for government action, yet we expect governments to hold the line on spending. Programs which are currently being cut back were originally implemented because they had a constituency. If the constituency no longer exists or is now relatively weak, the government can reduce programs and can even abandon them. For example, Prime Minister Trudeau could easily and quite arbitrarily decide upon abolition of Information Canada—who, after all, was he going to antagonize by doing this? However, this situation would seem to be a rare case. It is quite likely that, even as some programs are cut, others will be devised to meet problems identified by a significant number of voters. For example, Canadians used to take their physical environment largely for granted. In recent years, and rather suddenly, there were "problems" of air and stream pollution, simply because a significant number of people insisted there were. There are now bureaucracies at all three levels of government dealing with these problems. Similarly, a concern for consumerism led very rapidly to elaborate bureaucracies at all three levels of government.

This process will probably continue in that as industralization proceeds and as society changes, certain situations and conditions will become defined as "problems." People will demand government action, and government will respond with policies requiring further bureaucracy for their implementation. In this sense, if there is a problem of bureaucracy in Canada today, we have created it for ourselves and will perpetuate it.

As a final point, there is the question of the extent to which people want bureaucracy *per se*, as opposed to creating bureaucracy as a by-product of their demands and needs. The demand for bureaucracy as such is discussed in an excellent article by John Markoff on 18th century France.[53] He suggests that the process of bureaucratization is invariably seen as something which occurs from above, the government itself supplying the spark and generative force. That is, although the reasons ascribed to government for doing so vary considerably from writer to writer, the government bureaucratizes itself for its own purposes. As a result, bureaucracy is imposed on the people, who are the beneficiaries or the victims, depending on the viewpoint. There is very little indication in the literature that under certain circumstances "bureaucracy" may be demanded from below, that public opinion may require bureaucratic rule from the government.

While Markoff points to a very wide variety of historical examples which suggest a demand for bureaucracy as such, the major example he cites, due to its specificity, concerns the *cahiers de doléance* presented to the Estates General in 1789. The *cahiers* were statements of complaint and grievance, and also included suggestions and proposals. They were drawn up by various assemblies of parishes, guilds, and towns as well as by the nobility and clergy. The entire nation, in effect, gathered in assemblies to record grievances, aspirations, and demands for change.

According to Markoff, if one reads the *cahiers* with Max Weber's list of bureaucratic characteristics in mind, one gains the eerie impression that the authors had read Weber before composing the documents. There is, he says, a remarkable resemblance between Weber's characteristics and the requests of the *cahiers*, in that virtually everything which Weber proposed as a defining characteristic of bureaucracy is demanded somewhere in them. For example, there are demands for abolition of ownership of public office, for specialized training for public servants, for demonstration of technical proficiency, for the end of irrelevant criteria used in hiring and promotion, and for careers open to talent.

While Markoff concedes that the idea of demands from below for creation of bureaucracy *per se* needs further study, he strongly urges that we not lose sight of this as a possibility, that we stop seeing bureaucracy always and inevitably as something imposed on us from above. For example, he argues that the bureaucratization of factories is typically viewed as a response by management to needs for efficient organization, or the wish for greater control over workers. This ignores the role that unions have played in their efforts to protect members from arbitrary powers of hiring, firing, payment and so forth. In their fight for written contracts and formal rules the unions definitely contributed heavily toward bureaucratization. In fact, he suggests that it is possible that all sorts of groups who see themselves denied certain rights or who feel they are subject to arbitrary and perhaps illegitimate authority, will *demand* rules, predictability, and formalization of role relationships. That is, they will demand bureaucracy, even though they may themselves be ideologically anti-bureaucratic.

Summary and Conclusions

The relationship between bureaucracy and society is quite problematical. We are not agreed upon why bureaucracy exists nor on the extent to which it should exist. Even when we agree that there is a "problem of bureaucracy" we cannot agree on either the reasons for it or on the strategies necessary to cope with it. The most "restraint based" governments in Canada today do not seriously advocate a total retreat into some idyllic, non-bureaucratic past. In actual practice it is probable that at best governments will hold the line for a period of time, and that gradually political demands for material benefits or for bureaucracy *per se* will recommence the trend toward bureaucratic expansion. A large number of people will continue to be alienated from bureaucracy, and both normative and other arguments about bureaucracy will continue in their problematical vein.

For Further Reading

BOOKS AND REPORTS

Albrow, Martin. *Bureaucracy*. London: Macmillan, 1970.

Benveniste, Guy. *Bureaucracy*. San Francisco: Boyd and Fraser, 1977.

Blau, Peter M. and M. W. Meyer. *Bureaucracy in Modern Society*. New York: Random House, 1971.

Coleman, James S. *Power and the Structure of Society*. New York: Norton, 1974.

Crozier, Michael. *The Bureaucratic Phenomenon*. Chicago: University of Chicago Press, 1964.

Downs, Anthony. *Inside Bureaucracy*. Boston: Little, Brown, 1967.

Dvorin, Eugene P. and Robert H. Simmons. *From Amoral to Humane Bureaucracy*. San Francisco: Canfield Press, 1972.

Gouldner, Alvin Ward. *Patterns of Industrial Bureaucracy*. New York: Free Press, 1967.

Hall, Richard H. ed. *The Formal Organization*. New York: Basic Books, 1972.

Hegedus, Andras. *Socialism and Bureaucracy*. New York: St. Martin's Press, 1976.
Hill, Michael J. *The Sociology of Public Administration*. London: Weidenfeld and Nicolson, 1972.
Hummel, Ralph P. *The Bureaucratic Experience*. New York: St. Martin's Press, 1977.
Jacoby, H. ed. *The Bureaucratization of the World*. Berkeley: University of California Press, 1973.
Jaques, Elliott. *A General Theory of Bureaucracy*. London: Heineman, 1976.
Kamenka, Eugene and Martin Krygier, eds. *Bureaucracy: The Career of a Concept*. London: Edward Arnold, 1979.
Mainzer, Lewis C. *Political Bureaucracy*. Glenview: Scott, Foresman, 1973.
Mouzelis, Nicos P. *Organization and Bureaucracy: An Analysis of Modern Theories*. London: Routledge and Kegan Paul, 1975.
Niskasen, William A. *Bureaucracy and Representative Government*. Chicago: Aldine, Atherton, 1971.
Peters, B. Guy. *The Politics of Bureaucracy: A Comparative Perspective*. New York: Longman, 1978.
Presthus, Robert V. *The Organizational Society*, 2nd ed. New York: Knopf, 1978.
Schuman, David. *The Ideology of Form: The Influence of Organizations in America*. Lexington, Mass.: Lexington Books, 1978.
Sofer, Cyril. *Organizations in Theory and Practice*. New York: Basic Books, 1972.
Swingle, Paul G. *The Management of Power*. Hillsdale, N.J.: L. Erlbaum Associates, 1976.
Thompson, Victor A. *Bureaucracy and Innovation*. University, Ala.: University of Alabama Press, 1969.
———. *Bureaucracy and the Modern World*. Morristown, N. J.: General Learning Press, 1976.
———. *Without Sympathy or Enthusiasm: The Problem of Administrative Compassion*. University, Ala.: University of Alabama Press, 1975.
von Mises, Ludwig. *Bureaucracy*. New Rochelle, N. Y.: Arlington House, 1970.
Warwick, Dennis. *Bureaucracy*. London: Longman, 1974.

ARTICLES

Anderson, Barry D. "Bureaucracy in Schools and Student Alienation." *The Canadian Administrator*, Vol. XI, 3 (December 1971), pp. 9-12.
Angus, W. H. "The Individual and the Bureaucracy: Judicial Review — Do We Need It?" *McGill Law Journal*, Vol. XX, 2 (July 1974), pp. 177-212.
Balutis, Alan P. "Normative Aspects of Comparative Administration: Some Introductory Comments." *Journal of Comparative Administration*, Vol. V, 1 (May 1973), pp. 3-14.
Brecht, Arnold. "How Bureaucracies Develop and Function," *The Annals of the American Academy of Political and Social Science*, Vol. 292 (March 1954), pp. 1-10.
Buchanan, Bruce II. "Red Tape and the Service Ethic: Some Unexpected Differences Between Public and Private Managers." *Administration and Society*, Vol. VI, 4 (February 1975), pp. 423-44.
Carney, T. F. "Two Contemporary Views of a Traditional Bureaucracy." *Journal of Comparative Administration*, Vol. I, 4 (February 1970), pp. 398-427.
Carson, Clarence B. "The Bureaucratic Incubus." *The Freeman*, Vol. XXVI, 1 (January 1976), pp. 10-20.
Currie, G. N. M. "Efficiency vs. Service in Public Administration." *Canadian Public Administration*, Vol. XII, 2 (June 1964), pp. 165-72.
Deaton, Rick. "The Fiscal Crisis of the State and the Revolt of the Public Employee." *Our Generation*, Vol. VIII, 4 (1972), pp. 11-51.

Desroches, Jacques M. "The Developing Irrelevance of Formal Organization Patterns." *Optimum*, Vol. I, 1 (1970), pp. 6-12.

Deutsch, John J. "The Public Service in a Changing Society." *Canadian Public Administration*, Vol. XI, 1 (1968), pp. 1-8.

Diamant, Alfred. "Anti-Bureaucratic Utopias in Highly Industrialized Societies." *Journal of Comparative Administration*, Vol. IV, 1 (May 1972), pp. 3-34.

Dimock, Marshall E. "Administrative Law and Bureaucracy." *The Annals of the American Academy of Political and Social Science*, Vol. 292 (March 1954), pp. 57-64.

Finkelman, Jacob. "Government by Civil Servants." *The Canadian Bar Review*, Vol. 17 (1939), pp. 166-77.

Foreman, James. "The Professionalization-Bureaucratization Dilemma: The Case of the Funeral Director." *International Journal of Contemporary Sociology*, Vol. XI, 4 (October 1974), pp. 229-44.

Frederickson, H. George. "The Lineage of New Public Administration." *Administration and Society*, Vol. VIII, 2 (August 1976), pp. 149-74.

Friedman, Milton. "The Threat to Freedom in the Welfare State." *Business and Society Review*, No. 21 (Spring 1977), pp. 8-16.

Friedrich, Carl J. "Bureaucracy Faces Anarchy." *Canadian Public Administration*, Vol. VIII, 3 (1970), pp. 219-32.

Grey, Rodney. "Bureaucracy and Ottawa." *Queen's Quarterly*, Vol. 57 (1950-51), pp. 88-98.

Hodgetts, J. E. "The Liberal and the Bureaucrat." *Queen's Quarterly*, Vol. 62 (1955-56), pp. 176-83.

Hylton, John H. "Bureaucratic Skills and Social Work." *The Social Worker*, Vol. XLV, 1 (Spring 1977), pp. 25-32.

Jaffary, Karl D. "The Role of the State in a Technological Society." *Canadian Public Administration*, Vol. XV, 3 (1972), pp. 428-40.

Johnson, Walter S. "The Reign of Law Under an Expanding Bureaucracy." *The Canadian Bar Review*, Vol. 22 (1944), pp. 380-90.

Kernaghan, Kenneth. "The Ethical Conduct of Canadian Public Servants." *Optimum*, Vol. IV, 3 (1973), pp. 5-18.

Kuruvilla. P. K., "Administrative Culture in Canada: Some Perspectives." *Canadian Public Administration*, Vol. XVI, 2 (1973), pp. 284-97.

Lemoine, B. Roy. "The Modern Industrial State: Liberator or Exploiter?" *Our Generation*, Vol. VIII, 4 (1972), pp. 67-95.

Markoff, John. "Governmental Bureaucratization: General Processes and an Anomalous Case." *Comparative Studies in Society and History*, Vol. 17 (1975), pp. 479-503.

Perrow, Charles. "The Bureaucratic Paradox: The Efficient Organization Centralizes in Order to Decentralize." *Organizational Dynamics* (Spring 1977), pp. 2-14.

Schneck, Rodney, Douglas Russel and Ken Scott. "The Effects of Ruralism, Bureaucratic Structure, and Economic Role on Right Wing Extremism." *The Canadian Journal of Political Science*, Vol. 7 (1974), pp. 155-65.

Sheriff, Peta. "The Sociology of Public Bureaucracies 1965-75." *Current Sociology*, Vol. XXIV, 2 (1976), pp. 1-115.

Toren, Nina. "Bureaucracy and Professionalism: A Reconsideration of Weber's Thesis." *The Academy of Management Review*, Vol. I, 3 (July 1976), pp. 36-46.

Vaison, Robert. "'Administrative Culture' and Understanding Administration." *Optimum*, Vol. V, 1 (1974), pp. 17-22.

van Poelje, G. A. "The Theory of Public Administration as the Theory of the Means Towards the Realisation of Social Ideals." *International Review of Administrative Sciences*, Vol. XXIII, 2 (1957), pp. 146-55.

Wurzburg, Frederic. "Bureaucratic Decay." *Journal of Comparative Administration*, Vol. I, 4 (February 1970), pp. 387-97.

ENDNOTES

1. Martin Albrow, *Bureaucracy*. (London: Macmillan, 1970), p. 72.
2. *Time* (Can. ed.) February 23, 1976.
3. *Our Generation*, Vol. VIII, 4 (1972), pp. 3-9.
4. Douglas Fisher, "Incompetence is Our Hallmark," *Executive*, Vol. XVIII, 12 (December 1976), p. 50. This is only one example of Fisher discussing bureaucracy, and many other articles in this magazine reflect, to varying degrees, similar sentiments.
5. John van der Feyst, "Ouch!" *Canadian Business* Vol. XLVIII, 12 (December 1975), pp. 14-16 and 18.
6. *Globe and Mail*, May 6, 1977.
7. It is probable that quite a number of Canadians actually believed that the CBC Ombudsman was "for real." I have read several student essays which discuss the usefulness of the office of Ombudsman and proceed to cite the CBC version as a good example of the office in practice.
8. J. E. Hodgetts, "The Liberal and the Bureaucrat," *Queen's Quarterly*, Vol. 62 (1955/56), pp. 176-183.
9. Gerald Baldwin, "Government Threatens the Auditor General," *Canadian Business Magazine*, Vol. XLIII, 6 (June 1970), pp. 38-40.
10. Hugh L. Keenleyside, "Public Service as a Career in Canada" *Civil Service Review*, Vol. XXIII, 2 (June 1950), pp. 174-76, 181-82, and 184-86.
11. Discussion of Marx to this point is based on David McLellan (ed. and trans.), *Karl Marx: Early Writings* (Oxford: Basil Blackwell, 1971), pp. 68-70; and Andras Hegedus, *Socialism and Bureaucracy*, New York: St. Martin's Press, 1976, pp. 9-16.
12. Albrow, pp. 68-72.
13. Max Weber, *The Theory of Social and Economic Organization*, trans. A. M. Henderson and Talcott Parsons (Glencoe: The Free Press, 1947), pp. 337-39.
14. For these tendencies see Weber, *The Theory . . .* , pp. 338-341.
15. Robert Michels, *Political Parties* (New York: Dover Publications, 1959), p. 401.
16. *Ibid.*, p. 389.
17. For this discussion of government bureaucracy see *Ibid.*, pp. 184-201.
18. *Ibid.*, p. 373.
19. Hewart of Bury, *The New Despotism* (London: Ernest Benn, 1945), pp. 13 and 153.
20. *Ibid.*, pp. 11-14. His antipathy toward "scientism" of this nature is particularly interesting if one recalls from the preceding chapter the zealous advocation of it in vogue at the time.
21. *Ibid.*, p. 21.
22. *Ibid.*, p. 43.
23. *Ibid.*, p. 154.
24. Walter Johnson, "The Reign of Law under an Expanding Bureaucracy," *Canadian Bar Review*, Vol. 22 (1944), pp. 380-90.
25. Frederick Hayek, *Road to Serfdom* (Chicago: University of Chicago Press, 1944).
26. *Ibid.*, p. 70.
27. Hayek's views as indicated here are to be mainly found in the chapter "Planning and Democracy," *Road . . .* , pp. 56-71.
28. "The Threat to Freedom in the Welfare State," *Business and Society Review*, No. 21 (Spring 1977), pp. 8-16. "A government bureaucrat is seeking to serve his private interest just as you or I or the ordinary businessman."
29. Jacob Finkelman, "Government by Civil Servants," *The Canadian Bar Review*, Vol. 17 (1932), pp. 166-77.

30. Vol. VIII, 4 (1972), pp. 3-9.
31. Alvin W. Gouldner, "Red Tape as a Social Problem" in Robert K. Merton *et al.* (eds.), *Reader in Bureaucracy* (New York: The Free Press, 1952), pp. 410-18. See also Peter Blau, *Bureaucracy in Modern Society* (New York: Random House, 1956), chapter "Bureaucracy and Democracy," pp. 101-18.
32. Herbert Kaufman, "Administrative Decentralization and Political Power" in Joseph A. Uveges, Jr., *The Dimensions of Public Administration: Introductory Readings* (Boston: Holbrook Press, 1971), pp. 551-67.
33. Alfred Diamant, "Anti-Bureaucratic Utopias in Highly Industrialized Societies" *Journal of Comparative Public Administration*, Vol. IV, 1 (May 1972), pp. 3-34.
34. Robert L. Kahn *et al.*, "Americans Love their Bureaucrats," *Psychology Today* (June 1975), pp. 66-71.
35. For these various findings see *To Know and be Known* (Ottawa: Queen's Printer, 1969), pp. 68-81. The Gallup Poll reports from time to time have data on opinions about government which have a bearing on this general area.
36. The discouraging complexity of this kind of situation is very aptly portrayed by Victor A. Thompson, *Without Sympathy or Enthusiasm* (University, Alabama: University of Alabama Press, 1975).
37. Robert K. Merton, "Bureaucratic Structure and Personality" in Merton (ed.), *Reader*. . . , pp. 361-71.
38. *Ibid.*
39. Gideon Sjoberg *et al.*, "Bureaucracy and the Lower Class" in *Sociology and Social Research*, Vol. L, 3 (April 1966), pp. 325-37.
40. Joseph Bensman and Bernard Rosenberg, "The Meaning of Work in Bureaucratic Society" in Maurice R. Stein *et al.* (eds.) *Identity and Anxiety: Survival of the Person in Mass Society.* (Glencoe: Free Press, 1960), pp. 181-197.
41. The following is taken from Felix A. Nigro and Lloyd G. Nigro, *Modern Public Administration*, 3rd ed. (New York: Harper and Row, 1973), pp. 64-65. On the concept of "culture of poverty" see, in particular, Oscar Lewis "The Culture of Poverty" and Jack L. Roach and Orville R. Gurselin "An evaluation of the Concept 'Culture of Poverty'" in W. E. Mann (ed.), *Poverty and Social Policy in Canada* (Toronto: Copp Clark, 1970), pp. 26-35 and 35-47, respectively.
42. Sjoberg *et al.*, "Bureaucracy . . .".
43. The problems of both "sides" in this type of situation are well portrayed in the movie "Up the Down Staircase."
44. Sjoberg *et al.*, "Bureaucracy . . .".
45. This suggestion of modern sociology is not unlike the bureaucracy-clientele relationship described by Marx.
46. Ralph P. Hummel, *The Bureaucratic Experience* (New York: St. Martin's Press, 1977), p. 23.
47. A good example of the "maverick" which seems to enjoy enduring popularity is the television "Doctor" series, such as Casey, Kildare, Welby and Quincy. A common theme of these programs concerns an individual doctor identifying with his patient on an emotional level and then successfully bucking the hospital bureaucracy and medical legislation in order to "properly" treat his client.
48. Eugene P. Dvorin and Robert H. Simmons, *From Amoral to Humane Bureaucracy* (San Francisco: Canfield Press, 1972).
49. Diamant, "Anti-Bureaucratic Utopias . . .". See also F. Marini (ed.), *Toward a New Public Administration: The Minnowbrook Perspective* (London: Chandler, 1971).
50. Orion F. White, Jr., "The Dialectical Organization: An Alternative to Bureaucracy" *Public Administration Review*, Vol. XIX (January/February, 1969), pp. 32-42.
51. Peter M. Blau, *Bureaucracy in Modern Society* (New York: Random House, 1956), p. 115.
52. Jo Freeman, "The Tyranny of Structurelessness" in *Ms.*, July 1973, pp. 76-78 and 86-89.
53. John Markoff, "Governmental Bureaucratization: General Processes and an Anomalous Case," *Comparative Studies in Society and History*, Vol. 17 (1975), pp. 479-503.

CHAPTER FOUR

The Theory and the Practice of Public Policy-making in Canada

Introduction

In recent years much interest has been shown within public adminstration, political science and most other social sciences in the study of public policy. New journals have been launched, policy institutes established, academic programs in policy studies begun and numerous books and articles written setting forth theories and analyses of policy-making and policy results. While nothing like a coherent discipline of public policy studies has yet emerged, there have been significant theoretical and methodological advances in the study of public policy over the past several years.[1] In addition to being a rapidly growing field of academic study, policy analysis is also an applied discipline and governments in the 1960s became increasingly interested in the application of social sciences to the solution of societal problems.

Notwithstanding the apparent success of policy studies, beginning students should question the assumptions and the appropriateness of this approach to the study of bureaucratic behavior and the wider political process. The policy approach makes the assumption that it is useful to employ policy problems as the principal unit of analysis—how they get to the agenda of government, how they are acted upon once there, what solutions are applied, and what happens as a result of these events. However, other approaches are available. The institutional approach which predominated in an earlier period tended to focus on the structures and formal-legal features of the political system, but the linkages between important institutional arrangements and the content of public policy were largely ignored. Thus, there were lengthy discussions of the proper constitutional role of the bureaucracy within the Canadian political system, but little attention was paid to the impact of bureaucracy on the type of policy developed. The institutional approach is reflected to some extent in our later chapters on budgeting and accountability.

More recently, the behavioral approach had a great impact on the academic study of public administration. Rather than concentrating on the principles of administration, this school of thought moved into the area of applied behavioral research and social psychological theorizing. The emphasis was upon the individual and the human factor in public organizations, including "irrational" elements in that environment. Unlike those who used the institutional approach, which was often reformist in outlook, the behavioralists tended to skirt normative questions of how the bureaucracy "ought" to behave in favor of the so-called value free analysis of actual bureaucratic behavior.

The point here is not to decide which perspective is in some sense the best, for they are to a large extent complementary rather than competing, but rather to alert readers to the fact that the policy emphasis in public administration is relatively new and represents only one alternative but nonetheless valuable way of looking at the political and administrative processes.

Because of the growing popularity of policy studies, there has been some resistance from established disciplines. The objection has been raised, for example, that social problems are so complex that social scientists cannot fully analyse them or predict with accuracy the consequences of policy choices without becoming experts in a host of disciplines. In other words, policy studies might become an excuse for amateurish muddling in policy problems and the academic home of the dilletante. Behavioralists object that, by emphasizing social relevance, the policy approach foresakes the objectivity and neutrality which is central to the scientific enterprise in favor of advocacy and political activism. In any case, it is argued that policy analysis cannot resolve the value conflicts which are inherent in pluralist societies; that it has been oversold as a "technological fix" for the essentially political task of developing support for policy alternatives and applying sanctions and/or rewards to competing individuals or groups within society to obtain compliance. Finally, more conservative observers would argue that by portraying themselves as heroic problem-solvers, policy analysts exaggerate the capacity of governments to change society through their policies. New policies usually create new sets of problems and governments are always constrained in their behavior by powerful factors within the environment of their operations.

While such criticisms may cause us to temper our enthusiasm for policy studies, it should be remembered that there is an element of professional jealousy involved in them as the established disciplines seek to resist the gravitation of a growing number of students to this new field.

The Definition of Public Policy

The newness of the policy approach has led to disagreement about the appropriate scope, conceptual framework and methodology to be followed. The controversy is reflected in the debate over a definition for public policy. Definitions abound. Most writers appear to approach a definition like the judge who said of obscenity: "I don't know how to define it, but I know it when I see it." In other words, researchers define public policy in terms of what they study. Many of the definitions offered tend to be broad, potentially encompassing all of the relationships between the society and the state. For example, a widely quoted source defines public policy as "the authoritative allocation of values for the society."[2] Reading further we discover that only government can allocate values for the whole society and that everything that the government chooses to do or not to do results in the allocation of values, either material or symbolic. While this definition has the virtue of comprehensiveness, it establishes an enormous research task for students of public policy and several of the basic concepts are difficult to apply in a concrete fashion.

A simpler, more straightforward definition by Thomas Dye states that "public policy is what governments choose to do or not to do."[3] This definition summarizes the consensus of most writers that public policy consists of the actions of government. Several implications of the definition should be noted, however. First, Dye treats policy as the decisions of governments. Other writers maintain that it is artificial to view policy-making as a series of discrete, isolated events. Rather, policy should be seen as the outcome of a long series of more or less related activities and their consequences. In other words, we should conceptualize policy-making as a prolonged course of action, taking place over time and involving a large number of decision points rather than as individual acts of decision-making. This is more than a mere semantic quibble because, by focussing on decisions, we may neglect how the wider, underlying political forces are interacting, how the values of decision-makers may change over time and how the perceptions of the outcomes by the participants may vary.[4]

A second thing to be noted about Dye's definition is that it includes the concept of "*non-decisions*."[5] A decision by government to ignore a problem is in some sense a policy decision because it tends to favor perpetuation of the status quo. Therefore, a complete measurement of power within a society should consist not only of the ability of various groups to initiate and to modify policy, but should also include their ability to prevent government action on certain issues. In other words, the concept of non-decisions refers to the recognized fact that, while at any given time there are thousands of demands being made upon governments, only a small portion receive active, serious attention from policy-makers. What, then, accounts for the fact that some issues never make it beyond the general discussion agenda of the society on to the more specific and concrete institutional agenda of governments?

Bachrach and Baratz have suggested that all political systems involve a "mobilization of bias" defined as "a set of predominant values, beliefs, rituals and institutional procedures (rules of the game) that operate systematically and consistently to the benefit of certain persons and groups at the expense of others."[6] In this view, policy-makers may anticipate the reactions of powerful groups within the community and avoid certain issues. Or they may actively seek to suppress certain issues by threatening the use of sanctions (e.g., cutting off funds to protesting Indian organizations), harassment (e.g., RCMP investigations and infiltrations of radical groups) or even the outright use of force (e.g., the past use of provincial police against strikers). More subtle ways of keeping issues off the policy agenda include: delay (e.g., the appointment of royal commissions); the co-opting of leaders of protest movements through the offer of positions and benefits; and the launching of propaganda campaigns to combat complaints.

While the concept of non-decisions and the related idea of the political agenda are interesting, unfortunately at this stage we know too little about the process of agenda-setting in Canadian government to say whether powerful groups are completely or partially successful in limiting debate to safe issues which do not threaten their interests. Critics have maintained that the study of non-decisions is more an exercise in metaphysics than a scientific enterprise because it is inherently impossible to determine empirically the existence of non-decisions. We cannot, it is argued, draw conclusions about the exercise of power solely from non-occurrences. For example, if governments fail to deal with industrial accidents and illness, it may be tempting to conclude that industry has blocked effective action. However, in the absence of clear evidence, there could be other plausible explanations; for example, governments may simply be unaware of the gravity of the situation or union leaders may be ambivalent towards worker health and safety, preferring higher wages or job security over improved working conditions. It is difficult to determine from non-events what should or would have happened. And, how should researchers select from the multitude of non-decisions by governments which are the most important to be studied?

While the notion of non-decision poses serious research problems, it seems safe to conclude that most public policy-making does not conform to the model implied in traditional democratic theory. That theory assigns public opinion working through competitive political parties and elected representatives in legislatures a crucial role in determining which issues receive serious consideration. However, available studies suggest that such a "grassroots" conceptualization of the policy process is too simplistic and somewhat naive. Political leaders and appointed officials often take the initiative to convert certain problems into "live" issues. They do not act simply as passive receptors of cues from the public, but instead shape and mould public opinion. Because public servants possess expert knowledge and give continuous attention to problems, they play a critical role in determining which issues elected politicians will consider. Government agencies interact regularly with specialized interest groups who may be able to pressure officials to place an item on the agenda.[7] The mass media have played an increasingly important role in forcing policy-makers to add an issue to the agenda. Earlier media research sought to measure the persuasive effects of media messages, but more recent studies stress the order in which the media place issues before us for public discussion. Through selection and emphasis the media help to determine which issues will become important. In short, the mass media "may not be successful in telling us what to think, but they are stunningly successful in telling us what to think about".[8] Adept use of the media by individuals outside of government has caused governments to deal with problems. A mass media discussion of an issue can cause a widespread arousal of public opinion and bring issues to the attention of policy-makers. Isolated and unexpected events within the society, such as natural catastrophes (e.g., floods and hurricanes) or human events (e.g., the FLQ kidnappings of 1970), compel decision-makers to give urgent attention to policy responses. In fact, such crisis decision-making may represent a departure from more routine procedures which are the basis for most theories of policy-making.[9] As this brief survey suggests, the sources of policy are many and it is clear that policy-makers cannot always limit controversy to so-called "safe" issues.

Another aspect of the problem of applying the concept of non-decision arises from the identification of public policy only with the actions of governments. A non-decision by government occurs when policy-makers avoid an issue because of the anticipated reactions by influential groups. However, decisions on the issue may still be made by non-governmental or private bodies. Returning to our previous example of industrial health and safety, inaction by governments means that decisions on improvements in working conditions are left to the industries involved. In this case, and in many others, the cumulative impact of a series of decisions of private groups could in one sense be considered "public" policy.[10] Such decisions are public in the sense that they affect a significant segment of the public.

So what we have finally are two possible definitions of the "public" component of public policy. One can say that the word signifies only actions of government officials or it can signify action done to or for the public regardless of who is performing it. As the public and private sectors become more interdependent in modern society and various intermediate bodies come into existence, the case for defining public policy in the second, broader, sense becomes more persuasive. However, for our purpose of generally discussing the topic, we will continue to treat public policy as synonymous with the activities of government.

Another point to be raised about our definition is its lack of reference to the objectives or goals held by governments. Most other definitions suggest that all policy-making is purposive, i.e., done in the pursuit of certain goals. In practice, however, the goals of most government policies and programs are vague, multiple, unstable and often conflicting.[11] Some goals of policies, such as the desire to be re-elected, probably cannot be admitted publicly. Moreover, the lack of reference to government goals permits us to include within the scope of policy studies the unintended consequences as well as the formally announced goals of government action. For example, a guaranteed annual income scheme may be intended to eliminate poverty and to reduce the welfare bureaucracy, but it could conceivably have second-order effects upon such other social and economic phenomena as family stability, rural outmigration, minimum wage levels and the general cost of living.

Having decided not to define public policy exclusively in terms of the pronouncements of governments, it seems useful to include within the scope of our concern the symbolic impact of policies.[12] A formal statement of goals (e.g., fair taxation, strict pollution control or tough competition laws) could mask the realities of policy as actually implemented. Since most of us, most of the time, are passive spectators to political events, we are not well enough informed to judge the efficacy of proposed courses of actions, yet we may be symbolically reassured that the government had taken charge of a problem. Therefore, when we study public policy we must pay attention to the original statements of government goals and the resulting legislation, the administrative implementation of policy and its real world effects, and what various segments of the public believe is being accomplished by the action.

As a final point, while there is broad, strong interest in studying public policy, this interest tends to be the only consensual element within and among the various disciplines engaged in the study. As noted, definitions and conceptualizations abound, and when we cannot agree on what public policy *is*, then it should come as no surprise that there is much controversy over how we should go about studying it.

Approaches to the Study of Public Policy

It is obvious from the above discussion that the study of public policy is an ambitious and challenging undertaking that encompasses far more than the study of bureaucracies and involves many disciplines other than public administration and political science. To help us to simplify and clarify our thinking about a complex phenomenon, social scientists have developed numerous theories, models, and concepts for the analysis of policy-making. To prevent aimless meandering, such theories must direct our attention to the more important relationships that are believed to exist and to the underlying causes of government action. They should be neither so broad that they are not easily applied to political reality nor so narrow that they are unable to tell us anything about the significant aspects of policy-making. Finally, they should suggest explanation, that is, the causes and consequences of policy, rather than simply consist of descriptions.

Richard Simeon has presented a useful typology of the potential approaches to the study of public policy. He begins from the assumption that "the political machinery and the policy-makers at any point in time work within a framework which greatly restricts the alternatives they consider and the range of innovations they make." This framework, according to Simeon, defines "a set of problems considered to be important, a set of acceptable solutions or policy responses, a set of procedures and rules by which they will be considered."[13] Five general, complementary and not mutually-exclusive approaches to an explanation of this public policy framework are identified. Each can be described only briefly here to emphasize the scope of the enterprise rather than to provide a full explanation or assessment.

First, policy is seen as the consequence of underlying environmental forces.[14] The *types and levels* of policies adopted by governments are presumed to be conditioned by the basic socio-economic features of the society (such as geography, industrialization, urbanization, affluence and education) and by certain political system characteristics (party competition, voter turnout, representation, the size of the bureaucracy and the like). Initial comparative studies of public policies in American states suggested that wider socio-economic forces were far more significant than political factors in explaining the variations that existed among different jurisdictions. Such findings were contentious in the United States and have not been fully supported in similar analyses of interprovincial differences in Canada.[15] More appropriate measures of public policy (other than simply levels of government spending which happen to be readily available), more thorough elaboration of political-system characteristics (for example, provision for the factor of shared-cost programs within the federal system), and more sophisticated statistical techniques for analyzing the relationships among factors have been developed.

However, the relationships identified still remain statistical in nature rather than being clear cause-effect statements. In other words, it cannot be determined on the basis of these studies how social and economic changes caused changes in policy outcomes. Existing studies have been weak in specifying a theoretical explanation for the translation of environmental factors into particular policies. For example, increasing urbanization and industrialization undoubtedly contributed to the emergence of the various programs covered by the phrase "the welfare state" by generating a set of policy demands; but how these demands reached and were acted upon by governments is usually not specified in such studies. Moreover, while environmental changes may condition what issues are dealt with by governments, they do not completely determine how the issues will be defined and what policy responses will be considered. "To the extent they do shape policy, it is as they interact with cultural and ideological predispositions, with the distribution of political resources among social groups and the like."[16] Moreover, policy may feed back upon any or all of the following factors: the environment, political perceptions and demands, and even the structures and processes of the political system. In short, environmental factors may be a good starting point for the study of policy-making but they cannot provide complete explanations.

The second approach suggests that the key to understanding policy is power. One such view is that the policymaker is like the physicist charting and measuring conflicting forces at work in a situation. He then proceeds to allocate costs and benefits in accordance with the strengths and intensity of the various demands being presented. As was indicated earlier, however, the conceptualization and measurement of power is a complicated and controversial matter. There has been a long-standing debate in political science between pluralists and elitists. Pluralists insist that power is widely diffused within society and that most policy is a compromise based upon shifting coalitions among various groups active on different issues; the elitists argue that interconnected elites sharing similar values dominate most policy-making and limit policy to marginal changes that do not upset the status quo.[17] The concept of non-decision introduced earlier further complicates this debate.

We obviously cannot resolve these issues here. However, much current policy analysis consists of inferences about the relative power or influence of different participants in the policy process based upon what appears to be the distribution of the costs and benefits involved in the outcomes. An assumption of both the pluralist and elitist schools is that individuals act strictly or mainly on the basis of self-interest, but it may be the case that key policy-makers have a sense of responsibility to protect the interests of others. The type of policy at stake, including how it is perceived by different groups, will help to determine whether different interests are aroused and whether coalitions among groups can be formed.

A third approach suggests that policy reflects the dominant ideas, values, theories and beliefs in the society. Such factors are both procedural and substantive in nature. Procedural values refer to the accepted rules of the game. Studies have shown, for example, that Canadians generally are more deferential towards government elites and less aggressive in political participation than are Americans.[18] This may mean that Canadian decision-makers are not as subject to mass pressures and have more room to bargain with organized groups. Substantive values relate to the scope and purpose of government activity. Again, opinion surveys suggest that Canadians are less wedded to free enterprise values and are more willing to use the instrument of the state for collective purposes. These value differences may contribute to the wider scope of government activity in Canada than in the United States, as is indicated in Chapter 6 on public budgeting.

When talking about the impact of ideas upon policy-making it seems essential to distinguish between the values of the political and bureaucratic elites and those held by the general public. Are elites essentially self-interested or do they regard the interests of others as important? Do they see citizen participation as a useful way to widen the policy debate or as ill-informed and time-consuming? What attitudes do politicians and bureaucrats hold on the use of government to effect a redistribution of wealth within the society? Does the ideology of different parties which come into office affect the types of policies governments adopt? In understanding individual policies, elite orientations are probably more important than those of citizens generally. But even elite and mass values combined do not provide complete explanations. Because such ideas are broad and general they more often help to define problems and the range of policy alternatives considered, rather than providing the basis for the content of specific policies.

The fourth approach concentrates on the impact of the institutional structure on the policy process. The way authority and power are distributed within the political system serves to determine partially how issues are defined, handled and resolved. For example, the Canadian federal system decentralizes considerable authority and power to provincial governments. As a consequence, issues tend to be debated in terms of federal versus provincial responsibilities. Thus, poverty is not seen mainly as a redistributive issue between the "haves" and the "have nots," but instead, the debate rages over whether Ottawa or the provinces should deal with it. Similarly, the fact that the constitution concentrates authority in the cabinet, prescribes for the bureaucracy a role of undivided loyalty to the government of the day, and fosters the operation of Parliament on the basis of disciplined political parties, means that there are fewer points of access to key policy-makers than in the American political system. The American system operates on the constitutional principles of separation of powers and checks and balances in which power is diffused, including within Congress, and in which the organizational loyalties of government agencies are more divided. Successful interest groups in this country recognize that it is usually vital to have their input before policy moves from the executive arena into the parliamentary arena.[19]

While institutional arrangements thus structure political competition, they are themselves influenced by environmental forces. When economic and technological change occurs within society the equilibrium among various groups may be disrupted and demands made for new government initiatives. For example, increasing economic concentration threatened the viability of small businesses, causing the formation of new organizations like the Canadian Federation of Independent Businesses, and eventually governments were obliged to establish new agencies and programs to assist such enterprises. It is very difficult to separate the independent policy effects of institutional arrangements from the wider social, economic and political forces which are mediated through such structures. However, despite the problematical nature of the relationship between structures and policy outputs, governments in the last decade have placed considerable faith in structural reforms as the way to obtain improved public policy. More will be said on this point later in this chapter and in the next chapter on budgeting.

Fifth, almost indistinguishable from the institutional approach is the process approach. Much of the available policy literature is concerned with describing the process by which so-called "proximate" policy-makers — politicians, bureaucrats and interest group leaders — interact in the development of policy. While earlier analyses of the policy process usually stopped when a bill was passed or an agency was created, more recently there has been a recognition of the need to follow items completely through the policy cycle, including the implementation phase. It has been found in several studies that implementation is far more than a brief interlude between a bright idea and the achievement of policy goals. It is often a stage crucial to the success of programs. At this point politicians are very dependent on the ability and willingness of bureaucrats to follow through on the general intentions established in legislation, and in the process of implementing policy it is often discovered that modifications to both ends and means are required.

As Simeon points out, the virtue of the process approach is that it captures the dynamic of policy-making.[20] It seeks to show how environmental factors, competing interests and ideas, and different institutional factors interact to produce policy. While drawing upon other approaches, this perspective also serves to highlight the independent effects of decision-making patterns upon the types of policies produced. There are a variety of conceptual frameworks available which seek to describe how governments reach decisions, but before turning to some discussion of these it is necessary to repeat that full understanding of the policy-process must involve a wider sweep of coverage than simply characteristic patterns of decision-making. Each of the five approaches discussed above contributes something to that wider understanding. Public policy is a complicated phenomenon and the research task facing students of the policy process is vast.

Theories of Decision-Making in Government

Policy-making typically involves many decisions, some procedural and some substantive, some routine and some fundamental. Rarely will a policy consist of a single decision, but rather will be the result of a series of related decisions. Moreover, successful policy-making consists of much more than simply following the right steps to reach the best decision; it also involves the mobilization of public understanding and support for the outcomes.[21] In focussing upon decision-making in this section, we are isolating a portion of the wider policy-making process. Four theories of decision-making that focus on the activities involved in making a decision will be discussed. Unfortunately, it is often not made clear whether the statements of these theories are presented as descriptions or prescriptions. In other words, there is confusion over whether the theories are intended to describe how governments actually make decisions or whether they are statements of how decision-making *ought* to occur.

Comprehensive Rationality

The most widely accepted theory of decision-making in governments is *comprehensive rationality*. This theory presents a neat, logical process of decision-making consisting of the following steps:

1. The rational decision-maker is faced with a given problem that can be separated from other problems and considered in comparison with them;
2. The rational decision-maker first clarifies his goals or objectives in relation to the problem and then ranks those goals in terms of their importance;
3. He then proceeds to list all the possible ways of achieving those goals;

4. Next, he lists all the possible consequences that could conceivably follow from each of the alternative policies;
5. He then compares each alternative, with its attendant consequences, with all other alternatives;
6. Finally, the decision-maker chooses the policy alternative that maximizes the attainment of his goals or objectives.[22]

The result of this process is a rational decision, one that most effectively achieves a desired end. Even if all the precepts of comprehensive-rationality cannot be fulfilled, many advocates of this approach seem to suggest that it represents an ideal which decision-makers should strive to approximate as closely as possible.

Disjointed Incrementalism

There has been substantial criticism of this rational theory. One influential critic, Charles Lindblom, argues that the theory ignores the limitations on decision-making in the real world.[23] In practice, according to Lindblom, decision-makers are not faced with a *given* problem, instead they have to identify and define the nature of the problem. The way in which a problem is defined will greatly influence the decision about the best policy to adopt and "misdefined" problems will almost certainly lead to policy failure. For example, poverty may be seen initially as insufficient income, but further refinement of the problem reveals that economic need arises from a variety of circumstances — limited education and job opportunities for poorer families, low earnings for the so-called "working poor," or inadequate retirement income for old age pensioners, to name just a few. A policy problem may also represent a new opportunity. Cable television, for example, threatens the economic viability of conventional broadcasting, but offers the opportunity for wider viewer choice. For various reasons, therefore, there is room for controversy over what the problem is and how best to deal with it.

Lindblom also argues that, even with the recent helpful advances in decision-making techniques (systems analysis, computers and social forecasting), the analytical requirements for rational decision-making cannot be completed. We still do not understand fully the linkages between particular government actions and their impact on society. The information required to consider all possible alternatives and all their consequences simply will not be available. Most government decision-making occurs under pressures of time and often the timeliness of a decision is as important as the thoroughness with which it has been considered. Some attention must also be paid to the costliness of full analysis in terms of the staff and financial resources devoted to the task.

An even more fundamental limitation upon rationality, according to Lindblom, is the difficulty of weighting and ranking the values to be sought through policy. In a pluralistic society involving multiple interests, values are likely to be in conflict. At a high level of abstraction we may all agree (for example, we all support the preservation of human freedom) but policy-makers have to descend to the concrete and practical level where certain values must be sacrificed to achieve others. Frequently decision-makers must trade off competing values — they might, for example, accept some additional level of unemployment caused by reduced government spending in order to combat inflation. Agreement on which values should predominate in policy-making is difficult to achieve and will likely delay action on problems. For these reasons decision-makers seldom engage in a review of the basic values which guide their choices or of all the possible policy options they might consider.

Faced with the bewildering complexity of modern public policy, governments adopt an "incremental" style of decision-making, according to Lindblom. *Incrementalism* is a more realistic, intuitive, unstructured and unsystematic approach than rationalism. Intuition, hunches and insights play an important part in this kind of decision-making. It is policy-making through small or incremental moves on particular problems rather than a comprehensive reform program. Choice is made from among a series of closely-related alternatives not substantially different from past policies and without evaluating all possible ramifications. Incrementalism is exploratory in the sense that goals and means are adjusted in the light of experience and it is continuous in the sense that there is no single decision or right solution to a problem.

The resourceful incrementalist uses a number of strategies to cope with complexity.[24] He "*simplifies through omission*," ignoring non-incremental policies, not exploring all possible consequences and discarding objectives that are not attainable by present means. Secondly, he engages in "*satisficing*" by adopting policies that will satisfy the demands being made and will suffice for the present. He does not engage in an exhaustive search for maximum goal fulfillment because the search is not worth the costs involved. Thirdly, he adopts a *remedial approach*, seeking to eliminate known social ills rather than producing some desired, future state of affairs. Fourthly, the creative incrementalist makes use of "*feedback*" and "*next chance*." He does this by deliberately choosing a policy that leaves open the possibility of doing better in a subsequent effort and builds in feedback to allow for better choice on the next chance. Finally, the incrementalist makes use of "*bottlenecks*" *or delays*. In the rationalist's view of decision-making, unwarranted delay is evidence of the breakdown of the process, but to the incrementalist it represents time to clarify problems and to decide whether to act on them. To many, the incrementalist may seem to be a timid compromiser and an indecisive procrastinator, but to Lindblom he is "a shrewd, resourceful problem-solver who is wrestling bravely with a universe that he is wise enough to know is too big for him."[25]

It seems clear that Lindblom endorses incrementalism as the best approach to government decision-making, rather than simply offering it as a realistic description of how such decision-making now occurs. Incrementalism is desirable because it allows for desirable outcomes. Not only does incrementalism help decision-makers to master the complexity of the real world, it also adds flexibility and resilience to the political system. Conflict is heightened when decisions involve major policy shifts causing great gains or losses by different participants, and part of the aim of public policy-making is to reduce and to manage conflict. Incrementalism, it is argued, is congruent with political reality. In pluralist societies like Canada, what is feasible politically are policies which are only incrementally or marginally different from what has gone before. Policy is the outcome of a process of give and take, of compromise, or what Lindblom calls "partisan mutual adjustment." Political parties compete for votes by agreeing on fundamentals and offering only incrementally different policies. Because parties fail to offer coherent, long-range programs in elections, they are unlikely to approach policy-making in a comprehensive, rationalistic manner once in office. Instead, they will lapse into a managerial style of governing, driving bargains with specialized interest groups as political and administrative convenience dictates. Limits on the available budgetary resources and the capacity of government organizations to resist attempts to dismantle their programs also contribute to incremental outcomes in government decision-making. The extent to which the incrementalist theory corresponds to actual patterns of decision-making within the Government of Canada is examined later in this chapter.

Mixed Scanning

A variety of criticisms of incrementalism have been raised, the most influential perhaps being those voiced by the sociologist Amitai Etzioni, who offers his own theory of mixed-scanning as a compromise between rationalism and incrementalism. Etzioni agrees with Lindblom that the requirements for complete rationality cannot be met, but he sees incrementalism as inherently too conservative.[26] By stressing limited change, the theory does not take account of major social innovations. In short, it mistakes routine decision-making for all decision-making and does not include those situations when decision-makers are prepared to expend the costs in terms of time, personnel and effort in order to make more fundamental decisions. In addition, the incremental theory ignores the fact of an unequal distribution of power within society. By stressing that the "best" decision is often the one on which political agreement can be found, the incrementalist accepts that privileged and well-organized groups will determine most public policies.

Etzioni distinguishes (unfortunately, not too precisely) "*contextuating*" or fundamental decisions from "*incremental*" or bit decisions. While marginal changes in policy greatly outnumber fundamental changes, the latter may be of greater significance. Most incremental decisions, in fact, reflect or anticipate more fundamental decisions. In order to assess the success of incremental policies, we must have some evaluative framework in mind. And at times, a more fundamental review process takes place. At such points, the scanning or review of alternatives is mixed in the sense that only a few aspects of a problem and only a few alternatives are selected for intensive analysis. According to Etzioni, this fundamental review process occurs when there is rapid change in a society or when a crisis occurs because of prolonged neglect or mistaken treatment of a problem.

The mixed-scanning theory alerts us to the fact that decision-making within governments varies in scope and magnitude. It may be that in the lower echelons of the bureaucracy, routine, incremental decision-making is the predominant style, whereas at higher levels a more encompassing scanning of alternatives may occur. Incrementalists would argue that mixed-scanning is within their tradition because they do not insist that *all* decision-making processes and outcomes are purely incremental and they do not disparage the use of rationalistic techniques when the situation allows. However, mixed-scanning does seem to provide for greater theoretical recognition of those occasions when bold, forthright policies are possible. Unfortunately, Etzioni does not tell us clearly how mixed-scanning would operate in practice.[27]

A second prominent critic of incrementalism and a proponent of rationalism is Yehezkel Dror, who argues that Lindblom's "science of muddling through" is based on three closely interrelated conditions that are by no means always met in decision-making solutions.[28] First, for incrementalism to really work in practice, present policies must be basically satisfactory so that marginal changes to them are all that are necessary in order to achieve desired results. That is, if the results of present policies are quite "unsatisfactory," then incremental change in policy will in no way lead to "satisfactory" policy results. What is needed in this instance is a "radical" change, a change with which the rationalist approach *is*, and the incrementalist approach *is not*, prepared to cope. Second, the nature of the problem must remain more or less constant. If the problem is to be dealt with only incrementally, the problem itself can only change incrementally as opposed to fundamentally. The most obvious difficulty for incrementalism on this point occurs when there simply is no previous policy, while at the same time a problem, even a crisis, has arisen and must be dealt with. And, third, in order for incrementalism to be relevant, there must be strong continuity in the available means for coping with problems. In this case, if the decision-makers have in their possession basically new technology and/or new knowledge related to the problem, unless they ignore these they cannot realistically make incremental decisions regarding the policy. In short, in Dror's view the "science of muddling through" has at best only limited validity — it is really a position advocating inertia.

Policy Types: Substance and Process

These disagreements may be partly explained by the fact that there is not a single, monolithic policy process which cranks out all policy and the advocates of the various theories focus on different types of decision-making. This view, that there are a variety of patterns of policy-making depending partly on the level and nature of the policy involved, is mainly the contribution of Theodore Lowi, who argues explicitly that "policies determine politics."[29] What is at stake, both objectively and in terms of the perceptions of those groups affected, determines the scope and nature of the political conflict which will arise. This perspective requires us to classify policies in terms of their real or anticipated impacts upon society. Discarding more conventional subject-matter categories (e.g., agriculture, education, health, and so on), Lowi advances a classification scheme involving "distributive," "regulatory," "redistributive" and (subsequently) "constituent" policies and argues that each of these policy types produces a distinctive policy process. The basis for distinguishing among policy types is the degree of conflict and coercion involved and whether there are readily identifiable winners and losers. Lowi maintains that we can predict certain patterns of political behavior if we know the kind of policy involved.

There is not the space here to examine Lowi's typology in depth, but its main outlines can be presented and assessed briefly. His first category of "distributive" policies is said to involve decision-making in which governments distribute benefits to particular groups on a highly individualized basis. The costs of such benefits are usually absorbed through the general revenue system and hence are distributed broadly across the larger population so that the cost is small for any particular individual or group within that population. The fact that there are no clear winners and losers means that there is a low-level of political conflict and competition associated with distributive policies. Patronage and subsidies to particular regions or groups are usually said to epitomize distributive policy-making.

By contrast, regulatory policy-making involves a more deliberate choice as to which groups will be indulged and which will be deprived as the result of government decision-making. It should be noted that Lowi uses the term "regulatory policy-making" more broadly than is the usual convention within the public administration literature. For him, not all regulatory policies and actions need be administered by regulatory agencies; regulation may, for example, take place through the taxation system. What is distinctive about regulatory policies according to Lowi is the fact that they involve clear winners and losers and therefore groups have an incentive to press their demands openly and policy tends to be the outcome of group conflict. This policy type arouses wider, more varied, interests. Coalitions are built among related interests to pursue particular policy objectives and are then dismantled once an issue is dealt with by government. For example, industries may come together temporarily to oppose changes to labor relations laws and then revert to competition among themselves on other public policy issues.

Like regulatory policies, redistributive policies are held to involve clear winners and losers, but the groups involved in the policy process are not so numerous—essentially the conflict is between the "haves" and the "have-nots" within society. The battles over the emergence of the welfare state in the 1930s and 1940s are usually seen as the classic example of a redistributive policy clash. The conflict involved essentially two broad social groupings or classes, one group which would benefit and the other which would lose as a result of redistributive measures. Because the economic power of different groups is at stake in such conflicts the coalitions that emerge tend to be permanent rather than shifting as in the case of regulatory policy. (We will omit discussion of "constituent" policy-making here because it appears to have been an afterthought by Lowi and is not as well developed as the other categories.)

In assessing Lowi's categories it quickly becomes apparent that they are so broad and lacking in explicit detail as to pose serious problems for any researcher seeking to apply the scheme.[30] Many decisions can be expected to contain at least some characteristics of each of Lowi's types, but there is little guidance for determining how a policy is to be classified in any but the simplest case. It could be argued that a particular policy is predominantly of one type or another, but Lowi compounds the problems of classification by insisting that the perceptions of policy held by various participants should be taken into account. As has been noted, "there is simply no objective way to determine which set of perceptions should be dominant in classifying a policy when there is substantial disagreement among the participants themselves about what is at stake."[31]

Several studies of American public policy have with some success employed Lowi's scheme, although some "squeezing and shoving" to fit particular policies into his categories seems to have been required. The most useful category has been distributive policy-making. In fact, it has recently been argued that the fragmentation of political power involved in the American constitutional system and the related development of numerous specialized interest groups provides the basis for an underlying bias toward distributive policies in the United States.[32] However, Canadian readers might speculate on whether distributive policy-making is less common here (though not unheard of) because of the greater concentration of authority and power found in our cabinet-parliamentary system. For the same reason, Lowi's categories may not be exhaustive. Because he assumes the diffusion of power characteristic of the American system, it has been argued that he ignores "positional politics."[33] The phrase refers to attempts by groups to gain standing or access to governments rather than specific benefits. Since there are fewer points of access for groups within the Canadian political system, an institutionalized recognition of a group's right to have input in a particular policy field can be a valuable policy achievement.

Of course, all of these various models and decision-making theories are merely abstractions of political life meant to simplify and clarify what is a very complex process. Furthermore, most models and theories are derived from observation of the policy process in the United States. The next section examines the extent to which certain of these theories are capable of accurately describing and explaining the decision-making process at the national level in Canada.

Public Policy-Making and Bureaucracy in the Government of Canada

In order to achieve policy objectives, governments employ a variety of "policy instruments" or means of achieving a desired impact on society. The most familiar are Acts of Parliament and ministerial policy statements, but other important policy instruments are regulations, tax incentives, crown corporations, departmental memoranda and practices, and even the manner in which a minister or an official settles an individual problem or case. The less-well-known forms of policy-making are discussed later in Chapter 8 dealing with accountability, and here we will concentrate upon the higher level policy-making usually associated with the cabinet and the upper echelons of the departmental bureaucracy.

Even in the case of what we usually think of as government policies, there is no single pattern by which issues arise and are dealt with by government. Any attempt to develop reliable generalizations runs into the problem that the process is exceedingly complex and crucial aspects of it are shrouded in secrecy. However, while the process is complicated, most observers are agreed that it does not correspond to the traditional constitutional model of a supreme Parliament exercising continuous control and supervision over the cabinet and the bureaucracy, on behalf of an informed and active electorate. Instead, the consensus among most students of the process is that throughout most of this century real decision-making power has been moving from Parliament to the cabinet and in turn from the cabinet to the bureaucracy because the environment of the political system is such that highly specialized knowledge gathered by large organizations is required to find solutions to current problems.[34] In this view, bureaucrats are not deliberately usurping the legitimate power of elected representatives, but it is flowing into their hands because they have the technical expertise required for contemporary policy-making.

Bureaucratic power and influence is a pervasive theme throughout this book. There is disagreement among commentators on whether the administrative apparatus of the modern state has a monopoly on power or whether it only influences decisions taken by the people's representatives, the politicians. Further disagreement arises concerning the sources of bureaucratic power or influence and the relative significance of such factors. Still, it would be the height of equivocation to imply that there is not a strong consensus among commentators that bureaucratic involvement in policy-making has grown substantially during this century. Some of the sources of this growth are common to all western political systems, while others are more specific to the Canadian situation. Here we wish to present these factors almost in a "shopping list" fashion and readers will find throughout the book elaborations of the points mentioned here.

As was suggested above, expert knowledge is a primary source of bureaucratic influence in policy-making. The rise of a professional public service during this century has meant that it is the bureaucracy which is the major source of information concerning the technical, administrative and financial feasibility of the policy alternatives considered by the politicians, who are usually only "enlightened amateurs" in the various fields of public policy. All departments and agencies of government are deeply involved in the formulation of policy during its initial stages. To this end, they are in regular contact with organized interest groups in their policy fields. Such contacts serve to increase the specialized knowledge possessed by the bureaucracy and add to the legitimacy of the advice offered to the politicians since departmental recommendations are seen to be based upon prior negotiations with the interests most directly affected. In this way, the "mere" provision of advice can become much more than a neutral exercise since public servants are in a good position to determine what alternatives their political "masters" will consider and how these alternatives will be defined. The fact that politicians change offices regularly, either through electoral misfortune or through shifts in ministerial responsibilities, contrasts with the greater permanence of public servants within particular fields of public policy and administration. Continuity in office and the fact that public servants can give continuous attention to policy development and implementation, without the numerous other distractions which fill the hectic schedules of cabinet ministers, allows them a closer working knowledge of policy issues than that likely to be acquired by the politicians whom they serve.

Delegation of rule-making authority, as elaborated on in Chapter 3, to public servants within departments and agencies is also a source of an enlarged policy role for the bureaucracy. For various reasons, such as lack of parliamentary time, lack of parliamentary knowledge on technical matters and the need for flexibility in the administration of laws in an era of rapid social and economic change, the cabinet and Parliament have found it necessary to pass general, "skeletal" legislation and to entrust to the bureaucracy the responsibility for filling in the specific content of such legislation through regulations and other forms of subordinate law-making. Chapter 8 deals with the problems of accountability posed by the grant of such rule-making authority. Suffice to say here, that most acts passed by Parliament now provide for wide powers of delegated legislative authority and this is the basis for an immense amount of submerged, relatively invisible policy-making at the lower-levels throughout departments and agencies of government.

The importance of expertise in policy-making and the need for delegation of legislative authority are sources of bureaucratic influence in all western political systems. Among the factors more specific to the Canadian situation is the inter-governmental dimension of most policy-making. Chapter 7 explores federal-provincial relations in depth, and here we will simply mention that federal-provincial committees at the bureaucratic level have played an increasingly important role in the setting of policy priorities in Canada. Ministers must permit their officials some freedom to negotiate on inter-governmental matters and will probably be reluctant to alter the agreements which are the product of long and delicate negotiations.

Bureaucratic influence may be further enhanced by the relatively non-ideological character of the Canadian party system. The two main political parties at the national level, the Liberals and the Conservatives, are pragmatic and opportunistic.[35] Traditionally, they have not spent much time or resources on the formulation of policy, instead they have made leadership the principal focal point of their appeals to the electorate. Since the parties do not usually come to office with strong ideological convictions, a well-defined policy blueprint or even a precise electoral mandate, it is harder for them to impose a sense of direction upon the administrative branch of government. Instead the bureaucracy moves in to fill the vacuum which exists in terms of the definition of future policy options. The result, it is alleged, is a strong tendency towards an apolitical, technocratic approach to governing.[36] The fact of one-party government, with the Liberals holding office during most of this century, further contributes to the predominance of a "managerial approach" within government. As the "Government Party," the Liberals have developed close working relationships with the senior bureaucracy, indeed the ranks of the bureaucracy have been a fruitful source of ministerial talent for successive Liberal governments. The similarity of the social backgrounds and the professional values held by political and bureaucratic elites in this country has led to a closer merger of roles and to greater influence for the bureaucracy.

Prime Minister Trudeau's Philosophy of Policy-Making

During the 1960s Liberal governments in Ottawa initiated a series of organizational reforms intended to halt the perceived drift towards bureaucratic policy-making based upon existing departmental structures that did not always correspond to over-all governmental goals and ignored the interrelatedness of most policies. While the ideas behind many of these reforms pre-dated the leadership of Prime Minister Trudeau, it was his accession to power in early 1968 that led to their full expression in changes within the executive-bureaucratic arena. While his predecessor, Lester Pearson, was a product of the federal bureaucracy with extensive contacts throughout it, Trudeau was a newcomer to "official Ottawa." He believed that the bureaucracy had acquired disproportionate influence over policy determination at the expense of the role of elected politicians in cabinet.

Moreover, Trudeau brought a coherent philosophy of policy-making to the office of Prime Minister. This philosophy stressed clear definitions of goals, systematic analysis of policy options, the monitoring of the progress of programs and an anticipation of societal trends — in short, rational and comprehensive planning.[37] John Langford has suggested that the Trudeau government attempted to improve the performance of government in terms of goal achievement by establishing three specific administrative values throughout the bureaucracy.[38] The first such value was "responsiveness," defined not so much in terms of meeting public demands, but, instead, the ability of the bureaucracy to respond to the directions of the cabinet. The emphasis was on integrated, "top-down," policy-making. Departments and agencies of government should develop policies and programs to serve national priorities as set down by cabinet rather than pursuing their own narrow visions and quests for organizational power. Second, the Trudeau government sought "innovative planning" from departments in the form of the capacity to foresee the nation's needs several years ahead rather than simply responding to events and defending programs already in operation. The third administrative value pursued was "effectiveness," defined generally as the measurement of government performance in relation to declared goals. The tight budgetary situation of the federal government in the late 1960s implied that the termination of out-dated and ineffective programs was necessary in order to release the funds for new, more effective programs serving the present priorities of the cabinet.

A series of reforms to achieve these rationalistic aspirations were begun in the late 1960s and early 1970s. Many were heralded as ushering in a new era in national policy-making. To the extent that they were oversold, disappointment was perhaps inevitable, but after discounting for the hyperbole which usually accompanies administrative reforms the structural changes introduced by the Trudeau government can perhaps fairly be seen as a mixture of limited success and a greater measure of failure.

The attempts to rationalize and better manage the policy process were expressed in several ways. An important aspect were the changes to the expenditure budget process, involving the introduction of the Program Planning Budgetary System (PPBS) and a strengthening of the Treasury Board as the expenditure management committee of cabinet. These changes are discussed at length in Chapter 5 dealing with the budgetary process. In this chapter we will describe and assess the following other manifestations of the Trudeau government's rationalistic pursuits: changes to the cabinet committee structure, the expansion of the "prime-ministerial" bureaucracy, the introduction of new coordinative portfolios of government, and the increased use of more inclusive departmental structures.

Cabinet Structure and Operations

The cabinet committee structure was reorganized by Prime Minister Pearson between 1963 and 1968, but his successor, Trudeau, gave the system enhanced importance in executive decision-making.[39] Pearson had employed 10 standing cabinet committees and a variety of ad hoc committees, but all the final decisions continued to take place in the cabinet itself. And in the committees, the system really amounted to a loose confederacy of departments, each going its own separate way. In full cabinet, the prevailing norm was deference to the recommendations coming from the individual ministers and their departments. As a result, most legislative and budgetary policy-making in the Pearson era corresponded to the incremental model. Ministers presented proposals to committees in final form. Their cabinet colleagues either had to approve or disapprove; there was little chance to examine alternatives or to recommend changes. After 1968 Prime Minister Trudeau sought to restore cabinet as an instrument for collective decision-making, to overcome the increasing "departmentalization" of policy-making and to ensure more rational consideration of interrelated issues.

Trudeau employed the same number of standing committees (10) as Pearson, but kept the number of ad hoc committees to a minimum. Proliferation of such committees in the past, it was felt, had led to confusion, disorganization and attempts by wily ministers to escape the more rigorous review process within the regular committees. Five of the standing committees covered broad areas of government activity — Culture and Native Affairs, External Policy and Defence, Economic Policy, Government Operations, and Social Policy. There were also four important coordinating committees — Priorities and Planning, Legislation and House Planning, Federal-Provincial Relations, and the Treasury Board — about which more will be said shortly. Finally, there was a Security, Intelligence and Emergency Planning Committee. The Prime Minister assigned ministers to three or four committees based mainly upon the nature of their departmental responsibilities, but also so as to ensure balanced regional and linguistic representation. Formerly, the membership of such committees remained confidential but after Joe Clark established the precedent during his brief tenure as Prime Minister of releasing the names, Trudeau adopted the practice when he returned to power in February, 1980. The cabinet committee structure as it existed in March, 1981 is illustrated in the following diagram.

Under Trudeau, committees became more active than in the Pearson period and a fixed schedule for meetings of full cabinet and committees was established. In 1978, for example, the cabinet met 56 times, usually on Thursday mornings, and committees held 207 meetings, with the leader in terms of the number of meetings held being the Government Operations Committee.[40]

Another important change from the Pearson system was that the committees no longer just made recommendations. Instead, they made

CABINET COMMITTEE SYSTEM

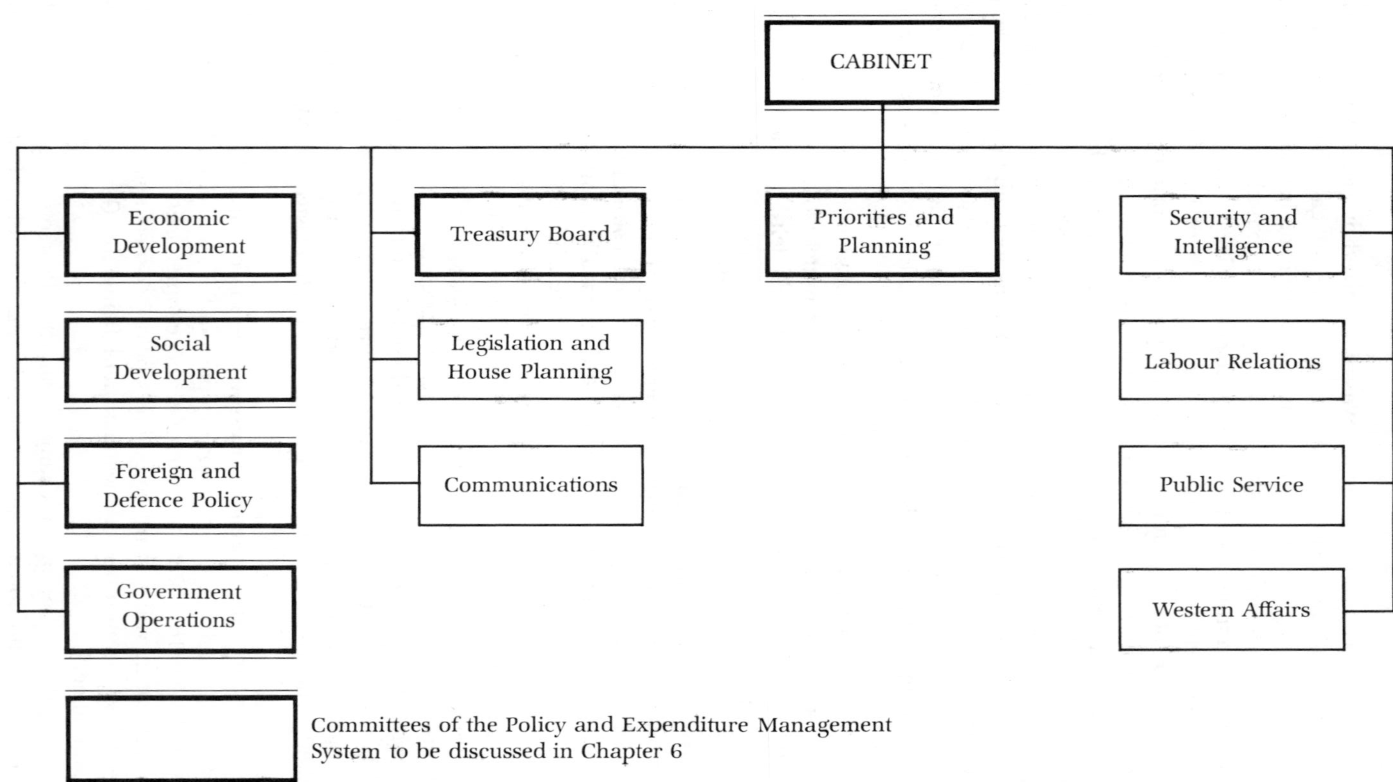

provisional decisions which were attached as an appendix to the agenda for the next cabinet meeting and were approved automatically unless a minister requested some discussion. Two main types of documents were used for cabinet decision-making.[41] Proposals for new programs would be submitted as *Memoranda to Cabinet*, signed by the responsible minister. In 5 to 10 pages, such memoranda would outline the background to an issue, the various considerations bearing on it, and the recommendations for action. In support of these relatively short documents, there would be prepared longer *Discussion Papers*. Such documents contained a more extensive discussion of the background, factors bearing on the issue, and the alternatives considered. Since Memoranda contained highly sensitive material (which might, for example, destroy the appearance of cabinet solidarity), they could not be publicized for 30 years, but the Discussion Papers could be circulated publicly after a cabinet decision was made and if their substantive content allowed. The matter of the confidentiality surrounding cabinet decision-making is discussed at some length in Chapter 9, but it can be noted here that the Trudeau government by employing after 1977 this distinction between the two types of cabinet documents sought to expose to public scrutiny and debate more of the considerations upon which policy was based. The flurry of paper caused by this rationalistic decision-making approach is revealed by the fact that in 1978 cabinet was presented with 483 Memoranda, 226 Discussion Papers, 89 draft bills, and 731 cabinet decisions were recorded.[42]

The functions of three of the four coordinating committees of cabinet deserve brief mention here; the Treasury Board as the cabinet committee dealing with expenditure management will be discussed in the next chapter. The most important cabinet committee under Trudeau has been the Priorities and Planning Committee. Chaired by the Prime Minister, its members were usually his more senior and trusted cabinet colleagues. Originally, the committee was to be concerned principally with the general direction of the government and to provide the planning capacity missing in Pearson cabinets. In practice apparently, formal planning occupied only a small part of the time of the Priorities and Planning Committee. While the Committee has played a role in legislative, budgetary and personnel planning, its weekly workload consisted mainly of urgent and politically-sensitive matters. It has, for example, often been used as a forum for settling policy disputes among ministers and deciding trade-offs among program objectives.

Towards the end of the second Trudeau administration the Priorities and Planning and the Federal-Provincial Relations committees were virtually identical, with much of the same membership and the Prime Minister as chairman of both. This arrangement provides testimony to the fact that in practically every field of public policy there is a federal-provincial dimension and the most sensitive issues in recent years (e.g., constitutional reform and energy policy) have involved federal-provincial bargaining. It is not unreasonable to suggest that one of the principal constraints on comprehensive rational policy-planning at the federal level is the need to secure provincial agreement. Detailed discussion of federal-provincial relations is found in Chapter 7.

The Legislation and House Planning Committee, chaired by the President of the Privy Council who serves as the leader of the government in the House of Commons, has performed two principal functions. The first is the development of the government's legislative program. In response to cabinet decisions, the Committee instructs departments to prepare draft legislation and these drafts (after review by the Justice Department) are returned to full cabinet via this Committee. The second part of its job is to advise and assist the President of the Privy Council in the complicated task of planning and managing the parliamentary portion of the policy process. According to two former insiders, past governments have not devised adequate means of forcing departments to comply with the requirements of legislative planning and there has been inadequate coordination of the several stages of the policy process.[43]

The Security, Intelligence and Emergency Planning Committee has the functions its name implies. The sensitive nature of its work means that most of its documents remain highly classified. Its work is not integrated with that of other cabinet committees.

The "Prime Ministerial" Bureaucracy

Under Trudeau there has developed a group of specialized support agencies designed to cope with the complex machinery of government and to assist in the better management of the policy process. The so-called "central agencies" of the Privy Council Office (PCO), Prime Minister's Office (PMO) and the Federal-Provincial Relations Office (FPRO) were to assist cabinet decision-making and to act as counterweights to the advice coming from regular, line departments.[44] One term used to describe their functions is "counter bureaucracies," reflecting the creation of bureaucracy to cope with bureaucracy.

The staff of the PCO expanded in size in response to the changes in the cabinet committee structure. By 1978, it consisted of 350 staff members, approximately 80 of whom were professional-level personnel.[45] With one exception, PCO officials are public servants, appointed by the Public Service Commission without regard to their political opinions. The exception is the Clerk of the Privy Council and Secretary to the Cabinet, who is appointed by the Prime Minister. The current (July, 1981) occupant of the post is Michael Pitfield who was first appointed in 1975 but temporarily vacated the position during the brief tenure of the Clark Conservatives. Past occupants of the post have included such legendary Ottawa mandarins as Gordon Robertson, Jack Pickersgill, Robert Bryce and Arnold Heeney. As the senior deputy minister within the Government of Canada, the position is clearly the top bureaucratic prize the Prime Minister has to offer and when Prime Minister Trudeau first gave it to Pitfield, who was only 36 at the time, there was apparently some resentment among more experienced deputy ministers.

The prestige of the position relates to the function of the PCO under Trudeau. In effect, the Office became "the lead agency for strategic planning."[46] Its Plans Division housed the key policy analysts grouped into secretariats, who supported the various committees of cabinet. Privy Council officials provided the Prime Minister with policy advice on programs. They worked with the ministers and officials of regular departments to integrate seemingly conflicting departmental objectives and programs. These tasks led to complaints that the "whiz kids" in the PCO were meddling in departmental affairs and second-guessing the expert advice of departments. In fact, because of the relatively small size of the PCO's professional staff, there is the danger that the agency will stretch its analytical resources too far. From time to time the PCO did prepare policy papers on "priority" problems. However, its defenders insist that it did not normally initiate and submit proposals to cabinet on its own, but merely commented on the plans of other agencies. Such a description tends to understate the influence that the PCO exercised because it lay astride the decision-making process. Ministers and departments had to frame their proposals in a form satisfactory to the PCO and presented them to cabinet committees in an order determined by the Office. As the "gate-keeper" for cabinet decision-making, the PCO was able to keep the Prime Minister informed of all the proposals coming through the system and this arrangement necessarily increased the influence and power of Trudeau.[47]

However, by far the greatest amount of time of PCO officials was taken up with keeping the government machinery running smoothly. PCO officials drew up, in consultation with the ministers chairing committees, agendas for cabinet committee meetings. They arranged for the circulation of documents in advance of meetings and kept minutes of cabinet and committee meetings. They reported cabinet decisions to departments and monitored their implementation. The emphasis on these "housekeeping" aspects of the PCO's operations led one former Clerk of the Privy Council to describe its role as being "non-partisan, operationally oriented and yet politically sensitive."[48]

By way of contrast, the Prime Minister's Office (PMO) was described as "partisan, politically oriented, yet operationally sensitive."[49] It grew from 60 staff members in 1969 to over 90 by 1972, but only 20 of the latter personnel were "policy advisers," with the remainder being junior clerks and secretaries. In charge of the PMO is the Principal Secretary, who in recent years, until July, 1981, had been Jim Coutts. In addition to increasing the size of the PMO, Trudeau gave it more the appearance of a personal advisory system by bringing in outside advisors rather than using public servants on a term basis as had been done in the past. He also created a number of new positions within the PMO. He originally appointed a Programme Secretary to link government activity to party goals and opinion; after the 1974 election this post was replaced with a secretariat entitled Policy, Plans and Programmes.

He experimented during his first term of office with several Regional Desks to improve communications with the various regions, but these were abandoned after the near defeat of the Liberals in the 1972 election and the related complaint that the parliamentary caucus was a more effective sounding board for regional public opinion than any bureaucratic structure. Finally, he created a Nominations Division within the PMO to advise him on the hundreds of order-in-council appointments which he makes.

A recent study of the PMO's operations suggests that its role is less glamorous than all the media speculation about "supergroups" would imply. Its initial strong role in policy-making during the early Trudeau years waned and increasingly it performed what has been described as "switchboard functions."[50] These included: the organization of the Prime Minister's scarce time, the conduct of media relations, the monitoring of the political situation, the handling of daily communications in all forms with the Prime Minister's Office, and advising on appointees to such public offices as the Senate. Only occasionally did PMO officials seek to mediate policy disputes between departments or seek to promote their own policy concerns.

The Federal-Provincial Relations Office (FPRO) began its organizational life within the PCO, but became a separate department under the Prime Minister in February 1975. By 1978 the FPRO had grown to over 40 professional staff members, directed by a secretary of the cabinet, who at that time was Gordon Robertson, a former Clerk of the Privy Council. In September, 1977, the office acquired its own Minister of Federal-Provincial Relations, but after its electoral defeat (May 1979) and fast recovery (February 1980) the Trudeau government abolished that cabinet portfolio. The FPRO existed principally to service the cabinet Committee on Federal-Provincial Relations. It was also responsible for developing the federal government's campaign in the May, 1980, referendum on the future of Quebec within Canadian Confederation and the preparation of the Liberal government's proposals for constitutional reform.

In summary, the expansion of the PCO, PMO, and FPRO was a response to the increased scope and complexity of modern government. It also reflected Trudeau's personal belief that he required alternative sources of information and political advice to that provided through the traditional channels of ministers and their departments. The new system allowed the Prime Minister to obtain a better overview of all that was going on within his government and gave him the opportunity to head off political disputes among ministers before they reached full cabinet. Reforms to the cabinet committee system and the central agencies strengthened the role of the cabinet as a vehicle for the collective determination of government policies, at a cost to individual ministers of much time and effort and some loss of the independence in policy-making that they previously enjoyed. Despite media impressions to the contrary and based upon the testimony of most former ministers, Trudeau adopted a consensual approach to cabinet decision-making. On most issues, rather than imposing his own views, Trudeau went to great lengths to ensure that all viewpoints were presented before cabinet decided. The requirement that a consensus be obtained often led to delays on what seemed to be routine decisions. Yet on issues that were of strong personal interest to him or were deemed urgent, Prime Minister Trudeau could be aggressive and creative in leading cabinet to agreement on solutions. For example, in the fall of 1978 the Prime Minister announced a number of economic initiatives which, according to most close observers of official Ottawa, were designed almost wholly by his personal advisers and represented decisive prime ministerial leadership.

While the reforms reinforced the cabinet's role as a vehicle for strategic planning, Trudeau fell short of fully realizing his rationalistic aims in this area. Complete "top down" policy-making was not achieved for several reasons.[51] First, the government was unclear about its goals and therefore could not provide explicit directions to departments. Instead, departments would prepare their own legislative and expenditure plans separately and then retrospectively slip them into the nebulous goal categories laid down by the cabinet. Second, events intervened to cause governments to set aside their longer-term plans in favor of responses to immediate problems. For example, the War Measures Crisis in October 1970 and the Parti Québécois victory in 1976 forced the cabinet to modify its agenda to find ways to solve the problem of national unity. "Urgent" problems took precedence over others which were merely "important." Third, the Prime Minister had to continue to grant individual ministers some freedom to engage in personal policy-making within their respective departmental domains so as to assist their separate political careers and to ensure their continued support for his leadership. Despite this, several ministers left the government complaining that they lacked the independence to develop and promote departmental plans. Finally, there was the factor of federal-provincial negotiation which pervades the policy-process in Canada and makes the idea of a coherent, national blueprint for action in any policy field seem almost utopian.

Even with the growth in the support services provided by the central agencies we have not witnessed the establishment of prime ministerial government in this country. The basic constraints of limited time and information make it impossible for any Prime Minister today to exercise complete personal control over the policy process in its numerous dimensions.[52] Seen in this perspective, Trudeau's reforms barely enabled him to keep pace with the growth and changes occurring throughout the rest of the governmental machinery. The central agencies remained heavily dependent on the information supplied by the departments and relied on them to follow through on cabinet decisions. Still, the emergence of a fairly elaborate prime ministerial bureaucracy financed by public funds raises some difficult constitutional issues of ministerial responsibility to Parliament and the public for the behavior of key political administrators. These issues are discussed in subsequent chapters.

The Use of Coordinative Portfolios

Another manifestation of the Trudeau government's rationalistic bias was the increased use of horizontal, coordinative portfolios in cabinet, discussion of which requires some definition of terms. A minister's *portfolio* refers to the totality of agencies for which he is responsible. Included in this is his *department*, the full-time management of which he entrusts to a deputy minister. The deputy minister has less authority with respect to other portfolio agencies. Thus the Minister of Energy, Mines and Resources has responsibility for his own department and also reports to Parliament on behalf of such independent or semi-independent agencies as the National Energy Board, the Atomic Energy Control Board, Atomic Energy of Canada Limited, and the Cape Breton Development Corporation. While the distinction between the department and the wider portfolio of the minister is important in constitutional terms, it does not represent an absolute difference in practice. Many departments are so large and extensive in the scope of their operations that they pose almost equal problems of surveillance and control for the minister and his deputy as do the independent agencies outside the departmental structure.

The Government Reorganization Act of 1971 produced several categories of ministerial portfolios.[53] First, there were the traditional "vertical constituency" portfolios that provide programs and services to a particular segment of the society. Departments like Agriculture, Energy, Mines and Resources, Labour, and Veteran's Affairs fall into this category. Because their mandates are relatively narrowly focussed, the ministers in charge of such departments have relatively fewer opportunities to intervene in the wider aspects of government operations.

Second, there are traditional "horizontal coordinative" portfolios which afford their ministers the highest number of strategic opportunities to intervene in any policy issue. Examples of such portfolios are the Prime Minister and the Ministers of External Affairs, Finance, Justice and the Treasury Board. Ministers in such positions deal with the interrelated, overlapping or horizontal dimensions of government policy. Thus, the Minister of Finance has always been considered, at least until very recently, the preeminent economic minister who was responsible for ensuring that departmental programs and expenditures were consistent with the economic, monetary and fiscal policy goals of the government in any given period. In other words, the legitimate concerns of such ministers cut across departmental boundaries and this gave them considerable influence in cabinet decision-making. In Doern's view these ministers formed a functional inner cabinet but, as he points out, they were not an inner cabinet in formal, legal terms.[54] Creation of a constitutional inner cabinet occurred after May, 1979, when Joe Clark served briefly as Prime Minister and more will be said about that experiment shortly. Within the category of established coordinative portfolios there are also less prestigious ministries which coordinate more at the administrative than the policy level of government activities. Such departments as National Revenue, Public Works and Supply and Services usually have less political influence because they tend to deal with the "nuts and bolts" of government operations, providing "common services" (taxation collection, buildings, furnishings, etc.) to the other departments.

The most striking category of new portfolios were the ministries of state. In introducing the Government Reorganization Act of 1971 D.M. Drury noted that in the future there were potentially to be two types of such ministers: ministers of state and ministers of state for designated purposes.[55] Ministers of state would be appointed to assist departmental ministers and would receive powers, duties and functions. The first Minister of State was appointed in 1972 and was to assist the Secretary of State with multicultural policy. As of June 1980 there were the following six Ministers of State in the Trudeau cabinet: Multiculturalism, Finance, Canadian Wheat Board, Small Businesses, Trade and Mines. So far none of these portfolios has become a leading cabinet position and the Prime Minister has usually given them to younger, promising, first-term cabinet ministers. In many ways this type of minister is the old-style minister without portfolio, but simply with a changed title.

The more interesting category for this discussion was the ministries of state for designated purposes, because they reflected Trudeau's desire to institutionalize rational analysis and planning in place of the traditional interplay of departmental interests and power as the basis of policy-making. Such ministers would provide greater flexibility in the executive structure to capture the interrelated aspects of departmental efforts and to coordinate the impact of programs on priority policy problems. It was not intended that these ministries were to become massive bureaucracies involved in actual delivery of numerous programs. Along with limited program capability, they would have limited budgets and they would not exercise budgetary control over regular departments. Their ability to coordinate and in general their influence on other departments was to be based on the excellence of their policy analysis. In traditional public administration language, they were to perform a staff function, providing policy advice and recommendation to their cabinet colleagues across several fields of public policy. In more contemporary public language, they were to perform something akin to Etzioni's mixed-scanning function within government. In any event, the important point to bear in mind is that they relied upon a different basis of cabinet influence than the traditional bases of program capability and/or the expenditure control function exercised by the Department of Finance and the Treasury Board. Another unique characteristic of these organizations is that they were to be transitory in nature, rather than existing indefinitely as most bureaucratic agencies seem to. When the priority problems for which they were created were solved these organizations were supposedly to ride off into the bureaucratic sunset.

The actual experience with ministers of state for designated purposes has not been all that impressive. Two such ministries were created originally;

one has since been disbanded and two others formed. A brief word about the experience of the two older ministries will reveal some of the problems they faced in their policy formulation and policy coordination roles.

The Ministry of State for Urban Affairs (MSUA), arose out of the widespread public concern about urban problems in the late 1960's, the appointment of a federal minister without portfolio responsible for housing and the creation of a task force and other studies on housing and related urban problems.[56] These studies called for an integrated "total federal approach" to urban problems and the creation of institutions to ensure joint planning among the federal, provincial and municipal governments in the urban field. In June, 1971, the creation of MSUA was announced. Between then and early 1978 when the ministry was disbanded, it had five different ministers, none of whom could be considered a political heavyweight in the federal cabinet lineup. On the administrative side, the ministry lost its first couple of secretaries (equivalent to the deputy minister in a regular departmental structure) in a short period and underwent several internal reorganizations. It began its operation by establishing the Policy Research wing, a step which, according to one study, contributed to its limited initial success.[57] It would have been better, according to the study, to begin by creating the Coordination and Development wing because the ministry's influence depended heavily on the cooperation of the provincial governments and other federal departments.

In the early 1970s, the ministry staged two tri-level conferences involving the three levels of government and a series of conferences with the provinces alone, but these efforts at joint planning in the urban field eventually floundered, apparently because of provincial sensitivities about federal intrusions into this supposedly provincial domain and because of Ottawa's refusal to put up additional funds for urban projects. MSUA did operate some small programs such as the Railway Relocation Scheme and the Neighborhood Improvement Program. It also conducted some useful research, such as the development of a set of urban indicators. By the 1975-76 fiscal year, it had a budget of approximately $22 million (in a total federal budget at the time of over $40 billion) and about 300 employees. However, the difficulties with the provinces and the worsening budget picture of the federal government, led to budget cuts within MSUA beginning in 1976 and to the merger, in the same year, of the ministry with the Central Mortgage and Housing Corporation under a single permanent head. The reorganization also led to a significant downgrading of the research function within MSUA. These events presaged its eventual disappearance in 1978, when further financial restraint was imposed in official Ottawa and the federal government retreated to its earlier pre-1970s position of adopting a low profile within urban affairs. Although the MSUA experiment can hardly be judged a resounding success, it did record some modest accomplishments, and some further discussion of the obstacles it faced will be presented after we have examined the similar, somewhat checkered history of the Ministry of State for Science and Technology (MOSST).

MOSST began its organizational life at the same time as MSUA.[58] There had been considerable discussion of the federal government's role in science policy before the 1970s; a Science Secretariat in the PCO had been established in 1964, the Science Council of Canada had been created as a public advisory body in 1966, and there had been both domestic and external reports calling for a ministry of science to provide centralized direction to the federal government's activities in the field of science and technology. Therefore, there appeared to be strong governmental and parliamentary support for MOSST when it began operation in 1971 as a horizontal planning agency with the mandate to develop a coherent science strategy out of the existing fragmented efforts of the various federal departments.

However, as a new ministry without any clear mandate to implement programs, MOSST was heavily dependent on the cooperation of other departments and in this regard it labored under several handicaps. First, the Prime Minister appointed mainly junior cabinet ministers to head the ministry and there have been seven ministers who have held the job since 1970. However, strong senior ministers with the clear backing of the Prime Minister would have been required to ensure successful coordination of other departments. Second, MOSST as an administrative organization suffered because there was a shortage of trained scientists who also possessed the managerial and political skills necessary to survive in the bureaucratic jungle of official Ottawa. There has been rapid turnover at the top. There have been five different Secretaries and in the three Assistant Secretary positions there were no fewer than seven incumbents in a two-and-one-half year stretch. Moreover, in its initial three years of operation MOSST underwent three ministry-wide reorganizations. Third, MOSST began life without a clear mandate. As the key strategic planning agency in support of the cabinet, the PCO wanted MOSST to produce a comprehensive, interlocking science policy, but the Treasury Board Secretariat, as another central agency, wanted the ministry to assist it with the budgetary evaluation of scientific programs. The government was not clear, according to Aucoin and French, whether science policy was a goal in itself or an instrument for the achievement of other goals.[59] Finally, there was the problem that MOSST lacked a homogeneous and unified clientele outside of government. The scientific community was, instead, split up into many organizations with diverse interests and no one body was able to speak with authority as a representative of the hundreds of groups working on science problems in industrial, government and academic settings. When it tried to discuss national scientific objectives in academic research with university representatives, some provinces challenged federal involvement in this field and insisted upon a greater say in the uses to which federal research money would be put in provincial universities.

Despite these serious constraints, MOSST was not entirely without accomplishments. It launched important research studies (e.g., on industrial innovation and technological forecasting), played a role in three major federal policy initiatives (the development of the so-called "contracting out" policy of federal scientific research, the development of an oceans policy, and the formulation of a space policy) and persistently lobbied other departments to pay greater attention to the scientific implications of their activities. But as the Senate Science Committee which has monitored its progress has reported, MOSST's main role has been to assist other departments in the preparation of their scientific programs and it has lacked the political power to direct and to change policies. Based upon the Committee's recommendations made in 1973, MOSST was given, beginning in the 1975-76 fiscal year, the authority to review and comment on the scientific expenditures of other departments and was instructed to prepare a total science budget for the federal government. While these steps brought MOSST more into the executive decision-making arena, the Senate Committee has since reported that most departments submitted their estimates to MOSST at the same time that they went to Treasury Board. This practice left too little time for the ministry to review and comment on the spending plans. Therefore, the Senate Committee recommended that departments be required to submit estimates earlier to MOSST before Treasury Board consideration and that a science advisor be appointed in each department to act as a liaison agent with MOSST. In recent years there has been much talk about an enhanced federal commitment to scientific research, but the science minister has not always been chairman of the relevant cabinet committee and apparently was never a member of the influential Priorities and Planning Committee. Currently (July, 1981) the occupant of the post is also the Minister of the Environment. In general, therefore, the situation may have in fact worsened since 1977 when the Senate Committee concluded that "the vacuum at the centre of science policy decision-making has not been completely filled."[60]

The Trudeau Government has since added Ministers of State for Economic Development (MSED) and for Social Policy (MSSP).[61] The former position is of interest for two reasons. First, in establishing the ministry, the government appears to have learned from the experiences of the earlier two ministries. Without the leverage of extensive program responsibilities or a budgetary control function, MSUA and MOSST had become "hostages to the power of the line departments."[62] For them, knowledge and bright ideas were not a sufficient basis to overcome the entrenched patterns of power brokerage and horse-trading within cabinet and inter-departmental decision-making. The proclamation establishing the new economic ministry sought to overcome these constraints by assigning MSED a strong role in the integration and coordination of all policies and programs related to industrial and regional development. The minister was to be chairman of a new Cabinet Committee on Economic Development and was "to lead and coordinate the efforts of the Government of Canada to establish cooperative relationships with the provinces, business and labour."[63] Even more significant in terms of the leverage of the new ministry, the new minister was, with the advice of the Cabinet Committee, to recommend to the Treasury Board "on the allocation of financial, personnel and other resources" to programs dealing with economic development. From the outset, therefore, the new ministry was given an explicit role in the budgetary process. The combination of policy formulation and expenditure control in a single cabinet committee presaged the eventual emergence of the new Policy and Expenditure Management System, which is discussed in Chapter 5 on the budgetary process.

It is too early to predict whether the two new ministries of state will be more successful than their forerunners in breaking down the prevailing attitudes and norms of departmental exclusiveness within policy-making. To do so, they will likely require the political support of the Prime Minister and so far they have not been particularly well served in this regard. The present (July, 1981) Minister of State for Economic Development is a member of the Senate, appointed by the Prime Minister to bolster cabinet representation from Western Canada, and as an unelected member of the appointed upper house of Parliament, it is questionable whether Senator Olson carries the political clout some had hoped to see in the new portfolio. As for the Social Policy ministry, it is presently (July, 1981) headed by the Minister of Justice, who chairs the Social Affairs Committee of Cabinet. However, during the present Trudeau administration, the Justice Minister has been preoccupied with the constitutional review process and the ministry has been almost invisible. If, as some have suggested, the latest two ministries represent the wave of the future, the Prime Minister will have to assign them to senior cabinet members and not overload those ministers with additional responsibilities.

Rearranging Departmental Boundaries

In addition to creating various ministries of state, the Trudeau government created new departments and remodelled old ones in order to solve the so-called crisis of coordination in contemporary policy-making. Large omnibus departments, grouping as many related functions as possible under a single minister, were often the result. There is not the space here to describe these developments in great detail. However, John Langford has provided an excellent account of the task force study of the Department of Transport's objectives and operation which serves as a good example of the attempt to consolidate in order to coordinate and control widespread government activities.[64] In 1969 when the study was conducted, the Minister of Transport was responsible for a variety of semi-autonomous agencies in the form of commissions and crown corporations (Canadian Transport Commission, National Harbours Board, Air Canada, CNR, and the St. Lawrence Seaway) as well as a department which was one of Ottawa's largest bureaucratic units. The department lacked an overall set of national transportation objectives and the minister, through his own office, was unable to integrate the operational, regulatory and developmental components of his ministry into a package serving the general priorities of the government. The task force recommended a radical reorganization of the portfolio along the lines of a ministry system.

Once approved by the cabinet, the reorganization plan took another six years to implement and Transport Canada was eventually denied the title of a ministry. Yet its new organizational format contained many features of the ministry model: a "ministry executive" composed of the minister, the deputy minister, and two assistant deputy ministers; a small "ministry staff" to support the ministry executive by coordinating the flow of information and planning research among the several components of the portfolio; four relatively autonomous operational administrations within the department, whose activities were to be coordinated through interlocking advisory boards; and a "transportation council" composed of the minister and the senior administrators from most of the units within the portfolio.

While this brief account does not fully describe the changes which occurred, the intention of all the changes was to strengthen the political direction given to the portfolio, to link its operational, regulatory and developmental components and to increase the attention given to the intermodal aspects of transportation planning. According to Langford, the reorganization did not produce a dramatic increase in planning coordination between the departmental and research groups within the CTC, CNR and Air Canada. Too much of the time of the Ministry Executive was taken up with "fire-fighting" and too little time was spent on longer-term strategic planning. Some closer scrutiny of the capital expenditure plans of the CNR and Air Canada has occurred and the Evaluation Branch established in 1975 within Transport Canada has conducted some useful assessments of programs. Despite all attempted and actual changes the transportation portfolio remains one of the most difficult in terms of policy management in the federal cabinet.

Other examples of this tendency towards consolidation can be mentioned more briefly. In a recent study, Anthony Careless provides an account of the formation, in 1969, of the Department of Regional Economic Expansion through the consolidation of programs operated previously through several different departments and then brought under one minister.[65] Apparently DREE has had limited success in interjecting regional development considerations into other national policy fields and has had difficulty in working towards joint planning with the provinces. Cultural agencies at the federal level were increasingly brought under the umbrella of the Secretary of State and Bernard Ostry has described efforts made to coordinate the vast number of cultural activities involving federal participation.[66] Finally, there was the Department of the Environment created in 1971 to bring together the numerous environmental programs of the federal government previously dispersed to several departments. While a full organizational history for this department is not yet written, it should be noted that the government recently hived off a portion of its operations to create a Department of Fisheries and

Oceans and there have been repeated calls for a separate department dealing with forests.[67] These additions to the bureaucratic landscape reflect more than just a penchant for rational policy formulation based upon neater, more logical, structures; they also represent "positional policies," which signal to affected groups and the attentive public that emerging problems have been recognized and are being dealt with.

Concluding Thoughts on Rationalism and Institutional Reform

In recent years the earlier infatuation with comprehensive rational planning has waned greatly in official Ottawa. The institutional reforms of the late 1960s and the 1970s have not been abandoned, but there is greater realism about what can be accomplished through changes to structures alone. There is also a recognition of some of the costs involved in a rigid adherence to the norms of rational decision-making. We have already mentioned the delays and heavy demands in terms of time imposed upon ministers by the collegial approach to cabinet decision-making. The submergence of the political individuality and visibility of cabinet ministers has caused some resentment and may have stifled creativity. It has been alleged that the Trudeau cabinet system has, in effect, transformed cabinet members from politicians into administrators.[68] The result of an excessive reliance on the functional cabinet committees and the various so-called scientific management routines has been to reduce the cabinet's traditional role of assuring that all regional and sectional interests are borne in mind in the formulation of national policies. Regional ministers with strong political skills continue to be important in cabinet decision-making and there is a requirement that federal-provincial implications be highlighted in submissions to cabinet, but these features do not entirely offset the apparent decline of the cabinet as a forum for regional and ethnic accommodation.

The mellowed attitude towards rational policy-making is also a product of the restrained budgetary situation of the federal government in recent years and the apparent growing public skepticism concerning the probability of success of large-scale government initiatives. The heyday of the policy analyst was the 1960s and early 1970s when ideas of social reform were in the air, government deficits were not seen as an overriding problem and there was confidence that governments, with the benefit of new social technologies, could formulate and apply solutions to social problems on a wide scale. Today that optimism about the possibilities for creative social change is gone, partly in the face of depressing (though highly disputatious) cost/benefit findings done on the program initiatives of the 1960s. The onus is now on the innovator to prove that his proposed programs will actually work. Increasingly in the ascendancy throughout the bureaucracy are the evaluators, who can provide assessments of on-going programs to identify those which are ineffective and might be terminated. More discussion of this change in the prevalent mood towards government spending is found in the next chapter dealing with the budgetary process.

Somewhat similar arguments to these are advanced by Richard French in his recent study, *How Ottawa Decides: Planning and Industrial Policy-Making, 1968-1980*.[69] According to French, Prime Minister Trudeau's limited success in realizing his rationalistic ambitions was due to the co-existence of three planning systems whose interactions frustrated rather than fostered cohesion in natural policy-making. The cabinet planning system (described above), the Treasury planning system (described in the next chapter) and the Finance planning system, each represented a different perspective on the planning enterprise based upon their own organizational history, position and role within the governmental structure and their own disciplinary bias. The cabinet planning system represented innovation and initiation, as opposed to the conservatism of the Finance planning system and the emphasis on termination and reallocation of revenues within the Treasury planning system. Each perspective was represented by intelligent and forceful individuals at the senior management levels and the clash of their operating styles and personalities made an integration of the three planning perspectives more difficult.

The conclusion of a recent study, that "In Canada we have created the structures of rational policymaking but incrementalism predominates within them," is one that would be endorsed by most observers of the policy process at the national level.[70] Perhaps the ultimate reason why rationalism has failed is that planning and politics do not co-exist comfortably. There seems to be much truth in Aaron Wildavsky's insightful argument that politics involves its own form of rationality.[71] According to Wildavsky, planning advocates envisage a technocratic process involving comprehensive rationality to override the messy, illogical, decentralized decision-making that now takes place. Planning is thus perceived as an antidote to politics. Ultimately, planning must succumb to the constraints of politics. Once we reintroduce the factor of human ignorance and recalcitrance into any planning situation, and remove the unrealistic assumption of complete knowledge and control, then we are back essentially to talking about politics. One then plans, says Wildavsky, the way one governs; by coping with situations as they arise and hoping for improvement as circumstances change. Some call this "adaptive planning"; Wildavsky prefers the phrase "muddling through."[72] Other writers have argued that where planning must be bold, comprehensive, long-term and goal-oriented, politicians are necessarily cautious, concerned with compromise and bargaining, preoccupied with short-term (i.e., electoral considerations) and hostile to explicit goals.[73] In this view, the logic of planning and the logic of politics are inherently inconsistent.

No doubt for some readers the above attacks misrepresent planning and therefore belittle it unfairly. Few scholars or practitioners of planning today would hold to an "apolitical" definition, making it a completely technocratic and value-free exercise. Planning has acquired multiple meanings over time and these include planning as intervention and social action as well as the more traditional definitions of physical design and systems analysis.[74] All planners are not, as Wildavsky insists, "dead set against spontaneity and so insistent upon control." They do not envision themselves as aloof experts, hovering above a debased political process. Wildavsky anticipates these criticisms by arguing that more recent, fashionable forms of planning — called, at different times, adaptive, participatory, and advocacy planning—are mixtures of "pure planning" and "pure politics" and hence are indistinguishable from most other methods of decision-making.

There was some confusion over what style of policy-making Trudeau was seeking and he contributed to the confusion by some apparently contradictory remarks. On the one hand, his changes within the executive-bureaucratic arena implied a more formalized, centralized and bureaucratized policy process. His stress on rational functionalism came through in a speech early in his first term as Prime Minister: "We . . . are aware that the many techniques of cybernetics, by transforming the control function and the manipulation of information, will transform our whole society. With this knowledge, we are wide awake, alert, capable of action; no longer are we blind, inert pawns of fate."[75] While this remark suggests the rejection of spontaneity, the need for neutral expertise and the desire for control which Wildavsky mentions as characteristics of planning, in other contexts Trudeau and his advisers were talking about "participatory democracy" and the "just society." Speaking in 1971 following the War Measures Crisis (October 1970), Trudeau commented: " . . . it may well be that a solution for the phenomenon of violence lies only in thorough democratization of all our institutions and social structures. Indeed this is why, in the past three years, I have emphasized the need for participatory democracy. . . . In a democracy, the people would be sovereign not merely once every four years at election time, but all times."[76] And the Trudeau government went beyond mere slogans to implement changes apparently designed to increase citizen involvement and influence in policy development. Such changes included: reforms within Parliament (e.g., changes to the committee system and increased staff support for MPs) designed to provide elected representatives with greater input into policy; the greater use of task forces and discussion papers as vehicles for gathering citizens' reactions to government plans; the establishment of Information Canada (since disbanded) as a public clearinghouse for information on government activities; the provision of public funds towards the costs of election campaigns; and the financing of social animators among disaffected youth, native peoples, tenants and others.

Critics insist that there was more "shadow than substance" in these changes and that more fundamental reforms (such as a Freedom of Information Act) were avoided. One observer suggests that the new activities represented the response of an insecure government, increasingly out of touch with its environment and anxious to strengthen the linkages between citizens and decision-makers in order to fulfill the precepts of an optimal policy-making system which required more complete information on citizen preferences. Better information would allow decision-makers to respond to and mould the preferences and demands of citizens. In the view of critics, the new procedures were essentially manipulative in nature. For example, Donald Smiley has argued that the Trudeau government's commitment to participatory democracy was similar to General Motors' devotion to consumer sovereignty in the sense that it arose from a common desire "to mitigate the uncertainties of oligopolistic competition."[77] Whether these were the Liberal government's actual motives is impossible to determine, but it seems clear that Trudeau was not proposing a transfer of real decision-making power to the people. At one point in response to a reporter's question, Trudeau shot back with an illuminating remark: "I think you are making the usual mistake of confusing participation and decision-making. To participate does not mean that you are going to make the decision."[78] Despite Trudeau's occasional philosophizing as a former academic about sovereign voters, there was little disposition on his part as a practising politician to make fundamental changes in the system of cabinet-parliamentary government which clearly granted initiative and control in the policy process to the party in power. Within limits Trudeau sought to open up the policy process and at the same time to make it more efficient, but he did not seek to transform it completely. This entire discussion of participatory democracy will be returned to in Chapter 10. Here, it is sufficient to suggest that comprehensive rationality and participatory democracy are at best uneasy partners and in fact may be antithetical to each other.

Many participants in national policy-making apparently share a weariness after all the administrative innovations that took place in the 1960s — one has identified what he describes as "signs of a saturation psychosis." But governments are unlikely to abandon their search for an "organizational fix" to the difficult problems of modern policy-making. For example, the Conservatives came to power in 1979 and immediately established a formal inner cabinet and a new expenditure management system, the latter discussed in the next chapter. As for the inner cabinet, it was not a new idea and had been rejected by successive prime ministers on the grounds that it would violate the principle of regional representation in cabinet decision-making and would blur individual ministerial responsibility.[79] Indeed, when the complaint was made that British Columbia had been left out of Prime Minister Clark's inner cabinet, he was forced to increase its membership by one (to a total of 12) in order to provide that representation. There remained the question of who was to be held responsible for policy and administrative innovations, the junior minister in actual charge of a department or the coordinating minister who served in the inner cabinet. Under the Clark system, the inner cabinet could make final decisions and the full cabinet would meet infrequently. There was also concern that issues would increasingly be bumped up to the inner cabinet, often on appeal by a minister who had lost the argument at the lower level, causing repetition of discussions. Prime Minister Clark assured a parliamentary committee that this tendency was not pronounced, but in his brief tenure it may simply have not had a chance to develop.[80] In any case, the reinstated Liberals under Trudeau continue to avoid this innovation, preferring instead to free ministers from departmental administration to give them time for policy development through the appointment of additional ministers of state and parliamentary secretaries.

The Wider Policy Process – The Public Service

To this point in our examination of the policy process within the government of Canada we have been concentrating mainly on decision-making within cabinet and to a lesser extent within departments. However, the reforms undertaken at the "centre" by the Trudeau administration had a significant impact on departmental operations. The insistence upon goal clarification and top-down coordination set off a chain reaction of developments and processes within departments. At the same time, many departmental mandates were being redefined and broadened. Life for senior public servants was further complicated by the practice followed by Prime Minister Trudeau of regularly rotating ministers and deputy ministers among the various portfolios of government.[81] While such movement of personnel may have lessened the likelihood of stagnation in particular departments and might have served to develop a cadre of public service managers capable of transporting their administrative skills from one location to the next, it did add to the turbulence of the public service environment over the last decade. Not all departments were equally affected by these developments. Some, such as Public Works, Supply and Services and National Revenue, were more oriented to "administrative" functions rather than to "policy-making" and were, therefore, less affected by the changed approaches to policy-making. All this points to a cautionary note: in the discussion which follows, while it is necessary to generalize, the reader should bear in mind that the public service is not a single uniform body, but rather a conglomeration of very diverse entities.

A government department is headed by a cabinet minister, who is formally responsible for all actions of the department and its officials. The actual extent of ministerial involvement in departmental affairs will depend to a large extent on his personality and skills, but ministers are forced to leave most administrative matters to the permanent officials under them. The consequence of this pattern of behavior for accountability within government is discussed in Chapter 8.

For both policy advice and administrative supervision, the minister relies greatly upon his deputy minister, who is the administrative head of the department. Deputy ministers are appointed by the Prime Minister. Although most are career public servants, upon appointment they become part of the "Governor-in-Council group," separate from the public service proper.[82] They hold office "at pleasure", which means that at any time the Prime Minister can replace them. When governments change, an incoming Prime Minister may insist that certain deputies resign because they are too closely identified with the policies of the former government. It is seen as essential that the minister have the confidence of the permanent head of the department. Automatic, wholesale replacement of deputies with a change of government has not occurred in Canada and the few departures which have taken place have reflected professional disagreements rather than straight partisan considerations.

The deputy minister is a crucial figure in the policy process because he is the link between the transient political leadership in the form of the minister and the permanent career public service. The deputy's role defies simple description. It is clear that he plays an active role in policy-making. He is also the principal administrator in the department. As will be discussed in Chapter 8, recent studies suggest that, in the past at least, deputy ministers have placed greater stress on their policy advisory roles than on their administrative responsibilities. This orientation reflected the fact that ministers received more political credit for launching new programs than for successfully administering existing ones and therefore they looked to the deputy mainly for policy advice. Since the deputy was there to serve his minister and probably because policy development was inherently more exciting, departmental management apparently received less attention.

The relationship between a deputy and his minister is highly personal and depends for its success upon the development of mutual confidence, trust and candor. There is no organizational formula that can describe or prescribe the optimal working relationship. That relationship depends greatly upon the personalities and basic operating styles of the two individuals involved. The deputy is clearly involved in the policy process: he talks to interest groups, assesses issues, formulates alternatives and makes recommendations. Undoubtedly, some ministers become the "captives" of their deputies because they lack expertise or because they are denied full information to make judgements.[83] But, according to former deputies, this kind of situation rarely occurs because senior public servants accept the legitimate right of the elected politician ultimately to decide on policy. Obviously, the deputy's role involves a delicate balance between deference and obedience to the minister on the one hand and frankness and independence on the other.

In response to the requirements of the new policy-making system launched by Prime Minister Trudeau, the major departments of the federal government during the late 1960s and 1970s rushed to establish their own policy planning capability. Michael J. Prince and John A. Chenier have recently analysed the rise and fall of policy units during this period.[84] They argue that the appearance of policy units within departments was a response to the new "rationalism" represented by systems analysis and PPBS within the budgetary process. The PCO and Treasury Board began to insist upon greater quality in departmental submissions. To cope with and perhaps to neutralize the new demands from central agencies, departments proceeded to establish policy planning units. Initially these were located near the top of the organizational hierarchy, usually at the level of the assistant deputy minister. Units established later were brought closer to the operational sides of the departments involved. By the mid-1970s, according to Prince and Chenier, there were at least 3,500 planners in the major departments of the federal government.[85] The expectations for policy units were very high in these early years of their development.

By 1980, however, the policy planning units within departments were on the decline. According to Prince and Chenier, they became "the victims of organizational infighting, slowly losing any effectiveness in the policy process, while at the same time acquiring a more passive, less visible role".[86] The factors contributing to this decline included: "the absence of agreed criteria for determining the essential elements of good policy; the difficulties of recruiting suitable personnel; the lack of attention to different departmental needs; the problems seemingly inherent in line-staff differentiation; and the absence of sustained commitment and support from senior management."[87] For further elaboration of these points, readers should consult the Prince and Chenier article. We would only suggest that the onset of an era of financial restraint within government and the importance of the new enterprise of "evaluation" within government, are probably additional factors accounting for the waning of the policy planning function.

Much goes on within departments which escapes the notice of both the minister and his deputy, and does not involve upper-level policy planning units. The daily decision-making that occurs throughout the various levels of the department can be said, in a certain sense, to constitute "policy". As noted earlier, governments today are increasingly forced to draft legislation in very broad general terms and leave it up to the bureaucracy to provide the actual contents of policy in the form of regulations or similar less-publicized forms of policy-making. The problems which such subordinate law-making presents in terms of traditional principles of accountability are discussed in Chapter 8. Here we want to stress the importance of this "implementation phase" of policy-making to the actual success of policy.

Until recently, implementation was almost completely ignored in the study of the policy process or it was simply treated as a brief interlude between the passage of legislation and the opening of the door of a government agency to provide service. However, studies have revealed that the best laid plans of legislators can go awry if there is not adequate, advance consideration given to the requirements for successful implementation of programs. It has been discovered in such studies that the carrying out of public programs is itself a complex political process. Most of these studies originated in the United States and may reflect problems endemic to that system.[88] Canada, however, is unlikely to be entirely immune from them.

Canadian political parties may be more cohesive than their American counterparts, but as has already been mentioned they are not programmatic parties with clear ideological goals. The legislative enactments which they sponsor when in office reflect their desire to broaden their support as widely as possible. As a result, vague legislative mandates put a generous amount of discretion in the hands of public servants. And while the Canadian bureaucracy may be more subject to unified political direction and control than is the American bureaucracy, there is still the danger that latent bureaucratic goals will displace manifest program goals. For example, a desire to expand their bureaucratic territory may lead departments to interpret the goals of programs as broadly as possible. This could create a further obstacle to successful implementation, namely, conflict with other administrative agencies over the appropriate scope of programs. Control agencies in government (for example, the Treasury Board as the cabinet watchdog over finances and the Public Service Commission as the supervisor of government-wide personnel policies) may also inhibit the implementation plans of government agencies. For example, the Canadian Human Rights Commission created in 1977 had a difficult time in convincing the Treasury Board that the classification of professional officers being requested by the Commission for its regional offices was in fact necessary and this may have adversely affected the Commission's capacity to fulfill its legislative mandate.

Forces outside the executive-bureaucratic arena may also affect the implementation process so as to modify or even to negate program goals. In Canada (even more so than in the United States), the success of many programs depends upon administration by provincial bureaucracies under the mantle of shared-cost or joint federal-provincial programs. It is often assumed that such programs create a superior-subordinate relationship with Ottawa "buying" provincial compliance with its goals and methods simply by offering to share the costs. As is discussed in Chapter 7, the actual relationships that emerge under joint programs are far more complex and problematic than just Ottawa "paying the piper and calling the tune." Federal grants often serve only to establish an opportunity for national politicians and bureaucrats to negotiate with their provincial counterparts over how programs should be implemented.

Because the statutory mandates for administrative agencies grant public servants considerable discretion, the actual content of policy may be modified by advice and complaints received from pressure groups. While these groups recognize the importance of having input early in the policy process, they are also aware of the value of persistence. Regulations passed to implement new legislation will often determine its actual impact and groups will lobby for rules that they can "live with". Pressure groups may try to convince the public servants administering legislation not to pursue their mandates too zealously or they may campaign for the actual repeal of legislation or regulations. To a lesser extent than in the United States where power is more decentralized, the courts and the legislatures may also influence the implementation process. Courts may declare regulations invalid as going beyond the scope of the authorizing legislation. Parliamentary committees may review program operations and recommend changes. However, both judicial and legislative review of the uses of bureaucratic discretion are subject to significant constraints, as will be discussed in Chapter 8 on accountability.

In summary, the conversion of legislation into actual programs is far from a routine and automatic process. A variety of participants affect the implementation of policy. At the implementation stage the bureaucracy plays a crucial role in determining the success of programs. Finally, any neat analytical distinction between policy formulation and policy implementation as two completely different and separate forms of activity soon begins to break down when applied to the real world of government decision-making. To a great extent the two processes are inseparable and share common characteristics.

Pressure Groups in the Policy Process

Pressure groups have become a ubiquitous presence in the national policy process. Several hundred national associations are represented full-time in Ottawa, including business, professional, labor, agricultural, cultural and social organizations. In addition, there are full-time lobbying firms, consultants, law firms and lawyers, MPs and Senators, and party officials who spend time representing "clients" before government.

A precise definition of lobbying is difficult and therefore a count of the actual number of organizations and individuals involved is next to impossible. Does political gossip over coffee with a bureaucrat constitute lobbying or do we wish to confine use of the term to more explicit attempts to influence public policy through briefs and direct representations? Much lobbying apparently occurs behind closed doors and is not subject to public scrutiny. If, previously, political scientists underestimated the importance of such activity this is no longer the case for there has been in recent years a proliferation of general literature and case studies of pressure groups.[89] Only the main findings of these studies can be presented here.

There seems to be general agreement in the literature that in terms of targets for pressure group activity the cabinet and the middle and upper levels of the bureaucracy clearly are favored by groups deemed to be most influential. For example, Robert Presthus, in his various studies, determined that business groups found it more effective to allocate most of their time to the public service and the cabinet, with the legislature ranking far behind as a target.[90] It is interesting to note that contact with departments was ranked slightly ahead of the cabinet by business representatives. Labor and social policy groups turned mainly to the legislature and secondarily to the public service. Often business representatives share high social and economic backgrounds, as well as common political values and attitudes, with senior public servants and ministers. Business groups tend to use lobbying tactics requiring the most political sophistication, particularly personal representations made to key decision-makers. Hence, the interaction between such private sector and public sector elites is said to involve limited confrontation and consists mainly of a pragmatic process of mutual accommodation.

Not all groups enjoy such a close relationship with key policy-makers. Organizations representing lower socio-economic groups are often poorly financed, have limited or no permanent organization, and little specialized knowledge to offer government decision-makers. They may be perceived by ministers and officials as politically and economically marginal, as not having sufficient political power to warrant special consideration. While they may have a chance to confront cabinet ministers with the annual submission of a brief, they do not usually enjoy the continuous access to power acquired by more affluent, better organized groups. Consequently, they have less chance of knowing early on what policies are being developed that may affect their interests. They must rely on making an impact through opposition parties in the legislature, protest rallies or through the media in order to have influence in the policy process. The disproportionate access enjoyed by some groups to government power and information, it has been argued, leads most policy-making to consist of piecemeal and incremental changes that do not upset the existing distributions of political and economic power.[91]

The tendency for pressure groups to focus their efforts on the executive-bureaucratic arena reflects some of the trends within the policy process described earlier, namely, the concentration of power in the cabinet and the bureaucracy and the relative decline of the legislature. Recent institutional reforms to the cabinet and the House of Commons have apparently caused some changes to the context in which pressure groups operate. Peter Aucoin has argued optimistically that the rise of central advisory agencies (described above) means that pressure groups are not given *a priori* the opportunity to dominate the input stage of policy-making, that now they are frequently confronted with advisors who must see beyond the specialized concerns of individual groups, and within the budgetary process their claims for expenditures on their behalf have become more visible.[92] In short, pressure groups must now rely less upon long-standing clientele relationships with departments and must argue more explicitly why they should receive benefits. On the legislative side, the procedural reforms introduced in the House of Commons in the late 1960s, which transferred the detailed consideration of legislation and spending to the standing committees, has probably served to increase the amount of pressure group activity directed at Parliament.

Appearances by pressure groups before such committees are used mainly as an appeal mechanism to contest issues lost earlier in the executive-bureaucratic arena. They are also used to seek detailed legislative changes and simply to publicize the viewpoint of an organization. The enhanced role of the committees has undoubtedly increased the exposure of MPs to the process of pressure group-bureaucratic interaction and may have increased thereby their own frustrations at being excluded from these earlier, usually crucial, stages of policy determination.

According to Robert Presthus, the claims of interest groups "provide much of the energy that activates the formal political structure and often determines the ends to which it is put."[93] Yet other writers maintain that the bureaucracy dominates most relationships that develop between departments and clientele groups in the private sector.[94] The apparent contradiction between these two general viewpoints may not, in fact, exist if we conceptualize the policy-making process as a series of "sub-governments" constructed along the lines of policy fields (agriculture, health and so on) where public and private elites interact on the basis of shared outlooks and interests to create policy. Aggressive promotion of its memberships' interests by pressure group representatives, which might, if pushed too far, cost them continuing access, is not necessary because of the basic similarity in outlook between the two groups. Obviously, individual cabinet ministers and senior public servants cannot be completely oblivious to wider policy considerations and the recent strengthening of the cabinet's collective policy role may counter the specialized pressure on individual ministers. It is also true that public servants may disagree with groups over what is in "the public interest" or in the interests of their departments. Strong lobbies may serve in some instances to create strong counterlobbies. However, despite these qualifications, the tendency for policy-making to evolve on the basis of subject-matter specializations that correspond closely to departmental structures and related patterns of pressure group activity remains very strong indeed.

Parliament and the Policy Process

All legislation must be approved by both houses of Parliament, the House of Commons and the Senate, and receive Royal Assent. While, in theory, Parliament is supreme, in practice its role in the actual formulation of legislation is limited. Most of the time of both Houses is spent on the examination of legislative and expenditure proposals that originate with the cabinet. While Parliament rarely initiates legislation, it could conceivably influence policy by amending bills presented by the government. In practice this rarely occurs, both because party discipline inclines MPs in the governing party to support measures presented by their cabinet colleagues and because members lack the expertise to make detailed changes to legislation. It has been argued frequently that Parliament is simply a rubber stamp for proposals prepared by the cabinet and the bureaucracy, but this view is perhaps too pessimistic.

The actual influence of the House of Commons and the Senate is subtle and difficult to measure precisely. While neither body regularly defeats or amends government bills in a substantial way, this no doubt partly reflects the fact that the more contentious features of such bills have been eliminated in the pre-parliamentary process of negotiation with pressure groups and the provinces. Successful passage of all its measures relatively unscathed may simply mean that a government has anticipated intense parliamentary hostility toward certain proposals and has withheld those bills. Occasionally, bills will be abandoned by the government before all the stages in the parliamentary process have been completed, perhaps because of opposition within the caucus of the governing party, which reflects in turn the concerns of outside groups. Therefore, any ratio of the number of government bills approved in Parliament in a session over those introduced will always be very high, but this should not be taken as complete or conclusive evidence that Parliament has no influence whatsoever on the outcomes of the policy process.

Parliament does play a role in refining government legislation. Beginning in 1969 the detailed examination of government bills by the House of Commons was transferred to the standing committees. This procedural change gave ordinary MPs a marginally better opportunity to contribute to policy determination by allowing them to specialize in various fields and to hear the testimony of expert witnesses. However, the government still controls the committees quite closely through the appointment (in effect) of the chairman who is a member of its own party and through its majority on the committee. As one of the authors of this text has written elsewhere, governments have remained protective of the essential features of their legislation and committee influence consists mainly of amendments to specific and limited features of bills.[95] From the government's perspective the changes had the salutory effect of making the House of Commons into a more efficient legislative machine. A recent study of Senate operations described that body as a "lobby from within" and argued that influential senators on certain key committees are able to use a process of detailed amendment to promote changes favorable to business interests which they represent.[96]

Thus, although constitutionally Parliament is supreme, in practice its influence has diminished with the accretion of effective power and control in the executive branch. The best prospect for enhanced parliamentary influence appears to involve the study of discussion papers issued by the government, where committees are not faced with a "take it or leave it" proposition and the government's prestige is not perceived to be on the line. Increased access to government information would also greatly improve the effectiveness of the parliamentary process.

Summary and Conclusions

Even the rather extended discussion above does not include all of the potential participants in the policy process. We have concentrated our attention on the principal structures and actors involved therein. Other actors who contribute to policy-making include: royal commissions and task forces, advisory bodies to governments, the mass media, independent research institutes and the universities, and to a limited extent (as revealed in Chapter 10 on citizen participation) the general public. The policy process is complex and multi-faceted. While the cabinet is at the centre its options are narrowed as it seeks to reconcile the numerous competing demands originating from the bureaucracy, pressure groups, the provinces, Parliament and others. The adjustment of interests which must occur often means that the policy results are less bold, comprehensive and rationalistic than outside observers would wish. Changes to the machinery of government will never completely offset, it seems, a process which is by definition, incremental, piecemeal and illogical.

Another recurrent theme in the above discussion is the importance of personality in the policy process. Most discussions of the policy process, this chapter included, fail to incorporate adequately the role played by personality and spontaneity. The personalities of key players within the inner circles, how they interact, and the ideas and actions of creative individuals are irreducible elements within the policy process.[97]

The policy process is almost always continuous. Cabinet decides on legislation and has it approved by Parliament, the bureaucracy applies the legislation and discovers on the basis of feedback from affected groups that it does not work in all respects, recommendations are then made to the minister and eventually to cabinet for amendments to be made to the original legislation and the whole process begins again. Similarly, adjustments are constantly being made to "policy" at the administrative level in the form of changes to regulations or department practices based upon feedback and evaluation. Few, if any, problems of any magnitude are settled permanently; they are constantly being redefined and policy is being redirected.

The policy studies field is a challenging one. It provides useful insights into the nature of the administrative process and the political process generally. This type of study can yield knowledge that has both a theoretical and practical significance and as this chapter makes clear there is plenty of room for disagreement and controversy.

For Further Reading

BOOKS AND REPORTS

Anderson, James E. *Public Policy-Making*, 2nd ed. New York: Holt, Rinehart & Winston, 1979.

Aucoin, Peter and Richard French. *Knowledge, Power and Public Policy.* Ottawa: Science Council of Canada, 1974.

Campbell, Colin, and George J. Szablowski. *The Superbureaucrats: Structure and Behavior in Central Agencies*. Toronto: Macmillan, 1979.

Doern, G. Bruce, and Peter Aucoin eds. *Public Policy in Canada: Organization Process and Management*. Toronto: Macmillan, 1979.

Doern, G. Bruce, and V. S. Wilson. *Issues in Canadian Public Policy.* Toronto: Macmillan, 1974.

Doerr, Audrey D. *The Machinery of Government in Canada*. Toronto: Methuen, 1981.

Dye, Thomas R. *Understanding Public Policy.* Englewood Cliffs, N.J.: Prentice Hall, 1979.

Edelman, Murray. *The Symbolic Uses of Politics*. Urbana Ill.: University of Illinois Press, 1967.

Edwards III, George C. and Ira Sharkansky. *The Policy Predicament: Making and Implementing Public Policy.* San Francisco: W. H. Freeman & Co., 1978.

French, Richard D. *How Ottawa Decides: Planning and Industrial Policy-Making, 1968-1980*. Toronto: James Lorimer, 1980.

Hockin, Thomas A. ed. *Apex of Power: The Prime Minister and Political Leadership in Canada*, 2nd ed. Scarborough, Ont.: Prentice-Hall, 1976.

Jackson, Robert J., and Michael M. Atkinson. *The Canadian Legislative System*. Toronto: Macmillan, 2nd ed., 1980.

Lindblom, Charles E. *The Policy-Making Process*. Englewood Cliffs, N.J.: Prentice-Hall, 1968.

Neilson, W. A. W., and J. C. MacPherson eds. *The Legislative Process in Canada: The Need for Reform*. Toronto: Butterworth/Institute for Research on Public Policy, 1978.

Presthus, Robert. *Elite Accommodation in Canadian Politics*. Toronto: Macmillan, 1973.

Pross, A. Paul ed. *Pressure Group Behaviour in Canadian Politics*. Toronto: McGraw-Hill Ryerson, 1975.

Van Loon, R. and M. Whittington. *The Canadian Political System*, 3rd ed. Toronto: McGraw-Hill Ryerson, 1981.

Wildavsky, Aaron. *Speaking Truth to Power: The Art and Craft of Policy Analysis*. Toronto: Little Brown & Co., 1979.

ARTICLES

Etzioni, Amitai. "Mixed Scanning: Third Approach to Decision-Making." *Public Administration Review*, Vol. XXVII, 5 (December 1967), pp. 385-92.

Greenberg, George D., et. al. "Developing Public Policy Theory: Perspectives from Empirical Research." *American Political Science Review*, Vol. LXXI, 4 (December 1977), pp. 1532-43.

Jackson, Robert J. "Crisis Management and Policy-Making: An Exploration of Theory and Research." *The Dynamics of Public Policy*, Rose, Richard, ed. Beverly Hills, Calif.: Sage, 1976, pp. 209-36.

Laframboise, H. L. "Moving a Proposal to a Positive Decision: A Case History of the Invisible Process." *Optimum*, Vol. IV, 3 (1977), pp. 31-42.

Lowi, Theodore. "American Business, Public Policies, Case Studies and Political Theory." *World Politics*, Vol. XVI (July 1964), pp. 677-715.

———. "Four Systems of Policy, Politics and Choice." *Public Administration Review*, Vol. XXX (July-August 1972), pp. 298-310.

MacDonald, F. "The Minister and Mandarins." *Policy Options*, Vol. I, 3 (September-October 1980), pp. 29-31.

Nadel, Mark V. "The Hidden Dimensions of Public Policy: Private Governments and the Policy-Making Process." *Journal of Politics*, Vol. XXXVI, 1 (February 1975), pp. 2-34.

Prince, Michael J., and John A. Chenier. "The rise and fall of policy planning and research units: an organizational perspective." *Canadian Public Administration*, Vol. XXIII, 4 (Winter 1980), pp. 519-41.

Simeon, Richard. "Studying Public Policy." *Canadian Journal of Political Science*, Vol. IX, 4 (December 1976), pp. 548-80.

"Symposium on 'Muddling Through'." *Public Administration Review*, Vol. 39 (November-December 1979).

"Symposium on Policy Analysis in Government." *Public Administration Review*, Vol. 37 (May-June 1977).

Wise, C. R., and G. H. Frederickson. "Symposium on Administering Public Policy." *Policy Studies Journal*, Vol. 5 (Autumn 1976).

ENDNOTES

1. See the discussion by Peter Aucoin, "Public Policy Theory and Analysis," in G. Bruce Doern and Peter Aucoin (eds.), *Public Policy in Canada, Organization Process and Management* (Toronto: Macmillan, 1979), pp. 1-26. Another source employed here is Charles O. Jones, *An Introduction to the Study of Public Policy* (Belmont: Wadsworth, 1970).
2. David Easton, *A Framework for Political Analysis* (Englewood Cliffs, N. J.: Prentice-Hall, 1965).
3. Thomas R. Dye, *Understanding Public Policy*, 3rd ed. (Englewood Cliffs, N. J.: Prentice-Hall, 1978), p. 3.
4. Richard Simeon, "Studying Public Policy," *Canadian Journal of Political Science*, Vol. IX, 4 (December 1976), pp. 548-80.
5. On this concept, see Peter Bachrach and Morton S. Baratz, *Power and Poverty: Theory and Practice* (New York: Oxford University Press, 1970), Chapter 3. For discussion see Geraint Parry and Peter Morriss, "When Is a Decision Not a Decision?" in Ivor Crewe (ed.), *British Political Sociology, Vol. I* (London: Croom Helm, 1974), pp. 317-36.
6. Bachrach and Baratz, p. 43.
7. See Robert Presthus, *Elite Accommodation in Canadian Politics* (Toronto: Macmillan, 1973) where it is argued that the initiative in policy-making is shared to a considerable extent with groups in the private sector. On the concept of the political agenda, see George C. Edwards III and Ira Sharkansky, *The Policy Predicament: Making and Implementing Public Policy* (San Francisco: W. H. Freeman & Co., 1978), pp. 102-8.
8. Two excellent sources on the agenda-setting role of the mass media are Steven H. Chaffee (ed.) *Political Communication: Issues and Strategies for Research* (Beverly Hills: Sage, 1975) and Donald L. Shaw and Maxwell E. McCombs, *The Emergence of American Political Issues: The Agenda Setting Function of the Press* (St. Paul: West Publishing Co., 1977). The quotation is from Bernard C. Cohen, *The Press and Foreign Policy* (Princeton: Princeton University Press, 1963), p. 13.

9. See the interesting article by Robert J. Jackson, "Crisis Management and Policy-Making: An Exploration of Theory and Research," Richard Rose (ed.) *The Dynamics of Public Policy* (Beverly Hills: Sage, 1976), pp. 209-36.
10. Mark V. Nadel, "The Hidden Dimensions of Public Policy: Private Governments and the Policy-Making Process," *Journal of Politics*, Vol. XXXVI, 1 (February 1975), pp. 2-34.
11. For some possible reasons why this is usually the case, see Richard Rose, *Managing Presidential Objectives* (New York: Free Press, 1976), Chapter 1.
12. See Murray Edelman, *The Symbolic Uses of Politics* (Urbana: University of Illinois Press, 1967) and Murray Edelman, *Political Language: Words That Succeed and Policies That Fail* (New York: Academic Press, 1977).
13. Simeon, p. 555.
14. For a good summary and critique of this body of literature see Joyce M. Munns, "The Environment, Politics and Policy Literature," *Western Political Quarterly*, Vol. XXVIII (December 1975), pp. 646-67.
15. For some Canadian examples of this approach, see W. Chandler, "Canadian Socialism and Policy Impact: Contagion from the Left?" *Canadian Journal of Political Science*, Vol. X, 4 (December 1977), pp. 755-80; D. Falcone and M. Whittington, "Output Change in Canada: A Preliminary Attempt to Open the 'Black Box'," a paper presented to the Canadian Political Science Association Annual Meeting, 1972, mimeo; W. Mishler and D. Campbell, "The Healthy State: Legislative Responsiveness to Public Health Care Needs in Canada," *Comparative Politics*, Vol. X (July 1978), pp. 479-97; Conrad Winn and Douglas McCready, "Redistributive Policy," in C. Winn and J. McMenemy *Political Parties in Canada* (Toronto: McGraw-Hill, 1976), pp. 206-27.
16. Simeon, p. 568.
17. A good summary of the elitist model of policy-making is found in Thomas R. Dye, pp. 25-28.
18. See Robert Presthus, Chs. 2 and 11, and John Meisel, *Working Papers in Canadian Politics*, 3rd ed. (Montreal: McGill-Queen's, 1974).
19. See the contributions by Paul Pross, Helen Dawson and Peter Aucoin in A. Paul Pross (ed.), *Pressure Group Behaviour in Canadian Politics* (Toronto: McGraw-Hill, 1975).
20. Simeon, p. 576.
21. G. Bruce Doern, *Political Policy-Making: A Commentary on the Economic Council's Eighth Annual Review and the Ritchie Report* (Toronto: Private Planning Association, 1972), p. 2.
22. James E. Anderson, *Public Policy-Making*, 2nd ed. (New York: Holt, Rinehart and Winston, 1979), pp. 9-10.
23. Charles E. Lindblom, *The Policy-Making Process* (Englewood Cliffs, N.J.: Prentice-Hall, 1968), Ch. 3, and David Braybrooke and Charles E. Lindblom, *A Strategy of Decision: Policy Evaluation as a Social Process* (New York: Free Press, 1970), Part One.
24. See Lindblom, *The Policy-Making Process*, Ch. 4.
25. *Ibid.*, p. 27.
26. Amitai Etzioni, *The Active Society* (New York: Free Press, 1968), Chs. 11 and 12, and Amitai Etzioni, "Mixed Scanning: Third Approach to Decision-Making," *Public Administration Review*, Vol. XXVII, 5 (December 1967), pp. 385-92.
27. For one attempt to operationalize something like Etzioni's mixed-scanning approach see, C. Wiseman, "Selection of Major Planning Issues," *Policy Sciences* Vol. IX, 1 (February 1978), pp. 71-86.
28. See Yehezkel Dror, *Public Policy-Making Reexamined* (San Francisco: Chandler, 1968).
29. Lowi has written three articles developing this theme. See Theodore Lowi, "American Business, Public Policies, Case Studies and Political Theory," *World Politics*, Vol. XVI (July 1964), pp. 677-715; "Decision-Making vs. Policy-Making: Toward an Antidote for Technocracy," *Public Administration Review*, Vol. XXVIII (May-June 1970), pp. 314-25; and "Four Systems of Policy, Politics and Choice," *Public Administration Review*, Vol. XXX (July-August 1972), pp. 298-310. An interesting application and modification of Lowi's scheme in a Canadian setting is presented by John Shiry, "Distributive and Regulative Policy in Ontario: A Test of Lowi's Arenas of Power Scheme" (a paper presented to the Canadian Political Science Association Annual Meeting, 1976).
30. A good review of efforts to apply Lowi's typology is found in George D. Greenberg, Jeffery A.

Miller, Lawrence B. Mohr and Bruce C. Vladeck, "Developing Public Policy Theory: Perspectives from Empirical Research," *American Political Science Review*, Vol. LXXI, 4 (December 1977), pp. 1532-43.

31. *Ibid.*, p. 1535.

32. John Clayton Thomas, "Governmental Overload in the United States: A Problem of Distributive Policies?" *Administration and Society*, Vol. 11, 4 (February 1980), pp. 371-91. Canadian examples of the use of the distributive category are Robert Best, "Youth Policy," in G. Bruce Doern and V. S. Wilson, *Issues in Canadian Public Policy* (Toronto: Macmillan, 1974), Ch. 6, and Donald E. Blake, "LIP and Partisanship," *Canadian Public Policy*, Vol. II, 1 (Winter 1976), pp. 17-32.

33. Peter Aucoin, "Theory and Research in the Study of Policy-making," in G. Bruce Doern and Peter Aucoin (eds.), *The Structures of Policy-Making in Canada* (Toronto: Macmillan, 1971), pp. 10-38.

34. This is the thesis presented in R. Van Loon and M. Whittington, *The Canadian Political System* (Toronto: McGraw-Hill, 1976) — perhaps the most widely used textbook in Canadian political science courses.

35. See Hugh Thorburn (ed.), *Party Politics in Canada*, 4th ed. (Scarborough: Prentice-Hall, 1979) for a series of articles which develop this point.

36. See John Porter, *The Vertical Mosaic* (Toronto: University of Toronto Press, 1964), Ch. XIII, especially pp. 407-12.

37. See G. Bruce Doern, "The Policy-Making Philosophy of Prime Minister Trudeau and His Advisers," in T. Hockin (ed.), *Apex of Power: The Prime Minister and Political Leadership in Canada*, 2nd ed. (Scarborough: Prentice-Hall, 1976), pp. 189-96.

38. John W. Langford, *Transport in Transition: The Reorganization of the Federal Transport Portfolio* (Montreal: McGill-Queen's, 1976), Ch. 1.

39. Useful sources on the Cabinet committee system include: T. Hockin *Apex of Power*; W.A. Matheson, *The Prime Minister and the Cabinet* (Toronto: Metheun, 1976), pp. 83-91; George Radwanski, *Trudeau* (Toronto: Macmillan, 1978), pp. 145-78; and Mitchell Sharp, "Decision-Making in the Federal Cabinet," *Canadian Public Administration*, Vol. XIX, 1 (Spring 1976), pp. 1-7.

40. Robert J. Jackson and Michael M. Atkinson, *The Canadian Legislative System*, 2nd ed. (Toronto: Macmillan, 1980), p. 62.

41. An excellent discussion of Cabinet decision-making and the role of support agencies is: Richard D. French, "The Privy Council Office: Support for Cabinet Decision-Making," in Richard Schultz, Orest M. Kruhlak and John C. Terry, *The Canadian Political Process*, 3rd ed. (Toronto: Holt, Rinehart & Winston, 1979), pp. 363-94.

41. Jackson and Atkinson, p. 63.

43. Ibid., pp. 71-80.

44. There is a dispute among comentators about what constitutes a central agency and who qualifies therefore as a "central agent."

45. Colin Campbell and George Szablowski, *The Super-bureaucrats* (Toronto: Macmillan, 1979), p. 76.

46. Ibid., p. 33.

47. J.R. Mallory, "The Two Clerks: Parliamentary Discussion of the Role of the Pricy Council Office," *Canadian Journal of Political Science*, Vol. X, 1 (March 1977), pp. 3-19.

48. Gordon Robertson, "The Changing Role of the Privy Council Office," *Canadian Public Administration*, Vol. XIV, 4 (Winter 1971), pp. 487-508, quotation at p. 507.

49. *Ibid*., p. 507.

50. Campbell and Szablowski, p. 60.

51. Jackson and Atkinson, pp. 67-69.

52. Richard Schultz, "Prime Ministerial Government, Central Agencies and Operating Departments: Towards a More Realistic Analysis," in T. Hockin, *op. cit.*, pp. 229-36.

53. The following discussion relies greatly upon G. Bruce Doern, "Horizontal and Vertical Portfolios in Government," in G. Bruce Doern and U.S. Wilson (eds.), *Issues in Canadian Public Policy*, pp. 310-336.

54. Ibid., p. 316.

55. See Canada, House of Commons, *Debates*, June 21, 1971, pp. 7165-7174.

56. See Donald Higgins, *Urban Canada: Its Government and Politics* (Toronto: Macmillan, 1977), pp. 76-86; David Cameron, "Urban Policy," in Doern and Wilson, *Issues in Canadian Public Policy*, pp. 228-252 and N.H. Lithwick, "Political Innovation: A Case Study," *Plan Canada*, Vol. XII, 1 (1972) pp. 45-56.

57. David Cameron, *op. cit.*, p. 245.

58. The following account is based largely on Peter Aucoin and Richard French, *Knowledge, Power and Public Policy* (Ottawa: Science Council of Canada, 1974).

59. *ibid.*, p. 34.

60. Canada, Senate, Special Committee on Science Policy, *Report*, Vol. 4, "Progress and Unfinished Business," August 4, 1977, p. 27. For MOSST's own interpretation of its history see a Brief to the Senate Special Committee on Science Policy," *Minutes of Proceedings*, December 3, 1975, pp. 43-98.

61. The Ministry of State for Economic Development was created by Order-in-Council in December, 1978, and the Ministry of State for Social Policy was established by the same method in June, 1980. For a preliminary assessment of MSED see G.B. Doern and R.W. Phidd, "Economic Management in the Government of Canada: Some implications of the Board of Economic Development Ministers and the Lambert Report" (a paper presented to the Annual Meeting of the Canadian Political Science Association, Saskatoon, May 30, 1980).

62. Aucoin and French, pp. 78-79.

63. Order-in-Council creating the Ministry of State for Economic Development, December, 1978.

64. John W. Langford, *Transport in Transition*, *op. cit.*

65. Anthony G.S. Careless, *Initiative and Response: The Adaptation of Canadian Federalism to Regional Economic Development* (Montreal: McGill-Queen's, 1977).

66. Bernard Ostry, *The Cultural Connection: An Essay on Culture and Government Policy in Canada* (Toronto: McClelland & Stewart, 1978).

67. See R. Brian Woodrow, "Resources and Environmental Policy-Making at the National Level: The Search for Focus," in O.P. Dwivedi (ed.), *Resources and the Environment: Policy Perspectives in Canada* (Toronto: McClelland & Stewart, 1980), pp. 23-48.

68. See Blair Williams, "The Para-Political Bureaucracy in Ottawa" (paper presented to the CPSA Annual Meeting, 1978); A.W. Johnson, "Creativity and Bureaucracy," *Canadian Public Administration*, Vol. XXI, 1 (Spring, 1978), pp. 1-15.

69. Richard D. French, *How Ottawa Decides: Planning and Industrial Policy-Making 1968-1980* (Toronto: James Lorimer, 1980).

70. Jackson and Atkinson, p. 67.

71. See Aaron Wildavsky, *Speaking Truth to Power: The Art and Craft of Policy Analysis* (Toronto: Little Brown & Co., 1979) where this theme is developed throughout an excellent collection of articles.

72. See "Between Planning and Politics: Intellect vs. Interaction as Analysis," *Ibid.*, p. 128.

73. See Peter H. Schuck, "National Economic Planning: A Slogan Without Substance," *The Public Interest*, No. 45, (Fall 1976), pp. 63-78.

74. See Y. Manor and G. Sheffer, "Can Planning Be Salvaged?" *Public Administration*, Vol. LV (Summer 1977), pp. 221-25 for a more optimistic assessment of the prospects for planning.

75. Quoted in K.J. MacDonald, "Cabinet and Administrative Secrecy in a Participatory Democracy," in Jean-Pierre Gaboury and James Ross Hurley (eds.), *The Canadian House of Commons Observed* (Ottawa: University of Ottawa Press, 1977), pp. 201-202.

76. *Ibid.*, p. 202.

77. Donald V. Smiley, "The Dominance of Withinputs?: Canadian Politics," *Western Political Quarterly*, 1975, p. 280.

78. K.J. MacDonald, *op. cit.*, p. 204.

79. See W.A. Matheson, *The Prime Minister and the Cabinet*, *op. cit.*, pp. 65-68, and Edwin R. Black, "Turning Canadian Politics Inside Out," *The Political Quarterly*, Vol. LI, 2 (April-June 1980), pp. 141-53.

80. See Canada, House of Commons, Standing Committee on Miscellaneous Estimates, *Minutes of Proceedings and Evidence*, November 15, 1979.

81. Audrey Doerr has calculated that there were 5.3 ministers per portfolio during the period 1968-1979 — or roughly a change of ministers per portfolio every two years. See Audrey D. Doerr, *The Machinery of Government in Canada* (Toronto: Methuen, 1981), pp. 18-19.

82. *Ibid*., p. 79.

83. See Hon. F. MacDonald, "The Minister and Mandarins," *Policy Options*, Vol. I, 3 (September-October 1980), pp. 29-31 for a discussion of the alleged "entrapment devices" used by the Department of External Affairs during 1979 when Miss MacDonald was briefly minister before the fall of the Clark government.

84. Michael J. Prince and John A. Chenier, "The Rise and Fall of Policy Planning and Research Units: an Organizational Perspective," *Canadian Public Administration*, Vol. XXIII, 4 (Winter 1980), pp. 519-541.

95. *Ibid*., p. 529.

86. *Ibid*., p. 540.

87. *Ibid*., p. 534.

88. See E. Bardach, *The Implementation Game* (Cambridge, Mass.: MIT Press, 1977), J.L. Pressman and A. Wildavsky, *Implementation* (Berkley: University of California Press, 1973) and the "Symposium on Successful Policy Implementation," *Policy Studies*, Vol. VIII, 4 (Special Issue 1980).

89. See Robert Presthus, *Elite Accomodation in Canadian Politics* (Toronto: Macmillan, 1973); A. Paul Pross (ed.), *Pressure Group Behaviour in Canadian Politics* (Toronto: McGraw-Hill Ryerson, 1975); and the article by W.T. Stanbury, "Lobbying and Interest Group Representation in the Legislative Process," in W.A.W. Neilson and J.C. MacPherson (eds.), *The Legislative Process in Canada: The Need for Reform* (Toronto: Butterworth Institute for Research on Public Policy, 1978), pp. 167-207, which is followed by commentaries and a bibliography of additional sources.

90. Robert Presthus, pp. 150-154. It should be noted that this study has been the object of some strong theoretical and methodological criticisms, but these do not appear to be sufficiently devastating to undermine the validity of Presthus' main findings.

91. *Ibid*., pp. 348-52.

92. Peter Aucoin, "Pressure Groups and Recent Changes in the Policy-Making Process," in A. Paul Pross (ed.), *op. cit.*, pp. 174-89.

93. Robert Presthus, pp. 71-72.

94. A. Paul Pross, "Pressure Groups: Adaptive Instruments of Political Communication," in A. Paul Pross (ed.) *op. cit.*, pp. 1-26.

95. Paul G. Thomas, "The Influence of Standing Committees of Parliament on Government Legislation," *Legislative Studies Quarterly*, Vol. III (November, 1978), pp. 683-704.

96. Colin Campbell, *The Canadian Senate: A Lobby from Within* (Toronto: Macmillan, 1978).

97. See H.L. Laframboise, "Moving a Proposal to a Positive Decision: A Case History of the Invisible Process," *Optimum*, Vol. IV, 3 (1973), pp. 31-42.

CHAPTER FIVE

The Theory and Practice of Public Budgeting

Introduction

Budgeting is the most important annual ritual of government – "the World Series of Government," or perhaps "the Grey Cup of Government" within the Canadian context. Like those events in the sporting life of each nation, the coming of the budget is a sign of the passing seasons in bureaucratic life. Much of the rhythm of government derives from the budget process. Before the big event, much time is spent preparing for budgetary decisions and afterward there are the inevitable reactions, adjustments and post-mortems. Public budgeting involves both the raising and the spending of tax dollars, although it is the latter which will mainly concern us here.[1]

Politicians and public servants know the importance of the budget to themselves and to their programs. Budgets are the life blood of departments, supplying the transfusions of cash necessary for programs to operate, salaries to be paid, and public agencies to survive. Those cabinet ministers and public servants who do not recognize the crucial importance of the budget are destined to have short or low-profile careers.

While politicians and bureaucrats appreciate the significance of budgets, the general public tends to look upon them as a dry and dusty domain ruled over by accountants and economists. Prodigious and unintelligible documents, written in arcane "bureaucratese," appear to be designed more to obscure the probability that spending and taxes will rise rather than to shed light and understanding on government performance. In the face of such complexity, stoic acceptance seems for many citizens to be the only sensible posture to adopt. The budgetary process is, indeed, complicated and is constantly evolving as governments attempt to adapt institutional structures and expenditure management approaches to changing economic and political circumstances. Therefore, even those individuals whose interests lead them to serious, constant study of public budgeting can find themselves ignorant of obscure but nonetheless significant changes.

The budget is crucial because it states in dollar terms what value the society places on various public sector activities. It states who is to get what in any given year as a result of a complex series of government decisions, and it is therefore a tangible expression of the wider political process within government and the society. In other words, the public budget is the nuts and bolts of all public policy, and seeing it as a neutral, technical exercise is a fundamental distortion of reality. As the ultimate expression of politics, the public budget means far more to the actual welfare of citizens than does any of the beautiful rhetoric, replete with promises, which abounds in politics. The dry and dusty public budget puts values on words and converts ideas into action — an elementary fact of life which bureaucrats and politicians recognize but which often seems to escape public cognizance.

This chapter briefly examines the growth of government activity in Canada, as well as commonly advanced reasons for the growth. Even in what, on the surface, would appear to be a reasonably non-contentious area of discussion, there is profound disagreement. This disagreement over something so basic obviously contributes to controversy over such things as procedures either utilized or recommended in public budgeting. The chapter then analyzes the evolution of the budgetary process as it has been adapted to meet the pressures of more active government. This leads to the main interest of the chapter, which is a description and assessment of the objectives and procedures of the current expenditure budget process in the government of Canada. Dissatisfaction with budgetary procedures is a hardy perennial of administrative life and there are always reform proposals challenging existing practices. In the past two decades, the Planning-Programming-Budgeting System (PPBS) and Zero-Based Budgeting (ZBB) have come to the fore as the principal challengers to traditional, annual, incremental budgeting. Both PPBS and ZBB represent an effort to implement a rationalistic approach to budgeting. However, despite having some influence upon governments, these newer approaches have never in any jurisdiction really displaced the traditional approach. In seeking to explain the persistence of incremental budgeting, we return to the rationalist-incrementalist controversy discussed in the previous chapter.

The debate over how budgets are made, interesting though it may be, should not obscure the crucial fact that budgets involve resources and power in society and that any "reforms" which threaten the political equilibrium will be difficult to achieve. Put differently, if the public budget indeed states in dollar terms who is to get what in any given year or number of years, then any budgeting philosophy and/or actual procedures must be congruent with the basics of the political system; or, on the other hand, the budgeting philosophy/procedures or the political system must somehow be altered.

How Big Has Government Grown?

Governments in Canada today seem to be involved in every activity conceivable, from the operation of an airline and a broadcasting network, to the provision of social services and income support, to the delivery of mail (sometimes without great haste, it seems to many), down to the regulation of the content of potato chips and the labels placed on dog food tins. The total impact of governments on the lives of Canadians cannot perhaps be measured, but their influence has definitely grown and is now pervasive. Nostalgia for a by-gone era when life was less complicated and governments were not omnipresent will not by itself reinstate the good old days. There is at present an apparent strong anti-government and anti-bureaucratic mood among the general public. But while more individuals and organizations call for less government intervention and spending, what they often seem to mean is that governments should spend less on the guy next door. That is, while the costs of government are usually fairly clear, its benefits are less evident, often intangible or not clearly divisible among individual voters. It is, therefore, probably inevitable that exaggeration and distortion will be used on all sides of the controversy over the appropriate size and direction of government spending.

Governments at all levels in Canada in 1977-78 controlled approximately 40 per cent of the Gross National Product (GNP), an increase from 31 per cent just a decade ago, and an increase higher than in any other major western country.[2] The really explosive growth occurred from 1965 to 1975, when government spending reached the 41 per cent mark; since then the proportion has actually declined slightly. Provincial government spending rose more quickly than spending at the federal level.[3] To many observers such facts provide incontestable proof of the need for a taxpayers' revolt. Unfortunately for clarity, in this case the "facts" do not speak for themselves or at least they do not tell the whole story. Definitions of what constitutes the government sector and public spending have become blurred because of the great interpenetration of the "public" and the "private" sectors and the growth in numbers and size of organizations (like hospitals and universities) occupying a middle ground. While serving as a popular and handy yardstick, the government-spending/GNP ratio is not by itself very meaningful. It has to be interpreted. This statement is made in full awareness that it is just such "interpretation" which leads to arguments involving all sorts of "ifs," "buts" and "maybes."

First, to put the discussion in perspective, government spending as a percentage of GNP is higher in most Western European countries than in Canada, although it is lower in the United States. In relative terms then, Canadians may not be overburdened by big government, although this is an argument which is probably of small comfort to many. Moreover, Canadian governments at all levels have committed themselves since February 1978 to reducing the so-called "government take" from the economy. This popular phrase is also misleading because it does not distinguish the different component parts of government spending. Only a portion of government spending removes or uses up resources that would otherwise remain in the private sector. Direct government provision of goods and services would be an example of such "exhaustive spending." However, most of the increased spending in the decade from 1965 to 1975 occurred in the form of transfer payments to individuals, through higher unemployment insurance, family allowance and old age security payments.[4] Such transfer payments shift wealth among individuals within the society (though not so far, it seems, as to make the poor relatively much better off)[5] but they do not drain off funds from the private sector. Individuals, not governments, continue to decide how the money will be spent. A final qualification is that inflation hits governments as well as individuals. When government spending is adjusted to take account of the impact of inflation on the price of goods and services purchased by governments, the spending increases are far less impressive. Following a detailed analysis, Richard M. Bird concludes that "since 1970 the proportion of the economy's real goods and services 'used up' by the government sector in the course of its activity has actually *declined* slightly."[6] In short, the popular image of more interventionist governments steadily displacing private sector activity seems to be at least somewhat exaggerated.

However, analyses of direct public expenditures, such as those by Bird, do not capture the full impact of governments on the economy. For one thing, they usually exclude the revenues and expenditures of federal, provincial and even municipal public enterprises. No complete inventory of the number and size of such enterprises exists. Indeed, the federal government has trouble keeping track even of its own companies, primarily because crown corporations have been able to set up subsidiaries without approval from the Cabinet or Parliament. At last count, Canadians were the proud owners or part owners through their federal government alone of approximately 400 enterprises.[7] Apart from its possible impact on the economy, the expansion of the public enterprise sector compounds the problems of accountability in government, as will be discussed in Chapter 8.

In addition to spending directly on services or income support, governments also spend indirectly through what are called *tax expenditures*, that is, special tax exemptions or reductions to encourage socially desirable activity. Tax expenditures are an alternative policy instrument to direct budget outlays. They have grown in political popularity within governments, probably because they are a less visible means of pursuing policy objectives in a climate of financial restraint. They are now used by all governments to encourage investment, saving, regional development, housing, resource exploration and charitable giving. At the federal level alone, a recent estimate (December 1979) by the Department of Finance put the revenue loss at $32 billion for 1979 from some 190 exceptions, deductions and special tax incentives.[8] Elimination of just some of these tax concessions would have allowed the federal government to wipe out easily its projected $12 billion deficit for 1979-80. However, other means of reaching the policy goals served by tax expenditures would presumably then have to be found. In certain circumstances, tax expenditures are the simplest, most efficient way of pursuing objectives, but they also have the disadvantage of being more open-ended, permanent and less subject to regular review than direct expenditures. Other analysts find fault with them because they favor more affluent members of the society, offsetting whatever progressivity is present in the existing personal income tax system.[9] In this regard, indexing of personal income exemptions and rates in 1973 by the federal government was intended to counter the effects of general inflation which pushed individuals into higher tax brackets and thereby produced an automatic and easy revenue increase for governments. Probably no other recent fiscal policy decision did more to impose discipline on the spending habits of governments than the indexing of personal income tax.[10]

A third form of government intervention not at all fully reported by expenditure data is regulatory activity. The popular wisdom today appears to be that government regulation of economic and social activity has grown rapidly and has become excessively cumbersome and costly. At the same time, there are calls for still more government regulation. One can only conclude that there are good and bad regulations and what is good seems to be in the eye of the beholder. The topics of regulation and the accountability of regulatory agencies are discussed at some length in Chapter 8. At this point it is sufficient to indicate the extent of the growth of regulation by citing some of the findings of a recent report (November 1979) by the Economic Council of Canada:

- approximately 29 per cent of the Canadian Gross Domestic Product is subject to regulatory control compared to 26 per cent in the U.S.A.;
- between 1949 and 1978 the number of regulations passed under federal statutes increased by over 200 per cent;
- the average number of regulations per federal statute increased by almost 50 per cent between 1949 and 1978;
- in Ontario, just one province, there was an even faster increase in the number of regulatory statutes and pages of regulations than at the federal level;
- overlap, inconsistency and duplication of regulation by federal and provincial governments has meant confusion for citizens and corporations, problems of accountability, and increasing barriers to national economic integration.[11]

Much more work is needed to assess the direct and indirect costs and benefits of regulation, but the available evidence suggests that regulation has become one of the main areas of government growth in recent years. Governments pressured by the conflicting public demands for new government action but less spending and taxation may find regulation to be the least politically painful policy response since its costs are relatively hidden.

Further evidence of the growth of government is provided by the figures on public service employment. Creation of new departments to handle new initiatives in public policy, significant growth in existing departments and the proliferation of quasi-independent agencies in the form of crown corporations, regulatory boards and commissions have accompanied the extension of government activity. Increasingly large and professional public services at the federal and the provincial levels of government are the result; bureaucratic growth at the municipal level has so far been less dramatic. The greatest expansion of public sector employment took place early in the post-war period. Between 1946 and 1970 the number of federal government employees more than doubled from 116,657 to 259,495. By 1979-80, regular departments of the federal government employed approximately 300,000 personnel, but there had been virtually no increases in this figure over the preceding three years. However, there are approximately 200,000 additional individuals working within government-owned crown corporations.[12] Provincial civil services have grown at a high, steady rate in the last two decades and in 1975 three-quarters of the public employees in Canada worked for provincial and local governments.

Despite popular impressions to the contrary, Canada's rate of bureaucratic growth has not been abnormally high, being roughly comparable to the rate in the United States and other industrial countries. The impression in the public mind of uncontrolled bureaucratic expansion seems to persist despite the fact that the federal public service has experienced little or no growth in the last few years and several provincial jurisdictions have introduced hiring freezes. The Conservative Party apparently evoked a favorable public response (although not a favorable public service response) in the 1979 federal election campaign by its promise to cut the federal public service by 60,000 positions over the next three years.

On the other hand, to say that the growth of public bureaucracy in Canada is normal relative to that experienced by other countries may simply reflect the fact that *all* countries are overrun by bureaucracies. That is, from a certain perspective it can be quite reasonably argued that the constant increase in the scope of government activities and the attendant growth in public bureaucracies are signs of the ultimate demise of much of what is considered democratic and held dear by many Canadians. Furthermore, as was suggested in Chapter 3, while political parties may win elections with promises of restraint and retrenchment in government, their long-run ability and/or willingness to keep those promises remains in doubt. Perhaps a case in point is supplied by the Conservative government in Manitoba, whose electorally successful promise of "less government" in 1977 presaged others of like nature. While the Conservative government did considerable pruning of various departments, by late 1980 indications were that the bureaucracy would soon reach its pre-restraint numbers — and with an election in the offing the Government was placing less emphasis on restraint. Another example of the practical ability of governments to hold the spending line is perhaps supplied by the defeat in December 1979 of the Conservative government in Ottawa over its budget proposals.

In any event, at least as important as the quantitative growth in the public service is the qualitative change in its nature during the post-war period. The percentage of highly educated personnel falling into the administrative, scientific and professional categories has increased rapidly in recent years, particularly at the federal level.[13] This increasing specialization and professionalization of the public service, it is argued, was made necessary by the far greater complexity of the problems dealt with by governments. Most government employees are still clerks and administrators, but the stereotypical image of the bureaucrat as an individual with an eye shade, quill pen and rubber stamp performing routine tasks is clearly out of date.

A final popular charge is that public sector wages are out of control, causing government spending to rise and promoting inflation throughout the economy. The introduction of collective bargaining for public servants at the federal level in the mid-1960s and in most provincial jurisdictions supposedly led to a number of high profile wage settlements that touched off a round of wage inflation in the private sector. While this is not the place to go into the details of this debate, it should be noted that the best available evidence does not support the notion that public sector wages are out of control.[14] In the decade 1965 to 1975, with the major exception of the health area, total public sector wages increased on average slower than those in the private sector. And there is little evidence that high settlements in the public sector ignited a round of wage inflation throughout the economy. Governments in general have sought to control wage increases in recent years both through tough bargaining and legislative enactments; the political popularity of a tight-fisted approach to public service unions has not been unnoticed by them.

All the statistics and qualifications will not change the feeling on the part of many Canadians that government spending has increased unduly, that programs are not effective in reaching declared goals, that there is widespread waste and mismanagement in the public sector, and that public servants are underworked and overpaid.[15] At the federal level, recent reports from the Auditor-General, Parliament's financial watchdog, have called attention to the deficiencies in existing financial information and control systems within the government of Canada. His conclusion in 1976 that "Parliament — and indeed the government — has lost or is close to losing effective control of the public purse," received headline coverage and spurred the government to embark on a series of reforms.[16] These will be discussed shortly when the expenditure budget process is analyzed. First we will look at some of the factors contributing to the growth of governments.

Why Has Government Grown?

There is no single, widely accepted explanation for the growth of government in Canada. Rather, there are many explanations, some competing, and others complementary, each containing, no doubt, some element of truth. Douglas Auld offers the following list of factors as contributing to the post-war growth of government activity: the rising level of incomes; the effects of inflation; increased urbanization; ideological changes; technological changes; federal-provincial fiscal relations; and the nature of the political and bureaucratic structure.[17] Many of the determinants of government spending clearly lie outside of the political structure. Economists have tended to dominate debates on this topic and the theories they postulate tend to be very broad. Such theories usually purport to explain the total levels of government spending, not the allocation of spending among different sectors of government. Few of the economists have very much to say about the specific role of the various political institutions through which the budget must pass; it is as if the budgetary process were merely a conveyor belt for converting economic factors into government decisions. Not all economists, of course, take such a mechanistic view of the determinants of government spending, and some join with most political scientists in emphasizing the political behavior involved in the process.

It has been argued, for example, that the post-war expansion in government activity reflected a change in the public's conception of the appropriate role of the state from a restricted, negative one to an active, positive one.[18] The impact of growing industrialization, urbanization, the depression and the wars were contributing factors to this shift in attitudes. Another view is that, in a democracy, governments will grow because the poor are always more numerous than the wealthy and they will use their overwhelming voting power to secure more government benefits in the form of services and income support.[19] Politicians are forced to buy votes with the promise of new government initiatives. However, the available evidence provides little support for the view that majority demands have caused an expansion in governments. As is indicated in Chapter 10, dealing with citizen participation, governments in Canada are not subject to strong citizen pressures, and most lobbying is conducted by well-financed and well-organized elite groups, mainly business and professional organizations. Contrary to the popular view of the business community as wedded to free enterprise principles and always advocating limited government, recent historical studies indicate that often in the past business organizations have promoted government intervention as a stabilizing factor against such economic forces as so-called "destructive competition."[20]

Still another view is that pressures for the extension of the scope of public activity have arisen mainly within the governmental system itself. There are several versions of this basic argument. It has long been recognized that bureaucrats play an important role in policy-making, not least when decisions on public spending are involved. The motives and approaches followed by bureaucrats within the budgetary process have been variously analyzed and interpreted. Several economists recently have developed "self-interest" theories of the budgetary process.[21] There is not the space here to do justice to the range, subtleties and disagreements among such theories. Suffice it to say that, in the eyes of several distinguished commentators, departments and agencies of government naturally seek to maximize the size of their budget and seek to increase the demands of clients for their services. The budget-maximizing motivation leads organizations to expand their functions, perhaps at the expense of rival, adjoining departments and agencies. Institutional imperialism and growth for its own sake becomes, according to this view, the basis for bureaucratic expansionism and this drive then is reflected within the budgetary process. The Lambert Report gave some credibility to this interpretation when it reported that throughout the expansionary period from 1965 to 1975, nearly all the emphasis inside governments was on creating new policies and programs, little was placed on administration and financial management. The result was "a state of mind, permeating the entire system, that seriously eroded the old values of prudence, economy and restraint."[22]

There are, however, disagreements with this self-interest theory of bureaucratic behavior. First, not all government organizations gain influence and prestige by spending freely. So-called central agencies, such as the Treasury Board Secretariat and the Department of Finance, see their roles primarily in terms of expenditure restraint. As we will see shortly, the role and influence of such agencies have supposedly been upgraded in recent years. Moreover, it is not unheard of, though admittedly it does appear to be a rare occurrence, for a bureaucratic organization to resist increases in its functions, staff and budgets.[23]

The presumption of a uniform drive throughout the bureaucracy for larger budgets probably ignores, or at least underestimates, the significance of the wider political context in which budgets are prepared. When the general political perception is one of scarcity of public resources and there is a resulting emphasis on expenditure restraint, as has occurred in Canada in the late 1970s, then presumably public servants must adjust their expectations and behavior accordingly. Given the changed political context of fixed expenditure ceilings (except for a few selected areas of public spending), most government organizations can no longer expect the traditional annual increments in their spending. Skeptics would argue, however, that the long-term political commitment to restraint is missing and that meanwhile bureaucrats will shift to a defensive posture, seeking to minimize the potential damage to their programs. The failure of expenditure restraint exercises to produce major or permanent reductions in the amount of public spending will be taken as evidence of the continued influence of the bureaucracy. With an estimated 40 per cent of Canadian adults directly or indirectly on the public payroll, it is argued that there is a strong built-in resistance to any shrinkage in the public sector.

A more benign interpretation of the behavior of bureaucrats, whether they are on the offensive or the defensive within the budgetary process, emphasizes their professional commitment to the goals of public programs. Professionalism, not selfishness, is seen as the basic motive behind their actions. In this view, the professional experts within departments and agencies will at all times seek to achieve improved standards in public programs, not primarily for reasons of self-promotion and personal satisfaction, but because they see improved standards as in the interest of their clients and of society. Moreover, because they spend a great deal of time analyzing the operation of public programs, it is natural that they should be among the first to identify gaps or shortcomings and should argue for improvements.

A related explanation for the growth of public spending is said to be the asymmetrical character of most budgetary decision-making.[24] Budgets have traditionally been developed from the bottom up; that is, the decisive spending decisions were related to particular programs, not to the overall level of spending. Atomized decision-making by multiple actors throughout the bureaucracy has produced individually "rational" decisions in terms of the goals of program operators; yet the total level of public spending achieved was "irrational," in the sense that it was not set deliberately and may not have been wanted by the majority, both inside and outside of government. Budgeting was thus asymmetrical because "spenders" outnumbered "cutters," and spenders had more definite, positive arguments to present as opposed to a vague and negative commitment to keep spending within reasonable limits. As we will indicate momentarily, governments in Canada have recently undertaken structural reforms intended to offset this perceived inherent bias towards increased spending within the budgetary process.

The above explanations of the growth of government have been held to apply to most western industrial nations. An explanation more specific to Canada relates to the existence of a federal system in this country. It can be argued that federalism produces competition between national and provincial governments for jurisdiction and political credit for new initiatives. In many fields of public policy, pressure groups seeking government action on their problems find it possible to approach either or both levels of government with their demands. Two levels of government means that the number of pressure points for additional spending is multiplied. In the words of Alan Cairns: "Eleven governments pursuing visions instead of one, 200 ministers building empires instead of 25, several hundred departmental hierarchies of civil servants seeking expansion of their activities instead of a tenth as many — all these provide an extensive supplementary impetus to the normal pressures for the expansion of the public service which are present in politics."[25] Numerous joint programs, whose annual costs were largely determined by specialists within federal and provincial departments, have been a major source of recent expenditure growth. And, the accumulated, practical wisdom of treasury officials over the years has been that such shared-cost programs have been more immune to regular financial controls than are other programs. The recent (1977) major revision in federal-provincial fiscal arrangements, which ended open-ended cost-sharing on major health and education programs, put pressures on the provincial governments to keep future expenditures increases down.

In summary, explanations of a phenomenon as complicated and controversial as government spending are themselves very complicated and controversial. Even a brief sampling of the literature suggests definite limits to what can be accomplished by changes to budgetary procedures alone. It is essential to take into account the overall context in which budgeting occurs. That is, budgeting involves important relationships among government, society and the economy, and debates over the mechanics of budgeting too often ignore this wider context.

Budget Determination in the Government of Canada

In governments, budgeting serves at least four functions which are to some extent historically distinct.[26] Early budgeting in Canada emphasized financial *control* in terms of a strict legal accounting for the expenditure of funds. Control aspects of a budget seek to ensure that funds are spent according to legislative authorization and not diverted to other purposes. Strict auditing and reporting requirements ensure probity and accountability by lower-level bureaucrats.

Later, the function of effective *management* was added to the budgetary process. The budget was seen as a management tool to ensure the economical and efficient operation of departments and programs. Economy in departments is achieved when resources or inputs (personnel, buildings, materials) in suitable quantities and of good quality are acquired at the lowest price. Program efficiency refers to a ratio of outputs to units of inputs; for example, so many family allowance cheques processed by a given number of personnel over so many hours. In the early 1970s the Government of Canada began to install performance measurement procedures in departments so that managers could relate results achieved to resources used, and results achieved to results planned. Performance measurement is a long way from being applied throughout the public service and is most successful in relation to repetitive, production or process type of work. Eighteen departments and agencies provided performance measurement data in support of their budgetary requests for 1977-78 fiscal year. Only 25 per cent of the total work done in the government of Canada was then subject to performance measurement and the quality of the data presented even on that portion was most uneven.[27]

Over the years, as governments grew in size and the savings likely to be achieved through administrative efficiencies became miniscule compared to total spending, there was an increasing emphasis placed on the use of the budget to set long-range priorities and to evaluate existing programs. Emphasizing *planning* and *evaluation* in the budgetary process has been the most difficult of the four aims to achieve. In the budgetary context, as Shick has pointed out, "planning involves the determination of objectives, the evaluation of alternative courses of action, and the authorization of select programs."[28] In a climate of financial restraint, great emphasis has been placed on the evaluation and possible termination of programs as the way to reallocate funds or to release funds for new policy initiatives. Rational planning and program evaluation collide, however, with the entrenched incrementalism of the budgetary process, as is discussed below.

The budgetary process in the government of Canada is exceedingly complex. It is also a secretive process, its success depends to some extent on the frankness encouraged by confidentiality. Finally, it is a very changeable process, subject to the impact of such factors as the current political context, the relative power of different ministers, the personalities of the leading political and bureaucratic participants and the authority of different organizations involved. As such, the budgetary process is not a good subject for the development of sound, empirical generalizations. At best, we can only hope here to describe some of the mechanics of the process (which are themselves subject to regular changes) while still conveying the "flavor" of some of the important relationships involved.

There are eight institutions in the executive-bureaucratic arena directly involved with the development of the expenditure budget: the Treasury Board, particularly its President; the Treasury Board Secretary and his staff; the Comptroller-General; the Minister of Finance and his Department; the Government's Cabinet Committee on Priorities and Planning; five functional Cabinet Committees; the Privy Council Office (PCO); and the Prime Minister's Office (PMO). A brief word about each of these institutional actors and their interactions is useful at this point.

The Treasury Board is a six-member committee of Cabinet. In view of its role within the budgetary process one might expect that the leading economic ministers would serve on this committee. In practice, this is not usually the case. With the exception of the President of the Treasury Board, who chairs the committee, and the Minister of Finance, who is an ex-officio member and does not usually attend, the remainder of the membership normally consists of lower-profile, more junior ministers.[29] The Treasury Board is the only Cabinet committee which owes its existence and role to a statute, namely the Financial Administration Act (1951) as amended in 1966. Throughout the ensuing discussion, it is crucial to distinguish between the Treasury Board, as a statutory committee of Cabinet, and the Treasury Board Secretariat, which is the staff arm of the Board and does most of the actual work. The Cabinet Minister appointed as President of the Treasury Board directs and is responsible for the Treasury Board Secretariat, consisting in 1981-82 of 741 public servants who, with one exception, are appointed by the Public Service Commission.[30] The one exception is the Secretary of the Board, who is appointed by Cabinet and who holds one of the most demanding and important jobs in official Ottawa. Each of the occupants of the post tends to leave his own imprint on the operations of the Secretariat.

Traditionally the Treasury Board has performed three principal functions — until recently it acted as the expenditure committee of Cabinet, it still acts as the "general manager" within government to improve efficiency, and it acts for the government in its role as employer. These functions were more distinct in theory than in practice. Because our principal interest here is in the budgetary process itself, we will briefly describe the latter two functions first.

In its role as general manager for the government, the Treasury Board is concerned with administrative efficiency in departments. In practice, actual responsibility is usually delegated to the individual departments, specifically to the deputy ministers, with the Treasury Board performing a guidance and surveillance role to ensure that departments adopt acceptable financial and accounting systems, appropriate personnel policies, and controls over administrative transactions.

The Board's efficiency role has been shared since June 1978 with the Office of the Comptroller General.[31] The latter office was created in response to the criticisms of the Auditor General, reported earlier, that government spending was close to being out of control. The Comptroller General has the rank of a deputy minister and reports to the President of the Treasury Board. Broadly, his role is to ensure the quality of the financial administration systems and related practices used in the public service. He assists and directs departments in three areas: financial administration (accounting principles and practices, the content of financial reports and the development of financial officers); performance measurement (which all departments were supposed to implement by 1980); and program evaluations (in-depth investigations of the success of programs). The nucleus of the Comptroller-General's staff (a total of 178 individuals in 1981-82) was drawn originally from the Financial Administration and Efficiency Evaluation Branches of the Treasury Board Secretariat. While the Board continues to be concerned about where government expenditures are made, the Office of the Comptroller General is concerned with the how of the financial function. The office works with departments to improve performance measurement systems, program evaluation procedures, professional development programs for financial officers, and financial reporting practices.[32]

The third task of the Treasury Board is to act on behalf of the government in its role as employer. Principally, this involves the Board's representing the government in collective bargaining with its unionized employees. The Board, through its Personnel Policy Branch, also deals with non-negotiable fringe benefits (e.g., pensions), staff training, job classification, and personnel planning. Another branch of the Board is involved with implementing official bilingualism in the public service. While the employer role of the Board is of primary interest to personnel administrators, its importance for financial management is also obvious. For example, an increase in the cost of manpower may affect the efficiency of government operations and will definitely increase the costs.

While the above responsibilities are clearly important to the budgetary process, it is in its role as the expenditure committee of Cabinet that the Treasury Board is best known and has had its greatest impact. This function involves the allocation of funds among competing departments and programs.

CABINET COMMITTEES AND THEIR RESOURCE ENVELOPES

PRIORITIES AND PLANNING

FISCAL TRANSFERS

PUBLIC DEBT

ECONOMIC DEVELOPMENT

ENERGY

- Energy Programs
- Petroleum Compensation Program
- Agencies

ECONOMIC DEVELOPMENT

- Energy, Mines & Resources
- Industry & Technology
- Agriculture, Fisheries & Forestry
- Regional Economic Expansion
- Transportation
- Communications
- Labour; Consumer & Corporate Affairs

SOCIAL DEVELOPMENT

SOCIAL AFFAIRS

- Employment & Immigration
- National Health & Welfare
- Indian Affairs & Northern Development
- Canada Mortgage & Housing
- Veterans Affairs
- Secretary of State
- Environment

JUSTICE AND LEGAL

- Justice
- Solicitor General

FOREIGN POLICY AND DEFENCE

EXTERNAL AFFAIRS

- External Affairs
- Foreign Aid

DEFENCE

- National Defence

GOVERNMENT OPERATIONS

PARLIAMENT

- Senate
- House of Commons
- Parliamentary Library

SERVICES TO GOVERNMENT

- Executive
- National Revenue
- Post Office
- Public Works
- Supply & Services
- Statistics Canada

In the words of a former Secretary to the Treasury Board, it is the nuts and bolts of the budgetary process.[33] Under recent changes to the expenditure process, there has been some reduction in the scope of the Board's participation in this function as there has been an attempt to decentralize decision-making to Cabinet committees and to increase ministerial direction and control over expenditure decisions.

Following criticisms by the Auditor-General and the Royal Commission on Financial Management and Accountability about the lack of expenditure control, the newly-elected Conservative government announced in August 1979 the creation of a new expenditure management system.[34] With some slight modifications, the new system was retained by the Trudeau government when it returned to power after the general election of February 1980. The new system was intended to solve the basic problem of the old budgetary process which had an apparent entrenched bias in favor of increased spending.

Before the 1979 changes, the Treasury Board faced the difficulty of being the only Cabinet committee interested exclusively in controlling expenditures. The other functional committees of Cabinet were principally interested in launching new initiatives and were not forced to identify potential areas for reductions in spending to finance such initiatives. Under the old system, the Treasury Board's task was to take the broad expenditure priorities of the government, as originally set by the Cabinet Committee on Priorities and Planning but also approved by full Cabinet, and translate these into amounts to be spent on specific departments and policies. In other words, the Treasury Board decided where money would be spent, subject of course to final Cabinet approval.

In practice, most of the actual negotiations with departments over their budgetary requests for the ensuing fiscal year were conducted by the staff of the Treasury Board Secretariat. Disgruntled departments which felt that the proposed cuts in their "asking budgets" were too brutal could urge their ministers to appeal the Secretariat's recommendations to the Treasury Board itself, and this was done regularly.

Another problem with the old system was the opportunity it allowed for "end runs" around the Treasury Board. Regular departments recognized during the earlier Trudeau governments (1968–1974) that their spending plans would receive an easier passage if approved first by the Privy Council Office, the appropriate subject-matter committee of Cabinet, and then by full Cabinet, before submission to the Treasury Board for commentary. Changes became almost impossible at that late stage in the process. Moreover, policy development decision-making was separated under this old system from resource allocation decision-making. After 1976, departmental memoranda to Cabinet proposing new programs had to be reviewed first by the Treasury Board before appearing on the Cabinet agenda, but policy and expenditure planning still took place in two separate Cabinet committees.[35]

The new expenditure management system initiated in 1979 sought to ensure that groups of ministers who wanted to spend were also required to save.[36] It also sought to ensure that policy was decided and that expenditure limits were set at the same time and within the same Cabinet committee. A new Cabinet committee structure provided the framework for the system. When Mr. Clark was Prime Minister, an Inner Cabinet, which he chaired, established the overall expenditure limits and allocated resources among policy sectors in accordance with the broad priorities of government. Upon his return to power, Prime Minister Trudeau opted not to retain a formal inner Cabinet and the allocation of funds among policy sectors was done by the Cabinet Committee on Priorities and Planning. Ten policy sectors have been identified and these sectors are each given a "Resource Envelope" of dollars to spend. The 10 resource envelopes are managed by five Cabinet Committees, as is displayed in Figure 1. The chairmen of the policy committees serve, along with the Minister of Finance, the President of the Treasury Board, and several other ministers on the Cabinet Committee on Priorities and Planning, which is chaired by the Prime Minister.

On the basis of this structure and allowing for such 'abnormal' events as two changes of government in one fiscal year, which occurred during 1979-80, the annual expenditure process normally works as follows.[37] First, in September of each year, the Priorities and Planning Committee begins to establish the general expenditure priorities for the upcoming fiscal year and the ensuing four years. It will have before it a multi-year Fiscal Plan prepared by the Department of Finance which presents forecasts of total revenues, expenditures, fiscal deficits or surpluses, and borrowing requirements that might arise. The plan also outlines the Department's views on the necessity and magnitude of adjustments required to anticipated revenues and expenditures. After consultation with the President of the Treasury Board, and taking into account the policy sector plans developed in the five Cabinet Committees, the Minister of Finance recommends the amounts to be placed within the 10 resource envelopes over the next four years. While expenditure limits are identified for functional envelopes, firm, three-year budgetary ceilings for specific departments and agencies (as recommended by the Lambert Commission) are not published because such an approach would, in the Trudeau government's view, impose an excessive rigidity on expenditure decision-making.[38] In reviewing the Department of Finance's proposed Fiscal Plan, the Priorities and Planning Committee will also have from the President of the Treasury Board an update on the cost of existing programs. After approval, first by the Committee and then by full Cabinet, the multi-year Fiscal Plan will be tabled in Parliament as part of the Minister of Finance's budget presentation, which usually takes place in October.[39]

The resource envelopes set by Cabinet, on the advice of Priorities and Planning, are then transferred to the Cabinet Committees. There may also be issued specific advice to the Committee regarding which policies and programs should be emphasized over the four-year expenditure plan. The envelope which each Cabinet committee receives contains small reserves for cost overruns, but generally it is expected that new programs or expansions of existing programs will be financed only through program savings or the elimination of programs. Restricting ministers to what is available within their envelopes places pressure on the Cabinet committees to review programs within their policy sectors and to reallocate funds to more effective programs. Policy committees may, in turn, issue planning guidelines to departments.

The departmental response to the work of the policy committees is a document labelled a "Strategic Overview." Each department produces such an overview annually. While the form and content of such documents may vary somewhat among departments, generally they are expected to contain a review of departmental objectives, some discussion of different strategies for reaching those objectives, the costs of such options, and a summary of recent program evaluation findings. The Strategic Overview covers the four-year planning period and is submitted to the appropriate Cabinet committee on March 31st. A review by the policy committee will lead to the approval or modification of the department's medium-range strategy.

In addition to the Strategic Overview, departments must also produce a Multi-Year Operational Plan. Originally submitted in March each year, these documents are updated and resubmitted in October. While the Operational Plan has several elements in common with the Strategic Overview, it differs in that it is restricted to approved programs and therefore does not recommend new initiatives. The Multi-Year Operational Plan is also an evaluation instrument since it sets out the benefits and results (quantified, where possible) of programs and departmental plans for evaluating them. Detailed analysis of the Plan is carried out by the Treasury Board Secretariat in order to assist ministers in identifying the most efficient and effective means of reaching their policy objectives. When resubmitting their plans to the Cabinet committees in October, the departments include a "Budget-Year Operational Plan" which sets out in more detail the goals and the resource requirements for the upcoming fiscal year which begins five months later.

It would be easy for the newcomer to the budgetary process to be dazzled (and confused) by the array of documents used — the Multi-Year Fiscal Plan, the Strategic Overview, the Multi-Year Operational Plan and Budget-Year Plan. Because the new system has been in operation only since 1979, it is premature to offer any definitive judgments on its strengths and weaknesses; we can only indicate some of the apparent implications of the changes.[40] First, involving all ministers, instead of just the President of the Treasury Board and the Minister of Finance, in the search for efficiency and effectiveness in government spending, may result in greater expenditure control. Evaluation of continuing departmental programs began a few years ago on a selective basis through designation by the Treasury Board, but now such reviews are to be integrated into a more regular on-going process controlled by Cabinet. The extra discipline on spending induced by these changes may cause more conflict among ministers over available resources, but there appears to be a greater prospect that expenditure decision-making will become more top-down and collective in nature than it was in the past.

A second apparent consequence of the changes is to strengthen the role of the Minister of Finance and his department and to reduce somewhat the role of the Treasury Board. The Finance Department always wielded considerable influence in expenditure planning because it determined, virtually unilaterally, the total expenditures and influenced greatly additional discretionary spending.[41] The new system permits the Minister of Finance to advise on both the four-year Fiscal Plan (ie. aggregate expenditures and revenues) and on the composition of the Resource Envelopes. Previously the Treasury Board had been responsible for allocating funds among departments and agencies. Now the five policy committees of Cabinet have become, in effect, 'mini-Treasury Boards' in which the ministers themselves negotiate the amounts to be distributed to particular departments and programs. In the words of the Liberal Government's Guide to the new system, the Policy Committees are responsible for the program decisions "which will determine the allocation of available financial resources," whereas the Treasury Board will "determine the level of resources required to deliver efficiently the policies and programs approved by the Policy Committees."[42] Treasury Board, or more accurately the Treasury Board Secretariat, provides information on resource allocation options and identifies "cross-envelope" financial implications of proposals. Therefore, while there appears to be some loss of function from Treasury Board to Finance, this shift should not be exaggerated.[43] Finance has always had considerable influence within the process and Treasury Board's freedom to maneuvre in the past had been constrained by the expenditure ceiling set by Finance and by the substantial amount of permanent or statutory spending (about which more will be said shortly).

Two agencies also involved in the budgetary process which have not been discussed yet in this Chapter are the Privy Council Office (PCO) and the Prime Minister's Office (PMO). The general nature and role of these offices was described earlier in Chapter 4 dealing with public policy. Most of the activity of these two offices does not relate directly to budgeting; but because the agencies have been involved in the identification of priorities, it is obvious that they have some influence on expenditure decision-making. For example, because of its strategic role as the 'gatekeeper' of the flow of information in and out of Cabinet committees, the PCO is in a position to enhance or retard the spending prospects of departments. It could, for example, refer a department's proposal to the Cabinet committee most likely to be sympathetic to its plans. While the PCO seldom initiates policy proposals, it does offer commentary on the plans of other organizations within government. In the case of the PMO, although it gradually yielded over successive Trudeau administrations the principal role of central policy analysis to the PCO, it still occasionally promotes specific policy proposals and thereby has an impact on expenditure patterns.[44]

Having identified the principal actors within the executive-bureaucratic arena involved with the process, it is necessary to say something about their interrelationships and the dynamics of that process. Unfortunately, reliable and fixed generalizations are difficult to construct for, as Douglas Hartle emphasizes in his superb study of the budgetary process, many considerations are involved.[45] The political skills of individual ministers, their relationships with the Prime Minister, with their other cabinet colleagues, with their own senior officials, and their own reputations as politicians and departmental 'managers', may all have a bearing on the outcomes. In a government recently elected on the coattails of a dashing Prime Minister there will be some initial gravitation of power to the center. Cabinet ministers are never equal in talent, nor are they equally respected by their colleagues. While senior bureaucrats seldom, if ever, deliberately embarrass their ministers, they do lament from time to time their misfortune of being stuck with a dud. Ministers may feel obliged in such circumstances to promote 'hopeless causes' in order to win the respect or even the more active support of their officials. Differences in political and bureaucratic talent, together with different assessments of the strengths of various departments and programs, mean that there are always disagreements over how money could best be spent.

Timing can also be crucial to the success of budgetary proposals. For example, when Marc Lalonde as Minister of Health and Welfare appeared before Cabinet in 1975 with a $2.1 billion plan for income support and income supplementation to the working poor, he was defeated in spite of being a strong minister and a former Principal Secretary to the Prime Minister.[46] His inability to sell the plan was partly explained by the timing; it came shortly after several other expensive social policy reforms and the Cabinet's perception was that the budgetary "cookie jar" for social spending was empty. The same event illustrates how the content of proposals can affect their fate. In the case of Lalonde's plan, the redistributive implications of the scheme aroused the opposition of certain conservative elements within Cabinet and the shakiness of the cost estimates created doubts in the minds of other ministers. In summary, the power of the main actors within the budgetary process will fluctuate over time. Formal organizational charts and statements of responsibilities cannot capture the fluidity of a dynamic and varied process.

Coping With Complexity in Budgeting

The participants in the budgetary process must cope with enormous complexity. For 1981-82 the Main Estimates, known as the Blue Book, show planned expenditures totalling more than $67.5 billion.[47] Through thousands of pages the Blue Book identifies approximately 200 programs, lists thousands of objectives and sub-objectives of spending, and shows the authorized "person-years" for each department and agency. Looking every bit like a major metropolitan telephone directory and probably less fun to read, the Blue Book can be a gold mine of useful information, but only when in the hands of someone highly experienced in finding his or her way through its numerous rows and columns.

It is more than the sheer magnitude which makes the budgetary task so difficult; there is also the fact that at any given time the ministers on the Treasury Board and the staff of the Secretariat will be working on up to three sets of estimates simultaneously. For any given fiscal year the Treasury Board, or more accurately its staff in the Secretariat, was dealing with approximately 8,000 submissions annually from departments and agencies. Only about one-tenth of these were actually brought before the Treasury Board ministers at their weekly meetings.

Another complicating factor is the existence of numerous 'tax expenditures'. It will be recalled from earlier discussions that tax expenditures are incentives in the Income Tax Act intended to induce certain behavior on the part of individual and corporate taxpayers. Before 1979 the expenditure management system took tax expenditures into account only to the extent that they reduced total revenues available to government. However, when new or modified tax expenditures were introduced, the loss of revenue involved was not counted as additional support for a given policy area, even though tax expenditures are in many ways no different than direct budgetary outlays. In short, tax expenditures provided ministers with an indirect method of spending in their policy fields without having to reckon with the costs involved. The new expenditure-management system seeks to control spending through tax incentives by requiring that the revenue cost of any changes in tax expenditures reduce the Resource Envelope allocation for that particular policy area.[48] Before introducing any modifications or new tax expenditures, ministers must obtain the concurrence of the Minister of Finance, who still has final responsibility for the tax system. By treating both direct and indirect spending similarly, the new system theoretically removes the previous incentive to ministers to reach their goals through indirect tax expenditures. More practically, however, one wonders whether in political terms tax expenditures will ever be as visible and hence subject to as close scrutiny as direct budget outlays. For one thing, there is no forum within Parliament currently where the Tax Expenditure Account of the government of Canada receives a thorough and systematic review. Furthermore, there is little incentive for groups of ministers on Cabinet committees to recommend the elimination of any existing tax expenditures because there is no guarantee that the additional revenues captured for the treasury will, in fact, flow into their resource envelope.

A further constraint—which may in fact simplify somewhat the task of expenditure decision-makers—is the existence of so-called "statutory expenditures." These are some 60 different types of statutory expenditures for which permanent authorization is found in substantive legislation (such as the Old Age Security Act and the Medicare Act). While the amounts of such spending are presented annually in the Main Estimates so that Parliament and the public are made aware of them, they do not have to be voted annually by Parliament through Appropriation Acts. Short of amendments to the authorizing legislation, such spending is predetermined. According to the Report of the Royal Commission on Financial Management and Accountability, approximately 56 per cent of the Federal Government's total spending involves such statutory obligations.[49] For example, most social policy expenditures are both statutory in nature and indexed to inflation. In 1980-81 such "uncontrollable" social spending accounted for 40 per cent of the federal budget. According to the conventional wisdom around Ottawa, another 20 to 30 per cent of federal spending (beyond the 56 per cent statutory expenditure) cannot be easily cut back, at least over the short term, because it involves commitments to provincial governments or matters such as defence spending which offer little scope for saving. In short, regardless of the fiscal stance of the incumbent government and no matter how vigilant the Treasury Board Secretariat might be in identifying economies, the room for realizing dramatic savings or engaging in massive reallocations of funds seems very limited indeed.

To cope with the magnitude of their task, ministers and officials in the Treasury Board Secretariat resort to a number of short-cuts or rules of thumb. For example, they concentrate on expenditure changes, looking for unusual increases in departmental requests. The presentation of such requests in the *A* and *B* budget formats facilitates such a search. *A* budgets represent a continuation of existing programs at present levels with adjustments for inflation. *B* budgets represent requests for new programs or improvements in existing programs. It has been estimated that 90 percent of the total budget falls into the *A* category, which leaves the Treasury Board officials, and eventually the Ministers on Policy Committees, with the task of ranking the remaining 10 per cent of expenditures in terms of their relative contribution to the government's priorities. Few departments, of course, willingly volunteer programs for termination.

Another way that treasury officials make their jobs manageable is to work on the basis of past experience and trust. If certain departments or deputy ministers are known for their tendency to pad budgetary requests, then the Treasury Board will review their requests more critically. Detailed, specific probes may be used as the basis for reaching wider judgments about the efficiency of departmental operations. Trust in the competence and honesty of senior departmental officials means that every sum need not be recalculated. Informal chats can resolve apparent difficulties. Because the whole negotiation process occurs within severe time constraints, there is additional pressure on the participants to reach agreement. Irreconcilable differences will ultimately have to be resolved at the political level, either in Policy Committees or in full Cabinet, and departments may feel that a compromise reached among officials, where there is greater appreciation of the department's substantive concerns, is preferable to a solution based upon 'political' considerations.

Parliament and the Purse Strings

To this point we have concentrated on the budgetary process within the executive branch. This is appropriate since, under the Canadian system of responsible government, all spending must originate with the Crown, which means in practice the Cabinet. However, a second fundamental principle of the Canadian Constitution is that the government can make no expenditures except those approved by Parliament, in ways approved by Parliament. Governments obtain annually the funds to carry out their programs through the passage in Parliament of Appropriation Acts. These Acts are based upon the Main and Supplementary Estimates. In February of each year, the President of the Treasury Board presents the Main Estimates to the House of Commons for discussion and approval. Commonly called "the Blue Book" because of the color of its cover, the Main Estimates set out the Government's spending plans for the forthcoming fiscal year (April 1st-March 31st). It has become usual over the past several years for governments to present one or more sets of Supplementary Estimates to cover situations where initial funding proved to be inadequate or to deal with new, unforeseen circumstances. Although there is an opportunity for the House of Commons to debate and to vote on the Estimates, it is the Government's responsibility to accept or reject any changes in the Estimates which might arise as a result of parliamentary discussion. Consistent with the principle that spending must originate with the Crown, only motions to reduce the Estimates are allowed in these debates. In practice, such motions are rarely successful because they are treated as matters of confidence, and party discipline prevails.

Without intending to minimize its importance, therefore, one can say that parliamentary control of the purse really refers to a public review of Cabinet decisions. A system of actual parliamentary authorization of spending, including regular and significant revisions of the executive's plans (as is done by the American Congress) is alien to the Cabinet-parliamentary model. On the other hand, the fact that the Estimates are approved substantially unchanged is not a totally convincing argument for their dismissal as a largely meaningless formality. The process of obtaining parliamentary approval requires governments to at least explain in public before the House of Commons their intended expenditure plans and allows Commons' committees the opportunity to evaluate the efficiency and effectiveness of departmental programs and operations. Thus the process of "granting Supply", as it is called, is the foundation for the wider process of the accountability of ministers, both collectively and individually, for their performance in office. Many observers feel, however, that the deficiencies of the existing process of parliamentary scrutiny of public expenditure mean that governments are not required to render a full and adequate accounting of their achievements and failures in office.[50]

Probably no aspect of parliamentary procedure has been more resistant to change than the process of granting Supply.[51] It remained basically unchanged from Confederation down to December 1968. The new supply procedure adopted in 1968 clearly represents at least a marginal improvement over its century-old predecessor, but even it is not without problems. To understand the improvement involved, it is necessary to present a brief historical account of how the old supply process worked. When the Estimates were presented to the House of Commons, they were referred to what was called the Committee of Supply. This committee was actually the full House of Commons meeting under another name, with the Speaker (as the historical representative of the Crown) replaced by the Deputy Speaker, and the formal rules of debate relaxed somewhat. The motion to enter the Committee of Supply was debatable, amendable and votable. It usually launched a wide-ranging debate in which members were free to raise any subject, not necessarily of a financial nature. Eventually a vote expressing confidence in the government was held. While limits on the number of days that could be spent on "supply motions" were gradually introduced by governments, the whole process served to delay the actual consideration of the Estimates. The 'supply motion' debates did serve the political function of allowing spokesmen from various regions to voice complaints before the Parliamentary Press Gallery and even on occasion to extract concessions from the government.

The second part of the old supply process — the actual consideration of the Estimates once the Commons was in committee — also evolved into a characteristic pattern. For each department there was an item entitled "general administration vote," the consideration of which usually provoked a general discussion of departmental policies. Once past this, the committee took up further items in the estimates. Members often used these items to raise matters of concern to their constituencies and as a result the discussion lacked continuity. Since departmental officials could not answer questions in the House, two would be perched at a desk in front of the minister whose estimates were under examination and they would feed him answers to queries that arose. This facade helped to maintain the fiction that the minister had actual knowledge of and control over all departmental operations. The House would frequently find itself bogged down on early estimates and end up rushing through millions of dollars of spending near the end of the parliamentary session. Originally, the supply process operated without time limits and opposition parties used obstruction to extract concession from governments. Beginning in 1965 the number of days spent on supply was fixed and many observers believe that nothing did more than this change to eliminate any parliamentary influence on government spending.

The changes introduced in December 1968 reflected the belief of Liberal governments that they could not develop a record of legislative accomplishments when 75 to 80 days of each parliamentary session were devoted to supply. It was also felt that the Committee of Supply was not a forum in which the detailed scrutiny of the Estimates could be realistically attempted. Therefore, the new rules of the Commons transferred the detailed consideration of the Estimates into the standing committees of the Commons. There are approximately 18 standing committees whose terms of reference cover one or more departments and agencies of government. The Main Estimates are referred to the standing committees by March 1st. The ministers of departments appear before the appropriate committees to explain and defend their expenditure plans. Usually, they are accompanied by a team of departmental officials and, after an initial appearance by the minister, the officials will often be left to handle questions on their own about the administrative aspects of departmental operations. Shifting the estimates into the committees saves the time of the House for other government business. Members of Parliament have been given a greater chance to specialize through service on committees of greatest interest to them, to discuss with the responsible minister departmental goals and progress toward their achievement, and to receive an education about departmental operations from senior officials. More time is given to the actual examination of the Estimates than was possible under the old supply procedure.

If these are positive features of the new supply process, there is another aspect which detracts from its popularity in the eyes of spokesmen for the opposition parties. There are now fixed deadlines for the approval of the Estimates. For purposes of granting supply, the parliamentary year has been divided into three periods and Estimates referred to the committees during each period must be reported back to and approved by the House of Commons by specified dates. As a result, it is alleged that the committees are rushed to conclude their reviews of the performance of departments and cannot do an adequate job. Furthermore, the requirement that all Estimates be approved by certain dates means that it is no longer possible to delay supply indefinitely. Since ministers need only wait for the efflux of time in order to obtain their funds, they have become, according to the opposition parties, unresponsive to suggestions and criticisms.

In addition to the committee reviews, the new procedure preserved the right of opposition parties to criticize, on the floor of the Commons and therefore before the Press Gallery, the financial policies of the government through the device of what is called "opposition" or "supply days". These are 25 days, spread throughout the parliamentary year, on which the opposition parties get to select the topic for debate. Needless to say all motions submitted by opposition parties are critical of the government's performance and on six of the 25 days the debates end in a vote of confidence in the government. Thus the opposition is permitted to criticize with the press in attendance and to determine periodically whether the government enjoys the continued confidence of the House. While it was originally envisaged that some of the 25 supply days would be devoted to the debate of reports from the standing committees dealing with the Estimates, in practice this has rarely occured.

Part of the reason for the lack of such debate is that most committee reports consist of nothing more than a motion to approve the Estimates. This in turn reflects the usual close government control over the committees. If there is a majority government, the majority on the committee will consist of MPs from the governing party. Few such Members would wish to ruin their future career prospects by embarrassing their own minister through the disclosure of departmental mistakes. Chairmen of the committees are theoretically elected, but in practice they are chosen by the governing party, and they can steer investigations away from dangerous political ground. While it was once hoped that the adoption of the PPBS format would assist MPs in their duty of financial review, it is still the case that the 'Blue Book' hides most of the substance of departmental plans in a bookkeeping fog. Many of the financial studies prepared in the executive branch, such as cost-benefit analyses on the effectiveness of programs, are not made available to MPs. Ministerial attendance at committee hearings is frequently too short for MPs to have their policy concerns answered and the officials who substitute for the minister on other occasions are technically barred from answering policy questions.

Not only procedural and partisan factors account for Parliament's limited influence on government spending. There is also a problem with the attitudes of MPs themselves. Most are more interested in debating new policies than in reviewing the administration of on-going programs. Rather than specializing on one or two committees, many MPs prefer to move around from one committee to another following their own interests or the concerns of their constituents. The result is a very high substitution rate on most committees which prevents the development of subject-matter expertise among MPs. The frequency of committee meetings during the spring when most Estimates are under review compounds this problem. Only a minority of MPs work full-time within the committee system. The rest either believe that the process is futile or that more political credit is to be won by providing constituency services or participating in the more highly publicized debates on the floor of the Commons' chamber. The fluctuating membership on committees and the constituency concerns of many who attend mean that the hearings on the Estimates are often haphazard and disjointed in nature. Rarely, therefore, do committees have the time, the knowledge or even the inclination to review the financial management and administration of departments in any thorough and systematic fashion.

One committee which is somewhat better off is the Public Accounts Committee (PAC). It has responsibility for conducting a retrospective examination of government spending. The chairman of PAC is an opposition member and the committee is assisted by the work of the Auditor General, who has responsibility for scrutinizing the accounts of the government. The passage in 1977 of a new Act made the Auditor General more independent of the government of the day. His office was given the authority to report, not only whether the government spent its funds legally and efficiently, but also whether departments have established adequate procedures to measure the effectiveness of their programs. In other words, while the Auditor General will not himself conduct program evaluations, he will report to Parliament on instances where departments have failed to evaluate their own programs. It will be recalled from the earlier discussion, that the Auditor General's warning that spending was out of control led to the creation of the post of Comptroller General within the administration. He has since worked closely with the Comptroller General to introduce "value for money" accounting into the public service and to upgrade the quality of financial information being made available to Parliament. J. J. Macdonell, the Auditor General during the late '70s, argued strongly that "value for money" auditing would provide the financial discipline required in an organization like the government of Canada, which did not possess a bottom line of profitability. Others, however, are skeptical whether it is either desirable or possible for accountants to provide a measurement of the worth of public spending which the phrase "value for money" suggests. Should accountants, even those who serve the institution of Parliament, pronounce on whether the public received good value for the money spent on Old Age Security or Canada Assistance Plan payments? Or, how would an accountant evaluate the cost-effectiveness of the recent debate on the constitution, which has taken up a great deal of the time and energy of government? If the Auditor General becomes involved with such difficult value judgements, will he not inevitably be drawn into political fights between contending parties within Parliament or contending governments within the federal system? And finally, do accountants possess the skills and the information necessary to complete the comprehensive auditing which they are advocating? Douglas Hartle, former Deputy Secretary to the Treasury Board, thinks not. He argues that believing in value for money auditing is "an act of pure faith," that such an approach ignores the political and bureaucratic realities of the budgetary process, and that the sizeable increases in the Auditor General's staff to implement the new approach would fail their own test of a cost-effectiveness analysis.[52] Sharon Sutherland has argued that in the final analysis the Auditor General's approach would remove political control over the assessment of public spending and would entrench "philosophical conservatism" within government, a suspicion of government spending and a desire to cut back the scope of big government.[53]

In summary, while Parliament is theoretically central to the budgetary process, in practice it is a marginal actor. While Parliament cannot constitutionally control spending in the sense of determining the levels of expenditures on particular functions, a common argument is that it should be able to exact a more adequate accounting from governments concerning the use to which they put public funds. Spending continues to be looked at piecemeal and on a short-term basis by the House of Commons. Thorough investigations of the impact of programs seldom take place. Members' attitudes have not been appropriate to the performance of their surveillance task. The present weakness of parliamentary financial control deeply worried the Royal Commission on Financial Management and Accountability and in Chapter 8, dealing with administrative accountability, we will examine some of their proposals for reform.

The Sources of Incrementalism in Budgeting

Because of the process of political bargaining described above most budgeting is incremental. Attention is focused on the expenditure increases requested each year, while little effort is made to evaluate ongoing programs. From year to year, the budgetary changes that occur are marginal or incremental in nature. Decisions built into last year's budget are difficult to change because departments can always point to good works accomplished and can line up pressure groups ready to support such claims. Therefore, the budgetary base is treated as given. Departments rarely wish to evaluate the effectiveness of their continuing programs except perhaps to prepare a case for an enriched version of those programs.

Incremental budgeting is non-programmatic in the sense that budgetary information is organized according to inputs and functions – amounts spent on personnel, supplies, maintenance and so on – rather than according to program objectives. The objectives of spending, if they exist in written form, tend to be vague and rhetorical. No attempt is made under the incremental approach to bring together and to compare the effectiveness of programs serving the same or related objectives. Decision-making tends to be fragmented rather than comprehensive in nature. Alternative, perhaps less costly, means of reaching the same goals are not examined because analysis plays a limited role in incremental budgeting. The best decision seems to be the one on which most political agreement can be found. Some of the real goals of spending, such as ensuring the re-election of a government or the survival of a government agency, cannot be announced. Clear and precise objectives, towards which progress might be measured, could frustrate the achievement of such political goals.

Less cynically, it is argued that incrementalism represents a pragmatic response to the complexity of contemporary budgeting. In a pluralistic society of multiple competing values there will never be an overall evaluative framework that would enable decision-makers to weigh different values and the relative effectiveness of various programs in achieving those values. No less than a broad societal consensus about the purposes of government would be required to eliminate conflict over budgets. Furthermore, budgeting is done under great pressures of time, and trying to reach agreement on broad objectives would, it is argued, cause delays and lead to unproductive ideological conflict. Governments also lack the information and analytical capability to forecast the effects of all possible expenditure alternatives. Incremental budgeting may be fragmented and short-sighted, but these characteristics give it the appeal of simplicity, adaptability and congruence with the wider political process, according to advocates like Aaron Wildavsky.[54]

Beyond Incrementalism – PPBS

The appearance of new analytical techniques of policy analysis and later the reaction against the growth of spending, led governments to experiment first with Planning, Programming, Budgeting Systems (PPBS) and more recently with Zero Based Budgeting (ZBB) as alternatives to incrementalism. Both approaches emphasized the management and planning purpose of budgeting. Both sought to submit the expenditure base to regular scrutiny and to calculate the future in some rational manner. Neither has displaced incrementalism to any great extent. Recent evaluations of PPBS have ranged all the way from cynical pronouncements on its demise to sanguine declarations about its continuing, positive impact on governments. What seems clear, however, is that PPBS was oversold by its early advocates, and disappointment was inevitable. A balanced, retrospective assessment of PPBS suggests that it was neither a panacea nor a mirage in government. But the same mistake of placing extreme faith in the ability of any single mechanism or technique to settle budgetary issues is now being repeated with ZBB and sunset laws, more so in the United States than in Canada it seems.

PPBS was originally developed in the United States for public sector purposes in the Department of Defense under Secretary Robert McNamara. In 1965 President Johnson ordered all departments in the federal government to henceforth prepare their budgets along PPBS guidelines. During those years, according to one writer, PPBS had a "messianic spirit," with public officials all across the United States learning under academicians the "gospel according to Robert McNamara."[55] The "ultimate solution" aspect of the PPBS concept can also be seen in the rash of praise and criticism of it appearing in economic texts, learned journals, and books of readings on public policy.

At the federal level in Canada PPBS was being seriously studied during its development in the United States, and by 1970 the departmental budget submissions were in keeping with the PPBS perspective. The way had been paved not only by apparent initial success in the United States, but also by the Royal Commission on Government Organization (Glassco Commission) whose *Report* in 1962 strongly criticized the federal public service for not being more receptive to a wide range of new techniques successfully demonstrated in the private sector. Among these were budgetary and accounting systems which would create better control over financial resource allocations as well as performance measurements. Techniques such as cost-benefit analysis were pointed out as available for evaluating alternative courses of action and for designing and appraising methods and systems of operation. What was seen as necessary by the Glassco Commission was a systematic, as opposed to *ad hoc*, introduction of such techniques into the Public Service.[56] The influx of systems analysts, operations research experts and accountants into the Treasury Board in the post-Glassco era paved the way for the introduction of PPBS. Adoption of PPBS was also encouraged because it corresponded with Prime Minister Trudeau's own philosophy of policy-making which stressed "top down" direction of policy-making and the employment of rational analyses for long-range planning.[57]

PPBS was heralded as "budget breakthrough" by the Minister of Finance when it was introduced.[58] According to the Planning Programing Budgeting Guide issued by the Treasury Board, the features of PPBS were as follows: (1) setting specific objectives, (2) systematic analysis to clarify objectives and to assess alternative means of reaching them, (3) stating budgetary proposals in terms of programs to meet objectives, (4) projection of program costs for a number of years into the future, (5) formulation of plans of achievement on a yearly basis for each program, and (6) monitoring of program achievements and reassessment of program objectives and of the program itself in light of achievements.[59]

PPBS was, in essence, an effort to develop and use informational sources and technologies in order to bring more objective and quantitative analysis to public policy-making. It assumed the existence of an analytical support system, but most departments lacked the personnel and information to perform the analysis required.[60] For example, a popular feature of most PPB systems was cost/benefit analysis, but there was no way, except arbitrarily, that analysts could attach a value to different programs and then divide that value among the different people who make up the society. Defenders of PPBS admitted that the benefits and costs of some projects would be difficult to quantify, "but the very process of stepping through the analysis will be of great value to the decision-maker."[61] Some analysis is better than none at all, it was argued. Critics, however, went further to contend that the insistence on quantification was more than simply difficult, it was dangerous. Decision-makers would be given high benefit/cost ratios for certain programs whose benefits were easily quantifiable, while programs involving less tangible benefits (for example, the services provided by a social development agency) could not point to similar "success," especially in the short-term. Quantification would introduce a bias in the budgetary procedure in favor of programs delivering so-called "hard" or "physical" goods.

In addition to its analytical purpose, PPBS was intended to serve a projective purpose through its requirement for program forecasts and multi-year costing.[62] Planning was to be integrated with the budgetary process, with planning as the master and budgeting as the servant. The cavalier dismissal of the future entailed in incrementalism would be overcome, and it would thus be more difficult for departments to sneak in major long-term expenditures with an initial modest request. Making plans over three or five years would permit larger changes in spending to be effected in a more orderly way. There could, for example, be a shift from defence to social spending.

But such benefits presume an ability to predict with some accuracy the performance of the economy and hence the revenues anticipated by the government. Such predictions are notoriously difficult to make in practice. Multi-year budgeting also implies some loss of flexibility, making budgets less responsive to changing economic and political conditions. It is questionable whether governments have the political commitment to make long-term budgeting work the way it is intended. In its first budget the Clark Government presented Parliament with a five-year projection of its anticipated revenues and expenditures. The Liberal Government followed suit in this regard, but were careful to stress that the revenue and expenditure forecasts were highly vulnerable to events within a complex and ever-changing economic environment.

PPBS implied a centralizing of power within governments. The enhanced status of the Treasury Board, the PMO and PCO, and the increased role of Cabinet committees, especially the Priorities and Planning committee, were intended to give top-down direction to spending. However, according to the Auditor-General, departments did not in practice use their program forecasts to implement cabinet priorities. Few departments prepared long-range plans. Most program forecasts were based on detailed budgets prepared by individual managers throughout the departments. Budgets continued to be built from the bottom up and future spending was an extrapolation from the past with some provision for future departmental aspirations. "As a result, Program Forecasts submitted to the Treasury Board Secretariat often reflect an aggregation of current objectives of individual managers rather than a unified response to the objectives of the Cabinet."[63] Whether the new expenditure management system described earlier will change all of this can only be a matter for speculation at this stage.

PPBS was also intended to ensure accountability by presenting spending in terms of objectives and sub-objectives towards which progress could be measured. The new format for presenting financial information would raise the sights of decision-makers from the minutiae of amounts spent on furniture and trips to the big issues of the relative amounts spent on different functions of government. No longer would it be necessary for legislators, for example, to add up the amounts spent across departments to discover how much the federal government was spending on health. In practice, on the other hand, the process of clarifying goals of spending was protracted, controversial and incomplete. According to the Auditor General's 1976 Report, most departmental objectives were so broadly stated that they could not be challenged meaningfully, could not be measured and created serious auditing problems.

To incrementalists, this result was not surprising. Politicians want vague and rhetorical goals that make it easier for them to secure political agreement, to claim credit for bold action, and to take refuge in ambiguity when the results are less than promised. Along with their bureaucrats, ministers also want to define goals broadly so as to protect and to expand their jurisdiction. Still another problem arises in distinguishing between stated purposes of spending and its unintended effects. Should such effects be acknowledged, and if so, should they subsequently be incorporated into program goals? Finally, even if a list of objectives can be agreed upon, this does not settle the question of the appropriate level of funding. Ministers may agree that a program must continue even when they cannot agree as to why. One minister may believe in the program goals, but another may support continuation in order to ensure his own re-election.

PPBS has nowhere been completely and successfully implemented.[64] There are a variety of explanations, but probably the most powerful and widely accepted is the emphasis on the political and hence incremental nature of budgeting. The essence of PPBS is "logical-rational" in nature, and PPBS cannot be pursued in situations where stress is laid on "political rationality." The attempt to introduce analysis into government through the budgetary process may also have been a mistake. That process is too steeped in its own traditions and routines, too weighted in favor of past decisions, and operates under such serious time constraints that it cannot serve as the main vehicle for redirection of government activity but rather can record such shifts only after they occur. Most program innovation will probably remain extra-budgetary, occurring through royal commissions and task forces, legislation and in-depth departmental reviews of selected programs.

Disillusionment over PPBS is probably less pronounced in Canada than in the United States because we had somewhat more success with it. Our system of government is in the long-run probably more congruent with the requirements of PPBS. The American system of checks and balances and separation of powers, with the Congress remaining a very significant budgetary force, involves a dispersal of power that runs contrary to the centralizing bias inherent in PPBS. In Canada, where a majority government controls the House of Commons, there was a better prospect for the successful introduction of PPBS. Optimists argue that while some of the formal requirements of PPBS may be gone from the Canadian budgetary procedures, its residual impact on government decision-making can be seen. The precepts of rational planning may not have been fulfilled, but governments were forced to be more self-conscious about their goals. Arranging programs around goals, even vague ones, highlighted some overlapping, outdated and misguided efforts. There was a widening of the budgetary debate to include more systematic considerations of efficiency and effectiveness. Some of the incremental rules of thumb were weakened and more attention was paid to relative shares devoted to different functions of government. On the other hand, the more jaded observers argue that PPBS involved an enormous cost in terms of time and personnel, produced a mountainous amount of useless information, and led to very few program terminations or dramatic shifts in expenditure patterns. Anyone who did a cost-benefit analysis on the introduction of PPBS, it is argued, would be forced to conclude that it was not worth the effort.

Zero-Based Budgeting

No sooner was PPBS in disrepute than the budgetary reform movement found two new approaches to endorse. Zero-based budgeting and sunset laws both emerged in the decade of the 1970s, a period of tight budgets, of widespread disillusionment with the apparent ineffectiveness of government programs, and strong suspicion of unaccountable bureaucracies. Both concepts sought to challenge incremental ways of making budgets and public policies. Both began in government at the state level in the United States, spread to the national level in that country under the sponsorship of President Jimmy Carter and have attracted considerable interest in Canada. The Conservatives under Joe Clark promised during the 1979 federal election to implement both zero-based budgeting and sunset laws.

The "father" of ZBB is usually taken to be Peter Phyrr, who developed the procedure within Texas Instruments and in 1971 advised Governor Jimmy Carter on its implementation in Georgia, the first of about a dozen states to adopt ZBB. By an executive order in February 1977, Carter, then President of the United States, ordered all federal departments to use ZBB in preparing their budgetary requests for the 1979 fiscal year. Several governments in Canada have shown an interest in ZBB by contracting ZBB consultants and holding seminars on the subject. Despite some disillusionment with the rationalist-based perspective of PPBS, the also rationalist-based ZBB appears to be growing in popularity. The PPBS "gospel according to McNamara" is now the ZBB "gospel according to Phyrr."

ZBB does not represent a specific set of procedures, but a general approach to budgeting. Its inventor, Peter Phyrr, stresses its flexibility, arguing that the mechanics of the approach can be adapted to fit the specific needs of each user.[65] While ZBB comes in several formats, there are three basic steps or procedures common to all versions. The first step is to examine the structure of the organization in order to identify and define decision units. According to Phyrr, this is a straightforward process. "Decision units" may be based on traditional budgetary units, on a projects basis, or, most popular in governments, objectives to be accomplished through the performance of services. In the latter case, decision units could cut across departmental lines of authority since programs in different departments contribute to the same objectives. In practice, most governments have confined their decision units to the existing departmental structures.

The second step consists of the preparation of "decision packages" within each budget unit. As defined by Phyrr, a decision package "identifies a discrete activity, function or operation in a definitive manner for management evaluation and comparison with other activities. This identification includes purpose; consequences of not performing the activity; measures of performance; alternative courses of action, costs and benefits."[66] Managers must ask themselves three basic questions. Is this activity necessary? What is the best way to operate it? What different levels of service and cost are possible? It is this identification and evaluation of different levels of spending and services which is the unique feature of ZBB. By requiring managers to consider reduced levels of spending, budget attention is shifted from increments above the base to the effect on programs of possible reductions. Few working ZBB schemes in theory and none in actual practice require managers to justify their budget from scratch each year, although evangelists of the approach sometimes talk of beginning each year with a clean slate. What is usually undertaken is a form of marginal analysis. For example, Thomas Lauth reports that in Georgia budget officials rely heavily on past experience in considering departmental requests and analysis is concentrated on decision packages falling between 85 per cent and 110 per cent of the previous year's funding level.[67]

The third step in ZBB is to evaluate and rank each decision-package. The review process can be designed to fit the size and needs of the organization. In all cases, however, lower-cost decision packages must be accorded higher priority. In several state jurisdictions, decision packages are ranked at progressively higher levels up the organizational ladder until they reach the central budget office. Unlike PPBS, which was supposed to be budgeting from the top down, ZBB is budgeting from the bottom up, based on the assumption that program managers are in the best position to know what level of funding they can accept to operate viable programs. The final rankings by the central budget office and chief executive will depend partly on available resources and policy objectives. If funds are short, the decision may be made to eliminate lower-ranked programs and reallocate resources to programs of higher priority.

The advantages of ZBB are claimed to be numerous.[68] First, by requiring more justification for spending, ZBB would overcome incrementalism. It would induce a changed state of mind within government by establishing the habit of thinking about efficiency in spending and alternatives. It would improve the quantity and quality of information available to top decision-makers by requiring departments to submit more than just one budget proposal that must be accepted or rejected. Under ZBB choices could be made among several levels of service and costs. Better information would also result because ZBB provides for greater involvement by lower management personnel in the budgeting process and those same individuals have the greatest familiarity with how programs are actually operating.

Skeptics insist that ZBB will not live up to these inflated expectations. It will not result in significant cuts in budgets or dramatic reallocations because by itself any budgetary technique cannot override the much stronger incentives within the bureaucracy to seek larger budgets and expanded functions. ZBB relies on departments to supply information and few will voluntarily disclose information that might lead to negative decisions. Besides bureaucratic resistance, there will be wider political constraints on the operation of ZBB, such as the activity of pressure groups, the public expectation that most programs will continue, and statutory commitments to spend on certain programs. There are also the practical problems of insufficient time, a lack of performance data and a shortage of analytical talent to do the job of reviewing all programs each year during the short budgetary cycle. The sheer magnitude of the task will mean that, rather than the thorough assessments envisaged, the result will be a ritualistic fulfillment of the requirements of ZBB. For example, Allan Shick reports that the first two budgets produced by the Carter administration in Washington were the most incremental in recent years.[69] Similarly a recent review of the experience of four states concluded that neither shifts in funding nor spending reductions were accomplished under ZBB.[70] Given these outcomes and the enormous work involved, critics ask whether ZBB is worth the effort.

A balanced assessment would seem to suggest that ZBB is neither a panacea nor a fraud. It has provided budget makers with information not normally available under traditional budgetary procedures and has marginally increased their ability to assess competing demands for funds. Ranking decision-packages has facilitated the identification of overlapping programs and has led to the streamlining of government organization through the elimination or amalgamation of agencies. It is contended, for example, that 278 agencies were eliminated in Georgia during the first year of ZBB; but it should be noted that only 65 out of the 278 agencies were actually funded at the time and that a major executive reorganization was occurring simultaneously. Only one agency completely disappeared, the rest were subsumed within continuing organizations.[71] Over time, ZBB could lead to a redirection of spending and perhaps to greater program efficiency. However, there seems to be an emerging consensus that ZBB should be applied selectively, not universally, in combination with traditional incremental budgeting. For example, programs that did not present an adequate justification in one year or those that were changing direction, could be subject to fundamental and regular reviews, while the more stable and well-defended programs could be exempt from ZBB for perhaps five years.

Sunset Laws

The current rival to ZBB for the reformer's passion is the concept of the sunset law.[72] Sunset involves the automatic termination of government agencies, programs, regulations or other laws after a specified period of time unless the legislature first reviews and recreates them. The concept has been adopted by approximately 20 American states, was endorsed by President Carter and leading members of Congress, and in Canada was part of the Conservative Party's election platform in 1979. Where sunset laws exist, their coverage varies. Some cover all state departments and agencies (e.g., Louisiana), some only regulatory agencies (e.g., Colorado), while still others are quite selective (e.g., New Mexico's sunset law covers only occupational licensing agencies). The length of the review cycle also varies. Some states review agencies every four years, some use five years, and others six.

In the United States, sunset laws are seen as a legislative tool to restore the legislature's control over spending. They would complement ZBB, which is seen primarily as an executive tool. Sunset provisions would force legislatures to review programs on a regular basis. Being separate from the budgetary process, sunset would make the reallocation of funds easier since there is not the same pressure of time and the built-in tendency of the budget process to concentrate only on next year. Programs with a similar purpose are to be reviewed at the same time under some schemes. Conflicting or redundant programs could be dropped or merged more easily because the reviewers would be able to point to continuing programs that served the same purpose. The threat of possible termination and the fact that programs do not continue indefinitely would be an incentive to individual agencies and government as a whole to improve performance.

All these benefits are still hypothetical, of course, and many observers doubt whether they are realizable in practice. Legislative review of programs reflects the suspicion that administrative organizations, with a few notable exceptions, cannot be expected to evaluate themselves objectively. However, most legislative committees that would conduct the reviews would still depend greatly upon the agencies in question for their information. Since these committees are often advocates of additional rather than less spending, one can question how objectively they would approach their task. Even if the review of programs is staggered over a number of years, it is argued that legislatures would not be able to cope with the additional workload, given their already congested agendas. Because of the work involved and because of the inherent difficulties of meaningful program evaluation (such as the lack of clear statements of goals), there would be a tendency among legislators to conduct superficial, ritualistic reviews, except perhaps for those programs that were obviously in some kind of trouble. Critics even question how serious the threat of termination will be as a disciplining force on agencies. Some, perhaps most, agencies and programs would not be candidates for oblivion. Who, for example, would vote to wind down the operation of National Revenue which collects taxes? Departments would adopt strategies to deal with legislative reviews, such as setting easy program goals that they could easily attain, preparing lengthy and glossy reports which extoll their accomplishments, and lobbying with influential legislators to ensure continuing political support for their programs.

Transferring ZBB and sunset laws from the United States, where they originated, to the Canadian context would cause further problems because of the different nature of the two political systems, particularly the relative impotence of the Canadian Parliament within the expenditure process in comparison to the American Congress. As we have seen, in Canada the Cabinet exercises almost complete control over spending and Parliament must depend on governments for most of its financial information. Congress is far more of a political force to be reckoned with in the American system, especially since the passage in 1974 of the Budget and Impoundment Control Act. That Act created new House and Senate budget committees; the Congressional Budget Office to provide analyses of alternative fiscal budgetary and programmatic policies to those presented by the President; an Office of Program Review and Evaluation within the General Accounting Office controlled by Congress; and new provisions for controlling presidential impoundments, that is, cases where the President refused to spend the money authorized by Congress.[73] The changes, approved by huge margins in both houses, were intended to halt the shift in budgetary power to the President. They provide a dramatic illustration of the basic difference between the American and Canadian system. Institutions operating on the basis of a separation of powers, checks and balances, and weak party discipline diffuse political power within the American political system. This makes it possible for Congress to have considerable influence on spending, but it also makes it difficult for the electorate to pinpoint responsibility for the eventual budgetary outcomes. By contrast, the Canadian system concentrates constitutional authority over spending in the Cabinet and the legislature operates on the basis of strict party discipline. This means that the Commons exercises minimal influence on government spending, but the public presumably finds it easier to assign credit or blame for the outcomes since the Cabinet is in control of the budgetary process throughout.

Given these fundamental differences, ZBB would be even more an executive-dominated process in Canada than it is in the United States. An effective Freedom of Information Act (to be discussed in a later chapter) might improve the situation somewhat. As for sunset laws, all the practical problems already mentioned would arise and there would be the additional constraint of party discipline, which would mean in a majority government situation that the party in power could stifle most investigations judged to be politically dangerous to itself. However, the Royal Commission on Financial Management and Accountability, which rejected the notion of an omnibus sunset law for Canada covering all programs and agencies, did recommend that governments be required to review the mandates of all crown corporations and regulatory commissions at least once every 10 years and that the results of such reviews be published and made available to Parliament.[74] These and other recommendations of the Commission are discussed more fully in the chapter on accountability in government.

Some Concluding Thoughts

A final point concerns the possibility of rational budgeting proposals and practices having a "real goal" either replacing or supplementary to their "stated goals." This real goal could perhaps be regarded as the achievement of political rationality as opposed to logical-economic rationality. Readers will recall Prime Minister Trudeau's statement in the late 1960s that he had no interest in being Prime Minister if he could not control the bureaucracy. As we noted in our discussion, ministers previously used to deal with virtually completed budgets prepared by the bureaucracy into which they had little input, particularly in terms of establishing overall priorities. Cabinet may have had ultimate decision-making authority, but given the fact of completed budgets, plus the normal constraints of complexity and the pressures of time, the actual decision-making capability of ministers was limited. Thus the budgetary reforms adopted during the late 1960s and the 1970s can perhaps be seen as an attempt to impose political direction on spending.

The rationality sought was not primarily economic and logical in nature, but rather political. Politicians, not bureaucrats, were henceforth to decide the direction of spending. If this was the goal of the changes to the budgetary process, there are disputes over whether it has been realized. Some observers argue that a shift of power from the regular departments to the center occurred because individual departments must now work within the rather elaborate context of Cabinet committees, prescribed budgetary frameworks, and under the watchful eye and to some extent, the direction of central agencies such as the Treasury Board Secretariat, the Office of the Comptroller General, the PMO and the PCO. However, other commentators insist that departments have adapted to the complexity and increased political emphasis within the budgetary environment. According to Campbell and Szablowski, "Ten years of active participation (in Cabinet Committees and in dealings with central agencies) has produced officials highly sensitive to political considerations."[75] According to this view, the new system makes bureaucrats think and behave more like politicians and causes Cabinet ministers to become more like the administrators whom they are supposed to direct. The net result is that political influence has not been increased significantly and in the process we have created in the central agencies a new class of "political administrators" who occupy a sort of constitutional twilight zone and belong neither to the category of the traditional public service nor to that of full-fledged politicians with all the hazards of that occupation. More is said about the significance of this trend in our chapter on accountability in government.

The budgetary reform parade marches on, only the banners have changed. Pursuit of better public budgeting is a noble goal. However, reformers often display a surprising political naiveté when proposing new techniques by ignoring the wider context in which budgeting occurs. We will probably never agree on better budgeting because budget decisions will always benefit some of us to the detriment of others. The persistence of incrementalism is explained by its congruence with the wider political process. On the other hand, while negotiation and compromise characterize the decision-making process, the results over the longer term need not always be incremental. "By the early 1970s, for example, less than 5 per cent of total government expenditure was on defence, compared to the post-war peak of 28 per cent reached at the time of the Korean War in 1953."[76] The budgetary mills do grind slowly (and not exceeding fine, many would hasten to add) but shifts in spending do occur as political demands and support for those changes develop.

For Further Reading

BOOKS AND REPORTS

Bird, Richard M. *Financing Canadian Government: A Quantitative Overview*. Toronto: Canadian Tax Foundation, 1979.

Canada, Treasury Board. *Guide to the Policy and Expenditure Management System*. Ottawa: Supply and Services, 1980.

————. Treasury Board. *Accountable Management: A Progress Report to Parliament*. Ottawa: Supply and Services, March, 1981.

————. Treasury Board. *Planning, Programming, and Budgeting Guide*, rev. ed. Ottawa: Queen's Printer, 1969.

————. Royal Commission on Financial Management and Accountability. *Final Report*. Ottawa: Supply and Services, 1979.

————. Auditor General of Canada. *Annual Reports*. Ottawa: Supply and Services, various years.

Doern, G. Bruce and Allan M. Maslove, eds. *The Public Evaluation of Government Spending*. Montreal: Institute for Research on Public Policy, 1979.

Doern, G. Bruce, ed. *Spending Tax Dollars: Federal Expenditures, 1980-81*. Ottawa: School of Public Administration, Carleton University, 1980.

Gow, D. *The Progress of Budgetary Reform in the Government of Canada*. Ottawa: Special Study No. 17 for the Economic Council of Canada, 1973.

Hartle, D. G. *The Expenditure Budget Process in Canada*. Toronto: Canadian Tax Foundation, 1978.

————. *A Theory of the Expenditure Budgetary Process*. Toronto: University of Toronto Press, 1976.

Kroeker, H. V. *Accountability and Control: The Government Expenditure Process*. Montreal: C. D. Howe Institute, 1978.

National Finances, 1979-1980. Toronto: Canadian Tax Foundation, 1980.

ARTICLES

Hartle, D. G. "Techniques and Processes of Administration." *Canadian Public Administration*, Vol. XIX, 1 (Spring 1976).

Hicks, Michael. "The Treasury Board of Canada and its clients: five years of change and administrative reform, 1966-1971." *Canadian Public Administration*, Vol. XVI, 2 (Summer 1973), pp. 182-205.

Jordan, J. M. and S. L. Sutherland. "Assessing the results of public expenditure: program evaluation in the Canadian federal government." *Canadian Public Administration*, Vol. XXII, 4 (Winter 1979), pp. 581-609.

Reid, Timothy. "Federal Government Experience with Measuring Program Performance." *Optimum*, Vol. IX, 4 (1978), pp. 17-28.

Rogers, H. "Management Control in the Public Service." *Optimum*, Vol. IX, 3 (1978), pp. 14-28.

Steele, C. G. E. "Needed—a Sense of Proportion! Notes on the History of Expenditure Control." *Canadian Public Administration*, Vol. XX, 3 (Fall, 1977).

Sutherland, S. L. "On the audit trail of the Auditor General: Parliament's servants, 1973-1980." *Canadian Public Administration*, Vol. XXIII, 4 (Winter 1980), pp. 616-45.

"Symposium on the Report of the Royal Commission on Financial Management and Accountability." *Canadian Public Administration*, Vol. XXII, 4 (Winter 1979).

Thomas, Paul G., "Parliament and the Purse Strings." *Parliament, Policy and Representation*, Clarke, H. D., et al., eds. Toronto: Methuen, 1980.

ENDNOTES

1. On the taxation side of the budgetary process, see the informative study by David A. Good, *The Politics of Anticipation: Making Canadian Federal Tax Policy* (Ottawa: School of Public Administration, Carleton University, 1980).
2. Royal Commission on Financial Management and Accountability, *Final Report* (Ottawa: Supply and Services, 1980), pp. 15-16. Henceforth cited simply as the *Lambert Report* in honor of its chairman, Allan Lambert.
3. Richard M. Bird, *Financing Canadian Government: A Quantitative Overview* (Toronto: Canadian Tax Foundation, 1979), p. 14.
4. *Ibid*., p.
5. Irwin Gillespie, *In Search of Robin Hood: The Effect of Federal Budgetary Policies During the 1970s on the Distribution of Income in Canada* (Montreal: C.D. Howe Institute, 1978).
6. Bird, p. 20.
7. Treasury Board Secretariat, "Government Owned and Controlled Corporations," (Ottawa: Financial Administration Branch, 1977).
8. Department of Finance, *Government of Canada, Tax Expenditure Account* (Ottawa, December 1979). The second tax expenditure account, issued by the Liberal government in December 1980, does not provide an estimate of the total revenue foregone because of tax expenditures.
9. See Alan M. Maslove, "The Other Side of Public Spending: Tax Expenditures in Canada," in G. Bruce Doern and Allan M. Maslove (eds.), *The Public Evaluation of Government Spending* (Montreal: Institute for Research on Public Policy, 1979), pp. 149-58 for a discussion and analysis of other tax expenditure surveys.
10. Bird, p. 93.
11. Economic Council of Canada, *Responsible Regulation* (Ottawa: Supply and Services, 1979), p. 7.
12. *Lambert Report*, p. 328; W.D.K. Kernaghan, "The Role of the Public Service in the Canadian Democratic System," in W.D.K. Kernaghan (ed.), *Bureaucracy in Canadian Government*, 2nd ed. (Toronto, Methuen, 1973), pp. 6-7; and the excellent article by Richard M. Bird and David K. Foot, "Bureaucratic Growth in Canada: Myths and Realities," in G. Bruce Doern and Alan M. Maslove, *op. cit.*, pp. 121-48, are the sources for the statistics in this paragraph.
13. Bird and Foot, p. 139.
14. Douglas A.L. Auld, "Wage Behaviour and Wage Control in the Public Service" (Paper prepared for the Centre for the Study of Inflation and Productivity, Economic Council of Canada, Ottawa, November 1979).

15. In 1977, the Gallup Poll reported that "a majority of Canadians believe that federal civil servants here are under-worked and over-compensated." See the *Gallup Report*, Saturday, September 17, 1977 (The Canadian Institute of Public Opinion, Toronto, Ontario).
16. *Report of the Auditor-General of Canada to the House of Commons* (Ottawa: Supply and Services, 1976), p. 10.
17. D.A.L. Auld, *Issues in Government Expenditure Growth* (Montreal: C.D. Howe Research Institute, 1976), *passim*.
18. For example, W.K. Bryden, *Old Age Pensions and Policy Making in Canada* (Montreal: McGill-Queen's, 1974).
19. Allan H. Melzer and Scott F. Richard, "Why Government Grows (and Grows) in a Democracy," *The Public Interest*, No. 52 (Summer 1978), pp. 111-8.
20. For example, see the excellent collection of articles in Leo Panitch, *The Canadian State: Political Economy and Political Power* (Toronto: University of Toronto Press, 1977).
21. See the discussion in D.G. Hartle, *A Theory of the Expenditure Budgetary Process* (Toronto: University of Toronto Press, 1976), pp. 11-36 for an excellent exposition and assessment of these theories.
22. *Lambert Report*, p. 18.
23. See Richard Shultz, *Federalism, Bureaucracy and Public Policy*.
24. See Ole P. Kristensen, "The Logic of Political Bureaucratic Decision-Making as a Cause of Governmental Growth," *European Journal of Political Research* Vol. VIII (1980), pp. 249-64.
25. Allan Cairns, "The Other Crisis of Canadian Federalism," *Canadian Public Administration*, Vol. XXII, 2 (Summer 1979), p. 189.
26. See Donald Gow, *The Progress of Budgetary Reform in the Government of Canada* (Ottawa: Economic Council of Canada, 1973).
27. Timothy E. Reid, "Federal Government Experience with Measuring Program Performance," *Optimum*, Vol. IX, 4 (1978), pp. 17-28, and Hon. Robert Andras, *Performance Measurement, A Report to the House of Commons* (Ottawa: Treasury Board, November 1977).
28. Allen Shick, "Road to PPB: The Stages of Budget Reform," *Public Administration Review*, Vol. XXVI, 4 (December 1966), p. 244.
29. See Colin J. Campbell and George Szablowski, *The Superbureaucrats: Structure and Behaviour in Central Agencies* (Toronto: Macmillan, 1979), p. 161, which shows the Minister of State for Small Business, the Minister of Supply and Services, the Minister of Public Works, and the Minister of State for Fitness and Amateur Sport as serving, along with the President, on the Treasury Board in November 1977.
30. *Estimates for the Fiscal Year Ending March 31, 1982* (Ottawa: Supply and Services, 1981), p. 31-8.
31. See two papers by the first Comptroller General, Harry Rogers, "Management Control in the Public Service," *Optimum*, Vol. IX, 3 (1978), pp. 14-28 and "Program Evaluation in the Federal Government," in G. Bruce Doern and Allan M. Maslove, *op. cit.*, pp. 79-90.
32. See the testimony by Rogers to the House of Commons Standing Committee on Miscellaneous Estimates, October 25, 1979.
33. A.W. Johnson, "The Treasury Board of Canada and the Machinery of Government of the 1970s," *Canadian Journal of Political Science* Vol. IV, 3 (September 1971), p. 365.
34 See Department of Finance, *The New Expenditure Management System* (Ottawa: Supply and Services, 1979) for a description of how the budgetary process was supposed to work under the Conservatives. Late in 1980, the Treasury Board, *Guide to the Policy and Expenditure Management System* (Ottawa: Supply and Services, 1980) provided a description of the Liberal government's plans for the budgetary process.
35. Douglas G. Hartle, *The Expenditure Budget Process in the Government of Canada* (Toronto: Canadian Tax Foundation, 1977), pp. 43-4.
36. Department of Finance, *The New Expenditure Management System*, pp. 6-7.
37. The following description is based upon the Treasury Board, *Guide to the Policy and Expenditure Management System*, Chapter 3.

38. See President of the Treasury Board, *Accountable Management: A Progress Report to Parliament* (Ottawa, March 1981), p. 2.
39. This arrangement is based upon the recommendations of the Lambert Report. For some assessment of the possibilities for parliamentary scrutiny of the Fiscal Plan, see Paul G. Thomas, "The Lambert Report: Parliament and Accountability," *Canadian Public Administration* Vol. XXII, 4 (Winter 1979), pp. 557-570.
40. See G. Bruce Doern, "The Federal Expenditure Budget Decision Process," in G. Bruce Doern (ed.), *Spending Tax Dollars: Federal Expenditures, 1980-1981* (Ottawa: School of Public Administration, Carleton University, 1980), pp. 199-211.
41. Douglas G. Hartle, *The Expenditure Budget Process in the Government of Canada*, p. 8.
42. Treasury Board, *Guide to the Policy and Expenditure Management System*, pp. 17-18.
43. Doern, p. 202.
44. Campbell and Szablowski, pp. 59-69.
45. See Douglas G. Hartle, *The Expenditure Budget Process in the Government of Canada*, pp. 22-25 in particular.
46. Rick VanLoon, "Reforming Welfare in Canada," *Public Policy* Vol. XXVII, 4 (Fall 1979), pp. 469-504.
47. *Estimates for the Fiscal Year Ending March 31, 1982* (Ottawa: Supply and Services, 1981), pp. 20-21.
48. Treasury Board, *Guide to the Policy and Expenditure Management System*, p. 16.
49. *The Lambert Report*, pp. 100-103. The Lambert Commission recommends that a modified "sunset approach" should be adopted for future new statutory programs. This would require that funding for new statutory programs lapse five years after their introduction unless Parliament authorizes continuation.
50. See *The Lambert Report*, Part V, "Accountability to Parliament: Closing the Loop," pp. 369-419.
51. The following discussion of parliamentary financial control is based largely upon two articles: Paul G. Thomas "The Lambert Report: Parliament and Accountability," *Canadian Public Administration*, Vol. XXII, 4 (Winter 1979), pp. 557-70, and Paul G. Thomas "Parliament and the Purse Strings," H.D. Clarke, et. al. (eds.), *Parliament, Policy, and Representation* (Toronto: Methuen, 1980), pp. 160-181.
52. See Douglas Hartle, "Canada's Watchdog Growing Too Strong," *The Globe and Mail*, (January 10, 1979), p. 7.
53. S.L. Sutherland, "On the Audit Trail of the Auditor-General: Parliament's Servant, 1973-1980," *Canadian Public Administration* Vol. XXIII, 4 (Winter 1980), pp. 616-645.
54. See Aaron Wildavsky, "A Budget for All Seasons? Why the Traditional Budget Lasts," in G. Bruce Doern and Allan M. Maslove, *op. cit.*, pp. 61-78.
55. Thomas P. Murphy, "Congress, PPBS, and Reality," *Policy Analysis*, Vol. I, 4 (Summer 1969), pp. 460-478.
56. Canada, Royal Commission on Government Organization, *Report*, abridged edition, Vol. I (Ottawa: Queen's Printer, 1962), p. 46.
57. See John W. Langford, *Transport in Transition: The Reorganization of the Federal Transport Portfolio* (Montreal: McGill-Queen's, 1976), chapter one, for an excellent discussion of Trudeau's philosophy of policy-making.
58. Hon. Edgar Benson, "The New Budget Process," *Canadian Tax Journal* (May-June 1968), pp. 161-7.
59. Canada, Treasury Board, *Planning, Programming, Budgeting Guide* rev. ed., (Ottawa: Information Canada, 1969), p. 8.
60. Auditor-General of Canada, *Supplement to the Annual Report to the House of Commons, 1975* (Ottawa: Information Canada, 1975), pp. 54-60.
61. Treasury Board, *Guide*, p. 26.
62. See Douglas G. Hartle, *A Theory of the Expenditure Budgetary Process* (Toronto: Ontario Economic Council, 1976), pp. 37-46 for a discussion of the three related purposes of PPBS.

63. Auditor General, *Supplement to Annual Report, 1975*, p. 47.
64. Aaron Wildavsky, *Budgeting* (New York: Little Brown, 1977).
65. Peter Pyhrr, "The Zero-Base Approach to Government Budgeting," *Public Administration Review*, Vol. XXXVII, 1 (January-February, 1977), p. 2.
66. Susan Salasin, "An Interview with Peter Pyhrr," *Evaluation*, Vol. IV (1977), p. 44.
67. Thomas P. Lauth, "Zero-Base Budgeting in Georgia State Government: Myth or Reality," *Public Administration Review*, Vol. XXXVIII, 5 (September-October, 1978), pp. 420-9.
68. The literature on ZBB has rapidly become voluminous. Some of the readily available works are the following: Garry D. Brewer, "Termination: Hard Choices — Harder Questions," *Public Administration Review*, Vol. XXXVIII, 4 (July-August 1978), pp. 338-43; Stephen L. Gould, Alan A. Oldall and Fred Thompson, "Zero-base Budgeting: Some Lessons from an Inconclusive Experiment," *Canadian Public Administration*, Vol. XXII, 2 (Summer 1979), pp. 251-60; Donald F. Haider, "Zero-Base Federal Style," *Public Administration Review*, Vol. XXXVII, 4 (July-August 1977), pp. 400-7; George A. Neufeld, "Learning from Zero Base Budgeting (ZBB)," *Optimum*, Vol. IX, 3 (1978), pp. 40-52; Allen Shick, "Zero-Base Budgeting and Sunset: Redundancy or Symbiosis," *The Bureaucrat*, Vol. VI, 1 (Spring 1977), pp. 12-32; and the section on budgeting in Frederick S. Lane (ed.), *Current Issues in Public Administration* (New York: St. Martin's Press, 1978), pp. 301-36.
69. Alan Shick, "The Road from ZBB," *Public Administration Review*, Vol. XXXVIII, 2 (March-April 1978), pp. 177-80.
70. E.J. Clynch, "Zero-Base Budgeting in Practice: An Assessment," *International Journal of Public Administration*, Vol. I, 1 (1979), pp. 43-64.
71. Thomas Lauth, *op. cit.*, p. 426.
72. Once again the literature on sunset laws is large. The following works are relied upon here: Robert Behn, "The False Dawn of Sunset Laws," *The Public Interest*, Vol. XLIX (Fall 1977), pp. 103-18; Steve Charnovitz, "Evaluating Sunset: What Will It Mean?" *The Bureaucrat*, Vol. VI, 3 (Fall 1977), pp. 64-79; and James Davidson, "Sunset — A New Challenge," *The Bureaucrat*, Vol. VI, 1 (Spring 1977), pp. 6-20. The House of Commons debated briefly a private member's bill to establish a Canadian sunset law. See House of Commons *Debates*, February 16, 1979, pp. 3332-9.
73. See Dean Crowther, "The Public Evaluation of Public Spending: The American Experience," in G. Bruce Doern and Allan Maslove (eds.), *op. cit.*, pp. 111-119; and James A. Thurber, "Congressional Budget Reform and New Demands for Policy Analysis," *Policy Analysis*, Vol. II (Spring 1976), pp. 197-214.
74. Lambert Report, p. 325 and p. 353.
75. Campbell and Szablowski, pp. 155-59.
76. Richard M. Bird, p. 10.

CHAPTER SIX

The Meaning of "Merit" in Canadian Public Administration

*by Robert B. Best**

O that estates, degrees and offices
Were not derived corruptly, and that clear honour
Were purchased by the merit of the wearer! —

— Shakespeare, *The Merchant of Venice*, Act II, scene IX, line 41.

Introduction

Ask almost any public servant about the merit principle or the merit system and you will probably receive a knowing nod and a quick reply. In the reply you will quite typically hear terms such as "best qualified," "most deserving," "most capable" and "best suited" used to describe a desirable goal within the public service, and terms such as "objective," "accessible" and "equitable" used to describe the appropriate means to that end. Reference may also be made to skill, knowledge, experience, education, seniority and physical capability in the attempt to explain the essence of the individual's concept of merit. Ultimately, merit appears as both a laudable goal and a noble procedure within the public service — the deliberate, careful seeking out of that person most qualified to perform most effectively the duties associated with a given position.

Implicit in the relationship between "best qualified" and doing the job most effectively is the notion that the first condition will produce the second — that superior qualifications engender superior performance. If this is accepted — and it is indeed the basis of the whole idea of merit in administration — then matters appear at the outset to be extremely simple. One needs only to examine a candidate's qualifications in order to predict his performance in the position to be filled.

*Robert B. Best approaches the topic of merit from two different but quite inter-related perspectives: first, from his 15 years of experience in personnel selection with the Manitoba Civil Service Commission where he was Director of Personnel for the major part of that term; and, second, from his more recent experience as Executive Director of the Manitoba Human Rights Commission. Mr. Best is presently a senior personnel executive with The Great West Life Assurance Company. He holds a B.A. from the University of Manitoba and a M.P.A. from the University of Winnipeg.

The matching of applicant qualifications to position requirements in order to achieve the most effective job performance is carried on continuously in public services and it has come to be known as the *merit system*. So, for example, a merit system will typically consist of such factors as job analysis, internal issuance of job vacancy bulletins and placement of newspaper advertisements, written examinations for applicants followed by screening interviews, selection committee interviews and reference checks. The goal toward which this system works is the awarding of the position in question to the most qualified applicant in the expectation that this person will most effectively perform the functions of the position. This goal has come to be known as the *merit principle*.

Neither the merit principle nor merit system are confined to the selection of staff for public service. For example, one definition of the merit system states it is " . . . a fair and orderly process for hiring, paying, developing, promoting, retaining, disciplining, and retiring people on the basis of ability and performance."[1] However, while the idea of merit may pervade the entire personnel function in government departments, it has traditionally been most closely associated with personnel selection activities, and it is on these that discussion here will primarily, although not exclusively, be focused.

Given widespread acceptance of the need to have the merit principle in the public service, and determination to pursue that principle through the merit system, employee selection would at face value appear quite simple. One determines the functions of the position, establishes the skills and/or knowledge necessary to perform the functions well, examines all applicants to determine their relative merits, and then appoints accordingly. Unfortunately for ease of employee selection, however, selection in practice does not usually, if ever, even closely approximate the theory. For example, assuming that qualification criteria are agreed upon, there is the fact that job requirements vary considerably from position to position, and from organization to organization. Professional positions, for example, require substantially different skills and knowledge from those important in, say, the clerical field. Within a single field, skill and knowledge requirements will vary from position to position and from level to level. Determining the exact job requirements and their nature becomes, in practice, a very complex, tricky endeavour.

Furthermore, *assuming* that both qualification criteria and job requirements have been agreed upon, there remains the fact that, very typically, those who are doing the evaluation will assign different weights to the same item in the candidate's background. Even when they arrive at a unanimous conclusion, there is a good chance that each has made his choice for different reasons.

In practice, the underlying, constant problem in applying the idea of merit as the basis for selection in order to achieve most effective performance is the fact that examiners often do *not* agree on qualification criteria, on what is meritorious. At times, there is profound disagreement over the criteria. This disagreement has traditionally occurred and remains over the criteria of education and experience, although both these today are being increasingly challenged by a variety of other, specific criteria which one might label the "humanistic criterion." In order to see the bare tip of the merit iceberg, consider the following:

A manager or personnel officer faced with 50 applications for one vacancy may very well opt for educational criteria as the major determining factor in assessing qualifications. He may do this consciously, but it can easily be an unconscious bias. Educational accomplishments are, after all, so visible, sought after and objective that they are almost unassailable as a concrete qualification to point the way to choice and to defend that choice should it somehow later be challenged. So the manager sedulously screens out those applicants whose forms do not show evidence of some established educational designation. Pushed very far, this procedure leads to transformation of the "best educated" into the "best qualified"—all in the name of merit.

However, by no means do all public service managers and personnel officers subscribe to the theory that educational credentials are synonymous with merit. On the contrary, many believe firmly in the maxim that experience leads to competence. These managers will screen out all those candidates who have not worked at related jobs for "x" number of years. And who can fault them for seeking people with all that solid work experience? In this fashion, the "most experienced" is transformed into the "best qualified" and, once again, the merit system is at work.

To be fair, it should be noted that most personnel selection officials do not rely exclusively on a single standard such as education, but rather they make use of a combination of perhaps several selection criteria to assist them in identifying the most appropriate candidates. Nonetheless, the difficulties arise when individual selection personnel exercise their right to choose people on the basis of those objective criteria. In applying the various standards to real people who rarely match the ideal, officials will tend to favor one selection standard over the others, be it education, experience or whatever, and thus undermine the importance of the rest of the criteria.

Furthermore, increasingly in recent years still other hiring authorities will play down both educational and experiential standards in favor of criteria related to race, language, color, sex and so forth. Their aim is to employ staff who are somehow more representative of the population at large than would otherwise be the case if the other two traditional criteria were utilized. The idea here is that, if the public service is to serve all in the nation appropriately and equally, then public servants should be drawn from the various socio-economic categories that comprise the population. Who, that is, is better qualified to comprehend and administer to the needs of people in these groupings than those who are themselves from and of these groupings? The "most representative" candidate is thus transformed into the "best qualified" and, once more, the merit system has prevailed.

It is in this fashion that public service hiring authorities arrive at often outrageously different conclusions about whom should be selected for a position, thus raising very serious, practical questions. For example, in the name of merit should people be appointed to the public service because they come from a particular ethnic group, speak a certain language, or because they participated in a certain war? That is, are these bonafide, competence-related qualifications? Can we possibly begin to answer such questions on grounds other than our personal values? And there remain the traditionally acceptable criteria of education and experience. Why does one manager emphasize education while the other swears by experience? Why do they end up selecting different people for the same job if they are both using an objective, rational decision-making system? Can it be that the concept of merit is actually susceptible to subjective interpretation and personal manipulation, even if unconscious?

To suggest that merit is associated with anything but the most objective criteria is to revile a concept which has carried with it an air of sanctity for many years. The alleged purification powers of merit have really been quite extraordinary when one considers the countless public service decisions which have been made in its name. How many hundreds of thousands of people in Canada alone have been appointed, promoted, trained and so forth on the basis of the merit system? It has taken on a mythical, even religious aura, and has resisted critical examination from many quarters. And, when you get right down to it, what in the world could replace the merit principle and the merit system?

The anomalies associated with the concept of merit have developed over many years through attempts to replace hiring, promotion and other personnel practices defined as undesirable with others that are good and proper. In this development, social, political and administrative reformers have usually made little if any attempt to define their conception of the term merit. Undoubtedly, it has meant to them something good, but beyond that attempts at definitional precision have seldom ventured.

Since the concept of merit today is both in theory and practice surrounded by ambiguities arising over the years, it seems appropriate to provide a brief history of public service reform in this country, indicating in passing the reasons for the entrenchment of the idea of merit in our administrative practices to the point that, although it is not clearly definable, it nevertheless appears ineradicable. This history includes a brief survey of related developments in Britain and the United States, since administrative practices in these two countries have had significant impact on Canadian developments. Furthermore, Britain and the United States have each pursued a certain definitional emphasis concerning merit, the definition of one tending to preclude the practices of the other. That is, the concern here is not for appreciation of history *per se*, but rather through the historical discussion the reader will, hopefully, gain an appreciation of the options that have been, are, and will be open to Canadians. There are indications today in Canada that significant unease, even unhappiness, surrounds the concept of merit in the public services. Not only does there remain the older tension between the experiential and educational emphases, but the newer humanistic emphasis, opposed to both, has made very significant inroads in Canadian public administration. The history of the concept of merit in the three countries suggests that, in the case of many proposals for reform, we and/or others have already been there and were not too happy about it at the time.

Thus, the importance of merit in the historical context should not be underrated. A careful analysis of the history of these three countries will reveal that a relationship may very well exist between changes in the concepts of merit and changes in the economic, social, political and military events that occurred. In some respects merit was, and is, a reflection of the times, and its changing nature would suggest that it is not in fact an absolute, static concept but rather an evolving, relative one. It might be noted for instance, how the three merit systems operated differently during periods of national emergency — how "war time" merit was at odds with "peacetime" merit, or how bad economic times brought about alterations to the merit principle. Similarly, as various groups in society put sufficient pressure on politicians, the merit principle was enlarged, in theory at least, to accommodate the demands, particularly with respect to public service employment. When bureaucracies seemed to become too large and unwieldy, elected officials intervened with their task forces and commissions to call for administrative reforms which almost invariably further modified merit operations and definitions.

Merit in Canadian public administration has been inescapably linked to both British and American reform movements over the past century and a half. Drafters of the original Canadian merit system legislation admitted openly that they were influenced by the systems in those two countries. And for almost 75 years since then, Canadian politicians and public servants have carefully observed the unfolding character of merit as evidenced in Britain and the United States. For example, one such observation of the contemporary American scene has led Canada to the point where it too has chosen to give more serious consideration to a concept which is not new, but which seems to have received more compelling attention in recent years — representative bureaucracy. Representative bureaucracy, in turn, it will be seen, is a modern manifestation of the same idea that President Jackson attempted to implement over 150 years ago, in the United States. Other interesting cyclical occurrences will be detected as the reform histories are traced.

Before commencing this brief historical survey, a word of caution is indicated with respect to the idea of *reform* attached to the concept of merit. Reform tends automatically to imply something good or better, or more precisely, it implies a change from one state to a more desirable state. However, and unfortunately for ease of discussion, reform, like beauty and probably merit, tends to be in the eye of the beholder, varying from person to person, place to place, and over time. In discussion here, effort is made to use the term reform in a neutral sense, as a synonym for change, leaving to the reader the choice of whether particular changes constitute something better or something worse.

Britain and the United States: Similar impetus but different paths to merit.

Canada's public service has undoubtedly been influenced in its evolution by the inheritance of British traditions, while the proximity of the United States has also led to a discernible impact by that country. In addition, the public service has been influenced in its development by a variety of indigenous factors. The result has been a Canadian public service, not purely British or American, but rather an amalgam reflecting external and internal forces in such a way that a certain uniqueness is achieved.

The period from the 1600s to the late 1800s in Great Britain was marked by a civil service dominated by the aristocracy, the hereditary nobility. Public service appointments were conferred upon the landed gentry, not on the basis of competence or even political patronage, but rather on the basis of family status and attendant wealth. Government positions could be obtained for cash and/or services rendered, and many positions, having become the property of the holders, could in turn be bequeathed to relatives. Although traces of patronage began to appear toward the end of the 17th century, the influence of class rather than political affiliation remained very strong. Fortunately for these aristocratic civil servants, administrative demands were not particularly onerous, and politicians were able to handle much of the required business personally within the laissez-faire economic environment.

By the end of the 18th century, conditions in Britain had changed significantly and attention was being directed to the administrative branch of government and its capacity to function effectively. There was a clear need for an administrative structure to meet the demands of a growing and changing nation. By 1830, the civil service had become an entity relatively distinct from the political arena—a status it achieved as a result of the tremendous quantity and complexity of public administrative business which cabinet ministers were beginning to hand down to their officials. With the probably inevitable changes in the demand for civil service personnel, a corresponding alteration appeared in the hiring of government employees. Political patronage gained a fairly secure foothold on the appointment system, and as the commercial classes began to displace the landed gentry as the dominant force in the country, the bourgeoisie made inroads into the civil service at the expense of the aristocracy. But while one apparently objectionable appointment system was being removed, concern was expressed from many quarters about its replacement. Was it indeed preferable to appoint public servants on the basis of their political association as opposed to their family/class connections? Did political allegiance in any way suggest competence and dedication in the performance of public service work? Could such a reward system satisfy the burgeoning demand for civil servants with varied technical and administrative backgrounds? The answer to these questions came clearly in a call for public service reform.

In 1853, Sir Stafford Northcote and Sir Charles Trevelyan presented a report entitled "The Organization of the Permanent Civil Service" which was to have profound effect on the future course of public service appointments in Britain and eventually in Canada. It marked the first time that formal recommendations were made to establish a selection process designed to evaluate a candidate's ability. That process then was " . . . to provide, by a proper system of examination, for the supply of the public with a thoroughly efficient class of men."[2]

Although the Report did recommend the implementation of competitive examinations for appointment to the Civil Service, it went on to suggest that the examinations be *literary* in substance. This latter suggestion was perhaps as significant as the former in that it was the birth of an association between classical education and appointment to the higher British civil service — a relationship that has endured to this day. Since the proposed examinations were based on knowledge that could only be acquired at the old universities, and since only the very wealthy could afford to send their children to these institutions, recruitment to the higher civil service was effectively restricted to a very small minority. The insistence on education in the classics stemmed from the belief that it provided a broad background and outlook, qualities deemed to be well-suited for public service administration. This belief was to benefit and sustain the upper middle classes in the higher positions of the civil service for many years to come. Wealth had thus replaced title as the underlying pre-requisite for appointment to the top-level British civil service jobs, and varying forms of educational achievement dictated entry to the lower, more routine positions. The British merit system, based on the objective criterion of education, was taking form. The underlying class bias of this educational criterion is discussed later on in the present Canadian context.

From 1855, when the first Civil Service Commission was formed in Britain, to the beginning of the war in 1914, the principles of the Northcote-Trevelyan Report were gradually extended and implemented as reform measures. Recruitment for public service vacancies came to involve public notices, written examinations for candidates, and competitive interviews before Selection Boards — methods not unlike those currently in use in all three countries of concern here.

The World War had two major influences on the British public service appointment process, one temporary and the other considerably more persistent. During the war years, entry standards to the public service were relaxed to allow for the more expeditious processing of recruitment demands, and open competitions were suspended until several years after the termination of the War. Also, and more enduringly, one of the first forms of statutory preferential treatment in appointments appeared when the British civil service held special examinations for returning veterans and reserved almost all of the vacancies for them. To the criterion of education for assessing merit was added the criterion of military experience.

This strong, almost absolute preference for veterans endured until after World War II when a government committee established to consider recruitment during the reconstruction period, rejected the idea of total access of veterans to all vacancies, putting administrative efficiency ahead of national obligation to servicemen.[3] A clear conflict over who was most worthy had developed — the merit principle and system were feeling sharp growing pains. Should those who had fought for their country be accorded rewards in the form of appointment to all public service vacancies? Or should such a restrictive practice, which effectively reduced the potential pool of recruitment, have been abolished in favor of open competition which in turn tended very strongly to favor another category of applicants? Wherein lay true merit? The solution in this instance was a compromise: major portions of vacancies were reserved for the ex-servicemen, provided they possessed the required education and were able to pass the special examinations. In this compromise, the elusive essence of merit was not to be revealed, but rather was further obscured.

Important to Canadian developments, a basic concept evolved in British public administration through its education-based examinations was that the generalist-trained administrator was better equipped to carry out the responsibilities of a civil servant than was the specialist-trained administrator. This concept remained pretty well unchallenged until the Report of the Fulton Committee in the 1960s.[4] The Report was critical of the generalist approach and members advocated (with a dissenting view) that greater emphasis be placed on relating the subject matter of preparatory educational studies to the functions of the public service position for which the person was being considered. In other words, the report recommended that the basis for selection shift from a generalized career focus to a specific position emphasis. Merit, it was suggested, should be redefined to incorporate the concept of specific job-relatedness in educational background, the latter a factor more familiar to public services in North America.

Today, public administration in Britain is based on recruitment standards which allow opportunity for those in the lower grades to advance to the higher without benefit of wealth or political connections. However, neither political patronage nor, certainly, plutocratic patronage were eradicated by changes over the years. Furthermore, the generalist nature of the higher civil service has withstood contrary recommendations, and those who point with pride to the service as the best anywhere are quick to attribute its quality to the generalist training and disposition of its top-level members. Merit, in Britain, emphasizes not just education as its primary criterion, but a certain *kind* of education.

The early American public service was also composed largely of the landed gentry, in spite of the efforts of many to combat any characteristics or actions which could be associated with British administration during the colonial period. That is, the ideal was officially said to be appointment on the basis of competence, but the practice distinctly tended toward a civil service dominated by members of the upper classes. For example, George Washington stated, "I must be permitted . . . to nominate such persons alone to offices, as in my judgement shall be the best qualified to discharge the functions of the departments to which they shall be appointed."[5] These high-sounding words, which could just as easily have been uttered by a current Public Service Commissioner, acquired curiously subjective aspects as he practiced his merit system over a period of time. Social status and prestige, for example, were not ignored in assessing suitability for office. Moreover, Washington considered political orthodoxy as an element of fitness for office, so partisan appointments were deemed virtuous if all of the other factors related to fitness were also present.

Subsequent chief executives institutionalized the practice of partisan appointments to the public service. Removal from office of political appointees became common with each succeeding administration, and the political and loyalty criteria in selection appeared to be given more and more weight. The system of partisan appointments sustained the predominantly aristocratic composition of the American public service, and this characteristic was not seriously questioned until the election of Andrew Jackson in 1828.

Ironically, the man who has been most frequently associated with the "spoils system," actually attempted to dislodge these aristocratic elements in the public service and replace them with a group more representative of the American people as a whole. He attempted, in effect, to democratize the public service appointment system. Jackson's advocacy of the "removal from office" or "rotation" principle was in the interests of destroying the concept of property or ownership of public service positions. In his first annual message to the people in 1829, Jackson expressed his concern that " in a country where offices are created solely for the benefit of the people no one man has any more intrinsic right to official station than another." He was later to make a statement which became much more celebrated and erroneously reported: with respect to the duties of public office, Jackson declared that they were "so plain and simple that men of intelligence may readily qualify themselves for their performance . . . ." Rather than belittling the role of the public service, Jackson was implying that such positions ought not be the exclusive reserve of the affluent, propertied class. His ideas are closely related to the concept of representative bureaucracy, a concept which will be discussed later.

Whatever his intentions, President Jackson solidified the spoils system, a system which was to endure for several decades and which created growing public discontent. By 1871, several public-spirited reformers had made recommendations for alterations to the public service appointment system, and an Act was passed providing for a Civil Service Commission and competitive examinations. It was not until 1883, however, that the Pendleton Act was passed which firmly established the foundation for the introduction of the current merit system in the United States. One of the main provisions of the Act called for the political neutrality of civil servants, and for their appointment and promotion on the basis of merit through competitive examinations. A mechanistic process was created to screen out appointments based on political considerations. Much more explicitly than the British, the Americans emphasized the view that politics had no place whatsoever in the selection of the bureaucracy. Politicians were to do their political things, and public servants were to do their administrative things. The politics/administration dichotomy, which implicitly if not explicitly remains a pervasive myth in British, American and Canadian public services, received its clearest enunciation and serious attempts were made to institutionalize it in practice.

Thus, the modern American merit system was conceived in the same context as that of the British, and as will be noted shortly, the Canadian. A mechanism was purposefully created to preclude certain undesirable elements from entering the civil service. The emphasis was on negative rather than positive factors, due probably to the recency and pervasiveness of the spoils system. Merit, in effect, became an expression of what was *not* wanted —keep the rascals out—but it had little to say about what *was* wanted for the civil service.

As the years went by, the American government and accordingly, the public service, became increasingly involved in a multiplicity of matters concerning society. The requirement for technically trained personnel grew rapidly, and the specialization of functions advanced rapidly along with a centralization of policy-making. Key professional, managerial and administrative positions demanded highly-skilled people to fill them, and there developed increasing doubt that the passive, plodding and rigid mechanism which administered the merit appointment process would be capable of fulfilling these demands.

Under President Franklin Roosevelt's New Deal administration, the United States civil service experienced a major expansion, but the new appointments were largely made outside the merit system.[6] The protective devices of merit were essentially sacrificed to facilitate the expeditious launching of government programs to deal with the problems produced by the Depression. In effect, and similar to earlier British experience, the interests of efficiency in public service appointments assumed temporary priority over the evils associated with political patronage. However, having used this unfettered appointment process to recruit an extraordinary group of energetic and able civil servants, Roosevelt then devoted his efforts to reinforcing the merit system which many claimed he had abused.

The United States government reacted to veterans of World War II along the same lines as pioneered by the British. Congress passed the Veteran's Preference Act in 1944 which assured veterans of both preference in initial appointment and retention in the public service once employed. The American merit system, curiously, was being directed by legislative mandate for perhaps the first time to adhere to a specific criterion in the appointment of personnel. It was a return, however, to the reward approach — veterans were accorded preference in appointments in recognition of their service to their country rather than on the basis of any job-related qualification. Service to one's country, however, appeared a much more palatable concept than that of service to a political party, as the new twist to the merit system seemed to meet with almost universal approval in the immediate post-war years.

In the 1950s and 1960s in the United States, as a result of changing social attitudes and attendant legislation and court decisions, policies of nondiscrimination were introduced into the federal civil service. Applicants for government jobs were henceforth not to be refused on the basis of their color, race, religion or national origin — all of which had been grounds for non-appointment under the merit system. With the support of Presidents from Truman to Johnson, it became clear that the civil service was to make positive efforts to bring about greater equality in the appointment system and thereby in the society in general. The Civil Rights Act of 1964 embodied in law the concept that all persons had an equal right to be considered for employment on the basis of their individual qualifications. In response to this act and other subsequent legislation which further refined the principle, public service bodies across the United States began to develop *affirmative action programs*. Adopting a multitude of euphemisms to sanctify the process, systematic attempts were made to give preference in hiring to minority groups who had been traditionally excluded or underrepresented in the public service.

In 1971, the Supreme Court of the United States ruled in *Griggs v. Duke Power Company* that selection tests used by an employer must measure a person for the job and not the person in the abstract. This ruling had a significant impact on the use of many selection devices which had been assumed to constitute valid means of applying meritocratic standards. What it meant, basically, was that if minorities were effectively excluded from employment opportunities as a result of employment tests, the onus was on the employer to show that the tests were manifestly job-related. The Court recognized in this decision that the mere use of apparently objective devices did not guarantee a wholly objective selection choice.

As affirmative action programs in the United States became more widespread, reactions from members of majority groups, male whites for example, became common. Their concern was that less qualified minority individuals were being selected over better qualified majority persons. In another Supreme Court case, *Allan Bakke v. The Regents of the University of California*, a white male claimed he had been wrongfully denied admission to the medical school because of an affirmative action plan which reserved 16 places out of 100 in each class for qualified members of racial minorities. Bakke was rejected while special applicants were admitted with lower admission test scores. In a split decision in 1978, the Supreme Court upheld the constitutionality of affirmative action programs but declared the admissions program of the medical school unconstitutional because it set aside a fixed number of places for minorities. In ordering Bakke's admission to the school, it contended that race is a factor which may be considered in admission decisions but it must not be the sole criterion. The fate of affirmative action in the United States was not particularly enhanced by this somewhat ambivalent pronouncement.

To complicate matters further, the Supreme Court appeared to reverse its approach in a more recent case involving *Weber v. Kaiser Aluminum*. Brian Weber, a white male, was denied a position in a training program which reserved 50 per cent of its opening for black employees as part of an affirmative action program. The majority decision of the court in this instance was that such a race-conscious affirmative action plan was not prohibited in that it was a temporary measure intended to bring about a percentage of blacks in the plant which approximated the percentage of blacks in the local labor force.

In spite of the rather rocky and uncertain road being travelled by Americans in the pursuit of equal opportunities in employment, changes in the composition of the workforce are being brought about. Employers in the United States are faced with two options: they can take voluntary action to change their system to accommodate women and minorities, or they can wait until they get sued. And some of the suits which have been successfully made against employers who have not complied have been financially devastating. A minority person can initiate a "class action" against an employer who is suspected of discriminating against a particular group. Awards in the form of backpay for unrealized promotions for several minority members represented by one complainant are not uncommon.

The American methods which can come down so heavily on the uncooperative employer's pocket book, are being closely observed by Canadians who to date have resisted the introduction of legislation to force the institutionalization of selection methods and standards on employers. Affirmative action programs in Canada are currently encouraged by various government bodies, but it remains to be seen whether or not the very different experience in the United States will move Canadian legislators to install similar compulsory measures in this country.

Canadians are also watching an innovative program which was introduced into the United States civil service to provide, as President Carter claimed, "greater management flexibility and better rewards for better performance without compromising job security." A new merit pay plan was installed for senior level managers which was to be based on their performance and contributions to their organization rather than on their length of service. President Carter's Civil Service Reform Act of 1978 was a bold attempt to tackle, among other things, a perceived deterioration of the merit system in the United States civil service.[7] The Act called for some 9,000 senior executives to be given the opportunity to trade off job security for the prospect of increased financial rewards and promotions based on job performance. Of these executives, up to 10 per cent could be noncareer. More freedom was given to demote, transfer or reassign those executives who did not measure up to required performance standards. But because of this freedom, some claimed the system was being made more vulnerable to instances of patronage activities and hence politicization — the "outstanding" performers, for example, could be viewed as those who were sympathetic with partisan measures. Nonetheless, the changes to the Senior Executive Service apparently were sincere efforts to reduce the rigidity imposed by the safeguards which had developed in the merit system, and to give more tangible recognition of superior performance.

It is still too early to evaluate the effect of the Carter reform measures in the civil service. The codification of the merit principle in law, while perhaps a commendable step, did not provide a clarification of how the principle could be effectively and consistently applied.

It is also too early to assess the impact which President Reagan's new policies will have on the merit principle and its system in both the public and private sectors. His concept of "deregulation" would seem to suggest that certain merit-sustaining government activities may not be as vigorously administered as they have been in the past, and that the plight of minorities in employment will not be enhanced in the process. But history has shown that hard economic times in the United States have often produced correcting mechanisms which, in relation to merit, have added to the complex nature of the concept.

Merit and the Canadian Experience

The development of merit in Canada shows some similarity with both Britain and the United States, as well as some differences. In Canada, as far back as 1839, Lord Durham expressed his concerns about the incompetence of the colony's civil service.[8] Certain modest reform measures were subsequently instituted, such as the establishment of individual departments and the creation of a Civil Service Examining Board. In the case of the examining system, however, examination of entrants to the civil service was not compulsory, and for that matter the tests used were quite impractical for identifying competent candidates for civil service positions. Political patronage was unquestionably the principal basis for appointment.

In 1868, one year after Confederation, the Civil Service Act was passed.[9] While at the time its purpose was deemed commendable, like attempts at reform in Britain and the United States, its practical application was inconsequential. The Act was designed "to limit the age and ensure the proper qualifications of candidates for positions in the public departments, to establish a regular classification, to provide for judicious promotion, to check the unnecessary employment of extra clerks, and guard against an undue expansion for civil government".[10] In actual fact, the "proper qualifications" of candidates for civil service jobs were determined by the politicians who continued to insist on partisan appointments in apparent disregard of the legislation.

Calls for reform continued and in 1877 a Select Committee brought forward a report which was sharply critical of the appointment system. It recommended open examinations to be administered and selections to be made by a commission of men from outside the civil service. These proposals were not legislated by Parliament, however, nor were other, subsequent reform bills calling for changes to the civil service appointment system. It was not until 1882 that Parliament passed a new Civil Service Act, this time providing for a three-member Board of Examiners who were to draw up lists of qualified candidates from which appointments were to be made. The catch was that while the Board administered examinations, the ministers did the appointing, and given the rather weak standards applied, the resulting field of choice was sufficiently large that political patronage could not only be practised freely but also now had a hint of legitimacy. That is, the Board gave the examinations, the politician then stepped in to make the appointment using the successful passing of the examination to justify his choice.

The turn of the century brought greater demands on the Canadian government: an increasing population, a rapid growth in technology and economic concerns — all contributed to the need for a larger, more sophisticated and more competent civil service. Based largely on the recommendations of the Courtney Commission of 1907, the government passed the Civil Service Act of 1908, a document which marked the true beginning of actual civil service change in Canada. The Act established an independent Civil Service Commission with the power of appointment and protection from undue influence. The majority of appointments were to be made through open, competitive, job-related examinations. Once appointed, civil servants were prohibited from engaging in partisan activities related to a Dominion or provincial election. Defenders of the Act insisted in Parliamentary debates prior to enactment that they had considered both the British and the American systems in formulating the provisions, the idea being, supposedly, that this Act contained the strengths and avoided the weaknesses of both. The basic purpose of the legislation, as suggested by one of its main proponents, was "...to create a tone in the service...due to the stimulus of the better class of people..." who through rigorous examinations, would enter the service "... by their own merit and not by favour."[11] However, while the majority of the members of Parliament of the time supported, at least in principle, the merit concept as an alternative to the patronage system, several questioned the effectiveness of the proposed examinations to provide a basis for the selection and appointment of civil servants. For example, did the mere passing of an examination, they wondered, guarantee that the person would be a competent civil servant? The significant question was there, but neither then nor subsequently did it receive a generally acceptable answer.

Although promising in theory and in its stated objectives, the Civil Service Act of 1908 did not bring about the desired end to partisan appointments. The Civil Service Commission, in spite of its mandate, was weak when strength was clearly needed to force change on established patterns of behavior. Moreover, the Act provided virtually no protection for public service positions outside of Ottawa, known as the Outside Service, and these outnumbered the so-called Inside Service by at least five to one. As a result, when the Conservatives defeated the Liberal government in 1911, thousands of employees of the Outside Service were removed from their positions. The optimism which had been expressed by the politicians for public service reform apparently was not, if left up to them, to be quickly transformed into reality.

Whether despite, or due to, the unspectacular results of the Act of 1908, reform efforts persisted from within and outside Parliament through to World War I. While the war took attention away from the issue of reform, the deleterious effects of the war years on the Canadian civil service system were evidenced by frequent gross inefficiencies and scandal. Out of this came a renewed pledge on the part of Robert Borden's coalition government to eradicate political patronage and bring about reform.

Three Orders-in-Council were passed in 1918 which spelled out guidelines and temporary regulations relating to such reform, and they culminated in the passage of the Civil Service Act in the same year. Under the terms of the new Act, the Civil Service Commission was for the first time to be responsible for appointments to almost all the civil service, including the Outside Service. The merit system, utilizing competitive examination, was to be the basis of appointment. Emphasizing the politics/administration dichotomy, the idea of which was prevalent at the time, political activity by civil servants was prohibited. But these provisions, for the most part, had been included in the 1908 Civil Service Act. What was significantly new was that the independent Civil Service Commission was to replace cabinet ministers as the body responsible for appointment and promotion. The Commission was also given a mandate to reorganize the civil service in consultation with deputy heads, and to introduce a new job classification system. Furthermore, implementation of the classification system was to have a subtle but important impact on the merit concept: appointment to most of the 1,700 classes became contingent on the passing of specific technical, job-related examinations as opposed to the more general academic-oriented tests of previous years.[12] It was a move from the British approach emphasized earlier in Canada to what was to become a distinctively American approach.[13]

The new image of merit was further influenced by the inclusion in the Act of provisions for the employment of returning veterans. The rationale for such legislated preference appeared to be basically twofold. First, there was the reward element whereby those who had defended their country were to be recognized in a meaningful way by a grateful nation – and what was more meaningful to a returning serviceman than the offer of a job. Second, there was the "equalizing" argument which held that servicemen were at a disadvantage during the War in that they were unable to receive the education and training necessary to qualify them for civilian jobs. On the other hand, those who were not in the Service were able to avail themselves of that education. To bring about equal opportunity, the disadvantaged veterans were accorded special preference in public service hiring. It was to be one of Canada's first experiences with a crude form of affirmative action.

The heavy responsibilities given to the Civil Service Commission strained its capacity to respond, and tensions developed between this central personnel body and the line departments, resulting in many circumventions of the Commission's authority and control. For example, departments called for and received exemptions for certain job categories from the provisions of the Civil Service Act. This left them free to appoint staff in these areas without the involvement and direction of the Commission. By 1930, approximately one-third of the civil service was again effectively outside the jurisdiction of the Civil Serice Commission.[14]

The Depression years in Canada also took their toll on the civil service. Dwindling revenues led to reduced administrative expenditures and a general slow-down in the hiring process. Concerns for merit gave way to the more pressing need for fiscal restraint. The many personnel activities controlled by the Civil Service Commission came almost to a halt.

World War II unquestionably expanded operations and therefore swelled the ranks of government employees, but most of the wartime agencies which emerged were created under emergency authority derived from the War Measures Act, and the administration of the merit system was compromised in the process. As a consequence, the rationality of the civil service structure was considerably weakened, and numerous classification, pay and recruiting anomalies developed.

In the years following the war, increased national wealth and productivity and expanding government activities emphasized demands for a more diversified, efficient and competent civil service. Several commissions were appointed to analyse the organization and operation of the civil service and make recommendations for improvements, particularly in the personnel management area. Walter Gordon headed one such commission in 1946 which found that there existed conflicting roles and authorities between the two central government agencies, the Civil Service Commission and Treasury Board. The Gordon Commission called for greater managerial autonomy in the departments and for more of a service-oriented central agency structure. This point was later taken up by A.D.P. Heeney in 1958 in a study entitled *Personnel Administration in the Public Service*. In his report, Heeney recognized the dilemma of allowing more, and beneficial, managerial freedom in the departments while maintaining the necessary central control to protect the merit principle in personnel operations.[15] He felt the merit system should be preserved, but that its essentially negative and defensive characteristics should be given less emphasis. The personnel and staffing function in government had gone beyond merely guarding the merit principle, and according to Heeney, this fact enhanced the creative role for the Civil Service Commission. With regard to veterans' preference, Heeney recommended its retention but with several qualifiers including the condition that the preference option be used *one-time* only by the veteran.

In spite of a less than enthusiastic reception from the newly-elected Conservative government, many of the Heeney proposals were incorporated into the Civil Service Act of 1961. That is, while it was considered important to make selections on the basis of merit, it was also seen as important that the competence of those already in the service be developed and maintained, rather than simply assumed after the initial entry. In the meantime, the Royal Commission on Government Organization (Glassco Commission) was busily re-studying, among other things, the personnel management system in the Canadian civil service.[16] It too struggled with the problem of reconciling the need for departmental autonomy with the still relevant merit principle and central control. However, the Commission felt that the machinery created to operate the merit system was so cumbersome that it jeopardized, rather than protected, the merit principle. The excessive number of controls resulted in long delays in filling positions, often less than competent candidates, and thoroughly frustrated departmental managers.

To remedy the perceived ills that had beset the civil service, and in the name of efficiency, the Commission recommended that departments be authorized to recruit and select their own staff for those positions with salaries above a specific minimum amount per year. The Civil Service Commission would retain recruitment authority for more junior positions and would certify all initial appointments to the civil service. Implicit in these recommendations was the notion that line managers were in a better position to select people for their own areas of responsibility than the more removed (albeit more impartial) central agency personnel officers. It was the "let managers manage" idea and a departure from the more mechanistic approach of the central recruitment and selection body. It recognized the importance of further involving the line supervisor in the process of determining how prospective applicants would "fit" into the group, and implicitly questioned the value of written examinations to reveal such things as interpersonal skills. Taking these recommendations at face value, it would appear that determination of merit, if not merit itself, was to vary according to position in the hierarchy. The recommendation would, in effect, have excluded a large percentage of employees from the institutionalized operation of the merit system.

It was not until 1967 that the Canadian Parliament passed legislation incorporating several of the Glassco recommendations, although the main reason for doing so then was to implement collective bargaining in the newly named Public Service. The Public Service Employment Act and the amended Financial Administration Act of 1967 delineated the personnel responsibilities of the new Public Service Commission and Treasury Board. The latter agency became the employer for the vast majority of public servants and, as such, assumed responsibility for negotiating collective agreements and for maintaining the classification system. The authority to develop personnel policy was also vested in the more powerful Treasury Board. On the other hand, the Public Service Commission, having been stripped of many of its responsibilities, was left with recruitment and selection, common training and appeals related to staffing and dismissals. The ambiguous long reign of the Commission as the supreme personnel management body was over. What remained were the vestiges of that defender of the merit principle, that enemy of the spoils system, whose place now seemed to some to be rather anachronistic. A new dawn had arrived — the negativism of the traditional approach was giving way to the increasing demand for competence, productivity, efficiency and professionalism in the public service. There remained a role for the Public Service Commission, but in practical terms the Treasury Board assumed an enormously influential role in the personnel field.[17] This was not simply a jurisdictional shift from one government body to another. Rather, it represented a major shifting of personnel functions from the supposedly neutral, objective Public Service Commission to the potentially partisan-dominated Treasury Board.

The Changing Concept of Merit in Canada Today

Three years after establishing the Royal Commission on Bilingualism and Biculturalism in 1963, Prime Minister Pearson announced in the House of Commons that "the linguistic and cultural values of the English-speaking and French-speaking Canadians will be reflected through civil service recruitment and training."[18] This effectively meant that another criterion — language — was to enter officially into the already ambiguous, conflictive meaning of merit in Canadian public administration. Whether this criterion is seen as added or subtracted depends on one's point of view, but the difference was not and is not an idle one. The allegedly neutral merit system had been discovered to have a strong language bias in that it favored the anglophone educational system. Was the solution to subtract the language bias by revising the recruitment standards to make them genuinely neutral, or was the solution to be the addition of a new factor — ability to speak French — to the official meaning of merit? The Pearson government, and later the Trudeau government, adopted the latter solution. Rather than attempting to ensure genuine impartiality toward language differences and allowing staffing practices to depend on a "linguistic laissez-faire", they attempted to make the ability to speak French in particular, and the ability to speak both languages in general, positive factors in the official definition of merit, thereby hoping to improve the lot of francophones in the public service. A new Public Service Employment Act and the Official Languages Act of 1969 paved the way for change in the public service by recognizing the equal status of the French and English languages. Reinforcement for such reform came from Prime Minister Trudeau in 1970 when he confirmed the government's acceptance of the broad objectives of the Royal Commission concerning French as a language of work in the public service. Moreover, he declared " ... that Canadians whose mother tongue is French should be adequately represented in the Public Service — both in terms of numbers and in levels of responsibility."[19]

The statements of policy concerning the official languages programs and the many administrative directives which followed from the central public service agencies, had a profound effect on the recruitment and promotion of staff. Given the disparities which then existed between the numbers of francophones as opposed to anglophones in the various occupational categories, a recruitment program of catch-up for francophones was clearly indicated. In addition, the government recognized the importance of offering an increased opportunity for civil servants to acquire linguistic competence through a programme of language training. Through these two basic measures, it was hoped that the objectives could be met of allowing the public servant to work in, and the citizen to be served in, the official language of his or her choice. To round out the plan, the government began the difficult task of identifying those positions in the public service which would be designated bilingual and those where competence in one language was sufficient. To designate a job bilingual was to have the effect of immediately precluding certain public servants who might have had superior job-related qualifications, but who did not speak a certain required language. The new requirement for linguistic ability to do the job undoubtedly tipped the balance in favor of those who were bilingual. Recognizing this as a disadvantage for certain unilingual employees, the government placed heavy emphasis on language training in the public service. The problems associated with the implementation of the language training programs were well documented in the 12-volume report by Dr. Gilles Bibeau.[20]

The early initiatives to improve the situation for francophones were met with considerable resistance. Charges of "reverse discrimination" were common, and many public servants expressed the sentiment that the merit principle was being clearly perverted in the interests of one group — the francophones. On the other hand, it was pointed out that it was under the merit system that francophones had lost ground over the years. The legislation of 1918 which outlawed patronage actually worked against the involvement of the francophone in the civil service in that French Canadian members of Parliament were then no longer able to recommend appointees to government positions. This prohibition, combined with the fact that the civil service qualifying examinations were based on the anglophone education system, resulted in the steady decline of francophones who were products of the

French classical system of education. From a proportional representation of 22 per cent of the civil service population in 1918, francophones dropped to 13 per cent in 1946, and then as a result of the special affirmative action initiatives of recent years, the figure rose from 22.3 per cent in 1971 to 26.5 per cent in 1979.[21] The latter figure corresponds roughly with the current percentage of francophones in the Canadian population, but is no reason for the government to be completely satisfied with the results. According to the 1979 Annual Report of the Public Service Commission of Canada, francophones in the Senior Executive category accounted for only 21.3 per cent of the employees, and they represented only 19 per cent in the Scientific and Professional categories. By contrast, francophones occupied 31.1 per cent of the Administrative Support positions in the Public Service. In spite of these rather uneven distributions in the occupational groups, the affirmative action programs of the government have unquestionably assisted francophones in gaining entrance to most levels of the bureaucracy. Concern has been expressed, however, about whether the initiatives that have been taken will have sufficient momentum to continue to improve francophone participation. For example, some people have pointed out that francophones are not well represented in the replacement pools for senior executive level positions in the Public Service. Moreover, downturns in external recruitment because of economic restraint, combined with relatively high resignation rates among francophones in the middle management positions, have given rise to speculation that francophone representation may decrease in the future. Continued affirmative efforts from such agencies as the Office of Commissioner of Official Languages, Treasury Board Secretariat, and the Public Service Commission will likely be evident in the future.

Although the Government of Canada is still striving to achieve its goal of a fully bilingual public service, the programs which have been introduced to that end have resulted in incontrovertible gains for francophones. The francophone experience demonstrates that more equitable representation can be attained if the government is determined to bring about the change. What is not completely clear in this instance is the reason why the last few administrations have consistently and aggressively pushed for greater francophone representation. Were they truly attempting to build a bilingual public service which would be more responsive and effective in serving its citizens? Or, were they really intent on establishing a bureaucracy which provided a greater number of opportunities for francophones? Or, more simply and importantly, were they trying to hold a country together? Perhaps all of these reasons and others make up the rationale for their actions. Whatever the reasons, the merit system was dramatically altered to effect the desired changes, and in the process, the merit principle has acquired a new dimension.

Thus, the disturbing anomaly that the merit system had created disproportionate representation of Canada's peoples in the civil service, moved politicians to legislate additional criteria for the merit principle and establish corresponding administrative policy. Not since the enactment of Veterans Preference had the Canadian Parliament seen fit to pass legislation to produce a conscious distortion in the merit principle.

The Public Service Employment Act of 1967 also affected the operation of the merit system by clearly prohibiting discrimination on the basis of sex. Prior to that time, as Kathleen Archibald's later report *Sex and the Public Service* was to reveal, the public service merit system, while hiring women, had relegated them to the administrative support categories.[22] So although about one third of the federal employees were female, over two thirds of that group occupied the lower paid positions. Since then, there have been several developments in the federal civil service which have tended to increase opportunities for the more than 92,000 women (in 1979) who have traditionally occupied these lower-paid support positions. In 1971, Prime Minister Trudeau responded to the report of the Royal Commission on the Status of Women by announcing the designation of a cabinet minister responsible for matters relating to the status of women in Canada. Subsequently, the Public Service Commission established an Office of Equal Opportunities for Women, and Cabinet issued a directive to all deputy ministers to take steps to encourage the placement of more women into middle and upper level positions. In spite of the many well-intentioned programs, however, results to date have not been outstanding. Only 50 women have broken through to the 1,339 senior executive positions, and only five women in the public service earn over $50,000 a year, compared to 165 men.[23]

Perhaps one of the reasons for this apparently slow progress can be found in the equivocal pronouncements of the Public Service Commission in its 1973 Annual Report. While acknowledging that there had been past discrimination against women, the Commissioners resolutely rejected the remedial measure of preferential treatment, by claiming they had no Parliamentary mandate for employing that concept. Instead, they reaffirmed their faith in "...staffing according to merit" as the "... key principle guiding the Commission in its activities."[24]

What the Commissioners appeared to be saying was that previous practices had no doubt been discriminatory against women. These practices had been developed under the merit system—that system had not been neutral on the subject of sex. However, the merit system now was going to be neutral on the subject, as it was not proper to correct the imbalance under the merit system. Here, at this point, the Commission was inconsistent and its views stand as an excellent example of the problems and anomalies involved in the definition of merit. The Commission was, in fact, pursuing two different notions in regard to merit, in that one emphasized the positive and one the negative nature of the concept. As noted in the case of language, French-speaking Canadians had been discriminated against by the allegedly neutral merit system. Since this was the case, the Commission was charged with reversing the recruitment and promotional bias by affirmative action programs devoted to strengthening the position of the French language in the public service and thereby redressing the balance. In the case of sex, however, although women too had obviously been discriminated against in very similar fashion by the merit system, the Commission felt it wrong for itself to engage in positive steps aimed at redressing the balance. Language balance, apparently, was a more compelling criterion than sexual balance — at least at this point in time. In any event, early efforts to break down the traditional attitudes and stereotypes which had militated against women were pretty well confined to research and educational activities. The posters, brochures and discussion groups which carried the equal employment opportunity message did little to change the status quo.

In November 1975, Treasury Board President Jean Chrétien announced that approval had been given for new policy and program guidelines concerning equal opportunities for women in the public service. Departments and agencies were directed to plan and implement affirmative programs which would produce "identifiable results," and Treasury Board and the Public Service Commission were to provide assistance and do periodic reviews of the plans and progress reports.[25] However, in spite of the government's directives, many departmental officials found it difficult to reconcile the concepts of representativeness and merit in theory and in practice.

The relatively short-lived Canadian Human Rights Commission has added to the push for improved conditions for women (and natives and other minorities) in the Public Service of Canada.[26] By investigating and attempting to settle complaints of discrimination in public sector employment, the Commission heightens the awareness of hiring officials with respect to the observance of bona fide occupational qualifications in the selection process. It has been argued, however, that the threat of the Commission's potential intervention has simply reinforced the safe reliance on credentials as a selection standard.

A secondary, but equally important role of the Canadian Human Rights Commission, has been to advance the principles of equal opportunity through educational and, at times, advocacy activities. As such, the Commission "consults" with the Canadian Public Service on such topics as affirmative action, and in so doing, performs a function analogous to that of an external pressure group.

Still another affirmative action program, one for native people, reveals an added dimension to the dilemma that has been developing with merit. A report in 1976 on Native People and Employment in the Public Service of Canada pointed out that while there was no strong evidence to indicate that the merit system purposely discriminated against the Native, " . . . the heavy emphasis on educational qualifications has undoubtedly played a major role in discouraging possible Native government employment."[27]

To deal with this problem, the federal government two years earlier had launched a Northern Careers Program with the purpose of achieving greater representation of native people in the public service north of the 60th parallel.[28] Native recruits were assigned conditionally to the Public Service

Commission where they received on-the-job training as well as formal education for a period of up to two years. After that, they competed for management jobs in the several departments in the North. For the purposes of entry, the Commission waived certain merit system requirements, especially those related to education. This move was particularly significant in that it recognized criteria other than education and job experience as being meritorious. In their place, substitutional qualifications such as knowledge of native customs, ways and languages were accepted, and for many of the positions which were under consideration, the substitutions were argued to be more legitimate — i.e., meritorious — selection criteria than those suggested by the older merit system.

Then, in 1978, the government approved another policy aimed at hiring natives in jobs throughout the Public Service. By June 1980, however, not even half of the federal departments had complied with requests for action plans, and the number of natives in public service jobs had not increased significantly. Disappointed with the results and the apparent apathy of the bureaucrats, Treasury Board President Donald Johnston suggested that deputy ministers' performance evaluations should be based in part on the number of indigenous people hired in their departments.

As recently as August 1980, the Government of Canada announced the development of a more general affirmative action strategy which is to involve, initially at least, three public service departments: Treasury Board, Secretary of State and Employment and Immigration. The plan is to improve the representation of women, indigenous people and the handicapped in the public service at all levels, and is to involve a comprehensive audit of existing employment barriers, and the design of new policies and programs to correct the effects of past discrimination. Treasury Board President Donald Johnston made it clear that the affirmative action initiatives would not include quota systems, but rather would incorporate *targets* for the employment of the designated groups.

Other public service programs for blacks and handicapped persons round out the general government objective to increase the participation of certain groups in the various activities of the federal bureaucracy. This raises the whole question of what is termed *representative bureaucracy* and its very problematical relationship to the concept of merit.

Representative Bureaucracy

We know from the administrative histories of Britain, the United States and Canada, that governments in the past have adopted measures to rid the public service of, or prevent the appointment of, certain elements: landed gentry, plutocrats, political partisans and incompetents. Emphasis has been on the negative — "keep the rascals out." More recent developments in public personnel administration have been related to more positive efforts to bring certain people into the public service. First it was the technician and professional (in North America at any rate), then it was the trained public administrator. In each instance, there was a planned effort to recruit people whose specific qualifications somehow corresponded to the demands and functions of the individual public service position.

In keeping with the trend toward positive recruitment initiatives in the public service, another phenomenon has surfaced which has created enormous implications for the merit principle. That phenomenon is known as "representative bureaucracy" and it is manifested in the numerous affirmative action and equal employment opportunity programs across North America which have been designed to bring about a more representative public service.[29] A representative bureaucracy is one in which there is an approximate correlation between the composition of the public service and that of society as a whole (or at least as it pertains to the constituency served). In other words, it would be expected that the public service would be made up of people whose group characteristics were present in a ratio which corresponded roughly to the societal group characteristics.

Several arguments are made for the rationale behind representativeness of appointed government employees.[30] Some claim that citizens from all groups have a right not only to be considered for employment in the public service, but to be served by public servants who come from their groups, who assist in the development and administration of public policy. Two positive accomplishments are claimed in the process: first, that the appointment system is made more "democratic" as the overrepresentation of the white, English-speaking middle classes is reduced, and secondly, that public policy is conceived with input from those who will be affected by the policy. In other words, the current preponderance of middle class representation in the public service presents a problem in the eyes of some. If power is in fact shifting to the bureaucracy from the hands of elected politicians and if bureaucrats are increasingly performing functions similar to those attributed by constitutional theory to politicians (e.g., acting as a broker of competing interests and making value judgments), is it not significant that public servants are drawn from a relatively narrow segment of society? Actually, the thrust of this notion is not new, as it essentially reflects the concern of early reforms in Britain and the United States to rid their public services of the aristocratic stamp. In this present case, the dominant element is the white, male, middle-class as opposed to the white, male, upper-class of earlier years, but the principle of representativeness is the same.

Implicit in the concept of a representative public service is the assumption that the public servant will actually function on behalf of, or in the interests of, the group from which he or she originally came. Since one of the justifications for the concept is that public policy will be developed and administered by someone who is intimately familiar with the group's problems and wishes, it should follow that that representative does indeed respond to those concerns. Otherwise, the apparent value attributed to representativeness is largely lost. What remains is an apparently democratic appointment system.

In order to derive much of the benefit of a representative system, then, the public servant must become a kind of advocate for his or her group of origin. But how far down into the social structures of society does one reach for adequate representation in the bureaucracy? What about subcultures and groups within groups, do they not have a democratic right in this system to be represented in the policy-making process? In what numbers and to what degree? If all of the group representatives in the public service are pulling for the interests of their own groups, who is looking out for the broader national issues which touch all citizens? And perhaps most significantly, who resolves the multifarious disputes and contentious claims upon the limited resources of the state?

There must also be some element of doubt in the proposition that persons chosen to represent certain interests in the public service can be expected to maintain that advocacy role indefinitely. After all, they become part of another group — the bureaucracy — in the process, and who is to say they will not undergo a further socialization which will alter their perceptions and priorities. Results of an empirical study done on the United States civil service revealed that " . . . apparently, agency socialization tends to overcome any tendency for the supergrades to hold attitudes rooted in social origins."[31] This whole idea related to the strongly middle class nature which is alleged to characterize bureaucracy, is discussed in Chapter 3. It could be argued, however, that the nature of the public service position could determine how long and how closely the public servant identified with his or her group of origin. Public servants who deal frequently with members of their group in a direct service capacity, might retain their values and sympathies longer than those who occupied higher-level and more isolated positions. Social workers, for example, could conceivably be more effective in dealing with members of their own group by virtue of their basic understanding of the cultural and social norms. Nevertheless, there is a lingering doubt as to whether or not the representatives would faithfully and accurately reflect the wishes of their groups in the public service. Many would say that such functioning is not important, that what is significant is the fact that the composition of the public service is tied to the make-up of the people served, and that government employment is truly made accessible to the members of all groups.

How does this concept of a representative public service fit in with the merit principle and its "system"? To answer this question we first should examine the group characteristics of those employees who currently comprise the many public services across the country. In most, if not all of the jurisdictions, we would find severe imbalances of group representation, particularly at the senior levels.[32] We might question how such uneven distributions have come into being—through discriminatory hiring practices? Or are those public servants in fact the best qualified to perform the jobs, even though they almost all belong to the majority class in their society? Does that fact, by corollary, make the unrepresented minority group members less qualified to do those public service jobs? In a sense there may be some substance to all of these propositions, albeit in a perverse way.

In the first place, modern merit systems lean heavily on education as a selection criterion. Education enjoys the advantages of relative objectivity, achievement orientation, easy identification for selection officials and popular acceptance as a selection standard. It was the apparently objective nature of education that appealed to public service reformers of the past who wanted to introduce measures to preclude favoritism in the hiring process. Moreover, it became one of the few tangible traits that could be assessed by hiring officials and later used to justify their choices.

The one disadvantage arising from the use of education as a selection criterion is that the members of many minority groups, for whatever reasons, have not obtained the same levels of training in the same numbers as those in the majority groups. The result has been that public service hiring systems, using the apparently objective educational criterion, have produced an uneven distribution of representatives in the bureaucracy. However, this apparent anomaly could be as much an indictment against the social and educational systems as against the public service appointment system. If in fact the members of certain groups in a society have greater access to the institutions of higher learning for reasons other than their basic intelligence, it follows that those groups will be appointed to the public service in greater numbers than those who do not have the same opportunity for advanced education.

To remedy these inequities in the interests of a more democratic public service, governments could consider two alternatives. They could focus on the educational system itself and try to transform it into something much more accessible and desirable in the hope that people of all different origins and means would avail themselves of the opportunities for education. Or, governments could reexamine the need for formal education as a selection criterion in public service appointments. In both cases the differentiating function of education in the selection process would diminish—but what would replace it?

Some people would suggest that related job experience be substituted for education as a selection criterion. But how does one get started in a particular career if only those who have done the job before are considered for public service vacancies? Here, indeed, is a Catch 22 situation. And are years of experience necessarily synonymous with competence? How about those people who have been only marginal performers for decades, but nobody will terminate them because of their seniority? Are they the best qualified to receive the higher bureaucratic positions?

Advocates of a representative public service would press for the appointment of more persons from various groups who are not proportionately represented. In essence, they would be recommending the use of ascriptive criteria such as ethnic, racial and/or religious backgrounds to determine the selection decision. Yet it was the use of such ascriptive criteria which historically created the problem in the first place and which led to the adoption of the merit system. It seems we have come full circle.

Nonetheless, for certain public service positions, a case could be made perhaps for considering the ethnic or racial backgrounds of people if they were required to deal closely with clients of the same origin. In this instance, however, the rationale for appointing such persons would be that the ascriptive factor is job-related—that public servants with backgrounds similar to those they served would in fact do a more effective job.

The seemingly difficult task of reconciling the concepts of merit and representative bureaucracy is evident in the Canadian government attempts to increase the participation rates of minorities in the public service over the past decade. Reflecting on those frustrations, the Public Service Commission of Canada observed in its 1979 Annual Report that the administration of the merit system was becoming progressively more difficult " . . . because of language issues, elaborate procedures and regulations in documentation and the aspect of human rights."[33] If the merit system were an objective and precise instrument for identifying those most worthy to work in the public service, would not human rights be automatically respected, and would not the public service be in fact a truly representative organization? Is acknowledgment of the latter statement an admission that the current system, because it has not produced a representative bureaucracy, has used biased and discriminatory methods of selection? The answers are by no means clear, and there is little to suggest that substantial clarification will come in the near future. In the meantime, the debate about merit and representativeness continues.

The Influence of Recent Special Reports

In the past couple of years, two important government studies have taken place which could conceivably alter the way in which the merit principle is administered in the Canadian public service. The first of these was a study done by the Royal Commission on Financial Management and Accountability, and the resulting Lambert Report of March 1979, which recommended that the historically sacred staffing function of the Public Service Commission be transferred to a Board of Management (a new name proposed for a reorganized Treasury Board). Legislation of 1967 had already removed many of the personnel management responsibilities from the Commission, but now its last major function was being placed in peril by the recommendation. The Royal Commission claimed that this move was necessary to clarify central management responsibilities and to bring about a closer tie between personnel and financial operations.[34] A denuded Public Service Commission would retain the appeal function and would monitor appointments according to the proposal, but would otherwise lose control over the central recruitment, selection, appointment, transfer, promotion, demotion and release of public servants. Implicit in the recommendation was a deduction that political patronage no longer represented a significant threat to the merit system, and as such, did not require an independent body to be responsible for discouraging political appointments to the public service.

Although the Lambert Report did suggest structural changes which could affect the merit system, it left the more difficult task of an in-depth analysis of the merit principle to the Special Committee on the Review of Personnel Management and the Merit Principle under the Chairmanship of Guy R. D'Avignon. After almost two years of work, which consisted largely of interviewing and meeting with hundreds of people across the country representing employees, unions, interest groups and central agencies, the committee presented its report to the government in September 1979.

The Committee concluded that the many regulations and administrative operations that had developed in the name of the merit principle had become dysfunctional in that they were placing the efficiency and effectiveness of the public service in peril. They called for the retention of the merit principle, but they believed the merit system which had been used for years was in need of a transformation, and this necessitated a "reinterpretation of merit."[35] One recommended change was for the determination of merit to be based on a candidate's qualifications to assume broader public service career responsibilities in addition to the job for which he or she was initially being considered. This constituted a distinct shift toward the British recruitment system.

A point made several times in the Report is that "sensitivity to the public" is a critical constituent of merit, and that it should be considered as a selection standard for appointment and promotion. Undoubtedly prompted by the popular and persistent perception of the bureaucracy as impersonal, uncaring and unresponsive toward the individual citizen, they recommended that public servants be selected and evaluated partly on the basis of how successfully they deal with the public.[36] In this regard, a public servant performing a "giving" function such as awarding a government contract to a company or handing out a welfare cheque to an individual is in a decidedly better position than the public servant who must perform a "taking" or regulatory function such as collecting taxes or frisking potential smugglers at border crossings. The latter group of employees could be charming, patient, understanding and flexible and still be the subjects of virulent condemnation by the citizen recipients of the service. And consider the problematical nature of measuring such sensitivity in the public servant—a formidable task for any manager.

Despite the obvious difficulties associated with the question of sensitivity to the public, it is a matter of very real concern for public service managers. But if this characteristic or behavior of the employee is to be encouraged, it is only fair that the attendant consequences of rule-bending, regulation-stretching and preferential treatment would not be unduly discouraged while he is attempting to ingratiate himself with, or be sensitive to, the public.

Of particular interest was the way in which the Special Committee dealt with the perplexing concept of a representative public service. First of all, they acknowledged the legitimacy of the concept, then they offered a novel suggestion for its implementation. Merit, they claimed, "...can and should be temporarily suspended by parallel provision for special treatment of members of designated groups in support of eventual real equality of opportunity."[37] So in this instance, the merit principle was not being further expanded to encompass equal employment objectives, but rather it was being temporarily set aside in order that the other principle could operate. The Committee went further in its efforts to enshrine the new principle of special treatment for the members of certain groups. They recommended amending the Public Service Employment Act to allow preference in appointment for members of designated groups with minimum qualifications, and for the "suspension of certain qualifications" which could later be obtained through training on the job.[38] The merit principle, according to the Committee, was to remain, but it was to operate along with other principles such as equality of opportunity, efficiency, effectiveness, sensitivity, responsiveness and equity.[39] In addition to these criteria, seniority was to be considered in those situations where other basic qualifications were considered approximately equal.

By characterizing these principles as coexistent with the merit principle, however, the Commissioners did not really come to grips with the problem that there were basic conflicts among them. The merit system, for example, could not readily accommodate the principle of representative bureaucracy. Moreover, the complicated administrative machinery necessary to provide *equity* for employees did not fit easily with the *efficiency* principle. The system allowing for appeals on selection decisions, for example, has seriously prolonged and encumbered the recruitment and selection process. Moreover, it has created the need for an ever-more precise definition of merit, lest the appeal body be accused of second-guessing the original decisions unfairly. And not insignificantly, the possibility of a selection decision appeal has perhaps made those responsible for selecting staff too "credential" oriented in their approach and more concerned about the consequences of an appeal than the acquisition of a competent employee. Something has to give. If equity is emphasized, efficiency, and perhaps merit, may suffer; if efficiency is eagerly sought, the principle of equity is jeopardized. (Of course, this all depends to a significant degree on just how we define efficiency. See Chapter 3.)

In a way, the Committee fell prey to the same disease which they claimed had plagued the public service: an inability to define goals so as to make them clear and unequivocal. In their attempt to embrace all of the various principles they felt were worthy of recognition, they neglected to follow through on the implications of their recommendations. If they thought public servants were confused before, they might be disappointed to learn that their suggested reforms would likely not serve to elucidate the major roles of the public service in a practical way. The ambiguity pervading the report may, in fact, lead to more rather than less confusion among public service personnel.

This is not meant to imply that the D'Avignon Report was not an earnest effort to grapple with a multi-faceted problem in the public service in a manner which recognized the changing times. The future activities of the Public Service of Canada with respect to the merit principle will probably not be uninfluenced by the work of this Special Committee. However, in these times of economic restraint and unemployment coupled with public service declines in population, the definition of merit is likely to remain a matter of considerable contention. With the battle over language rights in the public service not definitively won in favor of bilingualism, the federal government has begun to ease out of the expensive bilingual programs. There is bound to be continuing, perhaps even severe, tension over the matter. Much more obviously, the struggle for sexual equality has to date achieved little concrete redressing of the male bias in the public service, and one suspects this will be a contentious point for years to come. Native rights to public employment will surely continue in a problematical vein. In fact, the whole exercise of the D'Avignon Committee points to the continuing problematical nature of the allegedly neutral concepts of the merit principle and the merit system. Merit indeed appears to be in the eyes of the beholders, and not only do present beholders disagree profoundly on the subject, through replacement of generation by generation constantly changing emphases can be expected to occur.

Conclusions

The merit system was developed primarily as a mechanism to prevent the appointment of first privileged and then politically partisan persons to the public service. It was conceived in recognition of a politics/administration dichotomy which held that politicians alone determined policy matters and public servants alone executed those policies. In other words, the political process and the administrative process were assumed to be separate. Public servants, it was thought, had no business in the activities of policy-making and conversely, politicians had no role to play in administration. To bring about these conditions, public servants had to go about their duties in a quiet, neutral fashion, and politicians had to be effectively excluded from the selection of these employees. It was within this context that our current merit system began to emerge almost a century ago.

Interestingly enough, this anti-politics aspect of the merit system has persisted to this day in spite of an almost universally accepted view that a politics/administration dichotomy does not in fact exist, that bureaucracies do influence policy-making and that politicians do become involved in administration. Today it is just not reasonable to imagine senior public servants, for example, not making significant inputs into the various public policies which are ultimately announced by elected officials. And yet the merit system vigilantly guards the appointment process to ensure that the politicians are totally uninvolved in the selection of those people upon whom they will be relying for crucial policy-related information and advice. There is an implicit assumption that if the politicians were involved, they would automatically choose political "hacks"—people whose only claim to fame was their political allegiance.

While this kind of patronage was unquestionably prevalent during the period when the modern public service was taking form, there is some argument that it would not repeat itself today. First, the public service has grown so large that cabinet ministers would find it very difficult to become actively involved in making patronage appointments to departments, many of which contain thousands of employees. Second, it is also contended that the tremendous advances made in the communication media make it exceedingly difficult for politicians to commit any serious errors which are not detected and broadcast to the nation within hours. Such careful scrutiny of their actions would probably have the effect of keeping blatant and objectionable partisan appointments by politicians to a minimum. Third, many of the positions in the public service today are far more sophisticated and demand much more training, skill and experience than those which existed before the turn of the century when patronage was fashionable. The poorly qualified political appointee of today, it is argued, is much more apt to become recognized and censured for his or her incompetence, and is usually the victim of termination somewhere down the line.

In view of the commonly held contemporary perception that public servants are in fact real, though perhaps invisible, participants in the policy-making process, and given the fact that politicians have a vested interest in seeing that policies are carried out in an effective way and will become involved in administration to that extent, it becomes evident that the politics/administration dichotomy is indeed a myth. In these circumstances, the original rationale for the merit principle and system is considerably weakened. In earlier times, merit was seen simply as non-political appointment in the public service. Today, as noted, merit has assumed much broader and much more complex characteristics and meaning. But the original prohibitive nature of merit which remains to this day, has created an interesting one-way street: bureaucrats freely participate in the policy process on a regular basis, but politicians, because of the merit system, are prevented from participating in the selection of the bureaucrats and, in some instances, are even impeded in their attempts to direct the public servants who work for them. An important exception to this, of course, is the right of Cabinet to select and appoint deputy ministers of their choosing. Nonetheless, at least some of the frustrations which elected officials and the public experience with the bureaucracy stem from the negative vestiges of the merit system.

As merit began to take on a more positive aspect in its meaning and application, the number of problems did not diminish. The virtuous, rather Diogenical, quest for the "best qualified" created a brand new set of difficulties. In spite of the many endeavors to make the merit selection system an objective one, unconscious distortions invariably crept into the works. Written examinations were used, selection committees were formed, reference checks were made, but in each instance, the subjective element was present. Those who took pride in using this marvellous objective merit instrument to select public servants did not realize the extent to which they were injecting their own cultural/social norms into the measuring process. Studies conducted on the results of employment interviewing, for example, reveal that selectors are influenced in their decisions by biases and stereotypes, and that the traits of the interviewers are more important in the selection decision than are the traits of the applicants.[40]

In the Canadian Public Service, various systems were put in place to ensure that equity prevailed in the appointment process. An elaborate appeal mechanism, for example, was installed to provide redress for those disappointed employees who felt that they should have been selected for the job, that their merit had been improperly or inadequately judged. An inevitable reaction from those doing the selecting was to identify criteria which might not have been directly relevant in terms of predicting job performance, but which were eminently suitable for defending their decisions. Formal education was greatly emphasized for almost all jobs in the public service. Its clean, clear, concrete and objective qualities were very useful to point to if one was called upon to justify a disputed selection. For many, even to this day, the "best qualified" has become synonymous with the "best credentialled," and while there are some public service positions for which extensive and specific graduate education is required, the emphasis on the criterion of education even for manual jobs, has bordered on the ludicrous.

From a certain perspective, the biggest embarrassment of the merit system has been its failure to produce a public service that is even remotely representative of the various groups which make up our society. Special programs have had to be devised in order to bring unrepresented and underrepresented groups into the public service, and even these affirmative measures have not as yet resulted in significant gains for those so designated. It could be argued that both francophones and women populate the public service in numbers which approximate their ratio in the total population, but they still occupy, to a large degree, the lower echelons of the hierarchy. Thus, the D'Avignon Committee recognized the practical difficulty of marrying representativeness with merit and recommended that the principle of equality of opportunity be considered "supplemental to merit."

It is interesting to speculate just what would happen if all of the major social collectivities that had experienced problems of access to public service positions in Canada were accorded representative privileges, and representatives were to perform advocacy functions on behalf of their groups. Pluralists would have us believe that such a situation would be an appropriate, logical outcome of the political/administrative process. Out of the interaction of the various represented groups would emerge the public good. Opponents of pluralism would not accept the prediction that the bargaining and competing of represented groups would be self-correcting, and that one group would be checked by another. Instead, the result would be imperfect competition in which a small number of powerful groups would still dominate. In any event, the answer may never be known given the impracticality of the suggestion that all social groups in Canada *could* be represented in the public service.

In the final analysis, merit is largely a matter of who defines it and who uses it at any given time. The merit system does contain certain physical elements which have remained basically unchanged—the competitive examination, for example—but the actual substance of merit probably changes each time some one person or a group of people set out to select a candidate for a job vacancy in the public service. Human beings are not automatons who respond entirely objectively to situations, they are people who have strengths and weaknesses, passions and prejudices, and vastly different points of view. As long as this is the case, and as long as people continue to be responsible for the evaluation of other people, the concept of merit will remain suspect. In this regard, one need only consider the incredible, enduring nature of the personal interview in the selection process, in spite of its questionable value as a predictor of successful performance. Properly fed computers could surely more objectively and effectively choose the best qualified candidate for the job. But the "chemistry" would be missing — that inexplicable feeling that one human being has about another— and the whole process would somehow be rendered rather inhuman.

As a guiding principle the concept of merit has been unassailable; as a working system it has had its fair share of hurdles to overcome. Its inherently problematical nature does not bode well for consistent future application in the Canadian public service in spite of the well-intentioned efforts of many officials and interested observers to refine merit to its most workable form. It may even come to pass that, in the face of seemingly unfulfilled expectations, frustrations and deficiencies, the entire concept of merit will be removed from the public service. However, what could possibly replace it is unstatable in the absence of a crystal ball.

For Further Reading

BOOKS AND REPORTS

Archibald, Kathleen. *Sex and the Public Service*. Ottawa: Queen's Printer, 1970.

Beattie, Christopher. *Minority Men in a Majority Setting*. Toronto: McClelland and Stewart, 1975.

Bendix, Reinhard. *Higher Civil Servants in American Society*. Westport: Greenwood Press, 1949.

Blau, Peter M. and M. W. Meyer. *Bureaucracy in Modern Society*. New York: Random House, 1971.

Campbell, Colin and George Szablowski. *The Superbureaucrats: Structure and Behaviour in Central Agencies*. Toronto: Macmillan of Canada, 1979.

Campbell, G. A. *The Civil Service in Britain*. London: Duckworth & Co., 1965.

Canada. *Report of the Special Committee on the Review of Personnel Management and the Merit Principle*. Ottawa: Supply and Services, 1979.

———. Royal Commission on Financial Management and Accountability. *Final Report*. Ottawa: Supply and Services, 1979.

———. Royal Commission on Government Organization. *Report*. 5 vols. Ottawa: Queen's Printer, 1962.

———. Civil Service Commission, *Personnel Administration in the Public Service*, Ottawa: Queen's Printer, 1958.

———. Royal Commission on the Civil Service, *Report*, Ottawa: King's Printer, 1907.

———. Royal Commission on the Status of Women, *Report*. Ottawa: Information Canada, 1970.

———. Public Service Commission, *The Employment of Women in the Public Service of Canada*, Ottawa: Supply and Services, 1973.

———. Treasury Board. *Increased Indian, Metis and Non-Status Indian and Inuit Participation in the Public Service of Canada*. Ottawa: Supply and Services, 1977.

———. Native People and Employment in the Public Service of Canada. *Report*. Ottawa: Impact Research, 1976.

———. Honorable Marc Lalonde. *Status of Women in Canada*. Ottawa: Information Canada, 1975.

———. Royal Commission on Bilingualism and Biculturalism, *Report*, Ottawa: Queen's Printer, 1965.

Canadian Federation of Government Employee Organisations. *Merit Recruiting in the Public Services of Canada*. Halifax: The Federation, 1965.

Carpenter, W. S. *The Unfinished Business of Civil Service Reform*. Princeton: Princeton University Press, 1952.

Cayer, Joseph. *Public Personnel Administration in the United States*. New York: St. Martin's Press, 1975.

Chapman, Richard A. *The Higher Civil Service of Britain*. London: Constable, 1970.

Chartrand, P. J. and K. L. Pond. *A Study of Executive Career Paths in the Public Service of Canada*. Chicago: Public Personnel Association, 1970.

Civil Service Department. *Report — on The Civil Services of North America*. London: Her Majesty's Stationery Office, 1969.

Cohen, E. W. *The Growth of the British Civil Service 1780–1939*. London: Archon Books, 1965.

Cole, Taylor. *The Canadian Bureaucracy*. Durham: Duke University Press, 1949.

Corson, J. J. and R. S. Paul. *Men Near the Top: Filling Key Posts in the Federal Service*. Baltimore: John Hopkins Press, 1966.

Dawson, R. MacGregor. *The Civil Service of Canada*. London: Oxford University Press, 1929.

Donovan, J. J. ed. *Recruitment and Selection in the Public Service*. Chicago: Public Personnel Association, 1968.

Downs, Anthony. *Inside Bureaucracy*. Boston: Little, Brown and Company, 1966.

Dunnette, Marvin D. *Personnel Selection and Placement*. Belmont: Brooks/Cole, 1966.

Fish, Carl. *The Civil Service and Patronage*. New York: Russell & Russell, 1963.

Gardner, J. N. *Excellence: Can We Be Equal and Excellent Too?* New York: Harper, 1961.

Gerth, H. H. and C. W. Mills. *From Max Weber: Essays in Sociology*. New York: Oxford University Press, 1946.

Gladden, E. N. *Civil Services of the United Kingdom*. New York: Augustus M. Kelley, 1967.

Harvey, Donald. *The Civil Service Commission*. New York: Praeger, 1970.

Hodgetts, J. E. *Pioneer Public Service: An Administrative History of the United Canadas*. Toronto: University of Toronto Press, 1955.

———. *The Canadian Public Service: A Physiology of Government 1867-1970*. Toronto: University of Toronto Press, 1973.

———, et al. *The Biography of an Institution, The Civil Service Commission 1808-1967*. Montreal: McGill-Queen's University Press, 1972.

Hoogenboom, Ari. *Outlawing the Spoils*. Urbana, Ill.: University of Illinois Press, 1968.

Judek, Stanislaw. *Women in the Public Service*. Ottawa: Queen's Printer, 1968.

Kelsall, R. K. *Higher Civil Servants in Britain*. London: Routledge and Kegan Paul, 1955.

Kernaghan, Kenneth, ed. *Public Administration in Canada: Selected Readings*, 3rd ed. Toronto: Methuen, 1977.

———. *Bureaucracy in Canadian Government*. Toronto: Methuen, 1969.

Kingsley, J. Donald. *Representative Bureaucracy: An Interpretation of the British Civil Service*. Yellow Springs, Ohio: The Antioch Press, 1944.

Kranz, Harry. *The Participatory Bureaucracy*. Lexington: Lexington Books, 1976.

Krislov, Samuel. *Representative Bureaucracy*. Englewood Cliffs: Prentice-Hall, 1974.

Mainzer, Lewis. *Political Bureaucracy*. Glenview, Illinois: Scott, Foresman, 1973.

Meriam, Lewis. *Personnel Administration in the Federal Government*. Washington D.C.: Brookings Institution, 1937.

Milton, Charles R. *Ethics and Expediency in Personnel Management: A Critical History of Personnel Philosophy*. Columbia: University of South Carolina Press, 1970.

Mosher, Frederick C. *Democracy and the Public Service*. New York: Oxford University Press, 1968.

Niskanen, W. *Bureaucracy and Representative Government*. Chicago: Aldine-Atherton, 1971.

Olsen, Dennis. *The State Elite*. Toronto: McClelland and Stewart, 1980.

Parris, Henry. *Constitutional Bureaucracy*. London: Allen and Unwin Ltd., 1969.

Peters, B. G. *The Politics of Bureaucracy*. New York: Longman, 1978.

Ponting, J. R. and Roger Gibbins. *Out of Irrelevance: A Socio-Political Introduction to Indian Affairs in Canada*. Toronto: Butterworths, 1980.

Porter, John. *The Vertical Mosaic*. Toronto: University of Toronto Press, 1965.

Rose, P., S. Rothman and W. Wilson. *Through Different Eyes*. New York: Oxford University Press, 1972.

Rowat, Donald C. *Basic Issues in Public Administration*. New York: Macmillan, 1961.

Sayre, W. S., ed. *The Federal Government Service* (The American Assembly). Englewood Cliffs: Prentice-Hall, 1965.

Shafritz, Jay M. *Public Personnel Management*. New York: Praeger, 1975.

Stahl, O. Glenn. *Public Personnel Administration*, 6th ed. New York: Harper & Row, 1971.

Stewart, Frank M. *The National Civil Service Reform League: History, Activities and Problems*. Austin: University of Texas, 1929.

The Committee on the Civil Service (Fulton Committee) *Report*, Cmnd. 3638, London: HMSO, 1968.

Van Riper, Paul. *History of the United States Civil Service*. New York: Row Peterson, 1958.

Webster, E. C. *Decision Making in the Employment Interview*. Montreal: The Eagle Publishing Co., 1964.

Young, Michael. *The Rise of the Meritocracy*. Middlesex: Thames & Hudson, 1958.

ARTICLES

Bach, Hollis B. "The Merit Track in Local Government: Abused and Diffused." *Public Personnel Management*, Vol. VI, 2 (March/April 1977), pp. 116-120.

Blumrosen, Alfred W. "Strangers in Paradise: Griggs v. Duke Power Co. and the Concept of Employment Discrimination." *Michigan Law Review*, Vol. 71 (November 1972).

Campbell, Alan K. "Civil Service Reform: A New Commitment." *Public Administration Review*, Vol. XXXVIII, 2 (March/April 1978), pp. 99-103.

Carson, J. J. "Bilingualism in the Public Service." *Canadian Public Administration*. Vol. XV, 2 (1972), pp. 190-93.

________. "Where Did We Go Wrong, Or Did We?" *Optimum*, Vol. IX, 2 (1978), pp. 14-23.

Cloutier, Sylvain. "Senior Public Servants in a Bicultural Society." *Canadian Public Administration*. Vol. XI (Winter 1968), pp. 397-98.

Collins, D. J. "Recruitment and Selection for Public Administration: the Last Ten Years." *Canadian Public Administration*, Vol. VII (June 1964), pp. 197-204.

Couturier, Jean J. "The Quiet Revolution in Public Personnel Laws." *Public Personnel Management*, Vol. V, 3 (May/June 1976), pp. 150-167.

Downs, Anthony, "A Theory of Bureaucracy." *American Economic Review*, Vol. 55 (1965).

Dunnett, Sir James. "The Civil Service: Seven Years After Fulton." *Public Administration*, Vol. XXX (Summer 1977), pp. 293-313.

Goode, William J. "The Protection of the Inept." *American Sociological Review*, Vol. XXXII (February 1967).

Heisel, W. Donald. "The Personnel Revolution: An Optimist's View." *Public Personnel Management*, Vol. V, 4 (July/August 1976), pp. 234-38.

Howard, L. "Civil Service Reform: A Minority and Woman's Perspective." *Public Administration Review*, No. 4 (July-August 1978).

Kaufman, Herbert. "Administrative Decentralization and Political Power." *Public Administration Review*, Vol. XXIX, 1 (January/February 1969).

Kernaghan, Kenneth. "Representative Bureaucracy: the Canadian Perspective." *Canadian Public Administration*, Vol. XXI, 4 (1978), pp. 489-512.

Kranz, Harry. "Are Merit and Equity Compatible," *Public Administration Review* (September/October 1974).

________. "How Representative is the Public Service?" *Public Personnel Management* (July-August 1973), pp. 242-55.

Krause, Robert D. "Public Personnel in a Changing World." *Public Personnel Management*, Vol. VIII, 5 (September-October 1979), pp. 340-343.

Larson, Arthur D. "Representative Bureaucracy and Administrative Responsibility: A Reassessment." *Midwest Review of Public Administration*, Vol. 7 (April 1973).

Levine, C. "Unrepresentative Bureaucracy." *Bureaucrat*, No. 4 (April 1975).

Lipset, Seymour M. "The Rigidity of a Neutral Bureaucracy," *Agarian Socialism*. Berkeley: University of California, 1950.

Long, Norton. "Bureaucracy and Constitutionalism." *American Political Science Review*, Vol. 46 (September 1952), pp. 808-18.

Love, J.D. "Personnel Organization in the Canadian Public Service: Some Observations on the Past." *Canadian Public Administration*, Vol. 22 (Fall 1979), pp. 402-14.

Marsh, John J. "Personnel Employees' Perceptions of a State Merit System." *Public Personnel Management*, Vol. VI, 2 (March-April 1977), pp. 93-97.

McDermott, F. Arnold. "Merit Systems Under Fire." *Public Personnel Management*, Vol. V, 4 (July-August 1976), pp. 225-33.

Meier, K. John. "Representative Bureaucracy: An Empirical Analysis." *American Political Science Review*, Vol. 69 (June 1965).

———. and L. C. Nigro. "Representative Bureaucracy and Policy Preferences: A Study in the Attitudes of Federal Executives." *Public Administration Review*. Vol. 36 (July-August 1976).

Nachmias, David and D. Rosenbloom. "Measuring Bureaucratic Representation and Integration." *Public Administration Review*, (November-December 1973).

Nethercote, J. R. "Comments on the D'Avignon Report." *Optimum*, Vol. XI, 1 (1980), pp. 5-15.

Owen, Thomas. "Public Service Morale and Merit System." *Optimum*, Vol. IX, 1 (1978), pp. 61-68.

Porter, John. "Higher Public Servants and the Bureaucratic Elite in Canada." *Canadian Journal of Economics and Political Science*, Vol. 24 (November 1958), pp. 483-501.

———. "The Bureaucratic Elite: A Reply to Professor Rowat." *Canadian Journal of Economics and Political Science*, Vol. 25 (May 1959).

Reeves, E. J. "Equal Employment and the Concept of the Bureaucracy as a Representative Institution." *Midwest Review of Public Administration*, Vol. 6 (1972).

Rich, Harvey. "The Canadian Case for a Representative Bureaucracy." *Political Science*, Vol. 27 (July/December 1975), pp. 103-8.

Rosen, B. "Merit and the President's Plan for Changing the Civil Service System." *Public Administration Review*, No. 4 (July-August 1978).

Rosen, S. M. "Credentials — Two Strategies," *Social Policy*, Vol. 6 (March 1969).

Rosenbloom, David H. "Forms of Bureaucratic Representation in the Federal Service." *Midwest Review of Public Administration*, Vol. 8 (July 1974).

Rowat, Donald C. "On John Porter's Bureaucratic Elite in Canada." *Canadian Journal of Economics and Political Science*, Vol. 25 (May 1959).

———. "Representativeness Does Not Include Partisanship." From a review of Paul Van Riper's "History of the United States Civil Service." *Canadian Journal of Economics and Political Science*, XXV (May 1959).

Saltzstein, Grace. "Representative Bureaucracy and Bureaucratic Responsibility." *Administration and Society*, Vol. X, 4 (February 1979).

Santos, C. R. "Public Administration as Politics." *Canadian Public Administration*, Vol. XII, 2 (1969).

Savas, E. S. and S. G. Ginsberg. "The Civil Service: A Meritless System?" *The Public Interest*, Vol. 32 (Summer 1973).

Sheriff, Peta. "Unrepresentative Bureaucracy." *Sociology*, Vol. 8 (1974).

Sigelman, Lee and W. G. Vanderbok. "Legislators, Bureaucrats and Canadian Democracy, the Long and the Short of It." *Canadian Journal of Political Science*, Vol. 10 (September 1977).

Sjoberg, G. and R. Brymer and B. Farris. "Bureaucracy and the Lower Class." *Sociology and Social Research*, Vol. 50 (April 1966).

Subramaniam, V. "Representative Bureaucracy: A Reassessment." *American Political Science Review*, Vol. 61 (December 1967), pp. 1010-19.

Thompson, Frank J. "Minority Groups in Public Bureaucracies." *Administration and Society*, Vol. 3 (August 1976).

Wilson, V. S. and W. A. Mullins. "Representative Bureaucracy: Linguistic/Ethnic Aspects in Canadian Public Policy." *Canadian Public Administration*, Vol. 21 (Winter 1978), pp. 513-38.

Wilson, Woodrow. "The Study of Administration." *Political Science Quarterly*, Vol. 2, Bobbs Merrill Reprint, 1887.

ENDNOTES

1. Bernard Rosen, *The Merit System in the United States Civil Service: A Monograph* (Washington: U.S. Government Printing Office, 1975), p. 7.
2. Richard Chapman, *The Higher Civil Service in Britain*. (London: Constable), p. 26.
3. See G.A. Campbell, *The Civil Service in Britain* (London: Duckworth & Co., 1955), p. 57.
4. *The Civil Service*. (The Fulton Report) (London: HMSC, 1969).
5. From Carl Fish, *The Civil Service and Patronage* (New York: Russell & Russell, 1963), p. 7.
6. By 1934 Congress had exempted 60 agencies and some 100,000 positions from the merit system. See Paul Van Riper, *History of the United States Civil Service* (Evanston Row: Peterson), p. 321.
7. For further details on this program, see Alan K. Campbell, "Civil Service Reform: A new Commitment," *Public Administration Review* (March/April 1978) pp. 99-103; and Bernard Rosen, "Merit and the President's Plan for Changing the Civil Service System," *Public Administration Review* (July/August 1978).
8. See J.E. Hodgetts, *Pioneer Public Service: An Administrative History of the United Canadas, 1841-1867* (Toronto: University of Toronto Press), pp. 12-23 for a more detailed description of this period.
9. For an excellent analysis of the evolution of the Canadian civil service, the reader is referred to J.E. Hodgetts et al., *The Biography of an Institution: The Civil Service Commission*, 1908-1967 (Montreal: McGill – Queen's, 1972) and J.E. Hodgetts, *The Canadian Public Service: A Physiology of Government 1867-1970* (Toronto: University of Toronto Press, 1973).
10. Royal Commission on the Civil Service, Canada Sessional Paper, 1892, p. xvii.
11. S.A. Fisher, *Debates of the House of Commons*, June 25, 1908. p. 11378.
12. R. MacGregor Dawson, *The Civil Service of Canada* (London: Oxford University Press, 1929), p. 96.

12. Hodgetts et al., *The Biography of an Institution*, p. 69.

14. The "Spinney Amendment" of 1921 allowed the Governor in Council on recommendation of the Civil Service Commission to exclude certain categories from the Act. See Hodgetts, *The Canadian Public Service*, p. 270.
15. *Report* of the Civil Service Commission of Canada (Ottawa, 1958), p. 5.
16. See the *Report* of the Royal Commission on Government Organization, abridged edition (Ottawa: Queen's Printer, 1962).

17. In fairness, it should be pointed out that both representatives of Treasury Board and the Civil Service Commission expressed reasonable satisfaction with the reallocated responsibilities. See Hodgetts et al., *Bibliography of an Institution*, p. 325.
18. House of Commons *Debates*, April 6, 1966, p. 3915.
19. House of Commons *Debates*, June 23, 1970, p. 8487.
20. For a comprehensive review of the historical development of language programs in the civil service and the role of Commissioner of Official Languages, see Gilles Bibeau, *Report of the Independent Study on the Language Training Programmes of the Public Service of Canada*, 1975.
21. *Annual Report*, Public Service Commission of Canada, 1979, vol. 1, p. 21.
22. Kathleen Archibald, *Sex and the Public Service* (Ottawa: Queen's Printer), 1970.
23. *Annual Report*, Public Service Commission, 1979, vol. 2, p. 2 and p. 22.
24. *Annual Report* of the Public Service Commission of Canada, 1978, p. 17.
25. See the *Report*, "Women in the Public Service," compiled by the Office of Equal Opportunities for Women, Public Service Commission of Canada, 1976, p. 6.
26. The government of Canada created the Human Rights Commission in 1977.
27. *Report* on Native People and Employment in the Public Service of Canada, prepared by Impact Research, Ottawa, 1976, pp. 28-29.
28. The federal government's efforts to involve native people more in the public service have not been limited to only the Northern Careers Program. For an account of other more recent initiatives see J. Rick Ponting and Roger Gibbins, *Out of Irrelevance: A Socio-political Introduction to Indian Affairs in Canada* (Toronto: Butterworths, 1980), pp. 140 ff.
29. For an excellent discussion of "representative bureaucracy" and how it relates to the Canadian scene, see Kenneth Kernaghan, "Representative Bureaucracy: the Canadian Perspective," and V. Seymour Wilson and Willard A. Mullins, "Representative Bureaucracy: Linguistic/Ethnic Aspects in Canadian Public Policy," in *Canadian Public Administration*, vol. XXI, 4 (Winter 1978), pp. 489-538.
30. For a fuller examination of some of these arguments and their counter-arguments, the reader should consult Donald J. Kingsley, *Representative Bureaucracy: An Interpretation of the British Civil Service* (Yellowsprings, Ohio: Antioch Press, 1944); Samuel Krislov, *Representative Bureaucracy* (Englewood Cliffs, N.J.: Prentice-Hall, 1974); Norton Long, "Bureaucracy and Constitutionalism" *American Political Science Review*, (September 1952); Peta Sheriff, "Unrepresentative Bureaucracy" *Sociology*, vol. 8, (1974); V. Subramanian, "Representative Bureaucracy: A Reassessment," *American Political Science Review* (December 1967); and Frederick C. Mosher, *Democracy and the Public Service* (New York: Oxford, 1968). There are several other references which can be found within the works cited.
31. See K.J. Meier and L.C. Nigro, "Representative Bureaucracy and Policy Preferences: A Study in the Attitudes of Federal Executives," *Public Administration Review*, vol. XXXVI (July/August 1976), pp. 458-69.
32. Several empirical studies have been conducted which support this conclusion. See for example, John Porter, *The Vertical Mosaic* (Toronto: University of Toronto, 1965) and Dennis Olsen, *The State Elite* (Toronto: McClelland & Stewart, 1980). Both make the point that senior bureaucrats in particular are drawn from a narrow segment of society and that this elite tends to perpetuate itself through the meritocratic system (Olsen, p. 69). Of some 224 deputy and assistant deputy ministers at the federal level, Olsen discovered that 92 per cent possessed university degrees, and 61 per cent had post-graduate degrees (Olsen, pp. 70-72). The same group, excluding 22 members who were born outside of Canada, had 171 from upper or middle-class origins (p. 81). Olsen found ethnic representation in 1973 was a little more balanced in the federal bureaucracy than Porter had found it to be in 1953, but it still showed an overrepresentation of members of British origin. Finally of the 224 bureaucrats studied, only six (or three per cent) were women (Olsen, p. 76).
33. *Annual Report* of the Public Service Commission of Canada, 1979, vol. 1, p. 10.
34. See the *Report* of the Royal Commission on Financial Management and Accountability (Ottawa: Supply and Services, 1979, pp. 118-126.
35. Guy D'Avignon, *Report of the Special Committee on the Review of Personnel Management and the Merit Principle*, 1979, p. 8.

36. The "impersonal" character of bureaucracy was seen in a constructive light by Max Weber. Later, Victor A. Thompson in *Without Sympathy or Enthusiasm* (University of Alabama Press, 1975) and the final chapter of his *Bureaucracy and the Modern World* (General Learning Press, 1976) makes the point that compassion is illegal and will lead us back to an earlier era of patronage and favoritism.
37. D'Avignon, *Report*, p. 90.
38. *ibid.*, p. 108.
39. *ibid.*, p. 92.
40. See for example a somewhat dated but probably still applicable study by E.C. Webster in *Decision Making in the Employment Interview*, (Montreal: Industrial Relations Centre, 1964).

CHAPTER SEVEN

Federalism and the Administrative State

Introduction

The anecdote is told that at the pearly gates to Heaven there is a sign especially to welcome recent arrivals from Canada. The sign reads: "This way to a debate on whether Heaven is a Federal or a Provincial Responsibility." The joke reveals the extent to which the fact of federalism pervades public life in Canada. Debates over the respective jurisdictions of the two levels of government have become such a popular, national indoor sport that they are often broadcast live to bemused television audiences, who seem never quite sure whether to applaud or to bemoan the performances of their federal and provincial spokesmen.

It is practically impossible in Canada today to identify a field of public policy which does not have some degree of intergovernmental involvement. Regardless of the job or the level of government for which they work, most public servants are in regular contact with other governments. For example, thousands of provincial public servants meet daily with their federal counterparts to negotiate and to administer policies related to transportation, regional development, communications, water management, taxation and on and on. Even city and municipal officials get caught up in the web of intergovernmental relationships when they seek to communicate their financial and other needs to the so-called "senior levels" of government or seek to take advantage of federal and/or provincial programs. Because the actions of any one level of government can have great significance for the affairs of another level, public administrators must be aware of what other governments are doing or planning, and must strive to maintain good working relationships with officials of those governments. Modern federalism necessarily involves close collaboration among governments, but it can also produce intergovernmental conflict, as Canadians are well aware.

In short, a large part of the job of public servants today is to understand the complex intergovernmental environment and to manage it effectively so as to avoid pointless conflict and possible federal-provincial deadlocks. To this end, there has developed in Canada a class of public officials whose specialization and full-time occupation is to operate the intergovernmental machinery that has become so extensive and important within the Canadian political system.

This chapter seeks to explain our system of intergovernmental relations and to outline the role played by public officials within that system. There is ample literature available which describes and analyzes the constitutional, financial and political history of Canadian federalism.[1] Much less, however, has been written about the administrative features and implications of federalism. Therefore, while the chapter places recent intergovernmental relations in an historical perspective by tracing the evolution of the Canadian federal system, its principal concern is the structure, role and problems of the intergovernmental bureaucracy. Particularly since the end of World War II there has developed an extensive array of mechanisms for federal-provincial consultation and collaboration, involving at the summit elected politicians and below them a wide variety of appointed officials from various levels in the administrative hierarchy. Concentrating on the relationships among officials, the chapter addresses a series of questions or issues.

Does the federal-provincial relationship, at both the political and administrative levels, involve mainly cooperation, competition and conflict, bargaining, or some other format? To what extent can we generalize about such interactions or must we distinguish among issues and over time? Does increased interdependence and competition among governments increase the size of government, the cost of government, the extent of government regulation and the proliferation of certain kinds of bureaucratic structures? How has the formal machinery of intergovernmental liaison developed? What types of committees now exist? Is the formal machinery more often successful when used as a means for allowing officials to reach agreements on technical problems of mutual concern and does it break down when the basic political interests of participating governments are in conflict? There is an extensive range of informal, often bilateral, contacts among governments on almost a daily basis. Do such dealings relate primarily to administrative matters and how effective are they as a means of ensuring policy and program coordination and of resolving disagreements?

Since the 1960s we have witnessed the appearance within the federal and certain provincial governments of bureaucratic units whose principal mandate is to conduct and to coordinate intergovernmental relations. What has been the impact of such units on the federal system? Have they, as some writers allege, contributed to heightened conflict within the system? And relatedly, what has been their impact on the internal operations of governments? For example, do the regular line departments resent the rise of central agencies which are assigned the task of supervising federal-provincial dealings? Or, in terms of the more traditional concerns of public administration, does the need for joint decision-making in most areas of domestic policy-making enhance bureaucratic influence at the expense of control by elected politicians? Does the widespread practice of federal financing for programs which are administered mainly by provincial governments compound the problem of achieving accountability within the system? Are intergovernmental relations dominated by the ministers and public servants and is there sufficient democratic accountability through legislatures for the conduct of those relations? Does the emergence of several layers of intergovernmental structures and processes contribute to public confusion about where responsibility for specific matters resides? Does this make the political system less accessible and hence less responsive to citizen concerns and needs?

These questions are more easily asked than answered. In this field, as in the others which we have examined, there is much room for disagreement. Furthermore, understanding the intricate system of intergovernmental dealings is made more difficult by the secretive and dynamic nature of the federal-provincial process. In the concluding section of this chapter we speculate briefly on the problems of managing federalism in the 1980s and beyond.

Concepts of Federalism

A federal state is usually defined as a structure which divides powers between national and regional governments in such a way that each level of government is independent within its assigned sphere of authority.[2] For many authorities on the subject, the essence of federalism is legal and constitutional. In practice, however, modern federal states derive their most important features from political and administrative processes. Although the constitution is still important in interpreting federalism, more attention is now paid to the "politics" of federalism. More traditional, formal and legal approaches to federalism tended to downgrade the significance of underlying political, economic and social forces which were not adequately represented or "captured" by constitutional theories. Moreover, such legalistic approaches gave federalism a static quality, whereas in practice it is inherently a dynamic process. Let us offer the following definition of federalism that seems to fit the Canadian situation. M.J.C. Vile has described federalism as "a system of government in which central and regional governments are linked in a mutually interdependent political relationship."[3] The essence of this relationship is bargaining since neither level of government can dictate the decisions of the other. Vile goes on to state that while functions will be allocated initially by a constitutional document, thereafter the "real" working relationship will be mainly a product of the political process. This is not to deny entirely the importance of the constitution for it may have a continuing impact on the perceptions of the participants in the federal system and provide a basis for bargaining.

This definition stresses the dynamic of the federal process. Intergovernmental relations represent a fluid, changing, evolving process, as we will see momentarily. An additional attraction of the definition is its emphasis on the competitive aspect of the federal system. While the question of whether most federal-provincial dealings are competitive is left for later examination, the definition draws our attention to the fact that all governments in Canada have their own constitutional, financial and political concerns that shape their behavior in intergovernmental dealings, negotiations and bargaining. In this view, the mere existence of a federal structure serves to create vested interests which support its retention.

Economic, social and technological changes in our society have led to new demands on governments and changes within the federal system. Changing interpretations of the constitution by the courts have also contributed to shifts of authority between the federal and provincial governments. Federalism in Canada has been a flexible, largely pragmatic system of power sharing. However, not all changes to the federal balance originate outside of government in the shifting social, economic and political circumstances. Governments themselves have the capacity to mould their environments. As Alan Cairns has noted, the existence of provincial governments provides a focal point for the organization of political parties and interest groups. "Each government's policies," according to Cairns, "pull the affected interests into relationships of dependence and attachment to the power centre which manipulates their existence."[4] According to this perspective, the 1980 energy pricing dispute between Ottawa and Alberta should not be seen simply as the provincial government representing the interests of the dominant business class within that province. Instead, provincial authorities, both elected and appointed, represent a political-bureaucratic elite separate from the oil and gas industry. This political-bureaucratic elite is anxious to protect the provincial constitutional claim to resource ownership and to embark upon ambitious plans to diversify the Alberta economy. While there may be an alliance of interests here between government and industry, it has been argued persuasively that within the alliance provincial authorities have their own motives, besides a desire to protect the future of the oil and gas industry, for fighting Ottawa hard on the pricing issue.[5]

As the Alberta example suggests, the relationship between societies and the federal structure is complicated and problematical. However, the relationship is definitely a two-way street, with national and regional governments not only reflecting underlying social and economic forces, but also becoming actively engaged in shaping the economy and society, including public perceptions about what is the appropriate role of each level of government. Another consequence of federalism may be to produce "overload" or "overgovernment," a possibility already suggested in our chapter on budgeting. Obviously, by the simple fact of dividing legislative and executive authority between two levels of government, a federal system implies a need for additional administrative manpower. However, it may also harbor the potential for the expansion of government activity. At the administrative level, increased functional specialization and professionalism within the bureaucracy can produce harmony and cooperation among program specialists across governmental levels, which in turn leads to the proliferation of programs. If the federal-provincial relationship is more political and competitive in nature, the same result could still ensue when governments seek to maximize their jurisdiction and to claim political credit for increased activities.

When it is recognized that by the end of 1976, the federal government employed approximately 300,000 public servants and all the provinces combined employed close to 600,000 public servants, we can see how entrenched bureaucratic ambition to maintain and expand their respective jurisdictions could lead to conflict within the federal system.[6] The alignment of particular outside interests behind either level of government could further serve to reinforce competition and conflict within the system. Large, interventionist and competitive governments in Canada will probably mean that for the foreseeable future most public issues will continue to be debated in federal-provincial terms.

A popular metaphor to describe the historical evolution of Canadian federalism has been that of the swinging pendulum. At various times the pendulum of power is said to have swung to the federal government, to the provinces and back again. Other observers insist that the trend, during this century at least, has been towards more provincial power, with the notable exception of periods of war and the Depression when national authority was briefly reasserted. Such disagreement reflects the difficulty of deciding the most appropriate indicators of centralism and provincialism within the federal system. At any point in time, for example, it is difficult to make unequivocal judgments about the relative importance of the functions performed by each level of government. Is health, (which is primarily a provincial responsibility) more important than international trade (which is primarily a federal responsibility)? What do we mean by importance in this context? Even if we could agree now, the perceived importance of various functions would likely shift as social needs changed.

Moreover, today neither level of government performs its functions in separate water-tight compartments. If at an earlier stage federalism was described as a "layer cake" of separate national and regional program activity, a more appropriate metaphor today is that of a "marble cake" with the two levels of government involved in extensive interlocking activity.[7] Discerning who has power, initiative and control in such relationships is never easy. Take the case of shared-cost programs about which more will be said later. In such programs Ottawa puts up a portion of the money, but the provinces do the actual spending. Is this an instance of centralization of power on the principle that "he who pays the piper calls the tune" and Ottawa is therefore able to insist upon the adoption of national program goals and standards? Or, are the provinces legally and politically free to reject such assistance and is Ottawa, therefore, merely gaining an opportunity to bargain with the provinces rather than buying their compliance? These questions will be investigated later but for now they serve to illustrate the difficulty of making unequivocal statements about the relative degree of centralization/decentralization within the federal system.

The Evolution of Canadian Federalism

PHASE ONE: Quasi-Federalism

It is possible to discern a number of historical stages in the evolution of Canadian federalism.[8] To understand and interpret contemporary federal-provincial encounters some appreciation of past events is necessary. The following brief look at the history of intergovernmental relations reveals several competing perspectives on federalism and the appropriate roles to be played by each level of government.

At the outset of Confederation in 1867 the preference was clearly for a highly centralized federal structure. Indeed, during the first 20 years, the system was really "quasi-federal" in character, with the national government showing little respect for the supposed independence and autonomy of the provincial governments. The framers of the British North America Act had assigned the national government the bulk of the public revenues along with the major spending responsibilities then assumed by governments. Health, education and welfare were provincial responsibilities, but during this early period such services were limited and/or were provided by private charitable organizations. The federal government was granted a number of constitutional controls over provincial actions and made frequent use of such powers. For example, it was given authority to reserve or to disallow provincial legislation and used these powers on numerous occasions. In the case of the western provinces, the federal government retained control over their natural resources until 1930. The fact that the first 20 years of Confederation coincided with a period of one-party dominance in national politics gave additional strength to the national government within the federal structure. While there were examples of intergovernmental cooperation in the 19th century, to a much greater extent than became the case during the 20th century, the two levels of government operated in relative isolation from one another. Such relationships as there were tended to be highly formal and ceremonial in character.[9]

PHASE TWO: Power to the Provinces

The time from about 1896 to 1914 we label the "Power to the Provinces" period. It featured a movement towards a more genuine federal state in which there was a greater balance of power between the two levels of government. Court interpretations of the constitution favorable to the provinces were one of the reasons for the shift.[10] The appearance of strong and demanding premiers in several provinces, such as Oliver Mowat in Ontario and Honoré Mercier in Quebec, led to a provincial rights offensive and the first inter-provincial conference in 1887. This in turn led to provincial demands for a renegotiation of the financial arrangements of Confederation. In 1906, almost 40 years after the birth of Confederation, the first conference of federal-provincial First Ministers took place and produced increased financial subsidies for the provinces. By the turn of the century, Canada was enjoying strong economic development and prosperity and it no longer seemed as essential for the national government to exercise strict economic direction and control. Disallowance was resorted to less frequently and was used mainly in relation to legislation passed in British Columbia to exclude Asian immigrants. After 1896 a Liberal government in Ottawa under Prime Minister Wilfred Laurier was electorally committed to ensuring provincial autonomy and found it easier to work with Liberal governments that gradually appeared in provincial capitals. The national government began to consult regularly with the provinces on matters of mutual concern. Federal grants-in-aid or shared-cost programs in the fields of agriculture, technical education and transportation were begun during these pre-war years. All of these factors contributed to the breakdown of the original highly centralized version of federalism practised since Confederation.

PHASE THREE: Emergency Federalism

World War I ushered in a period of "emergency federalism." To ensure successful prosecution of the war there was at the national level a vast delegation of authority by Parliament to the executive and Ottawa assumed sweeping control over the economy, and over matters of property and civil rights which in peacetime belonged to the provinces. Because of the emergency, the courts gave their blessing to the near obliteration of the normal division of powers. During the war, the federal government began for the first time to levy direct personal and corporate income taxes. It also applied wage and price controls and prohibited strikes in vital wartime industries. For the duration of the hostilities, at least, Canada was virtually transformed into a unitary state.

PHASE FOUR: Provincial Power, Cars and Booze

Once the war was over, however, the courts reverted to their earlier interpretation of the constitution which favored the provinces. We label the decade of the 1920s "Provincial Power, Cars and Booze" because it featured a notable upswing in provincialism. Provincial power was the product of many forces. It reflected the increasing urbanization and industrialization of Canadian society and the related demand for services which fell mainly within the provincial sphere. During the 1920s the provincial responsibility for health, education and welfare assumed far greater social importance than had been imagined at the time of Confederation. In addition, the invention of the automobile led to demands for the development of provincial highway systems. These and other developments placed a strain on provincial budgets and treasurers set to searching for new sources of revenue to exploit. Provincial governments moved into the personal and corporate income tax fields in a bigger way. New revenues were gained from automobile licenses, gasoline taxes, resource royalties and the sale of alcohol through provincially-controlled liquor outlets. Over time the statutory subsidies from the federal government gradually assumed minor significance (approximately 10 per cent) in provincial budgets. Yet, even with these new areas of direct taxation, most provincial treasurers found little room for financial manouevring in the face of the new demands being made upon their governments.[11]

PHASE FIVE: Return to Emergency Federalism — Depression and War

The precariousness of the provincial financial situation was revealed by the Depression's devastating impact. The Prairie and Maritime provinces were hardest hit and their governments came close to bankruptcy. Eventually the federal government had to step in to provide financial support to all provinces, to assist with relief measures (welfare and unemployment services) and to ensure continuation of essential services (such as public health). One result of the economic crises of the 1930s, therefore, was to enlarge the number of mutual concerns of federal and provincial governments, but rather than an effective structure of liaison there developed a large number of "makeshift intergovernmental arrangements to meet the urgent needs of individuals and families."[12] A second impact of the Depression was to produce chaos within the tax system as governments at all three levels scrambled to find additional sources of revenue. The result was the so-called "tax jungle," with governments levying double or even triple taxation on the same income.

Several commissions of inquiry were launched to discover solutions to the economic crises of the 1930s, but none of their elaborate blueprints were implemented. However, many of the general ideas contained in those reports later became the basis for post-war actions by governments. The Rowell-Sirois Commission on Dominion-Provincial Relations reported in 1940 and called for greater centralization of power within the federal system. Generally it was skeptical of collaborative arrangements between governments. "Where legislative power over a particular subject is divided," the report stated, "it is ordinarily desirable that these powers should be pooled under the control of a single government in order to secure a unified effort in administration."[13]

Apparently the Commission was led to this conclusion by a study done by J.A. Corry. Corry studied four areas of joint regulatory activity and concluded that the quality of administration was inadequate because competition, rather than cooperation, characterized relations between the two levels of government. Administrative rivalry arose within the context of shared-cost programs because there were seldom agreed-upon and clear objectives for programs and criteria for judging success. Each set of officials sought to master the resulting ambiguity in their own favor and there was no hierarchical superior to resolve the resulting disputes between two bureaucracies. Corry was probably too deterministic and pessimistic in his view of bureaucratic behavior because during the next two decades relations between federal and provincial public servants involved with joint programs were more cordial and constructive than he had predicted.[14] We will examine some reasons for such harmony shortly.

The Report of the Commission on Dominion-Provincial Relations was not acted upon, partly because of World War II, but mainly because the wealthier provinces felt that they had a great deal to lose under its centralized financial scheme. Nevertheless, to support the war effort, the provinces agreed to give the federal government complete control over the personal and corporate income tax fields. Supposedly, this arrangement was to last only until the cessation of hostilities, but by then Ottawa was convinced that it should retain these major sources of revenue.

Two factors contributed to this development.[15] First, there was the impact of the economic theories of Lord Keynes. Keynes' most famous work, *General Theory of Employment, Interest and Money* (1936), argued that national governments must ensure economic growth, employment and reasonable price increases through the manipulation of the economic environment. Officials in the Department of Finance, who had absorbed the Keynesian philosophy, believed that Ottawa must ensure economic stability through management of the money supply by the Bank of Canada created during the interwar years, and through tax cuts and additions to government spending in a period of economic downturn. Secondly, just such a recession was feared in the post-war period and to forestall this eventuality Ottawa sought to embark on a program of post-war reconstruction and social spending. Blocked in its attempt to secure general provincial agreement for its ambitious plans, Ottawa was nevertheless successful in achieving many of its objectives in a gradual, piecemeal fashion through bilateral negotiations with the provinces.

PHASE SIX: Father-Knows-Best Federalism

The late 1940s and the 1950s were a period of relative centralism within the federal system. Ottawa assumed a national leadership role in economic management and led the way in the development of the so-called welfare state. Accordingly we have labelled this period "Father-Knows-Best Federalism" because of the extent to which Ottawa assumed a paternalistic role within the federal system. Several factors accounted for Ottawa's predominance.[16] The war effort had had a unifying effect, on English Canadians at least, and they looked to the central government to provide the transition to peace time prosperity. Keynesian economic theory provided the rationale for federal leadership in the management of the economy. The fact that more Canadians were mobile, moving from one region to another, led to pressure on Ottawa to ensure roughly comparable services in different parts of the country. The growing interdependence within the society and the economy caused the rise of national organizations, whose primary pressure targets were the cabinet and the bureaucracy in Ottawa.

Within these same corridors of power, there was the belief, held to a lesser extent throughout the country, that the national government had greater program expertise than was found in the provincial capitals. This belief in Ottawa's superior bureaucratic competence was based partly upon the perceived hesitancy of the provinces to come to terms with the Depression compared with the take-charge approach of the national government during the war. It also reflected the actual state of development of the bureaucracies of the two levels of government. While Ottawa might have exaggerated its own level of competence, it was true that provincial public services, especially in the less affluent provinces, were still small and possessed a narrow range of professional expertise, limited mainly to the fields of public works and accounting.

A paternalistic approach was also encouraged by the entrenchment of the Liberal Party in a majority government position through several federal elections and the fact that Ottawa was often dealing with Liberal administrations in provincial capitals. A final, crucial factor was the posture of the government of Quebec during this period. Under Premier Maurice Duplessis and the Union Nationale Party, Quebec opposed all federal initiatives that appeared to compromise provincial independence. It refused, for example, to cooperate in several joint programs. But while Quebec conducted an ongoing battle with Ottawa, its approach was essentially a negative one; it sought to remain aloof, but seldom had alternative, constructive proposals to counter Ottawa's plans.

These were the factors, then, that led to Ottawa's dominance during the decade following the war. The extent of that dominance can be seen from the fact that in 1955 Ottawa collected 75 per cent of all the taxes paid by Canadians, whereas the provinces and municipalities combined collected only 25 per cent of the total.[17] These relative revenue shares reflected the two principal mechanisms by which Ottawa achieved its predominance. First, by means of a series of five-year Tax-Rental (and later Tax-Sharing) Agreements signed with the provinces — the first ran from 1947 to 1952 — the federal government acquired control over the personal and corporate income tax fields. The conclusion of these agreements restored order to the tax system which had earlier been upset by excessive competition among governments and it had the additional advantage of promoting administrative simplicity since there was in most instances only one tax collector (Ottawa) and one form to complete. Against these benefits there were some disadvantages. Both Ontario and Quebec refused to rent out their tax fields to Ottawa and the anomalous position of these two provinces outside of the agreements was to become a source of tension later. A greater problem, however, was the surrender of provincial autonomy involved in the tax rental scheme. Throughout all the agreements, Ottawa insisted that the participating provincial governments accept the definition of taxable income (the so-called tax base) and the taxation rates laid down in the national Income Tax Act before Ottawa would collect taxes on their behalf.[18] In other words, at least for the duration of each agreement, at which point the provinces could negotiate changes, provincial governments gave up control over the tax base and the tax rates to be used within their boundaries.

The second principal feature of the "Father-Knows-Best" era of Canadian federalism was the extensive use of the conditional grant-in-aid to support certain shared-cost programs.[19] Under such arrangements the federal government provided financial assistance, either in the form of a lump sum or a fixed ratio of the cost of a program, on the condition that the provincial governments provide certain services. While the BNA Act makes no explicit provision for the use of conditional grants, over the years the federal government has used them to involve itself in virtually all areas of provincial jurisdiction. Despite the apparent violation of provincial autonomy involved, the consensus among constitutional authorities is that the federal Parliament can make conditional (or unconditional) grants for any purpose provided that it does not attempt to legislate or to regulate provincial behavior. In Frank Scott's words, "Generosity in Canada is not unconstitutional. If grants are undesirable, it must be for non-legal reasons."[20]

The heyday for the use of the conditional grant to emphasize national leadership was during the 1950s. The conditional grant also served to bridge the gap which had developed between the expensive constitutional responsibilities held by the provinces and Ottawa's control, by reason of its dominance of the main tax fields, over the greatest portion of the public revenues available in Canada. The tight financial situation of most provinces, especially the poorer ones, led them to acquiesce in federal intrusions and sacrifice a measure of provincial autonomy, in order to obtain the revenues involved with joint programs. Only Quebec initially raised constitutional objections to the use of federal spending power in this way.

As a result, federal intrusions into provincial fields spread rapidly during the 1950s and early 1960s. Nine categorical programs in the health field were started in 1949. Federal grants to provincial universities were begun in 1952. In the field of social welfare, joint programs were continued or launched to provide financial assistance to the elderly, disabled, blind and those individuals who were unemployed, but did not qualify for unemployment insurance. In 1964, these and other categorical assistance programs were combined into the Canada Assistance Plan, which provided for a federal-provincial equal sharing of the costs. In 1957 a national hospital insurance plan was established to be administered by the provinces. There was federal aid for vocational education in 1960. And a national medicare scheme, which all provinces eventually joined, was passed in 1967. In addition to these major shared-cost programs, there were hundreds of others established in agriculture, forestry, rural development, housing, transportation and others. By the 1960s the conditional grant payments to the provinces had surpassed the unconditional payments made under the Tax Sharing

Agreement in terms of aggregate dollars within provincial budgets. In 1967 conditional grants accounted for 83 per cent of all federal payments made to the provinces. From about $58 million in transfers in 1946, the federal government's bill for conditional grant payments had risen to $1.5 billion in 1968.[21]

The proliferation of shared-cost programs during the 1950s and early 1960s reflected and contributed to harmonious relations within the federal system. Little attempt was made to adjust constitutional arrangements to changing economic and social realities and there were only limited efforts to develop formal machinery at the political-executive level as the basis for wider, political agreements. Instead, adjustments were made largely by officials on a pragmatic, functional basis. Provided that agreement existed among program specialists and that there was a low level of public interest in the programs, politicians granted the program operators a large measure of autonomy.

D.V. Smiley has suggested four influences at work in shared-cost relationships which served to inhibit conflict.[22] First, the various program specialists (highway engineers, foresters, social workers and so on) tended to share a common frame of reference such as might result from common professional backgrounds, attitudes and values within their particular policy fields. Shared knowledge and attitudes provided a basis for resolving disputes which might arise. A study done at Queen's University, based upon interviews with ministers and officials involved with intergovernmental matters, listed as one of its general observations that the more technical or specialized the area of consultation, the more harmonious consultations were likely to be, whereas when consultations touched upon broad policy matters, the more difficult they tended to be.[23] Administrative consultations among officials over particularistic items tended to involve low levels of conflict.

Federal-provincial cooperation was also facilitated by long-standing acquaintanceship, often friendship, developed among officials. Not only were many of them graduates of the same educational institutions, they also met frequently at conferences, served on advisory committees together, and read the same professional journals. Through extensive interacting, many senior officials came to know one another on a "first-name" basis and could better judge in a given situation what another party was likely to be able to accept. The Queen's study concluded that "the greater the development of personal understanding (particularly among officials) the more chance there is of harmonious relationships."[24]

Cooperation was also encouraged because specialists tended to share a commitment to particular programs and were prepared to support each other against attempts by politicians and other generalist administrators (perhaps in central agencies) to impose budgetary and other controls on programs. Certainly treasury officials at both levels of government have long suspected that shared-cost programs are more immune to the normal budgetary controls than other programs. There was an incentive for program specialists to resolve their disagreements "within the guild," rather than to permit the intrusion of wider political and budgetary considerations.[25] Their own sense of professionalism, combined with self-interest to see programs expand, led program specialists to protect their relative independence from political and central administrative controls.

In summary, the relationships among officials under the mantle of many shared-cost programs became symbiotic. They shared common outlooks, met frequently, created programs that expanded their authority, developed client and special interest-group support and often appeared to circumvent control by elected policy-makers. In the United States this model of intergovernmental relations has been described as "picket fence" federalism because the main competition is between the "pickets" or program areas within governments, not between the two levels of government.[26] As we will see, during the late 1960s and 1970s the existence of these functional fiefdoms was challenged by developments within and among governments.

Despite the proliferation of joint programs, and partly because of Ottawa's financial dominance, the formal, organized machinery of intergovernmental relations grew slowly during the 1950s. For its part, the national government saw the possibility of a more institutionalized partnership as potentially weakening its dominant position, whereas the provinces, particularly the less affluent ones, tended to be more concerned with obtaining financial aid than with developing collaborative mechanisms. As has already been suggested, most of the interactions were of an informal, unstructured nature and involved program specialists. There were, of course, examples of formal, continuing organizations in fields of overlapping activity. The Dominion Council of Health was one such body. Founded in 1919, the Council consisted of deputy ministers from all governments plus representatives from some outside groups. It provided a forum for federal-provincial consultation in health and submitted recommendations to federal ministers. Its advice greatly influenced the decision in 1948 to introduce a scheme of public health grants.[27] There were similar bodies in other fields of public policy, but generally the formal, consultative mechanisms were far fewer than became the case during the 1960s and 1970s. In 1957, a list of federal-provincial committees contained only 64 items, a small number by comparison to what exists today.[28]

In the field of fiscal or economic policy because of its obvious importance, there was a greater interest shown in the creation of effective liaison devices. The experience of negotiating the recurring taxation agreements no doubt also led governments to look for additional methods of consultation. The first practical step in this direction was taken in 1955 with the formation of a working committee of federal and provincial officials who were to provide technical information and support as background for an intergovernmental conference planned for October. At that conference, the preparatory committee was transformed into a permanent body called the Continuing Committee on Fiscal and Economic Matters. Representation on the committee consists of deputy ministers from all governments, with the deputy minister of finance from the government of Canada as chairman. The committee meets twice a year or more often depending upon the work referred to it by the conferences of finance ministers. Its work has been described as follows: "The committee members agree on facts, clarify problems, discuss memoranda submitted by members, but make no independent decisions, take no votes, exercise no executive powers as a committee, do not lobby as a body and do not bind their principals in any way."[29] In spite of its subordinate, advisory status, the committee did serve to fill a gap which existed by providing a forum for the exchange of information and opinion over the broad and crucial fields of fiscal and economic policy. Much of the real work in paving the way to political agreements on contentious financial matters (such as tax-sharing arrangements) has been done within this committee.

PHASE SEVEN: Cooperative and Double Vision Federalism

Only against the background of this post-war period of initial federal dominance within the political system, can we understand the more recent trends in intergovernmental relations and the conflicts which have surfaced. We label the period from the early 1960s onwards as "Cooperative and Double Vision Federalism," a reference both to the movement towards a greater partnership basis for operating the federal system and to the emergence of a more nationalistic Quebec government and society within Confederation, acting on the assumption that two nations comprise Canada. What we have witnessed as a result of these two developments has been the gradual dissipation of the dominance which Ottawa had established during the decade following the war. The reverse swing was precipitated by a number of factors. First, there appeared to be a decline in the relative importance of Ottawa's constitutional responsibilities and a growth in importance of provincial responsibilities in such fields as health, education, welfare and resource development. To some extent the conditional grant mechanism which served as an instrument of federal leadership contained the seeds of its own destruction because it helped to create larger, more competent and more confident provincial public services in many of the program fields mentioned above. No longer was it true and/or accepted that Ottawa possessed a real superiority of administrative talent and ability.

Another factor in Ottawa's decline was its poor record of economic management. According to a 1967 royal commission report, national fiscal and monetary policy in the post-war period had been inappropriate to the prevailing economic circumstances about half of the time.[30] Moreover, Ottawa often failed to take account of the regional incidence of its policies and had ignored the related problem of regional economic disparities. When Ottawa eventually did move in the mid-1960s to develop policies to assist particular regions and specific industries, the provinces, because of their constitutional responsibilities, inevitably became more influential in economic matters.[31] A series of minority governments in Ottawa from 1962 to 1968 was a further factor weakening the national role.

However, the most crucial catalyst of change within the federal system during the 1960s was the rise of a more nationalistic, dynamic and aggressive provincial government within Quebec. Unlike its predecessors, the Quebec government elected in 1960 under Liberal leader Jean Lesage was determined to use the instrument of the state to develop the Quebec economy and society so as to ensure French Canadians a more equal opportunity and to promote the community's culture. Almost overnight the provincial government's role was transformed from one of minimal intervention to an active and expansionist one. A stronger, more nationalistic government in Quebec began to demand an end to federal intervention in provincial affairs, a greater share of the available revenues within the federal system, and the introduction of constitutional changes which would make the provincial government the chief protector of French-Canadian interests and aspirations.[32] The success of Quebec in achieving some of its demands undoubtedly encouraged other provinces to adopt a similar course.

The popular cliché for referring to the 1960s, when the centralized variant of federalism was breaking down, was "cooperative federalism." This is a vague phrase and at times the relations between the two levels of government seemed anything but cooperative. Part of the problem stemmed from the different understandings of cooperative federalism. For provincial officials, both elected and appointed, the concept implied joint decision-making on matters of mutual concern. In this view, consultation between the two levels of government should precede decisions and should be genuine and open. For the federal government, cooperative federalism was less a matter of joint decision-making and more a commitment to listen to provincial views after a national policy had been developed.[33] Obviously, the latter view gave the initiator of policy actions, which in most cases was Ottawa, a considerable advantage in federal-provincial dealings. In essence, then, cooperative federalism was a process of negotiation and bargaining among governments of relatively equal political status, a process much like that described in the earlier definition provided at the outset of the chapter.

Shifting Financial Power

While cooperative federalism was mainly a state of mind and a general process, it was reflected in three institutional changes within the federal system. First, in fiscal arrangements, there was a change after 1957 from tax rental to tax sharing and a steadily increasing amount of room was granted to the provinces to levy their own taxes. For example, beginning in 1957 each province was granted 10 per cent of the personal income tax collections within its boundaries, nine per cent of the corporate taxable income, and 50 per cent of the estate taxes in the province.[34] A province could, if it wished, levy its own taxes in these fields (after 1962, even beyond the tax room vacated by Ottawa) and have the national government collect these taxes, provided that the province in question adopted the national definition of taxable income. In subsequent negotiations of the five-year financial agreements, Ottawa was forced to acquiesce to the constant provincial demands for greater control over the three main tax fields consistent with their growing expenditure responsibilities. By 1977, under the Fiscal Arrangements Act, which was to run until 1982, the provinces received 44 per cent of personal income tax collections, 12 per cent of corporate taxable income and had, since 1972, enjoyed complete control over the estate tax or succession duties field.[35] Only two provinces in 1980 actually levied succession duties, but most levied personal and corporate income taxes beyond the tax room vacated by Ottawa. Quebec collected its own tax in both these fields, Ontario had collected corporate income tax for a number of years, and in 1980 the Alberta government announced that it would establish its own corporate income tax system beginning the following year. In other words, Canada seemed to be moving away from the unified tax system developed in the post-war years, which had avoided the confusion and duplication of separate taxation regimes in all 11 jurisdictions. Moreover, there had been a considerable shift in financial power within the federation. The situation had changed from one in which, in 1955, Ottawa collected three-quarters of all public revenues, to a situation in 1980 in which the provinces and municipalities combined collected about 53 per cent of total tax revenues.[36]

Complaints Against Conditional Grants

The second indication of the swing in favor of the provinces was the declining use of shared-cost or conditional grant programs.[37] Beginning in the early 1960s, all provinces, led by Quebec, began to raise various objections to such programs on both philosophical and practical grounds. In justifying such programs, Ottawa had often argued that they were in the "national interest." In provincial eyes this type of argument often involved the implicit assumption that Ottawa was either better able to reflect the national and local will and/or was capable of reaching sounder decisions than the provinces. In either case, the attitude smacked of an outdated paternalism which took no account of the improvements in the competence of provincial public services.

A more sophisticated, but really no more acceptable argument in provincial eyes, was that the federal involvement in provincial fields was justified because the effects of many programs spread beyond the territorial boundaries of a given province. Because of such "spillovers," a province might be reluctant to spend an adequate amount on a given government function. If, for example, the Government of Manitoba recognized that many of its recent university graduates were moving to Alberta to work rather than joining the Manitoba labor force, what incentive would there be for the province to spend more money on higher education? The government of Alberta might also conclude that it was cheaper to import talent than to train all skilled personnel within its own boundaries. The overall effect of such provincial decisions could be to create an undersupply of skilled manpower (recent shortages of engineers and business administration graduates may be an example) in relation to overall national needs and, therefore, the federal government, with its constitutional responsibility for the overall management of the economy, would be obliged to show some interest in the matter.

A second provincial objection to conditional grants was that they allegedly distorted provincial budgetary priorities. By announcing that it would participate in the costs of a particular program, Ottawa increased its importance within the provincial budgetary process. The provinces, of course, were not forced to join such programs. In practice, however, they could rarely afford, either financially or politically, to reject federal offers. If they refused a federal grant, citizens in their province would still be taxed to pay for the program but would not receive the benefits. Moreover, there was usually some interest group(s) operating in the province which favored the proposed program and would publicize the fact that the provincial government was denying voters benefits for which they were going to pay anyway. A classic case of this type of situation was the medicare debacle of 1966-1968, when all but one of the provinces objected to the immediate implementation of a national medicare program. At that time, the provinces felt the need to hold the budgetary line and that they were being dragged into another expensive, but politically popular program, simply to enhance the reputation of the national government and the federal Liberal Party.[38]

It might be expected that the poorer provinces would be most vulnerable to this form of "federal interference" because they would be least likely to be providing the service at all or at an acceptable level at the time of the federal offer. Since it would be more difficult for them to resist the inducement of federal funds and since they had to provide their own matching share of program costs, such poorer provinces could be forced to allow other, non-aided functions to go undernourished. The question arises: What remained of the political freedom of action of a province like Prince Edward Island which received over 60 per cent of its total budget in federal transfer payments in the late 1960s?[39]

A related complaint from the poorer provinces was that conditional grants were inequitable because in most cases Ottawa reimbursed at a uniform rate. This practice ignored the differences in the relative capacity of provinces to raise their share of the costs and differences in the need for certain services. While it might be theoretically possible, as is done in many conditional grant programs in the United States, to build in explicit equalization, Ottawa usually found this politically difficult because of having to gain support from the richer provinces for such programs. The more affluent provinces argued that all equalization should take place under the grotesquely complicated formula contained in the financial agreements signed between the two levels of government.[40]

There was a further set of more minor, administrative problems associated with shared-cost programs. Frequent federal-provincial disputes occurred over which provincial costs were shareable and to what extent. Curious anomalies arose. For example, Ottawa agreed to share the costs of general hospitals, but not of tubercular and mental hospitals. Or, federal-provincial officials might argue 45 minutes over whether replacement light bulbs for vocational colleges were a "capital" or an "operating" expense (which involved a lower federal sharing ratio), which is what one critic might have meant by "the Chinese torture of cooperative federalism". The "red tape" which Ottawa insisted upon tended to upset its provincial counterparts. Inspection and audit controls, filling out of numerous forms and delays in the processing of provincial claims for federal funds occasionally caused ill will. Finally, there were complaints that Ottawa would act unilaterally to terminate programs or would introduce so-called minor changes to the sharing provisions and simply expect the provinces to take up any financial slack created thereby.

Not all provincial officials objected to the alleged federal interference involved with joint programs. While program specialists (e.g., veterinarians, foresters, welfare workers) might occasionally chafe under Ottawa's control, they also recognized the advantage of having their programs upgraded in the eyes of budget decision-makers because the national government supplied a portion of the cost. Besides, as provincial public services developed greater program expertise, they would not just acquiesce in federal directions on program standards or funding simply because Ottawa was supplying a portion of the funds. Although Ottawa had the superior financial resources, it depended on provincial cooperation to implement program ideas. Because of the secrecy surrounding federal-provincial negotiations, we cannot determine precisely the extent to which Ottawa was able "to buy" provincial compliance, but it seems unlikely that the situation was always that of a federal master dangling a carrot in front of the provincial donkey. Especially in the case of wealthier provincial governments, a more apt image might be that of a sophisticated consumer bargaining with a rich merchant anxious to make a sale.

During the 1960s provincial criticisms of conditional grants became more frequent. Largely to accommodate Quebec, Ottawa in 1965 granted the provinces the right to "opt out" of certain larger, well-established, shared-cost programs and to receive compensation in the form of additional tax room to finance its own programs.[41] In other words, in relation to a limited number of programs, a province would no longer suffer a financial penalty for non-participation and it only had to meet two conditions to qualify. It was required during a transition period to maintain programs at their existing levels and it had to participate on intergovernmental committees established to coordinate program activities. As it turned out, only Quebec took advantage of the "opting out" procedure. While this step was seen outside Quebec as a generous concession to the distinctive role of the province, inside the Quebec government it was viewed as a token, minimal and overdue step to return to provincial hands legitimately-owned constitutional responsibilities.[42]

For its part, Ottawa was not entirely happy with the shared-cost schemes either. During the 1960s the conviction grew within the federal government that it was not receiving sufficient political credit for its share in the financing of such programs, yet was expected to assume the political blame for collecting the revenues which paid for them. Moreover, the programs represented a large, uncontrollable item in the federal budget. Provincial actions determined the size of Ottawa's bill for its many open-ended shared-cost commitments. In 1966, partly under the influence of the constitutional philosophy of Pierre Trudeau, who had recently entered national politics, the federal government embarked on an approach leading to a stricter version of federalism which would end the movement of Quebec towards a "de facto" special status within Confederation.[43]

Ottawa tried over the next decade to "disentangle" itself from some of its numerous shared-cost commitments. In the early part of the 1970s, it acted unilaterally to impose ceilings on its annual contributions to the vital shared-cost programs of hospital insurance, medicare and post-secondary education. Finally, in 1977, Ottawa achieved a major "disentanglement" through the negotiation with the provinces of the Established Programs Financing (EPF) portion of the Fiscal Arrangements Act of 1977, which expires in 1982.[44] Under EPF, Ottawa extracted itself from the open-ended commitment to pay about half of rapidly-growing provincial costs in the fields of hospital insurance, medicare and post-secondary education. In return, Ottawa granted the provinces additional tax room under the tax-sharing provisions of the Fiscal Arrangements Act, plus an additional cash payment determined by a complicated formula which need not be discussed here.

In addition to satisfying provincial complaints about federal intrusions and helping Ottawa to put its own budgetary house in order, it was hoped that EPF would induce more cost-consciousness in the three program fields since the provincial governments could no longer, as previously, simply pass on half their costs to Ottawa. The 1977 Fiscal Arrangements Act (including EPF), involving as it did approximately $9 billion in public revenues in 1977-78, was probably the most significant financial agreement in the post-war period and signalled the culmination of a real shift in financial power within the federation in favor of the provinces.[45] It should also be noted that in recent constitutional discussions Ottawa has offered to restrict the future use of conditional grants only to situations where a "national consensus" in favor of such programs exists, such a consensus being expressed by the passage of affirmative resolutions in a weighted majority of the provincial legislatures.[46]

Given the traditional opposition of Quebec, joined now by more affluent provinces which wish to go it alone, the prospects for any major new national shared-cost programs seem remote.

The Machinery of Executive Federalism

In addition to the adoption of tax sharing and the mounting attack on conditional grants, a third indication of the growing role of the provinces was the development of extensive intergovernmental machinery for policy development, coordination and implementation. This development reflected the growing interdependence of the two levels of government and the provincial insistence upon prior consultation. Ottawa could no longer simply take the provinces for granted, instead it had to interact, bargain and negotiate with them. A related development was occurring inside governments at both levels. In response to the impact of new decision-making technologies and mounting budgetary pressures, efforts were made to formalize and to rationalize the policy-making process. An attempt was also made to counterbalance the "departmentalization" of policy-making (which was caused partly by the earlier growth of categorical shared-cost programs) by restoring cabinets to the role of collective leadership within governments. The institutional expressions of this "rationalistic" urge—the creation of cabinet planning systems, the rise of central agencies, the introduction of new structures and PPBS in the budgetary process and the creation of new omnibus departments with broad mandates—have been described elsewhere in this book. These developments went further in Ottawa and some of the larger provincial governments, but the basic purpose was present within all governments: a desire to re-establish political control and to achieve the horizontal coordination of program activities of departments which previously operated in a more autonomous fashion.

According to several observers, the impact of the new rationalistic approaches within governments was to produce more conflict among governments. Functional collaboration and incremental adjustments among program specialists sharing similar outlooks, which was the predominant form of intergovernmental relations during the 1950s, was replaced by the clash of grand policy designs, conceived often by new-style "political administrators" in the central agencies. Donald Smiley has coined the phrase "executive federalism" to describe this most recent variant of Canadian federalism.[47] Relatively fewer intergovernmental matters were handled by program officials lower down in the administrative hierarchy; instead, intergovernmental relations were conducted and supervised by cabinet ministers and senior administrators in central agencies. This made it "less likely that alliances in policy-making will cut across governmental lines." Instead, conflicts were channelled through to cabinets and to senior officials of the governments with the result that policy conflicts became mixed with the institutional and status concerns of governments.[48] Intergovernmental relations became more "politicized" and conflict was heightened.

The majority of intergovernmental contacts continue to take place at the administrative level among officials. However, their efforts at collaboration can be inhibited by the more general attitudes and strategies towards federalism being adopted by their governments at the time. In other words, the shift in concern from particular, programmatic decisions in an earlier period to the current emphasis on bargaining and the relative power of the units within the federal system has contributed to increased conflict. Of course, conflicts of aims and ambitions are inherent to some extent in any federal system. If governments view federal-provincial relations as only a struggle for power or purely in terms of partisan political rivalries, no structure of liaison, however elaborate, can be made to work successfully. While recognizing this obvious qualification, governments beginning in the 1960s, placed greater reliance on the capacity of intergovernmental committees to define problems, identify compromises and, in general, channel the inevitable political conflict in the direction of more positive purposes. If at times the structure of liaison displayed striking weaknesses, it is probably because the political will to make it operate effectively was missing.

The structure of liaison has, in fact, become quite elaborate. Intergovernmental committees became more numerous and began to meet almost constantly. With so many politicians and officials coming and going between Ottawa and provincial capitals, the wonder of it is how Air Canada was able in any given year to chalk up a deficit! Contrast, for example, 1957 when there were only five federal-provincial liaison bodies at the ministerial level and 59 at the administrative level, with 1977 when there were 31 ministerial groupings and 127 involving appointed officials.[49] By one count in 1975 a total of 782 federal-provincial meetings were held. They involved first ministers (six meetings), ministers (173) and officials (386), and they took the form of 490 bilateral, 45 regional and 247 multilateral meetings.[50]

The formal machinery of intergovernmental relations took on a variety of forms. There are now federal-provincial meetings among ministers, committees of officials, advisory bodies and several organized forums for federal-provincial dealings. It is not possible to examine each of these types in detail, but it is useful to indicate in a general way the nature and role of these bodies.

In the first category of federal-provincial committees, the best known bodies are the Federal Provincial Conferences of First Ministers.[51] Since the initiation of constitutional discussions in 1968, these meetings have assumed a much higher profile and their frequency has increased. Before this period, the first ministers conferences dealt mainly with the financial relationships between governments. After 1971, when the first round of constitutional negotiations collapsed with Quebec's rejection of the Victoria Charter, the first ministers moved on to energy, inflation, pollution and other important topics. Later, in October 1978, the quest for a new constitutional order was resumed, culminating in a series of nationally televised meetings held over four days in September, 1980. Once again these meetings failed to produce an agreement and the Trudeau government proceeded unilaterally with its own constitutional plans.

The government of Canada convenes the first ministers' conferences and has considerable leverage over the agenda, although in recent years prior consultation with the provinces has normally been the practice. While other ministers often attend the conferences and may intervene on specific topics, it is the first ministers who dominate the proceedings. The conferences are primarily a forum for discussion and persuasion since decisions are reached through consensus rather than by voting. According to Richard Simeon, "much of the important work of the conference is done outside the formal session, at dinner, in the lobbies of hotels, and so on."[52]

The staff work done in support of first ministers conferences has grown in size and improved in quality over the years. A common practice in recent years has been for the full conference to refer subject matters to committees of ministers and/or senior bureaucrats to work out problems between plenary sessions. For example, on the constitutional issue, the Continuing Committee of Ministers on the Constitution was established in October, 1978.[53] It consisted of Ministers of Intergovernmental Affairs and the Attorneys-General from the federal and provincial governments. It sought to refine the main constitutional issues and subsequently presented to a first ministers' conference a list of "Best Effort" draft proposals.[54] The Canadian Intergovernmental Conference Secretariat (created during the 1968-1971 period under the title, Secretariat of the Constitutional Conference) provided the background documentation for this exercise and intergovernmental units from both federal and provincial governments also contributed. In summary, the first ministers meetings have become the central arena of federal-provincial bargaining. They have become national media events, although the participants have decided to hold portions of their meetings *in camera* to facilitate bargaining.

At the ministerial level, there is a vast array of federal-provincial meetings. For nearly every federal portfolio there is a counterpart at the provincial level and the ministers who occupy these offices meet regularly, in most cases at least once a year. In the financial field, the Ministers of Finance and the provincial Treasurers have for more than a decade met annually in October to receive reports on the economic outlook and to exchange views on what fiscal and monetary policies should be followed. While this process has not gone so far as joint budgetary policies, it does allow governments to indicate their general budgetary intentions, which can be crucial given the increased importance of provincial spending and the interdependence within the economy. For example, the provinces have been insisting recently that they should have some input into the Bank of Canada's monetary policy. Agriculture is a field of concurrent jurisdiction under the BNA Act so that it is not surprising that for many years ministers in this field have met, at least once a year, to define federal and provincial roles and exchange views. Similarly in the health and resources policy fields ministers have been meeting regularly for a number of years. From 1973 to 1978 there was underway a series of federal-provincial meetings of ministers and officials concerned with reform to Canada's social security system.[55] In short, ministerial meetings have grown in number and importance.

A recent, but apparently short-lived innovation were the tri-level conferences involving the federal government, provinces and municipalities. These conferences were sponsored by the national Ministry of State for Urban Affairs, which as we noted in Chapter 5 was created in 1971 and disbanded seven years later.[56] There was always more enthusiasm within MSUA and within the Canadian Federation of Mayors and Municipalities for the tri-level conferences than there was among provincial governments. With constitutional responsibility for municipal government, some provinces were reluctant to encourage direct dealings with Ottawa. The first tri-level conference was convened in November, 1972. The participants agreed to a further meeting, but defeated a proposal to establish a tri-level secretariat. A second meeting commissioned a study of the financing of the three levels of government. The third planned conference never took place. Extensive formal and informal contacts between provinces and their municipalities continue, but tri-level conferences have disappeared, apparently because of the provincial governments' strong sense of their constitutional prerogatives in this area.

So far we have been describing federal-provincial meetings at the political level. Beneath this level there is a vast, submerged network of adminsitrative committees involving officials from the two levels of government. In 1972, Simeon estimated that 90 per cent of federal-provincial meetings took place at the official level.[57] The number of such committees has grown as the shared policy agendas of governments have expanded. These committees are so numerous and so varied in their roles that there is no easy way to describe or to classify them. Some are formally constituted and meet regularly, while othere are convened on an *ad hoc* basis and are not regarded as permanent consultative bodies, although it is generally recognized that they can be called together if required.

A large number of these committees are concerned with technical coordination in relation to shared-cost programs. Within such committees, public servants will be engaged at various times in policy formulation, monitoring and adjustment of continuing programs and the exchange of technical information. All of these activites can contribute to improved programs and to federal-provincial cooperation. We have already mentioned the important role in relation to economic policy played by the Continuing Committee on Fiscal and Economic Matters, which consists of deputy ministers and undertakes studies on behalf of the ministers of finance. In transportation, Langford identified over 30 federal-provincial committees and there are almost as many for agriculture.[58]

There are a number of bodies established by federal statute or order-in-council to serve in an advisory capacity to federal ministers, but with provision for provincial representation. The oldest of these is the Dominion Council of Health created in 1919. Its formal membership consists of deputy ministers, but the real work is done by a series of technical sub-committees which report back to the Council. Similar advisory bodies exist in agriculture, energy, forestry, manpower and welfare and so on. A rather unique body is the Canadian Council of Resource Ministers, which is formally incorporated and has its own staff to conduct research and advise governments on policy. Its work is directed by a committee of officials.

There are also interprovincial meetings at the political and administrative levels. The annual Premiers' Conference has been held since 1960 and has evolved from a social occasion to a working meeting, dealing in recent years mainly with national policies that affect provincial interests. A Council of Maritime Premiers (Nova Scotia, New Brunswick and Prince Edward Island) was created in 1971 and usually meets quarterly.[59] The Council is responsible for a number of joint activities, such as a higher education commission, a municipal training board and an energy corporation. Supported by a small secretariat it has had success at functional collaboration in areas such as the regulation of highway transportation. In contrast, the Western Premiers' Conference meets less frequently (once a year since 1971), has no bureaucracy of its own and has no joint ventures to direct. Nonetheless, it has become increasingly aggressive and successful in promoting regional concerns in relation to national policies. At one point, the Conference established a Task Force on Constitutional Trends, which was able to produce a list (the so-called "Intrusions Report") of 61 intrusions by the federal government into provincial jurisdiction.[60]

A final manifestation of the more complex federal-provincial environment is the emergence of bureaucratic units within governments to direct and coordinate their involvement. Quebec was the first to establish a separate Department of Intergovernmental Affairs in 1961.[61] Initially this portfolio was held by the premier, but after 1974 it was assigned its own minister. Because of Quebec's success in pursuing its interests in federal-provincial relations, Ontario created in the mid-1960s its own Department of Treasury, Economics and Intergovernmental Affairs, which was split in 1978, creating a separate ministry of Intergovernmental Affairs. An Alberta Department of Federal and Intergovernmental Affairs was established in 1972 and now has one of the largest staffs of federal-provincial relations experts in Canada. In 1979 the Saskatchewan government established a new Department of Intergovernmental Affairs, with its own minister who also serves as Attorney General. Previously federal-provincial relations were run out of the Saskatchewan Premier's Office, and this is still the case in Manitoba, New Brunswick, Prince Edward Island, Nova Scotia and Newfoundland. Since 1979 the British Columbia Cabinet has included a separate Minister of Intergovernmental Relations and in 1980 the establishment of a new department was underway. Several provincial governments now maintain full-time offices in Ottawa in order to monitor developments at the national level.

Within the national government there has been a rapid development in the machinery for federal-provincial relations. Until 1977, Prime Minister Trudeau chaired a Cabinet Committee on Federal-Provincial Relations, which was then merged with the Priorities and Planning Committee. In 1975 the Federal-Provincial Relations Office (FPRO) was established as a separate department. According to Campbell and Szablowski, FPRO has primary responsibility for the conduct of federal-provincial relations, but because the field is so wide and pervasive it cannot be managed without the assistance of many other organizations.[62] One such organization is the Federal-Provincial Relations and Social Policy Branch within the Department of Finance, which was created in May 1979. In 1977 the cabinet post of Secretary of State for Federal-Provincial Relations was established by the Trudeau government. A similar position existed within the Clark cabinet, and its incumbent chaired a cabinet committee on federal-provincial relations, but on his return to power Trudeau dropped the position.

The emergence of central units for intergovernmental affairs and the rise to prominence of the "process expert" in federal-provincial relations reflects the more extensive range of interlocking activity and the greater need for coordination among and within the participating governments. Most departments within the federal public service have created their own units for federal-provincial liaison. Although these organizational changes appear to be a necessary response to the complexity of the system, they can create some problems as well.[63] First, rationalization of policy development within areas of joint activity may increase conflict when the two levels of government approach one another with broad, preconceived plans. Secondly, "process specialists" in federal-provincial units may define their role exclusively in terms of enhancing the reputation of their governments and may approach all federal-provincial negotiations with the objective of "winning," rather than trying to identify a compromise solution. A third drawback of centralization may be increased conflict within governments, a point which we will return to momentarily when we discuss in more detail the administrative implications of federalism.

Federal-Provincial Conflict in the 1970s

The drive to rationalize policy-making and the increased "politicization" of federal-provincial relations produced a higher level of conflict among governments during the 1970s. The points in contention ranged from such central questions as constitutional jurisdiction over resources and tax sharing to seemingly more mundane issues of who will control lotteries or regulate the sale of video-TV games. Financial restraint has served to heighten the tension among governments. While "constitutional anarchy" would be too strong a term to apply to our current federal-provincial discontents, there is clearly a lack of consensus among political and bureaucratic elites about the respective roles each level of government should assume. Suffice to say, that federal-provincial relations became so acrimonious during the 1970s that the term "cooperative federalism" was largely dropped from our political vocabulary.

Probably the dominant image conveyed by the media and most academic writing in recent years is that of a beleaguered national government, reeling from successive provincial onslaughts, and about to go down for the count unless someone steps in to stop the action. It is true that recent public opinion surveys suggest Canadians identify more readily with their provincial governments and see Ottawa as somewhat remote and unresponsive.[64] However, other observers argue that this image exaggerates Ottawa's weakness within the federal system and ignores the residue of popular support which exists for a strong central government, especially in certain fields of activity.

Another view is that, rather than an attenuation of federal leadership, what we have witnessed recently is that Ottawa's influence on provincial decision-making has been achieved by more surreptitious and subtle means than the direct interference in provincial matters that was a common feature of the 1950s and early 1960s. In this view, there have been "no more medicares" since the mid-1960s when Ottawa acted directly contrary to the almost unanimous wishes of the provinces, but this fact does not rule out the possibility that federal authorities have been able to manipulate the "environments" of provincial governments in a less obvious way to constrain their decision-making.

An example of the federal government intruding in this more covert fashion might be in regional development. According to one Ontario public servant who was involved when the federal government first created the Department of Regional Economic Expansion (DREE) in 1969, no effort was made to include the provinces in development planning.[65] The situation appears to have changed since then with attempts by DREE to engage provincial governments in joint planning ventures under the umbrella of General Development Agreements.[66] However, during the earlier stages of DREE's operations, provincial officials saw it as part of a broader strategy by Ottawa to create new sources of political support within the regions. The use of direct spending through DREE, rather than the transfer of tax revenues to the provinces to permit them to operate their own economic development schemes, together with the insistence that all DREE projects be advertised as joint endeavors, reflected Ottawa's attempt to create new "constituencies" of support in have-not regions. Provincial departments became, according to this view, simply "administrative agents within federal policy."[67] It is argued that similar challenges to provincial authority occurred through such federal actions as: the decision in 1966 to take over adult occupational training; the establishment in 1971 of the ministries of state for urban affairs and science and technology; the creation of a Department of the Environment in 1970; the attempts, during the mid-1970s, to formulate a national mining policy and to make changes in national transportation policy.[68]

Interference tends to be a two-way street under modern conditions within the federation. At the same time as Ottawa was being accused of interfering in provincial matters, national spokesmen complained about the growing provincial involvement in matters which were constitutionally federal responsibilities. In this view, provincial governments used all available forums to provide input and criticism of federal decision-making on such "national responsibilities" as multinational trade negotiations, foreign ownership, grain marketing, ocean fisheries, transportation and the exploitation of uranium.[69] To some observers, it appeared that provincial representatives were seeking more than simply consultation on national matters which might impinge on their responsibilities; instead, they seemed to be insisting upon a provincial veto over certain federal decisions.

Government Regulation and Federalism

In its report entitled *Responsible Regulation*, the Economic Council of Canada called attention to the overlap and duplication of direct economic regulation by federal and provincial governments.[70] As was pointed out in Chapter Five, regulation has been one of the principal sources of the government growth in recent decades. As both levels of government became more interventionist through regulation, it was inevitable that their efforts would impinge upon each other's interests. Problems then arose because regulatory agencies enjoyed a measure of independence from direct political control. Thus, when federal-provincial interests clashed in a regulatory arena there was less possibility for federal-provincial bargaining to take place. According to Richard Schultz, the tension between regulatory independence and governmental interdependence is the source of several types of conflicts within the federal system.[71]

First, there are situations where only national regulation exists, but provincial interests are clearly affected. An example is the regulation of freight rates by the Canadian Transport Commission. In other instances, the sole regulatory authority is at the provincial level and regulations are enforced which limit the inter-provincial movement of goods, capital, or labor in such a way that the federal government becomes concerned about the impact on the national economy. Another form of interdependency arises when regulatory authority over a certain sector of economic activity is shared between the two levels of government, such as is the case in energy, transportation and consumer protection. Additional complications and further potential for conflict arise when public corporations are present within a field of regulated activity. Both the federal and provincial governments have created crown corporations to further development objectives which may clash with the regulatory approach of the other level of government.

Schultz maintains that national regulatory bodies have not exhibited sufficient sensitivity to the demands of the contemporary federal system.[72] He relates the complaint of provincial governments that regulatory agencies enjoy too much freedom to set policy within areas of federal-provincial concern. The provincial governments insist that independence may be necessary for the impartial adjudication of specific issues of a quasi-judicial nature, but regulatory agencies should not have an independent policy-making function. Such a policy role has been allowed to develop when agencies were created on the basis of vague statutory mandates and were allowed to issue wide-ranging policy statements. In addition, the provinces object to being treated as "just another pressure group" for purposes of intervening before national regulatory bodies.

In seeking to resolve the legitimate complaints of the provinces, Schultz warns us against sacrificing to various forms of political control the measure of regulatory independence required to deal impartially with judicial or quasi-judicial matters.[73] A balance must be struck, he argues, between the needs of the federal system and those of the regulatory system. More specifically, he recommends that the federal cabinet be granted authority to issue binding policy directives to all national regulatory agencies and that regulations should require either ministerial or cabinet approval before taking effect. He also suggests that provincial governments should be granted, by statute, "standing" before all federal regulatory agencies and that they should participate in the appointment of members to such bodies. In the chapter on accountability, we point out that the Trudeau government is proposing to amend the statutes creating several regulatory agencies to provide itself with the power to issue binding policy directives. And, in the context of the constitutional negotiations, Ottawa has indicated its willingness to discuss with provincial governments the means by which they might have input into regulatory appointments.

The Canadian Federal Experience: Brief Summary

In our survey of Canada's experience with federalism, we have covered a considerable amount of historical ground and catalogued a bewildering variety of institutions and processes. The persistent reader deserves a reward in the form of some general observations. First, in summarizing the history of Canadian federalism, it can be stated that the system has proven quite adaptive to changing social, economic and political circumstances. Most adaptations have been pragmatic, *ad hoc* and, until recently at least, administrative in nature. In other words, to date we have somehow "muddled through" in managing the federal system. Despite the pressures for change, grand constitutional designs for the reallocation of expenditure responsibilities and revenue sources have not been accepted. But given the increased interdependence of governments and the more "politicized" nature of federal-provincial dealings recently, the question is whether we have reached the limits of the piecemeal, remedial approach. There appears to be increasing criticism of the capacity of the existing institutions and processes to cope with future changes.

A related observation is that the substance of federal-provincial dealings and the effectiveness of the institutions and processes are closely related. As areas of overlapping activity have increased, the potential for conflict has grown because there is more at stake. In response to this greater complexity and to enhance their bargaining positions, governments have created new institutions and processes. These arrangements shape to some extent the perceptions of the participants within the intergovernmental process. As indicated earlier, more elaborate structures do not necessarily contribute to greater harmony; they may, in fact, serve to increase tension.

So far we have tended to portray federal and provincial governments as monolithic entities representing a single viewpoint in the intergovernmental process. However, there is evidence to suggest that this is not always the case. Disagreements over policy and its implementation *within* governments can have significance for the relationships which exist *among* governments. The "bureaucratic politics" model focusses on bargaining within governments. Richard Schultz employs it to provide an insightful case study of regulation of highway transportation in Canada.[74] It was Ottawa's hope in the late 1960s to assume regulatory control over interprovincial trucking by implementing Part III of the National Transportation Act (1967). However, it realized it needed provincial cooperation since trucking until then had been regulated by provincial authorities. According to Schultz, Ottawa failed to implement Part III because of the struggle between the Department of Transport and the Canadian Transport Commission. Internal conflict weakened the federal government as an effective negotiator and that is why the provinces won out, not because of their own effectiveness.[75]

Schultz's study shows that governments will not always behave as "unitary actors" for purposes of intergovernmental dealings. Even the recent rise of coordinating units, like the Federal-Provincial Relations Office in Ottawa or the new departments of intergovernmental affairs at the provincial level, do not guarantee that governments will always approach negotiations with a single, unified position. Schultz maintains on the basis of his case study that intergovernmental affairs units may be weaker in relation to regular line departments within their own governments than is often assumed. He presents several observations to support this view. First, despite the recent growth of central agencies, the staffs remain relatively small, while the scope of their responsibilities for monitoring programs and activities is broad. Secondly, while central agents may be "specialists in the 'machinery of government' or in intergovernmental relations," they "are essentially amateurs and generalists when it comes to specific policy issues."[76] Thirdly, given the small size and stretched capability of the central agencies they are often dependent upon regular departments for specialized knowledge and advice on policy alternatives. Since departments may be suspicious and resentful of the "whiz kids" in the central agencies, they may cooperate less than fully by withholding information, presenting biased information or not submitting proposals until the last moment when there is no time to investigate alternative approaches. While Schultz would not deny that central agencies have significant influence over policy-making, because of their strategic location, he speculates this may, in fact, be waning as operating departments establish their own intergovernmental relations units and begin to challenge the central agency "process" specialists.[77]

Two final themes can be identified from our earlier discussions. First, the available literature reveals considerable diversity in the intergovernmental process. The exercise of power, both by politicians and by public servants, appears to depend greatly on the issue under consideration. The relations at the political and administrative levels can be conflictual or cooperative, although harmony among program specialists is more likely for the reasons cited earlier.

A second observation is that, within limits, individual personalities and actions can be crucial factors in intergovernmental relations. For example, it appears that Tom Kent, as principal secretary to the Prime Minister, played a critical role in Ottawa's takeover of adult occupational training in the late 1960s. Later he was influential in the launching of the Department of Regional Economic Expansion.[78] In a similar, though perhaps less positive manner, Jack Pickersgill as President of the Canadian Transport Commission helped to scuttle Ottawa's plans to assume regulatory control over interprovincial trucking.[79] The key role played by a small number of appointed officials within the intergovernmental process leads us to a discussion of the implications of federal-provincial relations for responsible and responsive government.

Responsible and Responsive Government and Federalism

The intricate system of intergovernmental committees and contacts described above poses real challenges to the achievement of responsibility and responsiveness within the political system. Of necessity, public servants have a considerable role to play in operating the structures and processes of federalism. In an excellent paper, Ken Kernaghan has argued that the sources of bureaucratic power in the intergovernmental field are the same as in other fields: specialized knowledge, experience, contacts with interest groups, and discretion to formulate and to implement policy.[80] Diplomatic and bargaining skills can be important for bureaucratic success throughout government and they can be particularly critical in the intergovernmental field. Inevitably, politicians must entrust to their officials the freedom, subject to their instructions, to negotiate agreements on their behalf, particularly regarding technical questions like the taxation agreements. Kernaghan also indicates that in multilateral negotiations, involving all 11 governments, the balancing of competing interests can become extremely complicated and ministers may be reluctant to reject tentative agreements unless their objections are substantial and/or they have an alternative to offer.

In the conduct of negotiations, officials must, of course, remain sensitive to the wishes of their ministers and the cabinet as a whole. To a certain extent such officials become emissaries and spokesmen on behalf of their governments. And because the federal-provincial bargaining process has become more prominent in recent years, the officials involved have lost some of their traditional, bureaucratic anonymity. Bureaucrats who participate in well-publicized, federal-provincial clashes may become so publicly identified with a particular approach to federalism generally or to specific policy issues that their usefulness to subsequent governments, attempting to follow different policy approaches, can be impaired. At least this was the view of Gordon Robertson, who left the post of Secretary to the Cabinet for Federal-Provincial Relations in order to prevent possible embarrassment to the new Conservative government, which was seeking a different approach toward the provinces. According to Robertson, his close identification with the constitutional philosophy and approaches of previous Trudeau governments would inhibit Prime Minister Clark's efforts in this direction.

An additional concern about the current system is that it further weakens the role of legislatures within the policy process. As the phrase "executive federalism" implies, the intergovernmental process is dominated by cabinet ministers and their senior administrators.[81] Legislators have very little input into federal-provincial decision-making. There are few opportunities for legislators to examine intergovernmental issues before legislation incorporating agreements reached at federal-provincial conferences is presented to the legislature. Because the agreements enshrined in such legislation are often the product of long and complicated negotiations there is a natural reluctance on the part of the cabinet ministers involved to accept changes at the legislative stage with which other governments may disagree. Besides being excluded from participation, legislatures may not even be able to obtain a full accounting from the executive for its actions within the intergovernmental arena. For example, it is notable that neither the federal Parliament nor most provincial legislatures have developed standing committees on intergovernmental relations, despite the crucial importance of such relations within the policy process. Part of the reason for this failure, in addition to the natural reluctance on the part of cabinets to expose their actions to opposition criticism, is that the scope of the work of such committees would be potentially limitless since federal-provincial relations touch on almost every policy field.

A related concern about the intergovernmental process is the secrecy which it generates.[82] The current emphasis on conflict and negotiations within the federal system encourages the participating governments to play issues "close to the vest" so as not to give their adversaries advance knowledge of their policy positions and strategies. Closed federal-provincial conferences mean that legislators and the public are prevented from knowing what considerations went into the reaching of agreements. The complexity of the issues and the technical language ("opting out," "tax points," "fiscal equivalence," and so on) used, make public understanding and participation even harder. Governmental concern about the "stakes" of the bargaining game may well lead to a competition from which interest groups are directly excluded. For example, in the recent federal-provincial clashes over mining and oil revenues, the industries complained about being the only interested parties not represented in the discussions which would determine their future. While many observers have lamented the inadequate scrutiny and the loss of accountability associated with the rise of "executive federalism," there are practical limits to any reforms that might be contemplated. As mentioned earlier, legislative committees on federal-provincial relations, while useful, potentially could overlap with all other policy committees. Freedom of information statutes at the federal and provincial levels might help, but significantly most such proposals would exclude documents related to current federal-provincial negotiations from the scope of such legislation.[83]

Managing Intergovernmental Relations in the 1980s

A recent survey of 100 federal senior executives revealed that they considered federal-provincial relations the single most important public service issue over the next five years.[84] The overall relationship between the central government and the provinces continues to change and there is disagreement over the exact direction in which it should go. Besides, the general relationship encompasses a great variety of contacts among governments. These range all the way from the highly political, widely publicized and conflict-ridden encounters in conjunction with the constitutional review and energy pricing down to the more mundane cases of administrative cooperation in fields where the division of labor between governments is fairly well established and the "high politics" of federalism are absent or muted.

In recent years there has been some movement towards "disentanglement" of the functions of the two levels of government through a reduction of overlapping and joint programs. The main example of this trend is the Established Programs Financing provisions contained in the 1977 Fiscal Arrangements Act. Some observers would like to see this process carried further because they view the current intergovernmental process as inherently inefficient and slow. Moreover, the present arrangement, in which one level of government raises money while another level spends it, leads to fiscal irresponsibility and compounds the problem of achieving democratic accountability for results. Coherent joint policy-making is often impossible because the political, financial and status concerns of the participating governments always intrude into discussions and warp the results.

However, other observers reject as unrealistic the call for a return to any "watertight compartments" version of federalism. Given the interconnections among policies in the real world and the fact that many policy instruments are widely shared among governments, there is little chance of their operating in splendid isolation from one another. While not hostile to "disentanglement" where possible, this view suggests that such possibilities are limited and must be assessed against the costs involved. If disentanglement is achieved by means of further decentralization of responsibilities and revenues to the provincial governments, there is a real danger that interprovincial disparities in the quality of services will arise and there could be a loss of the portability of program benefits which Canadians now enjoy. In this view, nationally sponsored joint programs may not always have been administered with sufficient sensitivity to regional needs and concerns, but this is not a convincing argument for abandoning them entirely since they have been the vehicle for social and economic progress, especially within the poorer regions. And in this view, also, Ottawa must continue to act as the redistributing agency of wealth from the rich provinces to the poorer ones. The Economic Council of Canada has recently warned, however, that because of the tax room Ottawa has granted to the provinces it is in a poor position to play a major role in economic management and to conduct major national policies.[85]

Complexity and controversy appear to be inherent and persistent features of the federal system. Policy and administrative issues frequently become joined in the intergovernmental arena. Basic objectives often seem to clash with one another. We want greater coordination of the diverse, often conflicting, goals and programs of the two levels of government, but not at the expense of the autonomy of one level. We want more constructive collaboration among intergovernmental officials, but such officials should not escape an "appropriate" degree of ministerial and parliamentary supervision and control. A more representative and decentralized federal bureaucracy may produce gains in terms of the policy responsiveness and the legitimacy of central decision-making, but what would it mean for the merit principle in recruiting and for ministerial responsibility for departmental actions? "Regulatory sharing" might promote greater intergovernmental cooperation, but would this be obtained at the cost of the traditional independence of regulatory agencies? Clearly the effective management of the federal system is a complex, difficult task involving the delicate balancing of different values and interests. The future promises plenty of challenges to the practitioners who must operate the federal system and the students who seek to analyze and understand it.

For Further Reading

BOOKS AND REPORTS

Black, E. R. *Divided Loyalties: Canadian Concepts of Federalism*. Montreal: McGill-Queen's Press, 1975.

Burns, R. M. *Intergovernmental Liaison on Fiscal and Economic Matters*. Kingston: Institute of Intergovernmental Relations, Queen's University, 1968.

Careless, Anthony G. S. *Initiative and Response: The Adaptation of Canadian Federalism to Regional Economic Development*. Montreal: McGill-Queen's University Press, 1977.

Dupré, J. Stefan, et. al. *Federalism and Policy Development: The Case of Adult Occupational Training in Ontario*. Toronto: University of Toronto Press, 1973.

Meekison, J. P. ed. *Canadian Federalism: Myth or Reality*, 3rd ed. Toronto: Methuen, 1977.

Moore, A. Milton, J. Harvey Perry and Donald I. Beach. *The Financing of the Canadian Federation: The First Hundred Years*. Toronto: Canadian Tax Foundation, 1966.

Morin, Claude. *Quebec versus Ottawa: The Struggle for Self-Government, 1960-1972*. Toronto: University of Toronto Press, 1976.

Schultz, Richard J. *Federalism, Bureaucracy and Public Policy: The Politics of Highway Transport Regulation*. Montreal: McGill-Queen's University Press, 1980.

———. *Federalism and the Regulatory Process*. Montreal: Institute for Research on Public Policy, 1979.

Simeon, R. *Federal-Provincial Diplomacy: The Making of Recent Policy in Canada*. Toronto: University of Toronto Press, 1972.

———. ed. *Confrontation and Collaboration — Intergovernmental Relations in Canada Today*. Toronto: Institute of Public Administration of Canada, 1979.

Smiley, D. V. *Conditional Grants and Canadian Federalism*. Toronto: Canadian Tax Foundation, 1963.

———. *Constitutional Adaptation and Canadian Federalism Since 1945*. Ottawa: Information Canada, 1970.

———. *Canada in Question: Federalism in the Eighties*, 3rd ed. Toronto: McGraw-Hill Ryerson, 1980.

Stevenson, Garth. *Unfulfilled Union*. Toronto: Macmillan, 1979.

ARTICLES

Beer, Samuel H. "Political Overload and Federalism." *Polity*, (November 1977), pp. 5-17.

Burns, R. M. "Intergovernmental Relations in Canada." *Canadian Public Administration*, Vol. XXXIII, 1 (Spring 1973), pp. 14-22.

Cairns, A. "The Governments and Societies of Canadian Federalism." *Canadian Journal of Political Science*, Vol. X, 4 (December 1977), pp. 695-725.

———. "The Other Crisis of Canadian Federalism." *Canadian Public Administration*, Vol. XXII, 2 (Summer 1979), pp. 175-95.

Dupré, J. Stefan. "Reflections on the fiscal and economic aspects of government by conference." *Canadian Public Administration*, Vol. XXIII, 1 (Spring 1980), pp. 54-59.

Dyck, R. "The Canada Assistance Plan: The Ultimate in Cooperative Federalism." *Canadian Public Administration*, Vol. XIX, 4 (Winter 1976), pp. 587-602.

Pratt, L. "The state and province-building: Alberta's development strategy." Panitch, L., ed., *The Canadian State: Political Economy and Political Power*, Toronto: University of Toronto Press, 1977.

Simeon, Richard. "Intergovernmental relations and the challenges to Canadian federalism." *Canadian Public Administration*, Vol. XXIII, 1 (Spring 1980), pp. 14-32.

———. "The Federal-Provincial Decision-Making Process." *Intergovernmental Relations*, Toronto: Ontario Economic Council, 1977, pp. 25-38.

Smiley, D. V. "Federal-Provincial Conflict in Canada." *Publius: The Journal of Federalism*, Vol. 4 (Summer 1974), pp. 17-24.

———. "Territorialism and Canadian Political Institutions." *Canadian Public Policy*, Vol. III, 4 (Winter 1977).

ENDNOTES

1. A collection of some of the most relevant material is found in the several editions of J. Peter Meekison (ed.), *Canadian Federalism: Myth or Reality*, 3rd ed. (Toronto, Methuen, 1977).
2. The best known example of the constitutional approach to the study of federalism is K.C. Wheare, *Federal Government*, 4th ed. (London: Oxford University Press, 1963).
3. M.J.C. Vile, *The Structure of American Federalism* (London: Oxford University Press, 1961), p. 199.
4. Alan Cairns, "The Other Crisis of Canadian Federalism," *Canadian Public Administration*, Vol. XXII, 2 (Summer, 1980), pp. 175-95.
5. This thesis is part of the illuminating study by John Richards and Larry Pratt, *Prairie Capitalism: Power and Influence in the New West* (Toronto: McClelland & Stewart, 1979).
6. Alan C. Cairns, "The Governments and Societies of Canadian Federalism," *Canadian Journal of Political Science*, Vol. X, 4 (December, 1977), p. 702.
7. Morton Godzins wrote: "As colours are mixed in the marble cake, so functions are mixed in the American federal system," in "The Federal System," in Aaron Wildavsky (ed.), *American Federalism in Perspective* (Boston: Little Brown & Co., 1967). Malcolm Taylor, *Health Insurance and Canadian Public Policy* (Montreal: McGill-Queen's, 1979), p. xi, argues for the relevance of the metaphor to the Canadian situation.
8. The following discussion is based upon J.R. Mallory, "The Five Faces of Federalism," in J. Peter Meekison (ed.), *Canadian Federalism: Myth or Reality*, 3rd ed. (Toronto: Methuen, 1977), pp. 19-30; G.V. LaForest, *The Allocation of Taxing Power Under the Canadian Constitution* (Toronto: Canadian Tax Foundation, 1967) and A. Milton Moore, J. Harvey Perry and Donald I. Beach, *The Financing of Canadian Federation: The First Hundred Years* (Toronto: Canadian Tax Foundation, 1966).
9. Edgar Gallant, "The Machinery of Federal-Provincial Relations," in J. Peter Meekison (ed.), *Canadian Federalism: Myth or Reality*, 2nd ed. (Toronto: Methuen, 1971), p. 255.
10. See Peter Russell, *Leading Constitutional Decisions: Cases on the British North America Act*, revised. (Toronto: McClelland & Stewart, 1973); Martha Fletcher, "Judicial Review and the Division of Powers in Canada," in Meekison, *op. cit.*, pp. 100-23, and Alan C. Cairns, "The Judicial Committee and its Critics," *Canadian Journal of Political Science*, Vol. IV, 3 (September, 1971), pp. 301-45.
11. Moore, Perry and Beach, p. 9.
12. D.V. Smiley, *Conditional Grants and Canadian Federalism* (Toronto: Canadian Tax Foundation, 1963), p. 3.
13. Canada, Royal Commission on Dominion-Provincial Relations, *Report*, (Ottawa: King's Printer, 1940), Book I, pp. 257-59.
14. See J.A. Corry, *Difficulties of Divided Jurisdiction* (Ottawa: King's Printer, 1939), Chapter 6, a study prepared for the Royal Commission on Dominion-Provincial Relations, and the assessment by D.V. Smiley, "Public Administration and Canadian Federalism," in J. Peter

Meekison (ed.), *Canadian Federalism Myth or Reality* (Toronto: Methuen, 1968), pp. 271-87.

15. See Donald V. Smiley, "The Federal Dimension of Canadian Economic Nationalism," *Dalhousie Law Journal*, Vol. I (October, 1974), pp. 551-79.
16. The following discussion is based upon E.R. Black and A.C. Cairns, "A Different Perspective on Canadian Federalism," *Canadian Public Administration*, Vol. IX, 1 (March 1966), pp. 27-45, and D.V. Smiley, *Constitutional Adaptation and Canadian Federalism Since 1945* (Ottawa: Information Canada, 1970), Chapter 3.
17. Smiley, *Constitutional Adaptation*.
18. The government of Quebec has remained outside the agreements since the outset and since 1952 Ontario has collected its own corporation income taxes.
19. On conditional grants see George Carter, *Canadian Conditional Grants Since World War II* (Toronto: Canadian Tax Foundations, 1971) and Donald V. Smiley, *Conditional Grants and Canadian Federalism* (Toronto: Canadian Tax Foundation, 1963).

20 F.R. Scott, "The Constitutional Background of the Taxation Agreements," *McGill Law Journal*, Vol. II (1955), p. 6.

21. Carter, p. 24-25.
22. D.V. Smiley, "Public Administration and Canadian Federalism," *op. cit.*, pp. 278-79.
23. R.M. Burns, *Report: Intergovernmental Liaison on Fiscal and Economic Matters* (Kingston: Institute of Intergovernmental Affairs, Queen's University, 1968), p. 122.
24. *Ibid.*, p. 123.
25. D.V. Smiley, "Public Administration and Canadian Federalism," *op. cit.*, p. 278.
26. See Deil S. Wright, *Understanding Intergovernmental Relations* (North Scitate, Mass: Duxbury Press, 1978), p. 62.
27. Malcolm Taylor, pp. 22-23.
28. K.W. Taylor, "Coordination in Administration," Proceedings of the Sixth Annual Conference of the Institute of Public Administration of Canada (Toronto, 1954), p. 253.
29. A.R. Kear, "Cooperative Federalism: A Study of the Federal-Provincial Continuing Committee on Fiscal and Economic Matters in J. Peter Meekison (ed.), *Canadian Federalism: Myth or Reality* (Toronto: Methuen, 1968), pp. 311-312.
30. Canada, Royal Commission on Taxation, *Final Report* (Ottawa: Queen's Printer, 1967), Vol. 2, pp. 93-103 and Vol. 6, pp. 188-201.
31. Donald V. Smiley, "The Federal Dimension of Canadian Economic Nationalism," *op. cit.*, p. 563.
32. The most comprehensive account of the rise of nationalism in Quebec and its more recent expressions is by Kenneth McRoberts and Dale Postgate, *Quebec: Social Change and Political Crisis* rev. ed. (Toronto: McClelland and Stewart, 1980).
33. See Richard Simeon, *Federal-Provincial Diplomacy: The Making of Recent Policy in Canada* (Toronto: University of Toronto Press, 1972), pp. 172-3.
34. For a detailed account of the series of five-year Tax Sharing Agreements see Moore, Perry and Beach, *op. cit*.
35. For more detail on the 1977 Fiscal Arrangements Act see Thomas J. Courchene, *Refinancing the Canadian Federation: The 1977 Fiscal Arrangements Act* (Montreal: C.D. Howe Institute, 1978) and David B. Perry "The Federal-Provincial Fiscal Arrangements Introduced in 1977," *Canadian Tax Journal*, Vol. XXV, 4 (July-August, 1977), pp. 429-40.
36. *The National Finances, 1979-1980* (Toronto: Canadian Tax Foundation, 1980), p. 25.
37. See Garth Stevenson, *Unfulfilled Union* (Toronto: Macmillan, 1979), Chapter 7 and Donald V. Smiley, *Constitutional Adaptation and Canadian Federalism*, Chapter 5.
38. See Malcolm Taylor, Chapter 6.
39. See E.R. Blac, *Divided Loyalties: Canadian Concepts of Federalism* (Montreal: McGill-Queen's, 1975). pp. 82-83 for a calculation of what he calls a "policy limitation" index.
40. See Carter, Chapter 3 for a extended discussion of equalization and conditional grants.
41. See ibid, Chapter 5, and J. Stefan Dupre, "Contracting Out: A Funny Thing Happened on the

Way to the Centennial," *Report of the Eighteenth Annual Tax Conference* (Toronto: Canadian Tax Foundation, 1965), pp. 209-18.

42. See the interpretation of this period by Claude Morin, former Deputy Minister of Intergovernmental Affairs in the Quebec Government, in Claude Morin, *Quebec Versus Ottawa: The Struggle for Self-Government 1960-1972* (Toronto: University of Toronto Press, 1976).
43. For Mr. Trudeau's constitutional philosophy see Pierre Elliott Trudeau, *Federalism and the French Canadians* (Toronto: Macmillan, 1968).
44. See George E. Carter, "Financing Health and Post-Secondary Education: A New and Complex Fiscal Arrangement," *Canadian Tax Journal*, Vol. XXV, 5 (September-October 1977), pp. 535-50 and Pierre Elliott Trudeau, "Established Program Financing: A Proposal Regarding the Major Shared-Cost Programs in the Fields of Health and Post-Secondary Education," in Meekison (ed.), *op. cit.*, pp. 246-258.
45. Courchene, p. 47.
46. See P.E. Trudeau, *Federal-Provincial Grants and the Spending Power of Parliament* (Ottawa: Queen's Printer, 1969) for a statement of the proposal and D.V. Smiley and R.M. Burns, "Canadian Federalism and the Spending Power: Is Constitutional Restriction Necessary," *Canadian Tax Journal* Vol. XVII, 6 (November-December, 1969).
47. D.V. Smiley, *Canada in Question: Federalism in the Eighties* (Toronto: McGraw-Hill Ryerson, 1980), Chapter 4.
48. *Ibid*, pp. 109-116.
49. See Gerard Veuilleux, "L'évolution des méchanismes de liaison intergouvernmentale," in Richard Simeon (ed.), *Confrontation and Collaboration: Intergovernmental Relations in Canada* (Toronto: Institute of Public Administration of Canada, 1979), p. 37.
50. "Federal-Provincial Administrative Liaison in Canada," in Kenneth Kernaghan (ed.), *Public Administration in Canada*, 3rd ed. (Toronto: Methuen, 1977), pp. 80-81.
51. See Richard Simeon, *Federal-Provincial Diplomacy*, pp. 125-32 for a discussion of First Ministers meetings.
52. *Ibid*. p. 129.
53. Douglas Brown, *Intergovernmental Relations in Canada: The Year in Review 1979* (Kingston: Institute of Intergovernmental Relations, 1980), pp. 39-40.
54. See, *Ibid*., pp. 40-47
55. See Rick Van Loon, "Reforming Welfare in Canada," *Public Policy*, Vol. XXVII, 4 (Fall, 1979), pp. 469-504.
56. Donald Higgins, *Urban Canada: Its Government and Politics* (Toronto: Macmillan, 1977), pp. 86-90 and Donald Higgins, "Tri-Level Consultation: The Passing of a (Brief) Era?" *Urban Forum*, Vol. III, 4 (November-December, 1977), pp. 6-9, 37-39.
57. Simeon, p. 134.
58. John W. Langford, *Transport in Transition: The Reorganization of the Federal Transport Portfolio* (Montreal: McGill-Queen's, 1976), pp. 194-95.
59. See A.A. Lomas, "The Council of Maritime Premiers: Report and Evaluation After Five Years," in J. Peter Meekison (ed.), *Canadian Federalism: Myth or Reality*, 3rd ed. (Toronto: Methuen, 1977), pp. 353-63 and Douglas Brown, *The Federal Year in Review: 1977-78* (Kingston: Institute of Intergovernmental Relations, Queen's University, 1979), pp. 99-101.
60. See Brown, pp. 101-102 and M. Westmacott and P. Dore, "Intergovernmental Cooperation in Western Canada: The Western Economic Opportunities Conference," in J. Peter Meekison (ed.), *op. cit*., pp. 340-52 for some historical background.
61. D.V. Smiley, *Canada in Question*, pp. 97-98.
62. Colin Campbell and George Szablowski, *The Superbureaucrats: Structure and Behaviour in Central Agencies* (Toronto: Macmillan, 1979), pp. 49-51.
63. D.V. Smiley, *Canada in Question*, pp. 111-116.
64. See Harold S. Clarke, Jane Jenson, Lawrence LeDuc and Jon H. Pammett, *Political Choice in Canada* (Toronto: McGraw-Hill Ryerson, 1979).
65. Anthony G.S. Careless, *Initiative and Response: The Adaptation of Canadian Federalism to Regional Economic Development* (Montreal: McGill-Queen's, 1977).

66. See. T. Brewis, "Regional Economic Policy in Canada," in E. Hansen (ed.), *Public Policy and Regional Economic Development* (Cambridge, MA: Ballinger, 1974), pp. 305-33.
67. Careless, p. 207.
68. See J. Stefan Dupré *et. al.*, *Federalism and Policy Development: The Case of Adult Occupational Training in Ontario* (Toronto: University of Toronto Press, 1973) and the excellent articles in R.B. Byers and Robert W. Redford (eds.), *Canada Challenged: The Viability of Confederation* (Toronto: Canadian Institute of International Affairs, 1979).
69. Gordon Robertson, "The Role of Interministerial Conferences in the Decision-Making Process," in Richard Simeon (ed.), *Confrontation and Collaboration*, pp. 80-83.
70. Economic Council of Canada, *Responsible Regulation* (Ottawa: Supply and Services, 1979).
71. Richard J. Schultz, *Federalism and the Regulatory Process* (Montreal: Institute for Research on Public Policy, 1979), pp. 26-27.
72. *Ibid.*, Chapter 5.
73. *Ibid.*, p. 69.
74. Richard J. Schultz, *Federalism, Bureaucracy and Public Policy: The Politics of Highway Transport Regulation* (Montreal: McGill-Queen's, 1980).
75. *Ibid.*, p. 169.
76. *Ibid.*, p. 183.
77. *Ibid.*, p. 187.
78. Dupré *et. al.*, pp. 41-44 and Careless, pp. 61-63.
79. Schultz, *Federalism, Bureaucracy and Public Policy*, Chapters 5 and 6.
80. Kenneth Kernaghan, "The Power and Responsibility of the Intergovernmental Officials in Canada," (Paper presented to the Annual Conference of the Institute of Public Administration of Canada, Winnipeg, August 31, 1979).
81. See the remarks by Hon. Robert Stanfield, "The Present State of the Legislative Process in Canada: Myths and Realities," in W.A.W. Neilson and J.C. MacPherson, *The Legislative Process in Canada: The Need for Reform* (Toronto: Butterworth, 1978), p. 44.
82. Richard Simeon, "The Federal-Provincial Decision Making Process," in *Issues in Intergovernmental Relations* (Toronto: Ontario Economic Council, 1977), p. 35.
83. See Chapter 9 on "Administrative Secrecy."
84. Seymour Isenberg, "Profile of the Senior Management Environment in the Federal Public Service," *Optimum*, Vol. X, 1 (1979), pp. 5-20.
85. Economic Council of Canada, *Two Cheers for the Eighties* (Ottawa: Supply and Services, 1979), p. 57.

CHAPTER EIGHT

Accountability in the Administrative State

Introduction

Accountability has become a buzz word in government circles. Everyone seems to agree that there is not enough of it around, though not everyone agrees on what it is or why it is in short supply. The recent Royal Commission on Financial Management and Accountability likened accountability to electricity, being difficult to define but possessing qualities that make its presence immediately detectable. It should permeate and discipline governments, obliging the participants, both elected and appointed, "to pay attention to their respective assigned and accepted responsibilities."[1] This chapter examines the origins of the current quest for accountability in government and several alternative approaches to ensuring its presence within the political system.

Accountability is important in a democracy because of the need for the governed to be protected, in some manner, from the arbitrary use of power by the governors. With government activity growing so extensive in scope and so technical in content, there is a great concern that the future will involve an administrative state ruled by the bureaucracy. Must we continue to delegate increasing authority to administrative bodies staffed by experts? How can the administrative state be legitimized through effective democratic control? To what extent should the opinion of the experts in the bureaucracy be subordinated to the "inexpert" and partisan opinion of practising politicians? What is to stop public organizations from developing and exercising a will of their own separate from that of the political leadership in the society? These are enormous and difficult questions for which there are no easy answers.

In a democracy citizens seek to control their elected representatives who, in turn, are supposed to control the bureaucracy. To be successful such control must obviously consist of more than just formally installing elected representatives in government offices. If accountability is absent or weakly enforced in the relationships between Cabinet and the bureaucracy or between Parliament and Cabinet, then administrative actions will not be subject ultimately to popular, democratic control. Therefore, the ideal model of accountability in a cabinet-parliamentary system can be portrayed as follows; the lighter, upper arrows indicating the flow of accountability and the broader, lower arrows indicating the lines of control:

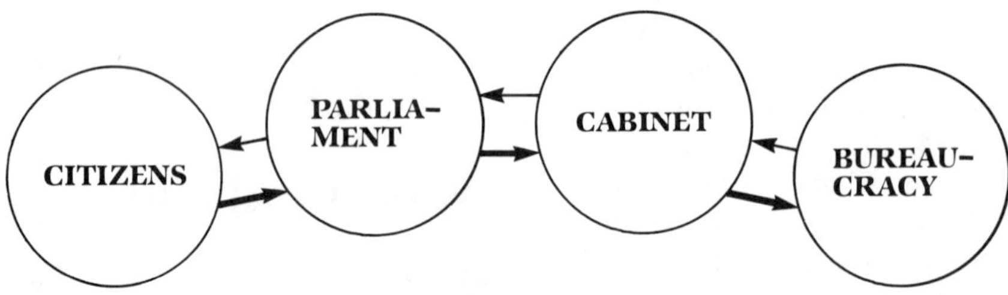

This simplified diagram obviously hides the many complexities and ambiguities of accountability relationships which exist in the real world, but it provides a starting point for thinking about the prevailing Canadian approach to bureaucratic accountability.

While control by elected representatives over bureaucratic actions is a basic constitutional principle in Canada, beyond a certain point, political interference in actual administrative operations is considered undesirable. Canadians, for example, want their bureaucracies to be loyal and responsive when new parties come into office, and one way of achieving this would be through large-scale dismissal of existing public servants and appointment of others whom the party has clear reason to trust. However, we also value the continuity and stability provided by a permanent, career public service. Similarly, we want ministers to provide leadership to government departments, but we also want judgment and originality in the bureaucracy. We want our public servants to obey their ministers, but they should not acquiesce automatically to improper, illegal or erroneous demands. Ministers must be sufficiently aware of the administrative operations of their departments, but they should not meddle unduly with the daily responsibilities of their officials. "Obedience and independence, stability and adaptability, power and restraints on power, cooperation and resistance — the problem of political control of the bureaucracy is obviously one of relative dilemmas."[2]

Some clarification of terminology seems necessary here. Definitions for the words "accountability" and "responsibility" have been the subject of lengthy debates in public administration and political science literature.[3] There is no space here to review the numerous semantic disagreements, but it should be noted that they contribute greatly to the problematical nature of accountability. We have selected a definition presented by Frederick Mosher that is sufficiently broad to incorporate the leading ideas represented in the debate.

Mosher distinguishes between objective and subjective responsibility. Objective responsibility "connotes the responsibility of a person or an organization to someone else, outside of self, for some thing or some kind of performance. It is closely akin to accountability or answerability. If one fails to carry out legitimate directives, he is judged irresponsible, and may be subjected to penalties."[4] Subjective responsibility, on the other hand, focuses "not upon to whom or for what one is responsible (according to law and the organization chart) but to whom and for what one feels responsible and behaves responsibly."[5] This second meaning is more synonymous with identification and loyalty, rather than with accountability and answerability. The latter definition highlights the importance of the value systems and professional norms of public servants to the achievement of administrative responsibility. This subjective responsibility can complement objective responsibility (accountability) and it can also short-circuit it. In either case, this can be to social benefit or to social detriment, or to both. We deal with this problem toward the end of the chapter.

Beginning then with objective responsibility, some additional distinctions should be noted. We must distinguish the *political* responsibility of elected politicians from the *administrative* responsibility of public servants. Both groups of actors are subject to external and internal controls and influences. Control refers to a superior-subordinate relationship in which one individual or organization is able to direct on the basis of his authority the behavior of another individual ot organization. Influence is a more general phenomenon in which individual or organizational behavior is shaped by the words or actions of others, but there is no formal authority relationship involved.[6] As we explore the current Canadian approach to controlling the bureaucracy, the significance of these distinctions will become clear.

Ministerial Responsibility in Canada

The doctrine of ministerial responsibility is central to cabinet-parliamentary government in Canada and provides the basis on which Canadians seek to control the bureaucracy. There are two dimensions to this doctrine. First, members of the Cabinet are *collectively* responsible to Parliament for the overall performance of the government and may remain in office only as long as they retain the support of a majority in the House of Commons. Under modern conditions, Cabinet takes the initiative for presenting legislative and spending proposals to Parliament for its approval. Individual ministers must either support Cabinet's plans, stifle their dissent, or resign. To preserve the image of unity and to encourage uninhibited discussion, decision-making at Cabinet level occurs in private. Cabinet solidarity and confidentiality allegedly facilitate the assignment of responsibility within the political system. Parliament directly and the public indirectly know that both credit and/or blame for policies rests with the Cabinet. The doctrine of collective ministerial responsibility is primarily a convention, rather than a legal requirement, but it has become essential to the democratic control of the use of political power.

Individual ministerial responsibility, the second dimension of the doctrine, is equally essential to Canada's system of accountability. A minister is personally responsible for the activities carried out under his authority and he must answer to Parliament for the actions of his department. The statutes creating departments provide for the appointment of a minister and give him responsibility for the management and direction of the financial and public service resources deployed in it. The pure theory of the doctrine implies that every act of a public servant shall be regarded as an act of his minister, and in the event of a grave error by his department the minister must resign.

It is important to recognize that the doctrine of ministerial responsibility has both political and administrative significance. Politically, it requires that elected politicians, rather than appointed officials, will take final responsibility for the policies of government. The government is responsible to Parliament — and so to the electorate — for its actions. Ministers may be questioned in Parliament on all aspects of administration for which they are responsible. Both individually and collectively, the ultimate sanction for error or abuse of authority may be the loss of political office for cabinet ministers.

Administratively, the corollary of this complete political responsibility for policies is the notion of an anonymous, impartial, career public service. Public servants do not take public credit or blame for the decisions and policies of ministers. They have a duty to advise, warn, criticize and object if they feel strongly about their minister's plans. However, after a public servant has made his views known in frank, confidential discussions and once departmental policy is settled, he must stifle his disagreements and implement the policy faithfully. Public servants must also avoid certain kinds of partisan political activity that might destroy their potential usefulness to future governments. In return for this partial sacrifice of their political rights, public servants theoretically enjoy immunity from public criticism since ministers will accept responsibility for policy and administrative errors, and public servants also enjoy security of tenure during good behavior and satisfactory performance. Public servants, in short, are accountable to Parliament only indirectly through their ministers.

Several important points arise out of this discussion of the political and administrative implications of ministerial responsibility. The first is that the doctrine rests on a distinction between policy and administration which, as we have noted in an earlier context, has been strongly criticized as artificial and incapable of application in the real world of government decision-making. According to many observers, it is unrealistic any longer to portray the bureaucracy merely as an instrument of the politicians. We will return to this debate shortly.

A second point is the interrelated nature of the doctrine of ministerial responsibility and the separate notion of a permanent public service. These ideas complement and reinforce one another. Thus, ministerial responsibility requires that the public servant ultimately subordinate his personal views on policy to those of the minister. The concept of a career public service requires that the public servant not become personally identified with contentious or partisan issues. This neutrality reinforces loyalty to the minister by requiring from the public servant a silent execution of his obligations.

The complementary nature of the two concepts poses a serious problem for reformers who wish to modify current constitutional philosophy to correspond more accurately to contemporary realities of government. Changing one part of the interrelated and logically coherent set of ideas has consequences for the remainder of the accountability system. Diagnosis of the problems of accountability, therefore, is easier and evokes more agreement than does prescription for reform.

Criticisms of ministerial responsibility are directed at both the political and administrative aspects of the doctrine. Many commentators have argued that changing political reality has undermined the viability of the device as a means of democratic control. First, it has been argued frequently that governments (cabinets) are no longer effectively accountable to Parliament because of the rise of disciplined political parties and the consequent disappearance of the ultimate political sanction of defeat of a government on the floor of the House of Commons. While the nature and consequences of party discipline in the House of Commons cannot be investigated here, it is worth pointing out that such a criticism presumes the existence of a majority government whereas Canadians elected six minority governments in the 10 elections held between 1957 and 1980. Presumably the withdrawal of support by the Commons is a more real prospect in a minority situation, and therefore such governments are supposedly more responsive to opinion in the Commons than are those with large majorities. Nonetheless, few observers would disagree with the argument that the rise of disciplined political parties has weakened the democratic control exercised by Parliament on behalf of the electorate.

A second development which calls into question individual ministerial responsibility is the far greater scope and technical nature of departmental operations today as compared to the 19th century when the concept was adopted in Canada. No longer is it realistic to assume that a minister can be aware of all actions taken in his name. In large departments the minister is able to see only a few of the most important or politically sensitive matters handled by his officials. There are heavy demands on a minister's time arising from his roles as a member of Cabinet and its committees, a member of a political party, a constituency representative and a Member of Parliament. He must, therefore, delegate management authority to his senior officials, particularly to the deputy minister. And since it is unrealistic to expect ministers to possess detailed knowledge of departmental operations, they are no longer willing to assume full responsibility for actions taken under their authority. The convention has become that their liability extends to flaws in policy with which they are personally identified and to major administrative errors which can be traced directly to their instructions. Minor administrative errors or even serious blunders of which they had no prior knowledge are not deemed to fall within the scope of ministerial responsibility. Since it is difficult, if not impossible, for Parliament, the media and the public to discover whether a minister approved of, or was involved in, a faulty or improper administrative action, the minister can usually escape blame by denying personal knowledge, promising to correct the mistake and discipline the offending public servants.

Cases do arise where the personal culpability of the minister is clear, but even in such situations there is no longer an automatic obligation on a minister to resign. His fate depends upon situational factors and partisan considerations.[8] Illegal, unethical and immoral acts will usually lead to resignation.[9] Lesser offences by a minister, for example, a failure to correct maladministration in his department, will not cause a resignation. T. Denton reports that he was unable to find any Canadian examples (with one possible exception) of ministers being forced out of office by parliamentary criticism of their public servants.[10] The existence of disciplined political parties means that Parliament no longer has the clout to enforce ministerial responsibility in terms of forcing ministers to resign. In actual practice, the decision on whether a minister will leave or stay in the face of serious criticism rests with the Prime Minister, and he decides the question — perhaps after receiving the advice of Cabinet and caucus — on the political grounds of whether the minister represents a net asset or liability to the government. As Brian Chapman has observed: "A minister resigns, or is effectively dismissed, if he really becomes too embarrassing to have on the front bench, or if he manages to earn the overwhelming hostility of his own party's backbenchers . . . , or if he becomes too closely associated with a policy which events prove either disastrously wrong or likely to lead to electoral suicide."[11] A more common, less humiliating fate is a demotion of the minister to a less important Cabinet post, probably with a strict warning to watch his step.

The limiting of ministerial responsibility to purely personal transgressions and the inability of Parliament to enforce the ultimate sanction of resignation has caused many observers to conclude that the doctrine of ministerial responsibility has entirely lost its utility as an accountability device. While this is probably too strong a conclusion to draw, the modifications in practice to the convention carry with them several significant implications. First, a weakening of parliamentary control is implied. If ministers, enlightened but harried amateurs, can no longer direct and control their large, specialized bureaucracies, then they are not in a position to give Parliament the assurance that bureaucratic power has been exercised responsibly. Second, if scarce ministerial time is spent increasingly on policy development and party work, then the views and actions of ministers will provide less and less guidance to individual public servants in their daily activities. As ministerial involvement in department operations slackens, other actors and other procedures will have to provide the basis for accountable behavior if such is to exist. Third, if ministers decline to accept full responsibility for departmental actions, the likelihood of public servants becoming the targets of criticism increases. Under current constitutional conventions they are largely defenceless targets since they have taken an oath of silence and are not free to answer charges. If ministers can escape being accountable, the public servant becomes a perfect scapegoat.

Regarding the last point, there is some indication that ministers are not entirely loath to shift the blame to public servants rather than shielding them from public criticism as convention requires. For example, in 1978, Jean-Pierre Goyer, then Minister of Supply and Services, charged before the press that an official in his department was guilty of gross negligence. A suit for libel ensued and the official was awarded $10,000 in damages as a result of Goyer's statement. The judicial decision included the following pertinent commentary:

> ... no matter how advanced the state of erosion of public service anonymity ... a minister should not be able to blame or castigate personally any civil servant of a department under his control in public and then fall back on the defence of qualified privilege. If that were the case and the civil servant were defamed he would be in the peculiar position of being prevented from obtaining vindication for spurious allegations by a minister.[12]

Public criticism of specific officials remains the exception, but it could become more common as public recognition grows that certain senior bureaucrats play a crucial role in policy formulation and implementation.

Most commentators argue that the changed situation described above does not mean that the doctrine of ministerial responsibility is now entirely defunct and useless. They agree that the emphasis has shifted from *complete liability* of the minister for departmental actions to *complete answerability* of both ministers and officials. The optimists see no weakening of the political significance of the doctrine. Thus the Privy Council Office under the Trudeau government in 1979 made the argument that the principle did not depend for its effectiveness on the threat of dismissal from office:

> The fact that a minister will probably not lose office as the result of the exposure of a particular instance of mismanagement, or even the misuse of authority by officials does not detract from his constitutional responsibility or his obligation to ensure that such instances do not occur. Indeed, his responsibility is honed by the ever-present possibility that in particular circumstances the minister may be embarrassed, suffer loss of prestige weakening himself and the government, jeopardize his standing with his colleagues and hence his political future, or even be forced to submit to public enquiry possibly resulting in censure and loss of office....These possibilities underpin the constitutional responsibility of ministers, which forms the basis for accountability throughout the system.[13]

Even if the above quotation exaggerates the normal peril of ministers, perpetuation of the myth of ministerial responsibility may still have the salutary psychological effect of restraining those in power.[14] Political reputations are quickly won and lost in the House of Commons and being forced to admit error or neglect in the performance of one's departmental duties will undoubtedly hurt a minister's political career. This is the real sanction of ministerial responsibility. Acceptance of the need to defend actions regularly before Parliament and the media undoubtedly requires ministers to pay some attention to departmental management and helps to focus accountability. Nevertheless, the ease with which ministers evade responsibility for mistakes and their refusal to name the guilty officials leaves the public with the impression that no one accepts blame for the serious blunders which do occur from time to time.

Thus far we have discussed the political dimension of ministerial responsibility, but there are also criticisms of the administrative side of the doctrine where changing practices have led to a strain on orthodox ideas. The first trend to be noted here is the decline in the traditional anonymity of public servants. This is the result of several developments. Reforms to the standing committees of the House of Commons and the procedures for handling the estimates of departments mean that public servants now regularly appear before such bodies to explain, and even on occasion to defend, departmental actions. The rise of a vast network of intergovernmental meetings dealing with federal-provincial concerns means that individual public servants are increasingly identified as representatives and spokesmen for their respective governments. The pressure to consult in advance on policy has meant that public servants more frequently discuss policy with interested groups or appear in public forums to explain departmental actions. In general, there is a growing recognition that public servants should share their knowledge with a wider audience than in the past and hence there has been a gradual relaxation of the previous restrictions on public commentary. This point takes us into the complicated issue of administrative secrecy, which is discussed at length in the next chapter, but we must draw attention here to the implications of this trend.

Even if it is acknowledged that, in the interests of more open government, officials should play a greater role in explaining government actions, such a role must still be reconciled with ministerial responsibility. The problem is to strike an appropriate balance among such values as democratic political control, openness in government and public service anonymity. For example, if specific public servants become identified with particular issues they could forfeit or at least impair their usefulness to subsequent governments. A higher profile for public servants will also mean a greater chance that they will be the subject of press commentary and public praise and blame. The end result might be the disappearance of an impartial and anonymous public service.

A second administrative problem related to ministerial responsibility is the stress placed upon meeting the minister's needs in departmental operations. To fulfill the principle of ministerial responsibility, departmental structures emphasize a clear chain of command up the administrative hierarchy to the minister. This is an extension, at a more specific level, of the accountability-control relationship discussed in general above. Memoranda which have a policy significance are checked not only for their intrinsic merits, but also for their political safety. What must be avoided at all cost is the major *faux pas* that might embarrass the minister. However, the overriding consciousness of the political environment has its price. Deputy ministers respond to the concerns of their minister, and the tendency of ministers is to focus on policy matters. As a consequence, management and administrative considerations tend to receive short shrift. The upwardly mobile public servant tends to perceive that the road to career advancement is in the policy advisory field. Thus, a survey of deputy ministers revealed that, while presenting a balanced set of management and policy responsibilities, more deputies ranked "supporting my minister" and "ensuring that my department is responsive to the policy thrusts of the government" as their first or second most important responsibilities.[15]

In addition to this negative impact on administration, the emphasis on serving the minister may have other dysfunctional effects.[16] By emphasizing hierarchy and formal lines of authority, it may cause disenchantment for public servants at the middle and lower levels of the bureaucracy. They may lose a sense of making a personal contribution. Too often, in their view, ideas become "lost in the pipeline" up to the minister, or they are appropriated for personal use by their superiors, or the ideas are judged by partisan rather than professional considerations. The emphasis on hierarchy also leads to organizational rigidity, making it difficult for officials in related areas to cooperate in policy development. It encourages an attitude of departmental exclusiveness. Since the collective attention of the department is focussed on serving the minister, and since bureaucratic rewards reinforce this tendency, the function of serving the public tends to be neglected, undernourished and centered in junior levels. This is deemed to be inappropriate by many who argue that governments must become more responsive to the public.

These consequences do not flow solely from ministerial responsibilities — and many would argue that the tendencies are not as pronounced as implied above — but the emphasis on a clear chain of command has been a major influence on department organization. This relates to Chapters 2 and 3, in that insistence upon stringent control of bureaucracy (i.e., subordinates) may have the unintended dysfunctional consequences of both destroying their initiative and flexibility and also creating a situation of goal displacement whereby the means become the end.

As the main link between the transient political leadership and the permanent public service, deputy ministers are crucial to the accountability formula. The traditional doctrine implies an exclusive duty on their part to serve their minister. In practice, however, they are involved in a confusing array of accountability relationships which belies the simplicity of this earlier definition. First, deputies in Canada as compared to their British counterparts seem to display a greater loyalty to the government as a whole, this collective loyalty arising out of several facts of the Canadian situation. First, the appointment of deputy ministers is more in the hands of the Prime Minister than is the case in the United Kingdom and hence deputies sense that they are answerable to the Prime Minister for their department's contribution to the overall goals of the government.[17] Second, the collective loyalty is encouraged by the increased participation of deputies in interdepartmental committees, including certain meetings of Cabinet committees. Further ambiguity arises because deputy ministers are subject to direction from a growing number of central agencies such as the Privy Council Office, the Treasury Board Secretariat, the Comptroller General, the Public Service Commission and the Official Languages Commissioner. These central agencies are seen as essential to collective responsibility. They enable the confederacy of separate departments to work by "synthesizing and co-ordinating, occasionally leading."[18] However, there is clearly the potential for conflict between departmental goals (including the minister's personal views) and the collective decisions of the system. The deputy minister will often be faced with reconciling the differences between departmental interests and the broader interests of the collectivity. Stated differently, the doctrine of ministerial responsibility has both a collective and an individual component, and the requirements of the first may, in practice, detract from ability to achieve the second.

These internal links do not exhaust the deputy minister's accountability relationships. As a leader of a department, he must also have a sense of responsibility for the motivation and morale of his employees. As a member of a cadre of senior officials in government, he may have a strong sense of responsibility to certain professional norms. Through appearances before parliamentary committees, he may develop a sense of responsibility to that body. He may also have a strong sense of responsibility to the public, particularly to the organized groups who are the main clientele for the department's programs and services. The establishment of elaborate advisory networks to government departments and the increase in the number of active pressure groups means that senior officials must work within a broad range of sometimes conflicting interests pressing for the attention of the ministers. Officials are inevitably involved in assessing and weighing the opinion of such interests in relation to some subjective definition of the "public interest." "Thus, responsiveness may on occasion conflict with accountability to political and administrative superiors."[19]

Administrative Rule-Making and Democratic Control

In modern government there are large areas of what might be called "middle-range" and "lower-level" policymaking where there is limited legislative or ministerial direction to guide public servants in their decision-making. For a variety of reasons – such as lack of technical knowledge, shortage of time, need for flexibility in new policy fields and simply force of habit – legislatures have increasingly passed legislation in broad, general terms and delegated to departments and other government agencies the authority to provide the actual content of policy. Traditional notions of parliamentary supremacy and the rule of law have tended to obscure the extent to which such administrative rule-making under delegated legislative authority has replaced the more familiar parliamentary statute as the main vehicle for government action in the 20th century.

In 1969, the Special Committee on Statutory Instruments found that of the 601 Acts of Parliament (constituting substantially all of the statutes then in force), 420 provided for delegated legislation or subordinate rule-making authority. Moreover, departmental replies to the committee's questionnaire revealed that the statutory powers to make regulations had been used extensively.[20] Examples cited by the committee revealed the very wide powers granted to departments through delegated legislative authority. There are understandable and justifiable reasons for most such delegations of power, but the widespread nature of the phenomenon creates serious problems of democratic control and accountability.

Delegation of legislative authority can be to regular departments of government or to independent or semi-independent regulatory agencies. In the case of subordinate law-making by departments the accountability of ministers is theoretically clear-cut, although in practical terms it is usually impossible for the minister to be aware of or assume responsibility for all policies adopted through departmental rule-making. As will be indicated below, the accountability of ministers for the behavior of regulatory agencies is even more doubtful.

One approach to the control of the broad discretionary authority granted to departmental officials is the preparation of manuals on administrative procedures and directives to guide officials in their decision-making. A few departments have developed systematic procedures to ensure that people affected by government decisions have a fair chance to register their views, that individual cases will be handled objectively, and that appeals of unfavorable decisions can occur. But a survey of 10 departments in 1977 revealed that "there was little general policy direction to ensure that complaints are handled systematically and fairly."[21] The handling of complaints about unreasonable or unjust administrative behavior apparently has not received much attention from senior managers because most of the bureaucratic incentives have rewarded policy formulation rather than serving the public. In any case, complaints would be reviewed, not by an impartial third party, but by officials of the organization involved. Government-wide procedures and standards, and a monitoring of departmental performance, might be an improvement, but it could also lead to elaborate, formalized and time-consuming procedures — and thus to more citizen complaints about bureaucratic red tape.[22] For this reason interest has grown in the establishment of an ombudsman to handle citizen complaints at the federal level, comparable to such offices which exist in most provincial jurisdictions. This idea is discussed later in this chapter.

Accountability and Regulatory Agencies

The problems of accountability become even more pronounced in the case of regulatory agencies. Much controversy has swirled around the topic of government regulation in recent years. Many observers believe that government regulation has become too extensive, complex, costly and has become less effective than it should be. At the same time governments are receiving demands to regulate certain economic activities more extensively. The subject of government regulation is obviously controversial, complicated and multi-faceted. A wide range of specialized knowledge (for example, from economics, law, political science, and public administration) would be required to study regulation comprehensively. Here we can only comment briefly on how regulation differs from other instruments of government, why it has become more popular as a policy instrument, and how the proliferation of regulatory agencies relates to the concept of ministerial responsibility.

Regulation is usually considered to be a distinctive form of government activity. However, as with so many terms in the literature of public administration, while definitions abound there is little agreement on the essential nature of regulation. For our purposes we use the definition offered recently by the Economic Council of Canada: "the imposition of constraints, backed by government authority, that are intended to modify the economic behavior of individuals in the private sector significantly."[23] Of course, virtually everything governments do involves the prescription of rules affecting individuals. Still, regulation seems to differ in one important respect from other policy instruments such as taxation, the provision of subsidies or services and the device of public ownership. The difference is that the costs and benefits, both direct and indirect, public and private, of regulation are less predictable and less readily identifiable than those of other government activity. There is no doubt that this quality of not producing readily identifiable winners and losers partly accounts for the popularity of regulation.

Regulation, then, represents one form of government intervention into what is normally perceived as a free enterprise economy. However, like ice-cream, regulation comes in many flavors. Agencies which perform the regulatory function are extremely varied and many simultaneously perform an adjudicative role among competing interests, a quasi-judicial role when disputes arise, an advisory role to governments and even, in certain cases, an expenditure role. Thus, given this diversity and multi-functional nature of regulatory agencies, generalizations about their genesis and behavior are rather hazardous. This point should be borne in mind as we proceed to discuss regulation in rather general terms.

Chapter 5 documented the proliferation of regulatory agencies over the last three decades.[24] There are a variety of reasons, both economic and political, for the spread of regulation. The most popular economic explanation is that regulation is required to correct so-called "market failures," that is, imperfections in the functioning of the competitive marketplace.[25] Such market failures can take several forms. Regulations are often introduced in situations of "natural monopoly," where the economies of scale in an industry are such that only one firm will emerge. To protect the public against unreasonable pricing by a single firm, government regulation of prices or rates will occur. An example is the regulation of Bell Telephone by the Canadian Radio-Television and Telecommunications Commission. A second form of market failure is what economists call "destructive competition." Too many firms engaged in cutthroat competition in certain sectors of the economy (e.g., the trucking industry or the marketing of agricultural products) cause prices to fall and companies to be driven out of business. The instability of supply of a service or product which results is deemed not to be in the "public interest" and regulation is therefore used to limit the entry of firms into the competition and to control their pricing policies.

Two other problems of market failure prompting government regulation are "spillovers" and "information limitations." The first occurs because the price mechanism of the market does not include the spillover effects of production. A classic example is pollution. In the past, producers treated the air and water as common waste disposal systems, using technologies designed to maximize production rather than to minimize negative environmental impacts. In effect, they paid little if any attention to what their activities were "costing" the society. Mercury pollution serves as an excellent example. The free market system also depends on consumers possessing sufficient information to make correct, informed choices. However, frequent changes in products and processes make it difficult for consumers to judge the safety and benefits of products and services. For example, the tobacco companies would not voluntarily tell consumers that cigarettes cause cancer so it was left to governments to require by regulation that health warnings be included on cigarette packages. In other cases, governments permit groups to be self-regulating. Without controls by doctors themselves, for example, the medical profession might be populated by "quacks" and the uninformed public would be placed in danger.

Not all regulation can be explained as attempts to correct alleged market failures. Some regulation involves the pursuit of social goals, in that regulation may be used to encourage subsidization of certain activities. For example, a regulatory agency may permit a railway freight service to earn excess profits (charging prices far above actual costs) to allow for cross-subsidization of a passenger service that would not otherwise be financially viable unless there were exorbitant charges to the passengers. Another example of the social purposes of regulation is the role played by the 30 to 40 provincial marketing boards engaged in the supply and price management of dairy, egg and poultry products. It is often alleged that such boards set prices too high, but part of their goal is to provide income protection to producers and ensure their continued presence in the society. In Canada, social goals regulation has also been prompted by our proximity to an economically powerful and culturally persuasive neighbor to the south, and a fairly wide range of regulations have been adopted to serve the goals of national economic independence and a distinctive national identity. For example, the Foreign Investment Review

Agency monitors the entry of foreign capital into Canada and the Canadian Radio-Television and Telecommunications Commission insists that television broadcasters carry a certain amount of "Canadian content" in their programming.

Because the elimination of market failures does not appear to be the sole or even the primary motivation for much regulation, the emphasis in research has recently shifted from economics *per se* to a search for more *political* theories of regulation. One popular perspective argues that the pursuit of self-interest by the main actors associated with the regulatory process accounts for the expansion of regulation.[26] According to this view, the *clients* of regulatory agencies (businesses and other producers) do not wish to face the uncertainties of free-wheeling competition. That is, while they may speak the rhetoric of free enterprise, they regard competition as healthy and beneficial only up to a point or when it is imposed on others. They want the security and advantage of limited competition, high tariff protection and so on. *Regulators* also respond to incentives leading to the expansion of regulation. For example, it is argued that the staff of regulatory agencies initially believe strongly in the regulatory purpose, they want to avoid the criticism that they are neglecting their regulatory mandate, and they want to protect or even to expand their jurisdiction. For them, regulation becomes as much an end in itself as a means of reaching other ends and hence we witness the phenomenon called "regulatory drift." That is, there is a constant, incremental extension of the domains of regulatory agencies for administrative reasons which may be either beneficial or detrimental (or both) to society.

According to the self-interested model, *politicians* can also benefit from regulatory action. Here it is useful to draw upon the insights of Murray Edelman's *Symbolic Uses of Politics*.[27] He offers a different perspective on politics in general and on regulation in particular. In his view, politics for most of us is less a fierce struggle for scarce resources and more a spectator sport in which we participate only vicariously. But because politics does visibly confer wealth, impose costs and even take life, it is a process upon which people displace private emotions, especially strong anxieties and hopes. The complicated nature of policy issues and the headline character of the news—lack of depth, detail and background—prevent widespread public understanding. Therefore in an anxiety-ridden and confusing world, politics has *symbolic* as well as realistic consequences. According to Edelman, much of politics consists of the manipulation of symbols to evoke public arousal or quiescence.

When this perspective is applied to regulation, the symbolic character of the regulatory process becomes apparent. When the public is aroused about a problem, politicians find it advantageous to advocate regulatory action and the initial public fervor will provide the political support necessary to obtain passage of legislation. However, once the regulatory agency is established, public interest will diminish. Many of the groups concerned are symbolically reassured that the problem has been handled and they therefore drop out of the active political arena. Over time, the grandiose promises of the original legislation may not be delivered. Adequate funds for the regulatory agency may not be provided. The attitudes of the agency's personnel may mellow and the agency may look to accommodation rather than confrontation with the interests it regulates. Eventually, it may end up adopting the values of the group it was established to regulate. At this point, the agency is mainly a symbol that has very little positive effect in terms of real regulation but serves to foster political quietism in an area of previous public concern.

The theory that regulatory agencies pass through an organizational life cycle and eventually are "captured" by the regulated interests was developed in the United States, but it was never held to apply to all regulatory agencies there, and may have even less relevance in Canada. Thus, Bruce Doern argues that the predominant style of regulatory policy-making in Canada is elite accommodation.[28] For him, this implies a process of mutual adjustment between the regulators and the regulatees rather than a one-way capitulation in favor of the industry's viewpoint. In other words, there would be a reasonable degree of aggressiveness throughout the life of an agency rather than just in its early years. A second problem with the so-called "captive thesis" of regulatory behavior is that it presumes a measure of independence from political control which is not found to the same degree in Canada as it is in the United States, a point which will become evident as we turn to an examination of the accountability of regulatory agencies. However, in saying this we do not want to imply that an over-identification by regulatory agencies with the client groups never occurs in Canada and that agencies never tend to become representatives rather than regulators of the client groups.

Accountability, Policy-Making and Regulation

Regulatory agencies have been described as "structural heretics" within a cabinet-parliamentary system because of their departure from the principle of ministerial responsibility. While individual ministers act as spokesmen for regulatory agencies in the sense of communicating information to the House of Commons, they cannot be held fully accountable for the decisions and actions of such bodies. In the case of regulatory agencies, Parliament has delegated directly to the commission or board certain duties and functions rather than entrusting them to a regular department. Very seldom does the government give up control and direction completely, but the degree of ministerial supervision and involvement varies widely and, therefore, so does the extent of ministerial responsibility. There is evidence that ministers are increasingly dissatisfied with their inability to control the policy-making functions of regulatory agencies, and legislators, in turn, are dissatisfied with the confusing accountability relationships that emerge.

Since the regulatory commission involves a departure from orthodox constitutional principles, there must be good reasons for its use. Two main explanations are usually offered.[29] First, it is considered desirable to separate the administration of certain activities, because of their nature, from the continuous ministerial control and constant parliamentary scrutiny that apply to departments. For example, in the case of economic regulation, inasmuch as it involves interference in the exercise of traditional property rights (e.g., regulation in the energy and transportation sectors) or competing applications for control of parts of the public domain (such as radio and television licenses), it is held necessary to insulate the function from political interference by entrusting it to independent, impartial agencies which are at arms-length from the government. A related argument is that regulatory agencies originally emerged to fill a need for policy innovation and flexibility in new and technical fields of government activity that could not be met by normal legislative enactments and within the confines of existing departmental structures. However, as the public service developed its expertise, a department could progressively assume the lead role in policy development. For example, the policy vacuum created by the development of radio broadcasting and, later, television, was initially filled by assigning authority to an independent body, but with the creation of the Department of Communication in 1971 there were more frequent challenges to the Canadian Radio-Television and Telecommunications Commission's (CRTC) virtual monopoly on policy-making in that field.

The second main reason for the use of the independent regulatory commission is to separate the administration of a function from the personnel and budgetary procedures and constraints that apply to departments. In the past it was argued that economic regulation, being highly complex and technical, required a type of specialized knowledge not normally found in departments. The argument was that businessmen, scientists and other specialists would not be attracted to regular departments because of the levels of remuneration, hiring and classification procedures, the constraints on decision-making and the pervasive influence of political considerations. Whatever its validity in the past, this idea has increasingly been challenged in recent years. A desire to relieve or at least not to add to the burden of ministerial supervision of administration seems to have been a consideration in some cases. Creating new departments instead of adding to existing ministerial workloads would increase the number of Cabinet members and make Cabinet a more unwieldy decision-making body than it had already become with over 30 members in recent years. The use of regulatory bodies where ministerial supervision was not continuous represented a compromise.

The actual autonomy of regulatory agencies from government direction and control varies widely. The essential characteristics of regulatory agencies which lead to their having more independence are: power to act on the basis of enabling legislation which is often vaguely worded; assured tenure of office (from three to 10 years) for the members of boards and commissions; the authority to make quasi-judicial decisions subject only to limited rights of appeal to the courts and in some cases Cabinet; and, in a few cases, power to enact subordinate legislation the form of regulations without the approval of

Cabinet.[30] In the case of most regulatory bodies, including those having a profound economic impact such as the National Energy Board, the Canadian Transport Commission and the CRTC, Cabinet has no power to provide policy direction short of amending the statute creating an agency or rejecting a regulatory decision. The first option of legislative amendment is time-consuming and, as for the second, even if individual decisions are rejected on policy grounds, there is no guarantee that the policy considerations of the Cabinet will set precedents with the regulators for future decisions.

The belief that regulatory agencies are often autonomous fiefs, making decisions that create policy, often on politically sensitive matters such as issues in federal-provincial relations, has led to the recommendation that Cabinet be given legislative authority to issue binding policy directives to such bodies. Such directives would apply only to general matters of policy and not to individual cases.[31] This restriction is urged to preserve the continued impartiality of commissions in the adjudicative or quasi-judicial function, while at the same time ensuring their responsiveness to the broad policy goals of the government in their legislative or policy-making role. The additional safeguards that regulatory agencies be consulted in advance on such directives, that public hearings on them be held, and that directives be tabled in Parliament would prevent undue political interference and promote greater openness surrounding the regulatory process.

Parliamentary Scrutiny of Regulatory Performance

Inadequate parliamentary attention has been paid to regulatory agencies in the past. The limited formal contact between MPs and commissions has occurred primarily through the Estimates process, usually before the Standing Committee on Miscellaneous Estimates or one of the other committees of the House of Commons. Not surprisingly, MPs have shown the greatest interest in the more important commissions (e.g., NEB, CTC and CRTC) and have not paid attention to others for years. Only when a regulatory decision requires political approval is the minister responsible in formal constitutional terms to Parliament. For the remainder of the work of commissions, the members of such bodies are themselves directly answerable to Parliament. However, in practice, all agencies and commissions present annual reports to Parliament and if such reports and testimony by agency officials reveal continuous problems within an agency, Parliament would probably not allow a minister to escape political blame by pleading ignorance. The presumption seems to be that ministers will remain generally informed about the activities of commissions without interfering in their day-to-day decision-making—a fine line for them to walk. A Commons' committee that sensed political interference or was not satisfied with the performance of a commission could issue a report calling for corrective action. However, since committee reviews of the performance of commissions are rare, so are reports.

Complaints about the growth of regulation and the apparent loss of accountability, led the Trudeau government to agree in May 1980 to the appointment of a House of Commons' Special Committee on Regulatory Reform. Its report was presented to Parliament in December 1980. Among other actions, it recommended that binding policy directives from Cabinet to regulatory agencies be allowed, that calendars of upcoming regulatory initiatives be published, that all proposed regulations be accompanied by an impact assessment statement, and that all departments and agencies review their existing regulations to identify those which are unnecessary or outdated. More specifically in relation to Parliament, the special committee recommended that the Standing Committees of the House of Commons be authorized to monitor the regulatory process of federal departments and agencies, to review the subject matter of new subordinate legislation, and to review specific regulatory activities, utilizing the evaluation reports prepared by departments, agencies, the Treasury Board or the Office of the Comptroller General. At the time of writing (October 1981) the special committee's recommendations have not been acted upon by the government.

Another parliamentary check on the use of regulatory authority is provided by the Standing Joint Committee on Regulations and Other Statutory Instruments. Created in 1972, the Committee consists of 20 members from the House of Commons and the Senate, with an opposition-party MP serving as the co-chairman. Since 1974 all orders-in-council, regulations, and other statutory instruments of federal departments, boards and commissions have been referred to the Committee. Statutory instruments are reviewed under 14 criteria, including whether they exceed the authority granted by the parent act, infringe the rule of law or principles of natural justice, impose a charge or payment without authority, are unclear, or violate the Canadian Bill of Rights. It is important to note that this scrutiny pertains only to the legitimacy of regulations, not to their effectiveness in achieving policy objectives. There is not the space here to delve deeply into the operations and influence of the Committee.[32]

Briefly, therefore, in its first substantive report (February 1977) the Committee complained that the Department of Justice had construed the legal definition of a statutory instrument so narrowly that the legislative review process was severely inhibited:

> There is no system whereby all orders that have legislative effect are tabled here in Parliament, are automatically referred to the standing joint committee and are also published so the public can know what is being done.
>
> There is a system only for regulations and not for all statutory instruments, many of which are effectively hidden, are unpublished and are unknown even to the Parliamentary Committee to which they stand permanently referred.[33]

For example, the Committee was denied the right to review the Immigration Guidelines issued to officers of the Department of Manpower and Immigration to guide them in the administration of the Immigration Act. The Guidelines apparently contained substantive rules, for example a definition of the crime of moral turpitude, the commission of which is grounds for exclusion from Canada.[34] The departmental manual in effect set immigration policy, but the parliamentary committee was not permitted to see it to determine whether the rules were consistent with original legislative intent, violated principles of natural justice or the other criteria. The government argued that since the Guidelines were advisory, not binding, they were not strictly speaking statutory instruments, even though immigration officers may in fact interpret them as binding.

In addition to the complaint about its jurisdiction and denial of information, the Committee also reported on the dangers associated with regulatory authority being further delegated to subagencies, regulations being dispensed with in individual cases and in particular circumstances on the basis of ministerial or administrative discretion, and the frequent use of vague regulatory authority as the means to raise and to spend funds without clear parliamentary approval. To date, the Committee's recommendations to limit the scope of administrative rule-making and to strengthen the parliamentary review process have not been adopted by government. However, even should the recommendations be implemented, Parliament will have time and inclination to review only a small portion of the total extent of bureaucratic policy-making that occurs through delegated legislative authority.

Accountability and Crown Corporations

The accountability dilemma posed by the use of crown corporations is similar, although not identical, to that involved with independent regulatory commissions. Crown corporations are institutions which are created by acts of Parliament or Cabinet orders and which while being wholly or partially owned by the government and ultimately accountable to Parliament, still enjoy some measure of independence from the government. In 1977 there were 54 crown corporations listed in the Appendix of the Financial Administration Act (FAA), the statute which sets out the general provisions for their relationships with government. However, this figure omits the hundreds of subsidiaries established by these corporations.

In general, crown corporations provide economic or social services on behalf of the government, ranging from nuclear reactor production, operation of the St. Lawrence Seaway, provision of unemployment insurance, and operation of a national lottery. Over 200,000 individuals are employed in crown corporations at the federal level in Canada and their expenditures from government revenues in 1977-1978 amounted to about one-seventh of the $38.9 billion spent by the federal government in that year. In addition, they generated revenues of their own close to $12 billion. They were, therefore, truly "a second public service."[35]

Most observers can discern no coherent or consistent philosophy that led to the present range of crown corporations.[36] The reliance upon public enterprise is usually seen as a pragmatic response to the necessities of the Canadian situation: a vast country, rich in natural resources but small in population living alongside a powerful and persuasive neighbor to the south. To serve the purposes of "nation-building" and more recently "province-building," governments at all levels have undertaken large investments in natural resource development, communications and transportation. However, the pursuit of broad economic and social goals does not account for the appearance of all crown corporations – some were created, for example, on the basis of more strictly political considerations – but it does provide the main explanation for why government intervention in this manner has gone further in Canada than in the United States.

In pursuit of these general goals, the device of the crown corporation, rather than the regular department which seems more appropriate in constitutional terms, has been considered desirable on several grounds.[37] First, it was a way to avoid direct political control of a sensitive function: when the function might be subject to abuse for narrow partisan purpose (e.g., broadcasting was placed under the control of the Canadian Broadcasting Corporation); when the function is regulatory (e.g., the regulation of nuclear energy by the Atomic Energy Control Board); when grants or subsidies are being allocated (e.g., the National Research Council) or when an advisory function is involved (e.g., the Science Council of Canada). A second reason for employing the corporate form was to avoid certain departmental procedures (such as the restrictions of the annual budget process or the control over personnel by the Public Service Commission), particularly when the activities performed are in competition with private enterprise. Higher salaries could be paid to key management personnel, there would be more direct and therefore better employer-employee relations in corporations than in departments, and in general crown corporations could perform more efficiently than regular departments because they were not so constrained by bureaucratic red tape. Relieving already overworked ministers of the burden of supervising the day-to-day operations of such enterprises was another consideration.

As might be expected, the degree of independence from ministerial control varies across the range of crown corporations. What we have, in effect, is a continuum ranging from those corporations over which the minister exercises almost continuous supervision and financial control (usually designated as "Departmental Corporations" under the FAA) to where such supervision and financial control is minimal (usually called "Proprietary Corporations"). There is also a group of corporations that fall into an intermediate zone ("Agency Corporations"). Even where ministerial involvement in corporate affairs is minimal, governments cannot entirely abdicate their responsibility for corporate activities. After all, the crown corporation is brought into existence by a government which determines what it will do, what administrative form it will take, who will serve on its board of directors and who will be the chief executive officers. Often the government provides an initial capital budget for the corporation and may support its operating budget. Moreover, in many cases there is considerable informal contact between the minister and the officials of the crown corporation, which means that their actual working relationships are much closer than is implied by legislation and other public documents.

Parliamentary Scrutiny of Crown Corporations

Therefore, although crown corporations are technically somewhat removed from elected politicians, the Cabinet must accept a degree of responsibility for their performance. The extent of such responsibility is contentious. A not infrequent occurrence in Parliament is to hear ministers disclaim responsibility as follows: "This is a matter involving an independent crown corporation and I can answer only insofar as the corporation sees fit to provide information." On the other hand, many observers would argue that ministerial responsibility must go far beyond simply answering questions or transmitting information. Another popular ministerial dodge is to employ the distinction between "long-term, general policy" (to be set or approved ultimately by the minister) and "day-to-day administration" (decided by the board and corporate managers). Since the line between policy and administration becomes blurred in practice, the minister often finds it convenient to take refuge in the resulting ambiguity of any situation that might prove embarrassing.

There are a number of potential parliamentary checks on the behavior of crown corporations, but none has proven particularly effective. Questions in the House of Commons can be useful as a spot check, but ministers will often refuse to answer on the grounds that questions relate to administration, would involve the disclosure of information damaging to the competitive position of the corporation, or would place an unreasonable burden on the corporation without corresponding benefits to the general public. Parliamentary debates suffer from the same shortcomings as questions. They tend to be infrequent, parochial or superficial. The use of parliamentary committees might allow for more systematic and thorough investigations, but only four Commons' committees — public accounts, broadcasting, transportation and agriculture — have regularly considered the annual reports of crown corporations. Only when controversy surrounds a crown corporation's operations or when its activities touch on the constituency interests of many MPs (such as the CBC and the CNR) can much parliamentary attention be expected. In general, therefore, Parliament has failed to invent new procedures for rendering crown corporations accountable for their performance.

Strengthening the Accountability of Crown Corporations

Several events in recent years have revealed the deficiencies of existing controls on the behavior of crown corporations exercised by both central executive agencies and by Parliament. In 1975 an inquiry revealed that Air Canada, through a subsidiary established without reference to Parliament, was undertaking a business that was not within the terms of its founding statute. In 1976 the Auditor General reported to Parliament that financial management and control in crown corporations was "weak and ineffective," that coordination and direction of their performance by central government agencies was "virtually non-existent" and that Parliament was presented with fragmented and incomplete financial reports.[38] To support these charges the Auditor General presented a parade of cases, but the one which caught the attention of opposition parties and led to an investigation by the Commons' Public Accounts Committee was the $10 million in expenses paid by Atomic Energy of Canada Limited to agents to push the sales of the CANDU nuclear reactor in Argentina and South Korea. There was no adequate accounting of the use of these funds by the overseas agents, and it was ultimately discovered that some of the money had been used to bribe government officials who were prospective buyers.

In response to these revelations, the Trudeau government published, in the form of a discussion paper (the Blue Paper of 1977), a set of proposals for reform to the existing system of accountability for crown corporations.[39] The underlying premise of the government's recommendations was that crown corporations, as major instruments of public policy, should be more responsive to the national interest as determined by the government. It was proposed, for example, that Cabinet should have the power to issue binding directives to crown corporations to ensure that their behavior conformed to the government's definition of the national interest. To ensure government accountability for such directives, they would be presented to Parliament. Where directives resulted in additional costs to a corporation, compensation would be paid by the government. It was also suggested that before a crown corporation could establish a subsidiary, approval would be required from the cabinet. In giving approval the cabinet would ensure that the business of the subsidiary was one which could be legally undertaken by the parent and that the financial statements of the subsidiary would be fully disclosed in the annual report of the parent company.

The boards of directors of most crown corporations serve "during pleasure," a legal phrase which means that the cabinet has the undisputed right to appoint and to replace them. According to the Blue Paper of 1977 there is a need to clarify the responsibilities of boards for the effective management of the corporation within the policy framework defined by the government and Parliament. To provide directors of crown corporations with clear standards upon which to base their conduct, the Trudeau government proposed to bring them all under the duties of the Canada Business Corporation Act. In general, that Act imposes two types of duties on directors:

a "fiduciary duty" to act in good faith and to avoid conflict of interest, and a "duty of care" to use skill, diligence, prudence and probity in their behavior. The Blue Paper also proposed that Cabinet be given greater control over the salaries paid to chief executive officers of crown corporations in order to ensure that compensation corresponded more closely to the prevailing practices within the public service.

This last proposal in particular has drawn considerable criticism on the grounds that in most cases Cabinet already has powers which in the private sector are exercised by the boards of directors, such as choosing the chief executive officer, determining the level of his compensation and approving certain expenditures. Extending such government controls would only increase decision-making costs by involving more actors and would introduce greater confusion into the ensuing accountability relationships. What is needed, according to the critics, is more precise legislative mandates for crown corporations which the boards would be responsible to Parliament for exercising, and in turn, stronger boards of directors should be freer from government interference to appoint management, to support and to monitor management's performance, and to replace management when required.[40]

The Blue Paper saw the annual budgetary process as potentially the single most important control mechanism over crown corporations available to the government. This is a sensitive area of the corporation-government relationship. On the government side, there is dissatisfaction with the content and the timeliness of corporate budgets presented for approval. On the corporation side, there is frustration with the delays involved in obtaining approval, which seem to rob the corporation of the virtue of flexibility, and there is also a sense of unwarranted intrusion on the prerogatives of boards of directors by central agencies. The Blue Paper's answer to this dilemma is proposed amendments to the Financial Administration Act that would allow the Treasury Board to determine the timing and the format of all budgetary submissions from crown corporations. In the case of operating budgets for corporations that are financially self-sufficient (i.e., they do not require appropriations from the Consolidated Revenue Fund), they would be presented to the Treasury Board for information only. Operating budgets involving government appropriations or subsidies would be subject to the same approval process that applies to departmental budgets. All capital budgets, whether they involved appropriations or not, would be subject to Cabinet approval. In addition, the Blue Paper proposed that corporation budgets be tabled in Parliament, that corporations prepare three to five-year "rolling" corporate plans outlining objectives, strategies and financial implications for approval by Cabinet, and that the information in the annual reports of crown corporations be upgraded. Other changes recommended were: the borrowing authority of certain crown corporations should be extended; there should be more consistency in the auditing of the financial statements of crown corporations; and the FAA should be made the governing statute for all corporations.

Most of these proposals have been favorably received, although it has been argued that the format for the budgets of corporations should be determined, not by the Treasury Board, but by each corporation's board of directors as they deem appropriate to the organization and consistent with the highest standards observed by similar enterprises in the same sector of the economy.[41]

In summary, rather than focusing on Parliament itself, the Trudeau government's proposals looked mainly to central administrative agencies (the Cabinet, the Treasury Board, and the Department of Finance) to bring about the required degree of control over crown corporations. However, tighter control over public enterprises by central agencies does not automatically mean more accountability to the general public and it places enormous faith in the ability of Cabinet ministers and boards of directors to determine what is in the "national interest." In contrast, the Report of the Royal Commission on Financial Management and Accountability paid more attention to parliamentary scrutiny of and influence over crown agencies. The Report suggested that at least once every 10 years the mandate and the policy performance of each crown corporation should be reviewed by the appropriate standing committees of the House of Commons.[42] The additional proposal to refer the annual reports of crown corporations to the same committees would permit Members to question on a continuous basis both ministers and corporation officials. In addition, the Commission recommended that the chairmen of the boards of directors and the chief executive officers of crown corporations should account regularly before the Public Accounts Committee for the management of their agencies.

However, while the suggestion of regular reviews every decade would force MPs to pay some attention to the activities of crown corporations, it is doubtful whether they will have the time or the inclination to provide the continuous surveillance envisaged by the Commission. To date, neither the Blue Paper's nor the Commission's recommendations have been implemented. Whatever their eventual fate, the proposals cannot be seen as final answers to the perennial problem of striking a balance between a measure of political control over crown corporations sufficient to ensure their responsiveness to broader public policy goals and the necessary autonomy to permit them to operate efficiently and effectively.

The Ombudsman and Bureaucratic Accountability

The expansion of government activities has meant that citizens are increasingly vulnerable to the decisions of public servants. When a citizen's interests are harmed by the bureaucracy, he can present his complaint in several ways. He might approach a legislator, for example his federal Member of Parliament, for assistance. While often helpful, investigations of complaints by legislators are not completely adequate. Legislators do not have the staff to deal with numerous complaints, they cannot compel departments to produce documents, if they are of the government party they may not wish to embarrass a minister by pressing hard and exposing maladministration in a department and, finally, one legislator may simply be more skilled than another in making the bureaucracy see the error of its ways. The result could well be different treatment of identical problems — citizen A might have his problem straightened out while citizen B might not.

The work of legislators as liaison agents with the bureaucracy on behalf of constituents can be supported and complemented by the increasingly popular newspaper "action line" columnists and similar reporters on radio and television. CBC television's "Ombudsman" program was probably the clearest example of how media intervention can often lead to a prompt and judicious redress of citizens' grievances based on government agencies' desire to avoid adverse publicity. However, the media face problems of access to relevant government information, a lack of time and staff resources, and a tendency to gravitate to a few dramatic cases and to sensationalize the events involved. Appeal to the courts to obtain redress is also open to a citizen, but as will be seen in the following section of this chapter, judicial review of administrative actions is limited in scope, expensive and time-consuming. Given the inadequacies of existing mechanisms for the resolution of citizens' complaints against the government bureaucracy, increasing interest has been shown in the idea of a government ombudsman.

The ombudsman has nearly a 200-year history in Sweden as a government office designed to assist citizens in reversing bureaucratic wrongs. The office of the ombudsman has been adopted with various modifications by about a dozen countries and by nine Canadian provinces. Several ombudsman bills have been introduced at the federal level in Canada — including most recently a government-sponsored measure (Bill C-43) introduced in April 1978 — but none has gone beyond second reading in the parliamentary process, apparently because of either government hostility, indifference or the press of other business.

In general terms, the ombudsman stands as an impartial intermediary between the bureaucracy and the individual citizen. His duty is to protect the public from bureaucratic errors, arrogance and inaction. Governments usually seek to confine ombudsmen to the handling of individual citizen complaints about *administrative* actions or inactions and exclude from their jurisdiction matters of broad *policy*. According to governments, intrusions by an ombudsman into matters of policy would involve serious damage to his personal credibility and to the impartial reputation of his office because he may be seen to be taking sides on partisan, political issues.[43] Academic observers, although far from unanimous, tend to view such an administrative/policy dichotomy as artificial and too restrictive. According to two critics of the recent government of Canada proposal for a federal ombudsman, "an ombudsman who concentrates exclusively on individual cases without watching for patterns of malfunctioning and their policy implications, and fails to probe questions of policy arising from his work, risks alienating his clients, the public and even a sector of the public service."[44]

The ombudsman is supposed to be independent from the executive branch of governments. His actual independence depends not only on his formal authority, but also on the manner in which he is appointed and removed, the way he is paid, his office is staffed and the personal qualities he brings to the job.[45] It is important to note that he normally does *not* have the authority to reverse administrative decisions. He can investigate citizens' complaints, he can compel the production of government documents and the attendance of witnesses, and he can bring a problem to the attention of the responsible minister. However, there are usually restrictions on his powers of investigation and if a minister fails to correct the offending action, the only course open to the ombudsman is to notify the complainant and make a report to the legislature. Therefore, the ombudsman's influence depends ultimately upon persuasion and publicity.

Some critics have concluded that asking people to place their faith in an ombudsman without real powers is akin to asking them to believe in Santa Claus or the Tooth Fairy. At best, it can only provide symbolic reassurance that the bureaucracy is under control and at worst, it could lead to complacency about the problem. Therefore:

> No useful purpose can be served by creating an office whose incumbent has no real powers, and the success of whose efforts depends on the illusory force of persuasive effort, because the cases in which he fails will be the very cases in which for his appointment to be effective, he should be able, but has not the power to succeed. Persuasion is a poor weapon against entrenched bureaucracy.[46]

The experience of various jurisdictions suggests that the above conclusion is far too pessimistic. Most ombudsmen find it advantageous to adopt a conciliatory rather than an adversarial approach in their dealings with government agencies since most officials are anxious to rectify mistakes that have been made. Often an indication of interest by the ombudsman is enough to cause a departmental review leading to a satisfactory solution. Even in more difficult cases where the department considers its actions to be completely appropriate, officials will usually prefer a quiet, objective hearing by the ombudsman rather than risk a possible debate in the legislature with attendant media coverage (usually dramatic and sensational) and probable embarrassment for their minister.

The fact that there has been no widespread public demand for the creation of a federal ombudsman has meant that governments, possibly not wishing to upset the constitutional status quo to their own disadvantage, have not felt compelled to assign the matter high priority. However, past federal governments have created a Correctional Investigator for Penitentiary Services, a Privacy Commissioner within the Canadian Human Rights Commission and a Commissioner of Official Languages, all of whom perform specialized, ombudsman-like duties. In addition, governments have recently proposed an Information Commissioner to defend the public's right of access to government documents. To continue to multiply the number of such separate agencies is likely to be cumbersome and confusing to the public. Therefore, some consolidation of jurisdiction and a close coordination of the operations of these specialized ombudsmen with any future general ombudsman at the federal level would appear to be desirable.

Judicial Review of Administrative Action

The courts also provide a check on administrative behavior. Judicial review and the right of appeal are two avenues of recourse open to an aggrieved citizen. Both involve complicated matters beyond the scope of this chapter, but a brief indication of the grounds for each should provide some appreciation of the limits of judicial supervision of regulatory and administrative activity. In general, the courts in Canada have not been as aggressive in supervising administrative rule-making as their American counterparts because tribunals in this country are more subject to Cabinet and legislative direction and accountability. Therefore, Canadian courts have been careful to distinguish proper judicial review of the legality of administrative action from inappropriate judicial interference in the formulation or evaluation of policy. "The courts will not look at the *substance* of a tribunal's decision from the viewpoint of whether it is wise or unwise, or helps or harms any person— the scope of judicial review at all levels of court is restricted to errors of law or jurisdiction."[47]

In seeking to thus limit the scope of their review, the courts have employed a three-fold classification of bureaucratic functions. Unfortunately, the categories are more precise in theory than in practice. First, in connection with the legislative or policy-making functions, the courts have seldom interfered on the grounds that Cabinet and Parliament can redirect agencies if it is felt that they have strayed in their subordinate law-making role from the intentions of the authorizing statute. The second category is the administrative function where the courts have intervened infrequently, normally only when agencies have exceeded the regulatory authority provided in the authorizing statute. Should the courts decide that an independent tribunal or even a department has exceeded its allotted powers, they can set aside a decision. But regulatory authority is frequently granted in such vague, sweeping terms that the courts have difficulty in challenging its use in practice. Phrases like "such regulations as are necessary to carry out purposes of the Act" or as "are deemed necessary and desirable" have become commonplace in authorizing statutes. The courts naturally have been reluctant to substitute their own subjective, "inexpert" opinion for the "expert" judgement of the members of a regulatory board or commission about what types and levels of regulations are required.

Most cases that come before the courts involve the judicial or quasi-judicial function of administrative agencies. Under the Federal Court Act of 1970 the grounds for obtaining judicial review of administrative decisions were expanded. The Trial Division of the Federal Court was given exclusive, original jurisdiction over complaints involving federal boards, commissions or other tribunals (there were over 120 such bodies in 1978). The main grounds for obtaining judicial review are that an agency exceeded its jurisdiction, committed errors in law or failed to apply the principles of natural justice in its proceedings.[48] While technically the Federal Court has the power to substitute its own decision for that of an agency, in practice this power is rarely used for the reasons of judicial self-restraint mentioned above. The usual practice is simply to set aside the decision of an administrative tribunal.

Judicial review is not exactly the same as an appeal from the decision of an administrative tribunal. There is not a general right of appeal of such decisions in common law. However, the statutes of many administrative tribunals were amended by virtue of the Federal Court Act of 1970 to provide for appeals, in the first instance, to the Federal Court. Where an appeal is available under statute, judicial review is unavailable to the extent that the scope of both actions are concurrent.

These complicated and somewhat esoteric matters should not divert our attention from the most significant point which is that only a very small portion of the thousands of administrative decisions issued annually are ever brought before the courts because the judicial review process is too complicated, expensive and time-consuming for most citizens to employ. It would be unrealistic, therefore, to rely greatly upon the courts to police the use of administrative authority.

Summary of the Diagnosis and Prescriptions for Reform

It seems inevitable that democratic responsible government will display enormous weaknesses given the scope and complexity of governmental activity today. It may be that the struggle for accountable government has been lost and that minor institutional reforms — such as more Cabinet committees, more central agencies, new budgetary systems, a strengthened Auditor-General, improved parliamentary committees, an ombudsman, and a Freedom of Information Act — singly or collectively will not resolve the problem of controlling bureaucratic power. As the body possessing the greatest measure of democratic legitimacy, the House of Commons remains vitally important within the political system, but it seems incapable in practice of fulfilling its prescribed constitutional role of holding Cabinet and its individual members accountable. Party discipline, the lack of relevant information and the sheer magnitude of the task are part of the problem. But it is also the case that ministers themselves lack the capacity to account for the administrative actions of their subordinates, even if the Commons had the political muscle to demand such an accounting.

The development of the Cabinet committee system and the rise of central agencies seem to have strengthened the collective control of ministers on the general direction of policy, but it has also compromised or qualified the extent to which individual ministers can be held responsible for the policies in their respective domains. Furthermore, while the emphasis on collective Cabinet decision-making recognizes the interdependence of departmental activities, it also imposes additional demands on scarce ministerial time. Twelve to 15 hours per week spent in Cabinet meetings, when combined with the time spent in the House of Commons, in caucus, in meetings with representatives of pressure groups, on constituency business and on party matters, leaves little ministerial time for departmental management. According to one estimate, "ministers can spare, at most, a working day a week for departmental business."[49] The inability of ministers to assume anything more than vicarious responsibility for actions which are not theirs seems obvious to many observers.

The need to delegate policy-making authority to independent or semi-independent crown corporations, regulatory agencies, boards and commissions further complicates the enforcement of the principles of collective and individual ministerial responsibility. Such arrangements necessarily weaken the ability of Cabinet to set and to achieve overall policy goals. Individual ministers usually have one or more regulatory boards or crown corporations within their portfolios of responsibility, but they do not exercise the same degree of control and supervision over their operations as in the case of regular departments. Paradoxically, at the time when many of these non-departmental agencies of government were created, there was a fervent desire to protect them from unwarranted political interference, while in recent years there has been growing concern that such institutions are not subject to sufficient political direction and accountability to Parliament. And as we have seen, a series of institutional reforms intended to achieve this result have been proposed. Whether they will be implemented and, if they are, whether they will be effective in achieving greater accountability, are questions for which there are no answers at present.

The inadequacies of the existing arrangements for holding the Canadian bureaucracy accountable have led some observers to conclude that radical reforms, rather than institutional tinkering, are required to ensure the preservation of responsible and responsive government. Not surprisingly, since Canadians are inundated by cultural spillover from the United States, increasing interest has been shown in importing congressional or quasi-congressional features into our system of government. Ironically, in the wake of Watergate and a series of lesser scandals, political reformers in the United States have talked widely about the virtues of the cabinet-parliamentary system which seem to them to provide more efficient and responsible government than Americans have enjoyed in recent years. Given the infatuation of reformers on both sides of the border with the alleged strengths of the neighboring system, it is useful to examine briefly the differences between the two systems and the extent to which it might be possible and/or desirable to transfer features from one to the other.

Canada and the United States represent two fundamentally different approaches to controlling the exercise of power.[50] The American constitution seeks to curb executives by dividing governmental power and making sure that it is not concentrated in one set of hands. The Canadian system, on the other hand, is designed to concentrate power in the hands of Cabinet and then provides means by which its members are supposed to be held directly and daily accountable for the way it is used.

The American constitution provides for a separation of powers among three distinct and independent branches of government; it provides for mutual checks and balances on the exercise of such powers by the executive, legislative and judicial branches; it divides powers within a federal system of national and state governments; and it provides for judicial review of legislative and executive actions. To these constitutional constraints are added a variety of informal and conventional mechanisms that further diffuse and fragment power. Decentralized and non-ideological parties, the different political constituencies of the President and Congress, the pluralism of the interest-group system, powerful and well-staffed congressional committees able to modify, delay and even to reject Presidential legislative and spending proposals — all these features of the American political system reflect and reinforce the dispersal of power which is basic to the American constitution. The cost of such a fragmentation of power is a great potential for deadlock and paralysis in the policy process and an obscuring of the clear lines of accountability to the public. According to William S. Livingston, "the American system is an institutionalization of buck-passing" and this feature makes it difficult to focus responsibility or to hold individuals personally accountable.[51] In any given area of policy there are a variety of actors in the administration as well as in Congress who share power, but there is often no one with final responsibility for the exercise of all the power necessary to take any action. By establishing countervailing centers of power throughout the system, Americans seek to preserve liberty by avoiding gross abuses of power.

The respective role of the bureaucracies within the two systems reflects these constitutional and political differences. The idea of a neutral, career public service able to supply advice and undivided loyalty to a succession of parties in office is far less firmly entrenched in practice in American government than in Canada. Theoretically the civil service is there to serve the President, but in practice organizational loyalties are divided.[52] Because power is widely dispersed, departments and agencies in Washington feel themselves accountable, not only to the President, but also to the congressional committees which authorize their spending, to their clientele groups outside of government, and to their own functional specialties and particular programs. Controlling these "iron triangles" or "sub-governments" is usually thought to depend upon presidential leadership, but there are numerous obstacles to such leadership. Presidents rarely arrive in office with a clear electoral mandate which could provide specific direction to the bureaucracy. Presidential teams in office tend to be disorganized. Members of the President's Cabinet are selected as much to meet political representation considerations as to provide managerial capability. While all Cabinet members owe a loyalty to the President, there are not at all the same incentives to Cabinet solidarity since governments do not fall based upon negative votes in the legislature. The constraints of time and information make it impossible for the President to provide leadership across the administrative branch. He must concentrate on what to him are *crucial* problems and leave to other executives those matters which are "merely important" to national policy. In other words, there are severe limits to what can be run directly from the White House. As Hugh Heclo has recently concluded, "if political leadership in the bureaucracy depends mainly on what the President can supply, there is unlikely to be enough to go around."[53]

The response of recent Presidents to these problems of political leadership in the bureaucracy has been to rely on the appointment of "team-playing loyalists" to strategic posts within the executive branch. As a result the politicization of the bureaucracy has been extended and the boundary line between political appointees and career public servants has become extremely blurred and variable over time. Depending on who is doing the counting, nine to 25 per cent of the top executive positions in Washington can be considered political appointments — a far higher percentage than the corresponding number in Ottawa. However, the approximately 7,000 top executives appointed by the President are in a relatively weak, uncertain position in relation to the permanent bureaucracy.[54] In Heclo's artful phrase they are "a government of strangers." They owe their appointments to diverse political sources and they are structurally divided and largely unknown to one another. There is no built-in incentive for them to coordinate the efforts of their departments. As temporary occupants of posts, political executives must depend heavily on the information, advice and follow-through of their departments. On the other hand, they must avoid being "captured" by their departments and still remain responsive to presidential goals where these exist. The result is a pervasive process of negotiation, bargaining and compromise among political executives and civil servants to determine which courses of action are to their mutual advantage. The American bureaucracy, therefore, is not a monolithic, unified center of power. It is pluralistic and internally competitive. And contesting elements in the bureaucracy regularly seek allies outside the bureaucracy—in the Congress and among the pressure groups. The Canadian system, by contrast, produces a more unified, symmetrical and less permeable bureaucracy based on the overriding idea of loyalty to the minister and to the government.

The American system emphasizes the personal responsibility of the bureaucrat and a preference for publicity surrounding the use of bureaucratic power. This contrasts with the Canadian emphasis on the anonymity of the public servant and the penchant for secrecy concerning bureaucratic decision-making.[55] As an equal branch of government, Congress has been concerned to preserve its prerogatives regarding the creation of administrative agencies and the supervision of their implementation of laws. To this end, Congress has developed far more opportunities and auxiliary organizations (such as the General Accounting Office, the Congressional Budget Office, elaborate committee staffs and so on) to ensure scrutiny of the uses of bureaucratic power. Cabinet secretaries and their deputies appear frequently before congressional committees to explain departmental policies and actions. While formally such actions are taken on behalf of the President, such appearances constitute, in effect, accountability sessions and in the end congressional committees will usually bring home to the bureaucrat his personal responsibility for his actions. Presidential attempts to shield public servants from rough treatment at the hands of Congress may occur, but they rarely succeed. The system also compels bureaucrats to share information more freely with the legislature than is the case in Canada. The American public servant who achieves real influence and prestige in the society is usually the one who breaks most completely the mask of anonymity. Other officials who seek careers as genuinely neutral civil servants find their aspirations blocked by the increasing politicization of the upper levels within the bureaucracy. By contrast, the most successful and respected public servants in Canada have usually been those individuals who are models of non-partisanship, discretion and anonymity.

These brief and rather oversimplified observations on the contrasts between the two systems lead us to the question of whether Canada would benefit from recognizing the important role played by the bureaucracy through some formal division of responsibility between ministers and their senior officials. The recent Royal Commission on Financial Management and Accountability argued that Canada should follow the example of the United Kingdom by making deputy ministers formally responsible to Parliament through the Public Accounts Committee. Deputy ministers would be held accountable for the probity and legality of expenditures, the economy and efficiency with which programs are run, and the effectiveness of programs in reaching policy goals.[56] According to the Commission, this assignment of responsibility would not impair the principle of ministerial responsibility, but would reinforce it by replacing theory with reality. Deputies would accept responsibility for the detailed operations of departments which are, in practical terms, beyond the minister's control. However, the idea of formal deputy ministerial responsibility was rejected by the former Liberal government on the following grounds:

> *Formal* and *direct* accountability of officials to Parliament for administrative matters would divide the responsibility of ministers. It would require the establishment of firm practices governing the sorts of questions for which ministers as distinct from officials would be

> answerable . . . .Experience indicates that such distinctions are artificial and that Parliament prefers not to recognize the informal division between the answerability of officials and of ministers for the very reasons that ministers are constitutionally responsible and the extent of their answerability is defined by political circumstance. Furthermore, theology aside, such divided responsibility would be unsound management.[57]

There might be a pragmatic relaxation of the traditional requirement of public silence to enable public servants to testify before parliamentary committees on administrative matters, but the idea of direct and personal bureaucratic responsibility is portrayed as an undesirable "congressional" import, even though Great Britain has practiced this form of accountable management for some years.

Other critics do not reject the Commission's argument for the need to update the pure version of ministerial responsibility to correspond more accurately to the complicated realities of contemporary public administration, but they insist that the idea of accountable management is pushed too far by the Commission's suggestion that deputy ministers assume liability for the effectiveness of programs. If deputies are only to ensure the productive use of funds (a ratio of outputs to costs) and the existence of the capability within their departments to evaluate programs, no major problems would arise. But to insist that deputies be responsible for the attainment of policy and program goals would be unrealistic and "unfair" since ministers prefer to state such goals in vague and rhetorical terms. Making deputies responsible for program effectiveness would allow ministers to shift the blame for program failures to officials who, under current conventions, could not present a public defense of their performance, and it could very well lead to them becoming the subject of partisan attacks in the House of Commons. Therefore, it is argued, ministerial responsibility should be modified only to the extent of recognizing the public and parliamentary responsibility of officials for narrow and clearly specified administrative duties (such as departmental efficiency and the use of delegated legislative authority).

Subjective Responsibility

Up to this point we have discussed ways to control bureaucrats to make sure they carry out their functions in accordance with the goals determined through the processes of representative government. We want to ensure that bureaucrats respect the wishes of elected politicians and therefore, in theory at least, the wishes of Canadian citizens. We want to ensure that they do not make decisions that violate individual rights. Most of the external political controls discussed above emphasize retrospective accountability for negative actions by the bureaucracy. But in a complicated and rapidly changing society, perhaps this emphasis on external control is misplaced. Perhaps administrative responsibility is more than just being held accountable for abuses of authority. Maybe a more positive and active definition of responsible bureaucratic behavior is required to assist public servants in dealing with the numerous ambiguous situations not covered by legislation, ministerial directives or departmental manuals, where at present they have only their professional judgment and personal conscience to guide them.

The argument that the bureaucracy has become too powerful to be controlled wholly by external institutions and that therefore bureaucrats need to possess a subjective or moral sense of responsibility has been made by a variety of writers over the last several decades. Unfortunately, there is little agreement on what such a code of responsible bureaucratic behavior should contain and on how the values it enshrines might best be nurtured in the public service. Based upon an analysis of the literature in the United States, Charles Gilbert has compiled a list of 12 values most frequently associated with a responsible bureaucrat. These values are responsiveness, flexibility, consistency, stability, leadership, probity, candor, competence, efficacy, prudence, due process and accountability.[58] Each of these values, of course, is subject to considerable interpretation and most probably they would clash with one another in any particular situation. That is, whiie they read as easily as do the Ten Commandments, making them operational is something else again.

Other writers have stressed that responsible administration in a bureaucracy demands that bureaucrats act in "the public interest." But what is the public interest? Does it exist for all issues? How are administrators to identify it? The debate over what constitutes the public interest has been protracted and vigorous in the political science literature. One group of writers identifies it as the result of the political process of aggregating, weighing and balancing a variety of competing interests.[59] For other writers the public interest consists of the common interests of all members of the society consistent with the prevailing values in the society.

A third group defines the public interest in terms of some transcendent value or values — which in some cases may not correspond to the temporary wishes of the citizens. For example, Dvorin and Simmons argue that bureaucrats should actively pursue the public interest defined as the enhancement of human dignity.[60] They admit that such a nebulous concept will entrust bureaucrats with difficult ethical judgments involving the reconciliation of competing values. But this is unavoidable in a conflictual and rapidly changing society. For them, the prevailing constitutional doctrines mask the powerful and creative role played by the bureaucrat in the formulation and implementation of policy and allow him thereby to abdicate responsibility for his actions.

A fourth approach to the public interest defines it in process terms, that is, the way in which decisions are reached. The processes of democratic decision-making, involving political executives, legislatures, interest groups and judicial review, produce decisions that are in the public interest, according to some writers. A somewhat different version of this argument is presented by Kenneth Kernaghan.[61] He maintains that public servants should be guided by the interplay of legitimacy, expediency and morality in their search for the public interest. Each of these concepts is open to interpretation in particular situations so that they do not provide precise guides to action, but their acceptance by public servants, he argues, could lead to more reflective administrative behavior.

The listing of these various definitions may have caused the more skeptical reader to conclude that the public interest is a will-o'-the-wisp that cannot possibly be the basis for responsible bureaucratic behavior. Other readers might be outraged at the suggestion that public servants employ their own normative definitions of the public interest since the result could be to sabotage the proper processes of popular democratic control through elected representatives.

In practice, the sources of the bureaucrat's values are many. They include all the elements of pre-career socialization as well as the forces that shape his outloook on the job. The institutional controls discussed earlier in this chapter undoubtedly help to mould the value system of the bureaucrat by convincing him to accept certain lines of authority and actions as legitimate and perhaps by alerting him to wider situational factors involved in decision-making. It has often been argued, however, that the reliance upon formal controls, given the political difficulties associated with their use, is inadequate and has meant that little thought has been given to means by which subjective responsibility might be nurtured in the bureaucracy. What interest has been shown has been sporadic and concerned mainly with the integrity of the public service in terms of the avoidance of malfeasance, conflicts of interest, the unauthorized disclosure of information and involvement in prohibited political activities. In response to a limited but well-publicized number of bureaucratic scandals, governments have rushed to legislate codes of ethics for public servants. Opinions on the efficacy of such devices range all the way from the view that they represent symbolic window-dressing to the view that they can be effective controls over administrative action. One major Canadian study of the value of such codes has concluded that they are not a cure-all for violations of public trust, but they can sensitize public employees to the need to adhere to high ethical standards. According to the study, the ideal code should be written rather than unwritten, should not rely excessively upon rigid, legal sanctions but should make liberal use of flexible administrative sanctions, and should aim for the greatest possible measure of clarity and precision.[62] Obviously drafting such a code involves striking a very precise balance since, for example, the final criterion may conflict with the previous two, and we have not even discussed the problem of wording the specific injunctions to public servants covering undesirable behavior.

However, according to other observers the greatest weakness of such codes (with their "thou shalt not" commandments) is that they miss the most difficult ethical issues involved in governing, namely the reconciliation of conflicts over values and policies. Theoretically, this is the exclusive domain of the politician, but in practice it seems that the public servant is inevitably forced to deal with such conflicts as well. Critics of mainstream public administration theory and public administration education insist that both pay too little attention to the value dilemmas of modern life. An educational process — both pre-career and in-service training — that is increasingly specialized and technocratic does not provide officials with the breadth of vision and the appreciation of the ethical ambiguities of situations. Frederick Mosher argues that most government recruitment and promotion policies emphasize technical and cognitive qualifications in the fields of specialization, whereas:

> Truly meritorious performance in public administration will depend at least equally upon the values, the objectives, and the moral standards which the administrator brings to his decisions, and upon his ability to weigh the relevant premises judiciously in his approach to the problems at hand.[63]

The response to such criticisms has been for schools of public administration increasingly to try to strike a balance between the transfer of technical skills (the "how to *do* it" of public administration) and the presentation of the wider issues of public policy formulation and implementation (the "what *ought* to be" of public administration).[64] In-service training has also featured such a shift in focus with, for example, public servants being introduced to various forms of "sensitivity training" designed to develop interpersonal skills of communication and to increase empathy with the needs of others. Needless to say, there has been resistance to these developments. Opponents argue that efforts to institutionalize feelings of compassion and identification with the wishes of clientele groups will subvert political control of the public service and may lead us back to an earlier historical stage where personal contacts and "pull" in the bureaucracy could lead to more favorable treatment.[65] There seems to be, therefore, no final solution to the problem of combining some measure of democratic political control with the reality of bureaucratic power. Probably the central question of future political and administrative life will be how active governments, wielding great and varied power and increasingly intervening in our daily lives, can be subjected to effective democratic control.

For Further Reading

BOOKS AND REPORTS

Canada, Royal Commission on Financial Management and Accountability, *Final Report*. Ottawa: Supply and Services, 1979.

———. Privy Council Office, *Responsibility in the Constitution*. Ottawa: Submission to the Royal Commission on Financial Management and Accountability, March 1979.

———. Privy Council Office, *Crown Corporations: Direction, Control and Accountability*. Ottawa: 1977.

———. *Report of the Committee on the Concept of the Ombudsman*. Ottawa: July 1977.

———. Economic Council of Canada, *Responsible Regulation*. Ottawa: Supply and Services, 1979.

———. Law Reform Commission, *Independent Administrative Agencies*. Ottawa: Working Paper No. 25, 1980.

———. Parliament, Task Force on Regulatory Reform, *Report*. Ottawa: Supply and Services, 1980.

Doern, G. Bruce and Peter Aucoin, eds. *Public Policy in Canada: Organization, Process and Management*. Toronto: Macmillan, 1979.

Doern, G. Bruce, ed. *The Regulatory Process in Canada*. Toronto: Macmillan, 1978.

Gelinas, A. ed. *Public Enterprise and the Public Interest*. Toronto: Institute of Public Administration of Canada, 1978.

Kernaghan, Kenneth. *Ethical Conduct: Guidelines for Government Employees*. Toronto: Institute of Public Administration of Canada, 1977.

Smith, Bruce L. R. and D. C. Hague, eds. *The Dilemma of Accountability in Modern Government*. New York: St. Martin's Press, 1971.

ARTICLES

Baker, Walter A. "Accountability, responsiveness and public sector productivity." *Canadian Public Administration*, Vol. XXIII, 4 (Winter 1980), pp. 542-57.

Cameron, D. M. "Power and Responsibility in the Public Service: Summary of Discussions." *Canadian Public Administration*, Vol. XXI, 3 (Autumn 1978), pp. 358-72.

Cornell, J. Peter. "Accountability." *Optimum*, Vol. VIII, 3 (1977), pp. 28-36.

Denton, T. M. "Ministerial Responsibility: A Contemporary Perspective." *The Canadian Political Process: A Reader*, 3rd ed., Shultz, Richard, Orest M. Kruhlak and John C. Terry, eds., Toronto: Holt, Rinehart and Winston, 1979, pp. 344-62.

Kernaghan, Kenneth. "Responsible Public Bureaucracy: a Rationale and a Framework for Analysis." *Canadian Public Administration*, Vol. XVI, 4 (Winter 1973), pp. 527-603.

———. "Politics, Policy and Public Servants: Political Neutrality Revisited." *Canadian Public Administration*, Vol. XIX, 3 (Autumn 1976), pp. 432-56.

———. "Changing Concepts of Power and Responsibility in the Canadian Public Service." *Canadian Public Administration*, Vol. XXI, 3 (Autumn 1978), pp. 389-406.

———. "Power, Parliament and Public Servants in Canada: Ministerial Responsibility Re-examined." *Canadian Public Policy*, Vol. V, 3 (Autumn 1979), pp. 383-96.

Mallory, J. R. "Responsive and Responsible Government." *Transactions of the Royal Society of Canada*, Series IV, Vol. XII (1974).

McLeod, T. H. "The Special National Seminar on Financial Management and Accountability: An Appraisal." *Canadian Public Administration*, Vol. XXIII, 1 (Spring 1980), pp. 105-34.

ENDNOTES

1. Canada, Royal Commission on Financial Management and Accountability, *Final Report* (Ottawa: Supply and Services, 1979), p. 9. Henceforth cited as *The Lambert Report*.
2. Hugh Heclo, *A Government of Strangers: Executive Politics in Washington* (Washington: Brookings Institute, 1977), p. 5.
3. A good review of the debate is found in Kenneth Kernaghan, "Responsible Public Bureaucracy: a Rationale and a Framework for Analysis," *Canadian Public Administration*, Vol. XVI, 4 (Winter, 1973), pp. 572-603.
4. Frederick C. Mosher, *Democracy and the Public Service* (New York: Oxford University Press, 1968), p. 7.
5. *Ibid*., p. 8.
6. Kernaghan, pp. 580-86.
7. The following discussion relies heavily on three excellent papers: H.V. Emy, "The Public Service and Political Control: The Problem of Accountability in a Westminister System with Special Reference to the Concept of Ministerial Responsibility," Paper for the Royal Commission on Australian Government Administration, *Report*, Vol. I; Kenneth Kernaghan, "Power, Parliament and Public Servants in Canada: Ministerial Responsibility Reexamined," *Canadian Public Policy*, Vol. V, 3 (Autumn 1979), pp. 383-396; and T.M. Denton, "Ministerial Responsibility: A Contemporary Perspective," in Richard Schultz, Orest M. Kruhlak and John C. Terry (eds.), *The Canadian Political Process*, 3rd ed. (Toronto: Holt, Rinehart and Winston of Canada, 1979), pp. 344-62.
8. Kernaghan, "Power, Parliament and Public Servants," pp. 9-10.
9. In the so-called "Judges Affair" of 1976, Charles Drury intervened with a Judge at the request of his fellow cabinet member, André Ouellet, against whom contempt proceedings were pending. After a judicial inquiry Drury submitted his resignation, which was refused by the Prime Minister, but Ouellet subsequently resigned. For details, see John Saywell (ed.), *The Canadian Annual Review, 1976* (Toronto: University of Toronto Press, 1977), pp. 16-18.
10. Denton, *op. cit*., p. 357.
11. Brian Chapman, *British Government Observed* (London: George Allen and Unwin, 1963), p. 34.
12. Quoted in Kernaghan, "Power, Parliament and Public Servants," p. 13.
13. Privy Council Office, "Responsibility in the Constitution," Submission I to the Royal Commission on Financial Management and Accountability (March 1979), p. 1-3.
14. See J.R. Mallory, "Responsive and Responsible Government," *Transactions of the Royal Society of Canada*, Series IV, Vol. XII, (1974), p. 210 for a brief discussion of what he calls the "homiletic value" of such myths.
15. *The Lambert Report*, p. 177.
16. H.V. Emy, *op. cit.*, pp. 35-39, has an excellent discussion of the potential administrative costs of ministerial responsibility.
17. See the article by J. Peter Cornell, "Accountability," *Optimum*, Vol. VIII, 3 (1977), pp. 28-36.
18. Privy Council Office, "Responsibility in the Constitution," pp. 1-33.
19. Kenneth Kernaghan, "Changing concepts of power and responsibility in the Canadian public service," *Canadian Public Administration*, Vol. XXI, 3 (Fall 1978), p. 403.
20. Canada, Parliament, House of Commons, Special Committee on Statutory Instruments, *Third Report* (October 22, 1969), pp. 1411-1508. Figures on p. 1417.

21. Government of Canada, *Report of the Committee on the Concept of the Ombudsman* (Ottawa, July 1977).
22. See Herbert Kaufman, *Red Tape: Its Origins, Uses and Abuses* (Washington: The Brookings Institute, 1977), Chapter 2, for an interesting discussion of how citizens generate "red tape" in government and then proceed to denounce it.
23. Economic Council of Canada, *Responsible Regulation* (Ottawa: Supply and Services, November 1979), p. xi.
24. See our Chapter 5 on "Public Budgeting."
25. The following discussion of the economic rationales for regulation relies heavily upon M.J. Trebilock, L. Waverman, and J.R.S. Prichard, "Markets for Regulation: Implications for Performance Standards and Institutional Design," in *Government Regulation: Issues and Alternatives* (Toronto: Ontario Economic Council, 1978).
26. While we are not employing Douglas G. Hartle's broad definition of regulation, he does present a persuasive argument for analyzing regulation as the outcome of the interplay of self-interested actors. See Douglas G. Hartle, *Public Policy Decision-Making and Regulation* (Toronto: Institute for Research on Public Policy, 1979), particularly Chapter 3. M.J. Trebilock *et. al.*, *op. cit.*, make a similar argument.
27. Murry Edelman, *The Symbolic Uses of Politics* (Urbana: University of Illinois Press, 1967).
28. G. Bruce Doern, "Regulatory Processes and Regulatory Agencies," in G. Bruce Doern and Peter Aucoin (eds.), *Public Policy in Canada: Organization, Process, and Management* (Toronto: Macmillan, 1979), pp. 158-89.
29. Privy Council Office, "Responsibility in the Constitution: Non-Departmental Bodies," *op. cit.*, Chapter 2, pp. 8-13.
30. Economic Council of Canada, *Responsible Regulation*, Chapter 5.
31. Both the *Lambert Report*, pp. 317-319 and the Economic Council of Canada, *op. cit.*, make this recommendation.
32. For reviews of the Committee's work to date see: Graham Eglington, "Scrutiny of Delegated Legislation in the Parliament of Canada," *The Parliamentarian*, Vol. LIX (October 1978), p. 273; J. Gary Levy, "Delegated Legislation and the Standing Joint Committee on Regulations and other Statutory Instruments," *Canadian Public Administration*, Vol. XXII, 3 (Fall 1979), pp. 349-65; and J.R. Mallory, "Parliamentary Scrutiny of Delegated Legislation in Canada: A Large Step Forward and a Small Step Back," *Public Law* (Spring, 1972), pp. 30-42.
33. Canada, Parliament, House of Commons, Standing Joint Committee on Regulations and Other Statutory Instruments, *Second Report* (Ottawa: February 3, 1977), p. 19.
34 *Ibid.*, pp. 18-19.
35. *The Lambert Report*, p. 328.
36. An important exception to this view is the argument of Herschel Hardin, *A Nation Unaware: The Canadian Economic Culture* (Vancouver: J.J. Douglas, 1974), that the range of crown corporations reflects Canada's "public enterprise culture."
37. John W. Langford, "Crown Corporations as Instruments of Policy," in G. Bruce Doern and Peter Aucoin (eds.), *Public Policy in Canada, op. cit.*, pp. 239-74.
38. Report of the Auditor General to the House of Commons (Ottawa: Supply and Services, March 1976).
39. Canada, Privy Council Office, *Crown Corporations: Direction, Control and Accountability* (Ottawa, 1977).
40. Professor Wilbrod Leclerc, "How Much Control Should Government Have Over Crown Corporations," *The Financial Post*, April 1, 1978, p. 16.
41. *The Lambert Report*, pp. 342-46.
42. *Ibid.*, p. 353.
43. Government of Canada, Report of the Committee on the Concept of the Ombudsman (Ottawa, July 1977), p. 20.
44. K.A. Friedmann and A.G. Milne, "The Federal Ombudsman Legislation," *Canadian Public Policy*, Vol. VI, 1 (Winter, 1980), p. 64.
45. For a detailed commentary on these aspects of the proposed federal ombudsman, see *Ibid.*, pp. 63-77.

46. R.M. Willes Chitty, "The Case Against the Appointment of a Federal Ombudsman," *The Globe & Mail*, July 7, 1966, p. 7.
47. Andrew J. Roman, "Regulatory Law and Procedure," in G. Bruce Doern (ed.), *The Regulatory Process in Canada* (Toronto: Macmillan, 1978), p. 71. Other useful sources on this difficult topic are: Peter Hogg, "Judicial Review: How Much Do We Need," *McGill Law Review*, Vol. XX (1974), pp. 157-76; J.E. Kersell, "Statutory and Judicial Control of Administrative Behaviour," *Canadian Public Administration*, Vol. XIX, 2 (Summer, 1976), pp. 295-301; and the *Second Report of the Standing Joint Committee on Regulations and Other Statutory Instruments*.
48. See Roman, *op. cit*., pp. 82-85 for a discussion of the principles of natural justice.
49. Denton, p. 356.
50. There have been few, if any, attempts at explicit comparisons of the Canadian and American approaches to ensuring accountable government. Two articles that use British and American contrasts are: William S. Livingston, "Britain and America: The Institutionalization of Accountability," *Journal of Politics*, XXXVIII (1976), pp. 879-94; and Wallace S. Sayre, "Bureaucracies: Some Contrasts in Systems," in Roy C. Macridis and Bernard E. Brown (eds.), *Comparative Politics: Notes and Readings* (Georgetown: Irwin Dorsey, 1972), pp. 350-60.
51. Livingston, *op. cit*., p. 882.
52. Hugh Heclo, *A Government of Strangers: Executive Politics in Washington* (Washington: The Brookings Institution, 1977) provides a thorough and insightful analysis of the problem of reconciling transient political leadership with permanent bureaucratic power in Washington.
53. *Ibid*., p. 14.
54. *Ibid*., p. 40.
55. Sayre, *op. cit*., pp. 357-59.
56. *The Lambert Report*, pp. 374-76.
57. Privy Council Office, *op. cit*., pp. 1-54.
58. Charles Gilbert, "The Framework of Administrative Responsibility," *The Journal of Politics*, Vol. XXI (August 1959), pp. 373-407.
59. A useful inventory of attempts at definition of the public interest is found in Douglas G. Hartle, *op. cit*., pp. 213-16.
60. Eugene P. Dvorin and Robert H. Simmons, *From Amoral to Humane Bureaucracy* (San Francisco: Canfield Press, 1972).
61. Kernaghan, *op. cit*., pp. 596-97.
63. Kenneth Kernaghan, *Ethical Conduct: Guidelines for Government Employees* (Toronto: Institute of Public Administration of Canada, 1977).
63. Mosher, *op. cit*., p. 218.
64. A. Paul Pross and V. Seymour Wilson, "Graduate Education in Canadian Public Administration: Antecedents, Present Trends and Portents," *Canadian Public Administration*, Vol. XIX, 4 (Winter, 1976), pp. 515-541.
65. See Victor A. Thompson, *Bureaucracy and the Modern World* (Morristown, N.J.: General Learning Press, 1976), Chapter 5, for an argument against efforts to establish a compassionate bureaucracy.

CHAPTER NINE

Administrative Secrecy

Introduction

During the 1980 Canadian federal election the following joke was being told:

> You may have heard the story of the Afghan who ran naked through the streets of Moscow yelling, "Brezhnev is a fool, Brezhnev is a fool." He was arrested, tried and sentenced to 98 years in prison — one year for indecent exposure, two years for insulting a leader of the Soviet Union and 95 years for revealing a state secret.

The Soviet Union, however, is not the only country in the world to have problems with protecting state secrets. On a visit to Canada in 1975, Henry Kissinger, then American Secretary of State, was unfortunate enough to have his private dinner conversation containing unflattering references to American politicans broadcast by an open microphone to the press at the back of a banquet hall. The accident led to a cartoon in *The Globe and Mail* in which Kissinger is seen reporting back to a worried-looking President Gerald Ford: "It's a beautiful open society. Why even their bugging system is amplifed and played live in all the corridors."

These anecdotes are not meant to trivialize a serious issue, but rather they serve to point to the suspicion and frustration of many Canadians with the prevailing norms of secrecy surrounding government operations. Canada, along with the majority of countries in the world, at present provides no general legal right for the public to obtain information possessed by their government. Instead, the government of Canada now practises what the leading Canadian authority on this topic has described as "discretionary secrecy"; that is, the government releases information if and when it decides to, and it controls the form in which such information is released.[1] Governments are free under the present system to withhold information, not only for legitimate reasons such as the protection of national security or personal privacy, but also for indefensible reasons, such as seeking to avoid political embarrassment or simply for administrative convenience.

While there is currently no statutory protection of the public's right to know at the national level, the administrative trend within the government of Canada has been towards greater openness. Three provincial governments — New Brunswick, Nova Scotia and Prince Edward Island — have enacted

Freedom of Information (FOI) statutes. However, only the New Brunswick legislation has generally won praise from commentators, while the other two statutes have been roundly criticized as imperfect and inadequate by most FOI advocates. At the national level, the short-lived Conservative government presented a FOI bill to Parliament and it was before a Commons' committee when the government fell. In July 1980, at the close of the first session of Parliament with the Liberals back in power a similar FOI bill was introduced. It is now under study before a parliamentary committee and it appears that Canada will have a national FOI Act in the near future.

It seems the time has come for freedom of information. Still it is useful to review the arguments for and against implementing the concept in various forms because it must be remembered that openness surrounding government operations is not an overriding political value.[2] As this chapter will try to make clear, in certain circumstances it may clash with other values, including some which Canadians have come to uphold strongly and aggressively in recent years, such as efficiency and effectiveness in government, social stability and security, and individual and corporate privacy.

The chapter begins by examining the nature and sources of administrative secrecy in Canada, including both the historical traditions of the political system and the more specific statutory expressions of those traditions. The recent liberalizing trends which have extended public knowledge of matters which were previously confidential are then examined as background to a subsequent discussion of the arguments for and against an expansion of publicity surrounding government operations. Included in this discussion is a brief assessment of the experience and relevance of other jurisdictions which practise more open forms of government. The specific practical arguments regarding a FOI Act at the national level will then be reviewed, particularly the two most contentious issues of exemptions from the general rule of publicity and the appeal mechanism to be used when governments refuse to release documents. Although departments are the main repositories of official information, especially of the more sensitive kind, important comparable information is also held by crown corporations and regulatory commissions. As will be shown, application of a FOI Act to such agencies is to some extent more complicated than is the case with departments.

There follows a section which speculates on the impact of freedom of information on the policy and administrative processes of Canadian government. Who will benefit from the operation of such an act? Will the general public use this mechanism which is supposedly adopted on their behalf, or will the act serve to increase the existing disparities in political influence by allowing well-heeled, sophisticated and strategically-located individuals and groups to take advantage of information sources not recognized by the general public? What will be the impact of an FOI Act on the behavior of public servants? Will they be more cautious in what they write? Will the more sensitive advice they offer be communicated orally? Following an examination of these kinds of questions, a brief concluding section serves to tie together the various themes and reiterates the point, stressed throughout the chapter, that in this new experimental field of public law the benefits and the costs of greater openness in government is more problematical than advocates on either side of the issue have been prepared to admit.

The Nature and Sources of Administrative Secrecy in Canada

Anyone who tries to cope with the voluminous amounts of information that pour forth from government offices in the form of departmental and parliamentary reports and studies might initially be skeptical of the complaint that there is too little information available about government operations. However, the fact that an individual can be swamped by government documents does not mean that he is necessarily in a better position to participate intelligently in debates about public policy or is better able to hold governments accountable for their actions. Much of the available material may be designed to extoll the accomplishments of government agencies, whereas information that is damaging to the reputation of the government as a whole or of individual departments may not be made available. We may, in other words, "be stuffed with information and starved for understanding."[3] At least this is the suspicion of FOI advocates, who insist that there are frequent abuses under the present rule of discretionary secrecy. They can point to many examples to support this contention, and only a sample of such a list will be presented here in order to provide the reader with some indication of the kinds of information recently denied to the public:

- Residents of Port Hope, Ontario, became concerned about the health hazard of radiation from Eldorado Nuclear, a crown corporation located in that community. The government conducted studies and assured citizens that there was no danger, but refused to release any reports on the grounds that they contained classified information.
- It was discovered that milkshakes being served in some restaurants in the Yukon did not meet federal health standards, but the Minister of National Health and Welfare refused to release the details on the ground that disclosure "would interfere with the working rapport" between federal health inspectors and restaurant owners. This case reflected the practice that test reports involving product safety are regularly withheld from public circulation.
- The Foreign Investment Review Agency established in 1974 to screen new foreign investment in Canada carries out its deliberations in secret. Little information on individual applications is made public, other than whether FIRA recommended cabinet approval or rejection of an application.
- Several consultant's reports on the operations of the Post Office were withheld from Parliament and the public even though unions within the

Post Office used excerpts from the reports in their public submissions calling for the transformation of the Post Office into a crown corporation.

- Bernard Maguire tried for three years to discover the reasons why he was fired from Canadian National Telecommunications. Eventually, he was allowed to see some personnel files to determine the unspecified security reasons for his dismissal but he was prohibited from divulging what he saw to anybody.

- In September 1976 the federal cabinet approved an order-in-council forbidding any person to speak of, or release documents on, any discussions held between 1972 and 1975 dealing with the production, refinery, use or sale of uranium. The penalty for breaking this ban was a fine of up to $10,000 and imprisonment for up to five years. The discussions involved government and industry representatives and were held to establish a world uranium cartel. There was such a public outcry against this so-called "uranium gag-law" when its existence was discovered that the government reluctantly lifted the ban on public discussion, but it had been in effect for over a year.

- Official manuals, internal bulletins and procedural memoranda are a major extension of statute law in Canada, but the "Secret law" which flows from these internal directives is not made public.[4]

Such a list of examples, while perhaps illustrative of the nature of the problem, does not provide conclusive evidence that the government of Canada practises excessive administrative secrecy. One should not exaggerate the picture of administrative secrecy by presenting a series of dramatic and sensational examples. Governments insist that most information in their possession is readily available to the public upon request. Conversely, critics, who perceive a pervasive veil of secrecy surrounding government, insist that upwards of 85 per cent of documents are routinely marked top secret or confidential. Such estimates are probably pseudo-scientific since it is virtually impossible to construct a precise estimate of the percentage of government information treated as confidential. The more important point, however, is that in the judgment of most informed observers a great deal more government information could usefully and safely be made public.

Turning, then, to a discussion of the factors that encourage administrative secrecy, the most important factor usually cited is certain traditions of cabinet-parliamentary government. Official secrecy is held to be endemic to cabinet-parliamentary government based on the principles of cabinet solidarity, ministerial responsibility, public service neutrality and anonymity, and an adversarial basis for the functioning of Parliament. Beginning with Cabinet solidarity, it is argued that the constitutional requirement that ministers accept collective responsibility for legislative and expenditure decisions means that Cabinet discussions must be confidential otherwise the image of a unified Cabinet might be destroyed and accountability for actions would become blurred. Prime Minister Trudeau experimented during his first term with the practice of allowing ministers to disagree publicly over policy options in advance of the government stating its official position. But once a Cabinet decision is taken, a dissenting minister must either suppress his opinions or resign from Cabinet.

Related to this requirement to preserve Cabinet unity, is the desire to encourage frankness in Cabinet discussions. Privacy helps to ensure that ministers will feel free to raise regional or purely political considerations in Cabinet decision-making and this is said to enhance the effectiveness of Cabinet as a forum for the reconciliation of the diverse interests within the country. For these reasons Cabinet ministers, as part of the Privy Council's Oath of Office taken when sworn into office, agree not to disclose any of the substance of Cabinet deliberations or to release documents which might reveal such deliberations or disclose the views of ministers on matters before Cabinet. Most records bearing on Cabinet decision-making are eventually transferred to the Public Archives of Canada and only released after 30 years (the so-called 30-year rule). Some remain classified indefinitely.

However, not all information and analysis presented to Cabinet must remain confidential. While secrecy might be justified to protect the confidentiality of advice and opinions, it need not cover background information and research. The difficulty then becomes how to distinguish between fact and opinion, a problem that is discussed later when we examine the recent procedures of the Trudeau government designed to liberalize access to Cabinet documents. In general, however, so long as we adhere to current constitutional principles, the Cabinet will remain "the best informed, yet least informative institution in our system of government."[5] And few, if any, advocates of freedom of information would favor departure from the rule of Cabinet secrecy.

Confidentiality has to go beyond collective Cabinet decision-making to include the process by which individual Cabinet ministers are advised both for their part in collective ministerial responsibility and the responsibility they assume for their individual portfolios. As was indicated in the preceding chapter on accountability, the concept of individual ministerial responsibility is closely related to the concept of a permanent, anonymous and neutral public service. The system requires that the role played by senior advisors to the minister and the nature of the advice they offer remain outside the area of political controversy; otherwise, the unity of purpose between the political and administrative sides of departments which the constitution presumes to exist might be broken. If a minister is seen to have rejected the advice of his experienced and expert officials, it is unlikely that opposition parties in Parliament would foresake the opportunity to gain political mileage from the case. Furthermore, once a public servant was identified with a particular policy and perhaps dragged into a political fight, his usefulness to subsequent administrations would likely be compromised, even severely undermined. Therefore, the principle of individual ministerial responsibility requires that discussions about actual or proposed policies — discussions involving ministers and public servants or public servants alone — should not be made public, for to do so would destroy the theoretical unity of the political and administrative sides of government.

Related to these concerns is the adversarial nature of parliamentary operations. Most participants and many commentators liken the House of Commons to a court where the contending parties present their best cases for the benefit of the electorate who are the jury.[6] For a successful clash of opinion to happen, prior decision-making must occur in private. Thus the previous Liberal government argued in its Green Paper (1977) on public access to government documents that:

> . . .our political system is an adversarial process, based on the belief that the public interest will be served by both government and opposition parties, presenting their views to public judgement as ably as they can.
>
> The effectiveness of this advocacy depends, at least to some extent, on the ability of parties to concert their plans in confidential discussions. Government and opposition are a little like football teams, who, in the huddle, prepare their plans out of earshot. To open up their advance planning to full public examination risks destroying their ability to put plans into action.[7]

The government probably regretted the use of this sports metaphor because it provoked considerable criticism on the grounds that it trivialized a serious process and seemed to imply (at least to some) that governments and people were adversaries rather than partners.[8] Nonetheless, the attitude it captured appears to be common among politicians in this country and is one additional restraint on openness.

The most significant barrier to greater openness in Canadian government appears, therefore, to be certain traditions of cabinet-parliamentary government. Secrecy is engrained or inherent in our system of government, according to many authorities. However, even if there was not the need to uphold certain constitutional traditions, it is often argued that a certain measure of administrative secrecy would still be required to ensure administrative vitality and effectiveness. According to K.W. Knight, if the public service operated under conditions of complete openness, public servants would begin to write for posterity or simply rely heavily upon oral communication.[9] The quality of advice received by ministers would decline because of the reluctance of public servants to record for public consumption unpopular or unconventional ideas. Therefore, the advice would be less frank, less imaginative and more cautious. Such an argument is contentious, as we will see momentarily, but for now it will be allowed to stand unchallenged as one of the interrelated sets of values that contribute to administrative secrecy.

The post-war expansion of the bureaucracy has meant that there has been a proliferation of communications in various forms that are considered internal and immune from public scrutiny. The increased size and specialization of the bureaucracy have also led to efforts to coordinate and control the flow of information. At one point, this resulted in the centralization of the public information function largely within a single administrative agency, Information Canada, which had as one of its principal duties the advancement of public knowledge and support for the activities of various departments. The rise and eventual demise of Information Canada is discussed below; the important point here is that even when the information flow has not been centralized in one location, many individual departments have sought to rationalize their own public information activities and the result has been a reduction in the number of information outlets.

Governments which have intervened more frequently in the economy have increasingly found it necessary or appropriate to adopt the prevailing norms of business secrecy as the basis of their own operations. The provision of government subsidies (in grant or loan form) requires that firms file financial records, marketing plans, expansion plans and so on with the government departments or agencies involved. Regulation of industries by independent commissions also requires that information on the internal operations of private companies be collected. In a competitive economy, according to businessmen, they could suffer financial and other damages (such as industrial espionage) if the growing volumes of information they provide to governments were brought into the public domain. As a result, a good deal of ordinary business secrecy has come to be assimilated into the procedures of government departments, commissions, boards and tribunals. However, the appropriateness of withholding at least certain portions of such information has come under question in recent years, as will be seen below.

In addition to corporate privacy, there is also a concern to protect individual privacy. The phenomenal growth of the ability of large public and private organizations to collect, aggregate and retrieve information poses a serious threat to personal privacy. Canadians pour out an almost continuous stream of information for government files — records for births, marriages, income taxes, the census, health services, social security payments and so on. Recently concern has been expressed about the growing use of the Social Insurance Number (SIN) in conjunction with a variety of government programs. The fear is that, because of computerization, SIN will enable governments to link data banks and to track an individual's complete file from cradle to grave.[10] Such a centralized government information system would represent a real threat to personal freedom, according to many observers. There are also legitimate concerns that unreliable or erroneous information will find its way into government files, that information will be used for purposes other than those for which it was collected, and that information could be inadvertently released or even stolen. Governments, it is argued, should provide information to citizens on what personal data files exist, allow citizens prompt access to such files and provide a way for them to correct erroneous information recorded therein. At the same time, precautions must be taken to protect the security of such files. Obviously, in the modern information society, we are faced with the delicate task of finding a balance between openness and privacy in government. Absolute openness and absolute individual privacy cannot co-exist. Later we will examine the Canadian effort to find the appropriate balance as expressed in Part IV of the Canadian Human Rights Act.

Another contributing factor to secrecy was the "Cold War" and the need to protect state secrets on the grounds of "national security."[11] The latter phrase has received a great deal of criticism recently because of its use or abuse as the basis for the cover-up of illegal actions both here and in the United States. In the present climate of relative detente in East-West relations it is tempting to heap ridicule on the classification systems and security procedures designed to protect the country against espionage in past decades. However, it is obvious that even in calmer international periods, some measure of confidentiality surrounding national defense and foreign policy decision-making will be required. The difficulty, then, lies in defining what constitutes national security and what types of information might be damaging to it. In Canada, the prevailing categories of classified information — top secret, secret, confidential and restricted — are based upon the presumed damaging consequences of disclosure. They were prepared in an earlier period of heightened world tensions, are based mainly upon military considerations, and are potentially sweeping in scope. Also, the present classification scheme has no statutory basis and there are no restrictions on the number of people in government who can classify material. The security classification system is operated in conjunction with a process of "security clearance," which requires that before a person is permitted access to material classified higher than "confidential" an investigation of his background by the RCMP must take place. Providing the legal background to both the classification systems and the security clearances is the Official Secrets Act, about which more will be said later.

According to many authorities, both security classification and clearance procedures have not been applied with appropriate discrimination and restraint. The main problem is that they have been applied outside the realm of "national security." That is, they have been used to protect information which should be public or should remain confidential on grounds other than national security. For example, the imprecision of the phrase "national security" has led to its use in relation to domestic police functions when it would appear to many to be more appropriate to develop separate criteria governing confidentiality in relation to law enforcement as distinct from espionage. There appears to be a degree of truth in the allegation that public servants follow the principle of: Classify everything in order to prevent improper disclosure. In 1969 and again in 1979 the classification policy and security procedures were reviewed by royal commissions, but neither recommended an abandonment or significant modification of the existing system.[12] The overall direction of both sets of recommendations by the commissions, according to civil libertarians, would be to drag us back into the murky depths of cold war secrecy and paranoia. More discussion of these reports and their impact is found in a subsequent section dealing with the recent liberalizing trends within government.

In summary, four general factors or considerations contributing to increased secrecy have been examined: the traditions of ministerial responsibility and the related concept of an anonymous public service; the expansion of the bureaucracy and the alleged need to ensure administrative vitality by protecting internal communication; the need to protect personal and corporate privacy; and the requirements for confidentiality based upon national security and law enforcement. There are other more specific considerations that give rise to secrecy in government—for example, the growing importance of *in camera* federal-provincial negotiations over policy and its implementation undoubtedly has increased the extent of secrecy practised in this country. However, the above four general trends within government seem to be the most important.

Statutory Restrictions on Access to Information

The historical nature of the several considerations that underlie administrative secrecy means that the government of Canada lacks a coherent approach to the control and provision of government information. The statutory landscape is littered with acts of Parliament which restrict or provide conditional public access to information. Much of the current legislation is seriously out of date. According to Richard French, if the government of Canada wishes to avoid administrative and legal chaos following adoption of an FOI Act, it will have to formulate a comprehensive information policy based upon a weighing of the various considerations mentioned above against the desired goals of public access and enhanced accountability.[13]

Every public servant employed by the federal government under the Public Service Employment Act must swear an Oath of Office and Secrecy that he "will not without due authority disclose or make known any matter that comes to (his/her) knowledge by reason of (his/her) employment." Administrative, rather than legal, sanctions support the oath.[14] Therefore, while no one can be prosecuted for a breach of the oath, an individual's career prospects could be damaged, even destroyed, by such an action. For example in 1973, Walter Rudnicki, a policy director for Central Mortgage and Housing Corporation, was dismissed for allegedly releasing without authorization a confidential Cabinet document on native housing to native leaders. Rudnicki insisted that the document in question was not a Cabinet paper and that the minister had authorized its circulation to native organizations. Forced to leave the federal public service, Rudnicki sued the government and eventually (July 1976) was awarded $18,000 in compensation for wrongful dismissal by the Ontario Supreme Court. Less severe administrative sanctions than dismissal presumably accompany less serious breaches of the oath, including the informal but very effective "blackball" device.

Some restriction on the freedom of public servants to release classified and privileged information is obviously required, but the present secrecy oath is judged by most observers to be too sweeping in its scope since it can be read to cover innocuous as well as classified and other sensitive information. It is alleged that the broad nature of the prohibition on the unauthorized release of information contributes to a climate of secrecy within the public service.[15] It also no doubt creates uncertainty in the minds of public servants who have been encouraged in recent years to be more accessible to interested groups to discuss programs and policy issues while still adhering to a restrictive oath of confidentiality. So long as the ground rules regarding the release of information remain ambiguous, public servants will naturally be somewhat inhibited in this role of communicating about public policy with parliamentarians, journalists, interest groups and the general public.

While no one can be prosecuted for breaches of the Oath of Office and Secrecy, this is not true of another statutory restriction on the flow of information — the Official Secrets Act. The Canadian Official Secrets Act was first passed in 1939, but it is based largely upon the British statute of 1911. The Canadian act has since been amended three times, but its language still reflects the concern over German espionage activity that led to its original hasty passage in Great Britain. The Act creates two separate, although sometimes related offences, espionage (Section 3) and leakage, i.e., the improper release of government information. Most of our concern is with the so-called leakage provision in Section 4. The Act prohibits communication with a foreign power "for any purpose prejudicial to the safety or interests of the State."[16] It is not necessary to prove that an accused person was, in fact, guilty of action prejudicial to the interests of the state if such a purpose can be deduced from the circumstances of the case, his conduct and/or his character. In other words, unlike ordinary criminal trials, in an Official Secrets case the burden of proof lies on the accused to establish his innocence if he is charged under the Act with contact with an agent of a foreign power.

An even more contentious part of the Section 4 makes simple possession of classified material an offence. Subhead (1) provides:

> Every person is guilty of an offence . . . who having in his possession or control any *secret official* code word or pass word, or any sketch, plan model, article, note, document or information . . . that has been entrusted in confidence to him by any person holding office under Her Majesty . . . (a) communicates (the above items) to any person, other than the person to whom he is authorized to communicate.[17]

The Act also makes it an offence for anyone to receive information, knowing or having reasonable grounds to believe that it has been received illegally, unless the recipient proves that the communication to him was against his wishes. Failure to take "reasonable care" of confidential material is also an offence under the Act. Even the suspicion that an offence has been committed under the Act is sufficient grounds to arrest an individual without warrant. A person charged under the Act may be tried *in camera* (though sentence must be pronounced in public) and, on conviction, can be sentenced for up to 14 years in prison.

No one disputes the need for some statutory restrictions on the flow of information as protection against potential subversion. But most authorities agree that the present Official Secrets Act is too sweeping in its coverage. As the First Report of the Commission of Inquiry concerning Certain Activities of the Royal Canadian Mounted Police (the McDonald Commission) indicated: "It is possible . . . that all government information, whether classified or not, is subject to Section 4. This is clearly the interpretation given to the comparable section of the British Act."[18] In other words, the section could potentially be read to cover innocent, unclassified information as well as classified material related to national security or law enforcement. At least initially, what constitutes a "secret" document is left to the government to decide. The Act itself does not discriminate; it is potentially all embracing. It can be made to appear ridiculous by saying that if a public servant tells his wife over breakfast what he plans to do at work that day, he may be guilty of violating the Act.

In real life, the facts are less dramatic. While theoretically the Act can be used to stop the circulation of all government information, in practice it has been used only in relation to national security and intelligence matters. Prosecutions under the Canadian Act have been fewer than in Great Britain. Well over half the Canadian prosecutions occurred as a result of Igor Gouzenko's defection in 1946 and his revelations of Soviet spying activities.[19] Most of the prosecutions have involved the espionage provisions of the Official Secrets Act, often in combination with similar offences under the Criminal Code. However, two recent cases involved prosecutions under the leakage section of the Act.

In one case, the *Toronto Sun* newspaper was charged with compromising national security through publication of an article based upon a secret 1976 RCMP report dealing with Soviet espionage activity in Canada. Originally, the federal prosecutors sought to prove damage to national security because publication of the information provided clues to counter-intelligence methods and would compromise RCMP sources. When defense lawyers countered that such a judgement must be based upon hearsay or second-hand evidence, the federal prosecutors shifted their main line of attack and argued that publication of a secret report alone (regardless of whether actual damage to national security occurred) constituted a violation of the Act. Eventually the court ruled that the *Sun* was not guilty of a violation since the information in question was already in the public domain, having earlier been used on a television program.[20] This case represents the first and only time in Canada that the Official Secrets Act was used against a newspaper.

The second case involved the prosecution of Peter Treu, a communications engineer with the Northern Electric Company who had done work for NATO on the European air defense system. Treu's security clearance for top secret defense work had been revoked when he changed companies, although he continued to be invited to top secret NATO conferences. The government charged that he had failed to take reasonable care of secret documents stored in his home after his security clearance had been revoked. The original trial, held in a sessions court in Quebec, took place *in camera*, based mainly upon the federal prosecutor's assertion (though no proof was offered) that publication of a certain document would reveal sensitive facts about the Chinese air defence system. After an original conviction and sentence of two years in prison, Treu appealed and in February 1979, the Quebec Court of Appeal declared him innocent. There was "no doubt" in the court's judgement that Treu had taken precautions to safeguard the documents in his possession.[21]

The failure of the government to prosecute successfully in these two instances does not lessen the conviction of most observers that the Official Secrets Act is in need of serious revision. Certainly the leakage provisions of the Act are in conflict with the objectives of any FOI legislation and Section 4 in particular would require modification. To the best of our knowledge, the impact of that section on the routine release of information by public servants has never been studied. Still, there is a legitimate concern that the Act serves as a subtle, but effective, form of political censorship, or, in the words of a British commentator, "it stiffens the secret spine of the bureaucrat and softens the vertabrae of the press."[22] Recent Liberal and Conservative governments have promised amendments to the Act designed to tighten the wording in order to confine its scope to state secrets and protection against espionage.

A third statutory barrier to openness is Section 41 of the Federal Court Act enacted in 1970.[23] This section governs use of the courts by citizens to gain access to government information. A citizen refused a document by a federal department can commence legal action in the Federal Court in order to obtain the document. However, according to one study, the obstacles to successful action under the Act "are most likely insurmountable."[24] The applicant must demonstrate that the public servant has a statutory duty to produce the document in question. But since most statutes establishing departments or programs are silent about such matters or explicitly prohibit disclosure, the requisite statutory obligation is lacking. Second, an individual must establish what is called "standing" before the Court, which means he must show that he would suffer a special injury by reason of non-disclosure beyond that experienced by the public in general.

Even if an individual can overcome these procedural barriers of access to the Federal Court, the government can still invoke "crown privilege," its inherent discretion to refuse a request for production of a document. Until recently, Canada's courts, based partly on British precedents, were prepared to accept without question a sworn affidavit from a Cabinet minister that production of a document was not in the public interest and therefore could not be made public. In the late 1960s, however, the courts began to demand more specific grounds for non-disclosure, such as reasons of national security, and the Federal Court Act codified the common law interpretation as it stood at that point. Subsection 1 of Section 41 of the Act upheld the right of the courts to look behind the ministerial affidavit and to balance the competing interests involved in the issue of disclosure. However, with respect to four classes of documents, the minister's word remains final. If the minister certified that the production of the document "would be injurious to international relations, national defense or security, or to federal-provincial relations, or that it would disclose a confidence of the Queen's Privy Council for Canada" (the Cabinet), then the courts can neither inspect the document to determine the degree of danger involved with its release nor weigh the public interests involved in such release. The absolute character of ministerial prerogative in these four areas is now inconsistent with evolving jurisprudence in Great Britain and the provinces where courts have been permitted to examine sensitive documents *in camera* and decide whether publication was warranted.[25] Because of this inconsistency, recent Liberal and Conservative governments have indicated their intention to amend the Federal Court Act to give the courts the final say over the disclosure of all documents after examination of ministerial statements of reasons for non-disclosure.

In addition to these general "secrecy" statutes, there are a wide variety of statutes administered by departments or other agencies which prohibit or limit public access to information. For example, Part IV of the Canadian Human Rights Act (1977) provides for access by individuals to government information concerning them. There are, however, a number of exemptions (Sections 53 and 54 of the Act) on the basis of which access may be denied by the responsible minister. The Act also allows for complaints arising from such denials to be reviewed by an ombudsman-type Privacy Commissioner. However, the Commissioner does not have the power to order the release of a document where he/she disagrees with the decision of a minister to invoke an exemption. According to critics, the purposes of the Privacy provisions and the work of the Privacy Commissioner have been frustrated by the wide and vague criteria for exemption that can be invoked by the government.

Section 53 of the Act allows "banks" or stores of personal information to be completely exempted by order-in-council from the operation of the access provisions of the Act, if disclosure of the information:

> (**a**) might be injurious to international relations, national defence or security, or federal-provincial relations; or
>
> (**b**) would disclose information obtained or prepared by a public investigative body
>
> (i) in relation to national security,
>
> (ii) in the course of investigations pertaining to the detection or suppression of crime generally, or
>
> (iii) in the course of investigations pertaining to particular offences against any Act of Parliament [(S. 53 (a)(b))].

Under these provisions, as of 31 December 1979, out of a total of 1,500 information banks, 22 banks had been completely exempted from access by individuals.[26] The exemption of a bank in its entirety supposedly rests on the overall purpose for which a bank is maintained. However, the Privacy

Commissioner (who was also initially denied access to such banks even for purposes of investigation, but who has since been granted conditional access) has argued that information properly belonging in an accessible bank might end up, inadvertently or otherwise, in a closed one.[27]

A second category of exemptions has been provided under Section 54, although there is much common ground between the two sections since they are intended to reinforce each other. Section 54 permits *complete* or *partial* denial of access on the same grounds as those specified in Section 53, plus the additional grounds that disclosure might: seriously disrupt an individual's prison or parole sentence, reveal information obtained on a confidential basis, result in physical or other harm to individuals, violate the privacy of another individual, impede the functioning of courts, quasi-judicial boards or commissions of inquiry, or might reveal privileged lawyer-client communications. As of December 1979, no information bank had been fully exempted under Section 54, but a total of 17 banks had been partially exempted. Exemptions under Section 54 were claimed in relation to 783 requests, but in all but 10 of these cases some information was released to the applicant.[28]

Other exemptions are provided in other sections of the Act, but Sections 53 and 54 have posed the greatest obstacles to the Privacy Commissioner in the performance of her duties. The Trudeau government has defended the continued complete exemption of certain banks on the grounds that such an arrangement prevents the release by mistake of sensitive information and it reduces the costs of administering the Act since the need for a detailed review of each document which is sought is eliminated.[29] Still, the government accepts the need to tighten the wording of the exemptions contained in Section 53 and it has also proposed that where the Privacy Commissioner and a minister disagree over whether or not information properly belongs in an exempt bank, the matter may be appealed to the Federal Court for review. These proposed changes and others of somewhat less significance would provide Canadians with much fairer and more effective protection of their privacy and access to personal information held by the federal government.

The long standing tradition of administrative secrecy is reflected in a multitude of other statutory provisions. A survey conducted for a joint parliamentary committee uncovered 30 statutory prohibitions on the disclosure of information.[30] All of these provisions could presumably be justified in terms of the broad considerations discussed at the outset of this chapter. The wording of several particular restrictions, however, can be challenged. For example, reports made under the Hazardous Products Act may be withheld if the minister decides, on the advice of the Board, that "the public interest would be better served" by non-disclosure.[31] Such broad discretionary authority is frequently argued to be inappropriate. Nevertheless, given the confidentiality clauses found in existing statutes, provision would have to be made for potential conflicts with any Freedom of Information Act that might be proposed. Parliament could decide simply to give an FOI Act precedence over all confidentiality clauses, except for a select few listed in an appendix, or it could acquiesce in the existing legal situation, thereby limiting the effect of any new access legislation, but respecting Parliament's past judgements.

The Recent Liberalizing Trend

Whatever the inhibiting effects of the various statutory restrictions may have been, they have not prevented a series of administrative and legislative changes during the 1960s and 1970s which have extended to some degree public knowledge of matters previously treated as confidential. To some observers, such a gradual and pragmatic approach to increased openness, based upon a recognition of changing conditions within government and changing values within society, is preferable to an abrupt shift in information policy produced by the passage of a single, all-encompassing piece of legislation establishing the "public's right to know" and entrusting to the courts the final responsibility for settling disputes that might arise. In the past Cabinet ministers and public servants may have been excessively cautious in their procedures, habits and attitudes towards the release of information, but some contend that this fact could not be accepted as an argument for erring in the opposite direction. In this view, access to information is a new, experimental field of public law, involving risks related to the inadvertent or premature release of sensitive information, and the last decade reveals that considerable progress can be achieved without sweeping and symbolic legislation.

On the other hand, while accepting that the trend in government has been towards greater openness, FOI advocates insist that the improvements achieved have been marginal. Besides, they insist that it is inappropriate in a democracy for the government to decide unilaterally where openness will end and secrecy begin. The present circumstances in Canada do not ensure that the requirements for secrecy in relation to particular kinds of information are weighed against other values through an open, political process.[32] Instead, public officials, both elected and appointed, have the power to dispose of citizen requests for information unilaterally and without an aggrieved person having an effective right of appeal. This is a situation that FOI legislation would correct, according to its proponents.

We will return momentarily to the debate over FOI, but both sides to that debate agree (although they quarrel about its significance) that there has been a shift in the last decade toward greater openness. The main reasons for the trend are usually considered to be: the relative detente in international affairs, which lessened the need for national security restrictions; the stress in government rhetoric, and to a much lesser extent, government practices, upon "participatory democracy," which required that citizens be better informed about government plans and policies; the influx during the 1960s of a large number of younger people into the federal public service, many of whom carried the prevalent ideas of social activism and reform and questioned established institutions and practices; the rise of an "adversary tradition" within the media, whose younger members in particular wanted to conduct "investigative journalism" and therefore began to promote their own professional interest in access to government information; and finally and more recently, the growing desire by governments to overcome the apparent alienation and mistrust felt by the public towards a large and seemingly unaccountable bureaucracy.

The campaign for improved access to information began slowly in the mid-1960s with the publication of several articles on the subject by Donald Rowat of Carleton University and the presentation in Parliament of several FOI bills sponsored by backbench MPs. In 1969, the Royal Commission on National Security submitted a series of recommendations to the Trudeau government, although its report did not offer much hope to the advocates of enhanced openness. The Commission recommended that stricter attention be paid to the "need to know" principle, i.e. the dissemination of security information only so far as necessary to the conduct of security operations. It admitted the vagueness of the existing classification system for security documents and recognized that there had been many complaints about over-classification, but it could not recommend a better system. The Commission did note that departments should be constantly reminded of the need to review and to downgrade the classification of documents. In general, the tenor of the report was conservative and cautious.[33]

Despite this emphasis, Prime Minister Trudeau announced in May 1969, that 30 years after their transfer to the public archives practically all departmental documents would be open to the public. This was a reduction from 50 years. The exception involved those documents whose "release might adversely affect Canada's external relations, violate the privacy of individuals or adversely affect national security."[34] More recently, in 1977, the Cabinet directed ministers to transfer public records to the archives as soon as practicable, but transfer would not occur sooner than the standard 30-year period if records contained "information the disclosure of which, in the opinion of the appropriate Minister, would be prejudicial to the public interest."[35] While these changes might facilitate archives research by historians and other social scientists they do not mean much to the average citizen.

Also in 1969, the Task Force on Government Information Services recommended that the government provide much more information to Canadians as the foundation for fulfilling their right to "full, objective and timely information."[36] The Task Force criticized the prevailing tradition of administrative secrecy. It suggested that more informative replies to parliamentary questions should be provided and that for this purpose guidelines should be prepared for departmental officials. Also, access by mass media representatives to public servants should be increased. Of greatest importance among the Task Force's 14 recommendations, however, was the suggestion that a central organization be created to coordinate the flow of government information and publications. Information Canada, which was the eventual title of the proposed agency, was also to serve the "function of public advocate in matters of access to federal information and timeliness of replies to citizens' queries."[37] In announcing the creation of Information Canada early in 1970, Prime Minister Trudeau endorsed the principle of the public's right to know and announced the government's acceptance of most of the 14 recommendations made by the Task Force. Significantly, the government rejected the suggestion that Information Canada be made a defender of the public's right to information on the rather weak ground that Parliament fulfilled this function, a claim which ignored Parliament's usual inability under majority governments to force disclosure.

There was a considerable suspicion by opposition parties at the time of Information Canada's creation that it would become simply a propaganda agency to extoll the accomplishments of the Liberal government's ministers and their departments. Part of the aim of the agency was to increase public awareness of government services and this inevitably involved some effort to enhance the public image of the departments involved. Critics complained that this new central agency would release only that information which brought political credit to the government. The line between legitimate publicity of government activities and partisan political propaganda is a subjective and difficult one to draw. As it turned out, however, Information Canada had a short and checkered existence. Most departments did not cooperate with it, arguing that they knew better than any central agency what their information policies should be. The agency's mandate was imprecise, it failed to attract sufficiently capable staff with suitable knowledge of government operations and its own operations were judged to be inefficient.[38] After a parliamentary inquiry revealed some of these difficulties, Information Canada was disbanded in 1977 and along with it apparently went the idea that the government could fulfill its publicity functions more effectively and economically through a single, central organization. It is very difficult today to identify and to measure the total cost of the information services because these are dispersed to the multitude of departments and agencies. However, it appears that those costs have grown since the demise of Information Canada as governments have become ever more conscious of the political value of good promotional activity.

In 1970, Parliament approved the Federal Court Act. As we have already seen, the Act has one serious flaw, but in general it enlarged the power of the courts to compel the production of official documents in the courts. In 1971, based upon the recommendations of a special Commons committee on statutory instruments, the Trudeau government agreed to the appointment of the Standing Joint Committee on Regulations and Other Statutory Instruments to review on behalf of Parliament and the public the use of delegated legislative authority. Once again there are problems with the terms of reference of the Committee, but since 1974 at least a portion of that vast, previously submerged body of subordinate law-making has been subject to some measure of public review and debate.[39]

In March 1973 the Trudeau government tabled in the House of Commons new guidelines to departments and agencies for the production of papers in response to motions and questions in Parliament. Government spokesmen insisted that adoption of the guidelines represented a reverse of the previous tradition of confidentiality. Previously, documents remained confidential unless cause could be shown as to why they should be released. Henceforth, unless the document in question fell under one or more of 16 listed exemptions, it would automatically be made public. Those 16 exemptions were criticized by the press and other observers as being too broadly worded, but in general they covered such traditional areas of confidentiality as national security, personal privacy, commercial confidentiality, the internal deliberations of government and legal opinions.[40] The guidelines were referred to the Joint Standing Committee on Statutory Instruments for study along with a private member's FOI bill sponsored by Gerald Baldwin (P.C.—Peace River), who had campaigned for more than a decade for such legislation.

As part of its proceedings the Joint Committee published an expurgated version of a Privy Council study prepared by D.F. Wall, former Assistant Secretary to the Cabinet for Security Matters. The study had been ordered following a series of embarrassing "leaks" of government documents. In 1971 a draft of the Gray Report on foreign ownership was revealed by a magazine. There followed in quick succession the publication in newspapers of cabinet documents dealing with funds for Indian schools, the potential use of the War Measures Act, northern policy development, aid to the publishing industry, low income housing, and so on.[41] Wall attributed the numerous leaks to a variety of factors. Rigid, pyramidal structures within the public service produced the conviction among younger, reformist public servants that their ideas would be "lost in the pipeline" and the unauthorized release of documents was the only way to bring serious attention to the shortcomings of government policies. Many of the existing security regulations were so restrictively worded as to invite abuse and ridicule. Finally, it was speculated that some of the leaks were deliberately staged by cabinet ministers in order to "float trial balloons" or in order to gain revenge in a dispute with Cabinet colleagues over a particular policy. Whatever the motives, Wall saw dangers in the growing leaks. There was the potential for harm to the public interest caused by premature or unwarranted disclosure, the possible distortion through media sensationalism of the definition of public problems or situations, and a costly disruption to the orderly processes of government.

In response to these concerns, Wall recommended stiffer sanctions to deal with the unauthorized release of classified documents. On the other hand, he also attempted to refine and make more precise the government's guidelines for the production of papers. He proposed a requirement that, when documents were classified, the criterion under which the material was classified must be noted. He also suggested that substantive portions of departmental files should be reviewed periodically to determine whether, when and in what form information could be released. Both these steps would have reduced slightly the acknowledged tendency of public servants to overclassify documents. However, Wall rejected for the time being at least a Freedom of Information law. Such a law in the United States, he said, had led to "an elaborate bureaucratic system of seeming to adhere to the letter of the law while avoiding much of its spirit."[42] He recommended instead a reformist approach, involving adoption of a new classification system, a review of security clearance procedures to ensure that their application was limited to areas where they were fully justified, a review of the pertinent legislation (the Official Secrets Act and Oath of Office and Secrecy) to ensure effective legal and administrative sanctions for the unauthorized release of information, and a full explanation by government of the damaging aspects of leaks. In view of his position as a security advisor to Cabinet, Wall's report naturally stressed the need for information control, but at the same time he did a creditable job in seeking to resolve the practical issues involved in reconciling secrecy with publicity in government.

In February 1976, Parliament adopted, with the unanimous support of all parties, the report of the Joint Committee (December 16, 1975) declaring approval in principle of the concept of FOI legislation. The government referred the subject matter back to the Committee for further study and recommendations. Meanwhile, in July 1977, Parliament passed the government's Canadian Human Rights Act, which contained in Part IV the so-called "privacy provisions" discussed earlier in this chapter. Establishment of the office of the Privacy Commissioner was seen by many observers as the Liberal government's model for the eventual creation of an information commissioner. Like the privacy commissioner, an information commissioner would have the power to publicize citizens' complaints regarding denial of access to information, but would not be permitted to overrule ministerial decisions regarding non-disclosure.[43] At the same time, the increased use of "white" and "green" papers as vehicles for the public discussion of policy options and the publication of proposals to create a federal ombudsman and to increase the public accountability of crown corporations, all seemed also to symbolize a government commitment to more open government.

Changing attitudes towards access to information and citizen participation can also be seen in changing practices and procedures in connection with regulatory activity. It will be recalled, for example, that since August 1978, the Treasury Board has required prior public notification and consultation in connection with all contemplated major regulations in the field of health, safety and fairness.[44] Individual regulatory agencies have sought to facilitate citizen participation in their proceedings. Probably a leader in this regard among federal regulatory agencies has been the Canadian Radio-Television and Telecommunications Commission. It has not simply sat back passively waiting for citizen participation to materialize, but rather has actively sought to encourage its development through innovative procedures and information practices. In 1978 it announced several changes in its procedures, including the following: an increase in the number of announcements of pending license renewals; regular notices during the term of licenses that stations filed with the CRTC at the time licenses were granted; and increased access by citizens to information available in a public file on licensees (e.g., the license, promise of performance, audited annual financial statements, CRTC rules of procedure and so on). In connection with financial information, the CRTC favored full disclosure, except when disclosure would result in *specific direct* harm to the company that would outweigh the benefits of disclosure. On the tricky issue of staff documents, the CRTC divided them into two categories. Those which added evidence not in the public file, but likely to be considered in Commission decision-making, would automatically be made public. Other staff documents, which did not add evidence but merely summarized evidence and discussed the applicability of regulation, would be released only at the discretion of the Commission.[45] These steps represented a substantial improvement over the situation existing in most other regulatory agencies where potential intervenors faced strong procedural and informational barriers to participation.

In 1977, as mentioned earlier, the Trudeau government established a new system of Cabinet documents, in which factual information was to be contained in one part (Discussion Paper) while the ministerial and civil service recommendations were to be contained in another (Memoranda to Cabinet). Under this system, some previously internal documents became public, although not all departments adapted to the spirit of the new arrangements by releasing their planning studies.[46] Despite this dragging of bureaucratic feet, however, there were several signs that the Trudeau government was heading, albeit too gradually and cautiously in the eyes of impatient reformers, toward a more open approach to governing.

In June 1977, this approach led to a statement in a government Green Paper, *Legislation on Public Access to Government Documents*, that "open government is the basis of democracy."[47] The Paper emphasized that the proposals it contained did not represent a fixed position, but were being presented for the purpose of public debate. It committed the Liberal government to introducing FOI legislation, although it seemed to favor reliance upon traditional parliamentary doctrines and practices of ministerial responsibility in order to enforce the proposed act. For this reason FOI advocates were disappointed and heaped criticism on the Green Paper, arguing in the words of one that it represented "a passionate attempt to avoid any meaningful legislation. By means of misleading appeals to ministerial responsibility and public service neutrality, the Government has clearly revealed its intention to perpetuate the paternalistic tradition of official secrecy in Canada."[48] In retrospect, however, the conclusion that meaningful legislation would not be forthcoming can be seen as perhaps unduly pessimistic.

When the government referred the Green Paper to the Joint Committee, the parliamentarians received a barrage of criticism about the inadequacies of the analysis contained in the government's discussion Paper. After listening to testimony from lawyers, journalists, interest groups and academics, the committee submitted its recommendations in June 1978.[49] The Committee disagreed with the position then being taken by the Liberal government on the two most crucial issues involved in the FOI debate, which had been taking shape over the preceding decade. These were the question of the list of exemptions to the general principle of access to documents and the review mechanism to be used in the event of a denial of access by a government minister.

The Canadian Debate Over An FOI Act

At first glance, creation of a statutory basis for public access to government information may appear to be a simple and laudable step. In practice, however, freedom of information raises a series of complex legal and administrative issues. Space does not permit a full exploration of these issues so we will concentrate on the two central ones which emerged in the Canadian debate over an FOI Act. In exploring these issues, we will also touch upon the relevance to the Canadian situation of the practices of the United States, a country usually cited by FOI advocates as a model of open government because there exists an FOI Act providing statutory protection of the public's right to government information.

The issue of the review mechanism involves the question of who will ultimately decide whether or not a particular document will be released. On this issue, the Liberal party apparently modified its position during its short stint in opposition between May 1979, and its return to office in the election of February 1980. When in office prior to 1979 it opposed the use of the courts to referee disputes over access to information, but now it seems prepared to accept some measure of judicial review of ministerial decisions to withhold certain documents.

The case for judicial review is usually developed along the following lines. First, access to information is seen as a basic human or civil right and the way to protect such rights is to establish legally enforceable claims. In the words of a study prepared for the Canadian Bar Association: "The history of the progress of fundamental rights in Anglo-Canadian jurisprudence has in fact largely been the conversion of discretionary political relief into statutory rights."[50] Reliance upon the traditional constitutional principle of ministerial responsibility and the parliamentary mechanisms of enforcement of that principle is no longer regarded as adequate. In practical, political terms, Parliament can no longer (if it ever could) force ministers to disclose information against their wishes. The rise of disciplined political parties means that in a majority government situation, the House of Commons will rarely approve a motion requiring ministers to produce documents because government MPs will not wish to embarrass their ministers in this way. Therefore, in effect the decision is left up to individual ministers and there is the real danger that they will substitute purely partisan considerations (Will the release of a document hurt the government's image?) or personal considerations (What will release of a document do to my own career prospects?) for the wider considerations of whether release of information is in "the public interest."

There is further danger that the natural tendency of ministers to be protective of official information will be reinforced by the advice received from senior public servants in their departments. These are some of the reasons why public servants might be expected to adopt a defensive, conservative approach toward the release of information: a desire to preserve their traditional anonymity; a concern to protect ministerial, departmental and personal reputations; a fear of giving "ammunition" to rival departments; and, in general, a desire to avoid the nuisance of having to explain actions publicly, the complications and subtleties of which parliamentarians and the public may be unable or unwilling to grasp. Public servants will often be successful in convincing ministers that life would be simpler for them as well if they did not go too far in the practice of open government. Therefore, any access system based upon ministerial responsibility will lack credibility and legitimacy with the general public, who will have little if any confidence in it. And for that reason, according to advocates of judicial review, the new citizens' right of access to information created by an FOI Act should not be subject to ministerial whims and discretion, but like other civil rights it should be enforceable in the courts.

The second argument made on behalf of judicial review is that it is not alien or foreign to Canadian constitutional traditions, as opponents claim. In Canada, unlike the United States, there is not a coherent concept of "political questions," on which the courts should avoid passing judgment.[51] Indeed, in Canada, in several areas, the courts are already involved in the settlement of issues with clear political overtones. For example, the courts participate in political matters when they act as referees of federal-provincial disputes. The national Parliament has enacted a Bill of Rights (1960) encouraging the courts to scrutinize its legislative enactments and declare them void if they impinge upon fundamental freedoms. The same Parliament can now permit the courts to weigh a minister's refusal to grant access to documents against the declared principle of openness in government. In this instance, the courts would simply be performing their familiar role in a new context.

The third argument on behalf of judicial review is that the kinds of questions faced by the courts under a FOI Act will be mainly legal and procedural in nature rather than political and substantive. Again, in the words of the Canadian Bar Association's study:

> What one is discussing is essentially akin to a procedural decision on whether certain information or documents ... should be produced, based on criteria which can be carefully spelled out by Parliament.[52]

The same study goes on to reject the assertion contained in the Liberal government's Green Paper (1977) that judges cannot be made fully aware of all the considerations — economic, social and political — that justify non-disclosure. This argument, according to the CBA, assumes that either ministers would not present the courts with substantive and sound arguments in defense of non-disclosure or the Green Paper insults the intelligence of the judiciary by suggesting that the courts lack the capacity to understand and weigh the arguments for and against publicity of particular documents.[53]

The final argument in favor of judicial review is that "there is no alternative social institution to which the Executive would conceivably surrender documents of a sensitive nature for the detailed scrutiny required."[54] Presumably, governments would not allow a parliamentary committee to study such documents for fear that opposition MPs would take advantage of perceived opportunities to embarrass the government without due regard for the possible social harm caused by the release of information. Courts could use an *in camera* procedure to safeguard such sensitive information. And because judges would be aware of the dangers of unwarranted release of certain information, they would not be aggressive in overturning ministerial decisions to withhold documents. In the words of the CBA study: "Ironically, if one wanted to choose a class of persons more likely to be sympathetic to the claim that politicians must have access to fair and candid advice and that certain documents should not be disclosed, one would find it difficult to choose a more appropriate group than the judiciary."[55] The process of selection of judges in this country ensures that they will hold political values very similar to those represented within the two main political parties.

The arguments against judicial review represent mainly counterpoints to the above positions. They were expressed most forcefully in the former Liberal government's Green Paper (1977), in the writings of certain senior public servants and in the commentaries of a few academics. The principal concern of this group is that use of the courts would involve a serious transgression of the principle of ministerial responsibility which is central to our system of government. In the words of the Green Paper (1977):

> A judge cannot be asked, in our system of government, to assume the role of giving an opinion on the merits of the very question that has been decided by a Minister. There is no way that a judicial officer can be properly aware of all the political, economic, social and security factors that may have led to the decision in issue. Nor should the courts be allowed to usurp the constitutional role that Parliament plays in making a Minister answerable to it for his actions.[56]

In our system of government, the task of balancing such desired values as social stability and individual privacy against the contending value of openness in government involves difficult and sensitive judgments better left to elected and accountable politicians than to appointed and unaccountable judges. Who, for example, would shoulder the blame if a judge ordered the release, against the advice of a minister, of a document that caused peril to national security? If real harm occurs, would the public understand and accept the explanation of a politician that he was legally bound to release a document? Insistence upon judicial review obscures the distinction between the political process of reaching broad judgments, for which governments are accountable before Parliament and in elections, and the judicial process, which should consist so far as possible of the application of laws determined by Parliament to individual cases on the basis of objective, legal criteria. According to this line of argument, while some measure of policy-making by judges cannot be avoided, we should not widen the scope of such judicial policy-making when that result is avoidable. Involving judges in the settlement of certain cases arising under a FOI Act would force them to substitute their judgment for that of a minister. This could weaken the traditional independence and impartiality of the judiciary under our constitutional system by making judicial decisions the subject of partisan debates and attacks.

The argument for court review, based as it usually is upon American examples and precedents, misunderstands the constitutional differences between the two systems. Canada has not followed the separation of powers principle adopted in the American constitution. In the United States the President is not responsible to Congress (except in the extreme case of impeachment) on a continuous basis in the same way that a Prime Minister and his Cabinet are responsible to Parliament. In the United States there is thus no alternative but to have the courts review decisions by the executive branch to withhold information. Based as the American constitution is upon a system of checks and balances among three separate branches of government, it is appropriate that their courts should act as referees in disputes that might arise between Congress and the President over the release of information.

The Canadian situation is different, however. Contrary to the assertion in the CBA study, there is an alternative institution to the courts which could enforce a FOI Act and that institution is Parliament or, at least, some auxiliary agency which Parliament might create. Because advocates of court review have little hope that executive predominance in the legislature can ever be overcome, they seek to transform essentially political questions into legal questions by transferring the matter into the hands of judges. This is a substantial constitutional innovation and it should not be undertaken lightly. It involves a significant departure from Parliament's traditional constitutional role of surveillance and holding the executive accountable. Moreover, such a step would not be consistent with the course followed in other areas, such as the creation of the offices of the Auditor General, the Commissioner of Official Languages, the Canadian Human Rights Commission (including the Privacy Commissioner) and the proposed federal ombudsman. In all these instances Parliament has deemed it inappropriate to create auxiliary institutions to assist it in the task of enforcing executive accountability. What would be wrong with following a similar course in relation to information by the creation of an Information Commissioner, who would publicize on behalf of Parliament and the public instances when the executive has withheld information? Even though an Information Commissioner might not have the authority to order ministers to release documents when they refused to do so, the normal political pressures (such as the daily Question Period and the related media coverage) would induce ministers to comply with the suggestions of the Commissioner in most instances. To describe such a Commissioner as another "civil servant," "an executive agency" or an "administrative tribunal" (as does the CBA study) is to misuse those terms to describe what would, in fact, be a parliamentary institution. To further argue, as did the CBA study, that public confidence would not be inspired by a tribunal appointed by the government of the day is to neglect the fact that judges are also appointed by elected governments. Defenders of traditional parliamentary mechanisms, therefore, ask why Canadians should have greater confidence in the judiciary than in the democratically responsive legislative branch.

In addition to these constitutional and philosophical objections, there are alleged to be practical problems associated with judicial review.[57] A question is raised about the appropriateness of judicial procedures and the judicial method in making decisions under a FOI Act. It is not suggested that judges lack the intelligence to make such decisions. Rather it is being pointed out that the methods of discovery used by the courts to acquire information and the normal rules of admissibility of evidence will inhibit judges in making decisions as to what should be made public. On the other hand, ministers will not be so restricted in the evidence which they can consider and weigh.

Further practical difficulties associated with judicial review involve the potential delays and costs of such a procedure. Use of the courts to adjudicate FOI disputes could greatly increase the existing congestion within the judicial system and lead to long delays in the provision of information whose value would partially depend on the timeliness of its availability.

Use of the courts would also require applicants on appeal to hire legal counsel and lawyers do not come cheaply. As a result, there is concern that financial barriers would mean that organizations with the resources to engage expensive legal talent would become the principal users of a FOI Act, as has been the case in the United States. For example, the Green Paper (1977) indicated that litigating an appeal under the American FOI Act costs on the average $10,000.[58] On the other hand, the CBA submission disputed the suggestion that similar costs would be faced in Canada. In their view, a Canadian FOI Act could provide for low-cost procedures and once experience was gained with use of the act the time and costs involved in processing routine cases would be reduced. As another way of reducing delays and costs, the joint parliamentary committee recommended a two-tiered review process.[59] In the first instance, an information commissioner would examine the document being sought *in camera*. He would then recommend to the minister whether it should be released and would simultaneously notify the complainant of his recommendation. The joint committee expected that, in most cases, the Commissioner's opinion would be accepted by the minister. However, regardless of the Commissioner's opinion and its impact on the minister, the committee favored the right of an applicant to appeal further to the courts. A special panel from the Federal Court would hear such cases, could if necessary examine documents *in camera*, and would ultimately have the power to order the release of documents.

The two-tiered approach might overcome some of the practical problems of delays and costs associated with straight judicial review. Of course, it still raises the question of whether judges should be allowed to substitute their judgments for those of elected politicians. There is the additional complication that "public interest" lobby groups are not nearly so strong in Canada as in the United States and public interest law is not as well developed here. It is feared that use of the courts as the first, or even the final, forum for appeal, will favor well-financed and well-informed groups. Corporate and other interests may use a FOI Act to pursue their own narrow, commercial interests in ways that do little to serve the values underlying the concept of the public's right to know.[60]

In its most recent (July 1980) proposed FOI Act the Liberal government accepted the two-tiered approach and accepted judicial review despite its earlier objections.[61] However, instead of making a complete review as to whether injury to the public interest as specified in the legislation (e.g., injury to national defence or international relations) would occur, the Court would decide only whether it was "reasonable" for the minister concerned to come to the conclusion that such danger would occur because of the release of documents. This formulation, it was felt, would avoid judges substituting their public policy judgements for those of the minister and therefore would be consistent with ministerial responsibility. If the Court found that the minister in claiming an exemption had not acted reasonably, it would order the release of documents so refused. Moreover, in the case of certain exemptions—such as whether disclosure would damage a company's competitive position or invade personal privacy—issues involving ministerial responsibility for protection of the public interest do not arise and the courts are as well equipped as ministers to decide such matters. In adopting this modified version of judicial review, the Liberal government seemed to be accepting the argument heard frequently that a more disinterested party than the minister had to have the final say on whether documents would be made public.

The second main issue in the Canadian FOI debate has been the list of exemptions to the general principle of publicity. Everyone seems to be agreed that such exemptions should be confined to areas where there is a genuine need for confidentiality, that these areas should be relatively few in number, and that in identifying these areas the statutory language used should be as clear and precise as possible. Beyond this, there is little agreement on the actual wording of the exemptions. Whether the bills have been presented by Liberal or Conservative governments, lawyers, opposition MPs and other FOI advocates have criticized the the list of exemptions as too long, and too broad in its coverage. A popular charge is that the exemptions are "so wide you could drive a truck through them" or they are so broad "bureaucrats could hide any information they wanted." While such rhetorical attacks may serve the useful political purpose of forcing the government to defend its chosen wording of the act, more specific criticisms and proposed amendments would obviously be more helpful. There is a penchant on the part of many lawyers to look for certainty and precision in the law, a tendency that minimizes the practical difficulties of specifying in advance exactly when the release of certain types of information might be dangerous or damaging. To meet the demand for greater precision, it may be necessary to include more and longer exemptions. Finally, critics who attack proposed wordings seem to assume implicitly that officials who administer the act will willfully misinterpret it in order to hide material. This assumption may be false and, in any case, the criticism ignores the fact that under the proposed bill the court would have the last word on the interpretation of the exemptions.

After admitting the difficulty of the drafting task involved, we should still pay close attention to whether the exemptions in any FOI Act are as tightly worded as possible. Exemptions fall into three categories: injury-test exemptions, class-test exemptions and mixed exemptions.[62] Injury-test exemptions identify public or private interests which must be protected from injury resulting from the disclosure of information. For instance, an exemption could protect information the disclosure of which would be damaging to federal-provincial negotiations. Because the interpretation of such exemptions is subjective, they are more likely to give rise to disputes. Class-test exemptions are intended to exclude certain categories of documents from publicity based upon their origins or content. For instance, Cabinet documents and advisory opinions prepared by public servants would qualify as exempt in order to protect the vitality of the decision-making process. Because such exemptions are more objective, they are less likely to give rise to disputes. Mixed exemptions combine injury and class tests. For example, an exemption regarding national security matters might contain a general injury provision (e.g., information the release of which would be injurious to national defence) followed by a list of categories of documents intended to illustrate the types of information which fall under the general provision. Not surprisingly, most of the criticism of previous drafting attempts by governments has been directed at the wording of the injury-test exemptions.

As a result of outside and parliamentary criticism, the wording of particular exemptions has been improved. While not all the exemptions can be discussed, perhaps a few examples will serve to illustrate the problem.

In the Liberal Green Paper (1977), for example, there was a general exemption for information which might be injurious to national defense or security.[63] In Bill C-43 (July 1980) this provision had been refined to cover only information "which could reasonably be expected to be injurious to the conduct of international affairs, the defense of Canada or any state allied or associated with Canada or the detection, prevention or suppression of subversive or hostile activities."[64] Not only does the new clause not take refuge in the ambiguous phrase "national security," which many feel has been abused in the past in Canada and in other countries, but the same clause proceeds to list the types of information covered by the clause, which could be used by the courts in interpreting the general provision and in assessing whether injury could be assumed. While some might criticize the list as too long and containing classes of information ordinarily not considered sensitive, such a criticism tends to ignore the fact that both the injury-test, as well as the class-test, must be met before a minister could claim the exemption for what might seem to outsiders to be innocuous information.

Another worrisome exemption covered federal-provincial relations. Since there is practically no field of public policy in Canada which does not involve a federal-provincial dimension, it was felt that any generally worded exemption in this area would cover a great deal of information which should in fact be made public. Bill C-43 (July 1980) improves upon earlier wordings by limiting the exemptions to sensitive documents discussing the substance or strategies of current or on-going federal-provincial negotiations, but not including past negotiations. There is also provision for protection of information provided to the federal government by the provinces, unless the latter consent to its disclosure.

A final example of an exemption which gave rise to concern is the protection for cabinet documents and advisory memoranda from public servants. Few, if any, advocates of a FOI Act would favor open Cabinet decision-making, but there was concern that a blanket exemption for Cabinet documents would prevent parliamentarians and others from understanding the considerations upon which public policy is based. Again, the recent bill represents an improvement upon its predecessors by limiting confidentiality only to actual decision-making documents for Cabinet and draft legislation before it is introduced in Parliament. In addition, Bill C-43 allows the Prime Minister to authorize at any time the release of particular Cabinet records and shortens from 30 to 20 years the period after which all past Cabinet records will come into the public domain. On the matter of advisory opinions from public servants, the bill provides for protection for 20 years. However, the exemption does not cover the reasons for the use of discretionary authority where the rights of a person are affected, nor does it cover consultants' reports. Product testing reports — a much sought-after item by consumers' groups — would be available only if disclosure would not prejudice the use or results of particular tests. Finally, the proposed bill contains what is called a "severability clause," which requires responsible officials to sever or to separate sensitive from non-sensitive information in order to allow for release of the latter.

Hopefully, this exploration of the "nuts and bolts" of three controversial exemptions intended to protect important public interests has revealed the difficulty of drafting "fair and effective" FOI legislation. Practically all of the exemptions contained in the proposed Canadian bill have their counterpart in the U.S. Freedom of Information Act and the Swedish Freedom of the Press Act.[65] In practice a great deal of the success of any such act depends upon its administration, and the fact that Bill C-43 makes ultimate provision for judicial review will likely lead critics to be somewhat less insistent that exceptions to the automatic rule of public access be spelled out precisely in advance.

The proposed bill covers practically all government institutions, as listed in a schedule attached to the bill. There had been some debate earlier over whether a FOI Act should apply to crown corporations and regulatory agencies. The Green Paper (1977) had argued on the following grounds against the application of access legislation to proprietary corporations (i.e. those which most closely approximate commercial private sector companies):

> Most proprietary corporations . . . could not reasonably be expected to comply with the requirements owing to the competitive business environment in which they function.[66]

The concern is that competitors would use a FOI Act for purposes of discovery of information (such as production and marketing plans) whose disclosure would harm the commercial success of the crown corporations. Therefore, in its bill the Liberal government excludes most of the proprietary corporations from the scope of the proposed FOI Act.

Against this reasoning, it has been argued that, for a variety of reasons, crown corporations should not enjoy the same business confidentiality accorded to private sector companies. Often part of the mandate of crown corporations is to serve public policy goals as well as commercial goals. In some instances (for example the CBC), crown corporations receive substantial public funds. In many cases, crown corporations operate in monopolistic or oligopolistic market settings where openness is required to protect the public interest. Finally, while ministerial responsibility for the performance of crown corporations cannot be as complete as for departments, ministers cannot be totally absolved of responsibility. In order to enforce the principle of responsibility, Parliament needs access to information about the operations of all crown corporations.

In the case of regulatory agencies there seems to be more agreement that they should be subject to a FOI Act. Both the Economic Council of Canada in its recent report on "Responsible Regulation" and the Canadian Law Reform Commission in its working paper on administrative tribunals have accepted the need for an effective FOI Act to ensure responsive and accountable regulatory agencies.[67] Consistent with the independent status of such agencies, it could be argued that each regulatory board or commission should have the flexibility to develop its own procedural rules and practices relating to confidentiality rather than being brought under an omnibus FOI Act.

Most observers reject the above argument on several grounds. First, a regulatory agency will still be able to argue through the responsible minister and before the Federal Court in favor of non-disclosure in individual cases. Like all other government agencies, it will simply have to prove that in each instance confidentiality is justified under one of the exemption clauses contained in the FOI Act. This would mean, in effect, that the Court would ultimately decide whether, for example, the provisions in the Anti-Dumping Tribunal Act designed to protect corporate privacy should be overridden by the openness requirements of the FOI Act. In reaching such a judgment, the Court might decide to hold hearings either wholly or partially *in camera* in order to minimize the potential commercial damage to the parties involved. If experience suggests to a particular commission that it cannot live with the requirements of the FOI Act, then presumably it could request from government, and eventually from Parliament, an amendment which would exclude a portion of its operations from the scope of the Act.

A second reason why the Liberal government did not exclude regulatory bodies from freedom of information provisions is that the general public would not understand much of what has just been said. Most citizens would not be aware of the distinctions between government departments and independent agencies and a decision to exclude the latter would produce public cynicism about the government's commitment to openness. Besides, there is a compelling necessity to ensure on the ground of procedural fairness that an individual affected by regulatory decisions has access to all the information considered in his case.

The Liberal government's bill contains a provision for regular reviews by a parliamentary committee, which could make recommendations to amend the FOI Act based on the lessons learned from administering the original legislation. At this stage, all commentators seem to presume that such reviews will lead to amendments taking us further along the road towards openness in government operations, correcting what are seen to be the deficiencies of the proposed legislation. While openness may be a highly prized political value, it is conceivable that the review will lead to a restriction rather than an expansion of the scope of publicity in government. Defensiveness and timidity on the part of governments and public servants are the most obvious, but not therefore the only or even the most plausible reasons for why this could occur. Parliament might discover in the light of practical experience that the costs of openness outweigh in some respects the benefits. It must be remembered that openness is not necessarily for all Canadians an overriding political value. In certain circumstances it may clash with other values, including some which Canadians have come to uphold strongly in recent years, such as efficiency and effectiveness in government, social stability and security, and individual and corporate privacy.

It seems highly probable that within the next year Parliament will enact a FOI Act along the lines proposed by the present Liberal government. Undoubtedly, there will be a period of adjustment for the bureaucracy as they establish the machinery and the procedures for meeting the requirements of the act. No doubt there will be pockets of resistance within the public service to the concept of open government. That is, the passage of legislation declaring the public's right to official information will not change overnight well-entrenched habits of discretionary secrecy built up over many decades. Still, the legislation will reduce the present presumption in favor of secrecy; no longer will individuals have to prove a special interest before being granted access to documents and no longer will requests be subject solely to the disposition of the responsible ministers. Over time, the operation of the act will undoubtedly have an impact on the prevailing customs and attitudes of public officials towards information in their possession.

At an early stage, the campaign for a FOI Act was portrayed as a battle for the rights of the public and the need for enhanced citizen participation in policy-making. Greater citizen involvement, based upon more complete information about the nature of the issues, would ensure that governments did not define issues too narrowly in terms only of the demands of sophisticated and articulate groups. A wider spectrum of opinion involved in the formulation of policy could ensure greater support for the outcomes. More recently, however, passage of a FOI Act has been seen less as a populist victory and more as a mechanism for ensuring political accountability and access for privileged groups. This perspective is said to be more realistic. It reflects the available studies on political participation, which reveal that sophisticated, well-heeled and strategically-located elite groups tend to dominate policy-making in this country. Provision of additional information will change this pattern only marginally. The benefits to the general public from a FOI Act will likely occur in a "trickle down" fashion. For the most part they will be won through the efforts of others and will be enjoyed only later. More discussion along these lines is found in the next chapter dealing with citizen participation.

While we have witnessed the emergence of an apparent consensus on the narrow issue of the desirability of a FOI Act, the wider problematical controversy of the need for and the extent of administrative secrecy within governments will never be fully resolved. Even with the existence of a FOI Act there will be differences over what matters can legitimately and safely be made public. The source of such disagreements lies in contending philosophies of democracy and the political process. As the next chapter makes clear, proponents of "participatory democracy" push for complete openness in government because they reject the benevolent elitism implied in other models of democratic decision-making. By way of contrast, advocates of what has been called "consociational democracy" insist that expert elites must be relatively insulated and immune from the pressures of mass public opinion, which is often ill-informed and volatile. In a diverse and weakly integrated society like Canada, it is argued, some freedom must be granted to political, economic and administrative elites to bargain in secret in order to reach the accommodations necessary to hold the country together. Given these contending philosophical perspectives, secrecy in government will remain enduringly problematical in Canadian public administration.

For Further Reading

BOOKS AND REPORTS

Canada, Secretary of State and Minister of Communication, *Access to Information Legislation*. Ottawa: A Cabinet Discussion Paper, 1980.

———. Hon. John Roberts, Secretary of State, *Legislation on Public Access to Government Documents*. Ottawa: Supply and Services, June 1977.

Fox, Larry. *Freedom of Information and the Administrative Process*. Toronto: Ontario Royal Commission on Freedom of Information and Individual Privacy, Research Study No. 10, 1979.

Franck, Thomas M. and Edward Weisband, eds. *Secrecy and Foreign Policy*. New York: Oxford University Press, 1974.

Friedland, M. L. *National Security: The Legal Dimensions*. Ottawa: Supply and Services, 1979.

Galnoor, I., ed. *Government Secrecy in Democracies*. New York: Harper and Row, 1977.

Kernaghan, Kenneth. *Freedom of Information and Ministerial Responsibility*. Toronto: Ontario Commission on Freedom of Information and Individual Privacy, Research Study No. 2, 1978.

Rankin, T. Murray. *Freedom of Information in Canada: Will the Doors Stay Shut?* Ottawa: Canadian Bar Association, 1977.

Rowat, Donald C., ed. *Administrative Secrecy in Developed Countries*. New York: Columbia University Press, 1979.

Smiley, D. V. *The Freedom of Information Issue: A Political Analysis*. Toronto: Ontario Royal Commission on Freedom of Information and Individual Privacy, Research Study No. 1, 1978.

ARTICLES

Abel, Albert S. "Administrative Secrecy." *Canadian Public Administration*, Vol. XI, No. 4 (Winter 1968), pp. 440-48.

French, Richard. "Freedom of Information and Parliament." (Paper presented to the Conference on Legislative Studies, Simon Fraser University, 1979.)

Knight, K. W. "Administrative Secrecy and Ministerial Responsibility." *Canadian Journal of Economics and Political Science*, Vol. XXXII, 1 (February 1966), pp. 77-84.

Mitchell, Heather. "Freedom of Information and Official Secrets." *Canadian Forum*, Vol. LX (February 1981), pp. 18-19, 33.

Robertson, Gordon. "Confidentiality in Government." *Archivaria*, No. 6 (Summer 1978), pp. 3-15.

Rowat, D. C. "Freedom of Information: The American Experience." *Canadian Forum*, Vol. LVIII (September 1978), pp. 10-13.

———. "A Freedom of Information Act: What It Is and Why We Need It." *Quarterly of Canadian Studies*, Vol. IV, 3 and 4 (1977), pp. 185-91.

———. "Administrative Secrecy and Ministerial Responsibility: A Reply." *Canadian Journal of Economics and Political Science*, Vol. XXXII, 1 (February 1966), pp. 84-87.

Thomas, Paul G. "Review Article: Secrecy and Publicity in Canadian Government." *Canadian Public Administration*, Vol. XIX, 1 (Spring 1976), pp. 158-64.

ENDNOTES

1. Donald C. Rowat, *Administrative Secrecy in Developed Countries* (New York: Columbia University Press, 1979), Chapter 11.
2. Donald V. Smiley, *The Freedom of Information Issue: A Political Analysis* (A study prepared for the Ontario Commission on Freedom of Information and Individual Privacy, 1978), pp. 28-31.
3. Richard French, "Freedom of Information and Parliament" (Paper presented to the Conference on Legislative Studies, Simon Fraser University, February 1979), pp. 15-16.
4. Compiled from House of Commons, *Debates*, June 22, 1978, and Donald C. Rowat, "Freedom of Information: The U.S. Experience," *Canadian Forum*, Vol. LVIII (September 1978), pp. 10-13.
5. D.F. Wall, *The Provision of Government Information* (Ottawa, Privy Council Office, April 1974. Printed as an appendix to the Minutes of Proceedings and Evidence of the Standing Joint Committee on Regulations and other Statutory Instruments, June 25, 1975), p. 59.
6. See Thomas Hockin, "Adversary Politics and the Functions of Canada's House of Commons," in O. Kruhlak et al., *The Canadian Political Process: A Reader*, 2nd ed. (Toronto: Holt, Rinehart and Winston, 1973), pp. 361-81.
7. Hon. John Roberts, Secretary of State, *Legislation on Public Access to Government Documents* (Ottawa: Supply and Services, June 1977), pp. 1-2. Henceforth cited as *The Green Paper, 1977*.
8. See T. Murray Rankin, *Freedom of Information in Canada: Will the Doors Stay Shut?* (Ottawa: Canadian Bar Association, 1977), pp. 133-43.
9. K.W. Knight, "Administrative Secrecy and Ministerial Responsibility," *Canadian Journal of Economics and Political Science*, Vol. XXXII (February 1966), pp. 78-80.
10. See J.M. Sharp, "The Public Servant and the Right to Privacy, *Canadian Public Administration*, Vol. XIV, 1 (Spring 1971), pp. 58-64. The Privacy Commissioner in the Canadian Human Rights Commission tabled a report on the use of Social Insurance Numbers within the federal government in January 1981. See, *Report of the Privacy Commission on the use of the Social Insurance Number* (Ottawa: Supply and Services, 1981).
11. See the collection of articles in Thomas M. Franck and Edward Weisband, *Secrecy and Foreign Policy* (New York: Oxford University Press, 1974).
12. See Canada, *Report of the Royal Commission on Security* (Abridged) (Ottawa: Queen's Printer, 1969), and Canada, The Commission of Inquiry Concerning Certain Activities of the Royal Canadian Mounted Police, *First Report, Security and Information* (Ottawa: Supply and Services, 1979), henceforth referred to as the *McDonald Report*.
13. French, p. 4.
14. See the Wall Report, and the testimony by R.G. Robertson, Secretary to the Cabinet for Federal-Provincial Relations, in Minutes of Proceedings and Evidence of the Standing Joint Committee on Regulations and Other Statutory Instruments, June 25, 1975, pp. 15-16.
15. Rowat, p. 211.
16. The following discussion is based upon the excellent study by M.L. Friedland, *National Security: The Legal Dimensions* (Ottawa: Supply and Services, 1979), Parts Two and Three.
17. Canada, Parliament, An Act Respecting Official Secrets, R.S.C., 1970, c. 0-3, Section 4(1).
18. *McDonald Report*, p. 22.
19. See Friedland, p. 34-36; Maxwell Cohen, "Secrecy in Law and Policy: The Canadian Experience and International Relations," in Thomas M. Frank and Edward Weisband (eds.), *Secrecy and Foreign Policy*, pp. 356-77; and Brian A. Crane, "Freedom of the Press and National Security," *McGill Law Journal*, Vol. 14 (1975), pp. 148-55.
20. Friedland, p. 35.
21. *Ibid*., p. 35.

22. Quoted in A. Seigel, "The Press and Parliament" (Paper presented to the Canadian Political Science Association, 1976), p. 4.
23. See Rankin, pp. 24-29.
24. *Ibid.*, p. 8.
25. See The Secretary of State and Minister of Communications, "Access to Information Legislation" (A Cabinet Discussion Paper, Ottawa, June 1980), pp. 29-30.
26. Canada, Treasury Board, *Report on the Operation of Part IV of the Canadian Human Rights Act* (Ottawa, 1979), p. 3.
27. See Canada, Annual Report of the Privacy Commissioner, 1978 and 1979 (Ottawa: Supply and Services, 1979).
28. Canada, Treasury Board, *op. cit.*, p. 6.
29. The Minister of Justice and Attorney General, "Privacy Legislation" (Cabinet Discussion Paper, Ottawa, June, 1980).
30. See Minutes of Proceedings and Evidence, Standing Joint Committee on Statutory Instruments and Other Regulations, March 11, 1975, Appendix, pp. 41-51.
31. *Ibid.*, p. 43.
32. See Smiley, *op. cit.*
33. See Canada, *Report of the Royal Commission on Security* (Abridged).
34. See House of Commons, *Debates*, May 1, 1969, pp. 8199-8200.
35. Friedland, pp. 65-66, and William Monopoli, "Prosecutors Say Publishing Secrets Is a Crime," *The Financial Post*, December 30, 1978.
36. Canada, Report of the Task Force on Government Information Services, Vol. 1 (Ottawa: Queen's Printer, 1969), p. 54.
37. *Ibid.*, p. 59.
38. See Canada, Senate, Standing Senate Committee on National Finance, *Report on Information Canada* (Ottawa: Supply and Services, April 1974).
39. See Gary Levy, "Delegated Legislation and the Standing Joint Committee on Regulations and Other Statutory Instruments," *Canadian Public Administration*, Vol. XXII, 3 (Fall 1979), pp. 349-65.
40. See editorial, "Tight as a Drum," *The Globe and Mail*, March 17, 1973, and Maurice Western, "Keeping the Public in the Dark," *Winnipeg Free Press*, March 17, 1973.
41. See *Wall Report*, pp. 43-45.
42. *Ibid.*, p. 48.
43. For an excellent discussion of a "parliamentary approach" to the provision of information, See Richard French, *op. cit.*
44. Economic Council of Canada, *Responsible Regulation* (Ottawa: Supply and Services, 1979). See Note 17, p. 113.
45. Canadian Radio-Television and Telecommunications Commission, "Proposed Procedures and Practices Relating to Broadcasting Matters," July 25, 1978, pp. 14-19.
46. Hugh Windsor, "Papers Freed by Ottawa May Not Be Exciting But They Are Seen as a Start," *The Globe and Mail*, October 15, 1977, p. 3.
47. *The Green Paper*, 1977, p. 1.
48. Rankin, p. 2.
49. Standing Joint Committee on Regulations and Other Statutory Instruments, *Fifth Report* (June 28, 1978), pp. 3-12.
50. *Ibid.*, p. 124.
51. *Ibid.*, p. 125.
52. *Ibid.*, p. 123 and p. 126.
53. *Ibid.*, p. 126.
54. *Ibid.*, p. 128.
55. *Ibid.*, Footnote 36, p. 127.
56. *The Green Paper*, 1977, p. 18.

57. See Smiley, pp. 75-78.
58. *The Green Paper, 1977*, *op. cit.*, pp. 25-28.
59. See Standing Joint Committee, *Fifth Report*, pp. 8-9.
60. This has been the experience under the American FOI Act according to one authority, Harrison Welfrod, "Rights of People: The Freedom of Information Act," in Norman Dorsen and Stephen Gillers (eds.), *None of Your Business: Government Secrecy in America* (New York: Penguin, 1975), p. 196.
61. Secretary of State and Minister of Communications, Access to Information Legislation, *op. cit.*
62. *Ibid.*, pp. 5-6.
63. *The Green Paper, 1977*, p. 10.
64. Secretary of State, Bill C-43, Section 15(1), First Reading, July 17, 1980.
65. Richard French, "Access to Government Information in the United States" (Ottawa, Privy Council Office, February 19, 1976), and Richard D. French, "Access to Government Information in Sweden" (Ottawa, Privy Council Office, January 9, 1976).
66. *The Green Paper, 1977*, p. 23-24. See Isaiah A. Litvak, *Information Access and Crown Corporations* (Toronto, Research Publication No. 14, Ontario Commission on Freedom of Information and Individual Privacy, February, 1980) for arguments on behalf of applying FOI legislation to all crown corporations.
67. Economic Council of Canada, *Responsible Regulation*, pp. 81-82, and Law Reform Commission of Canada, *Independent Administrative Agencies*, Working Paper No. 25 (Ottawa: Supply and Services, 1980), pp. 174-76.

CHAPTER TEN

The Administrative State and the Role of the Citizen

Introduction

For approximately the last 20 years there has allegedly existed in Canada a movement for citizen participation in both the general political system as well as in the more specific administrative sub-system. Since there is no agreed-upon definition in the social sciences of what constitutes a "movement," it is not surprising that there should be a quarrel over whether or not a movement has existed and/or does still exist. Some concede that it began but that it quickly lost its momentum and died by the early 1970s. Opinions on its success range from "substantively none" to "significant gains." There is also the view that, even if difficult to document, the movement still exists, but again opinions vary greatly on its actual as well as potential success.

For our purposes here, it is accepted that demands beginning in the 1960s for increased citizen involvement in and control of the political system were sufficiently widespread to constitute a "movement," that this movement had some impact on the operation of the political system, and that at least potentially it remains sufficiently strong to be of serious consequence for the political system. More problematical is whether the movement had or will have an impact representing something more significant and lasting than cooptation of some of its more influential spokesmen, and tokenism as opposed to substantive change. However, given the movement's aims, it is clear that if it enjoys or will enjoy even partial success it will seriously affect not only the present policy-making structures and processes in Canada, as discussed in preceding chapters, but will also have serious impact on the ongoing, day-to-day administration of policies.

This is a very problematical area of Canadian public administration theory and practice. Some regard the citizen participation movement as crucial to the maintenance of democracy in modern society. Citizen participation is a "good" and any increase in it is valued as an end in itself. Furthermore, increasing citizen participation is expected to help eradicate many wrongs in contemporary Canada. At the opposite extreme is the argument that any substantial increase in citizen participation in policy-making or implementation is neither necessary for basic maintenance of the democratic tradition nor desirable for the practical conduct of government affairs. Proponents of this view may even suggest that there is already too much impassioned, inexpert citizen input into difficult, complex policy areas (which is why Canada has so many pressing problems, even crises).

What is involved here is fundamental clash between opposing political philosophies. While contentions often focus on specifics such as the way Parliament operates, or political parties, or political leadership, or bureaucratic policy-making and so forth, they clearly involve the much more broadly-based value conflicts prevailing in Canadian society. For that matter, these value conflicts have existed in Western Civilization through the centuries. They revolve around differing conceptions of the nature of man in terms of his social, political and mental capabilities. They center, that is, on man's capability to act as a citizen.[1]

The concept of citizen participation is clearly attached to the broader notion of "democracy," and therefore citizen participation is inherently imbued with all the definitional, normative, and practical controversy surrounding the larger term. We have never agreed on exactly what constitutes democracy and similarly we do not agree either in qualitative or quantitative terms on precisely what is involved in citizen participation. With democracy, we typically attempt to resolve, but seem only to succeed in compounding, definitional problems by the addition of qualifying adjectives such as direct, indirect, liberal, tory, majoritarian, mass, representative, guided, socialist, capitalist, pluralist, consociational, contemporary, modern, viable, and many others. Similarly, to citizen participation, which is already ambiguous due to its attachment to democracy, we append such qualifiers as direct, indirect, popular, mass, reasonable, proper, affected interest, and so forth. Nor is this ambiguity in the least obviated by the fairly common usage of such couplings as participatory democracy and democratic participation.

We are not concerned here with participation *per se*, which can be loosely defined as any form of activity. Rather, the interest is with *political* participation, which involves the notion of activity of individuals, of citizens, directed toward ordering all other activities whether these be social, economic or aesthetic. Through this ordering, political or citizen participation denotes activity directed toward influencing public decisions and attendant actions. We participate politically when we somehow contribute to, when we somehow share in, the making of public choices.[2]

In attempting to refine this conceptualization of citizen participation, one must become rather arbitrary and suggest a certain bias which in turn tends to prejudge specific democratic perspectives as well as actual political conditions. For example, when a person consciously or unconsciously is politically *inactive* he nevertheless contributes to public choice by withholding his opinion, reasoning, and "vote" from public choice situations. In effect, he votes by not voting, a state of affairs which political scientists have in mind when they argue that political apathy supports the status quo or that it facilitates political system stability. Here, however, political apathy (quiescence, inactivity) is not regarded as political participation, but rather is seen as a genuine lack of it. Political or citizen participation as used here involves some identifiable activity directed toward influencing public choices.

This leads to the bias and prejudgement noted just above. It is precisely on this point of political activism and inactivism that basic views on democracy diverge. It would be nice if one could simply say that democratic theory emphasizes the need to promote citizen participation to the maximum possible extent, whereas authoritarian theory pushes toward the opposite extreme. Unfortunately, this is not the case today – if it ever was. Rather, as will be seen below, democratic theory and practice involve the notion that there must be citizen participation in order for democracy to exist, but both the quantity and the quality of such participation are matters of profound dispute.

We will attempt to clarify some of the major problematical aspects of this ongoing debate. From among a long line of "authoritarian" theorists we separate two, Plato and Ortega y Gasset, who are reasonably representative of a sub-group who have described and advocated what might be termed "benevolent elitism." It will be seen that many of the contentions related to citizen participation in Canada today are restatements of ancient arguments and can usefully be viewed in terms of an ongoing, historical dialogue. Furthermore, it will be noted that much, perhaps most, democratic theory today and a wide variety of practices related to that theory advocate or are based on views remarkably similar to those held by benevolent elitism. The overall intent of this approach is to depict something of the long-standing nature, depth, complexity, and significance of the controversy and thereby suggest the improbability of achieving any immediate and/or widespread agreement on the desirability/practicability of citizen participation in Canadian society.

Before proceeding to the specific concerns of this chapter it may be helpful to address briefly the question: What does all this discussion of citizen participation and democracy have to do with public administration? That is, is such a lengthy treatment of this topic really necessary in order to understand public administration in Canada?

While conceding that some of the interest here must reflect discipline bias, we nevertheless feel that the quantity and quality of citizen participation impinge heavily on the public service in any society. Beyond such normative questions as whether, how, and how much they should impinge, there is the fact that they do. Political activities of whatever form represent the presence of value conflicts within society, and despite the views and wishes of the mechanistic tradition it is impossible to believe that these conflicts do not pervade both the internal and external operations of the public bureaucracy. Public attitudes, beliefs, concerns and demands related to the public bureaucracy are present both implicitly and explicitly in all preceding discussion in this text. As discussed below, there is a close, although perhaps conflictual, relationship between arguments for increased citizen participation and those for participative management. Popular disillusionment with public bureaucracy affects in many ways the interaction between bureaucracy and clientele, among citizens, politicians and public servants. The controversies surrounding administrative secrecy, administrative federalism, and administrative representativeness are to a considerable extent the same controversies, stated in other contexts, as those involved in citizen participation. In Canada, for example, the entire concept of bureaucratic accountability becomes rather pointless if one removes the public from consideration in the accountability relationships. And public budgeting and policy-making relate at all times to the relationship between government and citizens. In short, whatever its specifics of quantity, quality and form, citizen participation is an integral component of public administration.

Three broad approaches suggest themselves for dealing with the topic of citizen participation. The first emphasizes the policy *making* aspect of public administration while the second stresses policy *implementation*. While neither approach necessarily subscribes to the notion of a politics/administration dichotomy, the first focuses on politics and citizen participation while the second stresses administration and citizen participation. The third approach attempts to combine both the first and second emphases.

In this chapter, we tend to concentrate on political stress while incorporating administrative aspects. This bias is pre-determined by the preceding chapters' orientation. It is generally conceded today that the public bureaucracy is integral to the policy process, its actual role variously assessed along a continuum ranging from "significant policy actor" to "dominant policy actor." Discussion of both the politicians and the bureaucracy as policy actors has received much attention in preceding chapters, most notably in Chapters 4, 5, 7 and 8. However, those chapters did not really address *the public* aspect of public policy. They did not, that is, especially discuss the public for whom all these policy actions allegedly occur in Canada. This chapter attempts to round out the picture.

However, policy-making and policy implementation are phases of a single process. The "public" of public policy must therefore be related to the implementation phase of the policy process. For the reasons just mentioned this implementation aspect does not receive the major emphasis here, but it cannot be ignored. Parts of the following discussion clearly indicate that in the entirely unlikely event that disagreement ended over the content of public policies, it would probably continue as hard as ever over policy implementation. As emphasized in Chapter 3, it is in the implementation of public policies that we as individuals are made most fully aware of the existence of policies, and the way in which policies are administered on a day-to-day basis is argued to have a great impact on our views of public bureaucracy and of public policy itself. This point was most clearly revealed in the discussions of alienation and of alternative forms to bureaucracy.

However, two further points should be noted. First, such things as bureaucracy and alternatives to it tend to be only abstractions. When we make them concrete through speech or action we move clearly into the political sphere. As an American political scientist has pointed out, concern for participation arises almost entirely as a result of real or imagined failure of government and its bureaucracy to respond appropriately to citizens; citizens feel that government response to their demands and needs would be more just had these received a fair hearing. In short, the controversy in whatever context it is initiated, ultimately boils down to criticism of the existing system of representation.[3]

Second, it is the assumption here that, by and large, individual citizens when they express desire to become more involved in the policy process are aiming at the *making* as opposed to the *implementing* part of the process. That is, while significant exceptions surely occur, we assume here that people normally do not want to get personally involved in program delivery (except as recipients), but rather seek involvement in the devising of programs to meet their needs. For example, we may want to participate in deciding whether there should be a park, where it should be located and what it should feature. We do not want to remove old buildings personally and plant lawns and trees. Thus, whether our demands for participation are aimed at politicians (a municipal council) or at administrators (a parks department) the demands are politically rather than administratively based because they aim at decision-making.

Benevolent Elitism, Old and New.

Much of today's literature concerning citizen participation, particularly that emphasizing its grass roots nature, reflects notions akin to those commonly attributed to the city state of ancient Greece. In this context, it is ironical that Plato, a citizen of such a state whose political philosophy has over the centuries greatly influenced Western political thought, denied the good of such concepts as the active citizen, political participation and public opinion. Plato did not think highly of common man's ability to govern himself.

In the *Republic*, Plato concluded that the "ideal state" is a state governed by knowledge, a notion not dissimilar to the rationalist perspective in public policy-making in Canada today. Following from the belief that society is the result of the need for division of labor in human affairs and the attendant specialization of function, government by knowledge is made possible by having as ruler(s) the one who possesses appropriate knowledge. Since philosophers are those most likely to possess this knowledge, unless philosophers become kings or kings philosophers, troubles will prevail in states and for mankind in general.[4] That is, as Plato saw it, the rational society is based on rule through intelligence free from the bonds of custom as well as from human stupidity and selfishness — intelligence capable of directing even human custom and stupidity toward a rational life.

There is distinct disagreement regarding the motivation behind Plato's argument. Sabine, for example, contends that this is a profession of faith by the intellectual who sees in knowledge and enlightenment the ability to achieve social progress.[5] Given the tendency in our culture to venerate knowledge, some democrats might concede that Plato was well-intentioned even if wrong. On the other hand, Wood and Wood, on the basis of lengthy discussion of Plato's life and times, conclude that Plato was simply attempting an elaborate justification for continuance of an aristocratic way of life in the face of democratic pressures.[6]

In any event, in Plato's scheme of things the individual is valued as an individual as well as a member of the citizenry — but he is valued for his contributions to society, not for his opinions on political matters. Society cannot exist without the contribution of all, but it also cannot function well if all attempt to govern.[7] The tradesman contributes to society through pursuit of his trade, not by attempts to govern. Therefore, public opinion and/or citizen participation in public policy-making as we know it today or, at least, as many would like to know it, simply did not exist in Plato's ideal state. In short, if we accept Plato's premise that rulers are qualified to rule because of their superior knowledge, then public opinion is either irrelevant or must be seen as a political safety valve holding in check the discontent of the governed.[8] Good government involves rule by dispassionate expertise as opposed to rule by passion and prejudice through citizen dominance.

Centuries later the Spanish philosopher José Ortega y Gasset, in *The Revolt of the Masses*, expressed the need for elite rule in the context of industrialization and the mass society. He believed that the 19th century had the grand distinction of bringing to fruition the highest type of public life yet known to the world. This life was based on pursuit of three principles: liberal democracy, scientific experiment and industrialization.[9] However, this very perfection of the 19th century led to the mass society, a society in which the masses demanded as "natural rights" those things which had been created for them only through pursuit of the three principles. In their thoughtless emphasis upon the natural correctness of their mass will, as Ortega y Gasset put it, the mob goes in search of bread and the means it employs generally results in the destruction of bakeries.[10]

He felt that what had occurred was the corruption of "real democracy" (liberal democracy) to "hyper-democracy" (mobocracy). In his view, human society, by its very nature, is aristocratic, dominated in public life by an elite, and it ceases to be a society when it ceases to be aristocratic.[11] The elite are determined not by birth or class necessarily — although these are important factors — but by the fact that a relatively few people do make great demands upon themselves, taking on many duties and striving toward perfection. Most people, however, are content to take things easy, demanding nothing special of themselves. They are average or, to use another term, mediocre.

Ortega y Gasset believed the growing dominance of the masses over the proper aristocracy had occurred through the corruption of democracy into hyper-democracy. Earlier, when democracy was the norm, the masses had realized that, with all their faults, the elite did have better understanding of public problems and so the masses were content to be ruled by them for the general good. This had changed during the 19th century, so that the commonplace mind, knowing full well its own commonplaceness, had begun to insist on its right to impose the commonplace wherever and whenever it willed. In short, the masses were, he felt, achieving total social power, despite the fact that they neither should nor could direct their personal existence or society in general. As a result of the masses' insistence on imposing their mediocrity on all aspects of society including government, Western civilization was undergoing the greatest crisis that could possibly afflict societies.[12]

Although such ideas today are not usually so bluntly expressed — there is a certain sanctity attached to the concept of "the masses" — they do have their theoretical as well as their practical adherents. In the Canadian context, this is seen in descriptions and advocacy of what is called *consociational democracy*.

One definition of consociational democracy is "government by elite control designed to turn a democracy with a fragmented political culture into a stable democracy."[13] The idea is that in a society characterized by a fragmented political culture the political schisms are so great or, conversely, the degree of consensus or felt commonality is so low, that group conflict is very intense and pervasive. Therefore, compromise on public policies cannot occur easily, if at all, and the political system is in a constant state of disruption. Thus the society itself faces the continuing strong possibility, even probability, of becoming a non-society, of destroying itself as a unified political entity. The political elite, drawn from the various groups, are regarded as being much more capable than are the rank and file of seeing the group benefits to be gained from retention of the whole. Therefore, the elite will work toward the common, overall goals through compromise on the various groups' more specific goals.

Implicit in this definition is the unquestioned value placed on *stability*, on persistence of the social system. The existence of the elite is justified in this particular type of democratic theory simply because they work toward stability.[14] And with stability of the political system is implied a positive value in retention of the status quo, the existing state of affairs at any point in time. The entire idea is given further theoretical justification by the argument that, while consociational democracy does violate the principle of majority rule, it does not deviate too much from the more common form of democratic theory in troubled times. That is, both majoritarian democratic theory as well as constitutions based on it, prescribe majority rule only when matters are not too "important"; in times of crisis majority rule is simply not adequate and is not practised.[15] For example the western democracies in World War II became near dictatorships in order to fight dictatorship.

In the book *Consociational Democracy*, the writers dealing specifically with Canada point to aspects of this particular form of democracy (or elitism, depending on how one views the theory) which have existed, do exist or should exist in this country. For present purposes, what is of interest is the concern expressed over the fact that consociational democracy has failed to become established, or firmly established, in Canada. For example, it is deplored that English Canada — and, therefore, French Canada — persists in working toward majoritarian democracy, this persistence being a constant danger to national unity.[16] The argument is that, if the elite were politically *more* dominant, if they were relatively *free* from citizens' pressures, they would be able to rise above these majoritarian concerns and, seeing the benefit of the whole, would develop compromise solutions to national problems. We would be saved despite ourselves.

In other words, while consociational democracy particularly relates to societies characterized by linguistic, cultural and regional cleavages (which Canada certainly has), its proponents nevertheless restate in a contemporary context the general concerns of benevolent elite thinkers such as Plato and Ortega y Gasset. And they stand in clear opposition to any current demands for significantly increasing citizen participation in the Canadian political system.

Looking at elitism from another perspective, John Porter in the *Vertical Mosaic* has emphasized the inevitability of elites in societies. Like death and taxes, elites are inevitable. A point he makes that is critical to many cherished notions of democracy is that there can be no total dominance by any one elite, providing other elites, defined along functional lines, continue to exist.[17] That is, while the elites by definition uphold the normative order of society — while they emphasize maintenance of the status quo — there is no total dominance provided competition among a number of elites prevails. Thus, political, social, economic and other changes can occur.

However, Porter argues that there is a fairly strong tendency toward non-differentiation among the Canadian elite. They are too homogeneous, too much of one camp, too much a group as opposed to a socio-economic category. Because of this, maintenance of the status quo is even more than normally secure and therefore Canada has a marked inability to resolve either internal or external problems. Because the elite do not have to compete strongly among themselves for particularistic ends, they do not have to worry too much about mass support. Thus there is relatively little concern for having to "pay off" the citizens of Canada, and social experimentation cannot occur.[18]

Unlike the proponents of consociational democracy, Porter suggests there is insufficient participation by the masses in today's society. The elite are relatively free from pressures largely due to the apathy of citizens. Twentieth century societies in general, he feels, are marked by widespread apathy, withdrawal and the absence of citizen participation in the making of public policy.[19] The conflict that does occur is among the "ins" rather than between the "ins" and "outs," and since the "ins" have a vested interest in the status quo, basic societal change does not occur easily, if at all. In short, while proponents of consociational democracy deplore majoritarianism which prevents compromise solutions to national problems from occurring in Canada, Porter argues that there is not sufficient citizen input and altogether too much easy, vested-interest compromise in our political system.

It should be emphasized, however, that Porter's is not what might be called a populist or participatory democracy argument. He does not advocate that the elite either can be or should be eradicated, but rather that the inevitable elite should be more differentiated so that they will be more amenable to citizen pressures. Artificial barriers to membership in the elite should be removed, allowing for new members with new ideas and loyalties, allowing democracy to re-emerge and flourish. In a sense, the idea is not that the masses should or should not expect to dominate the political system, but rather that there should be greater chance for individuals from the masses to rise to membership in the group which does dominate.

This perspective has a large number of supporters in the literature on democracy and it is often labelled *equilibrium democracy*. This, in turn, can be regarded as a sub-school within the more general school labelled *liberal democracy*.[20] However, whatever labels may be attached to specific arguments, this school of thought definitely limits the role of citizens in making public choices. In this view, as Joseph Schumpeter has argued, the role of the citizen in a democracy is to participate in deciding who will decide.[21] It is this emphasis on the normative and practical need for strong elites in democracies which leads one to attach much democratic theory, or *alleged* democratic theory depending on one's viewpoint, to the concept of *benevolent elitism*.

Perhaps a current, simplistic example will help clarify discussion to this point. In the case of the Quebec Referendum, Premier Lévesque attempted deliberately to involve the general populace of the province in making a major decision, as opposed to having input into the decision. This strategem was distinctly opposed to Canadian political tradition, since long-standing and constantly developing practice has been to refer such major items, if they cannot somehow be settled in a more informal fashion, to the formal federal-provincial conference.

Such a conference on whatever subject and at whatever level (whether premiers, ministers, deputy ministers) involves conflict resolution through elite accommodation. Thus, one encounters the argument that Canadian federalism means whatever the top political leadership decides it is going to mean. The term *bureaucratic federalism* has attached to it the belief that bureaucrats determine or help to determine the actual nature of federalism. We seldom know the details of such conferences, even the most publicized premiers' conferences, but it seems reasonably safe to say that they are attempts by the elite to reach basic policy decisions which are acceptable to the relatively limited number of participants. In both practical and normative terms, this can be viewed as consociational democracy.[22]

On the other hand, while we may not be made aware of the details, we are made aware through the mass media of the issues and many of the ramifications of possible decisions. Political leaders deliberately state their basic positions to the general public presumably in the hope of gaining support for them and thereby gaining strength in the bargaining situation. There is always the "re-election imperative" which incumbent politicians presumably must heed. The public, however, does not decide the issues; at most it influences decisions by its potential to elect new deciders in the next election should the present deciders not arrive at acceptable desisions. This, in practical and normative terms, can be seen as equilibrium democracy (or as contemporary, liberal, Schumpeterian, and so forth).

The referendum is different in that it involves citizens in actually *making* a decision. This practice departs from both the consociational and equilibrium models of democracy, relating more to a third model commonly referred to as *participatory democracy*. This relationship will be clarified in subsequent discussion. What is necessary at this point is some brief consideration of the extent to which the referendum represented a substantive change in political practice.

It is important to note that the citizens of Quebec did not have a right to decide on the matter under dispute. Their ability to participate directly was granted to them by the political elite of the province. That is, the political leadership decided to let the people decide. However, it was quite unclear what the provincial leadership would actually have done had the vote been "yes." Furthermore, at the national level, Prime Minister Trudeau emphasized that he would not feel bound to any course of action by the Quebec Referendum.

In the summer of 1980, just a few months after the Quebec Referendum (which he was not to be bound by), the Prime Minister was threatening provincial leaders with another referendum if the constitutional discussions did not, to his mind, turn out properly. Again, however, it is important to note that the citizens of Canada do not in practical terms have the right to decide such a basic question as the content of the Constitution which is intended to provide the framework governing their daily lives. In normative terms, one presumes the political leaders did not feel the public *should* have the right to decide on such a major issue, since only one group of leaders even suggested a referendum, and then only if the "proper" decisions could not be achieved at the elite level. For example, Premier Lyon of Manitoba, who has been in the forefront of provincial opposition to unilateral federal action in patriating the Constitution, does not argue that the people should decide. Rather, on his return from London where he attempted to influence necessary British legislative action, he stated in a televised speech (February 1981) that what is necessary is that the Prime Minister and all premiers sit down and consensually decide among themselves exactly what is to be done regarding the Constitution. In the face of an adamant federal government, the provincial position has since changed in some of its specifics but not in its basic philosophy. In April, 1981 the committee of eight premiers meeting in Ottawa was insisting that Prime Minister Trudeau and the premiers of the other two provinces join them in negotiations to resolve the constitutional issue without further recourse to the courts and without unilateral submission of the Liberal Party's constitutional package to the British Parliament. This package, among other things, includes a provision for referendum should constitutional matters in the future become deadlocked — an issue in great dispute with the premiers. The point of all this for present purposes is that neither the Prime Minister nor the premiers appear in the least to feel it necessary to ask the people now to resolve the matter. They insist that discussion among themselves ought to be the means to resolve the issue. The only reason that the issue is not resolved, and that the public have been brought into the controversy to the extent that both sides are actively seeking our support, is that they have failed to agree among themselves — at the elite level. One assumes that if they *had* agreed, we would not have been consulted at all.

This development would seem to relate to equilibrium democracy because of the extent to which elite preference determines citizen participation. Participatory democracy advocates would reject such elite dominance, while proponents of consociational democracy would deplore the majoritarian element that is involved. However, both consociational and equilibrium democratic theory are in favor of elite dominance and relatively limited citizen power. While this is variously justified, the basic idea is that the people are not to be trusted in making public choices. One thus encounters the view that widespread, continued political activism on the part of the citizens in a democratic society is really antidemocratic in nature because it contravenes the democratic order.[23] The idea is that modern societies are clearly vulnerable to mass politics simply because they encourage the entire citizenry, normally and historically politically quiescent, to engage in politics. Stated conversely, this means that in order to remain "democratic," democratic political systems should not encourage political activism on the part of the citizenry.

All this represents a shift from the "elite by knowledge" advocated by Plato and the "elite by dedication" advanced by Ortega y Gasset, to an "elite by election." However, while the normative bases of elitism and the means for determining the elite may have shifted somewhat, the fundamental reason for advocating elitism remains unchanged: people in general and as a mass are simply not capable of making good decisions.

There is still another line of argument concerning elitism and democracy that complicates discussion. This might be labelled the "real elite perspective." In general, the argument here is that, while there is indubitably a ruling elite, this elite is in whole (the extreme position) or in part comprised of non-elected persons. While this argument has mainly developed in the United States, for example, through C. Wright Mills and many subsequent writers, it certainly has its Canadian adherents. For example, Gad Horowitz has argued that what we have in Canada is not democracy even in contemporary terms. Those terms, as noted just above, at least give the citizen the right to decide on who will decide public policies. However, the Canadian political elite, our elected politicians, are not those who really make the major political decisions — the latter being defined as "those decisions which affect the community." Rather, such decisions are actually made by another elite — one might call them a super elite — who are in no way elected by us, who are therefore in no way accountable to us, and who therefore are in no way democratic. We do not, that is, have even elite-based democracy in Canada. We simply do not have democracy.[24]

Views differ concerning the membership of this real elite, but typically they are described as made up of big business, multi-national corporations and the bureaucracy. Wallace Clement,[25] for example, contends that the economic elite, and particularly the heads of multi-national corporations, are becoming predominant in public policy making in Canada. This does not mean that they heavily influence all decisions relevant to themselves, but rather that they tend to dictate or control such decisions. So, for example, one not uncommonly comes across the contention in discussion or in the media that petroleum interests ultimately control Canadian petroleum policy and therefore tend to control Canadian energy policy in general. In a variety of ways the same perspective is related to transportation policy, telecommunications policy, agricultural policy, and so forth.

It is impossible here to delve deeply into this real elite perspective, far less to attempt to prove or disprove its accuracy. The point is, the real elite perspective exists. As Virginia McDonald suggests, "in all analyses of the elitist strain in Canadian society there is recognition of the importance, if not predominance, of the corporate elite in symbiotic relation with political/bureaucratic elites."[26] The extent, if any, to which this perspective is an accurate picture of reality obviously has great relevance to any theory as well as practices attempting to promote citizen participation in public policy making.

The Sickness of Canadian Society and Politics – Diagnosis and Prescription

Throughout the 1960s and into the 1970s (and still today as a minor theme) there was the fairly common contention that "this land is sick."[27] Much of this sickness is said to be closely related to the elitist nature of Canadian society. Stated differently, lack of citizen participation in public policy making is symptomatic of a general sickness of society, particularly considering the extent to which our daily lives are affected by a seemingly infinite number and variety of government rules, regulations and activities. Given the diagnosis, the cure, not unexpectedly, is more citizen participation and therefore more control over ourselves through control of both public policy making and implementation.

Looking at actual citizen participation in Canada, there is an increasingly large body of empirical data on how, and to what extent, Canadians actually attempt to influence political choices. Much of this data is based on voting behavior, but some information is also available concerning such related political activities as expressing opinions, writing to legislators, membership in political parties. It has been found that Canadians, like citizens of other countries studied for similar activity, differ markedly among themselves as to their degree of participation. A fairly well-known scheme for categorizing these differences in terms of the degree of commitment and effort involved is the "hierarchy of participation" developed in the United States by Lester W. Milbrath.[28] At the lowest level of the three-tiered hierarchy are grouped the great majority of those identified as actual participants. This tier represents the lowest degree of commitment as expressed by the behavior attached to it and involves such participant activities as voting, discussing politics and being interested in politics. This tier is labelled "spectator." The top tier is termed "gladiatorial" and includes participants who are actively engaged in political party affairs, with the ultimate "gladiator" being the person who actually runs for public office. The middle tier is "transitional" between these two groupings of activities, and refers to such behavior as attending political meetings and contributing some time to political campaigns by, for example, addressing and stuffing envelopes.

In applying this scheme to Canada in an actual (1965) electoral participation survey, it was found that Canadian participation conforms to this hierarchical model. The data indicate that 4.4 per cent of Canadians could be called gladiators, 21.8 per cent transitional, and 73.3 per cent spectators. Canadian politics, on this basis, can indeed be considered a spectator sport. However, the lack of strong commitment to participate suggested by these figures is actually far greater, in that, as the author points out, approximately 40 per cent of all Canadians eligible to participate did not do so to the extent necessary to place themselves even in the lowest tier of the participation hierarchy. These people, in general, are of the lowest socio-economic categories, at or below the poverty line.[29] Because they provide virtually no input into the political system, it might be presumed they have no control over the outputs of that system.[30] (It can be argued, of course, that their interests are not necessarily ignored if the political/bureaucratic elite regard such interests as important and deserving of support).

Excluding the United States, Canada is deemed to have a relatively high degree of citizen participation compared to other countries, participation as expressed in voter turnouts as well as in terms of other indicators of political activism. However, perhaps due to unfavorable comparisons with the United States, or failure to meet standards held by various commentators on the subject, we are often said to have low political participation levels. For example, the data noted above can easily, depending on one's ideals about democracy, be said to represent a deplorable (also normal, reasonable or proper) situation.

There have been a wide variety of reasons suggested for the low levels of citizen participation in Canada. Some have empirical bases, while others are obviously more speculative, but none has been accepted as *the* explanation.

For example, it has been argued that Canadians have a colonial mentality evidenced by such things as slow evolution away from British dominance, retention of the monarchy, the lack until recently of a distinctively national flag. This mentality, it is suggested, is also indicated by a tendency toward national characteristics such as subservience, and dependent attitudes toward political leaders. A related argument points to weak national identity on the part of Canadians, and given this, there is low identification with the political system of the nation and therefore low participation in that system.

Another line of explanation points to specific structures and processes in the Canadian political system. Political parties are said to be weak devices for creating and maintaining citizen participation in Canada due to the way they are structured and operate. For example, the parties are said to be so disciplined that they allow for very little individual thought and action and therefore free-thinking individuals tend to back off from them. Political parties may want the citizen's support at election time, but they are alleged not to really want anything further from her/him and therefore not only make no effort to encourage further participation but, rather, seek to discourage it.[31] Furthermore, when parties do achieve office, other features of the political system are said to ensure that little if any effort is made to draw Canadians into further participation between elections. Thus, for example, there has been the rise of executive federalism epitomized by the meetings of first ministers, and also the apparent great unwillingness of political leadership to share basic information with the people — all, presumably, because they do not want, perhaps fear, activism on the part of the people should the latter have the information.

In general, there is nothing new about recent and current demands for citizen participation. Throughout the centuries there has been opposition to both elite theory and elite practice. In the 20th century, for example, there has been the phenomenon of national independence movements, justified by the general democratic aspiration of self-determination as opposed to the elitist nature of colonial dominance. The history of Western Europe, particularly in the 18th and 19th centuries, has quite typically been explained on the basis of growth in democratic theory and practices. The situation deplored by Ortega y Gasset was one of the natural, and desired by many, outcomes of the 19th century enfranchisement of groups previously excluded from the various electoral systems. Canada itself, in 1867, showed both the trend toward electoral egalitarianism as well as contemporary views on who should not have the right to vote. Women, for example, were initially excluded, and there were also certain significant property qualifications. These restrictions were gradually eliminated, the most recent major changes involving the enfranchisement of native people and of the age group 18-20.

Today, however, anti-elitism in Canada is not emphasizing enfranchisement of previously excluded groups, the right to vote apparently being generally accepted as sufficiently extensive. Rather, the emphasis is on increasing citizen participation and citizen impact on public policies by means beyond, and if necessary at the expense of, the normal devices. Stated differently, much of the concern expressed for increased citizen participation is directed toward basic change to the political system, as opposed to simply adding more elective offices to that system — although the latter course is not without its proponents.

One argument has it that this increased emphasis on other *forms* of political participation is the result of the fact that those institutions which are supposed to resolve conflict no longer do so. Since in this view the elite actually governing is not necessarily the same as the elected political elite, and since the institutions wherein decisions are really made are not necessarily those to which we elect our politicians, then it is natural enough that the democratic urge and desire to participate politically should take non-conventional modes of expression. Parliaments, that is, are not destroyed in this process, but rather are simply bypassed by the democratically-oriented citizen since they have already been bypassed by the decisional elite.[32]

It is also urged that contemporary democracy is really only an apology for or a facade to hide the elitism that prevails in Canadian politics. Horowitz,[33] for example, asserts that democracy, like many other terms in the twentieth century, has become subject to "doublespeak." This involves a process of adjusting ideals to reality as opposed to attempting to make ideals real. We do not state what democracy is to us in ideal terms, and then attempt to achieve some reasonable approximation of that ideal. Rather, we say that Canada is democratic, and therefore what characterizes Canadian politics is judged to be democratic. If Canadian politics is characterized by elitism, as opposed to widespread participation and control, we build elitism into our definition of democracy, label it contemporary democracy, or consociational democracy or whatever, and all is well.

The counter-view of democracy often advocated today is more akin to the older *direct* democracy of some of the Greek city states than to the *indirect* democracy characterizing systems of representation evolved over the years. It rejects the negativism attached to citizen participation by contemporary democratic theory and suggests its positive orientation by the term "participatory democracy." It holds that people can be and should be involved in deciding of all matters that significantly affect them.[34] "The overriding consideration is not what is conducive to the stability of institutions, but what is conducive to the well-being of people." Participatory democracy, that is, stresses the "logical and moral priority of independent men and women."[35] This perspective does not accept that a political elite is inevitable just because it exists, nor that an elite is justified simply because of the functions that it performs. In this view, a political elite is more or less antithetical to the entire notion of democracy.

While specific dates in an ongoing process must be viewed with caution, if one wishes to point to a time period in Canada in which this stress on citizen participation became a major political theme, the decade of the 1960s appears the most appropriate. During those years a significant emphasis was laid on the *sickness* of Canadian society. Although much of the discussion and attendant action originated south of the border and there took on more overtly dramatic overtones, Canada clearly experienced a similar phenomenon and, some might argue, while participatory democracy was never pursued so dramatically in this country, it was also not terminated so dramatically.

In the United States the desire for political participation on the part of groups previously excluded from having a meaningful political voice quickly became apparent during the early 1960s. Evidence of the occurrence of basic political change, and the need for it, had been pointed out by some academics and public figures, but it was not until the 1960s that the idea became fairly widespread. John F. Kennedy's New Frontier officially heralded the new view. Although the two years of his administration before his assassination did not accomplish all that much either legislatively or actually, they set the stage for the rest of the decade. The beginning of the 1960s was a rather euphoric period in American politics which to a certain extent became translated into specific actions. Kennedy's death and subsequent martyrdom provided an impetus under which Lyndon Johnson attempted to achieve the Great Society. By the mid-1960s various broad, humanitarian programs had been initiated which had as their goal the achievement of substantial socio-economic changes. Externally, for example, there were the Alliance for Progress designed to create basic socio-economic as well as political change in Latin America, and the Peace Corps, dedicated to sending Americans throughout the world to work as socio-economic missionaries of the good life. Internally, the major breakthrough was the creation of the Office of Economic Opportunity. This new bureaucracy was deliberately created to administer programs most of which could logically have been placed in established departments—for example, the Department of Health, Education and Welfare, and the Department of Justice. The older bureaucracies were by-passed and the new bureaucracy established, quite clearly in order to get away from the established, tried-and-true administrative methods and procedures and to allow for imaginative, creative people to tackle the newly defined problems in innovative ways.

The essential purpose of the OEO was to cure the newly perceived sickness existing in American society in the form of marked poverty and racial injustice. It quickly became the view that this task was to be accomplished with "maximum feasible participation" of the groups to be served by the programs. Whatever this term might have meant to Congress when first used in the Economic Opportunity Act of 1964, it came to mean operationally a very strong emphasis on government *by* the people, not just *for* the people. Through the OEO and its interactions with affected groups a host of specific programs were launched, many based on the idea of self help through citizen participation in creating and implementing them. They included legal aid, residential health care, "head starts" for disadvantaged children, adult education, day-care centers for the children of working mothers, residential improvements through the provision of recreational and leisure time facilities and services, and dozens of others. A domestic peace corps, the Volunteers in Service to America (VISTA), an organization funded and operated by the federal government, paid young people subsistence wages and sent them into communities to help people help themselves (knowing full well that these people would inevitably become involved in attacks against "the establishment").

It was a rather heady, euphoric period in much of American society; generally disadvantaged groups began to become more politically active, increasingly less apathetic and quiescent. Then came the assassination of Martin Luther King, Jr. which sparked race riots. Very quickly the 1960s, which had begun so optimistically, took on a note of gloom, even despair. Representing hard-core conservatism, Barry Goldwater had lost his bid for the Presidency in 1964, but Richard Nixon won in 1968 and his assumption of office heralded the end of a citizen participation movement consciously supported by government structures. The war on poverty quickly ground to a halt, if for no other reason than lack of government-paid "soldiers" to fight in it. The OEO and many of its programs became more-or-less defunct, the programs retained given over to the older bureaucracies. While this political reversion did not insist on eradicating all gains made by the disadvantaged groups, there clearly was no longer great interest in promoting further gains for them except in a very incremental, evolutionary as opposed to revolutionary fashion. America's home-grown "great leap forward" was aborted in mid-air.

Canada does not appear to have experienced anywhere near the same dramatic emphasis on elimination of poverty, concern for the disadvantaged and underprivileged groups and on citizen participation as did the United States. Our experience has, in fact, been described as the Pearson government's "watered-down war on poverty."[36] The Canadian equivalent of the Peace Corps was the Canadian University Students Overseas (CUSO) organization. The Company of Young Canadians (CYC) was created in 1965 along the lines of and with a philosophy quite similar to VISTA's. There was no OEO but the Special Planning Secretariat of the Privy Council Office was established to coordinate government actions in the anti-poverty area at all three levels of government – actions carried out essentially through ongoing bureaucracies such as the Secretary of State and the Department of National Health and Welfare. The Senate Committee on Poverty in 1969 began a systematic examination of poverty in Canada in order to recommend to Parliament ways of dealing with it. The Local Initiative Programs (LIP) for neighborhoods, the Opportunities for Youth (OFY) programs, and New Horizons for the elderly were commenced.[37] Throughout these developments emphasis was placed on citizen participation, whether by itself as a general term or as a major component of another concept very popular at the time, "community development."

There are a number of reasons advanced to explain why the emphasis on citizen participation arose in the 1960s. For example, the increased bureaucratization of Canadian society is pointed to by some as a major (even *the*) contributing factor. If one recalls the concerns of Chapter 3, which focuses on beliefs about and attitudes toward modern bureaucracy, a common contention is that growth in bureaucracy has led to a pronounced degree of alienation on the part of citizens both from the general society and from government specifically. While this bureaucratization is often pointed to as contributing to lack of participation, it has also been singled out as crucial to growth in participation. In this latter view, a number of factors are involved. There is, for example, the constantly rising level of education which makes people less accepting and more questioning of political events. Relatedly, the mass media provide these more educated citizens information they simply did not have in earlier eras, and the citizens tend toward action because of it. They feel more competent to speak and act politically. Further, they feel greater need to engage in politics by other means than elections because they more readily perceive the weaknesses in traditional mechanisms; at the same time they face accelerating changes in their way of life, toward many of which they stand opposed. People also have more time to devote to political activity due to developments in the world of work and to a decline in interest in other time-consuming areas of life such as religion, the community and even the family.

Particular reference is often made to the community, due to the extent to which citizen participation and community development became virtually synonymous terms. With clear echoes of Elton Mayo, the argument has frequently been advanced that people find little meaning in their lives either at work or beyond it. The answer has often been to restore the community to the full, older meaning of the term. However, attempts to do this almost invariably encounter government bureaucracy. People find that virtually everything they want to do is hindered, often prevented, by a plethora of rules and regulations made and enforced by a bewildering array of government agencies, controlled by a host of impervious and imperious bureaucrats apparently insensitive to people's needs, including the need to achieve something meaningful for themselves.

Citizen participation was advanced in a variety of forms as a certain cure for the sickness of Canadian society, a society which, according to some, needed to be constantly prodded and jolted to be responsive to human and economic challenges.[38] The very practice of citizen participation, and then its successes, would overcome the alienation and sense of being exploited felt by the down-trodden of our society.[39] Even those other than the clearly disadvantaged were to benefit from increased citizen participation in that their feelings of being unable to understand continuing events in their society, their feelings of helplessness and even hopelessness in a complex world would be ameliorated.[40] Both the relatively powerless middle class and the utterly powerless, victimized lower class would gain, through increased citizen participation, the ability to challenge the dominance of the rich and super-rich. The movement would refute the traditional view that the rich and the poor both "deserve" what they get, by helping the poor to get "more" and by challenging the system which underlies and is utilized by the rich to maintain their position in society to the detriment of others.[41] And according to one line of argument diametrically opposed to consociational democracy's emphasis on the cultural-linguistic elite, citizen participation would cross over such spurious cleavages as language because the poor are the poor whatever language they speak, just as capitalist dominance is dominance regardless of the language used by the capitalists.[42]

This thrust toward citizen participation was given explicit, "official" recognition in Canada by the *Report* of the Special Senate Committee on Poverty (*Croll Report*) published in 1971. Although it addressed itself to recommendations on the issue of poverty itself, much of its argumentation can easily be viewed in a broader participatory sense.

The *Croll Report* was very much in favor of participation by the poor in the development and administration of policies and programs relevant to themselves. It clearly echoed the American "maximum feasible participation" notion in its assertion that for too long the poor in Canada "have been people to whom and for whom things were done."[43] Its contention was that, while we pay lip service to user participation, we are really much too addicted to bureaucratic methods. That is, public servants who *speculate* on what people want and need are the ones to plan programs. Conversely, we tend not to allow users, for example, mothers in day care programs, who know what they want and need to participate in this process. However, the *Report* urged that it is both necessary and, fortunately, possible in a democracy to include users in all aspects of planning and organization of the services intended for them.

On this basis, the *Report* recommended the adoption of a consistent policy of including users of services on the boards of agencies in "consequential numbers"—"perhaps a third." This would provide genuine motivation for the formation and subsequent participation of citizen groups. These groups would have the opportunity to choose representatives, survey opinions, learn of decisions and research, point out needs, and suggest innovations.[44] This participation would continue beyond the policy planning and decision stages into the implementation of policies. Users would become an integral part of the entire policy process.

Further official recognition of the citizen participation emphasis was provided by the Task Force on Government Information, which pointed to a distinct and substantial potential problem for Canadian government should it fail to engage citizens in "relevant consultation."[45] The fear was that if citizens were not consulted to a significantly greater degree, then disaffection, alienation, apathy, and political ignorance would relentlessly increase.

Thus, by the end of the 1960's "Prime Minister Trudeau declared his allegiance to participatory democracy" and citizen groups were springing up all across Canada while Cabinet ministers and task forces toured the country seeking citizen reactions.[46]

This movement, it was argued, possessed strong overtones of millenarianism and messianism. Aryah Coperstock has called it the "New Religion of Citizen Participation,"[47] a religion spreading across the country and emphasizing the right of citizens to determine how they shall live. The new faith is described in the following terms: Its litany is "Power to the People"; its dogma is "Only local people can understand"; its mother church is the United States and its saints and martyrs are Martin Luther King and Malcolm X; its prophets are Stokely Carmichael and Saul Alinsky and its rites are sit-ins, marches, and confrontations; its ritual objects are buttons and picket signs; its deity is The People; and its devils are Vested Authority and The Establishment. He suggests other names for this new faith are community control, participatory democracy and grassroots democracy.

Less sardonically, Wilson Head[48] suggests that the ideology of the citizen participation movement in Canada as in the United States has been based on five assumptions. First, it is assumed that the ordinary citizen has the right to participate in the decisions that affect his life. Second, the disadvantaged groups have reached the point where they are ready to rebel against the system if their demands are not met. Third, the group that is organized represents, it speaks for, the citizens of the area or socio-economic category to which they, the group, belong. Fourth, activities of the group are non-political in the sense that they are above the bargaining and compromising of partisan politics. And fifth, the poor are not responsible for their position in life — they are there due to the operation of a system which discriminates against them while favoring others.

The all-embracing goal of the citizen participation movement in Canada can be summarized as the achievement of participatory democracy. Although this term is at times denigrated on the grounds that its two parts constitute a redundancy and therefore further confuse an already difficult concept, the adjective "participatory" is added to indicate a qualitative difference between itself and what is commonly called "representative democracy."

The Canadian political system allows the citizen to participate in selecting a party leader and party constituency candidates, and ultimately to vote on election day. The person thus elected "represents" the people of the geographic constituency. This representative idea has developed over the years to replace earlier forms such as that advocated and at times practised in the Greek city state and much later forms developed in North America which might be classified as "town hall democracy." Both the theoretical and practical justification for replacing these older, direct forms of democratic citizen participation with indirect participation through election of representatives has been and remains the increasing scope and complexity of government activities. It is quite impossible to get all the people of Canada or even all the people of a single province together in order to hold political discussions and arrive at policy decisions. Given increasing size and density, this is not possible even at the city level or, for that matter, at the city district level. Thus, it is argued that the election of representatives as it now occurs is the only practical way in which citizens of a large, modern, complex society can participate in their government.

However, the belief is frequently stated that the casting of one's vote has become a meaningless exercise. Some of the more typical arguments justifying this contention are: each political party in its attempt to gain the widest possible support at election time creates a platform so broad that it becomes indistinguishable from the other parties' platforms and we therefore are given no realistic alternatives for which to vote; if a party should provide real alternatives, we would probably be voting for certain items that we do not want in order to obtain those we do want; each party is dominated by an oligarchy and the citizen has no real voice in party affairs despite any democratic facade that may exist; and parties and individual candidates promise all sorts of things in order to get elected and, once elected, proceed blithely to ignore all their promises.[49]

Writing at the peak of the citizen participation movement Frederick Thayer stated that "a new theory of democratic government is emerging, one which defines 'participation' as the central right of all citizens." He contended that "voting, in *any* form, does *not* meet any meaningful definition of 'participation'." He suggested that as the right to meaningful participation gains in strength, electoral processes will diminish in importance. Also, "disenfranchisement" will come to mean depriving people of the new right to meaningful participation.[50]

Given belief in these kinds of arguments, new forms of citizen participation in political affairs become necessary if one is to remain convinced of the value and practicability of democratic government. That is, if one accepts the view that representative democracy is not in any meaningful sense "real democracy," then one can either give up on the whole idea of attempting to pursue democratic government in modern society or try to create new, or revive old forms for achieving meaningful citizen input.

In essence, the argument is that more and more Canadians are realizing that they are not receiving even minimally acceptable policies from the political system as it is at present constituted, and are attempting through creation of citizen participation to push their claims for what they consider to be their proper place in the sun. In a sense, citizen participation becomes a panacea in that through participation citizens can cure the sickness of Canadian society. Stated differently, while Canadians may have their bread and their circuses, they have the ability to define neither the flavor of the one nor the program of the other.

The Possible Significance of the Cure

There is obviously great significance for public administration if demands for citizen participation continue and particularly if they increase to the point that politicians and administrators must give serious heed to them. The making of public policy, both at the macro and micro levels, will include formally or informally, many other actors than at present. That is, affected, organized citizens in every policy area vociferously insisting on their right to participate meaningfully in public policy decisions is a situation that the present modes of policy making do not have to take into account. Routine administration of policies would also be greatly affected because, rather than simply delivering programs to recipients according to administratively-defined criteria and procedures, the administrator would face this organized public not only insisting on helping to devise the policies but also, presumably, insisting upon supervising and criticizing their implementation. In short, if the citizen participation movement is successful in gaining meaningful control over public policy making and implementation, the "blind and ruthless partisanship of red tape," would be seriously challenged.

However, there is ample room for doubt that the citizen participation movement will accomplish very much of genuine, lasting significance. There is even some room for doubt that the citizen participation movement, if it ever was indeed a "movement," is all that strong today.

There does not appear to be an overall, definable end goal held in common by various activated citizen groups. Terms such as the "just society," "social justice for all" and "participatory democracy" are fine in theory, but indefinable in practice. At times, given the vehemence of its advocates, one could legitimately conclude that citizen participation is being sought for its own sake. That is, since achievement of citizen participation is so greatly stressed, and since specific goals are often so poorly if at all articulated, citizen participation becomes *the* goal, not at all unlike the idea of learning for learning's sake or, more relatedly, voting for voting's sake — "It doesn't matter who you vote for, but vote."

In this respect, recall that Chapter 2 emphasized the extent to which values and value conflicts of the larger society invariably are reflected in the sub-society, the organization. One might assume, therefore, that participative management might bear a resemblance to participatory democracy. In actual actual fact, the resemblance is quite strong, in that a fair description of the latter term could be "macroscopic modern motivation theory."

In motivation theory a key element was participation in the management function by workers, *not* for the resulting greater material rewards, but simply for its own sake. Participation was seen in the theory as having a positive meaning in and of itself. The term "self actualization" is commonly attached to this notion. Similarly, the citizen in a democracy, entirely aside from material desires and thought of gain, is seen by many as self-actualizing when he/she participates meaningfully in the management of the community. That is, while policy outcomes with their attached rewards and/or deprivations cannot be ignored, the ability to participate meaningfully in deciding those outcomes is regarded as a desirable end goal in itself.[51]

In the macro-level literature on participation this distinction is stated in terms of "consummative" and "instrumental," or "subjective" and "objective." Instrumental or objective participation is essentially a means to an end. One participates in order to influence positively desired policy alternatives. Consummative or subjective participation, on the other hand, is seen as valuable in itself. One participates in order to somehow develop one's potential as a human being or, more specifically, to develop and to practise one's capabilities as a citizen. The distinction between consummative and instrumental participation is said to date back at least to Aristotle.[52]

However, while the distinction may sound fine in theory, and while attempts are occasionally made to provide examples of each in practice, nevertheless the distinction appears incapable of being put into operation. That is, organization theory is split as to actual motivations of people in work settings, as evidenced by the conflict between, say, modern human resource management theory and the literature emphasizing the bureaupathological behavior of people in large organizations. Similarly, it appears quite impossible to say what actually motivates people to participate politically.

For example, what is the motivation of people who spend a great deal of their time and mental and physical energy as members of "citizen boards"? Assuming that they receive no financial remuneration for this activity, which is normally the case, why do they pursue it? One answer, based on a positive-tending assumption about the nature of man, would be that they are somehow self-actualizing, finding personal satisfaction simply from doing something worthwhile. Another answer, however, based on a negative-tending assumption about the nature of man, would be that they are essentially on an "ego trip," that they are after personal prestige and/or power. The point is, however, that the validity of each assumption is equally questionable and the conflict between the two has not been resolved. To say that the truth lies somewhere between the two extremes is also not only questionable, but not very helpful.

However, despite any emphasis on citizen participation as an end in itself, it must also be seen as a means to other ends, however ill-defined and various these end goals may be.

This raises another serious potential problem for the movement. As long as citizen participation is being sought as an intermediate goal, it provides the heterogeneous groups with something in common; therefore they may have a good chance of achieving a definite, even if difficult to discern and describe, impact on the political system in Canada. However, the more this intermediate goal is attained, the less commonality will exist in the citizen movement as the various groups proceed toward attainment of specific goals which, in all probability, will come into conflict with one another and with overall system goals. The very commonality of the goal to participate will work toward self-destruction simply through its own attainment because, as it increasingly becomes a means, more specific goals will work against one another.

For example, a grey power group and a student power group may have in common the seeking of power for themselves, "power" to be regarded as a desire of old and young to participate in decisions affecting themselves. However, should the power goal be achieved by each, what do the old and the young then share in common? Such programs as, say, heavily government-subsidized housing for the elderly and free tuition for university students do not necessarily conflict — they are not logically, inherently opposed to one another. But funds are not limitless and government may not be capable of responding fully or even at all to the demands of the two groups, given all its other commitments. Both groups might get considerably less than they are demanding, and both will continue to be unhappy. Or one will be favored over the other, leaving the latter with feelings of injustice, even of hostility toward "the system." Furthermore, government must raise revenues in order to meet such demands, and in this activity quite easily may offend still other groups.

Or, for example, assume for purposes of argument that a capitalist elite dominates the Canadian political system. In this context, consider the demands for meaningful participation of minorities such as Canadian Indians, Eskimos, and "lower class whites" as well as of the majority middle-class white Canadians. Assuming that all these gained "meaningful political power" through severe curtailment of elite power, can we also reasonably assume that they would then pursue more specific common goals? It is extremely unlikely that they would. While Indians, Eskimos, and Metis may share in common the desire to gain political power to use as a means of escaping what in their view is hateful, unwarranted middle-class, white dominance, there exists at times great tension among themselves due to other factors manifested in specific issues.

Similarly, while lower- and middle-class whites, who clearly constitute a great majority of the total Canadian population, may share a desire for more meaningful participation in the political system, certainly they do not hold a world view in common and cannot realistically be expected to agree among themselves on many basic points. For that matter, as indicated in some of the arguments in Chapter 3, it is commonly contended that it is the middle-class nature of government in general and of bureaucracy in particular against which lower class people are said to be reacting—regardless of race. That is, while middle-class Canadians are often claimed to be reacting to such things as the very heavy taxation burden they carry in order for government programs to be carried out, the lower-class are seen as reacting to a great extent to middle-class dominance of themselves achieved by means of government programs directed at them.

Moreover it is a great distortion of reality to see such socio-economic categories as "white middle class" as "groups" in a unified, political-actor sense. While in a very generalized way they might be seen as a group demanding such a generalized goal as more citizen participation, beyond these extreme generalities the middle class includes the elderly, the young and the middle-aged, automobile users and transit users, urbanites and suburbanites, men and women, Maritimers and Albertans, French Canadians and English Canadians, public sector employees and private sector employees, union leaders and members and managers and entrepreneurs, and so forth *ad infinitum*. As voting data indicate, these are or can be significant political variables and one cannot simply dismiss them by referring to the "middle class," nor can one reasonably expect them to disappear in a spirit of one-for-all and all-for-one should the middle class be successful in achieving more meaningful political participation and therefore more actual political power.

Taking a different tack, the most (for better or worse) that might occur from demands for meaningful citizen input into public policies and administration is a greater degree of political pluralism. If public policy in Canada today is in fact dominated by relatively few political actors, then more significant actors would be added to the scene and public policies would reflect this. However, in practice political pluralism does not necessarily imply participation of all concerned in a pluralist society, far less does it imply equality in competition of all politically active groups. One of the major, constant criticisms of pluralist democracy is that it tends to assume some sort of equality among the competitors, whereas in practice groups are quite unequal, varying greatly in such things as membership numbers, financial resources, social prestige, leadership and group consciousness. That is, some groups compete from a very disadvantaged position, and pluralism, according to many, results in a strong bias toward maintenance of the status quo. If this is so, then one wonders what is to be gained by currently disadvantaged groups in Canada if they, through success of the citizen participation movement, find their potential political gains countered by the political gains of all the other groups?

As a specific example of this general problem, there is the area of urban politics and administration which remains the focus of constant proposals for increasing citizen participation. In this general context there has been much debate over proposals, plans and actual policies for "urban renewal" — the recreation of viable, "decent" living areas in the core sections of urban centers. Cities tend to expand outward through creation of new suburban areas, while the older residential areas tend to suffer a downgrading in actual value, often becoming outright slums comprised of what were once substantial homes. The controversy over such areas is multi-faceted, but one common aspect concerns the upgrading and maintenance — in general, the "proper" utilization — of these old homes. There has been much discussion of the role of citizen participation in deciding on the specifics in this issue, and a tendency to see this participation simplistically as being comprised of poor people attempting to make their life circumstances more congenial.

The notion of poor people being the primary participants, certainly the dominant participants, with the overall goal of urban renewal stated in their terms is much too simplistic. In fact, such citizen participation has definite, although by no means inevitable, potential for increasing rather than decreasing existing inequalities. Since such participation is typically of an "open shop" nature, there is a distinct tendency for those people who actually participate, are most articulate, take on leadership roles, and often dominate the situation, to have more education and income than are the norm. As a result, what might appear on the surface to be a populist phenomenon may in reality be manipulation, even if unconscious, of the majority by a minority. This, for example, is the situation which prompted the Committee on Government Productivity (in Ontario) to ask: For whom are the downtown neighborhoods being saved? Are they being saved for the "lower income people who have always lived there, or for nice young couples with jobs in universities and ad agencies with lots of bright ideas for renovating old houses?"[53]

In general, there is perhaps in the literature on citizen participation a blindness to genuine differences among socio-economic groupings. The middle-class groups can be, and in a generalized way probably are, supportive of the goal to eliminate poverty, of allowing other disadvantaged groups to participate equally in the benefits of Canadian society. However, the question of the extent to which this is an intellectual commitment that does not hold up in concrete situations can easily be raised. Examples of our failure to live up to our convictions abound. For example, the professional philosophy today in the care of the mentally handicapped, a philosophy apparently with generalized social support, is that such people should not be shut away, out of our sight in institutions, as they were in the past. They should, instead, be made a part of the larger community, allowed to function openly within their capabilities. However, when it comes to actually implementing this notion, trouble soon appears. If the route desired is to de-institutionalize by placing these people in group homes scattered through the city, the immediate, practical question soon arises: Where are these group homes going to be located and operated? Immediately there appears a reaction along the lines of: Sure, I'm all for integrating them, but I don't think my neighborhood is the best place. The same is true for group homes for juvenile delinquents, for subsidized housing for native people and even for little children who are wards of societies. As often as not it seems that a government, along Rousseauian lines, has to *force* us to live up to our ideals.

Another point to be thought about in this context is whether we, as citizens, have the right, moral as well as legal, to impose our views in situations which we can dominate. To say "yes" tends automatically to place us in the position of elite. We dominate and therefore our wishes will be pursued. To say "no" is to imply that either there is a still more dominant elite who will impose its will on the situation, or there is a higher morality than citizen morality. If the latter is the case, then there must be some sort of elite doing the defining, whether or not they are capable of enforcing the definition.

For example, it has been found that opinions are often held and expressed by large numbers of people virtually without information on the subject in question. Furthermore, people will form opinions in the absence of information, and will then select information conforming to their opinions, rejecting what does not. While this may in fact often be the case, it is quite another matter to take an evaluative stance and suggest that this type of opinion should not be used in policy formulation or in assessing what "the informed few" are likely to think or do.[54] This is essentially advocacy of elitism along Platonic lines. The elite is either the informed few or, perhaps more likely, it is those who define the membership of the informed few. For example, to exchange the informed few of the bureaucracy for the informed few of the general citizenry would not appear to contribute all that much to democratic aspirations — unless one adopts a markedly elitist concept of democracy.

All this relates ultimately to electoral behavior and ignores policy-relevant behavior of another kind. In this respect Canadians have many opportunities to participate in specific public policy fields if they would just avail themselves of them. For example, Children's Aid Societies across the country very often have difficulty in maintaining full membership on their boards. Community clubs frequently experience difficulty, even failure, in maintaining themselves as viable community enterprises due to lack of citizen interest. Task forces and commissions of enquiry are popular at all three levels of government, but their public hearings are typically poorly attended. This failure to participate can be argued to be symptomatic of a much more general social condition in that churches, unions and voluntary associations of all kinds experience similar failure. According to this view, we are perhaps fortunate to have even as much political participation as we do have — whatever that level actually is — because Canada, like other modern societies, is really not a participant society. We are all so self- and materialistically-oriented that we do not have the interest for any other-oriented activities.

On the other hand, there is the often emphasized notion of *meaningful* participation; it may be the case, as some contend, that to a great extent these democratic opportunities are facades in that they are not and are not intended to be conducive to genuine citizen participation in public policy formation or implementation.

Concerning this point, Sherry R. Arnstein[55] has advanced another tiered perspective of citizen participation which she calls the "ladder of citizen participation." While her concern is with those generally excluded from the forms of participation indicated in Milbrath's hierarchy, the ladder can also be seen to include many white, middle-class attempts to influence public policy. It is based on a distinction between the "empty ritual of participation" and "having the real power needed to affect outcomes." In this perspective, while citizens may be engaged in a variety of ways in participating in the public policy process, the critical question is: What *impact* do they really have in determining outcomes?

There are eight rungs in Arnstein's ladder, grouped into the three categories of "non-participation," "degrees of tokenism," and "degrees of citizen power." The non-participation category includes the first rung (manipulation) and the second (therapy). This kind of participation is not even intended to allow people to help plan and/or conduct programs, but rather is designed to enable those already holding power to "educate" and "cure" the participants. Rungs three (informing), four (consultation) and five (placation) are deemed "tokenism" in that they allow, and are intended to allow, citizens to be "heard," but are not intended to allow nor do they allow citizens to be "heeded." There is no real power for citizens in this kind of participation. The highest rungs of the ladder, apparently seldom attained, include degrees of actual citizen power to influence outcomes in public policy. Rung six (partnership) enables citizens to bargain meaningfully with ongoing power holders, while in the cases of rung seven (delegated power) and, ultimately, rung eight (citizen control) the citizens achieve at least "majority power" in public decision making situations.

Overall, then, in this view there are significant gradations of citizen participation in terms of decisional power, and these gradations enable greater understanding of demands for citizen participation. The argument is that, while there are many apparent opportunities for citizen participation, these seldom include *meaningful* participation and, it is implied, many people realize this. The government may have all sorts of citizen boards, may officially advocate citizen involvement in decision making but, according to this view, a great deal of this is rhetoric designed ultimately to provide a facade behind which the politicians and bureaucracy continue to do exactly what they have already determined to do.

Another factor to be considered is the possibility of lack of congruence between expressed desires for citizen participation and the ideas of current management theorists. While the two do not necessarily conflict, the potential for conflict is considerable. Their overall participation philosophy may, as noted above, be similar, but this very similarity may in practice lead to conflict as each attempts to pursue that philosophy.

As Chapter 2 attempts to clarify, the strong thrust of current "modern human resource management" theory and much practice is to treat employees as reasonable, intelligent, self-responsible and self-controllable human beings. Employees are, in this view, capable of being self-motivated, if the organization provides the proper environment and conditions so as to allow them to strive toward self actualization goals. This argument, of course, includes government employees. While the idea does not extend by any means to advocacy of anarchism within the organization, it certainly can be termed "organization democracy." Organizational imperatives remain, but within their broad parameters the employees should experience considerable freedom to pursue self-goals as a means of achieving organization goals. As citizens of the organization, the emphasis is to provide them with positive meaning in their work life.

On the other hand, as noted previously, citizens external to the organization are regarded in the same philosophical perspective. That is, they are seen as reasonable, responsible human beings who are self-starting and self-directed under the proper conditions. It is to be the goal of government to create these conditions, allowing citizens to pursue their interests and thereby to benefit not just materially but also spiritually. Within the broad parameters established by national imperatives, citizens are to be free. They are not to be dominated, either by a self-seeking elite or by a do-gooder bureaucracy. As a citizen of Canada one is to find positive meaning in life through participation in the resolution of one's own problems.

There are, then, two levels at which Canadians may be viewed in the same philosophical light — as employees and as citizens. One view is of the micro society, the organization, and the other of the macro society, the community.

Concerning potential problems, there is first the fact that while much of the literature dealing with the individual as employee sees public servants as reasonable and responsible, a great deal of other employee-centered literature sees him as a bureaucrat in the pejorative sense of that term. The citizen participation literature tends strongly toward the latter, the bureaupathological perspective, in that bureaucracy is regarded as sick and imposing its sickness on society. Thus arguments in this area tend to take on a further problematical nature, since, as argued in Chapter 2, these are two broad, fundamental assumptions about the nature of man in organizations and there is no clear evidence pointing to the overall validity of either. Stated differently, while there is ample evidence for the validity of both, this "evidence," however, is to a great degree determined by the ideology of the individual engaged in the evaluation.

If the bureaupathological argument is correct, there would appear to be an easy answer to the problem of the desire for meaningful citizen participation and the dominance of a cold, uncaring, perhaps even antagonistic bureaucracy. The citizens should so dominate the political system that their will is imposed on public bureaucracy, making it conform to citizen needs and wishes. However, this apparently easy answer, in addition to any consideration of how citizens can dominate the political system, is based on the operative word if. The great majority of Canadians engaged in formal employment situations are bureaucrats to one degree or another. Do we, as individuals, tend to see ourselves in the bureaupathological light? That is, do many of us see ourselves as sick in the bureaupathological sense? In all probability, most Canadians would answer "no" to this question. Some (and the numbers are quite debatable) might argue that if there is sickness then it is the organization that is sick, in that it is keeping us from performing as we would like to perform, preventing us from finding real meaning in our work.

If this view is accepted, then the solution can be restated: Somehow the organization must be revised so that it will not suffocate recipients of its services and at the same time allow its employees to self actualize. While this may seem reasonable at first glance, it does not really remove the problem of potential, even probable, conflict between citizen and bureaucrat. The solution assumes that the free citizen and the free public servant will want the same things, share common perspectives on problems, and arrive at common solutions. All will be sweetness and light.

However, the free citizen and the free public servant may easily come into conflict, in fact, they probably would. The public servant, for example, is an expert, trained and knowledgeable in his particular field. Will he have the same perspective on problems as do citizens with whom he interacts? He might, but in all probability, he usually would not. It is almost inevitable in such situations that the expert will perceive and assess many more and/or different factors in a situation than will the average citizen, and in general tend toward seeing the big picture while the citizen will tend to concentrate on his particular, immediate concerns. As a result, the turned-loose bureaucrat will probably arrive at solutions to problems which run counter to solutions seen by recipients of his services. Thus, the citizen cannot dominate if the dedicated public servant is to pursue his knowledgeable way, self-actualizing by doing good for others. On the other hand, the public servant cannot dominate if the citizen is to be free to pursue solutions to his own problems, gaining spiritual satisfaction in doing so.

Potential tension arising from the participative management being advocated in both organizational and social contexts can be easily seen in our school system. For example, an article in *The Canadian Administrator* in 1970 contended that two generalizations, supported by a variety of actual studies concerning teacher participation, were: 1) teachers want to assume responsibility for all activities directly related to instruction and 2) teachers favor increased autonomy for schools. The two generalizations are interdependent. The author argues that such wishes might be met by a change in administrative style — greater consultation with and sensitivity toward the teachers. Actually, he believes that fundamental change must come from genuine redistribution of power and influence in the school systems.[56] This involves decentralization of decision making from the upper, school board- and superintendent-level to the teacher level in the system.

On the other hand, the school system is often singled out as the ideal field for citizens to control to a significant extent one of the most important factors in modern society. It should be pointed out, that although major issues occasionally arise within a school district which create high levels of interest and participation, normally voter turnout for election of school boards is quite low, often extremely low. Candidates for board positions frequently win by acclamation.

It is often urged that we as citizens should change this, that we become heavily involved in school system policy making, not just in matters of budgets but in basic curriculum decisions, in determination of exactly what and how education will be delivered to our children. The end result of such urging, to the extent that it is effective, is to impose citizen control on the school district level which in the immediately preceding argument it is contended should be decentralized for the benefit of the teacher, not the citizen.

The point is, if we as citizens insist on dominating school policy, then that policy is not going to be decentralized in order to make teachers feel more useful. If decentralization does occur, teachers are going to resent and resist any push by citizens to force re-centralization of policy making in order to make citizens feel more useful. Of course, the positions here are stated rather dichotomously, and it is possible to suggest that a balance should be or can be sought between the two claims for influence. However, while this might be highly desirable and in theory possible, in practice the two thrusts tend to contradict one another.[57] School systems across Canada have indeed "been confronted with a rapidly expanding expectation from parents, teachers and other employees, and community members for participation in the making of a wide range of decisions." Furthermore, in spite of a general agreement that participation ought to occur in the field of education, "there is also a considerable degree of uneasiness and tension present concerning participation."[58]

One way around this type of conflict situation is to assign to the bureaucrat a rather saint-like nature and role similar to that ascribed to her/him by advocates of New Public Administration as discussed in Chapter 3. Thus, for example, in an article entitled "The Ethics of Participation"[59] the author suggests a distinction between the "official responsibility" of the bureaucrat and his "moral responsibility" toward his clients. On grounds of official responsibility the bureaucrat may refuse to allow the client to participate in any meaningful way in reaching decisions because he, the official, holds his job through competence and being assigned to it by superiors. Furthermore, he has not the right to delegate the task or part of it to someone without official status. On the other hand, the bureaucrat's moral responsibility is to help the citizen be a citizen, and should the citizen wish to feel himself morally responsible for participating in decisions, then it is the bureaucrat's moral responsibility to assist him to do so. That is, it is up to the bureaucrat, the possessor of competence and power, to do everything he can to help the seeker of participation to acquire similar competence and power. Thus, the bureaucrat is given not the negative role of saying, "You do not have the power or competence," but rather the positive one of saying, "I will help you gain power and competence."

The author concedes that while this may be the morality of the case, the politics of it will be different. And this idea does appear to call for a rather superhuman person. Moreover, the entire matter becomes entangled both practically and philosophically in the complexities not only between objective and subjective responsibility relationships, as discussed in Chapter 8, but also within each relationship. Certainly there is no obvious way of implementing the notion.

What is clearly involved is a very positive view of the nature of man, of man in his bureaucratic setting, and as Chapter 2 in particular emphasizes, there is great controversy between proponents of the positive view and those of the negative view. There is no way of proving either to the other's satisfaction, particularly since each is based on fundamental assumptions which are so "self-evident" to the believer that other views of reality are difficult to comprehend. Furthermore, even when one accepts a proposal such as the notion of the bureaucrat's moral responsibility, there remains the fundamental requirement for instrumental knowledge in order to operationalize it. That is, no matter how good an idea might be, it has no practical reality until we can somehow implement it. For example, one writer ascribes a rather heroic character to the unsung "fieldmen" of Canadian government, the front-line bureaucrats whose job is to help resolve social problems. They are the "front-line troops for democratic progress" who are urged to take on what amounts to an advocacy role for the people in the community they serve. They are to keep the upper echelons "well informed of the problems and frustrations encountered in the field" and are to act aggressively against hierarchical arrangements to remove "barriers that are impeding effective work in the community." The ills of bureaucracy are to be constantly guarded against, while they utilize bureaucracy to resolve social problems. "The fieldman — the frontline dispenser of social services — stands on strategic ground for the solution of this great dilemma of the modern industrial state."[60] However, while the writer very strongly states the case for what bureaucrats *should* do, his arguments are bereft of any practical, instrumental advice on *how* they can do this, given hierarchical constraints, complex accountability relationships, a disdainful public, politicians who may have a different view of reality, the existence of powerful organized groups whose interests might be inimical to bureaucratic solutions, and so forth.

There can be a real dilemma in this for the individual bureaucrat, the specifics varying from case to case but in any event leaving her/him with unpalatable choices. One must remember that, however its performance may be assessed, the merit system attempts to place competent people in government jobs. These jobs have formal constraints attached to them, and it is within these constraints and from a base of expertise that the bureaucrat must, legally, operate. For example, actions based on emotions such as liking and sympathy are, in bureaucratic terms, just as illegal as actions based on prejudice and hatred.[61] In this context, the individual bureaucrat must be prepared to defend his actions to his superiors in *job* terms, not in humanitarian terms. Furthermore, because of appointment based on competence the bureaucrat is an expert in his subject matter and will, typically, assess matters demanding decisions in terms of this expertise.

In the context of citizen participation, the great dilemma for the bureaucrats arises because of formal, objective responsibility requirements attached to their jobs, and demands for personal involvement with citizens as advocated in the notions of moral responsibility and front-line workers just described. What happens, in essence, is that both subjective and objective responsibility demands are placed on the bureaucrat. When these are compatible, all is relatively well. When these are incompatible, then the bureaucrat, in the vernacular, is caught between a rock and a hard place. When forced to choose, if he "goes by the book" he is the target of public ridicule, even hostility. If he accedes and perhaps goes against bureaucratic law and perhaps also against bureaucratic fact as embodied in his expertise he may, like Rudnicki of the CMHC (Chapter 9), find himself jobless or, as is more usually the case, find himself and his career shelved.

As an illustration, assume a hypothetical government program at its grass-roots, implementation phase. The program is to deliver a social service, and members of the community served constitute 50 per cent of a committee whose function is to determine exactly how the program is going to be implemented. This would include decisions on who would receive program benefits, the extent to which they would receive them, oversight of their use, and in general the oversight of the program's implementation so as to ensure that it achieves its purposes. The other 50 per cent of the committee is made up of government employees responsible for carrying out the decisions arrived at. Simplistically, the committee would appear as follows:

Now, on this committee superimpose the notions of accountability developed in Chapter 8. The situation would then be pictured as follows, again the broader arrows indicating lines of control and the lighter arrows the flow of accountability:

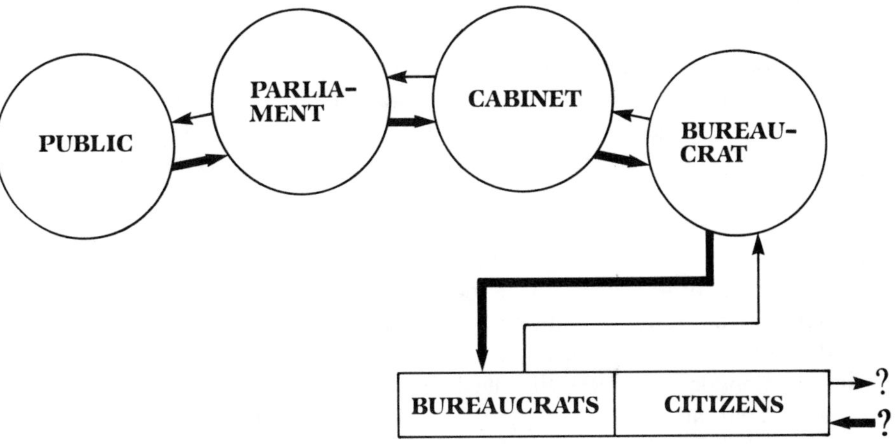

If one assumes that bureaucrats and citizens see exactly eye to eye then this relationship as pictured poses no problem. However, the extent to which bureaucrats and citizens *do not* see eye to eye determines the extent to which a problem of accountability will arise. Legally, the bureaucrat must be accountable to the larger department in the larger framework. He must, that is, at all times be aware of and predicate his decisions on the knowledge that he must account for them to the larger body. If the citizens are somehow elected by the community they will have an objective accountability relationship also, but not the same one as the bureaucrats must heed. If the citizens are not elected, then they do not have an objective accountability relationship to guide them. Furthermore, the two groups, to the extent that they are influenced by notions of subjective responsibility may not heed the same imperatives. The bureaucrat, remember, will have not only personal norms but also professional norms; but the citizen, while he would have personal norms would not, as a layman, have professional norms.

While this simplistic, hypothetical example does not suggest inherent conflict between the bureaucrat (the professional) and the citizen (the amateur), there is certainly great potential for it. The bureaucrat, because of his professionalism and the common human desire to feel "safe" has greater potential for seeing things differently than does the citizen. He is caught, then, between two forces: the force for accountability and the force for citizen participation — with limited ability to respond to both.[62]

One particular aspect of this situation leads to the general question of the extent to which we, as citizens, prefer public decisions to be rational. Chapters 4 and 5, it will be recalled, suggest that one way of assessing "proper" public policy making is to see it as falling along a rational-incremental continuum. The rationalist, systemic perspective insists that public policy making should be pursued with a clear definition of goal, definition and clarification of all alternative means for achieving the goal, evaluation of the various alternatives and selection and careful implementation of the best alternative. The decision is "right" because all relevant factors in the situation have been properly taken into account. The incrementalist approach, which is process-focused, suggests that public decisions should be made by the free play of political forces interacting in a compromising, bargaining fashion. In this view, public policy emerges, and it is assumed to be right because the process leading to it is right — that is, because the process is democratic the decision is good.

The proponents of citizen participation tend strongly toward the incrementalist perspective.[63] If they see present practice as leaning toward rationalism, then they argue it should be incremental in nature; or if they see it as incremental but dominated by powerful groups, then they feel it should be made open to all not just the relative few. In other words, advocates of citizen participation do not stress the need for "rational" (i.e., scientific) public decisions, but rather insist that public decisions be arrived at "democratically," incorporating the views and wishes of the public in general or, at the very least, of the affected groups.

Leaving aside the possibility that situations may be dominated by cynical, vested-interest elites, we must also take into account the opinion that it is exactly this catering to public whims, which has existed for many years, that has led to many of our current socio-economic problems. For example, it can be argued that "rational" approaches to the energy crunch become impossible if everyone is allowed to participate. This is because each person tends to approach such questions as oil conservation on the basis of "I'll consider you after I've looked after me."

Oil policy in Canada appears to be based on political rationality, which is a distinct component of incrementalism and is not to be confused with the rationality urged for public policy making in general. The Liberal Party claims to have a rational oil policy, but so too do the Conservatives and New Democrats, not to mention others such as the Alberta government. Each policy is claimed to be right, to be the best solution, and each is at present being sold to the Canadian public as parties pursue their views on political rationality.

In other words, one can argue that there is a strong element of incrementalism or "democracy" in decision making in the area of oil consumption or, conversely, energy conservation. This incrementalism clearly does not ignore popular preferences, tending to place heavy emphasis on interests of the moment rather than on future needs. On rational grounds — and there is no inherent contradiction between these and humanitarian interests — perhaps most Canadians do have concern for the future. However, it would appear to be quite secondary to our present desire to continue driving our own cars. This remains a constant, as we disagree over other matters such as federal versus provincial control of oil, sale of oil to the United States, and so forth. It all seems very democratic, but it is not necessarily rational in being what is best for us and for future generations of Canadians.

On the other hand, what acceptable alternative is there? If we do manage to consume all our oil in the next decade or so, then that is a decision that has been made by us as voting and consuming members of the public. That is, we vote parties into office, and if we do not ourselves stress conservation we cannot really expect the parties to pursue conservation *rationally*. Or, we may to some extent vote politically for policies leaning somewhat toward conservation, but we tend to counter this every time we vote with our dollars by buying more highly-taxed gasoline and driving our cars to work every day, usually just by ourselves.

Any alternative to this would somehow involve relinquishing some of our personal decisional powers. That is, if we are clearly not oriented toward conservation in a practical, personal sense, and if conservation is to become a fact, then we must somehow be forced to conform to conservational policies made "in the public interest" but not by us. These would involve careful consideration of a multiplicity of factors, evaluation of these to determine such things as the importance of each and their interrelatedness, and long-range government plans based on them.

Here, however, rationalism runs into great difficulty of a normative nature related to citizen participation. Every government planner, whether relatively specialized or generalized-comprehensive, must have goals to plan toward. That is, the planner cannot work in a vacuum and must have some conception of the public interest or national interest or interest of State. The comprehensive planner in particular must assume that his community's various collective goals can somehow be articulated and measured as to their relative importance. They then must be combined into a single hierarchy of community objectives.[64] Furthermore, the planner has to assume that people like himself can prescribe courses of action to achieve these objectives without negative side effects that would destroy the benefits to be gained through planning. And although planners themselves disagree over the extent to which they can be rational, by definition they must assume that they can be more rational, take more factors into account, than can other participants in decision-making situations. If they do not assume this, then there is no point in planning.[65]

If planners can indeed be more rational than politicians or the general public, then, of course, we would be well advised to heed their advice, to give it disproportionate weight in the making of public policies. That is, we should rationally concede that there ought to be a technocratic elite. However, this is not necessarily the case, and there are serious questions that can be raised on the matter. First and foremost, what does "planning for the public interest" mean when we cannot say unequivocally what the "public interest" is. Does "Canada" in an anthropomorphic sense want something? Or do "Canadians" want something? If Canadians do want something, is it in their overall interest to have it? An alcoholic or a drug addict, for example, wants alcohol or drugs, but is it in his best interest to have them? Children want many things which parents, in their best interest, deny them. Canadians want to continue to drive their own cars, but is it in their ultimate best interest to do so? Furthermore, is it at all realistic to say "Canada's interest" or "Canadians' interest"? How many citizens of Canada are involved in the statement "Canadians want to continue to drive their own cars"? Surely not all, because certainly not all Canadians drive cars or want to drive cars. So, if "public interest" is not 100 per cent, how great a percentage is it? Fifty per cent plus one, or 66 per cent, or 75 per cent? Conversely, does fifty per cent minus one not constitute a public interest, or 25 per cent or even five per cent? Questions of numbers aside, is the public interest to be determined only in terms of the present, or should it involve consequences for the future and the public of the future? If the latter, how much of the future should be included—our children, grandchildren? Do only those who are today old enough to vote get counted into the public interest? In short, both the normative and very practical questions surrounding such concepts as the public interest, which is itself necessary if we are to plan rationally to achieve it, can go on *ad infinitum* and the term has little if any operational value due to the inability to arrive democratically at answers to the questions.

This in turn leads to the argument that we *need* a knowledgeable elite along the lines advocated by Plato and Ortega y Gasset. Perhaps it is not so much a case of insufficient ability on the part of citizens to participate in the making of public policies, but rather a case of citizens having too great an ability to influence public policies with their passions and prejudices.

The dilemma is well illustrated by recommendations of the Economic Council of Canada in its Eighth Annual Review. On the one hand, it recommends that governments in Canada should become much more sophisticated in their use of data and decisional technology. They should, that is, become more rational, more scientific in their decision making. More specifically, there should be more training of government personnel in the policy sciences and universities should include more courses on the principles, processes and structures of government decision making. Special courses should be established for participants in public decision making.[66]

On the other hand, the Council points out that the ability to apply knowledge effectively is a basis of power, and therefore the concentration of such knowledge and ability should not occur only in government. Rather, private interest groups whenever possible should strengthen their analytical abilities so as to evaluate effectively government proposals and suggest their own alternatives. Their abilities would be greatly strengthened by governments clarifying and granting rights of access to government information so as to ensure that bureaucratic and political constraints do not inhibit the capacity to obtain and utilize relevant knowledge.[67]

Once again, however, this seems at best to point to a strengthening of political pluralism, and it does not appear to meet the case as stated by advocates of participatory democracy except in a peripheral fashion. Such advocates insist that the people are ready now to participate, and that they do not have to go back to school to do so effectively. Nor did the Council's recommendations resolve the question of who should participate. At face value, it was not recommending that only those who take training in such matters are to be allowed to participate. But unless some such notion is involved, the whole idea becomes rather pointless — unless one assumes that great numbers of us will voluntarily commit ourselves to pursuit of this academic effort, or the government will somehow compel us to obtain such knowledge so that we can participate effectively as citizens.

Conclusion

We return, then, to the basic question: Do we really want greatly increased citizen participation in policy making in Canada? On the one hand, many appear to be saying: While we feel as citizens that we can make good public decisions, it is in any event better to make less-than-good decisions ourselves than to be so limited as at present in making decisions at all. Many others seem to be insisting on a contrary position: We feel that it is better to have good decisions at the expense of citizen participation than to have poor decisions as a result of heavily increasing citizen participation. In the extreme, the one view insists that a public decision arrived at without public participation is almost by definition not a good decision, while the other contends that good public decisions almost by definition cannot be made by allowing the people actual choice in them. Furthermore, not only are we split among ourselves on this question, but as individuals, many of us are of divided mind. We may, that is, see desirability as well as practicability in both perspectives. Or we may accept the desirability of the one and the practicability of the other. We may normatively agree with the argument: "The overall consideration is not what is conducive to the stability of institutions, but what is conducive to the well-being of people."[68] On the other hand, we may in practical terms be inclined to accept Altshuler's viewpoint: "As the typical citizen values effective government much more than he values participation . . . the result of trying to involve and please everyone may be to please no one."[69]

In the middle stands the bureaucrat. Some, inclined toward the bureaupathological perspective, see the bureaucrat at best as a well-intentioned but anti-democratic influence, and at worst as a pernicious influence to be constrained if he cannot be eradicated. Others see the bureaucrat much more favorably, relying heavily on his expertise in helping to decide, at times even deciding, on solutions to pressing problems. Ultimately, the bureaucrat may, as W. Wronski suggests, face a dilemma leading to utter bewilderment.[70] As Chapter 8 portrays, the concept of accountability is extremely complex. If the bureaucrat attempts to obey his political master, the minister, he may irritate the public, and vice versa. If he pursues his conscience, he may please neither. His expertise may point to one path, and his need to survive may point to another.

For Further Reading

BOOKS AND REPORTS

Altshuler, Alan. *Community Control*. Washington: Urban Institute, 1970.

Clement, Wallace. *The Canadian Corporate Elite*. Toronto: McClelland and Stewart, 1975.

Connor, Desmond M. *Citizens Participate: An Action Guide for Public Issues*. Oakville, Ont.: Development Press, 1974.

Draper, James, A. ed. *Citizen Participation: Canada*. Toronto: New Press, 1971.

Government of Ontario. *Citizen Participation: A Working Paper*. Committee on Government Productivity, 1971.

Kornhauser, William. *The Politics of Mass Society*. New York: Free Press, 1957.

Kranz, Harry. *The Participatory Bureaucracy*. Lexington: Lexington Books, 1976.

McPherson, C. B. *The Life and Times of Liberal Democracy*. New York: Oxford University Press, 1977.

Mishler, William. *Political Participation in Canada*. Toronto: Macmillan, 1979.

National Voluntary Organizations. *The New Role of Voluntary Organizations in the Welfare State*. Ottawa: Report of the Second Annual Conference, 1976.

Pateman, Carole. *Participation and Democratic Theory*. Cambridge: Cambridge University Press, 1970.

Porter, John. *The Vertical Mosaic*. Toronto: The University of Toronto Press, 1965.

Schumpeter, Joseph. *Capitalism, Socialism and Democracy*. New York: Harper and Brothers, 1947.

Secretary of State, Canada. *Citizen Participation in Non-Work Time Activities*. Ottawa, 1974.

———. *New Citizens Organizations*. Ottawa, 1972.

Smith, Constance and Anne Freedman. *Voluntary Associations: Perspectives on the Literature*. Cambridge: Harvard University Press, 1972.

Smith, David and Valerie Ross. *Enhancing Citizen Participation*. International Association for Metropolitan Research and Development Secretariat, Intermet Working Papers Series, IWPS/Sec. C, 6 May 1973.

Thayer, Frederick, C. *Participation and Liberal Democratic Government*. Toronto: Committee on Government Productivity, 1971.

ARTICLES

Angus, W. H. "The Individual and the Bureaucracy: Judicial Review — Do We Need It?" *McGill Law Journal*, Vol. XX, 2 (July 1974), pp. 177-212.

Armitage, W. A. J. "A Structural View of Welfare Organizations." *The Social Worker*, Vol. XXXVII, 3 (July 1969), pp. 171-176.

Banovetz, James M. "Public Participation in Local Government." *Comparative Local Government*. Vol. VI, 1 (1972), pp. 54-60.

Bryden, Kenneth. "Some Observations on the Theory and Practice of Citizen Participation." (Paper prepared for the Annual Conference of the Institute of Public Administration of Canada. Halifax, September 1977.)

Childs, Richard S. "Citizen Organization for Control of Government." *The Annals of the American Academy of Political and Social Science*, Vol. 292 (March 1954), pp. 129-135.

Coperstock, Aryeh. "The New Religion of Citizen Participation." *Habitat*, Vol. XIV, 3 (1971), pp. 12-14.

Crenson, Mathew. "Organizational Factors in Citizen Participation." *The Journal of Politics*, Vol. XXXVI, 2 (May 1974), pp. 356-378.

Diamant, Alfred. "Anti-Bureaucratic Utopias in Highly Industrialized Societies." *Journal of Comparative Administration*, Vol. IV, 1 (May 1972), pp. 3-34.

Dion, Leon. "Participating in the Political Process." *Queen's Quarterly*, Vol. 75 (Autumn 1968), pp. 432-447.

Doyle, Robert U. "Perceived Effectiveness of Citizen Participation in Community Development." *The Social Worker*, Vol. XLI, 4 (1973), pp. 310-320.

Harding, W. M. "The Nature of Government and its Impact on Community Development." *Canadian Public Administration*, Vol. V, 1 (1962), pp. 117-126.

Henderson, Hazel. "Information and the New Movements for Citizen Participation." *The Annals of the American Academy of Political and Social Science*, Vol. 412 (March 1974), pp. 34-43.

Hollnsteiner, Mary Racelis. "People Power — Community Participation in the Planning of Human Settlements." *Assignment Children*, No. 40 (October-December 1977), pp. 11-47.

Kaufman, Herbert. "Administrative Decentralization and Political Power." *Public Administration Review*, (January-February 1969), pp. 3-15.

Krefetz, Sharon P. and A. E. Goodman. "Participation for What and For Whom?" *Journal of Comparative Administration*, Vol. V, 3 (November 1973), pp. 367-380.

Ladd, John. "The Ethics of Participation." *Participation in Politics*, Pennock, J. R. and J. Chapman, eds., New York: Lieber-Atherton, 1975.

Lemoine, B. Roy. "The Modern Industrial State: Liberator or Exploiter?" *Our Generation*, Vol. VIII, 4 (1972), pp. 67-95.

Lotz, Jim. "Citizen Participation, Innovation, and the Municipal Planning Process," *Habitat*, Vol. XIII, 4 (1970), pp. 16-23.

————. "Citizen Participation: Myths and Realities." *Optimum*, Vol. V, 2 (1974), pp. 53-60.

————. "Public Hearings — For Confrontation or Dialogue." *Optimum*, Vol. IX, 2 (1978), pp. 5-12.

McDonald, Virginia. "Participation in the Canadian Context." *Queen's Quarterly*, Vol. 84 (1977), pp. 457-475.

McNiven, J. D. "Bureaucratic Imperatives and Citizen Access: Some Theoretical Possibilities." *Optimum*, Vol. VII, 3 (1976), pp. 22-32.

Meade, Marvin. "'Participative' Administration — Emerging Reality or Wishful

Thinking?" *The Politics of the Federal Bureaucracy*, Altshuler, A. and N. Thomas, eds. New York: Harper and Row, 1977.

Meisel, John. "Citizen Demands and Government Response." *Canadian Public Policy*, Vol. XI, 4 (Autumn 1976), pp. 564-576.

Miklos, E. "Increasing Participation in Decision-Making." *The Canadian Administrator*, Vol. IX, 6 (March 1970), pp. 25-29.

Offe, Klaus. "The Ungovernability of Liberal Democracies." *Studies in Political Economy*, No. 3 (Spring 1980), pp. 5-16.

Perrow, Charles. "The Bureaucratic Paradox: The Efficient Organization Centralizes in Order to Decentralize." *Organizational Dynamics* (Spring 1977), pp. 2-14.

"Public Participation in the Federal Policy-Making Process." *Challenge*, Vol. XIX, 6 (1977), pp. 48-52.

Renshon, Stanley Allen. "Psychological Needs, Political Control, and Political Participation." *Canadian Journal of Political Science*, Vol. VIII, 1 (March 1975), pp. 107-116.

Rosenbaum, Walter A. "The Paradoxes of Public Participation." *Administration and Society* Vol. VIII, 3 (November 1976), pp. 355-383.

Saltzstein, Grace Hall. "Representative Bureaucracy and Bureaucratic Responsibility." *Administration and Society*, Vol. X, 4 (February 1979), pp. 465-475.

Smith, Richard Warren. "A Theoretical Basis for Participatory Planning." *Policy Sciences*, Vol. IV, 3 (September 1973), pp. 275-295.

Sproule-Jones, Mark. "A Description and Explanation of Citizen Participation in a Canadian Municipality." *Public Choice*, Vol. 17 (Spring 1974), pp. 73-83.

Stenberg, Carl W. "Citizens and the Administrative State: From Participation to Power." *Public Administration Review* (May-June 1972), pp. 190-197.

Stewart, Thomas R. and Linda Gelberd. "Analysis of Judgement Policy: A New Approach for Citizen Participation in Planning." *Journal of the American Institute of Planners*, Vol. XLII, 1 (1976), pp. 33-41.

Strange, John H. "The Impact of Citizen Participation on Public Administration." *Public Administration Review*, Vol. 32 (September 1972), pp. 457-470.

Van Meter, Elena C. "Citizen Participation in the Policy Management Process." *Public Administration Review*, Vol. 35 (December 1975), pp. 804-812.

van Poelje, G. A. "The Theory of Public Administration as the Theory of the Means Towards the Realisation of Social Ideas." *International Review of Administrative Sciences*, Vol. XXIII, 2 (1957), pp. 146-155.

Vauzelles-Barbier, Dorothee. "Public Participation in the Rehabilitation of Urban Centres." *International Social Science Journal*, Vol. XXX, 3 (1978), pp. 536-559.

Whalen, Hugh. "Democracy and Local Government." *Canadian Public Administration*, Vol. III, 1 (1960), pp. 1-13.

Wronski, W. "The Public Servant and Protest Groups." *Canadian Public Administration*, Vol. XIV, 1 (Spring 1971), pp. 65-72.

ENDNOTES

1. See Charles Taylor, "Power and Participation," in *The Pattern of Politics* (Toronto: McClelland and Stewart, 1975), pp. 97-127.
2. David Smith and Valerie Ross, *Enhancing Citizen Participation*. The International Association for Metropolitan Research and Development Secretariat, May 6 1973, pp. 2-3.
3. J.A. Riedel, "Citizen Participation — Myths and Realities," in *Public Administration Review*, May/June, 1972.
4. Francis MacDonald Cornford (trans.), *The Republic of Plato* (New York: Oxford University Press, 1960), p. 178.
5. George H. Sabine, *A History of Political Theory* (New York: Holt, Rinehart and Winston, 1961), p. 63.
6. Neal Wood and Ellen Meiksins Wood, *Class Ideology and Ancient Political Theory* (Oxford: Blackwell, 1978), p. 120.
7. Cornford, *The Republic of Plato*. See "Democracy," pp. 280-86.
8. Sabine, *A History of Political Theory*, p. 64.
9. José Ortega y Gasset, *The Revolt of the Masses* (New York: Norton, 1932), pp. 52-56.
10. *Ibid*., p. 60.
11. *Ibid*., p. 20.
12. *Ibid*., pp. 11-18.
13. Arend Lijphart, "Consociational Democracy," in Kenneth D. McRae (ed.), *Consociational Democracy* (Toronto: McClelland and Stewart, 1974), pp. 70-89.
14. *Ibid*.
15. *Ibid*.
16. Kenneth D. McRae, "Consociationalism and the Canadian Political System," in McRae (ed.), *Consociational Democracy*, pp. 238-61.
17. John Porter, *The Vertical Mosaic* (Toronto: University of Toronto Press, 1965), p. 212.
18. *Ibid*., p. 372.
19. *Ibid*., p. 27.
20. C.B. McPherson, "Model 3: Equilibrium Democracy," in *The Life and Times of Liberal Democracy* (New York: Oxford University Press, 1977), pp. 77-92.
21. Joseph Schumpeter, *Capitalism, Socialism and Democracy* (New York: Harper and Brothers, 1947).
22. Consociational advocates would not attach any legitimacy to the inclusion of the bureaucratic elite in this form of public decision making.
23. William Kornhauser, *The Politics of Mass Society* (New York: Free Press), 1957.
24. Gad Horowitz, "Toward the Democratic Class Struggle," in Trevor Lloyd and Jack McLeod (eds.), *Agenda 1970: Proposals for a Creative Politics* (Toronto: University of Toronto Press, 1968), pp. 241-55. See also Claus Offe, "The 'Ungovernability' of Liberal Democracies," *Studies in Political Economy*, No. 3 (Spring 1980), pp. 5-16.
25. Wallace Clement, *The Canadian Corporate Elite* (Toronto: McClelland and Stewart, 1975).
26. Virginia McDonald, "Participation in the Canadian Context," *Queen's Quarterly*, Vol. 84, 1977, pp. 457-75.
27. The term "sick" is deliberately used here because of the extent to which it appears as a description of Canadian society or aspects thereof in a wide variety of literature. In this context, one is reminded of the counterclaim summarized in the rather ill-fated Liberal slogan of the mid-1970s, "This Land is Strong."
28. Lester W. Milbrath, *Political Participation: How and Why People Get Involved in Politics* (Chicago: Rand McNally, 1965).
29. Rick Van Loon, "Political Participation in Canada: The 1965 Election," *Canadian Journal of Political Science*, Vol. III, 1970, pp. 376-399.
30. Milbrath subsequently refined his model in an attempt to be more precise. The earlier version is described here because it was the one related to the Canadian study by Van Loon.

The latter in turn is included here because it pertains specifically to the period of time during which the notion of "sickness" of Canadian society became most prominent. For a recent, extensive discussion of political participation in Canada see Wilson Mishler, *Political Participation in Canada* (Toronto: McMillan, 1979).

31. For example, see John Meisel, "Citizen Demands and Government Response," *Canadian Public Policy*, No. 4 (Autumn 1976), pp. 541-52.
32. Offe, "The 'Ungovernability' of Liberal Democracies."
33. Horowitz, "Toward the Democratic Class Struggle."
34. Carole Pateman, *Participation and Democratic Theory* (Cambridge: Cambridge University Press, 1970), pp. 110-11.
35. McDonald, "Participation in the Canadian Context."
36. Kenneth Bryden, "Some Observations on the Theory and Practice of Citizen Participation," (A paper presented at the annual conference, 1977, of the Institute of Public Administration of Canada, Halifax).
37. *Ibid*., and Jim Lotz, "Participation" *Habitat*, Vol. XIII, 4 (1970), pp. 16-23.
38. David Critchley, "Citizen Participation — Opiate or Opportunity?" *Canadian Welfare* (May-June, 1971), p. 13.
39. "The Montreal Citizens' Movement," *Our Generation*, Vol. X, 3 (1974), pp. 3-20.
40. Lotz, "Participation."
41. Ben Carniol, "Advocacy: For Community Power," *Canadian Welfare* (May-June, 1974), pp. 12-15.
42. B. Roy Lemoine, "The Modern Industrial State: Liberator or Exploiter?" *Our Generation*, Vol. VIII, 4(1972), pp. 67-95.
43. Croll Report, p. xviii.
44. *Ibid*., p. 97.
45. *To Know and Be Known* (Ottawa: Queen's Printer, 1969).
46. Critchley, "Citizen Participation — Opiate or Opportunity?"
47. Aryah Coperstock, "The New Religion of Citizen Participation," *Habitat*, Vol. XIV, 3 (1971), pp. 12-16.
48. Wilson A. Head, "The Ideology and Practice of Citizen Participation," in James A. Draper (ed.), *Citizen Participation: Canada* (Toronto: New Press, 1971).
49. The list of complaints is really quite extensive.
50. Frederick C. Thayer, *Participation and Liberal Democratic Government*. Committee on Government Productivity (Toronto, 1971). See also Alvin Toffler, *Future Shock* (New York: Random House, 1970), particularly pp. 416-30.
51. The integral relationship between the intra- and extra-organizational contexts of the same arguments has to date received relatively little explicit attention in either of the respective bodies of literature. For further discussion of the relationship see Marvin Meade, "'Participative' Administration — Emerging Reality of Wishful Thinking?" in A. Altshuler and N. Thomas (eds.), *The Politics of Federal Bureaucracy* (New York: Harper and Row, 1977); Pateman, *Participation and Democratic Theory*; and Bryden, "Some Observations on the Theory and Practice of Citizen Participation."
52. Bryden, "Some Observations on the Theory and Practice of Citizen Participation."
53. Committee on Government Productivity, *Citizen Involvement* (Toronto, 1972). For a case study of the poor and how they may relate to the citizen participation movement, see Maurice Pinard, "Poverty and Political Movements" in W.E. Mann (ed.), *Poverty and Social Policy in Canada* (Toronto: Copp Clark, 1970), pp. 250-64. This book provides excellent information and bibliography on the poor.
54. Richard J. Van Loon and Michael S. Whittington, *The Canadian Political System* (Toronto: McGraw-Hill, 1971), p. 78.
55. Sherry R. Arnstein, "A Ladder of Citizen Participation," *Journal of the American Institute of Planners*, Vol. XXXV, 4 (July 1969), pp. 216-24.
56. E. Miklos, "Increasing Participation in Decision Making," *The Canadian Administrator*, Vol. IX, 6 (March 1970), pp. 25-29.

57. A discussion of the two points is provided by W.D. Knill, "Community Decision Making in the Educational Area," *The Canadian Administrator*, Vol. VI, 5 (February 1967), pp. 17-20.
58. Rod A. Wickstrom, "Participation Revisited: Who Decides, When, and How Much," *The Canadian Administrator*, Vol. XIX, 2 (November 1979).
59. John Ladd, "The Ethics of Participation," in J.R. Pennock and J. Chapman (eds.), *Participation in Politics* (New York: Lieber-Atherton, 1975), pp. 98-125.
60. W.M. Harding, "The Nature of Government and its Impact on Community Development," *Canadian Public Administration*, Vol. V, 1 (1962), pp. 117-26.
61. For elaboration of this argument, see Chapter 3.
62. Some discussion of this is provided by Marry Racelis Hollnsteiner, "People Power," *Assignment Children*, No. 40 (October/December, 1977). See also Grace Hall Saltzstein, "Representative Bureaucracy and Bureaucratic Responsibility," *Administration and Society*, Vol. X, 4 (February 1979), pp. 465-75. For an excellent discussion on the utilization of citizen advisory agencies at the federal level, see C. Lloyd Brown-John, "Advisory Agencies in Canada: an Introduction," *Canadian Public Administration*, Vol. XXII, 1 (1979), pp. 72-91.
63. It should be noted that "incrementalism" as typically discussed in the literature on public policy and budgeting does not directly relate to citizen participation. The rationalist literature is often alleged to have an authoritarian bias, as opposed to the democratic nature of incrementalism. However, the latter seems to be related to ideas of *pluralist* democracy developed in the United States, and pluralist democracy, to some, is another way of saying elitist democracy.
64. See "Goals of Comprehensive Planning," *Journal of the American Institute of Planners*, Vol. XXXI, 3 (August 1965).
65. Richard Warren Smith, "The Theoretical Basis for Participatory Planning," *Policy Sciences*, Vol. IV, 3 (September 1973), pp. 275-95.
66. Economic Council of Canada, Eighth Annual Review, *Design for Decision-Making* (Information Canada, 1971), p. 229.
67. *Ibid*., p. 233.
68. McDonald, "Participation in the Canadian Context."
69. Alan Altshuler, *Community Control* (Washington: Urban Institute, 1970), p. 45.
70. W. Wronski, "The Public Servant and Protest Groups," *Canadian Public Administration*, Vol. XIV, 1 (Spring 1971), pp. 65-72.

CHAPTER ELEVEN

Summary and Conclusions

As the foregoing chapters emphasize, the field of public administration in Canada is ridden with problematical perspectives and contentions. There is great disagreement over the *facts* involved in studying public institutions as well as in studying the people who work within them. There is perhaps even greater dispute over *values* within the public bureaucracies, within the society which those bureaucracies serve and also between the bureaucracies and society. This situation is greatly exacerbated by the inter-relatedness of the various topical areas we have dealt with as well as the many areas which we have not specifically considered. That is, while one may, as we have done, select certain aspects of public administration and discuss each in relative isolation from other aspects, ultimately the whole must be at least partially perceived in order to understand the parts. This integral nature of public administration has been pointed to throughout this text, particularly in Chapter 10. Further consideration of the inter-dependence of the topical areas is the major concern of this final discussion.

In Chapter 2 discussion centered around differing assumptions about the nature of man in general and of bureaucratic man in particular. While these assumptions may be variously categorized and labelled, the approach utilized here was that of a pessimism-optimism continuum, with the argument that we tend, even if at times inconsistently, toward one side or the other of this continuum. It was then pointed out, using fairly commonly accepted terminology, that in earlier years administration was dominated in both theoretical and practical expression by pessimistic assumptions subsumed under the heading "the mechanistic tradition." Since the 1930s this tradition has lost much of its theoretical force and, to a definitely lesser extent, its practical force as well. It was replaced, at least in part, by humanistically based ideas and practices which, although they have changed in specifics over the years, are very much with us today. This humanism is based on a more optimistic perspective of human nature than prevailed in earlier years. The older, mechanistic perspective by no means ever fully died out. Partially out of its remnants and partially from other origins, another view of people in organizations has emerged. We have labelled this the "bureaupathological" perspective.

Thus we are left with two schools of thought, each with attendant voluminous and constantly expanding bodies of literature. The optimistic perspective, and practices based on it, tend to emphasize the inherent goodness, reasonableness and responsibility of people at work in large organizations, that is, of bureaucrats. Of course, the literature points to many problems in making these characteristics manifest, but nevertheless the underlying assumption about people here is clearly on the positive side. On the other hand, there is the pessimistic theory and a wide variety of practices based on it, indicating opposite-tending assumptions pushing toward quite different solutions to problems that appear in public administration. As an end result, the whole subject of people in public administration is pervaded by problematical contentions, appearing both very confused and confusing to the person attempting to understand its essential reality.

The reality of public bureaucracy was also the concern of Chapter 3 where discussion focussed on the broad assumptions apparently commonly held about bureaucracy and bureaucrats and their interrelationships with citizens and society. As with the nature of man notions in Chapter 2, the nature of bureaucracy discussion in Chapter 3 suggests change in perspective over time. In the later 1800s the predominant image of bureaucracy as expressed in the literature was generally quite negative. During the period between World Wars I and II this unflattering picture was modified to some extent, with public bureaucracy perceived in a more positive light. Since that period, however, bureaucracies have increasingly become the targets of cynicism and skepticism, particularly during the last decade. Whether pessimism is the current dominant public attitude toward bureaucracy is impossible to say with certainty due to the lack of hard research on the topic. Still, it is difficult to avoid the impression that there is quite widespread resentment of the alleged authoritarianism and lack of responsiveness of the faceless bureaucracy that appears to many to be accountable to no one. For example, John Meisel doubts whether any aspect of the federal government is as unpopular today as the public bureaucracy. It has grown phenomenally, and he contends that its salary scales exceed their counterparts in most of the private sector, that its members have "utterly unshakeable tenure," and that their very generous pensions which are indexed to the cost of living ensure that they, no matter what may happen to the rest of us due to economic vicissitudes, are safe. Furthermore, in his view the public bureaucracy is "also extremely powerful and possibly uncontrollable."[1]

This view of bureaucracy as essentially self-serving (and self-perpetuating) reflects the comments of early theorists such as Marx, Weber and Michels. Bureaucracy, in this view, is a malignant, dangerous force in society. Within the negative perspective, opinions seem to differ as to the exact nature of bureaucracy's autonomy and its role in society in general. Some, on a short-term and/or long-term basis see bureaucracy as essentially dominant in public affairs, others insist on the need to keep it under close observation, while still others feel that it is controllable and controlled by a variety of means. The discussion of the Canadian Monster in Chapter 3 and later the survey of accountability in Chapter 8 indicate great concern about ultimate control over bureaucracy.

The entire discussion in Chapters 2 and 3 is very general and based on extremely assumptive arguments compounded by pervasive, long-standing value controversies. As a result, little if anything can be regarded as "proved" or even "provable" in this area. Furthermore, values change and assumptive emphases shift over time, and any apparent agreement will most probably, judging from historical evidence, prove ephemeral in that there appears to be no single, enduring answer to questions based on the nature of man and on the nature of bureaucracy. As a final result, it is not uncommon to encounter in the literature on public administration the argument that such philosophical meanderings should be set aside in favor of "getting on with matters of substance."

This attitude is both understandable and valid in an academic and practical sense. However, the attitude misses much of the essential point, as it suggests that we act only on the basis of "facts" which are demonstrable and are more or less accepted as such. In our view, this is simply not the case. We contend that each of us acts on the basis of our personal ideology (as that term was defined in Chapter 1). Consciously or unconsciously we view bureaucrats and bureaucracies on the basis of generalized attitudes we possess which in turn are based on broad assumptions. These assumptions cannot be proved in one sense, but they are very real and important in our assessment of any aspect of public administration.

Therefore, the whole question of the validity of our assumptions about bureaucrats and bureaucracy is crucial to the study of public administration. As Stephen Bailey[2] points out, we perceive reality on the basis of the assumptions we hold, and if we intend to change any part of that reality, if we have any hope in general of controlling our destiny, then the validity of our assumptions about relevant people and institutions is crucial. The problem is, however, that this validity is neither demonstrable nor agreed upon.

The reader is challenged to view specific topics discussed in this text with the idea in mind of her/his personal assumptions. It should become apparent that, if one says, for example, that the ideas of New Public Administration are fine in theory but are quite impracticable, then one is operating on certain assumptions about the nature of man and/or of bureaucracy. Thus, because we differ in original assumptions, we often arrive at radically different conclusions on such specifics as the proper role of bureaucracy in public policy-making, the need for stringent financial accounting systems, the relative value of objective and subjective accountability, the necessary definition of the merit principle, the proper relationship among citizens, politicians and bureaucrats, the need for administrative secrecy, and on and on . . . .

As noted, interwoven throughout all this is conflict over basic values. That is, we not only disagree over reality, but also over what ought to be reality. On some discernible points there seems to be fairly broad agreement on the most general of values, but when we attempt to apply a value, to define it operationally, to reconcile it with other values, we typically are at odds with one another. For example, it seems reasonably safe to say that Canadians agree that government in our society should work in the public interest, but when we attempt to state exactly what the public interest *is* we quickly encounter difficulties. Furthermore, because we do not agree on the specific application of general values, we also disagree over the extent to which government is pursuing and realizing them in practice.

While terms such as "public interest" and "democracy" are perhaps outstanding examples of the problem, the same difficulties prevail regarding what would, at least at first glance, appear to be less encompassing, more precise terms frequently encountered in the literature on public administration. For example, as we have attempted to demonstrate here there is fairly widespread agreement that recruitment into the public service ought to be on the basis of merit. However, we do not appear to agree at all on what is meritorious. We insist that the public bureaucracy must be accountable, but apparently cannot agree on either the nature of accountability nor on such questions as for what and to whom and when. We seem to be agreed that in Canada there ought to be citizen participation in making public choices, but we disagree greatly over what constitutes participation. We might even agree, at this point in time, that there ought to be restraint in government spending, but we disagree over where in the public budget this restraint should appear.

Again, it can certainly be argued that we cannot validly generalize like this about people and that no perspective is consistently correct. Admittedly, one can find industrious, apparently goal-oriented public servants. After all, "some of our best friends are bureaucrats." However, one can also find lazy, self-oriented public servants, lazy and goal-oriented public servants, industrious and self-oriented public servants and so forth. But to admit that we cannot validly generalize is not to say that Canadians do not generalize. We do in fact tend to generalize, quite strongly. To put it differently, while it is possible rationally to say and believe that one cannot generalize about bureaucracy and bureaucrats, we insist here that most of us will tend to emphasize one perspective or the other, positive or negative. We will tend as supervisors to have generalized views about employees, and as employees, about supervisors. As politicians we will have general opinions about bureaucrats, and as bureaucrats, about politicians. As bureaucrats we will have views on the general ability of citizens to know, act upon and maintain what they want, while as citizens we will hold to ideas about bureaucratic efficiency or inefficiency, dedication or self-servingness, controllability or uncontrollability. Academics, for example, cannot agree even on what "bureaucracy" actually means. Martin Albrow points out that at least seven different conceptions of the term can be found in the literature.[3] More recently, another work on the subject, most appropriately sub-titled "The Career of a Concept," contends that the concept of bureaucracy "works as a Jack-of-all-trades and today it works overtime."[4]

It is not being suggested here that Canadians are always consistent in their attitudes and actions, either as individuals or as members of groups. In fact, the opposite is probably closer to the truth since as individuals we can very easily, if unknowingly, be quite inconsistent in our views. As noted in Chapter 3, for example, on the basis of a study of Canadians' politically-relevant attitudes, most of us apparently expect to be treated fairly by a sluggish, inefficient bureaucracy. Public services spend millions on a wide variety of personnel programs based essentially on optimistic assumptions, while politicians, who authorize the spending on these programs, talk blithely along pessimistic lines of bureaucratic fat and inefficiency. The advocates of citizen participation insist that the citizen, as common man, both can and should be trusted in matters administrative as well as political, while the politician and bureaucrat apparently are not seen as sharing these attributes since the same advocates insist on their untrustworthiness. Recognizing the need for expert knowledge in complex matters, we may insist on heavy bureaucratic involvement in devising good public policies, while at the same time we indicate strong suspicion about bureaucracy by insisting upon stringent accountability procedures — we rely on people we essentially cannot and do not trust. Along similar lines, it is probable that many Canadians believe that the merit principle (emphasizing competence) exists in the public service while at the same time they tend toward belief that the Peter Principle (emphasizing incompetence) reflects public service reality.

It is our belief that, as difficult to pinpoint as it may be, distrust of bureaucracy and bureaucrats is fairly prevalent in Canadian society today, whether despite or because of the fact that we are tremendously dependent on the bureaucracy and on bureaucrats in virtually every aspect of our lives. It is as difficult to find clear, unconditional statements of trust about Canadian bureaucracy and bureaucrats as it is to point to any significant aspect of our daily lives that is not somehow impinged upon by government legislation, attendant rules and regulations and government structures and personnel.

Take, for example, the concern about accountability which is such a perennially-blooming plant in Canada. Pursuit of accountability of this all-pervasive bureaucracy is perhaps the 20th century equivalent of the search for the Holy Grail in the Middle Ages, especially when accountability is seen in absolute terms. The democratic norm in Canada is that the bureaucracy should be accountable to the electorate through elected politicians. However, while subjective acceptance of this norm by bureaucrats may serve to restrain them in the use of their undoubted influence, the formal, objective procedures for ensuring accountability may continue to be less than satisfactory.

This concern is manifested in a wide variety of ways. For example, there is the constant argument by opposition members that bureaucracy under the party in power is running out of control, spending is rampant and accountability for that spending and all attendant actions is very weak, even non-existent. This view has been emphasized in *Reports* of the Auditor-General, and as a theme it pervaded the *Report* of the Royal Commission on Financial Management and Accountability. In addition, allegations of the loss of financial control and the usurpation of power by the bureaucracy provide headlines for many news stories and indignant editorials.

The introduction of a federal Ombudsman is seen by some as a modest, but essentially useful, palliative for the individual citizen aggrieved by the actions of public officials. Strengthened parliamentary committees with greater freedom to investigate departmental affairs, including the use of delegated legislative authority by officials, have been urged as an aid toward ensuring accountability. Many believe that a strong Freedom of Information Act is a prerequisite to achieving institutional reforms linked to the notion of accountability. And it should be noted that bureaucrats do not reject these and other proposals to enhance accountability; many bureaucrats are in the forefront on the pages of public administration journals and in conferences advocating such changes.

Ironically, all this occurs in the absence of any clear, commonly-accepted definition of accountability. In the case of politicians, the majority of Canadians *might* feel that political accountability occurs satisfactorily on election days, in that the party in power must somehow justify its past actions to at least a plurality of Canadians in order to be re-elected. However, the case is not at all so clear regarding bureaucrats. They are appointed, not elected, and therefore we have no direct access to them. Furthermore, since we apparently do not trust our politicians themselves to select competent people to staff the bureaucracy, we have established a neutral body to pursue a supposedly neutral selection process which ends in supposedly neutral competence — although, judging from impressionistic evidence, many if not most Canadians have doubts about the competence and perhaps about the neutrality as well.

In any event, once they are in office we insist that bureaucrats must be accountable to us through our politicians. However, relying upon elected politicians in cabinets to control departments and non-departmental agencies has perhaps become a matter of faith we should not question too closely if we wish to remain at ease. To what extent can politicians, who are essentially enlightened amateurs in the vast and complex world of public policy, really control huge, elaborate organizations pursuing specialized functions based on intricate programs? Furthermore, governments come and go, and even when they stay, ministers are frequently shifted from one portfolio to another. These are the individuals on whom we pin our hopes to exercise control over specialized bureaucrats who have large amounts of technical information at their fingertips and who have frequently worked continuously for many years in one area of government activity. And to complicate the matter, we also want some measure of independence for the bureaucracy, especially for the crown corporations and regulatory agencies. To provide this independence, we do not, for example, allow politicians into such personnel functions as selection and promotion.

It is difficult, and many insist it is virtually impossible, for politicians either individually or as a group to control bureaucrats. Cabinet ministers monitor program operations. The House of Commons has ultimate control over the spending function. However, as our chapters on policy making, budgeting, and accountability attempted to reveal, political control and direction are far from complete since departments, in addition to all other factors, can usually point to groups who are ready to defend existing programs. In the present public mood of retrenchment, governments have discovered that shifting spending into new categories or terminating ineffectual programs is as difficult a political process to manage as is creating new programs. There are almost inevitably segments of the public who will be upset by attacks on programs which serve their particular interests.

To emphasize this point, one wit has suggested that "Luxury is something your neighbor can do without." More seriously, Lester C. Thurow argues in his recent book, *The Zero-Sum Society*, that slower economic growth and the perception of impending scarcity, even economic doom, have increased political conflict over who gets what in government benefits and services. Because the public pie is not constantly getting bigger or, at least, is expanding very slowly, *everyone* cannot get more. Increasingly, then, we witness a zero-sum game in which there must be winners and losers. Governments, including bureaucracies, find it difficult under such circumstances to perform the brokerage role of reconciling competing interests because more groups and individuals are politically active and are less willing to accept what they consider to be losses.[5] No one, it seems, inside or outside government, appears willing to take less — everyone wants someone else to take the losses.

Furthermore, many of these ideas presuppose an essential trust in politicians (although not necessarily in bureaucrats). However, a significant number of Canadians trust *neither* the politician *nor* the bureaucrat. In this instance, assuming the individual does not opt out and refuse to be further involved in the whole idea of accountability and control, he will probably become an advocate of citizen participation and citizen control. But this does not really reduce the problematical nature of the idea. Rather, it shifts it to another focus, differing in emphases and major actors, but not essentially coming closer to resolution.

Furthermore, there is strong disagreement over just what accountability is all about. Is it (can it be, should it be) a rather mechanical process as pictured on page 2 of Chapter 8? For example, in the case of the minister, the mechanical ease of the accountability concept has been disintegrating for a number of years now, and it is impossible to predict whether a minister (or Cabinet, or party) will be *willing* to be held accountable according to the older conception of that term. Or, for example, in the case of the bureaucrat, while there may be widespread agreement that he/she should be accountable, there is great disagreement over normative specifics such as to whom, by whom, for what, how much, and when. Recently, for instance, it has become fashionable to insist that bureaucracies should be more responsive to the groups they serve, but such responsiveness may compromise ministerial responsibility. And not only do we fail to agree on the normative level, as the immediately preceding discussion points out, we do not achieve much agreement on the factual level either. Opinions appear to range from "need some further control" to "completely out of control."

Another major example of profound disagreement over matters which, although often stated simplistically, are extremely complex, is provided by Chapters 4 and 5 dealing with public policy making and public budgeting. Both chapters analyze recent efforts to reassert greater politicial (i.e., Cabinet) control over policy formulation and spending and in both instances the evaluations of recent institutional reforms are mixed, with majority opinion tending towards disappointment over the results achieved. Additional complications in the accountability equation were added when we looked at citizen participation (Chapter 10) and the impact of federalism on the policy and administrative processes (Chapter 7). Once again, the controversies involve both factual and normative matters.

Clearly, policy making, budgeting, federalism and accountability are closely interrelated, different aspects of the same process. Related to the search for greater accountability within governments has been the drive to achieve greater coordination both within and among governments in Canada. As governments have expanded, created new structural entities such as crown corporations and regulatory agencies, and consulted more regularly with affected groups and individuals, there has been perceived a greater need for coordination of the far-flung operations. Thus, intergovernmental relations constitute a major factor in policy making, and we have described some of the complex structures and mechanisms designed to achieve coordination. While the latter have developed, the influence and the size of the bureaucracies tend to fragment control, to divert attention to considerations of organizational survival and to pose serious challenges to political leadership. It is not too far-fetched to suggest that, because political parties and their leaders are constantly seeking a workable consensus, they cannot supply a strong sense of direction to government. As a result, Canadians may enjoy the benefits (and costs) not of one unified government, but of a group of competing governments within the federal system, within each of which there are a series of sub-governments pursuing narrow goals in terms of their own particularistic mandates and the interests of their clientele groups.

It is not difficult, for example, to come across literature suggesting that the entire political system, including the public bureaucracy, which is allegedly democratic is really a vast public show masking elite activities. Nor is it difficult to encounter literature praising the democratic nature of the

Canadian political system, including its bureaucracy. These disparate views relate to facts, in that they each purport to describe reality as the commentator sees it. And to say that, surely, the truth must lie somewhere between the two extremes does not, by itself, prove anything. A moderate view is not, by definition, the ultimate realistic view. Rather, it represents merely a third perspective, further complicating the actual truth of the matter. On the other hand, it seems fairly safe to insist that our personal view is the one we believe to be the realistic view.

More specifically, we do not agree on the extent to which the bureaucracy engages in policy making, whether the latter is stated in terms of goals or as strategies for the pursuit of goals. Again, it is not at all difficult to find the contention that bureaucracy dominates policy making, whether in the short-run and/or in the long-run. For example, there is Chapter 3 which discusses apparently fairly common beliefs about bureaucracy. On the other hand, we can also easily find arguments that, although the bureaucracy does engage in policy making in the form of loyally extending its information and best advice to the politicians, it does not actually *make* public policy.

When we cannot agree on the basic facts of the case, it is less than surprising that we disagree profoundly over the values involved in it. Preceding chapters offer many conflicting value perspectives on this point, as well as indicating the interrelatedness of facts and values in the controversy. Regardless of *how* public policy is actually made in Canada, there is the continuing question of how it *ought to be* made. Emerging from the older notion that there can and should be a science of administration (discussed in Chapter 2) which was connected to the belief that there can and should be a complete separation of political and administrative functions, there is the current belief that there can and should be a "policy science," whether or not it is based on the notion of a supra-discipline encompassing all the knowledge we at present possess. This is countered by the argument that there cannot be such a science due to the almost infinite complexities involved as well as the normative argument, along Orwellian lines, that we ought not even try to develop such a science.

Given the emphasis one finds today on the need for long-range, rational (good?) government planning, it can be argued that we should move away from older ways of deciding on public matters. Incrementalism, the oiling of squeaky wheels with public benefits, political patronage, emotionalism and intuition, in this view must give way to bolder, more comprehensive, scientific formulations of public policy. Given the rate and profound depth of change in so many areas of our lives today, older methods are essentially anachronistic. In this respect, and quite opposed to any emphasis on citizen participation (which is part of the noted anachronisms), we perhaps should allow the mantle of governing to fall on the experts, the trained and specialized professionals in the bureaucracy who are, if any one is, capable of understanding the nature and circumstances of problems. This is certainly not a new idea, as it was essentially expressed by, among others, St. Simon and

Carlyle over a century ago. However, it finds the consociational democratists as well as the advocates of citizen participation united in common cause. The former insist on rule by elected representatives and the latter on rule by the people — neither accepts technocracy.

The problem for many seems to be that they are uncertain about who to blame for those conditions which they, as individuals or as groups, define as problems in our society. That is, a situation may be agreed upon as a problem by a great number of Canadians who cannot agree among themselves on the direction in which the finger of blame ought to point. Some appear to lay the cause of most, even all, social ills on the politician, perhaps depending on his party but sometimes independent of party. Others stress the ineptness, blindness, and even iniquity of the public bureaucracies. Still others point to the insatiable collective greed of Canadians, our penchant for demanding more of all those things we define as good.

While many further examples could be offered to illustrate our point, perhaps we best restate it: Public administration in Canada is pervaded by problematical contentions. The concepts and practices associated with public administration (we have here attempted to address some of the major ones), demonstrate this fuzziness, this inability to say clearly either what *is* the case or what *ought to be* the case. Actually, to state the situation in terms of either/or as in the preceding sentence is too simplistic. What appears to be the case in every area we have discussed in this text is that questions of fact and questions of value seem almost invariably to be collapsed inextricably into one another with attendant compounding of confusion.

This is not to argue that understanding of our bureaucracies is necessarily beyond us. From a merely factual standpoint, public bureaucracies have grown dramatically in size and complexity in this century and perhaps they are essentially beyond our genuine comprehension. However, we have coped with profound advances in knowledge in many other aspects of our lives, and it is not unreasonable to believe that we are capable of similar understanding in public administration. The question of values is another matter. Canadians do not at this time appear to agree much on the basic values, and meanings of values, involved in the areas of public administration that we have discussed. Certainly, the environment of public administration in the last two decades has been turbulent. The public services have experienced rapid growth, unionization and considerable militancy among employees, forced bilingualism, a general affirmative action emphasis, new decision-making techniques, increased federal-provincial conflict, and other significant changes. Given the current mood of retrenchment, there is the possibility of stock taking and consolidation occurring with an attendant decrease in contention. Furthermore, values change, whether through elite, majoritarian or consensual preferences, and it is quite possible that at least some of these value controversies will abate, even terminate.

However, it is our view that while it is quite possible that the depth and scope of controversy may abate in a particular area we have discussed, it is impossible to believe that this condition could prevail generally. The differing perspectives with their accompanying disagreements are too fundamental and too complex for us to accept that they will significantly ease in the foreseeable future. Furthermore, while we have discussed certain controversial areas, we definitely do not want to leave the impression that these are the *only* areas in Canadian public administration subject to profound, fundamental dispute. For example, there is the problematical area of unionization and collective bargaining in the public services of Canada, here only peripherally touched upon. Unless one wants to assume that collective bargaining in the public service is not important, there is at the least the need to assess the employee and management perspectives, both in terms of is and ought to be. More specifically, there are such questions as: Do public service unions improperly use their right to strike? Are politicians given to cavalier treatment of collective bargaining in the public sector because the strike, when it occurs, saves money and can easily be blamed on the intransigence of the employees — thus fitting in nicely with the dim public view of bureaucracy? Should public employees have the right to strike at all? If not, why not? If so, are there to be conditions and what should these be? Another similarly contentious topic area involves the extent to which government can be (ought to be) "businesslike" in its activities, this debate quickly incorporating the extremely problematical term "efficiency" and what it can and should mean in government. Or, as a final example, there is the relationship between central and operating government agencies, which quickly tends to include the hoary but still pertinent arguments over the actual as well as proper role of line and staff units in organizations.

In this text we have attempted to leave our particular biases aside in order to present and assess neutrally the factual information as well as the controversies relevant to the various topic areas — although we realize that complete lack of bias is quite impossible. It would therefore be inconsistent and perhaps pedagogically undesirable at this point to inject our personal beliefs into the discussion. We have such beliefs, of course, based on our personal views of reality as well as of what ought to be reality — but that is all they are, our personal beliefs. Furthermore, it should be explicitly noted that "our personal beliefs" is quite intentionally stated in the plural. There are two of us, and we by no means interpret all public administration reality in exactly the same way nor, far less, do we achieve detailed agreement on what ought to be reality.

This statement, in fact, sums up the theme of our text. There is a good deal of accumulated fact regarding Canadian public administration which as such is not in particular dispute. However, there are areas of the discipline where our accumulated knowledge is extremely weak. Furthermore, interpretation of fact is crucial in creating problematical perspectives in any given area of the discipline. It is one thing to state, for example, the number of employees in the federal public service — although agreement on this "fact" is not as easy as it may appear due to differences of opinion over what should be included in the "public service." However, there remains the interpretation of the fact. What do the numbers imply? Do they reflect the emergence of the welfare state or the technocratic state, of both, of neither? Are they an indication of the increased dominance of the capitalist elite or of an emerging, government-sponsored egalitarianism in Canadian society? Do they suggest the need for greater, more stringently objective control measures over bureaucrats or do they point to the need for achieving greater subjective responsibility on the part of bureaucrats, or do they suggest the utility or futility of both?

Such questions are and will remain at the heart of the problematical nature of Canadian public administration, a nature which, we feel, is quite unlikely to change in the foreseeable future. The reader must, therefore, personally attempt to sort out what appears to be the reality and what ought to be the reality of the world of administration. While we cannot subscribe to the absolute statement that "knowledge is power," we do believe that knowledge can contribute to and serve power. To the extent to which one is either interested in and/or concerned about public administration in Canada, pursuit of such knowledge, as difficult as it may be, must be regarded as essential.

ENDNOTES

1. John Meisel, "The Federal Government: Can it Cope?" in *Walter Gordon Lecture Series, Vol. I, 1976-77* (Toronto: Canadian Studies Foundation, 1977).
2. Stephen K. Bailey, "Objectives of the Theory of Public Administration," in *Theory and Practice of Public Administration*, Monograph 8, (American Academy of Political and Social Science, October 1968).
3. Martin Albrow, *Bureaucracy* (London: Pall Mall, 1970).
4. Eugene Kamenka and Martin Krygier (eds.), *Bureaucracy: The Career of a Concept* (London: Edward Arnold, 1979), p. vii.
5. Lester C. Thurow, *The Zero-Sum Society: Distribution and the Possibilities for Economic Change* (Markham, Ontario: Penguin Books, 1980), Chapter 2.

Index